JavaServer Pages

DEVELOPER'S HANDBOOK

JavaServer Pages

DEVELOPER'S HANDBOOK

Nick Todd
Mark Szolkowski

DEVELOPER'S LIBRARY

Sams Publishing, 201 West 103rd Street, Indianapolis, Indiana 46290

JavaServer Pages Developer's Handbook

International Standard Book Number: 0-672-32438-5

Library of Congress Catalog Card Number: 2002105436

Printed in the United States of America

First Printing: May 2003

06 05 04 03 4 3 2 1

Sams Publishing offers excellent discounts on this book when ordered in quantity for bulk purchases or special sales. For more information, please contact

U.S. Corporate and Government Sales

1-800-382-3419

corpsales@pearsontechgroup.com

For sales outside of the U.S., please contact

International Sales

1-317-581-3793

international@pearsontechgroup.com

Trademarks

All terms mentioned in this book that are known to be trademarks or service marks have been appropriately capitalized. Sams Publishing cannot attest to the accuracy of this information. Use of a term in this book should not be regarded as affecting the validity of any trademark or service mark.

Warning and Disclaimer

Every effort has been made to make this book as complete and as accurate as possible, but no warranty or fitness is implied. The information provided is on an "as is" basis. The author and the publisher shall have neither liability nor responsibility to any person or entity with respect to any loss or damages arising from the information contained in this book.

Associate Publisher
Michael Stephens

Acquisitions Editor
Todd Green

Development Editor
Tiffany Taylor

Managing Editor
Charlotte Clapp

Project Editor
Andy Beaster

Copy Editor
Chip Gardner

Indexer
Sandy Henselmeier

Proofreader
Bob LaRoche

Expert Reviewer
Lance Andersen

Technical Editors
Alaric B. Snell
Marc Goldford

Media Developer
Dan Scherf

Team Coordinator
Cindy Teeters

Interior Designer
Gary Adair

Cover Designer
Alan Clements

Page Layout
Michelle Mitchell

Graphics
Tammy Graham

❖

From Nick Todd:

This book is dedicated to Sarah Todd.

From Mark Szolkowski

This is for my parents, who are always there.

❖

Contents at a Glance

Introduction **1**

I Core JSP

1 JSP, J2EE, and the Role of the Servlet **7**

2 The Basic Syntax of JSP **49**

3 Further JSP Syntax **87**

4 Deploying JSP in a Web Container **113**

5 The JSP Standard Tag Library **123**

6 JSP and Java Beans **165**

7 JSP Application Architecture **201**

8 Session Tracking Using JSP **235**

9 Developing Custom Tag Libraries **273**

II XML, Web Services, and Enterprise JSP

10 Utilizing XML from JSP **315**

11 Transforming XML Using XSLT and XSLFO **347**

12 Invoking Web Services from JSP **385**

13 Locating Resources Using JNDI **435**

14 Databases and JSP **461**

15 JSP and EJB Interaction **509**

16 Security and JSP **559**

17 Personalization and Web Applications **585**

18 Case Study **559**

III **Appendices**

A An XSLT and XPath Checklist **635**

B An Overview of XML Schema **645**

C A Checklist of the Tags in the JSP Standard Tag Library **655**

D Basic JSP Syntax Checklist **681**

E Debugging Tomcat and Running the Examples **693**

F The Java Community Process **701**

G J2EE Application Servers **705**

H Configuring Tomcat **713**

I Installing MySQL and WebLogic Server **727**

J Glossary **733**

Index **737**

Table of Contents

Introduction

I Core JSP

1 **JSP, J2EE, and the Role of the Servlet 7**

The Progression of Java and Web Applications 7

The Java 2 Enterprise Edition 10

The J2EE Standards 10

The J2EE Platform 12

J2EE Applications 13

J2EE Deployment 16

Java Servlets 17

The Servlet Lifecycle 18

The `HttpServletRequest` and `HttpServletResponse` 21

Installing Jakarta Tomcat 23

Starting and Stopping Tomcat 24

Creating Your First Web Application 26

Processing Form Data 28

Servlet Initialization 32

The `ServletContext` 35

Forwarding Requests to Other Servlets 38

Exception Handling in Java Servlets 39

`java.io.IOException` 39

`javax.servlet.ServletException` 40

`javax.servlet.UnavailableException` 41

Introducing the JavaServer Page 41

Web Application Scope 46

Summary 48

2 **The Basic Syntax of JSP 49**

JSP Defined 49

Comments in JavaServer Pages 50

The Expression Tag 53

The Declaration Tag 55
Embedding Code 59
JSP Directives 61
The Use of the `include` Directive 61
The Use of the `page` Directive 63
Basic Introduction to the `taglib` Directive 68
JSP Predefined Variables 69
The Roles of the JSP Predefined Variables 69
JSP Variables and ASP Variables 80
The JavaServer Pages Standard Tag Library (JSTL) 82
Introducing the JSTL 82
Using the JSTL 84
The JSP 2.0 Expression Language 85
Summary 85

3 Further JSP Syntax 87
The Standard Actions 87
Forwarding and Including 88
Templating Pages Using `<jsp:include>` 90
The Java Plugin 93
Using JavaBeans on Pages 97
Actions and Tag Libraries 97
The JSP Expression Language (EL) 98
EL Literal Types 101
The EL Operators 101
Accessing Objects and Collections 103
The EL Implicit Objects 107
Reserved Words 108
Expression Language Functions 109
Controlling Expression Language and Scriptlet Use 110
Summary 111

4 Deploying JSP in a Web Container 113
Configuring JSP in web.xml 113
Welcome Files 114
URL Mappings 114
Initialization Parameters 116

The Web Container 117

The Web Application 117

Deploying Web Applications 119

Deploying a Folder Structure 120

Deploying a WAR File 120

Summary 121

5 The JSP Standard Tag Library 123

The Need for Tag Libraries 123

The Challenges of Mixing Presentation Markup and Java Code 124

The Tag Library as a Solution 125

Using an Existing Tag Library 126

Introduction to the Core Tag Library 131

Scope in the Expression Language 132

The Core Actions 132

The XML actions 156

The SQL Actions 160

The Internationalization and Formatting Actions 160

Backwards Compatibility and Migrating from JSTL 1.0 to JSTL 1.1 161

Third-Party Tag Libraries 162

The Jakarta Taglibs Project 162

Summary 163

6 JSP and JavaBeans 165

What Is a JavaBean? 165

The Benefit of Component-Based Development 166

The Role of the Bean in Component-Based Development 167

The No-Argument Constructor 170

The `set` and `get` Methods 171

The Importance of Scope in a Web Application 174

The Role of Scope 174

When to Use the Different Scopes 176

Using JavaBeans from a JSP 177
Using JavaBeans from JSP with Standard Action Elements 177
The `jsp:useBean` Tag and Existing JavaBeans 190
JavaBeans and HTML Forms 193
Summary 200

7 JSP Application Architecture 201
The Model 1 Architecture 201
The Model 2 Architecture 202
Which Architecture to Use? 212
Introducing Frameworks 213
Jakarta Struts 214
An Overview of Struts 214
Installing the Struts Framework 216
Building an Application Using Struts 216
JavaServer Faces 230
General Guidelines 230
Separating HTML and Java 231
Encapsulating the Business Logic in Beans 231
Using the Most Appropriate Inclusion Mechanism 231
Stylesheets 232
Comments, Style, and Structure 232
Exception Handling 232
Summary 233

8 Session Tracking Using JSP 235
Using Cookies to Track Sessions 235
Interacting with Cookies from JSP 236
Cookie Versions 238
Cookie Comments and Cookie Security 239
Persistent Cookies 240
Cookie Limitations 241
URL Rewriting 241

The Session Object 243
Terminating a Session 248
Sessions and Events 248
`HttpSession` Object Summary 252
Keeping Track of Your Session Objects 253
Using a `SessionListener` 253
Session Failover 256
Shopping Cart Mini Case Study 259
The Beans 259
The Controller Servlet 262
The JSPs 265
Summary 272

9 Developing Custom Tag Libraries 273
Tag Extensions 273
Writing a Custom Tag 274
Expression Language Functions 274
An Empty Custom Action 276
An Empty Custom Action with Attributes 283
Repeated Processing of Body Content 292
Custom Actions with Body Content 297
Tags That Interact 303
Scripting Variables 303
Hierarchical Tag Structures 307
Summary 311

II XML, Web Services, and Enterprise JSP

10 Utilizing XML from JSP 315
Introduction to XML 315
XML Is Portable Data 315
Features of XML 317
XML's Syntax and Structure 317
DTDs and Schemas 324

Parsing XML 325
The DOM API 326
The Simple API for XML (SAX) 333
JDOM 341
Summary 345

11 Transforming XML Using XSLT and XSLFO 347
Introduction to XSLT 347
XSLT Input and Output 348
XPath 349
Single Template Programming (Exemplar Approach) 354
Using the Xalan XSLT Processor 357
Declarative Template Programming 360
Built-in Templates 362
Working with Subsets 363
Procedural Programming 366
Applying Browser-Specific Transformations 370
Transformation Using XSLFO 376
Formatting Objects 377
Cocoon 381
Summary 384

12 Invoking Web Services from JSP 385
Web Services Fundamentals 385
Java APIs for Web Services 388
Introducing Apache Axis 389
Installing Apache Axis 390
Deploying a Web Service to Axis 391
SOAP—Interacting with Web Services 393
Using XML Spy as a Client 395
Building Your Own Java Client 396
Passing Custom Objects 402
SOAP and JSP 408
The Web Service Description Language (WSDL) 413
The <types> Element 415

The <message> Element 416
The <portType> Element 416
The <operation> Element 417
The <binding> Element 417
The <service> Element 418
Generating WSDL 419
Generating Java from the WSDL 419
Accessing WSDL Programmatically 423
Universal Description, Discovery, and Integration (UDDI) 423
The UDDI XML 424
The UDDI API 428
Summary 433

13 Locating Resources Using JNDI 435
Naming and Directory Services 435
Overview of Naming Services 435
Overview of Directory Services 438
Naming Conventions 439
Why Use a Naming Service? 440
What Is JNDI? 440
The `javax.naming` Package 442
The `javax.naming.directory` Package 443
The `javax.naming.event` Package 444
The `javax.naming.ldap` Package 445
The `javax.naming.spi` Package 445
Using JNDI 445
JNDI and Sun's J2EE Reference Implementation 446
JNDI and JSP 455
Summary 458

14 Databases and JSP 461
JDBC Fundamentals 461
The JDBC Driver 462
The Driver Manager 463
Connections and Statements 465
The `ResultSet` and `ResultSetMetaData` 469

Modifying the Database 473
The `javax.sql.DataSource` 475
Accessing Databases Using the JavaServer Pages Standard Tag Library 479
The `sql:setDataSource` Action 481
The `sql:query` Action 482
The `sql:update` Action 486
The `sql:param` Action 487
The `sql:transaction` Action 488
Setting SQL Action Attributes Globally 490
Connection Pools 491
The `ConnectionPoolDataSource` Interface 493
The `PooledConnection` Interface 493
The `ConnectionEventListener` Interface 494
Content Caching 495
Caching JSP Output 495
Caching Database Content 495
The Shopping Cart Mini Case Study 496
Enterprise JavaBeans and Database Access 507
Summary 507

15 JSP and EJB Interaction 509
EJB Fundamentals 509
EJB Communication 512
Anatomy of an EJB 512
Accessing an EJB Remotely—What Goes On 514
The Client View of an EJB 515
Writing EJBs 517
Creating an Entity Bean 518
The Entity Bean Remote Interface 519
The Entity Bean Home Interface 519
The Entity Bean Implementation 521
The Entity Bean Lifecycle 524
Passivation and Activation 526
Deploying an Entity Bean 526
Running the J2EE Application 536

Session Beans 541
Creating a Session Bean 543
The Session Bean Home Interface 543
The Session Bean Remote Interface 544
The Session Bean Implementation 546
The Session Bean Lifecycle 550
Deploying a Session Bean 552
Web Application EJB Access Architecture 555
Summary 558

16 Security and JSP 559
Security Requirements 559
Security—From a Site User Perspective 559
Security—From the Site Perspective 560
The J2EE Security Model 560
Roles and Principals 561
Declarative and Programmatic Security 561
Authentication 561
HTTP Basic Authentication 563
Digest Authentication 564
Form-Based Authentication 566
HTTPS Client Authentication and SSL 569
Symmetric Key Encryption 569
Asymmetric Encryption 570
Digital Certificates 571
Digital Signatures 573
Java and SSL 573
Programmatic Security 576
Security in J2EE Applications 580
Unauthenticated Users 582
Java Authentication and Authorization Service (JAAS) 583
Single Sign On 584
Summary 584

17 Personalization and Web Applications 585
Introduction to Personalization 585
Using Persistent Cookies 586
Using Registration and Forms 586

A Personalized Application Example 587
The User Profile 587
Setting Up Login Using the Database 589
The Login Page 589
The Profile Object 592
Personalizing Pages 595
User Registration 598
Rule-Based Personalization Engines 600
Creating Rules 601
Summary 603

18 Case Study 605
Introduction to the Case Study 605
Case Study Architecture 606
The Page Architecture 607
The Course Information XML 609
Case Study Implementation 610
The Home page 610
Displaying the Course Information 611
The Controller Servlet 616
Processing the Form 619
Sending the Email 623
Interacting with the Database 627
Securing the Administration Pages 630
Summary 632

III Appendixes

A An XSLT and XPATH Checklist 635
XSLT Checklist 635
`<xsl:apply-templates>` 635
`<xsl:call-template>` 636
`<xsl:choose>` 636
`<xsl:if>` 637
`<xsl:otherwise>` 637
`<xsl:param>` 638
`<xsl:sort>` 638
`<xsl:stylesheet>` 639

<xsl:template> 640

<xsl:value-of> 641

<xsl:when> 641

<xsl:with-param> 642

XPATH Checklist 642

anElementName 642

/ 643

// 643

. 643

.. 643

* 643

@ 643

node() 644

| 644

Predicates 644

B An Overview of XML Schema 645

DTDs 645

XML Schema Introduction 646

XML Schema Namespaces 647

XML Schema Structure 647

Defining Elements 648

Datatypes 648

Attributes 650

Assigning XML Schemas 650

Multiple Schemas 651

Import and Include 653

Example Element Definition 653

C A Checklist of the Tags in the JSP Standard Tag Library 655

Tag Library URIs 655

Core Actions 656

The c:out action 656

The c:set Action 657

The c:remove Action 658

The c:catch Action 658

The c:if Action 658

The `c:choose` Action 659
The `c:when` Action 659
The `c:otherwise` Action 660
The `c:forEach` Action 660
The `c:forTokens` Action 661
The `c:import` Action 661
The `c:url` Action 662
The `c:redirect` Action 663
The `c:param` Action 663
XML Actions 664
The `x:parse` Action 664
The `x:out` Action 665
The `x:set` Action 665
The `x:if` Action 665
The `x:choose` Action 666
The `x:when` Action 666
The `x:otherwise` Action 666
The `x:forEach` Action 666
The `x:transform` Action 667
The `x:param` Action 668
Internationalization Actions 669
The `fmt:setLocale` Action 669
The `fmt:bundle` Action 669
The `fmt:setBundle` Action 669
The `fmt:message` Action 670
The `fmt:param` Action 670
The `fmt:requestEncoding` Action 671
The `fmt:setTimezone` Action 671
The `fmt:timezone` Action 671
The `fmt:formatNumber` Action 672
The `fmt:parseNumber` Action 673
The `fmt:formatDate` Action 674
The `fmt:parseDate` Action 674
SQL Actions 675
The `sql:setDataSource` Action 675
The `sql:param` Action 676
The `sql:query` Action 676
The `sql:update` Action 678

The `sql:transaction` Action 679
The `sql:dateParam` Action 679

D Basic JSP Syntax Checklist 681
JSP Directives 681
The `include` Directive 681
The `page` Directive 682
The `taglib` Directive 685
Comments in JSPs 685
JSP Predefined Variables 686
The JavaServer Pages Standard Tag Library 687
The JSP Expression Language 687
Standard Actions 689
Adding Java Code to JSPs 690
The Declaration Tag 690
The Expression Tag 691
The Scriptlet Tag 692

E Debugging Tomcat and Running the Examples 693
Debugging Web Applications and Tomcat 693
When I Start Tomcat, It Disappears After a Few Seconds 693
When I Try to Start Tomcat, It States That Port Number 8080 Is in Use 695
Tomcat Is Running, But I Cannot Get a Web Application to Work 695
General Debugging Tips 698

F The Java Community Process 701
Why Do We Need the Java Community Process? 702
Who Is Involved? 702
The Public 702
Community Members 702
Expert Group Members 702
Executive Committee Members 703
How Does a New JSR Evolve? 703
A Case Study—The JSP 2.0 Specification 704

G J2EE Application Servers 705

What to Look for in a Server 705

Integration 706

Money, Money, Money! 706

Standards Support 707

Extra Functionality 708

Integration with Development Environments 709

Scalability 710

Failover 711

H Configuring Tomcat 713

The Configuration File `server.xml` 713

Configuring Individual Applications 714

Configuring the Container 717

The Tomcat Servlets 721

I Installing MySQL and WebLogic Server 727

MySQL 727

Windows Installation and Setup 727

Linux Installation and Setup 728

Creating a Database 728

Running the Provided SQL Scripts 729

Setting Up the JDBC Driver 730

MySQL Issues 730

BEA WebLogic 730

Windows Installation and Setup 731

Linux Installation and Setup 731

J Glossary 733

Index

About the Authors

The authors of this book work for Content Master Ltd., a technical authoring company in the United Kingdom specializing in the production of training and educational materials. For more information on Content Master, please see its Web site at `www.contentmaster.com`.

Nick Todd B.Sc. PGCE has been with Content Master since 2000 and has been working in technical education since 1997. Prior to that, he was a Web designer, the lead developer on a Web site for a British university, and he also worked on a Web site for British Telecom. Nick has wide experience in providing training and consulting in Java, XML, and Internet technology to companies such as Sun Microsystems, Art Technology Group, Stilo Technology, and the UK eScience Institute based at Edinburgh University. In conjunction with Content Master, Nick has also written courses on Java technology for the Sun Microsystems global curriculum and also courseware on Web-related technology for Microsoft. When Nick is not sitting in front of a computer or standing in front of a technical class, you will often find him working in the Christian church that he leads in Bristol, England.

Mark Szolkowski, M.Eng was born in Manchester, England in 1972, and has a Masters degree in Microelectronic Systems Engineering. During his four years at UMIST, he spent the summers learning the wonders of writing 16-bit Windows software in C using nothing more than M and a command-line compiler. After leaving university, Mark worked as a System Administrator at a software house, which allowed him to feed his programming habit. Since 2000, Mark has mostly worked as an independent technical trainer and author, specializing in Java and XML technologies. Mark has been working with Content Master since 2001.

Acknowledgments

From Nick Todd:

I would like to thank Paul Hunnisett for all his hard work in helping construct the various demonstration applications and some of the appendixes. I would also like to thank Martin Bond, from Content Master, and Michael Fasosin for very insightful critiques of a number of the chapters in this book.

Finally, many thanks to my wife, Sarah, and the children, Alex, Abigail, and Zach, who had to put up with me working on this for so long!

From Mark Szolkowski:

My thanks first of all must go to Martin Gudgin, who first taught me to think like a developer way back in the days of 16-bit Windows software and the M editor!

I couldn't have made it to the end of this book without the support of my family and friends who have put up with my mood swings for the last six months. So, Mum and Dad, Ruth, Paul Spittle, and Clive: *na zdorovye*!

From Beverly Mullock—Project Manager, Content Master:

Content Master is grateful to Sams Publishing for giving us the opportunity to write this book. Special thanks go to Todd Green, Andy Beaster, and the rest of the editing team at Sams. I would also like to thank the authors, Nick Todd and Mark Szolkowski, for all their hard work to meet deadlines and taking the stress out of my job.

We Want to Hear from You!

As the reader of this book, *you* are our most important critic and commentator. We value your opinion and want to know what we're doing right, what we could do better, what areas you'd like to see us publish in, and any other words of wisdom you're willing to pass our way.

As an Executive Editor for Sams, I welcome your comments. You can email or write me directly to let me know what you did or didn't like about this book--as well as what we can do to make our books better.

Please note that I cannot help you with technical problems related to the *topic* of this book. We do have a User Services group, however, where I will forward specific technical questions related to the book.

When you write, please be sure to include this book's title and author as well as your name, email address, and phone number. I will carefully review your comments and share them with the author and editors who worked on the book.

Email: `feedback@samspublishing.com`

Mail: Michael Stephens, Associate Publisher
Sams Publishing
201 West 103rd Street
Indianapolis, IN 46290 USA

For more information about this book or another Sams title, visit our Web site at `www.samspublishing.com`. Type the ISBN (excluding hyphens) or the title of a book in the Search field to find the page you're looking for.

Introduction

JSP IS AT THE HEART OF MANY of today's existing Web sites. The technology has matured over recent years and has proven itself as an excellent building block for scalable and reliable enterprise Web applications. Now with the JSP 2.0 and Servlet 2.4 releases, Java Web developers can take advantage of a number of new significant features that have been added to their armory. This book has been written with these new features in mind.

Not only does this book cover the basics of JSP, but it also covers the more recent features of the new specifications such as the finalized JSP Standard Tag Library and the JSP Expression Language.

Who Should Read This Book?

The authors have years of experience between them in successfully equipping others to use this technology. This book should be read by anyone who needs to learn JSP. It will also be very valuable to JSP developers who need to get up to speed on the new features of JSP 2.0. All along, the aim has been to make it as accessible as possible to any Java developer who wants to learn JSP. The book also provides a great deal of sample code that can be used in existing applications.

What Do You Need to Know Before You Read This Book?

The book assumes that you have some knowledge of the Java programming language, and that you have a working knowledge of basic HTML. We cover the rest!

How This Book Is Organized

The book is divided into four core sections:

Part I—Core JSP

The first part of the book introduces all the core aspects of JSP. This includes the architecture, where JSP fits in J2EE applications, JSP syntax, JavaBeans, tag libraries, development environments, and session tracking.

Part II—XML, Web Services, and Enterprise JSP

Then, we'll move into the area of XML in the context of Web applications. In this part, we'll discuss how XML can be processed from pages by using APIs such as DOM and SAX, and also how you can interact with XML using the XML-specific tags of the finalized standard tag library of JSP 2.0. Then, this section introduces Web services, with discussion on WSDL, UDDI, and SOAP, and how Web services can be deployed on the Java platform, and then interacted with from JSP. The latter half of the book introduces in detail how JSP can be used as part of a distributed application. There will be focus on database interaction, EJB 2.0 and how JSPs can interact with EJBs, the role of JNDI, and also how Web applications can be secured. There is also a chapter in this section on how Web applications can be personalized when built using Java technology. Finally, in this section there is a case study, which is a demonstration application that brings together many of the strands that are discussed in the entire book.

Part III—Appendixes

There is a concise set of appendixes at the end of this book that is there to assist you with debugging, installations, and basic syntax of JSPs, tag libraries, XML schemas, and XSLT. There is also a glossary in this section.

How to Use the Sample Code

To learn any technology you need to work with it and try things out. Therefore, almost every chapter has a sample application to go with it, and almost every bit of code that you will see in this book is available to you within a fully functional Web application. These applications are available from the Web site that goes with the book. This Web site can be found by visiting `www.samspublishing.com`, and entering the ISBN number in the search field (0672324385). This will take you to the book Web site, which contains instructions on how to obtain the various applications.

You will also need the following software installed on your machine to try these demonstrations:

- Tomcat 4.1 or higher. Although you can use other Web containers, this is the one on which all the demonstrations were tested. Installation instructions for Tomcat are provided in Chapter 1 and configuration instructions are found in Appendix H. Tomcat is available for download from `http://jakarta.apache.org/`. The installation folder of Tomcat is referred to throughout the book as `<tomcat-home>`.

> **Caution**
>
> When the book was written, the JavaServer Pages Tag Library was in version 1.0. Version 1.1 was in development. The example applications are all written and tested with 1.0. The examples in the text have the URI for version 1.1. See Chapter 5, "The JSP Standard Tag Library" for more information.

- MySQL Database. This is the database that has been used throughout the book because of its availability (freeware) and its widespread use in many real-world applications. Instructions for installing MySQL for Windows and Unix-based platforms can be found in Appendix I, "Installing MySQL and WebLogic Server."
- BEA WebLogic 7. BEA WebLogic 7 has been chosen where a J2EE-compliant application server is required because of its substantial popularity and its comprehensive support of the latest standards. Instructions for installing BEA WebLogic for Windows and Unix-based platforms can be found in Appendix I.

Conventions Used in This Book

Features in this book include the following:

Note

Notes give you comments and asides about the topic at hand, as well as full explanations of certain topics.

Tip

Tips provide great shortcuts and hints on how to program more effectively with JSP.

Caution

Cautions warn you against making your life miserable and help you avoid pitfalls.

In addition, you'll find the following typographic conventions throughout this book:

- Commands, variables, directories, and files appear in `Monospace` font.
- Commands that you type appear in **`Bold Monospace`** font.
- Placeholders in syntax descriptions appear in *`Italic Monospace`* type. This indicates that you should replace the placeholder with the actual filename, parameter, or other element that it represents.
- XML elements and tags from tag libraries are frequently referred to within < > brackets to denote that they are XML elements.

I

Core JSP

1 JSP, J2EE, and the Role of the Servlet

2 The Basic Syntax of JSP

3 Further JSP Syntax

4 Deploying JSP in a Web Container

5 The JSP Standard Tag Library

6 JSP and Java Beans

7 JSP Application Architecture

8 Session Tracking Using JSP

9 Developing Custom Tag Libraries

1

JSP, J2EE, and the Role of the Servlet

THIS FIRST CHAPTER WILL INTRODUCE YOU to the big picture surrounding JSP technology. JSP technology is part of a bigger technology often referred to as J2EE, and in this chapter, you will see where JSP fits into the panorama that is J2EE.

After you have seen where JSP fits into the J2EE puzzle, you will be introduced to the core technologies that underline JSP, namely servlets. You will see what servlets are, and why your understanding of them is critical if you are to become a proficient JSP developer.

The chapter will then finish with an introduction to the basic syntax of JSPs themselves. This chapter is foundational to the rest of the book.

The Progression of Java and Web Applications

Java first made its mark on the IT world in the mid-1990s about a year after the Internet started making an impression. At the time, I was working as a Web designer for a software agency and started learning Java so I could write Java applets to improve the pages I was creating.

> **Note**
> *Java applets* are Java programs that run in Web pages using a Java virtual machine (JVM) within the browser.

Java's primary use back then was to make Web pages more interesting with the use of Java applets. Typical uses included image manipulation applets, scrolling text, and (for those of us who love tennis) the applet that gives us the Wimbledon scores.

Applets ran on the client machine and had no reliance on the server. If you wanted server-side processing, you used Common Gateway Interface (CGI) programs, which were often written in the Perl programming language. You could write CGI programs in

Java, but, frankly, it wasn't worth the trouble because a wrapper also had to be written to invoke the JVM that would then invoke your CGI program.

CGI had performance issues associated with it, however. Every request that came in to the server invoked the CGI application as a separate process in its own address space; this process serviced the request and then shut down. Large numbers of users resulted in many instances of CGI programs running concurrently, which can adversely affect the performance of your CGI program. This is illustrated in the left part of Figure 1.1. There was then a development by a company called Open Market, which enabled each CGI program to service multiple clients. It does still require a separate address space for each CGI program however. They still could not all operate within one running application.

Netscape, Apache, and Microsoft all published APIs that enable you to write server-side Web applications. For Microsoft and Netscape, these APIs are ISAPI and NSAPI, respectively. The Apache API is referred to as the Apache Web Server API. These APIs enable the developer to write much more efficient code. These server-side applications are multithreaded—meaning that the application could be permanently running, servicing multiple requests without needing multiple instances of the application running. Figure 1.1 contrasts CGI with the NSAPI/ISAPI model. However, the main drawback of these APIs is that they are tied into one specific server product.

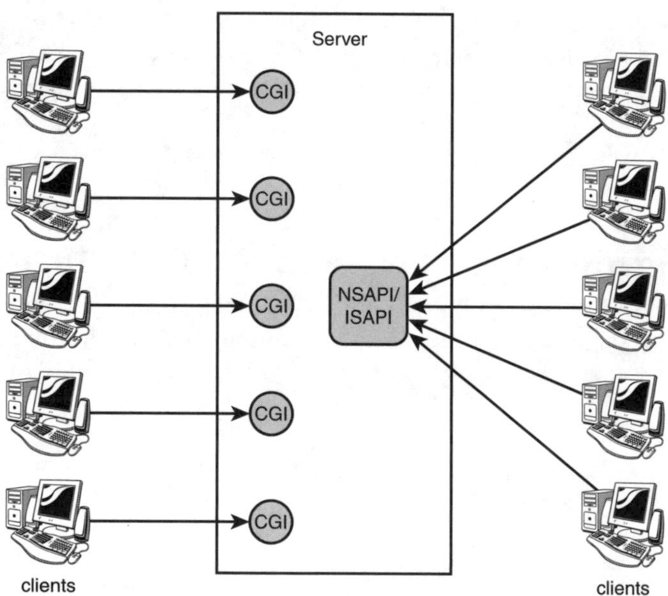

Figure 1.1 Contrast between single-threaded CGI and multi-threaded ISAPI/NSAPI.

Java programmers did however want to harness the platform independence of the Java programming language on the server, just as they had on the client with Java applets.

Many platforms are used to host Web sites. To see the spread of different Web servers currently in use visit `http://serverwatch.internet.com/netcraft/ncindex.html`.

The idea that you would be able to write server-side applications that could run on any server is very appealing.

Eventually, a mechanism was developed whereby Java could be used to write server-side programs without using CGI. The servlet was born!

The Java servlet is a server-side Java program that can be used to process a request and send a response. The Java servlet is multithreaded, and many servlets can be running within one JVM, processing many requests at any one time. The top half of Figure 1.2 demonstrates the basic servlet model.

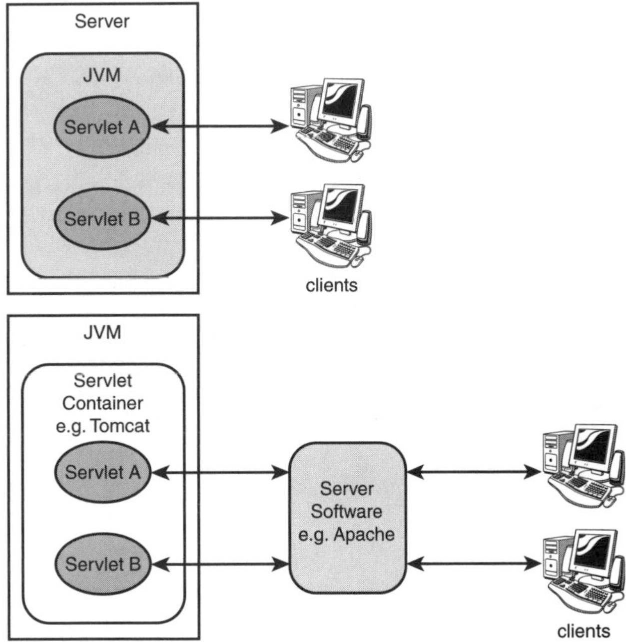

Figure 1.2 The servlet processing model.

Although the top half of Figure 1.2 demonstrates how multiple servlets can run within a JVM, and then how they can each service multiple clients, it is somewhat simplistic. Do the servlets run within the Web server, or is the Web server separate? Most Web server software cannot run servlets without an additional plug-in of some kind. As a result, various vendors came up with servlet containers that could be plugged into your existing Web server. For example, the Jakarta project came up with Tomcat for the Apache Web server, whereas Allaire came up with JRun for IIS.

Things have progressed a great deal since servlets were first developed. There were a number of significant initiatives going on at Sun, however, other than the servlet API. A new Java platform was emerging. When Java 2 was launched, it came out in three flavors: the micro edition for embedded devices, the standard edition for regular desktop type applications, and the enterprise edition for enterprise applications. The servlet API is in fact a part of the enterprise edition of Java 2 (or the J2EE as it is sometimes referred to).

The Java 2 Enterprise Edition

The J2EE platform is one of the most successful enterprise platforms available. It is worth stating that everything from the Java 2 Standard Edition (J2SE): GUI APIs such as Swing, standard language APIs such as the classes of the `java.lang` and `java.io` packages, and so forth are also available in J2EE.

J2EE builds on the standard edition with a significant number of other packages that are used specifically within distributed enterprise applications.

The J2EE Standards

J2EE is essentially a collection of APIs that can be used to build enterprise applications. Table 1.1 lists the APIs that are part of J2EE 1.4, and what they are for. It does not include the APIs that are also in the standard edition.

Table 1.1 **The Core APIs of J2EE 1.4**

API	Description
Servlets 2.4/JSP 2.0	APIs to enable the development of presentation logic within a Web application.
Enterprise JavaBeans (EJB) 2.1	APIs to define components that can exist within an EJB container. These components can be involved with data access, business logic, and messaging. Much of the enterprise functionality, such as transaction management, is handled by the container. New in EJB 2.1 over EJB 2.0, the ability to act as web service end points has been included, as has a new timer service.
Java Messaging Service (JMS) 1.0	An API for a messaging framework that can either interact with a non-Java–based messaging system, or be implemented in a 100% Pure Java environment.
Java Transaction API (JTA) 1.0	An API defining how transactions can be managed in an enterprise application.
Java Authentication and Authorization Service (JAAS) 1.0	Provides both declarative and programmatic security for Java applications.

Table 1.1 **Continued**

API	Description
Java Naming and Directory Interface (JNDI)	Provides a generic API for locating and naming resources within an enterprise application.
Java Mail 1.2	An API to enable the developer to send and receive email.
Java Database Connectivity (JDBC) 2.0 Extensions	The API for database access.
Remote Method Invocation over IIOP (RMI) and Java IDL	APIs to enable remote Java objects to interact across Java Virtual Machines, and also to interact with objects written in other programming languages.
Java API for XML Processing (JAXP) 1.1	Java APIs for the SAX, DOM, and XSLT processing of XML.
Java Activation Framework (JAF) 1.0	An API to support the conversion of MIME types into the Java platform.
Connector 1.5	An API to enable the connection of a J2EE application server to an enterprise information system (EIS)
Java API for XML Based RPC 1.0	New in J2EE 1.4, this API allows for the invocation of remote procedures using Simple Object Access Protocol (SOAP) and Web Service Description Language (WSDL) technology.
Java API for XML Registries 1.0	This API, also known as JAXR, is new to J2EE 1.4. It provides the ability to access registries based upon XML technology. These would often be Universal Description Discovery and Integration (UDDI) registries, and these registries are used for providing information on web service providers.
SOAP with attachments API (SAAJ)1.0	The API, typically used in conjunction with web services, to create and process SOAP messages. This API is also new in J2EE 1.4.

Each of these technologies is a standard in its own right and is developing and evolving; so for example, this book is being written about JSP 2.0 and Servlet 2.4. Within J2EE1.3, JSP is at level 1.2, and Servlets are at level 2.3, but in J2EE 1.4, there is support for JSP 2.0 and Servlet 2.4.

The big change though in J2EE 1.4 is the introduction of the APIs relating to web services. These are JAXR, SAAJ, Java API for Web Services, and JAX-RPC. These are new APIs that were not in J2EE 1.3. You shall learn more about web services in Chapter 12, "Invoking Web Services from JSP."

It is a challenge to keep up with all the different aspects of J2EE at the same time, but you can see what is happening with the different standards by visiting the Java Community Process Web site. These standards are developed by developers, and you can take part by going to `http://jcp.org`.

The Java Community Process is described in more detail in Appendix F, "The Java Community Process."

Let's look at what these APIs offer developers, and how they can be integrated together.

The J2EE Platform

Many of the APIs listed in Table 1.1 are little more than a number of Java interfaces. On their own, they don't do anything. However, vendors can implement these interfaces, and then release the implementation as a product. So, taking the Java Messaging Service (JMS) as an example, various implementations are available, all differentiating themselves on various aspects of specialization. FioranoMQ from Fiorano provides a C++ runtime library to access non-JMS messaging services, whereas MQSeries from IBM, has APIs to aid in the access of mainframe computers.

Some vendors implement the entire J2EE application framework. These applications are frequently referred to as J2EE *application servers*. These vendors again differentiate themselves with performance, ease of integration, personalization, and so on. These vendors have to ensure that their products do indeed fully adhere to the J2EE standards, and the products are tested using the J2EE Compatibility Test Suite from Sun. A list of implementations that fully support the J2EE standard is maintained on the Sun Web site at `http://java.sun.com/j2ee/compatibility.html`.

This open market approach has a number of benefits to the consumer. It results in healthy competition between the application server vendors because J2EE applications can be ported between application servers. Therefore, to maintain customers the server products must remain competitive.

> **Caution**
>
> Although it is possible to port applications from one application server to another, in practice it is not always that straightforward, especially when EJBs are involved.

This results in limited vendor lock-in, and vendors constantly improving their products. Vendors also put a significant amount of *value add* into their products. For example, the ATG Dynamo application server has a page format very much like JSP, called JHTML, to free the site developers from writing servlets. This was around before JSP had matured to where it is now. This JHTML innovation from ATG evolved and much of its technology became a part of the JSP—standard, the subject of this book!

As you can see, because of the constant development of the implementations, the J2EE platform is not something you simply go out and buy from Sun Microsystems (although they do provide the SunONE application server!).

> **Note**
> Sun Microsystems manages the J2EE standard, which is adopted by many vendors within their products. Sun also has a J2EE-compliant product called SunONE Application Server, which is part of its Sun ONE range. From what I have seen though, Sun has not attempted to use its strong influence on the standards to promote its products at the detriment of other vendors.

Let's examine what a J2EE application looks like.

J2EE Applications

A J2EE application can take many forms, but the classic J2EE application has a number of common components. The example used here will be for a Web-based application, but it is worth pointing out that J2EE applications do not have to involve the Internet.

J2EE applications consist of several layers or tiers. There can be any number of tiers, but Figure 1.3 shows the three main ones, and highlights the technologies involved in each.

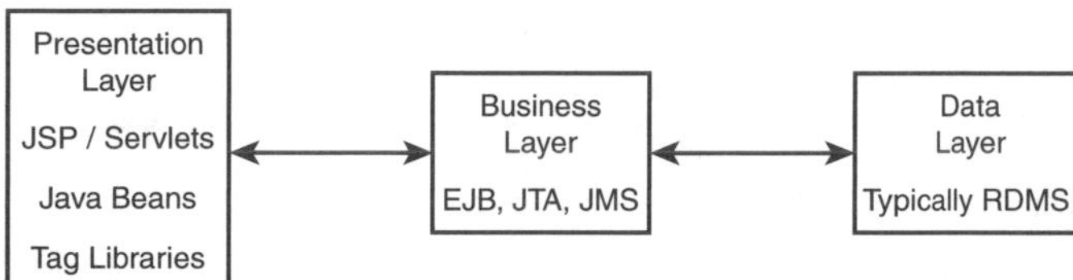

Figure 1.3 J2EE application layers.

One of the aims of the J2EE platform is to free the developer from much of the complexity of building disparate applications running over multiple tiers. Database access, for example, is required by nearly every enterprise application. To build database access into an application from scratch would require the developer to write code to both access the database and also manage any transactions that need to take place, and these may well be distributed transactions across multiple data sources. Although it is possible for the developer to do this, it is a fairly complex process required by all applications, so why not provide the functionality in the application server! In fact J2EE application servers provide a whole raft of services that the developer simply needs to use rather than build.

Both the presentation tier and the business logic tier live in what are referred to as *containers*. Containers enable the communication between the various tiers, and provide services to the components that exist within them. The presentation logic is within a *Web container*, and the business tier is within an *EJB container*.

All containers in a J2EE-compliant application server provide the following services based on the APIs listed in Table 1.1:

- *Java Messaging Services*—Messaging is vital to many disparate applications. A messaging service enables the application to send messages to other applications, even when they are offline. The messaging can also be asynchronous, meaning that the application thread does not have to wait for a response before continuing with its processing.
- *Transactions*—Transaction management can be very complex, especially when transactions span servers, and data sources. The transaction service provided within an application server can manage this process for you. You as a developer can determine when transactions start and end, and how transactions relate to other transactions, but the application server does the rest.
- *Java Naming and Directory Interface (JNDI)*—Within a system where components and services can be spread across multiple tiers, there needs to be a unified central place for these components and services to register themselves. This is what JNDI is, and it enables all the various parts of the application to find each other in a simple and consistent way.
- *Security*—All containers provide a security service to enable you to identify clients, and then limit access either programmatically or declaratively.

The differentiation between EJB containers and Web containers is as follows.

The EJB Container

The EJB container will not only provide the services just listed, but will also manage EJBs deployed within it. These EJBs have three discrete functions:

- *Entity Beans for Data Access*—To interact with databases, Entity Enterprise JavaBeans can be built that, when placed within the container, will enable the container to do all the database access for you, and manage the transactions associated with it. This means that your applications, although accessing databases, will not contain any JDBC code written by you. The access of the database is done by the container. You can also write entity Beans that contain all of the database interaction logic and transaction management yourself, but that is much harder work!
- *Session Beans for Business Logic*—Business logic components need to be managed somehow within an application. Imagine a straightforward component for accessing your bank account and returning your balance. In a traditional application, maybe you create one of these components when it is required, use it, and then garbage collect it. Then, the next client needs to create another one, and so on. You could alternatively have a whole raft of components that do this, but they might be expensive and take up precious resources. The container can manage the lifecycle of these business logic components for you. These business logic components take the form of Session EJBs. Session beans can also be allocated to specific clients where necessary. Session beans can also act as the endpoints for web services.

- *Message-Driven Beans for Asynchronous Messaging*—Until EJB 1.1 there were only session and entity EJBs. However, there was no easy way to get asynchronous messages to your EJBs, so in EJB 2.0, a new type of EJB was developed, the message-driven bean. These beans listen for messages from a messaging system that will come into the bean via the EJB container.

The developer can therefore build and deploy Enterprise JavaBeans within this container, taking full advantage of these provided services. Figure 1.4 shows the EJB container and its associated services.

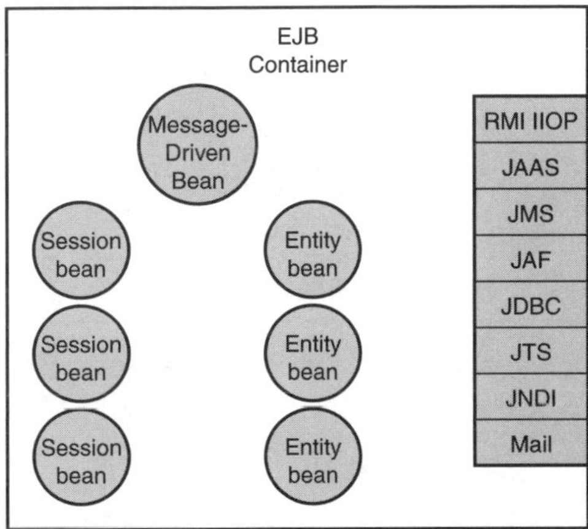

Figure 1.4 The EJB container.

Web Container

The Web container, where the JSPs are hosted, is where this book is largely focused. The Web container does not contain or run EJBs, but does need to include the client APIs for these services. It also hosts the presentation logic of a J2EE Web-based application and provides access to all the services already discussed. Presentation logic is built up using the following core technologies:

- *Servlets*—Discussed in more detail later, are Java programs that take in requests from clients, typically browsers, and send out responses.
- *JSPs*—Typically, HTML pages with dynamic content built in using Java code, JavaBeans, and tag libraries. Ultimately compiled to servlets, they take in requests from clients and send back appropriate responses.
- *JavaBeans*—JavaBeans can be used to contain the business logic for Web applications. They can be used instead of or in conjunction with EJBs running in an EJB container.

- *Tag Libraries*—These are HTML-like tags that can be placed into the JSPs to invoke Java functionality from the page without using Java code directly in the page, thus enabling the separation of Java and HTML code.

Figure 1.5 shows the Web container.

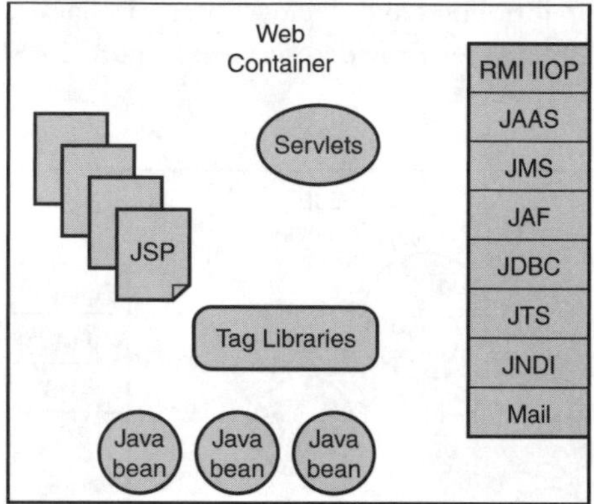

Figure 1.5 The Web container.

Applications that are built to run in Web containers are sometimes referred to as *Web applications*.

J2EE Deployment

How are application servers, already bristling with so much functionality, harnessed? How, for example, is an EJB deployed in an EJB container? How does a JSP, deployed in a Web container, locate a tag from a tag library also in the Web container? A significant part of the process of getting a J2EE application off the ground is the deployment process. J2EE applications need to be planned, then built, and then *deployed*. The deployment process involves creating a number of XML files called *deployment descriptors*.

So, for an EJB container, the EJB deployment descriptor is `ejb-jar.xml`. The classes can then be collated along with the deployment descriptor in a JAR file with the extension `.jar`. For a Web application, the deployment descriptor is `web.xml`, and the JSPs, servlets, tag libraries, and beans can be collated into a JAR file with the extension `.war` (Web application archive). To deploy a complete J2EE application, EJBs and Web applications can be deployed together. They have yet another deployment descriptor called `application.xml`, and they can be compressed into a JAR file with the extension `.ear` (enterprise application archive). Some application servers also need an additional deployment descriptor for their own specific deployment information. Figure 1.6 shows the various deployment descriptors involved in the different parts of a J2EE application.

The collation process is not mandatory, but there is a specific folder structure that all the various files must be put into. The deployment process will be discussed in more detail in Chapter 15, "JSP and EJB Interaction."

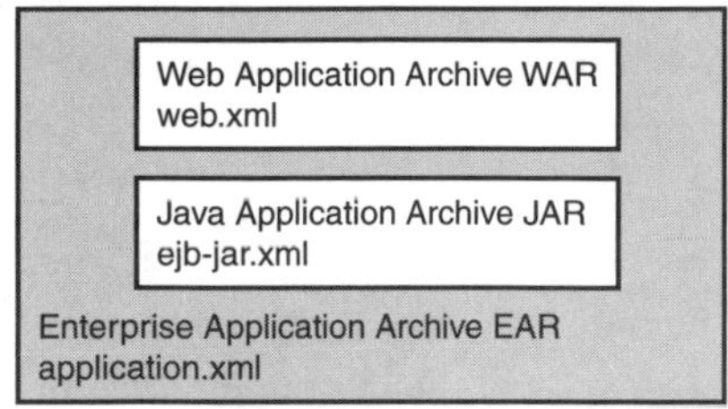

Figure 1.6 Deployment of J2EE applications.

Attention will now turn to the aspects of J2EE that are most important to JSP developers.

A Web application is made up of various parts as you have seen, but at the core of any Web application are Java servlets.

Java Servlets

Understanding how servlets work is vital if you are to understand JavaServer Pages. Although you could learn how to write basic JSPs without knowing about servlets, JSP makes much more sense when you have a clear grasp of Java servlets.

> **Caution**
>
> If you have very little understanding of Java Servlets, I encourage you to pay special attention to this section. In my experience as a JSP instructor, developers who understand servlets make much better JSP developers than those who do not.

Within the servlet API, there are a number of basic classes and interfaces. The main classes and interfaces we are interested in are in the following two packages:

```
javax.servlet
javax.servlet.http
```

The `javax.servlet` package is for writing generic servlets. These are servlets that are not specific to Web applications. Although not done a great deal, servlets can be written for other request/response paradigms in addition to Web applications. The `javax.servlet.http` package, on the other hand, contains the classes and interfaces specific to Web-based applications.

So, what does a servlet actually look like? All servlets must implement an interface called `javax.servlet.Servlet`. When writing Web-based servlets, you will typically extend a class that already implements this interface. This class is `javax.servlet.http.HttpServlet`.

> **Note**
> Some server products will encourage you to subclass a different superclass. This is typically because they have added additional functionality to an `HttpServlet` subclass. This would have an impact on portability.

The Servlet Lifecycle

Listing 1.1 is a basic servlet example that shows the lifecycle of a servlet when it is within a Web container. The methods that you can see in this servlet are overridden methods from the `HttpServlet` superclass.

Listing 1.1 `ServletLifeCycleMethods.java`

```
import javax.servlet.http.*;
import javax.servlet.*;
import java.io.IOException;

public class ServletLifeCycleMethods extends HttpServlet
{
  public void init(ServletConfig config) {
    super.init(config) ;
    // this method is invoked to initialize the servlet
    // when instantiated by the web container
    // the config parameter is there to encapsulate
    // any parameters that may need to be
    // passed to the servlet when it is constructed
    // you must invoke the superclass method when overriding this method
  }

  public void service(HttpServletRequest request, HttpServletResponse res) {
     // this method is invoked when requests come in
     // it then forwards requests based upon their type to other methods
     // such as doGet or doPost. You are not supposed to override this method
  }

  public void doGet (HttpServletRequest req, HttpServletResponse res) {
    // this method is invoked by the service() method when GET requests
    // are received
  }

  public void doPost (HttpServletRequest req, HttpServletResponse res) {
      // this method is invoked by the service() method when POST requests
```

Listing 1.1 **Continued**

```
        // are received
    }

    public void destroy() {
          // this method is invoked when the servlet is destroyed by the container
    }
}
```

The servlet lifecycle is as follows:

1. A client makes a request to a servlet.
2. Server instantiates servlet class, if not already running, using the constructor followed by the `init(ServletConfig config)` method of the servlet. The `ServletConfig` object encapsulates various parameters that can be passed to the servlet when it is created. This could be information about database connections, usernames and passwords, or whatever. This method does not need to be overridden if nothing specific needs to take place when the servlet is started. These parameters actually come from `web.xml`, which you will see later in the chapter.
3. The server then invokes the `service()` method of the servlet. This method is responsible for identifying what type of HTTP request has been received, and invoking the appropriate method. There are methods for all the different types of HTTP request, the most important methods being `doGet()` for `GET` requests and `doPost()` for `POST` requests. Note the two parameters that the `service()` method takes in—the `javax.servlet.http.HttpServletRequest` and also the `javax.servlet.http.HttpServletResponse`. These two objects encapsulate the request from the client and the response to the client. These parameters are forwarded to the appropriate method, such as `doGet()`.

> **Note**
>
> There are a number of different HTTP requests that can be made. As well as `GET` and `POST`, there are `PUT`, `TRACE`, `HEAD`, and `DELETE`. To find out more about these, visit the World Wide Web Consortium Web site at `http://www.w3c.org/Protocols`.

4. The `doGet()` or `doPost()` method will then process the request and decide what to do with the response. It may be to output some HTML, populate a database, or forward the request and response to another servlet or JSP for further processing.
5. After that first request has been processed, the servlet object is now running, and will be listening for further requests. It will not be instantiated by the container again for further requests unless it has been destroyed.

6. When the Web container is shut down, the server will call the `destroy()` method of the servlet and it will be removed. Some containers will also do this at other times, typically to conserve resources.

Figure 1.7 shows the process of dealing with a request to a servlet, and how the Web container responds.

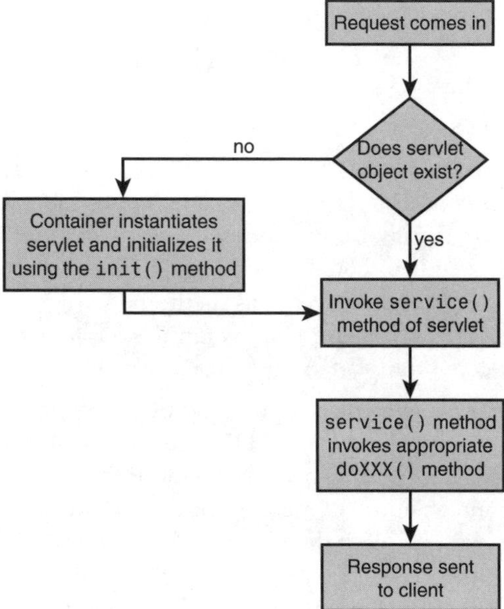

Figure 1.7 Web container process for handling a request to a servlet.

Multithreading

When multiple requests come to a servlet at once, new Java threads are created to service each client, each invoking the `service()` method. One common mistake servlet developers make is to use instance variables to hold data such as user information. Never do this because multiple users will share the same servlet instance!

> **Note**
>
> You can write Java servlets that are not multithreaded, and every client gets their own servlet instance. This is done by writing servlets that implement an interface called `javax.servlet.SingleThreadModel`. This is not encouraged, however, because it significantly affects performance.

The media loves to pick up on Web sites that result in users mysteriously viewing another user's data, such as credit-card numbers, and so on. If you write servlets with instance variables containing such data, your Web site could do the same thing!

So, what does a real servlet look like? Listing 1.2 shows a basic servlet that will output a response to a client.

Listing 1.2 `BasicServlet.java`

```
import javax.servlet.http.*;
import javax.servlet.*;
import java.io.IOException;

public class BasicServlet extends HttpServlet
{
  public void doGet (HttpServletRequest req, HttpServletResponse res)
                                  throws IOException
  {
    ServletOutputStream out = res.getOutputStream();
    res.setContentType("text/html");
    out.println("<html><head><title>Basic Servlet</title></head>");
    out.println("<body>Hello World</body></html>");
  }
}
```

`BasicServlet.java` has only one of the methods that can be seen in Listing 1.1. The other methods have not been overridden from `HttpServlet`. The method in this example is `doGet()`. The `doGet()` method is there to respond to `GET` requests from the browser.

When you enter a URL such as `http://www.myserver.com/BasicServlet` into your browser, it will issue a `GET` request to the server specified for the resource that you specified. In this case, the resource is our servlet in Listing 1.2. You should now understand what happens when this request comes in. First, the container sees if the servlet is instantiated. If not, the container invokes the constructor, calls `init()`, and then `service()`. Then, `service()` invokes a call to the `doGet()` method.

The reason that this URL invokes the servlet is not because the URL uses the classname. There is actually a mapping in the deployment descriptor, `web.xml`. You shall see this later.

If you examine the `doGet()` method now, you will notice the two parameters.

The `HttpServletRequest` and `HttpServletResponse`

These two parameters encapsulate both the request from the client and the response to the client.

The `HttpServletRequest` contains methods to access form data that is coming in from HTML forms. It also contains methods to access cookies, request headers, session information, and so on. The `HttpServletResponse` contains methods to access the `PrintWriter` used to write character data back to the client. It also contains methods to redirect the browser, as well as methods to modify the response headers and to add cookies to the response. Tables 1.2 and 1.3 list the key methods of the `HttpServletRequest` and `HttpServletResponse`, respectively.

Table 1.2 **Key Methods of the `HttpServletRequest`**

Method Name	Description
Cookie[] getCookies()	Returns an array of all the cookies that were sent with this request.
String getHeader(String name)	Returns the value of the specified header as a String.
java.util.Enumeration getHeaders()	Returns all the headers as an enumeration of Strings.
HttpSession getSession()	Returns the users' session if they are part of a session.
String getParameter(String name)	Returns parameters from the request, typically HTML form field values.
String[] getParameterNames()	Returns the names of all the parameters within this request.
String getRemoteAddr()	Returns the IP address of the client machine.

Table 1.3 **Key Methods of the `HttpServletResponse`**

Method Name	Description
void addCookie(Cookie cookie)	Adds a cookie into the header of the response.
void addHeader(String name, String value)	Adds the specified header into the response.
String encodeURL(String url)	Encodes a URL to contain the session ID.
void sendRedirect(String location)	Redirects the browser to the specified location.
void setStatus(int status)	Sets the status of the response. The various status codes are set up as constants within the class.
java.io.PrintWriter getWriter()	Returns the PrintWriter with which you can write character data to the client.
java.io.ServletOutputStream getOutStream()	Returns the ServletOutputStream so that you can write binary data to the client.
void setContentType(String mime)	Sets the content type of the output that will be coming from the servlet.

In Listing 1.2 you can see two methods of the `HttpServletResponse` object being used. One is to set the content type for the browser, and the other is to access the `PrintWriter`. The content type is set using a MIME type.

Note

MIME stands for Multipart Internet Mail Extensions. It is used by applications such as browsers to determine what to do with the content that is being sent to it. So, if you set the MIME type for your servlet to be text/html, you add an entry into the header so that the browser can act appropriately. The official list of MIME types can be found at `http://www.iana.org/assignments/media-types/index.html`.

`BasicServlet` sets the MIME type to text/html. The `PrintWriter` is then used to write output to the browser using `out.println()` statements.

Before this servlet can be run, a Web container will be required, and a mini Web application will need to be created.

Installing Jakarta Tomcat

Jakarta Tomcat is the Web container that we'll use throughout this book. This container has been selected because it is free, easily accessible, and implements all the latest standards. In fact, it is the reference implementation for the J2EE standards surrounding the Web container, that is, JavaServer Pages and servlets.

You will need to have a JVM installed, but you do not need a J2EE installation. A J2SE VM is all that is required. We strongly suggest that you use version 1.4 or higher; it will make the later parts of the book more straightforward for you. This is available from `http://java.sun.com/j2se/1.4/download.html`.

The instructions for installing this are available on the Sun Web site.

To download the latest version of Tomcat, visit the following URL: `http://jakarta.apache.org/site/binindex.html`.

This is the download page for the Jakarta project. From here, if you scroll down you will see the Release Builds section. This is where you can select the latest stable Tomcat. At the time of publication, this is Tomcat 5.

Caution

All the examples from the book have been tested using Tomcat 4 and a preview release of Tomcat 5 was also used. It is suggested that you use Tomcat 5 for all of the examples shown in the book. For the brave amongst you, feel free to use a later version. The applications will all continue to work, but it is possible that in some cases you may need to edit the Tomcat configuration files discussed in Appendix H, "Configuring Tomcat."

When you select the latest release of Tomcat, you get a page that looks something like Figure 1.8. This page gives a whole raft of possible things to download, which can seem a bit daunting at first.

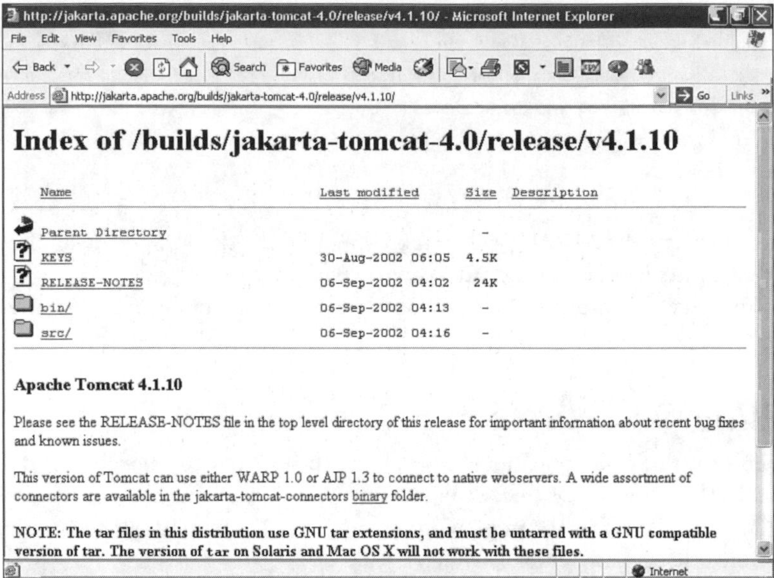

Figure 1.8 Jakarta Tomcat download page.

From the list of options, locate the `bin` folder link. This then takes you to a further page of options. From here, it will depend on your platform. If you are using a Windows platform, you can select an executable. If you are using a Unix-based platform, you will need to download a TAR or ZIP file.

After you have downloaded the appropriate file, on Unix you will need to extract the TAR file, and on Windows you can run the executable.

Starting and Stopping Tomcat

You can now locate the folder `<tomcat-home>\bin`. In there are a number of batch files and shell scripts.

> **Note**
>
> Within this section, and indeed throughout the book, you will see references to the following location `<tomcat-home>`. This refers to your Tomcat installation folder. This is equivalent to <catalina-home> referred to in the Tomcat documentation.

On a Windows platform you will need to launch `startUp.bat`. On Unix you launch the equivalent `startUp.sh`. This will open either a console or a command prompt window, which will have Tomcat running. Figure 1.9 shows the command prompt window that appears on a Windows platform.

```
Start Tomcat
09-Sep-2002 11:44:34 org.apache.commons.modeler.Registry loadRegistry
INFO: Loading registry information
09-Sep-2002 11:44:34 org.apache.commons.modeler.Registry getRegistry
INFO: Creating new Registry instance
09-Sep-2002 11:44:34 org.apache.commons.modeler.Registry getServer
INFO: Creating MBeanServer
09-Sep-2002 11:44:35 org.apache.coyote.http11.Http11Protocol init
INFO: Initializing Coyote HTTP/1.1 on port 8080
09-Sep-2002 11:44:35 org.apache.jk.server.JkMain init
INFO: Starting Jk2, base dir= C:\Java\Tomcat 4.1 conf=C:\Java\Tomcat 4.1\conf\jk
2.properties
09-Sep-2002 11:44:35 org.apache.jk.server.JkMain start
INFO: APR not loaded, disabling jni components: java.io.IOException: no jkjni in
 java.library.path
09-Sep-2002 11:44:35 org.apache.jk.common.ChannelSocket init
INFO: JK: listening on tcp port 8019
09-Sep-2002 11:44:35 org.apache.jk.common.ChannelUn init
INFO: No file, disabling unix channel
09-Sep-2002 11:44:35 org.apache.jk.server.JkMain start
INFO: Jk running ID=0 ... init time=80 ms
Starting service Tomcat-Standalone
Apache Tomcat/4.1.8-LE-jdk14
09-Sep-2002 11:44:44 org.apache.coyote.http11.Http11Protocol start
INFO: Starting Coyote HTTP/1.1 on port 8080
```

Figure 1.9 Running Jakarta Tomcat.

> **Note**
>
> If you have installed Tomcat on a Windows platform, you can also launch it from the Windows menu. It should be under `Programs\Apache Tomcat x.x\Start Tomcat`.

If your console or command prompt appear and then quickly disappear, something is wrong. Appendix E, "Debugging Tomcat and Running the Examples," contains a section on debugging Tomcat.

To test that your Tomcat installation has worked, you should now be able to visit the home page of your Tomcat installation. You do not need to install a separate Web server because Tomcat can act as a basic Web server.

If you now launch a browser with the following URL, you should see the Tomcat home page come up:

```
http://localhost:8080
```

Depending upon your version, the page will look something like Figure 1.10.

Figure 1.10 The Jakarta Tomcat home page.

Creating Your First Web Application

Locate the folder called `<tomcat-home>\webapps`, and create a new folder within it called `chapter01`. You should now have the following folder structure on your machine:

```
<tomcat-home>\webapps\chapter01
```

The `webapps` folder within Tomcat is where all the Web applications reside. Each folder represents an individual Web application. You have just created a new folder to hold your Web application.

Note

If you would rather not create all the various examples shown in this chapter, you can download the appropriate `war` file from the book Web site. In this case, it is called `chapter01.war`. This can then be placed in the `webapps` folder in Tomcat, or extracted using a tool such as `WinZip` into the `chapter01` folder you have just created. The war file can be found by visiting `www.samspublishing.com`, and entering the book ISBN number (0672324385) in the search box.

If you look again at Figure 1.4, you can see the various deployment descriptors mentioned for each of the different parts of J2EE applications. You are creating a Web application; therefore, you will need to create a file called `web.xml`.

Create a new folder within the `chapter01` folder called `WEB-INF`, all uppercase. Then, within this folder, create a new file called `web.xml`.

An example `web.xml` for the `BasicServlet` class, can be seen in Listing 1.3:

Listing 1.3 `web.xml`

```
<?xml version="1.0" encoding="ISO-8859-1"?>
<web-app xmlns="http://java.sun.com/xml/ns/j2ee"
   xmlns:xsi="http://www.w3.org/2001/XMLSchema-instance"
   xsi:schemaLocation="http://java.sun.com/xml/ns/j2ee
   http://java.sun.com/xml/ns/j2ee/web-app_2_4.xsd" version="2.4">
  <servlet>
    <servlet-name>BasicServlet</servlet-name>
    <servlet-class>BasicServlet</servlet-class>
  </servlet>
  <servlet-mapping>
    <servlet-name>BasicServlet</servlet-name>
    <url-pattern>/myServlet</url-pattern>
  </servlet-mapping>
</web-app>
```

The root element of the `web.xml` deployment descriptor is always `web-app`. Note that it contains a reference to an XML Schema which defines the elements and attributes used within the XML document. To deploy a servlet, there are two child elements that need to be specified. The `<servlet>` element defines the name you want to give your servlet with its associated class. The `<servlet-mapping>` element defines the URL that will be used to invoke the servlet.

> **Note**
> An XML Schema defines the structure of an XML document. The structure of `web.xml` has to adhere to a specific XML Schema and, therefore, must follow a set structure. If you want a quick introduction to XML Schema, one is provided in Appendix B, "An Overview of XML Schema."

The name of your servlet is set to be the same as the class name in Listing 1.3. The URL for the servlet named `BasicServlet` is then set to be `/myServlet`.

The last thing you will need to do to complete the Web application is to put the compiled servlet class into the folder structure. There is a specific place within a Web application where you are meant to place class files. Within the `WEB-INF` folder, you should create a new folder called `classes`, and place `BasicServlet.class` in there. Your completed Web application should now have the following form:

```
<tomcat-home>\webapps\chapter01\WEB-INF\web.xml
<tomcat-home>\webapps\chapter01\WEB-INF\classes\BasicServlet.class
```

If you start your Tomcat and browse to the following URL, you should see an output like Figure 1.11:

```
http://localhost:8080/chapter01/myServlet
```

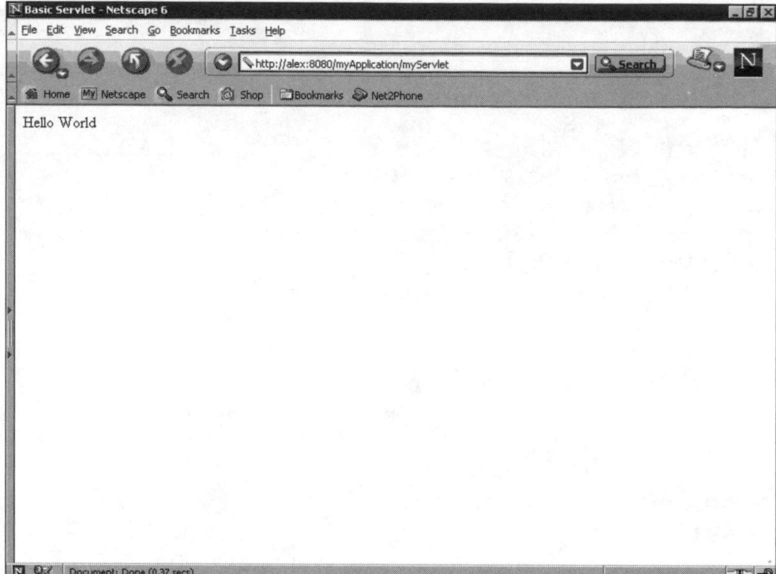

Figure 1.11 Output from `BasicServlet`.

Note

If you are having problems, you can turn to Appendix E, "Debugging Tomcat and Running the Examples."

Processing Form Data

You'll now see how to access HTML form data using a Java servlet. If you recall from Table 1.1, there are a number of methods in the `HttpServletRequest` object that are specifically relevant to accessing HTML form data.

Listing 1.4 is a basic HTML form.

Listing 1.4 **A Basic HTML Form**

```
<html>
<head>
<title> A Basic HTML Form</title>
</head>
<body>
<h1>Please enter your information</h1>
<form method="POST" action="formProcessor">
  Title: <select size="1" name="title">
  <option>Mr</option>
  <option>Mrs</option>
  <option>Miss</option>
```

Listing 1.4 **Continued**

```
  <option>Ms</option>
  <option>Other</option>
  </select><br>
  Name: <input type="text" name="name" size="20"><br>
  City: <input type="text" name="city" size="20"><br>
  Country: <input type="text" name="country" size="20"><br>
  Telephone: <input type="text" name="tel" size="20">
  <p>Please inform us of your interests:<br>
  <input type="checkbox" name="interests" value="Sport">Sport<br>
  <input type="checkbox" name="interests" value="Music">Music<br>
  <input type="checkbox" name="interests" value="Reading">Reading<br>
  <input type="checkbox" name="interests" value="TV and Film">TV and Film</p>
  <p>Your age
  <input type="radio" name="age" value="25orless" checked>Less than 25
  <input type="radio" name="age" value="26to40">26-40
  <input type="radio" name="age" value="41to65">41-65
  <input type="radio" name="age" value="over65">Over 65</p>
  <p><input type="submit" value="Submit"></p>
</form>
</body>
</html>
```

The HTML for the form uses different kinds of input field and looks similar to Figure 1.12 when displayed in a Web browser.

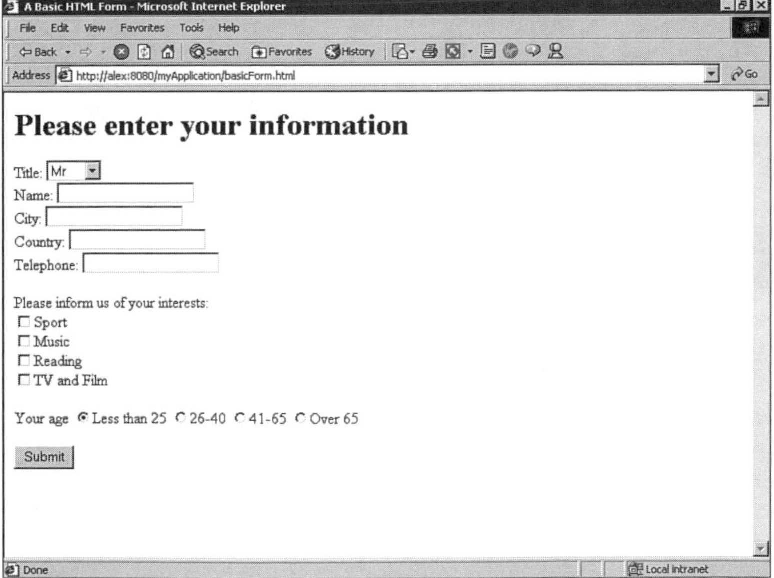

Figure 1.12 A basic HTML form.

To extract the data from this form and present it within a dynamically generated Web page, the servlet in Listing 1.5 could be used.

Listing 1.5 `BasicFormProcessor.java`

```
import javax.servlet.http.*;
import javax.servlet.*;
import java.io.IOException;

public class BasicFormProcessor extends HttpServlet
{
  public void doPost (HttpServletRequest req, HttpServletResponse res)
                                   throws IOException
  {
    ServletOutputStream out = res.getOutputStream();
    res.setContentType("text/html");
    out.println("<html><head><title>Basic Form Processor Output);
    out.println("</title></head>");
    out.println("<body>");
    out.println("<h1>Here is your Form Data</h1>");
    //extract the form data here
    String title = req.getParameter("title");
    String name = req.getParameter("name");
    String city = req.getParameter("city");
    String country = req.getParameter("country");
    String tel = req.getParameter("tel");
    String age = req.getParameter("age");
    // extracting data from the checkbox field
    String[] interests = req.getParameterValues("interests");
    //output the data into a web page
    out.println("Your title is "  + title);
    out.println("<br>Your name is "  + name);
    out.println("<br>Your city is "  + city);
    out.println("<br>Your country is "  + country);
    out.println("<br>Your tel is "  + tel);
    out.println("<br>Your interests include<ul> ");
    for (int i=0;i<interests.length; i++) {
              out.println("<li>" + interests[i]);
       }
       out.println("</ul>");
       out.println("<br>Your age is "  + age);
    out.println("</body></html>");
  }
}
```

The servlet in Listing 1.5 will process the data from the HTML form and write it out to a new Web page. Note the following features of this servlet:

- It overrides `doPost()` instead of `doGet()`. That is because the form data is being submitted using the HTTP `POST` method. Look at the `<form>` tag of the HTML Listing 1.4.

Note

Using `POST` avoids two key limitations that the `GET` method has. The `GET` method only supports a limited number of characters being submitted via a form, and the `GET` method does not allow for the encryption of form data as the data is appended to the URL. A benefit of `GET` on the other hand is that `GET` request URLs can be bookmarked in browsers.

- The `getParameter(String name)` method of the `HttpServletRequest` object is being used to extract the various form field values.
- For the check box data, a different method is used, called `getParameterValues(String name)`. This method is used because there can be multiple values submitted for the user interests. These can be extracted using the `getParameterValues(String name)` method. The method returns the values as an array of `Strings`.
- To output the data, the `PrintWriter` is used from the response object. All the HTML formatting is mixed in with the form processing logic.

The output from the servlet, in response to a completed form, would be as shown in Figure 1.13.

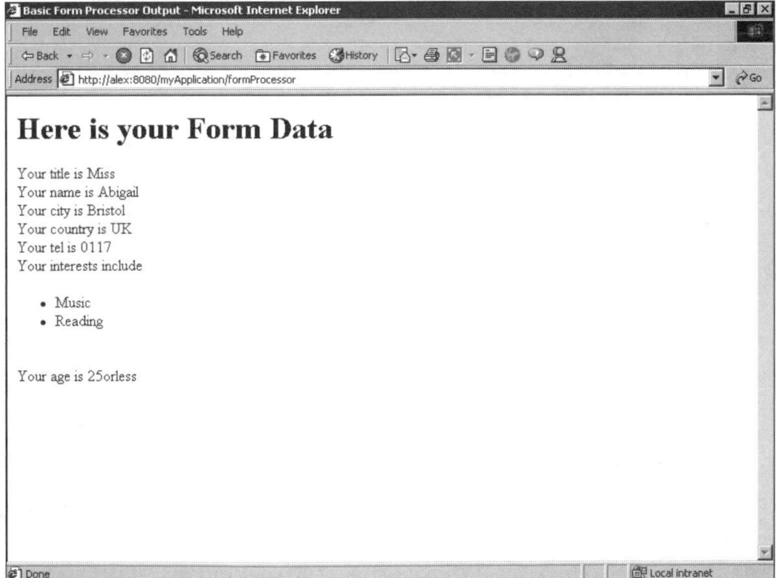

Figure 1.13 Output from `BasicFormProcessor` servlet.

The servlet would also need to be defined within the web.xml deployment descriptor. A modified version is shown in Listing 1.6.

Listing 1.6 `web.xml` **Defining the** `BasicFormProcessor` **Servlet**

```
<?xml version="1.0" encoding="ISO-8859-1"?>
<web-app xmlns="http://java.sun.com/xml/ns/j2ee"
   xmlns:xsi="http://www.w3.org/2001/XMLSchema-instance"
   xsi:schemaLocation="http://java.sun.com/xml/ns/j2ee
   http://java.sun.com/xml/ns/j2ee/web-app_2_4.xsd" version="2.4">
  <servlet>
    <servlet-name>BasicServlet</servlet-name>
    <servlet-class>BasicServlet</servlet-class>
  </servlet>
  <servlet>
    <servlet-name>BasicFormProcessor</servlet-name>
    <servlet-class>BasicFormProcessor</servlet-class>
  </servlet>
  <servlet-mapping>
    <servlet-name>BasicServlet</servlet-name>
    <url-pattern>/myServlet</url-pattern>
  </servlet-mapping>
  <servlet-mapping>
    <servlet-name>BasicFormProcessor</servlet-name>
    <url-pattern>/formProcessor</url-pattern>
  </servlet-mapping>
</web-app>
```

Because this file must adhere to a specific XML Schema, the `<servlet>` elements are defined before the `<servlet-mapping>` elements.

> **Note**
>
> When writing and editing J2EE deployment descriptors, it is very useful to have an XML editing tool available. One such tool is XML Spy, which is available from `www.altova.com`. You can try it for 30 days if you download it from here. It has templates for the J2EE deployment descriptors, and it checks them to make sure that they are valid documents before you try to use them. Some application servers such as the reference implementation from Sun provide GUI based tools to assist with the creation of deployment descriptors.

Servlet Initialization

Earlier, you were introduced to the `init(ServletConfig config)` method that is used to initialize the servlet. In this section, attention will be given to this process, and how you can pass parameter values into your servlet. Those of you familiar with applet programming or even using Java applets on Web pages will have seen the parameters that can be passed to a Java applet using <param> tags in the HTML. With servlets, parameter values can also be passed from web.xml to servlets that can be used often at initialization.

The javax.servlet.ServletConfig object is key to this functionality. It contains the following two methods that enable you to access these parameters:

```
String getInitParameter(String name)
String[] getInitParameterNames()
```

Listing 1.7 shows a web.xml file that contains parameters that are being passed into a Java servlet. Listing 1.8 then shows a servlet that is accessing these parameter values.

Listing 1.7 web.xml **Setting Servlet Initialization Parameters**

```
<?xml version="1.0" encoding="ISO-8859-1"?>
<web-app xmlns="http://java.sun.com/xml/ns/j2ee"
   xmlns:xsi="http://www.w3.org/2001/XMLSchema-instance"
   xsi:schemaLocation="http://java.sun.com/xml/ns/j2ee
   http://java.sun.com/xml/ns/j2ee/web-app_2_4.xsd" version="2.4">  . . .
  <servlet-name>ParameterServlet</servlet-name>
    <servlet-class>ParameterServlet</servlet-class>
      <init-param>
        <param-name>name</param-name>
        <param-value>John Doe</param-value>
       </init-param>
       <init-param>
         <param-name>password</param-name>
         <param-value>password</param-value>
       </init-param>
  </servlet>
  <servlet-mapping>
    <servlet-name>ParameterServlet</servlet-name>
    <url-pattern>/parameterServlet</url-pattern>
  </servlet-mapping>
  . . .
</web-app>
```

Listing 1.8 ParameterServlet.java **—Extracting Initialization Parameters from** web.xml

```
import javax.servlet.http.*;
import javax.servlet.*;
import java.io.IOException;
```

Listing 1.8 **Continued**

```
public class ParameterServlet extends HttpServlet
{
  private String dbName="";
  private String dbPassword="";

  public void init(ServletConfig config) throws ServletException  {
         super.init(config);
         dbName = config.getInitParameter("name");
         dbPassword = config.getInitParameter("password");
  }

  public void doGet (HttpServletRequest req, HttpServletResponse res)
                                                throws IOException
  {
    ServletOutputStream out = res.getOutputStream();
    res.setContentType("text/html");
    out.println("<html><head><title>Basic Servlet</title></head>");
    out.println("<body>Database username is  <b>" + dbName);
    out.println("</b><br>Database password is  <b>" + dbPassword + "</b>");
    out.println("</body></html>");
  }
}
```

`ParameterServlet.java` accesses the parameters set in `web.xml` from within the initialization method. These are then presented on a Web page to the user. The two parameters shown are a `username` and `password`. These parameters could be used for a database connection, for example. Notice also that the call to `super.init(config)` is present. This must always be there as the first line in the `init` function.

Note

The `ServletConfig` can also be accessed from anywhere else in a servlet by using the method `ServletConfig getServletConfig()`, inherited from `GenericServlet`, the superclass of `HttpServlet`.

There are two other methods in the ServletConfig class:

```
String getServletName()
javax.servlet.ServletContext getServletContext()
```

The `getServletName()` method simply returns the name of the servlet as defined in `web.xml`. The `getServletContext()` method, however, deserves a fuller explanation.

The `ServletContext`

The `ServletContext` is a very useful object, because it provides for a handle for the developer into the container. This is very important because it provides access to the following:

- Application-wide initialization parameters and application scoped attributes
- Web container log files
- Information about the Web container
- Information about URLs and MIME types, and the capability to forward requests to other servlets or JSPs

The main methods are shown in Table 1.4.

Table 1.4 **Key Methods of the** `ServletContext`

Method Name	Description
String getInitParameter(String name)	Obtains the value of the named initialization parameter.
Object getAttribute(String name)	Obtains a reference to an application-scoped object.
void setAttribute(String name, Object value)	Sets an application-scoped attribute.
void log(String message) or void log(String message, Throwable throwable)	Adds an entry into servlet log file with an optional stack trace from the Throwable object.
String getMimeType(String file)	Returns the MIME type of a specified resource.
java.net.URL getResource(String path)	Returns a URL to a specified path.
java.io.InputStream getResourceAsStream (String path)	Returns a resource as an input stream based on a specified path.
String getRealPath(String relativePath)	Returns the absolute URL for a relative path passed in.
String getServerInfo()	Returns name and version of the Web container.
RequestDispatcher getRequestDispatcher()	Returns a RequestDispatcher used for forwarding requests.

Application-Wide Attributes and Parameters

You have already seen how parameters can be passed to individual servlets through `web.xml`. You can also pass in parameters that are visible to all servlets within a Web application. So for example, in Listing 1.7 the parameters obtained are only available to that servlet. They might be relevant to a number of servlets, in which case they can be set as application parameters in the `web.xml` file. Listing 1.9 shows a `web.xml` file that is now setting application-wide parameters that are accessible throughout the Web application via the `ServletContext` object.

Listing 1.9 `web.xml` **Setting Application-Wide Parameters**

```
<?xml version="1.0" encoding="ISO-8859-1"?>
<web-app xmlns="http://java.sun.com/xml/ns/j2ee"
   xmlns:xsi="http://www.w3.org/2001/XMLSchema-instance"
   xsi:schemaLocation="http://java.sun.com/xml/ns/j2ee
   http://java.sun.com/xml/ns/j2ee/web-app_2_4.xsd" version="2.4">
  <context-param>
    <param-name>name</param-name>
    <param-value>John Doe</param-value>
  </context-param>
  <context-param>
    <param-name>password</param-name>
    <param-value>password</param-value>
  </context-param>
  . . .
</web-app>
```

Listing 1.10 shows a modified version of the `init()` method from the servlet shown in Listing 1.8. Instead of accessing servlet-specific parameters, the `init()` method shown here is accessing the application-wide parameters via the `ServletContext`.

Listing 1.10 **Modified** `init()` **Method of** `ParameterServlet.java`

```
  public void init(ServletConfig config) throws ServletException  {
          super.init(config);
          ServletContext context = getServletContext();
          dbName = context.getInitParameter("name");
          dbPassword = context.getInitParameter("password");
  }
```

Application-scoped attributes are different from parameters. Within any Web application there will be objects that ideally should be shared between all the parts of the Web application. Database connections and objects containing data that is required by all the servlets, such as product information on a commerce site, would be good examples. References to these objects can be stored in the `ServletContext` so that they can be referenced from any other part of the Web application.

The following lines of code can be used to add a new object of type `ProductList` to the `ServletContext`:

```
ServletContext context = getServletContext();
ProductList list = new ProductList();
context.setAttribute("products", list);
```

Then, from some other servlet, the object could be accessed in the following way:

```
SerletContext context = getServletContext();
ProductList list = (ProductList) context.getAttribute("products");
```

You will see these attributes used throughout the rest of the book.

Logging with the `ServletContext`

Web applications are up and running for long periods of time, and it is vital to gather relevant and helpful information. Logging is a part of the servlet specifications, so all Web containers must implement some kind of logging functionality. Tomcat places log entries into log files located in the following location:

```
<tomcat-home>\logs
```

The log file that gets written to has the name:

```
<servername>_log<date>.txt
```

So, an example on my machine would be

```
localhost_log.2002-04-24.txt
```

Listing 1.11 demonstrates a servlet that writes to this log file.

Listing 1.11 `LoggerServlet.java`

```
import javax.servlet.http.*;
import javax.servlet.*;
import java.io.IOException;

public class LoggingServlet extends HttpServlet
{
  private ServletContext context;

  public void init(ServletConfig config) throws ServletException  {
         super.init(config);
         context = getServletContext();
         context.log("Init has been invoked");
  }

  public void doGet (HttpServletRequest req, HttpServletResponse res)
                                       throws IOException
  {
    ServletOutputStream out = res.getOutputStream();
    context.log("doGet has now been invoked");
    res.setContentType("text/html");
    out.println("<html><head><title>Logging Servlet</title></head>");
    out.println("<body>Visit the <tomcat-home>\\logs and open the file);
    out.println("<servername>_log<date>.txt to see the log entries");
    out.println("</body></html>");
  }
}
```

Listing 1.11 puts the following entry in the log file:

```
2002-04-24 11:14:50 LoggingServlet: init
2002-04-24 11:14:50 Init has been invoked
2002-04-24 11:14:50 doGet has now been invoked
2002-04-24 11:18:26 doGet has now been invoked
2002-04-24 11:18:26 doGet has now been invoked
```

This log entry was generated by visiting a URL that invoked the servlet three times.

Forwarding Requests to Other Servlets

In Table 1.4, there are some additional methods associated with URLs and forwarding requests. The `java.servlet.RequestDispatcher` is an object that is made available to you via the `ServletContext`, and it provides you with the means to forwarding requests on to other servlets or JSPs. This is particularly important in sites that are using an architecture often referred to as the model 2 architecture, which will be discussed in Chapter 7, "JSP Application Architecture."

The key methods of the RequestDispatcher are

```
void forward(ServletRequest request, ServletResponse response)
void include(ServletRequest request, ServletResponse response)
```

The `forward` method is used when a request is going to be serviced by a resource other than the servlet. The `include` method includes the output from another resource in the eventual output to the client.

Figure 1.14 demonstrates what happens to the request when the `forward` method is used.

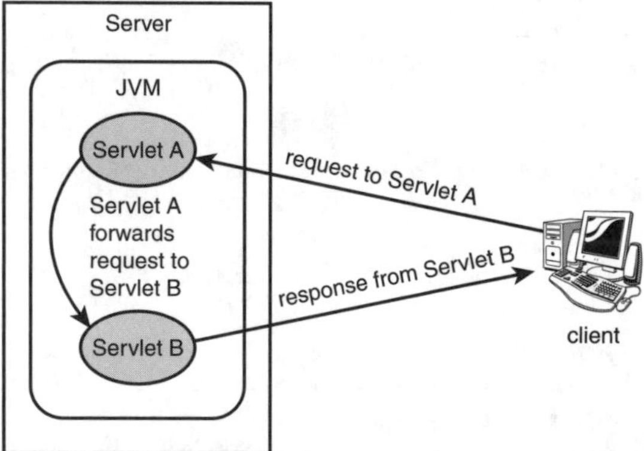

Figure 1.14 Forwarding requests.

The important thing to note is that this is *not* a redirection. The client only makes one request to the server. The fact that the response came from another servlet is transparent to the client.

Listing 1.12 shows a servlet that, when deployed, will forward the request to the basic servlet shown in Listing 1.2.

Listing 1.12 `ForwardingServlet.java`

```
import javax.servlet.http.*;
import javax.servlet.*;
import java.io.IOException;

public class ForwardingServlet extends HttpServlet
{
  public void doGet (HttpServletRequest req, HttpServletResponse res)
                          throws IOException, ServletException
  {
     ServletContext context = getServletContext();
     RequestDispatcher dispatcher = context.getRequestDispatcher("/myServlet");
     dispatcher.forward(req,res);
  }
}
```

If you set up this servlet within your Web application by providing a `<servlet>` and `<servlet-mapping>` entry in `web.xml`, you will find that when you invoke it, the URL in your browser does not change. The response to the browser is simply returned from the basic servlet in Listing 1.2.

The `include` method, on the other hand, simply includes the output from the specified resource. So, if in Listing 1.12 you used the `include` method, the output from `/myServlet` would be included in any output from the `ForwardingServlet`. In other words, it is a programmatic server-side `include`. In JSP, as you'll see later, this is achieved using tags.

Exception Handling in Java Servlets

If you look carefully at Listing 1.8, you will notice that the `init()` method throws a `javax.servlet.ServletException`, and the `doGet()` throws a `java.io.IOException`.

Why are these exceptions being thrown, and how are they handled? You never invoke these methods directly, so you have not written the exception handling code yourself; it is a part of the container.

In Web applications, the container will catch and handle three kinds of exception: `java.io.IOException`, `javax.servlet.ServletException`, and `javax.servlet.UnavailableException`.

`java.io.IOException`

These are thrown when there is a problem with the output stream to the client. The `doGet()` in Listing 1.8 uses a `PrintWriter` to output content to the client. Using the `println()` method, for example, throws an `IOException`. You can, therefore, pass this up to the Web container.

`javax.servlet.ServletException`

This is a general exception class that is thrown when the servlet cannot function correctly. The documentation says this about the `ServletException` class: "Defines a general exception a servlet can throw when it encounters difficulty."

What happens is that when an exception occurs within say the `init()` method of your servlet, a `ServletException` is created using a constructor that takes in both a `String` message and also a `Throwable` object type. This `Throwable` object will be the root cause of the problem. Listing 1.13 shows the output in the browser when a servlet fails because of a `null` pointer exception in the `init()` method. This would be displayed in the form of an HTML page. You can see in the second section that the root cause is shown. This root cause is from the `Throwable` object that was passed to the following `ServletException` constructor:

```
public ServletException (String message, Throwable rootCause)
```

> **Note**
>
> `java.lang.Throwable` is the superclass for all errors and exceptions in the Java programming language.

Listing 1.13 **The Output from a Servlet Throwing a `ServletException` from the `init()` Method**

```
javax.servlet.ServletException: Servlet.init() for servlet DeliberateException
                          threw exception
       at org.apache.catalina.core.StandardWrapper.loadServlet
                                                    (StandardWrapper.java:935)
 at org.apache.catalina.core.StandardWrapper.allocate(StandardWrapper.java:653)
       at org.apache.catalina.core.StandardWrapperValve.invoke
                                              (StandardWrapperValve.java:214)
       at org.apache.catalina.core.StandardPipeline.invokeNext
                                              (StandardPipeline.java:566)
        . . .
       at java.lang.Thread.run(Thread.java:536)

root cause

java.lang.NullPointerException
       at DeliberateException.init(DeliberateException.java:9)
       at org.apache.catalina.core.StandardWrapper.loadServlet
                                         (StandardWrapper.java:916)
       at org.apache.catalina.core.StandardWrapper.allocate
```

Listing 1.13 **Continued**

```
                                    (StandardWrapper.java:653)
      at org.apache.catalina.core.StandardWrapperValve.invoke
                                 (StandardWrapperValve.java:214)
       . . .
      at org.apache.catalina.connector.http.HttpProcessor.process
                                        (HttpProcessor.java:1012)
      at org.apache.catalina.connector.http.HttpProcessor.run
                                        (HttpProcessor.java:1107)
       at java.lang.Thread.run(Thread.java:536)
```

`javax.servlet.UnavailableException`

The `javax.servlet.UnavailableException` is thrown when the servlet is unavailable. This is often because of a configuration problem. You might encounter these `UnavailableExceptions` when you have made mistakes within the `web.xml` file.

That is enough about servlets for now. You will be returning to them throughout the rest of the book because they are so intrinsic to Web applications. We'll now turn our attention to the core subject of this book, the JavaServer Page.

Introducing the JavaServer Page

Servlets, although very efficient, are very awkward to develop. To be an effective servlet developer, you need to know the Java programming language, HTML, and be a good designer, so the output looks good. If you tried out some of the earlier listings, you may have found that you had errors because of typos in the `out.println()` statements. The servlets in the earlier listings have deliberately been kept very concise for clarity, but in real Web pages generated from servlets there could be reams of `out.println()` statements to write and maintain. For sites that use a large number of servlets, the relevant Java servlet class needs to be modified every time a change is needed to the output in the browser. It then has to be recompiled, and in many cases, the server has to be restarted to pick up the recently compiled Java class.

Shortly after the Servlet API had been developed, Microsoft launched Active Server Pages (ASP), which was much simpler to work with. ASP is a mixture of scripting and HTML, combined together to produce dynamic content. There is no compiling of code to be done by the developer. Issues such as portability, however, prevented many sites being developed and deployed on this platform. The only Java alternative was these rather cumbersome servlets.

Then, in the Java community, the JavaServer Page was invented, which has made the development of Web applications using Java far more accessible and straightforward. With each incremental release of a new JSP standard, JSPs have become progressively easier to develop, maintain, and work with.

A JavaServer page is an "inside-out servlet"; meaning, in a Java servlet, you have seen that there is Java code with HTML embedded in the form of `out.println()` statements. Just look at the servlet listings in this chapter to see what I mean! A JavaServer page is the opposite. It is not Java with HTML in it—it is HTML with Java functionality embedded in it. Take a look at the `basic.jsp` in Listing 1.14.

Listing 1.14 `basic.jsp`

```
<html>
<head><title>My Basic JSP</title></head>
<body>
<h1>A Basic JSP Example</h1>
<%
  for (int i=1; i<6; i++)  {
    out.println("<h" + i + ">Heading " + i + "</h" + i + ">");
  }
%>
</body>
</html>
```

Notice that in `basic.jsp`, there is normal HTML code, with a block of Java code in the middle of it. This will output the following HTML code to the browser:

```
<html>
<head><title>My Basic JSP</title></head>
<body>
<h1>A Basic JSP Example</h1>
<h1>Heading 1</h1>
<h2>Heading 2</h2>
<h3>Heading 3</h3>
<h4>Heading 4</h4>
<h5>Heading 5</h5>

</body>
</html>
```

In general terms, this JSP works by becoming a Java servlet. Look at Figure 1.15, which shows the lifecycle of a JavaServer page.

You will see from Figure 1.15 that the JSP is translated first into a servlet `.java` file, and then a `.class` file. This `.class` file is then instantiated to become a Java servlet object. If you want to test the JSP in Listing 1.14, all you need to do is copy it into the `<tomcat-home>\chapter01` folder, and visit the following URL:

```
http://localhost:8080/chapter01/basic.jsp
```

You do not need to modify `web.xml` when deploying JSPs. When you enter the URL, you will notice that it takes a while for the page to be displayed. This is because of the process that needs to occur to create the `.java` and `.class` files and to then instantiate the resultant servlet. If you open a second browser and visit the URL again, it will come up very quickly because the servlet is now running, listening for requests. In a production environment, you avoid this delay by precompiling all your JSPs, which will be discussed in Chapter 4, "Deploying JSP in a Web Container."

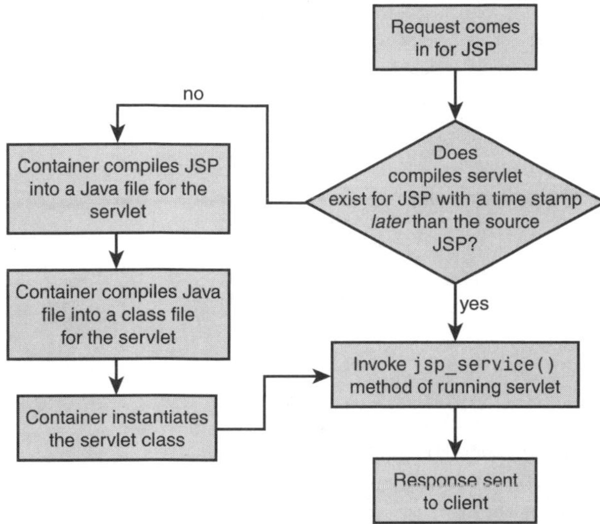

Figure 1.15 The JavaServer Page lifecycle.

If `basic.jsp` becomes a servlet, a reasonable question might be, can I see the servlet code? The answer is yes. All Web containers store the `.java` version of your JSP somewhere within their folder structure. Listing 1.15 shows the servlet that was created from `basic.jsp`. Listings similar to this will be shown throughout the book to demonstrate what is going on under the hood of your Web container when you add various syntax elements into your JSPs. Listing 1.15 was created by Tomcat 4. Be aware that different Web containers will produce slightly differing servlet output.

Listing 1.15 **Resulting Servlet from** `basic.jsp`

```
package org.apache.jsp;

import javax.servlet.*;
import javax.servlet.http.*;
import javax.servlet.jsp.*;
import org.apache.jasper.runtime.*;

public class basic$jsp extends HttpJspBase {
```

Listing 1.15 **Continued**

```
    static {
    }
    public basic$jsp( ) {
    }

    private static boolean _jspx_inited = false;

    public final void _jspx_init()
                        throws org.apache.jasper.runtime.JspException {
    }

    public void _jspService(HttpServletRequest request,
                        HttpServletResponse  response)
        throws java.io.IOException, ServletException {

        JspFactory _jspxFactory = null;
        PageContext pageContext = null;
        HttpSession session = null;
        ServletContext application = null;
        ServletConfig config = null;
        JspWriter out = null;
        Object page = this;
        String  _value = null;
        try {

            if (_jspx_inited == false) {
                synchronized (this) {
                    if (_jspx_inited == false) {
                        _jspx_init();
                        _jspx_inited = true;
                    }
                }
            }
            _jspxFactory = JspFactory.getDefaultFactory();
            response.setContentType("text/html;charset=ISO-8859-1");
            pageContext = _jspxFactory.getPageContext(this, request, response,
                            "", true, 8192, true);

            application = pageContext.getServletContext();
            config = pageContext.getServletConfig();
            session = pageContext.getSession();
            out = pageContext.getOut();

            // HTML // begin [file="/basic.jsp";from=(0,0);to=(4,0)]
                out.write("<html>\r\n<head><title>My Basic JSP</title>
```

Listing 1.15 **Continued**

```
                       </head>\r\n<body>\r\n<h1>A Basic JSP Example
                       </h1>\r\n");


        // end
        // begin [file="/basic.jsp";from=(4,2);to=(8,0)]

            for (int i=1; i<6; i++)  {
              out.println("<h" + i + ">Heading " + i + "</h" + i + ">");
            }
        // end
        // HTML // begin [file="/basic.jsp";from=(8,2);to=(10,7)]
            out.write("\r\n</body>\r\n</html>");

        // end

    } catch (Throwable t) {
        if (out != null && out.getBufferSize() != 0)
            out.clearBuffer();
        if (pageContext != null) pageContext.handlePageException(t);
    } finally {
        if (_jspxFactory != null) _
          jspxFactory.releasePageContext(pageContext);
    }
  }
}
```

You can view this output on your own machine by locating the folder `<tomcat-home>\work\localhost\chapter01`.

This `<tomcat-home>\work` folder is where all the Java source files for your JSPs end up. On other application servers it will be a different location. If you look carefully at Listing 1.15, you will see the `_jspService()` method. This is equivalent to the `service()` method of the servlets you saw earlier. The signature is the same as the `service()`, `doGet()`, and `doPost()` methods you saw in the regular servlet classes:

```
public void _jspService(HttpServletRequest request,
                        HttpServletResponse  response)
                        throws java.io.IOException, ServletException
```

If you look within the `_jspService()` method, you will note the following key lines:

```
out.write("<html>\r\n<head><title>My Basic JSP</title>
          </head>\r\n<body>\r\n<h1>A Basic JSP Example</h1>\r\n");
```

```
for (int i=1; i<6; i++)  {
                out.println("<h" + i + ">Heading " + i + "</h" + i + ">");
                }
out.write("\r\n</body>\r\n</html>");
```

These few lines are actually the content of our JSP file, `basic.jsp`. The HTML content is being written out to the browser using a writer of type `javax.servlet.jsp.JspWriter`; using this is the equivalent of using the `java.io.PrintWriter` used in a standard Java servlet.

The servlets that are created by a Web container from a JSP source must follow certain rules. The `javax.servlet.jsp` package, which `JspWriter` is a part of, contains a number of JSP-specific classes and interfaces that define the contract between the Web container and the servlet implementation class. If you look at Listing 1.9, note that the servlet class extends a superclass called `HttpJspBase`. This class is Tomcat-specific and is defined by the Apache project; from the package `org.apache.jasper.runtime`. The class will implement the `JspPage` interface from the `javax.servlet.jsp` package. If you were using a different server, the extended class would be different.

Web Application Scope

The last subject we need to discuss in this chapter is *scope*. This is an overview section that will be built on as you progress through the rest of the book.

Scope is integral to nearly every aspect of a Web application, so it is important that it is discussed in this foundational chapter. Earlier in the chapter, you saw an example that stored objects in the `ServletContext` object. The example referred to these stored objects as having *application scope*.

In Web applications, there are in fact four different scopes. The scope of an object indicates how long the object exists after it has been created. The lifetime of an object has a direct correlation to the JSPs that can access it. The levels of scope range from the entire lifetime of the Web container down to the lifetime of the individual page that uses an object. Objects that are stored in a particular level of scope are referred to as *attributes* of the scope.

The four scopes available to the Web developer are

- `application`
- `session`
- `request`
- `page`

Figure 1.16 shows the different scopes within an application running in a Web container. Figure 1.16 shows a client Web browser that makes a request for a page called `requestedPage.jsp`. This page includes a JSP called `includedPage.jsp`. The arrows that emanate from the two pages show which scopes are accessible to the pages. The next four subsections discuss the different scopes.

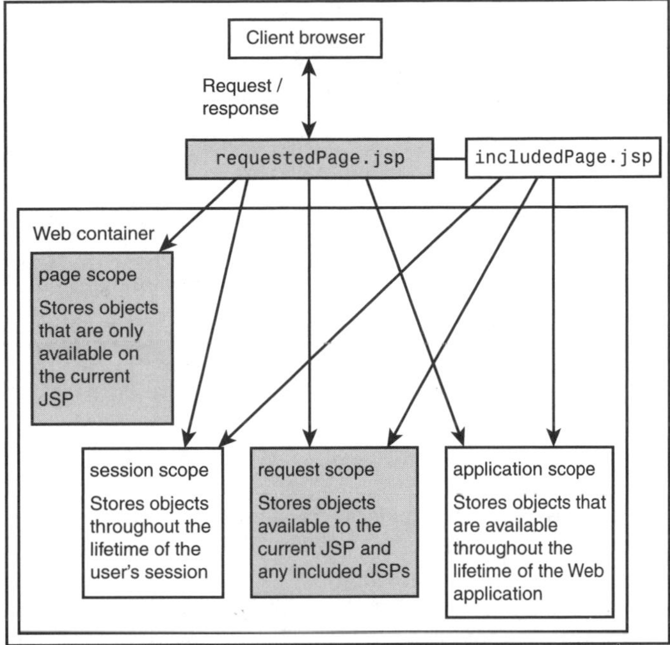

Figure 1.16 Scopes in a Web application.

The `application` Scope

Objects with application scope are stored in the `ServletContext` object. The `ServletContext` object is available to JSPs through a predefined `application` object.

The `ServletContext` object is shared by all servlets that are running in a given Web container. This makes the application-scoped objects available to any other JSP or servlet that is running in the Web container. This is true until the Web container is shut down. After a restart, the objects would have to be created again before they could be accessed.

The shared object can be accessed by using the `ServletContext` object's `getAttribute()` and `setAttribute()` methods as you saw when we discussed initializing servlets. An example might be a database connection pool where all objects within the container share the same pool of database connections.

The `session` Scope

Application-scoped components are ideal for things such as database connections, and so on, where they can be shared across the Web application. However, what about objects like shopping carts? You really need one for each user, not just one for the whole site! Objects such as this would be given `session` scope.

Objects that have a scope of `session` are stored by an object of type `javax.servlet.http.HttpSession`. It is available to all JSPs and servlets, and these objects bound to the session are available throughout the entire user's session. The concept of `session` scope will be discussed in more detail in Chapter 8, "Session Tracking Using JSP."

The `request` Scope

The `ServletRequest` object stores any objects that are declared to use the `request` scope. The `ServletRequest` object is available through the predefined `request` object that is available to JSPs and servlets.

The `request` scope is similar to the `page` scope in that the stored instance is discarded at the end of the page request. However, unlike the `page` scope, the stored object *is* available to any included JSPs. Form field parameters are examples of objects that are request scoped.

The `page` Scope

The default scope level is `page`. When an object has this scope, the instance is stored in the predefined `pageContext` object. However, the object reference is stored in the `pageContext` object only while the current request is executing. At the end of the current page request, the instance is removed from the `pageContext` object and is eligible for garbage collection. This means that this object is not available to any included JSPs.

You will see further examples of objects using these various scopes as we progress through the book. Assigning objects different scopes will be discussed in Chapter 6, "JSP and JavaBeans."

Summary

This chapter has introduced you to the J2EE platform. You should see that JSP is not a technology in isolation, but forms part of a standard that is used to build scalable, robust, enterprise Java applications. You have seen that JSPs are essentially servlets, and you have been introduced to how servlets work and how JSPs become servlets. You have also been introduced to the concept of scope within a Web application.

You have seen how servlets and JSPs run within the context of a Web container, and this container can interact with an EJB container. You have also seen how to set up the Web container that will be used for the rest of the book, Jakarta Tomcat.

In Chapter 2, "The Basic Syntax of JSP," you will be introduced to the basic syntax of the JavaServer page. You will learn how Java code can be used within pages, and how code can be separated from the pages by the use of technologies, such as tag libraries and JavaBeans, which have not been discussed so far.

2

The Basic Syntax of JSP

THIS CHAPTER COVERS THE BASIC SYNTAX that you can use to write a JavaServer Page (JSP). This chapter also introduces you to the JSP directives and shows you examples of their use. Then, you'll learn about the JSP predefined variables that are available, along with how and why you would use them. Finally, we briefly discuss the JavaServer Pages Standard Tag Library (JSTL) (you can find more information on the JSTL in Chapter 5, "The JSP Standard Tag Library").

It is useful when you first encounter page directives and page variables to see what effect their use has on the generated servlet. Therefore, at appropriate points, you will see sample code illustrating exactly what happens "under the covers."

JSP Defined

As you saw in Chapter 1, "JSP, J2EE, and the Role of the Servlet," JavaServer Pages (JSP) is a technology that enables you to serve dynamic content on a Web site. In the general case, requests for Web pages come from a client Web browser. The response to such a request is typically a page of HTML, although the content generated by a JSP can take other forms. For example, one common alternative data format is XML. You will learn how to create and manipulate XML from a JSP in Chapter 10, "Utilizing XML from JSP." You can also generate more advanced content, such as dynamic images and PDF documents. In Chapter 11, "Transforming XML Using XSLT and XSLFO," you will see a technology that allows you to do this from JSP.

To generate the content, several stages must occur:

1. The JSP itself must be written by a developer. Such a JSP is a mix of static HTML tags, JSP tags, and Java code, all of which are text and, therefore, can be authored in any text editor you choose. The Java code can be included directly in the page, although it is becoming common practice to partition the programming logic from HTML presentation. This will be discussed in Chapter 3, "Further JSP Syntax."

2. The JSP must be deployed inside a container that can process JSP. The deployment process is described for several popular servers in Chapter 4, "Deploying JSP in a Web Container."
3. When the JSP is requested for the first time, it must be translated to a Java servlet. The servlet is used to send the response back to the client. Thus, the actual content of the JSP on the server is *not* what the client sees in his Web browser. That is, the client sees the *result* of the server processing the JSP. Servlets are described in Chapter 1.

You might wonder where you can find the generated servlet source code. The answer is that different Web containers store the generated source code in different places. Some Web containers require configuring to keep the generated files. Tomcat stores files under `<TOMCAT_HOME>\work`. You should look in the documentation for your Web container to see where it stores the generated source code. A quick alternative is to do a recursive search for `*.java` files under the directory where your Web container is installed.

Comments in JavaServer Pages

Often, you want to document your JSP, and you can use *comments* to do this. A comment can take several forms, and depending on which you use, the comment might or might not be seen by the client if they use the View Source command in their Web browser. You will see exactly how the different comments behave.

As a Java programmer, you are no doubt familiar with at least two common forms for inserting comments into source code:

```
// this is a single-line comment
```

and

```
/*
    This is a multi-line
    comment.
*/
```

Consider the JavaServer Page in Listing 2.1, along with its generated servlet in Listing 2.2.

Listing 2.1 **Java Comments in JavaServer Pages**

```
<!-- Here is an HTML comment - copied to the output -->

<%!    // Single-line Java comments are copied to the generated servlet.

    /** This is a Javadoc comment, used to document Java functions */
    public void someMethod() {
           /* Multi-line Java comment, useful to comment out
              blocks of code during the development cycle.
```

Listing 2.1 **Continued**

```
            This sort of comment is copied to the generated servlet.
           */
        }
%>

<html>
  <head>
    <title>Comments in a JSP</title>
  </head>
  <body>
    <% // A Java comment inside a scriptlet - copied into the
           generated servlet %>
    The JSP that generated this page uses a combination of HTML,
    Java and JSP comments.
    <%-- A JSP comment - not copied to the servlet, nor the output --%>
  </body>
</html>
```

Listing 2.2 **Generated Servlet for the JSP in Listing 2.1**

```
public class jspComments extends HttpJspBase {
        // Single-line Java comments are copied to the generated servlet.

        /** This is a Javadoc comment, used to document Java functions */
        public void someMethod() {
                 /* Multi-line Java comment, useful to comment out
                    blocks of code during the development cycle.
                   This sort of comment is copied to the generated servlet.
                 */
        }

        ...

        public void _jspService(...) {
                 ...
                 out.write("<!-- Here is an HTML comment - copied to the ");
                 out.write("output");
                 out.write(" -->\r\n\r\n");
                 out.write("\r\n\r\n<html>\r\n  <head>\r\n    <title>");
                 out.write("Comments in a JSP</title>\r\n  </head>\r\n  ");
                 out.write("<body>\r\n");

                 // A Java comment inside a scriptlet
```

Listing 2.2 **Continued**

```
                out.write("\r\nThe JSP that generated this page uses ");
                out.write("a combination of HTML, ");
                out.write("Java and JSP comments.\r\n  ");
                out.write("</body>\r\n</html>");
                ...
        }
}
```

Upon inspection of Listings 2.1 and 2.2, you can see that the HTML comment from the first line of Listing 2.1 is written out as static text by the `_jspService` method and, thus, appears in the content that is sent back to the client:

```
out.write("<!-- Here is an HTML comment - copied to the output -->\r\n\r\n");
```

The Java comments from the declaration block of Listing 2.1 are copied into the generated servlet outside the `_jspService` method:

```
<%!    // Single-line Java comments are copied to the generated servlet.

    /** This is a Javadoc comment, used to document Java functions */
    public void someMethod() {
            /* Multi-line Java comment, useful to comment out
               blocks of code during the development cycle.
               This sort of comment is copied to the generated servlet.
    */
```

There should be no surprise here because you have already seen that the content of a declaration tag is copied in this way.

Any Java comment, such as the following, that occurs inside a scriptlet

```
<% // A Java comment inside a scriptlet - copied into the generated servlet %>
```

is used to document source code inside the `_jspService` method (see Listing 2.2, line 17):

```
// A Java comment inside a scriptlet
```

The only comment that does not appear in the output seen by the client takes the form:

```
<%-- comment content here --%>
```

You can see an example in Listing 2.1:

```
<%-- A JSP comment - not copied to the servlet, nor the output --%>
```

The HTML seen by a client for Listing 2.1 is shown in Listing 2.3. For example, the client could use the View Source command from a Web browser.

Listing 2.3 **HTML for the JSP in Listing 2.1**

```
<!-- Here is an HTML comment - copied to the output -->
<html>
  <head>
    <title>Comments in a JSP</title>
  </head>
  <body>
    The JSP that generated this page uses a combination of HTML,
    Java and JSP comments.
  </body>
</html>
```

With all these comments available, you are probably wondering which you should use! Because the JSP is the document that receives the most human attention, you normally use JSP comments within it. However, if you find yourself using large sections of Java code within the JSP, you might find it more readable to use Java comments within the scriptlets.

One thing that you normally do not want to do is place HTML comments within your JSP. The reason for this is that the HTML comments are embedded within the generated document and are not displayed to the user because most Web browsers ignore them. Thus, they just waste network bandwidth. The only time that you want to use an HTML comment within JSP is if you are certain that you want the comment to be visible to the users if they view the source of the document they are viewing.

The Expression Tag

The code in Listing 2.4 is for a simple JSP. It generates a value for a mobile phone's signal strength. You might have also encountered this kind of example before, masquerading as a random number generator.

Listing 2.4 **A Simple JSP** `simplePage.jsp`

```
<html>
  <head>
    <title>A Simple JavaServer Page</title>  </head>
  <body>
    <h1 align="CENTER">Mobile Phone Signal Strength Indicator</h1>
    <h3 align="CENTER">
      The current signal strength (0 to 10) is
      <font color="RED">
        <%= (int) (Math.random() * 10) %>
      </font>
    </h3>
    <h4 align="CENTER">(Refresh the page to see if the signal strength
                       changes...)</h4>
  </body>
</html>
```

If you are an HTML developer, the only part that might be unfamiliar to you is the following tag:

```
<%= (int) (Math.random() * 10) %>
```

This is an *expression tag*. Expression tags are used to embed the value that an expression evaluates to into the page.

> **Note**
>
> The expression tag of Listing 2.4 does not terminate with a ; character. That is, it is not a Java statement. Instead, it is a parameter passed to the `print` method of the `JspWriter` in the `_jspService` method of the generated servlet.

The content of the expression tag is passed as a call to the `print()` method of the `Writer` object, which is available to the `_jspService()` method that you saw in Chapter 1. All of the usual Java language rules for calling a `print()` method, such as `System.out.println()`, apply. Thus, in this example the value that is to be embedded is converted to a `String` for display. The JSP compiler is able to convert primitive types to `Strings`, and objects are converted by invoking their `toString()` method.

> **Note**
>
> The `java.lang.Object` class provides a `toString` method, and, therefore, all Java classes inherit this method. By default, the `toString` method returns the name of the class used to instantiate the object, followed by an @ character, followed by a 32-bit hashcode for the object. It is common practice to override this method on a per-class basis, usually for debugging purposes, and to return a string that shows the state of the important instance variables.

All that the expression tag in Listing 2.4 does is invoke the `random()` method of the `java.lang.Math` class. Because the method returns a `double` in the range 0.0 (inclusive) to 1.0 (exclusive), this return value is first multiplied by 10 before casting to an `int` to give a whole number in the range 0 to 9 as the value of the fictitious mobile phone signal strength. The output looks similar to what is shown in Figure 2.1.

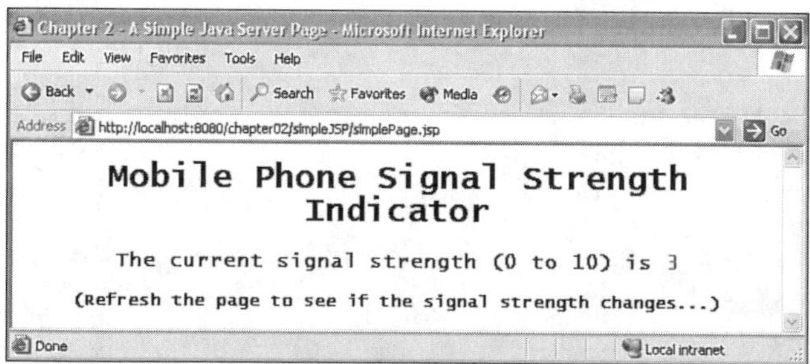

Figure 2.1 A simple JSP (`simplePage.jsp`).

It is helpful, when first learning JSP, to refer to the generated code to see exactly what is happening when the JSP is translated to a servlet. It is possible to look at the Java code that is generated by the container. For Tomcat, this is in the `<TOMCAT_HOME>\work` directory. For the example in Listing 2.4, the important lines from the generated servlet's `_jspService` method are shown in Listing 2.5. If you were to look at the whole file in your Web container, you would see many more than the few lines shown here. For example, `import` statements, constructors, and some servlet configuration that occurs at the start of the `_jspService` method. You could always, of course, write your own servlet in the first place, but that involves much more work.

Listing 2.5 **The `_jspService` Method for the JSP in Listing 2.4**

```
...
out.write("<HTML>\r\n  <head>\r\n    <title>A Simple JavaServer
          Page</title>");
out.write("\r\n  </head>\r\n  <body>\r\n    <h1 ALIGN=\"CENTER\">Mobile
         Phone Signal ");
out.write("Strength Indicator</h1>\r\n  <H3 ALIGN=\"CENTER\">\r\n      ");
out.write("The current signal strength (0 to 10) is \r\n<FONT COLOR=
          \"RED\">\r\n");

out.print( (int) (Math.random() * 10) );

out.write("\r\n </FONT>\r\n    </H3>");
out.write("\r\n    <H4 ALIGN=\"CENTER\">(Refresh the page to see if the
          signal strength ");
out.write("changes...)</H4>\r\n  </body>\r\n</HTML>");
...
```

The Declaration Tag

The code in Listing 2.4 uses an expression tag to insert a dynamic value into the JSP. It is also possible to embed Java code into the page. For example, you can declare methods and variables, and write code that makes use of them. This topic is discussed in much more detail in Chapter 3. However, consider the JSP in Listing 2.6 that generates output that looks as shown in Figure 2.5. The first four lines of the JSP form a *declaration tag*. Declaration tags take the following form:

```
<%! ... %>
```

They contain variables and methods that the `_jspService` method can make reference to. You will see shortly how to write code that is embedded into the `_jspService` method. The variables in a declaration tag can be any valid Java type. That is, any one of the eight primitive data types (`boolean`, `char`, `byte`, `short`, `int`, `long`, `float`, `double`), or a class type (user-defined or standard Java library). When declaring variables, they can optionally be initialized inline. For example, you could declare variables as follows:

```
<%!
    String name;     // not initialized
    int    age = 42; // initialized
%>
```

Listing 2.6 **Declaration Tag Example--Variables**

```
<%!
  String name = "Mark";
  String date = "8th April, 2002";
%>

<HTML>
  <title>Declaration Tag Example</title>
  <body>
    This page was last modified on <%= date %> by <%= name %>.
  </body>
</HTML>
```

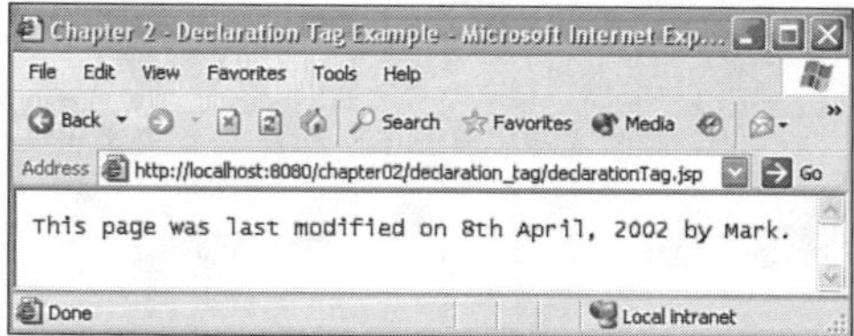

Figure 2.2 The declaration tag--variables

The code generated for the JSP in Listing 2.6 is shown in Listing 2.7.

Listing 2.7 **Generated Code for Declaration Tag Example--Variables**

```
public class declarationTag$jsp extends HttpJspBase {
    String name = "Mark";
    String date = "8th April, 2002";
    ...
    public void _jspService(HttpServletRequest request,
                            HttpServletResponse  response)
        throws java.io.IOException, ServletException {
    ...
        out.write("\r\n\r\n<HTML>\r\n  <title>Declaration Tag Example</title>");
        out.write("\r\n\r\n");
        out.write("  <body>\r\n    This page was last modified on ");
        out.print( date );
        out.write(" by ");
```

Listing 2.7 **Continued**

```
        out.print( name );
        out.write(".\r\n  </body>\r\n</HTML>");
        ...
    }
    ...
}
```

On the second and third lines of Listing 2.7 you can see the two `String` variables that were declared in the JSP of Listing 2.6. Note that the variables that were declared in the page are translated to *instance variables* of the generated servlet.

As described in Chapter 1, there is only one instance of a given servlet for a JSP, but multiple threads serving the client requests. Thus, you must take extra steps to ensure that any code you write to manipulate the generated variables is thread-safe. If you decide to use declared variables, you must provide your own thread safety. However, it is usually better to avoid using them in the first place. Some ways of doing this are described later in this chapter.

In addition to declaring variables inside declaration tags, you can also define Java methods. Any methods that are declared can be called by name from within the JSP, the reason for which will become clear when you see the code for the generated servlet. Methods are declared using the usual Java syntax:

```
optional_modifier_list return_type method_name (optional_parameter_list)
        optional_exception_list
{
  method_body
}
```

Consider the JSP in Listing 2.8.

Listing 2.8 **Declaration Tag Example--Methods** `declarationTag_Method.jsp`

```
<%!
  private String getNephewName() {
    return "Joshua Greenhough";
  }

  private int getNephewAge() {
    return 3;
  }
%>

<HTML>
  <head><title>Declaration Tag - Methods</title></head>
  <%= getNephewName() %>, age <%= getNephewAge() %>, is one funny kid!
</HTML>
```

When viewed, the page looks similar to Figure 2.3. The code that is generated for the JSP in Listing 2.8 is shown in Listing 2.9.

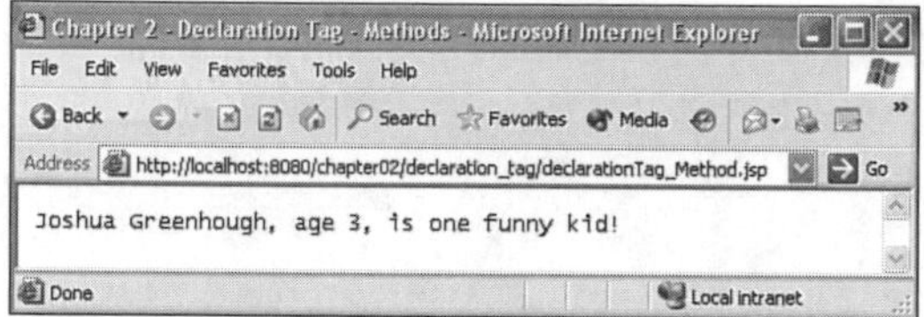

Figure 2.3 The declaration tag--methods

Listing 2.9 **Declaration Tag Example--Methods**

```
public class declarationTag_0005fMethod$jsp extends HttpJspBase {
    private String getNephewName() {
      return "Joshua Greenhough";
    }

    private int getNephewAge() {
      return 3;
    }

    public void _jspService(HttpServletRequest request,
                            HttpServletResponse  response)
        throws java.io.IOException, ServletException {
        ...
    out.write("\r\n\r\n<HTML>\r\n  <head><title>Declaration Tag");
        out.write("- Methods</title></head>\r\n\r\n  ");
        out.print( getNephewName() );
        out.write(", aged ");
        out.print( getNephewAge() );
        out.write(", is one funny kid!\r\n\r\n  \r\n</HTML>");
        ...
        }
    ...
}
```

As you can see from Listing 2.9, any methods that you declare in the JSP are translated into instance methods of the generated servlet:

```
private String getNephewName() {
  return "Joshua Greenhough";
}
```

```
private int getNephewAge() {
  return 3;
}
```

The methods can be called by name from the JSP itself as follows:

```
<%= getNephewName() %>, age <%= getNephewAge() %>, is one funny kid!
```

This equates to the `_jspService` method making calls to other methods defined within the generated servlet.

Embedding Code

It is possible to embed Java code into a page by using a *scriptlet*. Scriptlets are introduced here, but described in detail in Chapter 3. A scriptlet is a block of Java code that is copied into the generated servlet's `_jspService` method. The basic form of a scriptlet follows:

```
<% ... %>
```

A simple JSP that uses a scriptlet is shown in Listing 2.10. It simply uses some Java code to build a table from some data that is declared on the page. In reality, this data would probably be retrieved using a database API.

Listing 2.10 **Embedding Code in a JSP** `embeddingCode.jsp`

```
<%!
  String[] names = {"Ruth", "Matilda", "Millicent", "Micah"};
%>
<html>
  <head><title>Embedding Code</title></head>
  <body>
    <h1>List of people</h1>
    <table border="1">
      <th>Name</th>
      <% for (int i=0; i<names.length; i++) { %>
        <tr><td><%= names[i]%></td></tr>
      <% } %>
    </table>
  </body>
</html>
```

The following lines contain embedded Java code:

```
<% for (int i=0; i<names.length; i++) { %>
  <tr><td><%= names[i]%></td></tr>
<% } %>
```

You can see that the Java is intermingled with HTML tags. This is perfectly legal, but quickly becomes difficult to read in large pages. If you mix Java code and HTML markup, the editors of these pages will need to be able to work comfortably with both.

A valid question is, "Can Java code be removed from a JSP?" The answer is yes; separating business logic from presentation is a golden rule of any system. JSP was designed for use as the presentation layer. One technology that you can use to perform the logic is JavaBeans, covered in Chapter 6, "JSP and JavaBeans." Another option is to use the JSTL (see Chapter 5), or develop your own custom tags (see Chapter 9, "Developing Custom Tag Libraries").

When the JSP from Listing 2.10 is viewed, it should look like Figure 2.4. The important lines from the `_jspService` method are show in Listing 2.11.

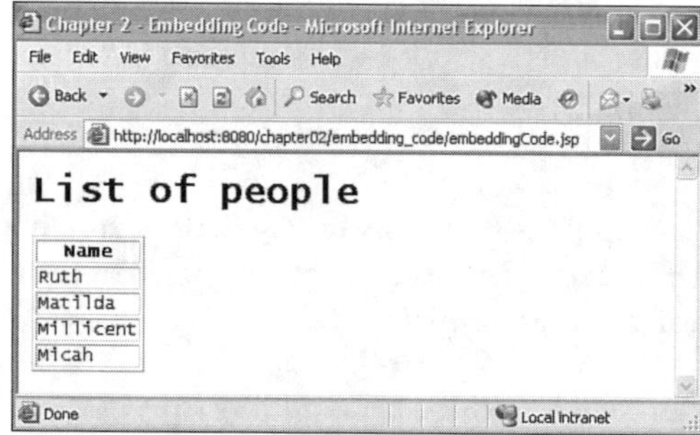

Figure 2.4 Embedding code in a JSP.

Listing 2.11 **Generated `_jspService` Method of the Servlet for the JSP in Listing 2.10**

```
public class embeddingCode$jsp extends HttpJspBase {

  String[] names = {"Ruth", "Matilda", "Millicent", "Micah"};
...

    public void _jspService(HttpServletRequest request,
                            HttpServletResponse  response)
        throws java.io.IOException, ServletException {
    ...     out.write("\r\n\r\n<html>\r\n  <head><title>");
    out.write("Embedding Code</title></head>\r\n\r\n  <body>\r\n    ");
    out.write("<h1>List of people</h1>\r\n    <table border=\"1\">\r\n      ");
    out.write("<th>Name</th>\r\n      ");
    for (int i=0; i<names.length; i++) {
           out.write("\r\n        <tr><td>");
```

Listing 2.11 **Continued**

```
            out.print( names[i]);
            out.write("</td><td>");
            out.print( ages[i]);
            out.write("</td></tr>\r\n      ");
    }
    out.write("\r\n    </table>\r\n  </body>\r\n</html>");
    ...
  }
...}
```

JSP Directives

Directives are tags that you can insert into a JSP document to give the JSP container information about the JSP itself. These tags directly affect the servlet code that is generated. You can use three directives in a JSP: `include`, `page`, and `taglib`.

The general syntax of a JSP directive is as follows:

```
<%@ directive_name directive_attribute(s) %>
```

or

```
<jsp:directive.directive_name directive_attributes />
```

The former approach is the original syntax that is probably easier to read and is backwards-compatible with older servers. However, you should be aware that since JSP 1.2, you can represent JSP using an XML syntax. As time goes on and more page authors learn XML, the latter XML-style will become the preferred syntax.

A directive has a name and a list of possible attributes. The actual attributes that you can use with a given directive depend on the directive itself. To put it another way, each directive has a different set of attributes.

The Use of the `include` Directive

The simplest of the directives is the `include` directive. Its purpose is to insert the text from another file into a JSP.

The syntax of the `include` directive is

```
<%@ include file="relative-url" %>
```

An absolute URL is one which has the following general syntax:

```
protocol://host:port/virtualPath?queryString
```

For example, in this book you will see URLs such as:

```
http://localhost:8080/chapter02/include_directive/MyAccount.jsp?id=1
```

However, when you use the `include` directive, the file that is to be included is specified using a relative URL, rather than an absolute one. This simply means that the protocol and host/port information is not specified, and that the required resource is identified by its relationship to something else, usually the current JSP.

For example, consider the case where a JSP called `page.jsp` includes a file called `banner.html`. If the `banner.html` file is located in an `includeFiles` subdirectory under the directory where the `page.jsp` file is located, the `include` directive would look like this:

```
<%@ include file="includeFiles/banner.html" %>
```

A common situation in which you might want to use the `include` directive is when you want to partition content into separate building blocks. You can then assemble Web pages that are built from these blocks. For example, you could write files that contain company logos, copyright notices, navigation bars, and so on.

The following example illustrates how you can use a standard banner on your JSP. The HTML in Listing 2.12 is included in the JSP page in Listing 2.13.

Listing 2.12 **Included File** `welcomeText.html`

```
<table width="100%" border="0">
  <tr>
    <td align="right" bgcolor="#FFFF99">
      <i><b>Welcome to your online account</b></i>
    </td>
  </tr>
</table>
```

Listing 2.13 **Main JSP** `MyAccount.jsp`

```
<html>
  <head><title>Example: include Directive </title></head>
  <body>
    <%@ include file='welcomeText.html' %>
    <P>
    This text appears after the included file
  </body>
</html>
```

The output is shown in Figure 2.5.

The `include` directive treats the file that is included as static text. That is, the file to be included is inserted into the JSP, and the result is translated to a servlet, which is then compiled and subsequently executed.

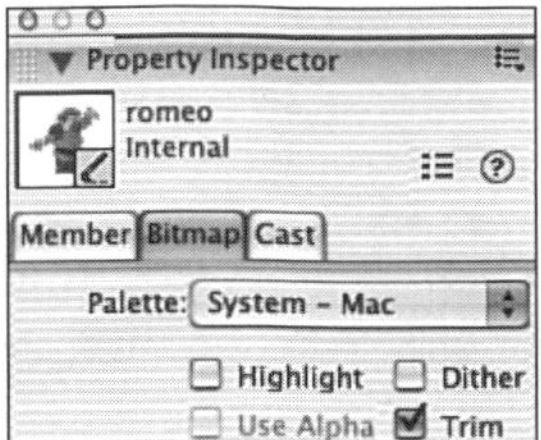

Figure 2.5 The result of using the `include` directive.

The important lines of code from the `_jspService` method of the translated servlet can be seen in Listing 2.14. These lines of code are generated to deal with the contents of the included file.

Listing 2.14 **The `_jspService` Method**

```
out.write("<html>\r\n  <head><title>Example: include Directive </title>");
out.write("</head>\r\n\r\n  <body>\r\n     ");
out.write("<table WIDTH="100%" border=\"0\">\r\n  <tr><TD align=\"right\");
out.write("bgcolor=\"#FFFF99\"><i><b>Welcome to your online account</b>");
out.write("</i></td></tr>\r\n</table>");
out.write("\r\n    <P>\r\n    This text appears after the included file\r\n");
out.write("  </body>\r\n</html>");
```

The included file in Listing 2.12 contains just HTML, without any JSP tags. However, it is possible to write included files that contain JSP tags.

An advantage of including content in the way described previously--rather than hard-coding the common content into each JSP--is that if you decide to modify the common content, the change is automatically reflected in the resultant JSP for all the pages that include it. However, there is an inconvenience associated with using the `include` directive: When the included file changes, it is necessary to update the time stamp on the including file or files before the user can see the change. Remember that the server only automatically recompiles a JSP if its time stamp does not correspond to the currently generated servlet. Different servers might provide a mechanism that monitors changes to included files, but the JSP specification does not mandate it.

As an alternative to using the `include` directive, you can use the `jsp:include` action to avoid having to modify the including file's time stamp. The content of the included resource is resolved in a dynamic fashion when the including JSP is requested by the user. You can find more information on the `jsp:include` action in Chapter 3.

The Use of the `page` Directive

If you want to set properties of a JSP, use the `page` directive. The properties that you can set are described in this section, such as the capability to indicate if there is another page to which the current page should forward errors, the MIME content type for the current page, and so on.

The page directive enables you to specify properties for a JSP by setting values for its attributes: `autoflush`, `buffer`, `contentType`, `errorPage`, `extends`, `import`, `info`, `language`, `isErrorPage`, `isThreadSafe`, `pageEncoding`, and `session`. These attributes are defined in Table 2.1. The attributes are case-sensitive, and the value must be enclosed in either single or double quotes.

Although you can use more than one `page` directive on a given JSP, you cannot duplicate any of the attributes, with one exception: You can specify the `import` attribute multiple times to specify which classes and interfaces you want to make available to the generated servlet. Alternatively, the `import` attribute can take a comma-separated list of values (see Table 2.1 for an example).

Table 2.1 **The** `page` **Directive Attributes**

Attribute nameName	**Value**	**Description**
autoFlush	Boolean true or false	Defines the behavior expected when the output buffer is full. If the value is true, the buffer is automatically flushed when full. If false, an exception is thrown when the buffer overflows. Default value: true Example: `<%@ page autoFlush="true" %>`

buffer	none or a number of kilobytes, for example, 64kb64KB	Enables you to set the size of the output buffer.
		Default value: 8KB
		Examples:
		`<%@ page buffer="none" %>`
		`<%@ page buffer="64kb" %>`

contentType	A MIME type, with an optional character encoding	Sets the MIME type for the output: text/html, text/xml, or text/plain. You should make sure that any value you specify for the optional character encoding matches the value specified in the pageEncoding attribute (see later in this table).
		Default value: text/html; charset=ISO-8859-1.
		Examples:
		`<%@ page contentType=`
		`"text/html" %>`
		`<%@ page contentType=`
		`"text/plain;charset=UTF-8"%>`

Table 2.1 **Continued**

Attribute nameName	Value	Description
errorPage	Relative URL	Sets the JSP page to which any Java exceptions thrown by the current page should be passed. Example: <%@ page errorPage= "myErrorPage.jsp" %>
extends	Fully qualified class name	Specifies the superclass of the servlet that is generated for the current JSP. *Use with care because the container may already be using its own class here.* Example: <%@ page extends= "com.foo.MyClass"%>
import	Classes and interfaces to import	Enables you to import from standard Java packages. Examples: <@ page import="java.net.URL" %> <@ page import="java.util.Calendar, java.io.*" %>
info	Textual message	Sets an informational string that can be retrieved from the generated servlet by invoking the getServletInfo() method that is defined in the javax.servlet.Servlet interface. Example: <%@ page info="A Currency Converter" %>
isErrorPage	Boolean true or false	Indicates whether the current page will receive exceptions from other pages. If so, the implicit exception object is made available (covered later in this chapter). Default value: false Example: <%@ page isErrorPage="true" %>
isThreadSafe	Boolean true or false	Dictates whether the generated servlet implements the SingleThreadModel interface (explained in Chapter 1). Use a value of false if your code handles multiple threads safely. Default value: true Example: <%@ page isThreadSafe="true" %>

Table 2.1 **Continued**

Attribute nameName	Value	Description
language	Programming language name	At the moment, there is only one valid name (java) for the programming language that can be used for the generated servlet. Thus, this attribute can be safely left to default to the value java. Default value: java Example: <%@ page language="c" %>
pageEncoding	Character encoding	The character encoding the JSP page uses for the response. Default value: `ISO-8859-1`. Example: <%@ page pageEncoding= "UTF-8" %>
isScriptingEnabled	Boolean `true` or `false`	If scripting is disabled (`false`) for this translation unit or page, then any declarations, scriptlets, or scripting expressions cause a translation error.Default value: `true`
isELEnabled	Boolean `true` or `false`	If the EL is disabled (`false`), then any EL expressions are ignored for this translation unit or page. If the EL is enabled (`true`), then any EL expressions are evaluated where they appear in either action attributes, or in template text.
`session`	Boolean `true` or `false`	Controls whether the current page needs access to session information. Default value: `true` Example: <%@ page session="true" %>

The code in Listing 2.15 shows a JSP page that sets values for the possible page directive attributes.

Listing 2.15 `PageDirective.jsp`

```
<%@ page autoFlush="true"
        buffer="16kb"
        contentType="text/html"
        errorPage="myErrorPage.jsp"
        extends="org.apache.jasper.runtime.HttpJspBase"
        import="java.sql.*"
        info="This page has a set of page directive attributes"
```

Listing 2.15 **Continued**

```
        language="java"
        pageEncoding="UTF-8"
        session="false"
%>

<html>
  <head>
    <title>Page directive attributes</title>
  </head>
  <body>
    The JSP page used to generate this content defined values for all of
    the page directive's attributes.
  </body>
</html>
```

The code that is generated is shown in Listing 2.16. Some of the code has been deleted for clarity.

Listing 2.16 **Generated Servlet for** `PageDirective.jsp`

```
. . .
import java.sql.*;
public class PageDirective extends HttpJspBase {
    public String getServletInfo() {
        return "This page has a set of page directive attributes";
    }
    . . .
    public void _jspService(HttpServletRequest request,
                            HttpServletResponse response)
        throws IOException, ServletException {
        . . .
        response.setContentType("text/html");
        pageContext = _jspxFactory.getPageContext(this, request, response,
            "myErrorPage.jsp", false, 16384, true);
    . . .
    }
}
```

Referring to Listing 2.16, let's examine the code and see which lines were generated by which page directive attributes.

This line is generated by the `import` attribute:

```
import java.sql.*;
```

The superclass on line 3 is specified by the `extends` attribute:

```
public class PageDirective extends HttpJspBase {
```

The next three lines are a result of the `info` attribute:

```
public String getServletInfo() {
    return "This page has a set of page directive attributes";
}
```

The content type (`contentType` attribute) is set as follows:

```
response.setContentType("text/html");
```

The next two lines set the error page (`errorPage` attribute); that the servlet does not participate in a session (`session` attribute); the output buffer size of 16384 bytes (`buffer` attribute); and that automatic flushing of the output buffer is required (`aut-oflush` attribute):

```
pageContext = _jspxFactory.getPageContext(this, request, response,
    "myErrorPage.jsp", false, 16384, true);
```

The Java programming language is the only one that can be used in declarations, expressions, and scriptlets (of which this page uses none). The `language` attribute is set to `java` to make this explicit.

Going back to the `include` directive for a moment, consider the case where you have a JSP that needs to import a long list of classes and JavaBeans from multiple locations. In such cases, you can use a separate file that contains a `page` directive, list the imported packages, and then include that file into the JSP. This helps you to keep the pages neat. Another good thing to put into the same included file is a reference to an error page that is shared across the whole site.

Basic Introduction to the `taglib` Directive

As well as the predefined tags (declaration, expression, scriptlet, and directive) that you can use in a JSP, you can also use third-party or even your own custom tags. A set of common tags is described in Chapter 5. You can find information about how to define your own tags in Chapter 9.

You can extend the functionality of a JSP by importing a tag library, which is simply a set of custom tags. The tags in the tag library can be used to replace sections of code in the JSP. Often, these tags are for pieces of reusable functionality, such as code that iterates through the result of a database query. In fact, one of the major benefits of tag libraries is that they enable you to partition roles between the Java developers and the HTML designers. Because it is possible to remove Java code from a page by using custom tags, it becomes a great deal easier for nonprogrammers to write dynamic pages using JSP.

Several steps are required before you can use a custom tag. First of all, some Java code needs to be written that performs the actual work of generating content for the page. The Java code is known as a *tag handler*. An XML document (tag library description, or TLD) is required that maps tag names to the relevant tag handler. Before you can use the tags in your pages, you must import the tag library using the `taglib` directive, whose syntax is

```
<%@ taglib uri="URI_TO_TAG_LIBRARY" prefix="TAG_PREFIX" %>
```

The uri attribute specifies the location of the tag library descriptor (TLD), using either a relative or absolute path. The prefix attribute is an arbitrary string of text that is used to uniquely identify the custom tags you want to use.

For example, if you had a tag library descriptor called MyCustomTags.tld in the same directory as a JSP, and wanted to use a predefined tag called processResultSet, you would do something similar to that shown in Listing 2.17.

Listing 2.17 **Tag Library Usage**

```
<%@ taglib uri="MyCustomTags.tld" prefix="foo" %>
<html>
  <head><title>Tag Library Usage</title></head>
  <body>
    ...
    <foo:processResultSet />
    ...
  </body>
</html>
```

JSP Predefined Variables

In this part of the chapter you will find the predefined variables that are implicitly available for you to use within your JSP. These variables are compared with those that are available in ASP, if you are familiar with that particular technology.

The Roles of the JSP Predefined Variables

There are nine predefined variables made available to you by the Web container. Such variables are known as *implicit objects*, due to the fact that you can use the variables by name within the Java code on a JSP, without ever having declared them yourself. To see exactly why this is the case, you will be shown the source code that is generated for the servlet that serves the JSP.

The nine implicit objects are application, config, exception, out, page, pageContext, request, response, and session. Some of these are defined in the servlet API (application, config, request, response, and session); the others are defined in the JavaServer Pages API (exception, out, page, pageContext).

At the start of a _jspService method, you will see code similar to that shown in Listing 2.18. All but the exception object are defined at this point, either as parameters to the _jspService method, or as local variables inside it. The exception object is only available in error pages. An error page is a JSP that uses the page directive with its isErrorPage attribute set to true.

Note that because the implicit objects are either parameters or local variables of the _jspService method, they are only available from within that method. The implication of this when writing a JavaServer Page is that the implicit objects are not available in declaration tags. Remember that declaration tags are used to declare variables and methods that belong to the generated servlet.

Listing 2.18 **A `_jspService` Method**

```
public void _jspService(HttpServletRequest request,
                        HttpServletResponse  response)
    throws java.io.IOException, ServletException {
    ...
    PageContext    pageContext = _jspxFactory.getPageContext(this, request,
                                                              response,
                                                         "", true, 8192, true);
    ServletContext application = pageContext.getServletContext();
    ServletConfig  config      = pageContext.getServletConfig();
    JspWriter      out         = pageContext.getOut();
    Object         page        = this;
    HttpSession    session     = pageContext.getSession();
    ...
}
```

The `application` Object

This object implements the `javax.servlet.ServletContext` interface. This interface provides methods that enable a servlet to query for information about its environment as well as write messages and errors to log files. For example, a servlet can query for the major and minor version numbers of the servlet API that is supported by the Web container. The `javax.servlet.ServletContext` interface is implemented by a service inside the Web container, and accessed by the servlet when necessary. When writing a servlet, you can obtain a reference to the `ServletContext` via the `ServletConfig` object that is passed to the servlet when it is initialized. You call the `getServletContext` method of the `ServletConfig` object to retrieve the `ServletContext`. The code in Listing 2.18 retrieves the `ServletContext` and `ServletConfig` objects via the `pageContext` object, discussed later.

A very useful feature of the `application` object is that it enables you to store objects by name. These stored objects are accessible by any JSP that is running as part of the application, and are therefore useful to share data between the pages.

The example pages in Listing 2.19 and Listing 2.20 illustrate how one page can create an object that is visible to any other page that is in the same application.

The second and third lines of Listing 2.19 create a `String` object that contains a message, and line 11 then creates a hyperlink to another page that retrieves the shared object and displays it. The JSP in Listing 2.19 looks like the screenshot in Figure 2.6 when viewed.

Listing 2.19 **Page Creating a Shared Object**

```
<%
  String theSharedObject = "JSP is cool";
  application.setAttribute("message", theSharedObject);
%>
```

Listing 2.19 **Continued**

```
<html>
  <head>
    <title>Application Object - Page 1</title>
  </head>
  <body>
    This page sets data that can be retrieved by other pages in the
    application.<P>
    Click <a href="application_page2.jsp">here</a> to see this in action.
  </body>
</html>
```

Listing 2.20 **Page Retrieving a Shared Object**

```
<%
  // getAttribute() returns a java.lang.Object, so need to cast
  String theSharedObject = (String) application.getAttribute("message");
%>
<html>
  <head>
    <title>Application Object - Page 2</title>
  </head>
  <body>
    This page retrieves the message that was stored in the <i>application</i>
   object  by another page.
  <P>
    The message is <b><%= theSharedObject %></b>
  </body>
</html>
```

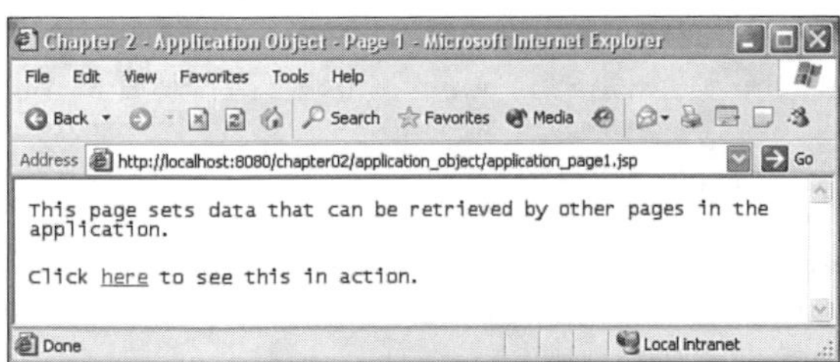

Figure 2.6 Page that creates a shared object.

The shared object created by the first page is retrieved by the third line of Listing 2.20. The following line 12, then, embeds the retrieved value into the current page:

```
The message is <b><%= theSharedObject %></b>
```

The output from the JSP in Listing 2.20 is shown in Figure 2.7.

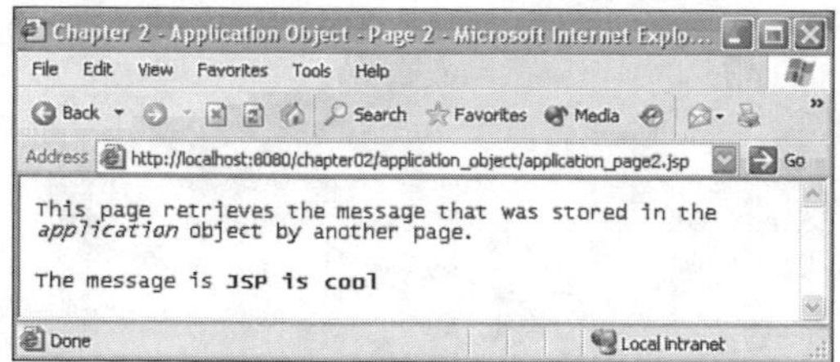

Figure 2.7 The shared object retrieved and displayed.

The code that is generated when you use the `application` object is shown in Listing 2.21 for the first page (Listing 2.19). Unsurprisingly, the code from the scriptlet in Listing 2.19 is simply pasted into the `_jspService` method immediately after the implicit object is set up (Listing 2.14).

Listing 2.21 `_jspService` **When Using** `application` **Object**

```
... // implicit objects are set up here
String theSharedObject = "JSP is cool";
application.setAttribute("message", theSharedObject);
out.write("\r\n\r\n<html>\r\n  <head>\r\n    <title>");
out.write("Application Object - Page 1</title>\r\n  </head>\r\n\r\n  ");
out.write("<body>\r\n    This page sets data that can be retrieved by other ");
out.write("pages in the application.<P>\r\n\r\n    Click <a href=\"");
out.write("application_page2.jsp\">here</a> to see this in action.\r\n  ");
out.write("</body>\r\n</html>");
... // end of _jspService method
```

Similarly, for the JSP in Listing 2.20, the scriptlet that retrieves the shared object is inserted into the `_jspService` method as is. In Listing 2.22, the second line retrieves the shared object, and the following line embeds its `String` value into the page:

```
out.print( theSharedObject );
```

Listing 2.22 `_jspService` **When Retrieving a Shared Object**

```
...
String theSharedObject = (String) application.getAttribute("message");

out.write("\r\n\r\n<html>\r\n  <head>\r\n    <title>");
out.write("Application Object - Page 2</title>\r\n  </head>\r\n\r\n  ");
out.write("<body>\r\n    This page retrieves the message that was stored in ");
```

Listing 2.22 **Continued**

```
out.write("the <i>application</i> object  by another page.\r\n  <P>\r\n    ");
out.write("The message is <b>");

out.print( theSharedObject );
out.write("</b>\r\n  </body>\r\n</html>");
...
```

The `config` Object

This variable is the `ServletConfig` object for the current page:

```
ServletConfig config      = pageContext.getServletConfig();
```

Thus, the `config` object provides methods that allow access to any initialization information provided to a servlet.

The `exception` Object

When writing application software, it is of the utmost importance to consider not just what you *expect* the user to do, but also what you do *not* expect! Users do not always follow the "rules" you have laid down for using the application.

So a Web application does not simply crash, it is important to write code that deals with unexpected situations during execution. The application programmer needs to decide at design-time what error-handling logic to put into place.

There are several ways that you can deal with such circumstances when writing the application code. For example, the C programming language provides a global variable to track errors. An alternative would be to check a return value from functions, as in the COM programming style, to determine if a function has executed correctly.

The downside of using either of the two techniques just mentioned is that there is no way to *force* the application programmer to use them! The Java programming language provides an *exception-handling* mechanism that is compiler-enforced (except for exceptions that are subclasses of `java.lang.RuntimeException`, of course).

This mechanism is extensible in that you can write your own exception classes that are usually subclasses of `java.lang.Exception`. You can then instantiate these objects when necessary, and *throw* them to indicate that an error has occurred in your application code. The question is then, "What happens next?"

From a JSP viewpoint, the standard Java exception mechanism rules are followed. If you do not provide a `try/catch` block on the page, the exception propagates up the call stack looking for an appropriate handler. This of course raises another question, "What if a handler is not found?" These questions are answered later with the aid of examples.

The way in which you can provide error handling in JSP is by writing *error pages*. You saw the `page` directive in Table 2.1 that can have attributes including `errorPage` and `isErrorPage`. An error page is simply a Web page that informs users that errors have occurred in a Web application.

During the development process, it is common for many pages to propagate errors to a single error-handling page that can prettify the exception and display it in a way that is helpful during the debugging process. When the Web application is deployed, it is also common to have multiple pages that use a common error page. This means that the error page should be sophisticated enough to deal with errors from multiple sources, and that the multiple sources are related in such a way that having a common error page is a logical choice.

The JavaServer Page in Listing 2.23 uses the `page` directive on the first line to specify that any exception that occurs during the processing of the page should be passed to the `processError.jsp` page located in the same directory (because the file is specified with a relative URL).

Listing 2.23 **A Page That Generates Exceptions** (`generateError.jsp`)

```
<%-- Declare the page to send errors to --%>
<%@ page errorPage="processError.jsp" %>

<%-- This scriptlet checks a hidden field to see whether
     or not to throw an exception
--%>
<%
  String hiddenField = request.getParameter("hiddenValue");
  if ( (hiddenField != null) && !(hiddenField.equals("")))
    throw new java.lang.NullPointerException();
%>

<html>
  <head><title>Generate Error</title></head>
  <body>
    This page generates an error when you click the button.<P>
    <FORM METHOD="POST" ACTION="generateError.jsp">
      <INPUT TYPE="HIDDEN" NAME="hiddenValue" VALUE="Bang!">
      <INPUT TYPE="SUBMIT" VALUE="Generate exception!">
    </FORM>
  </body>
</html>
```

The scriptlet checks to see whether a value has been specified for the hidden field:

```
<%
  String hiddenField = request.getParameter("hiddenValue");
  if ( (hiddenField != null) && !(hiddenField.equals("")))
    throw new java.lang.NullPointerException();
%>
```

Thus, the first time that this page is viewed, you see the message in Figure 2.8. When you click the `Generate Exception!` button though, the form submits a value for the hidden field back to the same page. When this value is submitted, the scriptlet throws a `java.lang.NullPointerException`. Any exception could be thrown at this point, including one that you write. A `NullPointerException` was chosen for this example simply to show the syntax without cluttering the example with extra code.

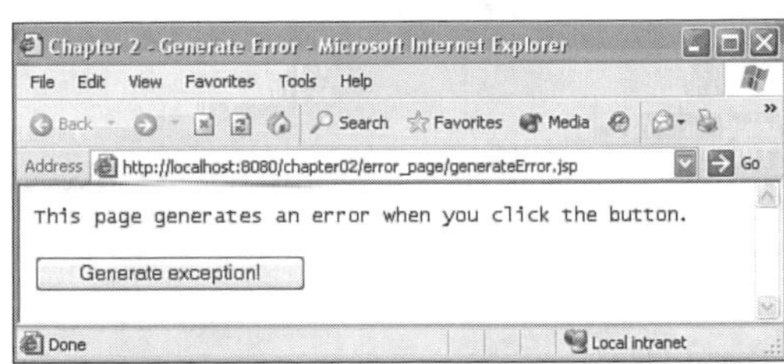

Figure 2.8 This page generates an exception.

As soon as the exception is thrown, it is passed to the `processError.jsp` page, as specified using the `page` directive. The reason for this becomes obvious when you examine the source code for the generated servlet (Listing 2.24). The `page` directive causes the error page to be set, and the scriptlet is as follows:

```
String hiddenField = request.getParameter("hiddenValue");
       if ( (hiddenField != null) && !(hiddenField.equals("")) )
           throw new java.lang.NullPointerException();
```

Thus, when the last line of the scriptlet throws the `NullPointerException`, it is caught by the `try/catch` block inside the `_jspService` method

```
catch (Throwable t) {
```

and handled by the `pageContext` object that is responsible for forwarding the exception to the `processError.jsp` page.

Listing 2.24 **Generated Servlet for Listing 2.19**

```
public void _jspService(...) {
    try {
        ...
        pageContext = _jspxFactory.getPageContext(this, request, response,
                        "processError.jsp", true, 8192, true);
        ...
        String hiddenField = request.getParameter("hiddenValue");
               if ( (hiddenField != null) && !(hiddenField.equals("")) )
                   throw new java.lang.NullPointerException();
        ...
```

Listing 2.24 **Continued**

```
    }
    catch (Throwable t) {
        ...
        if (pageContext != null)
                    pageContext.handlePageException(t);
        }
        ...
}
```

The page that receives the errors is shown in Listing 2.25. The first line uses the `page` directive to indicate that this is an error-handling page and, therefore, the implicit `exception` object should be made available. The error-handling logic itself is as follows:

```
<% if ( exception != null )
        out.write("\nAn error occurred. This page is to tell you what you did
                    wrong.\n");
    else
        out.write("\nYou have reached this page, but no error information is
                    available.\n");
```

A screenshot is not shown here because the output is trivial in this case; the same is true for the generated servlet. There is, however, something new at the beginning of the generated `_jspService` method:

```
Throwable exception = (Throwable) request.getAttribute(
                            "javax.servlet.jsp.jspException");
```

This line of code is a result of the `isErrorPage` attribute having a value of `true` (first line of Listing 2.25). Bear in mind that it is possible to view the `processError.jsp` page directly, which is why it is important to perform a check in the code to ensure that the `exception` object is available before trying to invoke any methods on it.

Listing 2.25 **Error-Handling Page (`processError.jsp`)**

```
<%@ page isErrorPage="true" %>
<html>
  <head><title>Process Error</title></head>
  <body>
    <% if ( exception != null )
          out.write("\nAn error occurred. This page is to tell you what you"
                  + " did wrong.\n");
        else
          out.write("\nYou have reached this page, but no error information"
                  + " is available.\n");
    %>
  </body>
</html>
```

Finally, if a JSP that did not specify an error page threw an exception, the Web container would generate some kind of error page similar to Figure 2.9. The code that generated this page is the same as Listing 2.23 with the omission of the `page` directive, and the logic of the `if` statement inverted to give

```
<%-- This scriptlet checks a hidden field to see whether or not
     to throw an exception
--%>
<%
  String hiddenField = request.getParameter("hiddenValue");
  if ( hiddenField == null || hiddenField.equals(""))
    throw new java.lang.NullPointerException();
%>

<html>
  <head><title>Generate Error</title></head>
  <body>
    You will not even see this, since the scriptlet throws an error immediately!
  </body>
</html>
```

Notice that in this example the body of the HTML page is not processed because the scriptlet throws a `NullPointerException` immediately.

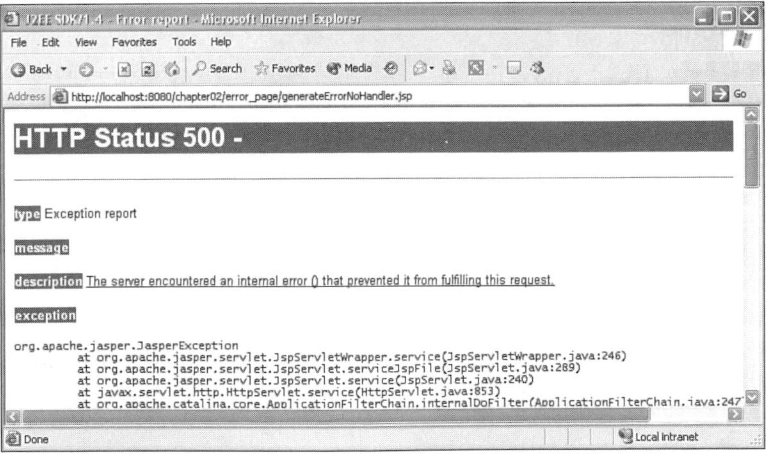

Figure 2.9 Unhandled page exception.

The `out` Object

You can send output back to the client by using the `out` object. You will notice from Listing 2.18 that the `out` variable is of type `JspWriter`. This class is a subclass of java.io.Writer, and provides a set of print methods that enable you to display primitives and String objects. The class inherits a set of write methods from its parent class, and in many of the examples in this chapter you see that the generated servlet uses both print and write methods. The print method tends to be used for anything that you embed into the page, whereas the write method is used to output the static text parts of the JSP. However, if you look at the source code for the JspWriterImpl class that ships with Tomcat, you can see that the print methods are implemented by delegating to the write methods. You can set the size of the output buffer of a JspWriter by using the page directive and its associated buffer attribute, as described earlier in this chapter.

The out object is only really used in practice from within scriptlets. For example, you do not need to use the out object when using expression tags, where you specify an expression that can be converted to a Java String object. If you refer to Listing 2.1, you see an example:

```
<%= (int) (Math.random() * 10) %>
```

Note that the expression to be embedded in the page does not terminate with a semicolon character (;). The generated code is shown in Listing 2.2, which does in fact call the out.print() method for you.

There have been several examples in this chapter that use the out object to display data, either directly or within the generated servlet code, so another example is not included at this point.

The page Object

This variable corresponds directly to the this reference in the generated servlet. The page object is not typically used when writing a JavaServer Page. The type of situation where it might be useful is when there is a script on the page that needs to call methods that take a parameter that is a reference to the page itself.

The reason for the existence of the page object is that in the future there might be programming languages other than Java that can be used as the scripting language for a JavaServer Page (see the page directive's language attribute in Table 2.1).

The pageContext Object

Although each JSP container has its own implementation for the implicit objects and page attributes, there is a uniform way to access them. The JSP container generates code inside the _jspService method to instantiate the pageContext object, that provides methods that enable you to retrieve references to the other implicit objects (see Table 2.2). It also enables you to store and retrieve objects via an attribute mechanism that uses a name/value pair. Forwarding and redirection of requests is also supported, and is how error handling is internally implemented. You saw this in Listing 2.24:

```
pageContext.handlePageException(t);
```

The pageContext object is an instance of a class that subclasses the abstract javax.servlet.jsp.PageContext class.

Table 2.2 **Convenience Methods of the `javax.servlet.jsp.PageContext` Class**

Method	Implicit Object
`getOut()`	`out`
`getException()`	`exception`
`getPage()`	`page`
`getRequest()`	`request`
`getResponse()`	`response`
`getServletConfig()`	`config`
`getServletContext()`	`application`
`getSession()`	`session`

The `request` Object

When a user makes a request of a JSP (or servlet), that request is usually modeled by an object that implements the `javax.servlet.http.HttpServletRequest` interface. The object is passed as a parameter to the `_jspService` method. The `HttpServletRequest` interface inherits from the `javax.servlet.ServletRequest` interface, and provides methods to

- Read the HTTP headers
- Acquire information about the request's content
- Identify client and server machines, plus the protocol used
- Crack open the querying URL into its constituent parts
- Access parameters and attributes
- Manage user security
- Access user session information

Requests with parameters can be made in a variety of ways. For example, you can have a hyperlink in an HTML page such as

```
<A HREF="displayDetails.jsp?name=Mark&age=30">Send details</A>
```

In this case, the `details.jsp` page receives two named parameters. The parameter `name` has the value *Mark*, and a parameter called `age` with a value of *30*. To make the request take dynamic values, you can use HTML forms with named input fields. In JSP, you can avoid passing parameters as strings on the query string by using a JavaBean that stores all the data. This is covered in Chapter 6.

The `response` Object

The `javax.servlet.ServletResponse` interface defines methods that enable a servlet to send a response back to the client. The `_jspService` method receives a parameter of type `javax.servlet.jsp.HttpServletResponse`, which inherits from `ServletResponse`. You can use the response object to

- Set content type (MIME type) and length
- Write binary and textual data
- Encode URLs with a session ID for robust session tracking
- Set HTTP headers
- Manage user session information

The `session` Object

The HTTP protocol is known as a *stateless* protocol because client requests are each opened over a separate connection, and the server does not maintain any contextual information that could form the basis of a conversation between the client and the server. Several solutions are commonly used today that get around this problem, two of which are cookies and URL rewriting.

Cookies are small files sent by a server to a client, which contain user identification information. Upon subsequent requests, a server can request the cookie from the client, and thus maintain server-side state on behalf of the client (such as the contents of a shopping cart).

Many users disable cookies, and a fallback mechanism that the server can use in such situations is URL rewriting. In this case, the client appends extra information to the end of the URL that it requests of the server. This extra information identifies the client to the server. For example, `http://server/page.jhtml?sessionid=FABBABE`.

However, writing the code that deals with cookies or URL rewriting is tedious and error-prone. The Servlet API provides a high-level solution that is generally implemented using cookies or URL rewriting. All three approaches are discussed in detail in Chapter 8, "Session Tracking Using JSP."

JSP Variables and ASP Variables

For those of you who are familiar with Microsoft's Active Server Pages (ASP) technology, this brief section mentions some of the similarities that exist between ASP and JSP. For example, they both use object-oriented, server-side scripting. ASP supports two main scripting languages: VBScript and JScript. ASP also has a set of intrinsic objects that are available for the scripts to utilize.

The ASP intrinsic objects that correlate to JSP implicit objects are listed in Table 2.3. You can see that there is a direct relationship between most of the variables. The only exception is that ASP provides the `Response.Write` method to provide access to the output stream, whereas JSP has the `out` object.

Table 2.3 **Implicit Objects in ASP and JSP**

JSP Implicit Object	ASP Intrinsic Object
`application`	`Application`
`out`	`Response.Write`
`request`	`Request`
`response`	`Response`
`session`	`Session`

Both JSP and ASP use the same syntax for directives (`<%@ ... %>`), expressions (`<%= ... %>`), and scripting (`<% ... %>`). The code in Listings 2.22 and 2.23 shows a simple example of ASP and JSP, and from them you can see how similar the two approaches are.

Listing 2.26 **ASP Example**

```
<%@ LANGUAGE="JScript" %>
<html>
  <head><title>ASP Example</title></head>
  <body>
    <h1>Quadratic Equation: y = x^2</h1>
      <table border="1">
        <th>x</th><th>y</th>
        <%
      for (i=0; i<5; i++)
            Response.Write("<tr><td width='100'>" + i + "</td><td width='100'>"
                           + (i*i) + "</td></tr>");
        %>
      </table>
  </body>
</html>
```

Listing 2.27 **JSP Example**

```
<%@ page language="java" %>
<html>
  <head><title>JSP Example</title></head>
  <body>
    <h1>Quadratic Equation: y = x^2</h1>
      <table border="1">
        <th>x</th><th>y</th>
        <%
      for (int i=0; i<5; i++)
            out.print("<("<tr><td width='100'>" + i + "</td><td width='100'>"
                      + (i*i) + "</td></tr>");
        %>
```

Listing 2.27 **Continued**

```
      </table>
  </body>
</html>
```

The HTML that is output from either example is exactly the same, and is shown in Listing 2.24.

Listing 2.28 **HTML output from Listings 2.21/2.22**

```
<html>
  <head><title>*SP Example</title></head>
  <body>
    <h1>Quadratic Equation: y = x^2</h1>
      <table border="1">
        <th>x</th><th>y</th>
        <tr><td width='100'>0</td>  <td width='100'>0</td></tr>
        <tr><td width='100'>1</td>  <td width='100'>1</td></tr>
        <tr><td width='100'>2</td>  <td width='100'>4</td></tr>
        <tr><td width='100'>3</td>  <td width='100'>9</td></tr>
        <tr><td width='100'>4</td>  <td width='100'>16</td></TR
      </table>
  </body>
</html>
```

The JavaServer Pages Standard Tag Library (JSTL)

So far in this chapter, JavaServer Pages have been introduced as consisting of directive, declaration, expression, and scriptlet tags. Although the scriptlet tag does afford you a great deal of control over the dynamic aspects of a page, the downside is that you end up with HTML and Java on the same page. In practice, this becomes very difficult to manage in short order.

Introducing the JSTL

As mentioned earlier in this chapter (in the "Basic Introduction to the `taglib` Directive" section), it is possible to write your own tags for use within JSP. For well-known tasks, such as conditional processing and iteration, it makes sense to have tested and reliable implementations of custom tags. This is where the JavaServer Pages Standard Tag Library (JSTL) comes in.

There are various tag library implementations available, but the examples in this chapter use the JSTL reference implementation from the Jakarta-Taglibs project at http://jakarta.apache.org/taglibs/doc/standard-doc/intro.html. You can download this and run it under Tomcat 4. Alternatively, you can go to Sun's Web site (http://java.sun.com/webservices/webservicespack.html) and download the Java Web Services Developer Pack that contains everything you need.

Consider the times that you want to iterate over the contents of a collection, or make a decision over what to embed into a page depending on the value of a variable. You saw an example of looping over the contents of an array in Listing 2.7, duplicated here for convenience, in Listing 2.25.

Listing 2.29 **Iteration Using a Scriptlet**

```
<%!
  String[] names = {"Ruth", "Matilda", "Millicent", "Micah"};
%>
<html>
  <head><title>Embedding Code</title></head>
  <body>
    <h1>List of people</h1>
    <table border="1">
      <th>Name</th>
      <% for (int i=0; i<names.length; i++) { %>
        <tr><td><%= names[i]%></td></tr>
      <% } %>
    </table>
  </body>
</html>
```

The following lines contain a mixture of Java code and HTML, which is difficult to read and therefore difficult to maintain:

```
<% for (int i=0; i<names.length; i++) { %>
  <tr><td><%= names[i]%></td></tr>
<% } %>
```

It also means that whoever is editing the page needs to be comfortable with both languages.

It is for situations such as this that the JavaServer Pages Standard Tag Library (JSTL) was designed. Rather than the page developer using scriptlets or third-party tags within a page, the JSTL defines a set of standard tags that can be used instead. The benefit here is that not only do you not have to use Java code in a JSP, but you only have to learn the replacement tag once and you can use it in many JSP containers. The JSP container implementations can of course implement the tags as they see fit, so different containers might perform better than others in different situations.

Using the JSTL

The example in Listing 2.25 can be rewritten so that it does not use a scriptlet, by using tags from the JSTL (see Listing 2.26). Several parts of the listing are new, but the details are not dwelt on in this example because they are covered in subsequent chapters (see Chapter 5 and also Chapter 9).

Listing 2.30 **JSTL Iteration Example**

```
<%@ taglib uri="http://java.sun.com/jstl-el/core"    prefix="c"    %>

<%!
  String[] names = {"Ruth", "Matilda", "Millicent", "Micah"};
%>

<html>
  <head><title>Embedding Code</title></head>
  <body>
    <h1>List of people</h1>
    <table border="1">
      <th>Name</th>
      <c-rt:forEach var="person" items="<%= names %>">
        <tr> <td><c:out value="${person}"  /></td> </tr>
      <c:forEach>
    </table>
  </body>
</html>
```

In this example, the first two lines are new and import tags, which are used later on, from the JSTL. Everything else is much the same, except the scriptlet has been replaced, and the following lines now use standard tags for iteration and output:

```
<c-rt:forEach var="person" items="<%= names %>">
  <tr> <td><c:out value="${person}"  /></td> </tr>
<c:forEach>
```

The `forEach` tag enables you to iterate over a collection of objects, and the `out` tag inserts text into the output stream.

The JSTL provides four groups of tags:

- Core tags for flow control, expressions, and URL management
- SQL tags for SQL database access
- Internationalization tags for formatting and parsing text
- XML tags for parsing, searching, and transforming XML documents

JSTL 1.0 provided two versions of the tag libraries: one that supported the Expression Language, and one that did not. The latter form supported request-time expressions and was provided so that you can use the standard actions without having to use the new Expression Language. Since JSP 2.0 contains the Expression Language, there is just one library in JSTL 1.1 that accepts both forms of expression. You can find more information about these tags in Chapter 5.

The JSP 2.0 Expression Language

JSP 2.0 introduces a new Expression Language. The rationale for this is that at the moment, whenever a page author needs to access a value of a JavaBean, he must use an expression tag of the form:

```
<%= someBean.getSomeValue() %>
```

When this syntax is used as an attribute value to any kind of tag, the result quickly becomes difficult to read:

```
<somePrefix:someCustomTag someAttribute="<%= session.getAttribute
                                         ("someValue") %>" />
```

The JSP 2.0 specification allows the use of a standard expression language for all custom tag libraries. The expression language enables the author of a page to use a simpler syntax to access objects. For example:

```
<somePrefix:someCustomTag someAttribute="${someValue}" />
```

As you can see from this line, expressions are enclosed inside curly braces `{...}`, and preceded with a `$` character so that the JSP container knows to process the expression rather than treating it as literal text.

The Expression Language is covered in detail in Chapter 3.

Summary

In this chapter you saw that JSP enables you to generate dynamic content using a mixture of static HTML and JSP tags. You saw the `expression` tag that enables you to insert a string into the output stream; the `declaration` tag that enables you to declare variables and methods for use within the page; the `scriptlet` tag for inserting code into the page; various ways of commenting parts of a JSP. For all these, you were shown the important parts of the servlet that is generated by the Web container. This is important when first learning JSP so that you can understand what is really happening when the client requests JSP.

You then saw the three JSP directives that affect the page that is generated, before covering the nine predefined variables that JSP provides. These were briefly compared to ASP variables for those of you that are familiar with that technology.

Finally, you were introduced to the JSTL, which provides a set of core functionality that is useful when writing JSP applications.

3

Further JSP Syntax

IN THE PREVIOUS CHAPTER, YOU WERE EXPOSED to the core of the JSP syntax. The chapter showed you how to embed Java code into your pages, it showed you the predefined variables, and it introduced you to the JavaServer Pages Standard Tag Library (JSTL).

In this chapter, see the role of what are known as standard actions, and you will be introduced to custom actions. The chapter will then progress to the Expression Language where you will discover how it can be used directly within pages, reducing further the need to have Java code embedded in your pages.

The Standard Actions

Since the earliest versions of JSP, there have been what are referred to as *standard actions*. These are special XML-like tags (XML is discussed in the introduction to Chapter 10, "Utilizing XML from JSP"). They take the form of an XML tag with a namespace-prefixed `jsp`, so a standard action always looks something like this:

```
<jsp:standardActionName . . . >. . .</jsp:standardActionName>
```

They are used for the following functions:

- Forwarding requests and performing includes in pages.
- Embedding the appropriate HTML on pages to invoke the Java plugin to be used within browsers to run Java applets.
- The interaction between pages and JavaBeans.
- The provision of additional functionality to tag libraries.

We'll look at these functions here, and you will see some being used in other contexts in later chapters.

Forwarding and Including

When a request is received by a JSP, it can be forwarded directly onto another relative URL from the same Web application to be processed. This must be a resource within the same Web application. To do this, you can use the `<jsp:forward>` standard action.

Forwarding is not the same as redirecting. Redirecting involves the browser being sent elsewhere for a resource, effectively resulting in the browser issuing two requests. Forwarding is the browser requesting a resource, and the response coming from the resource that has been forwarded to. Following is a basic page, which uses the `<jsp:forward>` standard action:

```
anything here will not appear in the browser
  <jsp:forward page="gotForwardedRequest.jsp"/>
anything here will not appear either
```

Pages that forward requests *cannot* send any content to the browser. In the very basic example shown previously, neither of the two fragments of text will appear in the browser because the request and response have been forwarded to `gotForwardedRequest.jsp`.

Use of the `<jsp:forward>` action creates the automatically generated code in the compiled servlet, as shown in Listing 3.1.

Listing 3.1 **Autogenerated Source from JSP Using** `<jsp:forward>`

```
// note that some code has been removed for brevity
public void _jspService(HttpServletRequest request,
                        HttpServletResponse response)
  throws java.io.IOException, ServletException {
    ...
    try {
          . . .
      out.write("anything here will not appear in the browser\r\n");
      if (true) {
        pageContext.forward("gotForwardedRequest.jsp");
        return;
      }
      out.write("\r\nanything here will not appear either");
    } catch (Throwable t) {
      if (out != null && out.getBufferSize() != 0)
        out.clearBuffer();
      if (pageContext != null) pageContext.handlePageException(t);
      ...
  }
}
```

You can see from Listing 3.1 that the standard action becomes a call to the `forward()` method of the `javax.servlet.jsp.PageContext` object.

In the example, the textual output in the forwarding page never gets written to the browser, as immediately following the `forward()` call, the `service` method returns. This is because the output is all in the buffer, and this is never flushed as the request is forwarded.

If the forwarding page has already committed output to the browser by flushing the buffer, then the forwarding will fail. The following modification will not allow the forwarding to happen:

```
anything here will now appear in the browser
<% out.flush(); %>
<jsp:forward page="gotForwardedRequest.jsp"/>
anything here will not appear as the output is flushed
```

This listing will display the first line of text and nothing else when viewed in a browser. No forwarding will take place. This is because of the presence of the `out.flush()` method call. This method will flush the JspWriter buffer, and after content is committed to the browser, a forward cannot be invoked. If it is tried, an `IllegalStateException` is thrown, and this is caught by the catch block that you can see in Listing 3.1.

The chapter download includes two JSPs, `getRequest.jsp` and `gotForwardedRequest.jsp`, which you can use to try this out.

So, you have seen how the `<jsp:forward>` standard action works, but why would you use it? Because it can only be used on pages that are not outputting anything to the browser, it is only really useful on pages that aren't being used to display any content—controller pages if you like. The concept of a controller is discussed in Chapter 7, "JSP Application Architecture."

Passing Parameters

It is also possible to pass parameters from one page to another when carrying out `forward` actions. To do this, another standard action is used—the `<jsp:param>` action. Take a look at the following listing, which passes these parameters:

```
<jsp:forward page="accessingParameters.jsp">
  <jsp:param name="myParam" value="John Doe"/>
</jsp:forward>
```

Here is the relevant fragment of the resultant servlet code:

```
. . .
if (true) {
  pageContext.forward
     ("accessingParameters.jsp" + "?" + "myParam=" + "John+Doe");
  return;
}
. . .
```

You might be able to identify what this `param` action has done. It has appended the parameter as a variable within the query string.

This is now accessible to the resource that the request was forwarded to using a basic statement like:

```
String value = request.getParameter("myParam");
```

This ability to pass parameters can be very helpful because the values of these parameters can be dynamic.

A complete example of this is part of the chapter download as pages `passingParameters.jsp` and `accessingParameters.jsp`.

Templating Pages Using `<jsp:include>`

The third standard action we will discuss is the `<jsp:include>` action. In Chapter 2, the `include` directive was introduced, which includes static content into your JSP.

The `include` directive is not always appropriate, however, because the included content is included as static text (see Chapter 2). The `include` standard action, however, processes any included files at runtime. In other words, when the servlet is invoked by a client, the included file is dynamically obtained. This results in the ability to include content that is being changed regularly, and also the ability to include output from other JSPs that are providing dynamic content.

The `include` action can be used to include the output from one JSP within another, and thus, you can build up templates of JavaServer Pages that make up complete Web pages. In fact, this is how the front ends of many Web sites are built. Figure 3.1 shows a diagram of what is meant by this.

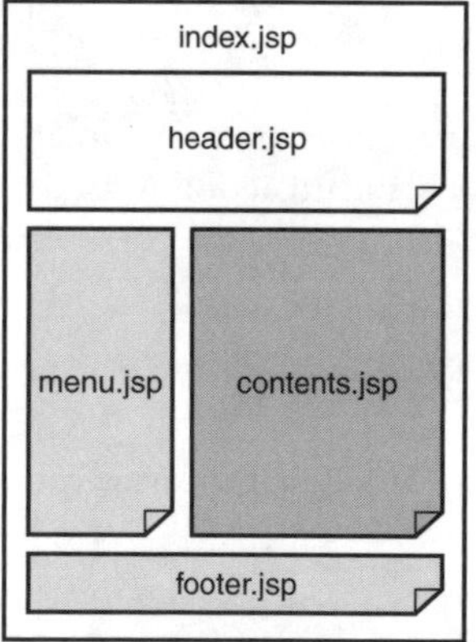

Figure 3.1 Templating using `<jsp:include>`.

Listing 3.2 shows a JSP that is built in this way with the use of includes.

Listing 3.2 `usingIncludes.jsp`

```
<html>
<head>
<title>Using Includes</title>
</head>

<body>
<!-- header page inserted here -->
<jsp:include page="tableheader.html" flush="true"/>

<!-- main content inserted here-->
<jsp:include page="maincontent.jsp" flush="true"/>

<!-- insert the footer here -->
<jsp:include page="tablefooter.html" flush="true"/>
</body>
</html>
```

As you can see from Listing 3.2, the `<jsp:include>` action has two attributes. The two attributes are shown in Table 3.1.

Table 3.1 **The Attributes of `<jsp:include>`**

Name	Description
`page`	This attribute specifies the page to be included. It must contain a relative URL.

`flush`	The flush attribute specifies what should happen to any buffered content that appears within the including page up until the include. See the short listing below:
	`content here could be buffered`
	`<jsp:include page="include.jsp" flush="true"/>`
	What happens to the text *content here could be buffered* can be determined by the value of the flush attribute. If the text is buffered, and the flush attribute is `true`, it will be flushed before the include is processed. If the flush attribute is set to `false`, any buffered content will not be flushed.
	The significance of this is that the buffer needs to be flushed for output to be sent to the browser, so most of the time, you set to `true`. There were some specific situations in JSP 1.1 a value of false was required.
	Note that the default is false, so you will need to specify a value of true.

As with the `<jsp:forward>` standard action, you can also pass parameters to included pages using the `<jsp:param>` standard action. A basic example is shown here:

```
<jsp:include page="accessingParameters.jsp" flush="true">
```

```
  <jsp:param name="myParam" value="John Doe"/>
</jsp:include>
```

This can be very useful when included content has features that are dependent on the including page. Consider Listing 3.3.

Listing 3.3 `usingIncludesWithParameters.jsp`

```
<html>
<head>
<title>This page passes parameters</title>
</head>
<body>
<!-- header from include-->
<jsp:include page="includeFileNeedingAParameter.jsp">
  <jsp:param name="department" value="Electrical"/>
</jsp:include>
Welcome to our electrical department. This <p>
area is packed with excellent deals on electrical
items.
</body>
</html>
```

Listing 3.3 shows a basic JSP for a department within a store. Each department has a name, which is passed to the included file for display. Here is the content of the included file:

```
<!-- the included file -->
<h1><%=request.getParameter("department") %> Department</h1>
```

> **Tip**
>
> A common mistake is to put HTML markup for the head and body, and so on, into an include file. This results in malformed HTML because these tags will be in the including page! Make sure that your include only includes the markup that is necessary.

There isn't much to see here because it is an included file. The parameter is passed as a `parameter` on the request object and is accessed using the `getParameter()` method as you saw with the forwarding example.

The output from this example is shown in Figure 3.2.

An alternative to using `<jsp:include>` is to use a new JSP2.0 feature that allows you to add headers and footers to groups of JSPs. There is a tag that can be used in `web.xml` to specify either a header or footer to be added to each page. Below is an example of this entry:

```
<jsp-property-group>
  <url-pattern>*.jsp</url-pattern>
```

```
  <include-prelude>/WEB-INF/includes/header.jspf</include-prelude>
  <include-coda>/WEB-INF/includes/footer.jspf</include-coda>
</jsp-property-group>
```

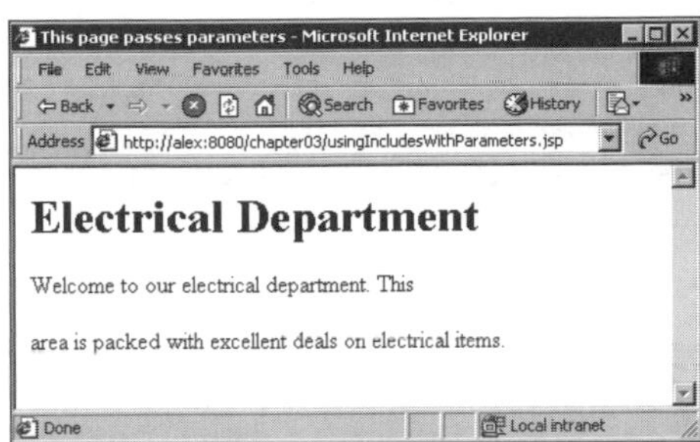

Figure 3.2 Output from `usingIncludesWithParameters.jsp`.

The `<jsp-property-group>` defines a group of pages, and within it you can set includes for the top of the pages `<include-prelude>`, and includes for the foot of the pages `<include-coda>`. This is ideal when you are using the same headers or footers on every single page. The `<url-pattern>` element specifies which JSPs are to be included in the group, in this case, all of them with the .jsp extension.

The Java Plugin

In this section, you will be introduced to three more standard actions:

- `<jsp:plugin>`
- `<jsp:params>`
- `<jsp:fallback>`

You will also see an additional use for the `<jsp:param>` element.

If you are planning to use Java applets within your application, you need to make sure that the client browsers support the applet you plan to use. One of the most frustrating aspects of applet development is the fact that you are reliant on the client browser virtual machine. Although Java is sometimes referred to as a "write once, run anywhere" language, in my experience, writing Java applets can be more like "write once, debug everywhere!" This is because the virtual machines in the browsers have various issues depending on the browser in use, and the platform on which the browser is running. Microsoft stopped shipping a Java virtual machine with its browser, requiring it to be downloaded separately; and on XP platforms, even that is no longer permitted. So, the reality is this: The more widely used browser (Internet Explorer) does not have very straightforward support for Java applets, and none at all in certain environments.

The traditional way to embed a Java applet into an HTML page is shown in Listing 3.4. This listing will not work in Internet Explorer where a virtual machine is not installed.

Listing 3.4 applet.html

```
<html>
<head>
<title>Not using the Java Plugin</title>
</head>
<body>
<h1>Applet running in the browser</h1>
<applet code="BasicApplet.class" width="90%" height="100">
  <param name="text" value="Hello from the applet">
</applet>
</body>
</html>
```

It is against this backdrop that the Java Plugin comes in. This neat little bit of software is a plugin to the browser; the same way that Shockwave or Real Audio can be installed as a plugin to your browser to provide support for complex animations or streamed media. The Java Plugin basically provides a Java virtual machine that can be used by browsers to run Java applets in a fully compliant virtual machine from Sun. Various plugins are available for various versions of the Java programming language.

The Java Plugin can be installed from `http://java.sun.com/getjava/`.

The fundamental problem with this is that going to this URL is fine for Java-savvy developers like you and me, but how many regular Internet users are going to want to "faff about" trying to find this URL simply so they can use your online calculator or whatever your applet does.

> **Note**
> *Faffing* is a British term often used to denote someone wasting time or not getting straight to the point.

The Java Plugin can be installed automatically if required, and this is achieved using some specific HTML that needs to go into your page. This is where the `<jsp:plugin>` include comes in really useful. Its role is to automatically put in the required HTML code to enable a browser to run your applet using the Java plugin, and also install it if it is not already present. Listing 3.5 demonstrates the use of the Java Plugin.

Listing 3.5 plugin.jsp

```
<html>
<head>
<title>Using the Java Plugin</title>
</head>
<body>
<h1>Applet running in the plugin</h1>

<jsp:plugin type="applet" code="BasicApplet.class" width="90%" height="100">
  <jsp:params>
```

Listing 3.5 **Continued**

```
    <jsp:param name="text" value="Hello from the applet"/>
  </jsp:params>
  <jsp:fallback>
      Your browser can't display this applet. Sorry
  </jsp:fallback>
</jsp:plugin>

</body>
</html>
```

> **Note**
> The sample application for this chapter has a basic applet that takes in a parameter and displays it. The code is available as part of the sample application, but is not shown because it is not relevant to the discussion.

The `<jsp:plugin>` standard action is the main action being used here. It specifies the applet class, and a number of other attributes—some are shown and some are not. The complete list can be found in the JSP 2.0 specifications available from `http://www.jcp.org/jsr/detail/152.jsp`.

The `<jsp:params>` action is optional and is required if the applet is to be passed any parameters. These parameters are then set using the `<jsp:param>` action that you have seen before.

Finally, the `<jsp:fallback>` action specifies what is to be displayed in the browser if the browser does not understand the `OBJECT` or `EMBED` tags that have been embedded into the HTML as a result of the `<jsp:plugin>` markup. The resulting HTML that is created from the JSP shown in Listing 3.9 is shown in Listing 3.6. This can be viewed by selecting `View/Source` in the browser.

Listing 3.6 **HTML Created by** `plugin.jsp`

```
<html>
<head>
<title>Using the Java Plugin</title>
</head>
<body>
<h1>Applet running in the plugin</h1>

<OBJECT classid="clsid:8AD9C840-044E-11D1-B3E9-00805F499D93"
   width="90%" height="100"
   codebase="http://java.sun.com/products/
             plugin/1.2.2/jinstall-1_2_2-win.cab#Version=1,2,2,0">
<PARAM name="java_code" value="BasicApplet.class">
```

Listing 3.6 **Continued**

```
<PARAM name="type" value="application/x-java-applet;">
<PARAM name="text" value="Hello from the applet">
<COMMENT>
<EMBED type="application/x-java-applet;" width="90%" height="100"
pluginspage="http://java.sun.com/products/plugin/"
java_code="BasicApplet.class"
 name="text" value="Hello from the applet"
>
<NOEMBED>
</COMMENT>

      Your browser can't display this applet. Sorry

</NOEMBED></EMBED>
</OBJECT>
</body>
</html>
```

The OBJECT tag is there for Microsoft Internet Explorer, and the EMBED tag is there for Netscape. When this page is running on a Windows platform, you will get a Java icon in your system tray. This is shown in Figure 3.3, which shows Internet Explorer showing this page.

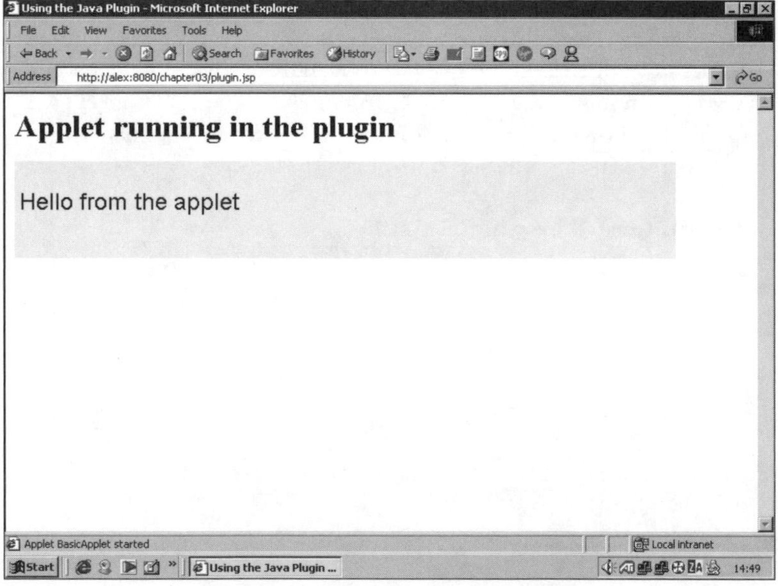

Figure 3.3 `plugin.jsp` in the browser.

Using JavaBeans on Pages

Three standard actions are associated with the use of JavaBeans on JavaServer Pages. JavaBeans are Java classes written to a certain specification which includes that they can have get and set methods for their properties. They also have a public no argument constructor. The standard actions allow the instantiation of beans, and also the setting and getting of their properties:

- `<jsp:useBean>` enables the use of JavaBeans within JavaServer Pages. It specifies the Beans to be used on a specific page.
- `<jsp:getProperty>` is used to access Bean properties from pages.
- `<jsp:setProperty>` is used to set properties from pages.

A basic example is shown here:

```
<!-- create an instance of the bean -->
<jsp:useBean class="Book" id="book" scope="session"/>
<!-- set the title property -->
<jsp:setProperty name="book" property="title" value="Treasure Island"/>
<!-- now display this property on the page -->
<jsp:getProperty name="book" property="title"/>
```

The use of JavaBeans on pages is vital if you are going to even begin to separate your business logic from your presentation. These standard actions associated with JavaBeans were the first step in the JSP specifications to enable this to be done. The subject of JavaBeans and their use in JavaServer Pages is discussed in detail in Chapter 6, "JSP and JavaBeans."

Actions and Tag Libraries

It is now also possible to create your own *custom* actions in addition to the standard actions that have been discussed. Custom actions are discussed in Chapter 9, "Developing Custom Tag Libraries," because custom actions are basically custom tags.

When using actions, there are some additional helper standard actions that you have available to you. One such action is the `<jsp:attribute>` action.

Consider the following code fragment:

```
<jsp:include page="includeFileNeedingAParameter.jsp"/>
```

The `<jsp:attribute>` action enables you to replace any attributes in your tags with `<jsp:attribute>` tags, with the attribute value now being element content:

```
<jsp:include>
  <jsp:attribute name="page">includeFileNeedingAParameter.jsp</jsp:attribute>
</jsp:include>
```

You might be wondering what the benefit of this would be. In this specific example there is no benefit, but, for example, when you have custom actions, you might want attribute values to contain XML-structured data. This would not be possible if you were using normal XML attributes because these cannot contain structured XML data. The `attribute` action also has an additional attribute called `trim`, which enables you to specify whether whitespace at the start and the end of the value is removed. The default value is `true`, which means it will trim the whitespace.

Another helper action is `<jsp:body>`. This element is used to explicitly specify the body content of a tag. The body content of a tag is the name given to the content between the opening and closing parts of a tag:

```
<jsp:someTag>here is the body content</jsp:someTag>
```

The body can be explicitly specified using `<jsp:body>` elements:

```
<jsp:someTag><jsp:body>here is the body content</jsp:body></jsp:someTag>
```

Clearly, this is somewhat superfluous, but when attributes have been specified using the `<jsp:attribute>` action, the body must be explicitly specified using this element because it is presumed the tag has no body content if it has `<jsp:attribute>` actions within it. An example of this is shown here:

```
<jsp:someTag>
  <jsp:attribute name="someAttribute">attribute value</jsp:attribute>
  <jsp:body>here is the body content</jsp:body>
</jsp:someTag>
```

You have now seen the standard actions available to the JSP developer. The chapter will now move on to look at the JSP 2.0 expression language.

The JSP Expression Language (EL)

The remainder of this chapter will discuss the JSP expression language. The expression language has been developed by two expert groups at the Java Community Process. One is the JSP Standard Tag Library expert group, and the other is the JSP 2.0 expert group. The reason for the involvement of both groups becomes clear when you realize that the EL is designed to be used both within JSP tags, and also in line within JavaServer Pages directly. In fact, the EL is part of the JSP2.0 specification as opposed to the JSTL 1.1 specification.

The following syntax identifies EL expressions within pages.

```
${ EL expression }
```

When used within the attributes of tags from the JSTL, for example, you end up with JSP code that looks like this:

```
<prefix:tag attribute="${EL Expression}" />
```

When used directly within pages, you could get code like this:

```
<body bgcolor="${EL Expression}">
```

Listing 3.7 shows a basic JSP that is using the expression language directly in the page.

Listing 3.7 `usingEL.jsp`

```
<!-- be aware that this listing will not work
in Tomcat 4.1, or any other JSP 1.2 container -->
<html>
<head>
<title>Expression Language Examples</title>
<%
  // set up a page context parameter for use later in the page
  // normally this would have been set within the context of
  // an application
  pageContext.setAttribute("pageColor", "yellow");
%>

</head>
<body bgcolor="${pageScope.pageColor}">

<h1>Welcome to the ${param.department} Department</h1>

Here are some basic comparisons:
<p>
Is 1 less than 2? ${1<2} <br>
Does 5 equal 5? ${5==5} <br>
Is 6 greater than 7? ${6 gt 7}<br>

<p>Now for some math:<br>
6 + 7 = ${6+7}<br>
8 x 9 = ${8*9}<br>


<hr>You appear to be using the following browser:
${header["user-agent"]}

</body>
</html>
```

The output of Listing 3.7 with the JSP 2.0 early access preview version of Tomcat appeared as shown in Figure 3.4.

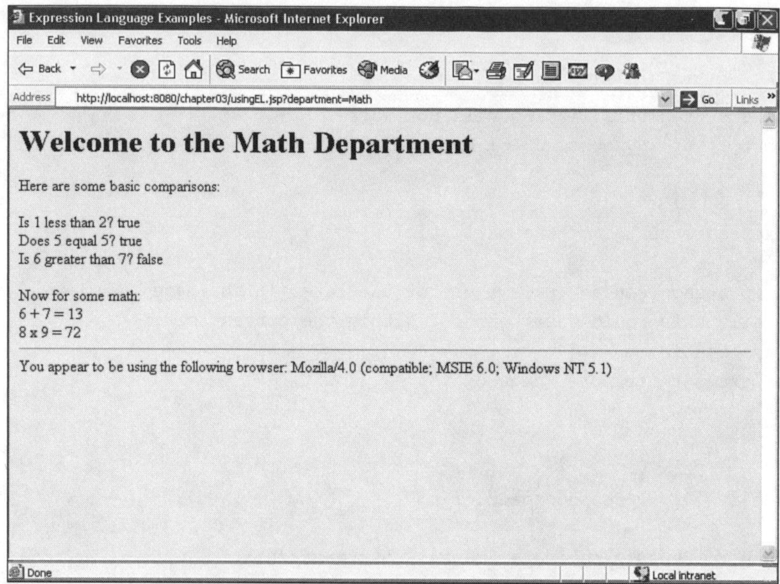

Figure 3.4 The output from `usingEL.jsp` in a browser.

Listing 3.7 will be referred to as we progress through the chapter. So, what does the EL look like? It draws its syntax from two other scripting languages: XPath and ECMAScript. XPath is used in XML applications and is discussed in Chapter 11, "Transforming XML Using XSLT and XSLFO." ECMAScript is mainly used as a client-side scripting language in Web applications, and is also commonly used in the development of Microsoft Active Server Pages.

> **Note**
>
> ECMAScript was developed within the context of the European Computer Manufacturers Association. It is essentially a standardization of Netscape's JavaScript, which has been widely used as a client-side scripting language in both Internet Explorer (implemented as JScript) and Netscape browsers.

The EL has the following features:

- It has a set of implicit objects available to it.
- It has a comprehensive set of operators.
- It can access collections and nested properties in an intuitive way.
- It has a selection of extensible functions mapping to static methods in Java classes.

EL Literal Types

The expression language has the following basic types that can be used for literal values:

- `String`—This is a value defined within double or single quotes.
- `Boolean`—Like Java, this type has only the possible values of `true` and `false`.
- `IntegerLiteral`—This type represents signed integral numbers. It is implemented as a Java long.
- `FloatingPointLiteral`—This type represents floating-point numbers.
- `NullLiteral`—This is the same as the Java `null`. The literal value for this is `null`.

The EL Operators

The EL has a comprehensive set of operators as you might expect. We will explore these in this section. As you'll see, many of them are the same as those found in the Java Programming language. The main difference, however, is that for many operators there is a textual equivalent. The most commonly used operators are discussed here; for a complete list visit the JSP 2.0 specification at `http://www.jcp.org/jsr/detail/152.jsp`.

The Arithmetic Operators

There are the expected operators here: `+`, `-`, `*`, `/`, `%`. You can also use the following for the `/` and `%` operators: `div` and `mod`. You can see examples of these being used in Listing 13.7:

```
<p>Now for some math:<br>
6 + 7 = ${6+7}<br>
8 x 9 = ${8*9}<br>
```

The Relational Operators

The relational operators are shown in Table 3.2.

Table 3.2 **The Relational Operators**

Symbol Version	Text Version
`==`	`eq`
`!=`	`ne`
`<`	`lt`
`>`	`gt`
`>=`	`ge`
`<=`	`le`

Notice that they all have a text version in addition to the more familiar symbol version. These are also used in Listing 13.7:

Here are some basic comparisons:

```
<p>
Is 1 less than 2? ${1<2} <br>
Does 5 equal 5? ${5==5} <br>
Is 6 greater than 7? ${6 gt 7}<br>
```

The Logical Operators

The logical operators are the same as the Java Programming Language, but they also have their textual equivalents within the EL. They are shown in Table 3.3.

Table 3.3 **The Logical Operators**

Symbol Version	Text Version
`&&`	`and`
`||`	`or`
`!`	`not`

The `empty` Operator

The `empty` operator allows you to test the following:

- Object references to see if they are null.
- Strings to see if they are empty.
- Arrays to see if they are empty.
- Lists to see if they are empty.
- Maps to see if they are empty.

You use the operator in the following way:

```
empty variableName
```

If any of the above conditions are met, then the operator returns true.

Operator Precedence

The operator precedence works from the highest precedence through to the lowest precedence, and then left to right - In other words, the same as the Java programming language. As with any other programming language, you can affect this precedence with the use of parentheses ().

The operator precedence table as defined by the JSP 2.0 specification is shown below in Table 3.4:

Table 3.4 **The Operator Precedence Table for the EL**

```
[] .
()
-(unary) not ! empty
* / div % mod
+ - (binary)
<> <= >= lt gt le ge
== !- eq ne
&& and
|| or
```

Accessing Objects and Collections

In the Java Programming Language, objects and their properties are accessed using `get` and `set` methods. This is because of encapsulation, and it is not considered good practice to access object properties directly.

So, for example, if there were a hierarchy of objects such as a bookstore, with a book, and the book had a chapter, the code would be something like

```
getBookStore().getBook().getChapter(“Ch03FurtherJSP”);
```

This can look quite messy, and although hiding the variables provides encapsulation, it is not clear to read, especially within JSPs in code like this:

```
<%= getBookStore().getBook().getChapter(“Ch03FurtherJSP”) %>
```

If this were a scripting language such as ECMAScript, it would be something like

```
bookStore.book.chapters.Ch03FurtherJSP
```

If you are familiar with ECMAScript, you will have seen how objects can be accessed in a variety of ways in that language. This is also the case in the EL. So, taking our basic chapter example one step further, using the EL, you can access this chapter object in the following ways:

```
bookStore.book.chapters.Ch03FurtherJSP
bookstore[“book”].chapters.Ch03FurtherJSP
bookstore[‘book’].chapters[“Ch03FurtherJSP”]
```

Essentially, what we are saying here is that there are two operators that can be used to enable you to access objects. One is the dot operator (.), and the other is the `[]` brackets. When using the brackets, you can place the name of a subproperty as a String in either double or single quotes within them, as shown. Using the dot enables you to step down through properties and the various subproperties.

> **Caution**
> In ECMAScript, you can also access objects by putting an index number in the square brackets. This is not possible in the EL unless the property is a collection of some kind.

This mechanism for accessing objects makes the development of JSPs substantially easier. This is especially true for Web designers, who will most probably already be experienced in the ECMAScript object access mechanisms, which are now available to the JSP developer.

The previous caution mentions that the use of the square brackets is also used to access collections. The EL can handle the various Java collection types, and it uses a generic syntax for accessing a collection, regardless of the actual collection implementation. So, the collection could be an array, a `List`, a `Vector`, and so on, but the syntax would be the same. Collections are accessed in a similar way to how an array would be accessed in the Java Programming Language; in other words, an index is placed within the square brackets. So, in the earlier simple example, if the chapters were stored as a `List` rather than individual named properties, you could access Chapter 3 in the following way:

```
bookStore.book.chapters[2]
```

If the collection were a `Map`, instead of an index number being placed within the square brackets, a key would be used:

```
bookStore.book.chapters["Ch03FurtherJSP"]
```

The access of objects from the EL is illustrated by the following worked example, starting with the JSP shown in Listing 3.8.

Listing 3.8 **ELAccessingObjects.jsp**

```
<!-- be aware that this listing will not work
in Tomcat 4.1, or any other container that does
not support the use of the expression language outside
of tags -->
<html>
<head>
<title>Expression Language Accessing Objects</title>

<p>Now lets use some objects. You will see more on the bean standard actions
in chapter 6. But for now, remember that here useBean instantiates beans
and setProperty sets the properties of beans.

<%-- create a single Person object --%>
<jsp:useBean id="man" class="com.conygre.Person">
<jsp:setProperty name="man" property="name" value="Nick"/>
<jsp:setProperty name="man" property="password" value="pass"/>
</jsp:useBean>
```

Listing 3.8 **Continued**

```
<p>Now we will use the expression language to access the properties.
The person is called ${man.name}, and the password is ${man.password}.

Now a list and a map is created as properties of the GroupPeople class.

<%-- create a GroupPeople object that contains a List and a Map --%>
<jsp:useBean id="group" class="com.conygre.GroupPeople"/>

The map is accessible using the following syntax:<br>
The first author is called ${group.mapPeople["authorA"]},
and the second author is called ${group.mapPeople["authorB"]}.

<p>The List is accessible also, but using the following syntax:<br>
The first author is called ${group.listPeople[0]},
and the second author is called ${group.listPeople[1]}.

</body>
</html>
```

In Listing 3.8, you can see the JavaBean related standard actions being used to set up two beans. One is a `Person` bean, which is based upon the Java class shown in Listing 3.9, and the other is a `GroupPeople` bean, shown in Listing 3.10.

Listing 3.9 **Person.java**

```
package com.conygre;
public class Person {

  private String name;
  private String password;

  public String getName(){
    return name;
  }
  public void setName(String s){
    name = s;
  }
  public String getPassword(){
      return password;
  }
  public void setPassword(String s){
      password = s;
  }
}
```

Listing 3.10 **GroupPeople.java**

```
package com.conygre;
import java.util.*;
public class GroupPeople {

  private List listPeople;
  private Map mapPeople;

  public GroupPeople()
  {
    listPeople = new Vector();
    listPeople.add("Nick");
    listPeople.add("Mark");
    mapPeople=new HashMap();
    mapPeople.put("authorA", "Nick");
    mapPeople.put("authorB", "Mark");
  }


  public List getListPeople(){
    return listPeople;
  }

  public void setListPeople(List s){
    listPeople = s;
  }

  public Map getMapPeople(){
      return mapPeople;
  }

  public void setMapPeople(Map s){
      mapPeople = s;
  }
}
```

The crucial lines within the JSP of Listing 3.8 are the ones that access bean properties using the EL. They are shown below:

```
The person is called ${man.name}, and the password is ${man.password}.
. . .
The map is accessible using the following syntax:<br>
The first author is called ${group.mapPeople["authorA"]},
and the second author is called ${group.mapPeople["authorB"]}.

<p>The List is accessible also, but using the following syntax:<br>
```

```
The first author is called ${group.listPeople[0]},
and the second author is called ${group.listPeople[1]}.
```

The first line in this snippet is accessing the `Person` instance with the `id` of `man`. It is accessing the `name` and `password` properties directly.

The remainder of this snippet demonstrates how maps and lists are accessed. The `GroupPeople` bean has a `Map` property and a `List` property set up with some `Strings` as content, as shown in Listing 3.10. The `GroupPeople` object `id` is set up as `group`. Therefore the code accesses the properties `listPeople` and `mapPeople` as you would expect. Notice that the `List` values are accessed by their indices, and the `Map` values are accessed by their `key` names.

The EL Implicit Objects

In the previous chapter, you were exposed to the implicit objects available to the JSP developer for use within your pages. The Expression Language also provides a number of implicit objects that can be used directly from within EL code. Table 3.5 lists these objects and what they can be used for.

Table 3.5 **The EL Implicit Objects**

Name	Description
`pageContext`	This is the page context object,. The the same object that is available as a JSP-implicit object. This was discussed in detail in Chapter 2.
`pageScope`	In the very last section of Chapter 1, the idea of scope was introduced. Page-scoped attributes can be accessed by name using this variable. This is because the variable is a `Map`. Here is an example of accessing a page-scoped object that we have called `pageColor`: `<body bgcolor="${pageScope.pageColor}">` or `<body bgcolor="${pageScope['pageColor']}">` This example can be seen in Listing 3.11.
`requestScope`	The `requestScope` is also a `Map` object, but it contains all the request-scoped attributes. It can be used in the same way as the `pageScope`.

`param`	The `param` object is another `Map` that contains any request parameters normally accessed using the `request.getParameter(String paramName)` method. This could be used as a more convenient mechanism for accessing parameters. The following fragment shown here could be rewritten from
	`<h1><%=request.getParameter("department") %> Department</h1>`
	To to a more simple
	`<h1> ${param.department} Department</h1>`
	This example can be seen in Listing 3.7.

Table 3.5 **Continued**

Name	Description
paramValues	This object represents the result of the call to `request.getParameterValues(String paramName)`. This method returns an array of parameter values based on a particular parameter name. The following would return all the values of a parameter called `favoriteColors`. `${paramValues.favoriteColors}`
header	This implicit variable contains a `Map` of all the headers along with their values. It returns the result of the method `request.getHeader(String headerName)`. The following example accesses the user agent, which details the client browser: `${header["user-agent"]}` This is visible in Listing 3.7.
headerValues	This object represents the result of the call to `request.getHeaders(String headerName)`. This method returns an array of header values based on a particular header name.
sessionScope	The `sessionScope` is a `Map` object that contains all the session-scoped attributes. It can be used in the same way as `pageScope`.
cookie	This variable provides access to the `Cookies` array that is available to JSP via the `request.getCookies()` method. Cookies are discussed in Chapter 8, "Session Tracking Using JSP."
applicationScope	The `applicationScope` is a `Map` object that contains all the application-scoped attributes. It can be used in the same way as `pageScope`.
initParam	This variable gives access to all the initialization parameters that may have been passed to the JSP when its corresponding servlet was initialized.

Reserved Words

There are also a number of reserved words for the EL. Many of these are textual versions of the operators listed in Table 3.6. Others are words that currently have no use, but have been reserved for future use. They are all shown in Table 3.7.

Table 3.6 **The Reserved Words**

lt	ge	le
eq	and	true
ne	or	false
gt	not	null
instanceof	empty	div
mod		

Expression Language Functions

The expression language also provides a number of functions, associated with string manipulation and for working with collections. These are shown in Table 3.7. Note that this list was taken from the JSTL 1.1 maintenance review proposals, and it is possible that this list is not the exact final list of functions.

Table 3.7 **Expression Language Functions**

Function	Description
`boolean contains(string, substring)`	Returns true if the specified String contains the sequence of characters in the specified substring.
`boolean containsIgnoreCase(string, substring)`	Returns true if the specified String contains the sequence of characters in the specified substring, but not taking account of case.
`boolean endsWith(string, suffix)`	Returns true if the string ends with the supplied string suffix.
`String escapeXml(string)`	Escapes any XML sensitive characters in supplied string (&, <, >, ', ") with the predefined XML entity equivalents and returns the result as a String. See Chapter 10, "Utilising XML from JSP" for more information on XML.
`int indexOf(string, substring)`	Returns the index within this string of the first occurrence of the specified substring.
`String join(collection, separator)`	This method takes in a collection, and concatenates the values together in a String, using the supplied separator.
`int length(collection)`	Returns the length of a `Collection` as an `int`.
`String replace(inputString, beforeSubstring, afterSubstring)`	Replaces the characters in a substring of the input string with the additional characters specified.
`String[] split(string, separator)`	Takes in a String, and converts the contents into a String array, with each new array entry beginning when the separator character is found.
`boolean startsWith(string, prefix)`	Queries a String to see if it starts with the supplied prefix.
`String substring(string, beginIndex, endIndex)`	Returns a substring from a string based upon the supplied beginning and end indexes.
`String substringAfter(string, substring)`	Returns a substring from a supplied string. The substring is the contents of the supplied string located after the supplied substring.

Table 3.7 **Continued**

Function	Description
`String substringBefore(string, substring)`	Returns a substring from a supplied string. The substring is the contents of the supplied string located before the supplied substring.
`String toLowerCase(string)`	Converts a supplied string to upper case.
`String toUpperCase(string)`	Converts a supplied string to lower case.
`String trim(string)`	Returns a copy of the supplied string with any leading and trailing white space removed.

In addition to the supplied functions, you can also create your own. This is done by exposing static functions present in Java classes. For example, if a static method had the following signature:

```
public static String returnNewString(String oldString)
```

You would be able to invoke it from a page using the following style of EL construct:

```
${myTagLibrary:returnNewString("the old string value")}
```

Any parameters that the method takes are passed in as a comma-separated list. How these functions are set up is discussed in Chapter 9, "Developing Custom Tag Libraries."

Controlling Expression Language and Scriptlet Use

It is possible to deactivate the processing of EL elements within a JSP with the use of the following entry in the page directive. This might be necessary if aspects of the content of a page actually contained output of the format `${xxx}`. To deactivate the expression language, you can disable it for entire groups of pages within a web application using an entry type in `web.xml` that is new in JSP 2.0. The entry is of the following format:

```
<jsp-property-group>
  <url-pattern>*.jsp</url-pattern>
  <el-ignored>true</el-ignored>
</jsp-property-group>
```

The `<jsp-property-group>`, discussed earlier in the chapter, is an element that can be used in `web.xml` to configure groups of JSPs. In the above example, the expression language will be disabled for all JSP files.

Alternatively, you can disable the expression language for an individual page by setting the `isELIgnored` attribute of the page directive.

```
<%@page isELIgnored="false" %>
```

Using the `<jsp-property-group>` element, you can also disable scripting elements. The following is an example of a `jsp-property-group` that does this:

```
<jsp-property-group>
```

```
  <url-pattern>*.jsp</url-pattern>
  <scripting-invalid>true</scripting-invalid>
</jsp-property-group>
```

This means that using these `<jsp-property-group>` elements, you can effectively enforce the use of the expression language instead of scriptlets using the two `<jsp-property-group>` elements shown above. This will enforce the separation of the Java from the JSPs.

Summary

You have been introduced to the standard actions used for forwarding and including, embedding applets, and interacting with JavaBeans. These standard actions will be used throughout the later chapters in this book.

Finally, the chapter introduced the Expression Language, and you have seen the syntax and rules associated with it. You will come across this language in various other places as you read the later chapters in this book. Remember though that the EL is new to JSP 2.0, and not all containers support it.

In the last three chapters, you have been exposed to what JavaServer Pages are, and where they fit into the wider Java 2 Enterprise Edition picture. You have also seen that JSPs are part of what are commonly referred to as Web applications. Chapter 4, "Deploying JSP in a Web Container," will discuss how these Web applications are deployed.

4

Deploying JSP in a Web Container

SO FAR IN THIS BOOK, YOU HAVE seen how JSP works, and you have seen much of the syntax involved in the development of JavaServer Pages. You have also seen how Java servlets work, and how the JSP becomes a Java servlet. What has not been explored in any significant detail is how applications built using JSP can be deployed within the Web container. This chapter will focus on the deployment process. Various Web containers will also be briefly discussed at the end of the chapter. If you are using Tomcat, you will want to pay special attention to Appendix H, "Configuring Tomcat," which explains in detail how Tomcat can be configured to run your Web applications.

> **Note**
> The examples contained in this chapter are all available as part of `chapter04.war`, which is part of the book download available from the book Web site. You can locate this by visiting `www.samspublishing.com`, and entering the ISBN number (0672324385) in the search box.

Configuring JSP in `web.xml`

In Chapter 2, you learned how servlets can be configured within the `web.xml` deployment descriptor. JSP can also be configured within this file. The following aspects of JSP can be configured in `web.xml`:

- Welcome files
- URL mappings
- Initialization parameters

Each of these will be discussed in turn.

Welcome Files

Suppose you enter a URL such as the following:

```
http://localhost:8080/chapter04
```

What gets displayed in the browser? If you are familiar with configuring Web servers, you will be familiar with the concept of a *welcome file*. The welcome file is what is presented to a user if no specific page is requested. It is the configuration of welcome files that enables you to enter domain names into the address bar of your browser without specifying the actual file that you want.

Welcome files can be set up for your Web application within `web.xml`. Listing 4.1 shows an example.

Listing 4.1 `web.xml` **Setting Up Welcome Files**

```
<?xml version="1.0" encoding="UTF-8"?>
<web-app xmlns="http://java.sun.com/xml/ns/j2ee"
   xmlns:xsi="http://www.w3.org/2001/XMLSchema-instance"
   xsi:schemaLocation="http://java.sun.com/xml/ns/j2ee
   http://java.sun.com/xml/ns/j2ee/web-app_2_4.xsd" version="2.4">
  <welcome-file-list>
    <welcome-file>index.jsp</welcome-file>
  </welcome-file-list>
</web-app>
```

As you can see, the core elements to enable the setting up of welcome files is the `<welcome-file-list>` element, which contains one or more `<welcome-file>` elements, each containing a relative URL for a specific welcome file.

URL Mappings

It is also possible to map JSP files to specific URLs other than the straightforward paths to the files that you have seen up to now. For example, in all the JSP examples you have seen, the URL is something like

```
http://localhost:8080/chapter04/index.jsp
```

The same file `index.jsp` could be mapped to an alternative URL, such as

```
http://localhost:8080/chapter03/home
```

This is done using `<servlet>` and `<servlet-mapping>` elements that you were introduced to in Listing 1.3 of Chapter 1, "JSP, J2EE, and the Role of the Servlet."

In Listing 4.2, the `<servlet>` tag is used as it would be for servlets (shown in Listing 1.7 of Chapter 1), but for a JSP, the `<servlet-class>` tag has been replaced by a `<jsp-file>` tag. Notice that the `<jsp-file>` and `<url-pattern>` elements must begin with a forward slash.

Listing 4.2 web.xml **Setting Up a URL Mapping for a JSP**

```
<?xml version="1.0" encoding="UTF-8"?>
<web-app xmlns="http://java.sun.com/xml/ns/j2ee"
   xmlns:xsi="http://www.w3.org/2001/XMLSchema-instance"
   xsi:schemaLocation="http://java.sun.com/xml/ns/j2ee
   http://java.sun.com/xml/ns/j2ee/web-app_2_4.xsd" version="2.4">
<servlet>
  <servlet-name>Index Page</servlet-name>
    <jsp-file>/index.jsp</jsp-file>
  </servlet>
  <servlet-mapping>
    <servlet-name>Index Page</servlet-name>
    <url-pattern>/home</url-pattern>
  </servlet-mapping>
</web-app>
```

This JSP can now be accessed by the following URL:

```
http://localhost:8080/chapter04/home
```

It is also worth mentioning at this point the `<url-pattern>` element can also be used to map multiple URLs to the same JSP or servlet. This is done with the use of the '*' as a wild card. So, you could set up a mapping as follows:

```
<servlet-mapping>
  <servlet-name>SomeServlet</servlet-name>
  <url-pattern>/folder/*</url-pattern>
</servlet-mapping>
```

In this example, the following URLs will all result in `SomeServlet` being invoked.

```
http://localhost:8080/appName/folder/index.htm
http://localhost:8080/appName/folder/subFolder/
http://localhost:8080/appName/folder/
```

This is because the '*' has been used to map any path that begins with the structure `/folder/`.

An alternative way of using the wildcard is to specify that any resource ending with a specific extension will be mapped.

```
<servlet-mapping>
  <servlet-name>SomeServlet</servlet-name>
  <url-pattern>/folder/*.html</url-pattern>
</servlet-mapping>
```

In the above example, any URLs that are for resources within `folder` with the extension `.html`, will result in `SomeServlet` being invoked.

```
http://localhost:8080/appName/folder/index.html
http://localhost:8080/appName/folder/test.html
```

You will see the wildcard used very effectively when we look at a JSP framework called Struts in Chapter 7, "JSP Application Architecture."

Because of the specifications in the `web.xml` XML Schema, the elements must be in the correct order. This means that all the `<servlet>` entries must precede the `<servlet-mapping>` entries.

Initialization Parameters

In Chapter 1, you saw how servlets can be passed initialization parameters from the `web.xml` file at startup, and because JSPs also become servlets, it makes sense to allow them to also access initialization parameters. Listing 4.3 shows a `web.xml` file that passes a parameter to a JSP called `initialization.jsp`.

Listing 4.3 `web.xml` **Passing Initialization Parameters to a JSP**

```
<?xml version="1.0" encoding="UTF-8"?>
<web-app xmlns="http://java.sun.com/xml/ns/j2ee"
   xmlns:xsi="http://www.w3.org/2001/XMLSchema-instance"
   xsi:schemaLocation="http://java.sun.com/xml/ns/j2ee
   http://java.sun.com/xml/ns/j2ee/web-app_2_4.xsd" version="2.4">
<servlet>
  <servlet-name>InitializationJSP</servlet-name>
    <jsp-file>/initialization.jsp</jsp-file>
    <init-param>
      <param-name>testParam</param-name>
      <param-value>hello from web.xml</param-value>
    </init-param>
  </servlet>
  <servlet-mapping>
    <servlet-name>InitializationJSP</servlet-name>
    <url-pattern>/Initialization</url-pattern>
  </servlet-mapping>
</web-app>
```

Listing 4.3 is remarkably similar to Listing 1.7 of Chapter 1, which demonstrates how initialization parameters are set for servlets. The `<init-param>`, `<param-name>`, and `<param-value>` elements are used in exactly the same way.

Listing 4.4 shows `initialization.jsp`, and how it can access the initialization parameter passed in.

Listing 4.4 `initialization.jsp`

```
<html>
<head>
<title>Initialization Parameters and JSP</title>
</head>
```

Listing 4.4 **Continued**

```
<body>
This page has retrieved the following initialization parameter from web.xml:
<br>
<%= pageContext.getServletConfig().getInitParameter("testParam") %>
</body>
</html>
```

The initialization parameter is accessible via the `ServletConfig` object for this JSP, and this is obtained from the `pageContext` implicit variable discussed in Chapter 2, "The Basic Syntax of JSP."

The Web Container

If you have read Chapter 1, "JSP, J2EE, and the Role of the Servlet," you will have seen that a Web application can consist of the following core component types:

- JavaServer Pages
- Java Servlets
- JavaBeans
- Tag Libraries

The web container is also capable of delivering other data formats such as HTML, graphics, and XML data to clients. As introduced in Chapter 1, the Web container, if it is J2EE-compliant, must be able to host these technologies and provide interfaces to a number of additional services such as JNDI. A diagram of the services that a Web container must be able to access is shown in Figure 1.5. It is important to note that the Web container is not required to host services such as JNDI, JMS, and so on. It must be able to interact with them, however.

The Tomcat Web container is one of the most popular Web containers available because

- It supports the very latest Servlet and JSP standards.
- It is the reference implementation for these technologies.
- It is free!

Other containers are integrated into application servers, which will also provide an EJB container as discussed in Chapter 1.

The Web Application

There is also a predefined folder structure for a Web application. That structure is shown in Figure 4.1.

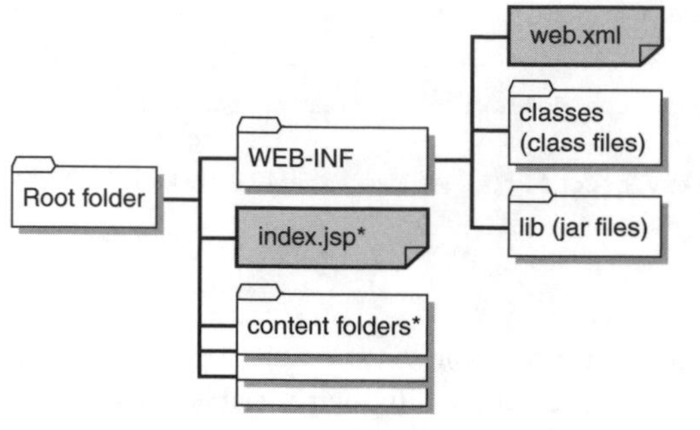

Figure 4.1 The structure of a Web application.

The main aspects of a Web application are as follows:

- The Root folder—This folder is the top-level folder for the Web application. It contains the entire structure of the Web application. If deployed as is, in Tomcat, that would mean putting the folder in the `<tomcat-home>\webapps` folder; the name of this folder is case-sensitive. It is worth pointing out that the entire contents of this folder can be placed into a JAR file, given the extension, .war, and then deployed in Tomcat by simply placing the .war file in the `<tomcat-home>\webapps` folder.
- The `WEB-INF` folder—This folder contains the configuration information for the application, and is the location for the folders containing any relevant JAR files and classes. The configuration information is located within the file `web.xml`. Tag Library Definition (TLD) files (discussed in Chapter 5, "The JSP Standard Tag Library") are also typically located in this folder.
- `web.xml`—This file contains the configuration information for the Web application. This includes initialization parameters such as those discussed in Chapter 1; for example, security constraints, references to EJBs, and so forth. You'll see many further examples of the elements that can be placed in this file as you proceed through the book.
- `WEB-INF\classes`—This folder contains all the classes that are used within this application.
- `WEB-INF\lib`—This folder contains any JAR files required by the application.
- `JSPs, HTML files` and any content folders—Any files and folders and files within the root directory apart from the `WEB-INF` directory are available to clients using HTTP requests. These files, which will make up the content of the Web application, can be arranged as desired by the Web developer into files and folders as you would for any Web site. There does not have to be any JSPs, HTML pages or content folders. If a Web application only contains servlets, for example, there may be

nothing more than the `WEB-INF` folder with the servlet classes and a `web.xml` configuration file.

It is worth commenting about the location of your class and JAR files at this point. You can put classes into the `classes` folder and JARs into the `lib` folder, as referred to earlier, but there are reasons for not putting them in those locations for certain specific situations. The benefit of putting them in those locations is that the Web application becomes self-contained, in that all the required classes and libraries are within the application. The reality is, however, that on some occasions they need to be placed within the classpath for the Web container itself.

> **Tip**
>
> Tomcat has its own locations for classes and library files. These two locations are
>
> ```
> <tomcat-home>\shared\classes
> <tomcat-home>\shared\lib
> ```
>
> Sometimes developers put classes or JAR files into `<tomcat-home>\common\lib` or `<tomcat-home>\common\shared`. This also works, although this is not advised because these locations are for classes internal to Tomcat as well as any deployed web applications.

The reasons for using these global locations for JAR files include

- Classes and libraries can be shared across multiple Web applications without the need for repeating them in each application.
- If you are using Tomcat 4 or lower, classes starting with the package name `javax` are not read when placed within individual Web applications. This is an issue when using the Apache Axis Web services engine, for example (see Chapter 12, "Invoking Web Services from JSP").

After an application has been built, a number of deployment methods exist.

Deploying Web Applications

Within the Tomcat Web container, there are four main ways to deploy a Web application. The first two mechanisms are discussed in this chapter. However, because not all readers of this book are going to be using Tomcat, the latter two mechanisms are discussed in Appendix H.

- Copy the Web application folder structure into the Web container folder structure.
- Copy a WAR file version of the application into the Web container folder structure.
- Set up a virtual folder containing your Web application folder structure.
- Use the manager servlet that comes with the container.

The manager servlet will be discussed later in the chapter.

Deploying a Folder Structure

In Tomcat, one of the easiest ways to deploy the application is to place the root folder of the application within the `<tomcat-home>\webapps` folder. After Tomcat has been restarted, the Web application will be detected by Tomcat and made available to clients with the URL to the application being

```
http://<server-name>:<portNumber>/<root-folder>/<content-folder>/<contentItem>
```

Other Web containers will also provide a location where you can deploy your Web applications in the same way.

Deploying a WAR File

To make the distribution of Web applications even more straightforward, you can JAR it up into a single file, a JAR file. As discussed in Chapter 1, this file can then be given the extension `.war`. This can be done using the `jar` tool that comes with the J2SDK or with tools such as WinZip on Windows platforms.

It is important when creating WAR files to ensure that the root directory is not stored within the WAR file. The top level of the WAR file should be the contents of the Web application root folder, not the root folder itself. Figure 4.2 shows the contents of the WAR file used in Chapter 1.

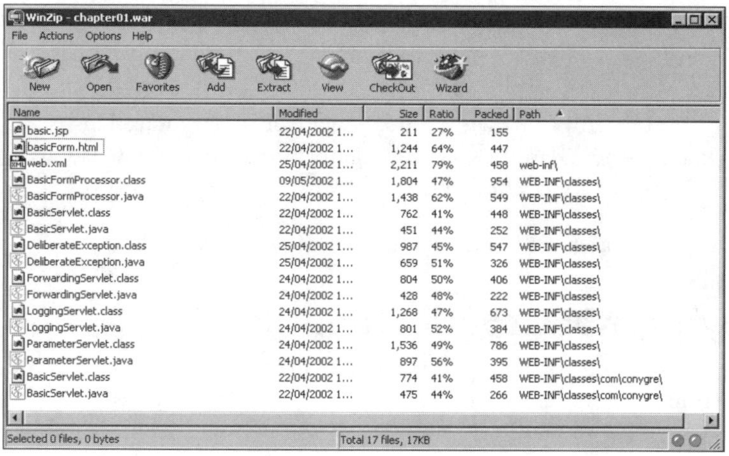

Figure 4.2 The structure of a WAR file.

If you are using Tomcat 4.1 or higher, you can deploy Web applications while Tomcat is running by dropping the WAR file in the `webapps` folder (or the expanded Web application). The control of this is discussed in Appendix H.

All other Web containers have mechanisms to make the deployment process as st
forward as possible. In Chapter 1, J2EE-compliant application servers were discuss
These servers enable you to deploy Web applications because they all provide a We
container. Many of these servers provide a Web interface to simplify the deploymen
process. Figure 4.3 shows the deployment interface for the BEA Web Logic server.

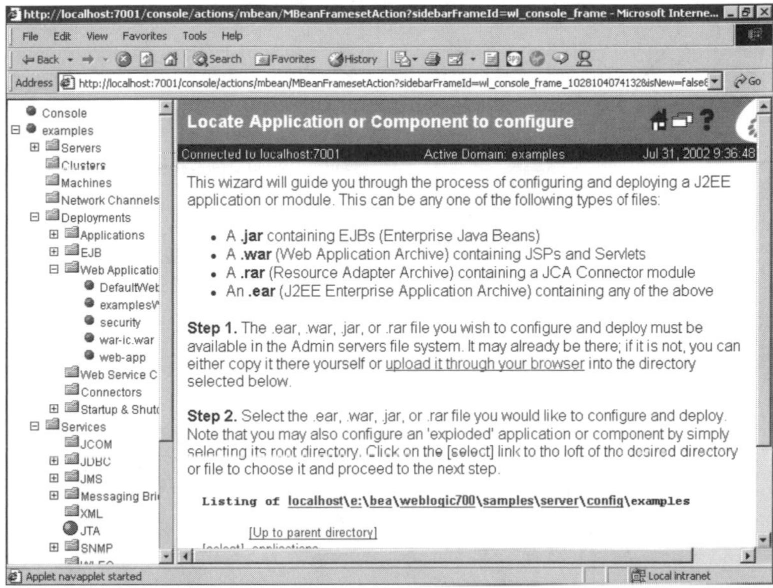

Figure 4.3 Deploying Web applications in WebLogic.

You'll see how to use this interface in Chapter 15, "JSP and EJB Interaction." More information about some of the different J2EE server products can be found in Appendix G, "J2EE Application Servers."

Summary

In this chapter, you learned what makes up a Web application, and how it can be deployed within a Web container.

In later chapters, you will discover more of what is involved in the configuration of a Web application. For example, in the next chapter, you will learn how to set up tag libraries. You will find out how to configure databases in Chapter 14 and you will learn to configure security in Chapter 16, "Security and JSP."

Finally, one of the most important things about this technology is its portability. Most Web applications can be ported between Web containers with relative ease. Nearly all the examples in this book will port with no modification whatsoever between Web containers. Basically, get your WAR file and choose a container!

So, let's now move on to tag libraries and learn how these can be incorporated into your Web applications.

5

The JSP Standard Tag Library

ONE OF THE MOST IMPORTANT RECENT DEVELOPMENTS in the world of JSP is the JSP Standard Tag Library (JSTL). This chapter explains how to use tag libraries from JSP and introduces the concept of a standard tag library. It will emphasize the key benefits of tag libraries, focusing on the capability to separate Java code from presentation markup.

The chapter begins by explaining the challenges faced by development teams of having Java code and presentation markup within the same files. It will then go on to explain how tag libraries can be used in JSP.

This chapter ends with an introduction to other tag libraries, specifically the Jakarta `taglib` project.

You can find a checklist of the actions that JSTL provides in Appendix C, "A Checklist of the Tags in the JSP Standard Tag Library." For more additional discussion of JSTL, you can also refer to the Sams book "JSTL: JSP Standard Tag Library Kick Start" (ISBN 0672324504).

> **Note**
>
> The examples contained in this chapter are all available as part of chapter05.war, which is part of the book download available from the book Web site. You can locate this by visiting `www.samspublishing.com` and entering the ISBN number (0672324385) in the search box.

> **Caution**
>
> When the book was written, the JavaServer Pages Standard Tag Library (JSTL) was in version 1.0. Version 1.1 was in development. The example applications are all written and tested with 1.0. The examples in the text have the URI for version 1.1. See the section in this chapter called "Backwards Compatibility and Migrating from JSTL 1.0 to JSTL 1.1" for more details.

The Need for Tag Libraries

Before you see how to use tag libraries from JSP, it is first important to understand why tag libraries are useful. In the next three sections, you will learn why tag libraries are created, as well as how to use an existing tag library from a JSP.

The Challenges of Mixing Presentation Markup and Java Code

As you saw in Chapter 1, "JSP, J2EE, and the Role of the Servlet," a servlet is a server-side Java program that can be used to process a request and generate a response. The Servlet 2.4 specification allows any protocol to be used for the request/response, but the HTTP protocol is still the only officially supported protocol. This of course presents no problem as far as writing JSP. However, in the section titled "Introducing the JavaServer Page" in Chapter 1, the point was made that to become an effective servlet developer, you must know Java, HTML, *and* be a competent Web page designer for the resultant Web page to look good to the user.

When Web developers first encountered servlets, it was common practice to put all HTML code into `out.println()` statements inside the `service()` method (or `doGet()`, or `doPost()`). There are several problems with embedding HTML code within a servlet. One problem is that the servlet very quickly becomes unreadable because of the sheer complexity of real-world HTML code that is used to generate today's Web pages. This in turn leads to a servlet that is difficult to manage.

More problems arise when the design department decides to change the content of the page. They come up with the HTML, but then the servlet developer must update the hard-coded HTML within the servlet. The editing itself can only be undertaken by somebody who is familiar with both the syntax of Java (for the servlet) and HTML (for the presentation code). Knowledge of one syntax without the other can lead to complications. For example, the HTML developer who edits the Java source code, but forgets—or removes—curly braces and semicolons and wonders what all the compilation errors are!

After the servlet has been successfully edited, it must be recompiled and redeployed. You must even restart some servlet containers before the new servlet is used to service client requests. This is inconvenient even when it is simply individual developers who are restarting their own personal development copy of the container.

> **Note**
>
> A solution to both of these problems is to store the HTML code in separate files that are dynamically processed by the servlet, before sending the result back to the client. Any changes necessary to the servlet can be carried out by a Java developer, whereas any changes necessary to the HTML can be carried out by an HTML developer.
>
> This is simply another example of separating the business logic from the presentation logic. This enables the different developers to go about their work with minimal dependencies on each other.

One solution to this problem is provided by templating libraries, which allow you to use templates from code. You write a template that contains HTML with additional tags that act as placeholders for dynamic content provided by your application. If you are interested in this approach, the following links are examples for Perl and Java, respectively: `http://html-template.sourceforge.net` and `http://html-tmpl-java.sourceforge.net`.

One of the golden rules of servlet development is to avoid putting HTML code directly into the servlet's code. When the JSP specification was first released and an easy alternative was available for generating dynamic content, it was very difficult for frustrated developers to resist going too far in the opposite direction. Page authors who were familiar with Java were tempted to embed great sections of Java code within the JSP. There are two disadvantages to going down this route. The first is that the JSP can only be edited by developers who are familiar with the Java programming language. The second is that it is difficult to reuse the Java code that is in the JSP.

The Tag Library as a Solution

JSPs were designed to enable page authors with no knowledge of Java to generate dynamic content. This is easy to forget, given the fact that JSPs are translated into servlets, and that the page author has access to the Java programming language from within the JSP itself.

For those page authors who are not familiar with a scripting language, there is always a need to access data and dynamically generate content for a page. Sun Microsystems developed *tag libraries* as a mechanism to help such people. This eventually led to the JavaServer Pages Tag Library (JSTL) Specification, which was developed by the JSR-52 expert group, under the Java Community Process (`http://jcp.org/`). Appendix F, "The Java Community Process," describes the Java Community Process. Before JSTL is discussed later in this chapter, it would be helpful to first examine tag libraries from a more generic viewpoint.

A tag library consists of a group of *custom tags*. A custom tag looks like an XML element, with optional attributes and body content. When a JSP that contains a custom tag is translated to a servlet, the generated servlet's `_jspService` method contains method calls to an associated *tag handler* object. As such, a custom tag is a construct that enables a Java developer to place Java code within a tag handler object and to *expose* the handler's functionality through tag names and attributes. When the custom tag is processed by the JSP container, the Java code within the associated handler object is executed. In this way, custom tags provide a page author the means to extend the functionality of a JSP without needing to embed any Java code within it.

Tag libraries and their custom tags can bring many benefits to your Web application. For example:

- Custom tags make it easier to write and maintain the JSPs. This is because the custom tags have an XML-like syntax that is easy for page authors who are familiar with HTML to learn. The resulting JSPs are cleaner because they are not cluttered with scripting code.
- One of the major benefits of custom tags is that they are reusable. Thus, you can write a custom tag of your own that provides a specific piece of functionality. After it has been tested and debugged, it can be used over and over again.
- The previous point leads to this one: Custom tags make the development of new Web applications quicker. After a page author has learned how a tag works, that knowledge can be reapplied to new JSPs. Also, because the custom tag has been

used before, new errors are not introduced as would be the case with the development of a new custom tag.

- If you decide that you want to change the way that the custom tag works, that change is automatically reflected in all the JSPs that use the tag. You do not need to modify any of the pages that use it. Having said that, it is possible to extend a tag with new attributes, rather than completely change the way it works. In this way, existing pages continue to use the old form of the tag until modified, but new pages can immediately use the new form with the extra attributes.

Using an Existing Tag Library

Chapter 9, "Developing Custom Tag Libraries," covers how to write your own tag libraries of custom tags. This current chapter covers the basic form of tag library descriptor (TLD) files along with how to deploy tag libraries, but look in Chapter 9 for more information.

There are two basic steps that you must take to use an existing tag library in a JSP:

- Make the tag library available to the JSP by importing it into the JSP.
- Insert the required tag into the JSP at the point that you need to use it.

Importing the Custom Tag Library

The process is really very simple, but this section shows you how the different pieces all fit together.

To import the tag library into the page you use the `taglib` directive that you saw in Chapter 2, "The Basic Syntax of JSP." The syntax of the `taglib` directive is

```
<%@ taglib uri="TAG_LIBRARY_DESCRIPTOR_URI" prefix="TAG_PREFIX" %>
```

The `prefix` attribute is an arbitrary string of text that is used to uniquely identify the custom tags you want to use. For example, if you specify a value of `c` for the `prefix` attribute, for the tag library in question you would use the syntax `<c:someTag ... />` for a tag called `someTag`.

Although this syntax looks similar to that used by XML namespaces, you should not confuse the two. XML namespaces enable you to bind a prefix to a namespace URI so that you can qualify element and attribute names in an XML document. You declare a tag library prefix in a different way, although the prefix also enables you to uniquely identify a tag.

The `uri` attribute enables you to specify the location of the custom tag library's *tag library descriptor* (*TLD*). A TLD is an XML file that describes the mapping between the custom tag and its tag handler.

There are two basic ways in which you can specify this mapping. One option is to specify a URL (relative or absolute) to the TLD file. The other option is to provide a logical name/URL mapping within the Web application's `web.xml` file, and then use the logical name as the value for the `uri` attribute in the `taglib` directive.

If you want to use the first option and specify a URL to the TLD file, you can use a `taglib` directive of the form

```
<%@ taglib uri="/WEB-INF/c.tld" prefix="c" %>
```

A downside to using a URL to locate a TLD file becomes apparent if the name or location of the file changes. You would have to change every JSP that contains the now incorrect URL. It is for this reason that the other method for specifying the location of the TLD file is preferred. With the preferred approach, a *logical name* is given to the tag library. This acts as a level of indirection because the JSPs can all use the logical name, and if the location changes, all you have to do is modify the `web.xml` file for the Web application that owns the JSP.

Another parallel with XML namespaces is that the logical name is usually specified by a URI because the URI specification gives a format for specifying unique names. Two common instances of URIs (Uniform Resource Identifiers) that you might have come across are URLs (Uniform Resource Locators) and URNs (Uniform Resource Names). URLs are more common, and when using JSTL you will see `taglib` directives that look like this:

```
<%@ taglib uri="http://java.sun.com/jstl-el/core" prefix="c" %>
```

When a JSP container translates a JSP to a servlet, the following process occurs:

1. The `taglib` directive specifies the logical name of the custom tag library.
2. The `web.xml` file maps the logical name to a TLD file.
3. The TLD file specifies handler classes for the custom tags within the tag library.
4. Within the generated servlet's `_jspService` method, method calls are generated to the appropriate tag handler.

What follows is a simple description of the major components of the `web.xml` and TLD files that must be configured to enable you to use custom tags within a JSP.

A Web application's `web.xml` file can map a particular tag library to its corresponding TLD file. For example, the `web.xml` file for the sample code for this chapter contains the following:

```
<?xml version="1.0" encoding="ISO-8859-1"?>


<web-app xmlns="http://java.sun.com/xml/ns/j2ee"
  xmlns:xsi="http://www.w3.org/2001/XMLSchema-instance"
  xsi:schemaLocation="http://java.sun.com/xml/ns/j2ee
  http://java.sun.com/xml/ns/j2ee/web-app_2_4.xsd" version="2.4">

    <description>
        Chapter 5 sample source code
    </description>
    ...
    <taglib>
```

```
        <taglib-uri>http://java.sun.com/jstl-el/core</taglib-uri>
        <taglib-location>/WEB-INF/c.tld</taglib-location>
    </taglib>
    ...
    <taglib>
        <taglib-uri>http://java.sun.com/jstl-el/xml</taglib-uri>
        <taglib-location>/WEB-INF/x.tld</taglib-location>
    </taglib>
    ...
</web-app>
```

For each tag library that your Web application uses, you specify a URI that is used to identify the tag library, along with a path to the TLD file that describes it. In the `web.xml` file for the sample source code for this book, there are `taglib` elements that use `taglib-uri` (for the tag library's logical name) and `taglib-location` (to specify the TLD file location) child elements for this purpose. The normal location to store the TLD files is in your Web application's `WEB-INF` directory.

> **Caution**
>
> Make sure that the value that you specify for the `taglib-uri` in your Web application's `web.xml` file matches the value for the `uri` element in the tag library's TLD file.

As mentioned previously, the TLD file is an XML document that describes the custom tags that make up the custom library. In Listing 5.1, you can see a subset of the TLD for some of the core tags from JSTL. The core tags are covered later in this chapter.

Listing 5.1 **The TLD for the Core JSTL tags (`c.tld`)**

```
<?xml version="1.0" encoding="UTF-8" ?>

<taglib xmlns="http://java.sun.com/xml/ns/j2ee"
    xmlns:xsi="http://www.w3.org/2001/XMLSchema-instance"
    xsi:schemaLocation="http://java.sun.com/xml/ns/j2ee web-jsptaglibrary_2_0.xsd"
    version="2.0">

  <description>JSTL 1.1 core library</description>
  <display-name>JSTL core</display-name>
  <tlib-version>1.1</tlib-version>
  <short-name>c</short-name>
  <uri>http://java.sun.com/jsp/jstl/core</uri>
  ...
  <tag>
    <description>
        Like &lt;%= ... &gt;, but for expressions.
    </description>
    <name>out</name>
    <tag-class>org.apache.taglibs.standard.tag.rt.core.OutTag</tag-class>
```

Listing 5.1 **Continued**

```
    <body-content>JSP</body-content>
    <attribute>
        <name>value</name>
        <required>true</required>
        <rtexprvalue>true</rtexprvalue>
    </attribute>
    <attribute>
        <name>default</name>
        <required>false</required>
        <rtexprvalue>true</rtexprvalue>
    </attribute>
    <attribute>
        <name>escapeXml</name>
        <required>false</required>
        <rtexprvalue>true</rtexprvalue>
    </attribute>
  </tag>
  ...
</taglib>
```

Listing 5.1 begins with an XML declaration that specifies the character encoding for the file:

```
<?xml version="1.0" encoding="UTF-8" ?>
```

The XML declaration is optional if the file is encoded using either UTF-8 or UTF-16.

Immediately after the XML declaration is the `taglib` element that specifies which XML Schema is used to constrain the logical structure of the TLD file:

```
    <taglib xmlns="http://java.sun.com/xml/ns/j2ee"
        xmlns:xsi="http://www.w3.org/2001/XMLSchema-instance"
        xsi:schemaLocation="http://java.sun.com/xml/ns/j2ee web-jsp-
taglibrary_2_0.xsd"
        version="2.0">
```

The top-level `taglib` element contains the following child elements:

```
  <description>JSTL 1.1 core library</description>
  <display-name>JSTL core</display-name>
  <tlib-version>1.1</tlib-version>
  <short-name>c</short-name>
  <uri>http://java.sun.com/jsp/jstl-el/core</uri>
```

This information gives details about the version of the tag library, the display name to be used by tools, and so on. The TLD file contains elements that describe the different custom tags that make up the tag library, such as

```
<tag>
  <name>out</name>
  <tag-class>org.apache.taglibs.standard.tag.el.core.OutTag</tag-class>
  <body-content>JSP</body-content>
  <description>
    Like &lt;%= ... &gt;, but for expressions.
  </description>
  <attribute>
    <name>value</name>
    <required>true</required>
    <rtexprvalue>false</rtexprvalue>
  </attribute>
  <attribute>
    <name>default</name>
    <required>false</required>
    <rtexprvalue>false</rtexprvalue>
  </attribute>
  <attribute>
    <name>escapeXml</name>
    <required>false</required>
    <rtexprvalue>false</rtexprvalue>
  </attribute>
</tag>
```

From the `name` element, you can see that this piece of XML describes the core `out` tag, which is similar to the JSP expression tag (`<%= ... %>`). You can see that there is an associated tag handler (from the `tag-class` element), as well as the different attributes that the `out` tag can have.

The actual custom tag libraries are usually distributed in JAR files. For example, JSTL contains the `jstl.jar` and `standard.jar` files. The JAR files are usually placed under the Web application's `WEB-INF/lib` directory. If you have an unpacked tag library, the files should be placed under the Web application's `WEB-INF/classes` directory.

> **Note**
>
> The `jstl.jar` file contains the JSTL API, whereas the `standard.jar` file contains the JSTL reference implementation. To run a Web application, both files must be available on the Web application's class path.

If a tag library is used by more than one Web application, under Apache Tomcat you can place the JAR files in the `<TOMCAT_HOME>/common/lib` directory. There is no need to modify the `web.xml` or TLD files if you do this. The JSP container automatically searches its `common/lib` directory.

Using a Custom Tag

After you have imported a custom tag library into a JSP, you can use its custom tags. Listing 5.2 shows an example page that uses custom tags to insert the user's name into a

JSP, and the total cost of the items in their shopping cart. There are more examples later in this chapter.

Listing 5.2 **Simple Usage of a Custom Tag**

```
<%@ taglib uri="http://java.sun.com/jstl-el/core" prefix="c" %>

<html>
  <head>
    <title><c:out value="${user.name}" />'s shopping cart</title>
  </head>
  <body>
      The total cost of items in your shopping cart is $
     <c:out value="${shoppingCart.total}" />
  </body>
</html>
```

The tag used in Listing 5.2 is `c:out`. It takes a single attribute called `value`, and has no body content (no child elements). However, it is perfectly valid for a tag to have either zero or many attributes, along with nested tags inside the tag's body. Attributes customize the behavior of a tag, and, in a sense, are like parameters that are passed to method calls. Attributes always appear in the *start* element for a tag, never in the closing element.

Introduction to the Core Tag Library

The goal of JSTL, as stated in the JSTL specification, is "to help simplify JSP authors' lives." To achieve this goal, one of the things that JSTL provides is a set of standard actions for often-required functionality.

JSTL is often referred to as *the* standard tag library. In fact, JSTL is made up of four tag libraries, each identified by its own namespace. A custom tag is also often referred to as an *action*, and this is the term that is used throughout the rest of this chapter. This chapter concentrates on the *core* actions, although the XML, SQL, and internationalization actions are introduced. You can find more information on the XML actions in Chapters 10 and 11, whereas the SQL actions are used in Chapter 14, "Databases and JSP."

An expression language is supported by JSTL, and is described in Chapter 3, "Further JSP Syntax." Together with JSTL tags, the expression language makes it easy to access and manipulate an application's data without having to use request-time expressions or scriptlets.

JSTL 1.0 provided two forms of the libraries: one that supported the expression language (EL), and one that did not. The latter form supported scripting expressions using JSP expression tags. These scripting expressions are known as runtime expression values, rtexprvalues, or just RT for short. The designers of JSTL envisaged that most page authors would use the EL libraries, which were the recommended ones. Support for scripting expressions was also provided to support those people that needed the ultimate performance and type safety in their expressions. It is possible to mix both kinds of tag within a JSP, some that are EL-based and some that are RT-based. However, since JSP 2.0 supports the EL, JSTL 1.1 has a single library that supports both EL and runtime expressions. This is because the JSP container evaluates whichever expression is present, and passes the result to the action. See the "Backwards Compatibility and Migrating from JSTL 1.0 to JSTL 1.1" section later in this chapter for more details. You might also wish to consult Appendix C that contains the JSTL 1.0 URIs."

The JSTL 1.1 URIs and common prefixes for the tag libraries are shown in Table 5.1. You can of course use any prefix you like in your JSPs.

Table 5.1 **Tag Libraries URIs (JSTL 1.1)**

Functional areaArea	URI	Prefix
Core	`http://java.sun.com/jstl-el/core`	`c`
XML	`http://java.sun.com/jstl-el/xml`	`x`
Internationalization-capable formatting	`http://java.sun.com/jstl-el/fmt`	`fmt`
SQL (relational database access)	`http://java.sun.com/jstl-el/sql`	`sql`

Scope in the Expression Language

JSTL uses slightly different names for the four levels of scope that you have seen so far. When writing expressions using the EL for use with JSTL, you use the following names for the different scopes:

- `pageScope` when you want to specify page scope
- `requestScope` when you want to specify request scope
- `sessionScope` when you want to specify session scope
- `applicationScope` when you want to specify application scope

The Core Actions

The core actions provide support for flow control and expressions, as well as a generic mechanism for accessing URL-based content that can be processed or included by a JSP. The core actions can be grouped into four main areas of functionality: general-purpose actions, conditional actions, iterator actions, and URL-related actions.

Most of the JSTL actions have attributes, whose values can always be specified dynamically except for a couple of exceptions. The first is for the name and scope of scoped variables to make it easier for vendors to produce development tools. The other exception is for the XML actions that use XPath expressions for attribute values.

General-Purpose Core Actions

The general-purpose core actions provide you with functionality to handle errors that can occur in a JSP, as well as to manipulate scoped attributes. The four actions that are described in this section are `c:out`, `c:set`, `c:remove`, and `c:catch`.

The `c:out` *Action*

The `c:out` action is similar to the JSP expression tag that you saw in Chapter 2. It evaluates an expression and inserts the result into the output. In its simplest form, it has the following syntax:

```
<c:out value="some_expression" />
```

The expression for the `value` attribute can be dynamic. That is, it can be either literal text, or an expression written using the Expression Language.

Consider the JSP in Listing 5.3. It contains a simple HTML form that enables a user to enter his first name, last name, and age. These details are then sent using the `POST` method to the next page, shown in a moment.

Listing 5.3 **An HTML Form That Prompts the User for Details (`createPerson.jsp`)**

```
<html>
  <head><title>Chapter 5 - Create Person</title></head>
  <body>
    <h1>Enter your details</h1>
    <form action="displayDetails.jsp" method="post">
      <table>
        <tr><td>First name:</td>
            <td><input type="text" name="firstName" /></td>
        </tr>
        <tr><td>Last name:</td>
            <td><input type="text" name="lastName" /></td>
        </tr>
        <tr><td>Age:</td>
            <td><input type="text" name="age" /></td>
        </tr>
      </table>
      <input type="submit" value="Submit details" />
    </form>
  </body>
</html>
```

Listing 5.4 shows the JSP that the details are sent to. This JSP displays the details in a table by using the `c:out` action.

Listing 5.4 **A JSP That Uses the `c:out` Action (`displayDetails.jsp`)**

```
<%@ taglib prefix="c" uri="http://java.sun.com/jstl-el/core" %>

<html>
  <head><title>Chapter 5 - Display details</title></head>
  <body>
    <h1>Your details (or, the details that you entered!)</h1>
```

Listing 5.4 **Continued**

```
    <table>
      <tr><td>First name</td><td><c:out value="${param.firstName}" /></td></tr>
      <tr><td>Last name</td> <td><c:out value="${param.lastName}"  /></td></tr>
      <tr><td>Age</td>       <td><c:out value="${param.age}"       /></td></tr>
    </table>
  </body>
</html>
```

You can use the implicit `param` object to access HTTP parameters, such as the ones from an HTML form. The three `c:out` tags in the JSP access the three form parameters with an expression of the form

```
${param.firstName}
```

The `c:out` action enables you to specify a default value that should be used when the expression evaluates to `null`, or if the expression fails to evaluate and throws an exception. The default value can be either literal text or a dynamic value that is computed when the JSP is processed. You can specify the optional default value using either of the following:

- An attribute called `default`.
- Body content of the `c:out` action. The body content can be any valid JSP code.

For example, perhaps you want to modify Listing 5.4 to display a value for the name of the user's partner. If the value is not passed by the HTML form, instead of a blank value in the table, you could specify a default value of `Unknown name` in the following way through an attribute:

```
<c:out value="partnerName" default="Unknown name" />
```

or, using body content instead:

```
<c:out value="partnerName">
  Unknown name
</c:out>
```

When you use the body content to specify a default value, the body content is trimmed in accordance with the `trim()` method in the `java.lang.String` class.

The only other attribute that you can specify to the `c:out` action controls whether certain XML characters are converted to entity references or character references. By default, such conversion takes place for the following characters:

- A `<` character is replaced with `<`.
- A `>` character is replaced with `>`.
- An `&` character is replaced with `&`.
- A `'` character is replaced with `'`.
- A `"` character is replaced with `"`.

This final, optional, attribute is called `escapeXml`, and takes a boolean value (`true` or `false`). The value does not have to be hard-coded into the JSP—it can be dynamically computed when the JSP is requested, although the default value is `true`. If you want, you can explicitly specify a value of `true` for the `escapeXml` attribute to make the JSP self-documenting. You can specify a value of `false` to disable the conversion process. Such a `c:out` action would look like

```
<c:out value="some_expression" escapeXml="false" />
```

In summary, the `value` attribute is mandatory, whereas the `default` and `escapeXml` attributes are optional. The complete syntax for the `c:out` action is therefore

```
<c:out value="some_expression"
       [default="default_value]
       [escapeXml="{true|false}"] />
```

or, with body content instead of a `default` attribute:

```
<c:out value="some_expression" [escapeXml="{true|false}"] >
   Default value
</c:out>
```

The `c:set` *Action*

You can use the `c:set` action to set the value of a scoped variable, known as an *attribute*. The scope can be any of the JSP scopes (that is, `page`, `request`, `session`, or `application`). The attribute is created if it does not already exist when the `c:set` action is processed.

The `c:set` action can take four forms. The first of these is

```
<c:set var="variable_name" value="expression"
       [scope="page | request | session | application"] />
```

This form of the `c:set` action specifies the exported variable's name and value, along with an optional scope (which defaults to a value of `page`). The scoped variable is identified by the values of the `var` and `scope` attributes. The type of the scoped variable (named by the `var` attribute) is whatever type the expression specified by the `value` attribute evaluates to.

As an alternative to using a value attribute to set the value of the scoped variable, you can specify the value by using any valid JSP code as the body content of the `c:set` action. Again, the body content is trimmed in accordance with the `trim()` method in the `java.lang.String` class. If there are any JSP elements in the trimmed content, these are then processed further.

The syntax for using body content to specify the value of the scoped variable is

```
<c:set var="variable_name" [scope="page | request | session | application"]>
  body content
</c:set>
```

For either form, the `scope` attribute is optional and defaults to a value of `page`. However, as mentioned earlier, the scope value and the variable name must be static, and you cannot dynamically assign them. Also, for either form, the scoped variable defined by the `var` and `scope` attributes is removed if the `value` expression evaluates to `null`.

Listing 5.5 shows a JSP that sets a session-scoped attribute, using a simple expression to compute a value for the attribute.

Listing 5.5 **Setting a Scoped Attribute from a JSP** (`setAttributes.jsp`)

```
<%@ taglib prefix="c" uri="http://java.sun.com/jstl-el/core" %>

<html>
  <body>
    This JSP stores the ultimate answer in a session-scoped variable where
    the other JSPs in the web application can access it.
    <p />
    <c:set var="theUltimateAnswer" value="${41+1}" scope="session"  />

     Click <a href="displayAttributes.jsp">here</a> to view it.
  </body>
</html>
```

The JSP in Listing 5.6 retrieves and displays the scoped attribute with a `c:out` action.

Listing 5.6 **Retrieval of a Scoped Attribute** (`displayAttributes.jsp`)

```
<%@ taglib prefix="c" uri="http://java.sun.com/jstl-el/core" %>

<html>
  <head>
    <title>Chapter 5 - Retrieval of attributes</title>
  </head>
  <body>
    The ultimate answer is <c:out value="${sessionScope.theUltimateAnswer}" />
    <br/>
  </body>
</html>
```

The other two forms of the `c:set` action are used to set the properties of target objects. In Chapter 6, "JSP and JavaBeans," you will see the `jsp:setProperty` action that enables you to set the values of JavaBean properties. You can also use the `c:set` action for this purpose. The syntax is very similar to the two forms already mentioned:

```
<c:set  target="object_name"  property="property_name"  value="some_value"  />
```

and

```
<c:set  target="object_name"  property="property_name" >
    body_content
</c:set>
```

These last two forms of the `c:set` action can also be used to add and set elements within an object of type `java.util.Map`. In this case, the `target` attribute specifies the `Map` object, the key in the map is specified by the `property` attribute, and the `value` attribute (or body content) specifies the object to be stored. If you want to remove an entry from the map, simply specify a `value` of `null` (or empty body content).

When you use either of these last two forms, an exception is thrown if you specify `null` for the `target` attribute. An exception is also generated if you specify an object that is neither a `java.util.Map` nor a JavaBean.

The `c:remove` *Action*

The `c:remove` action enables you to delete a scoped variable from the application. At a minimum, you must specify the variable's name, in which case the scopes are searched in order (page, then request, then session, and then application). You can optionally specify a value for the `scope` attribute to skip this search.

The syntax of the `c:remove` action is

```
<c:remove var="variable_name"
          [scope="{page | request | session | application}"] />
```

If you do not specify a value for the `scope` attribute, the scoped variable is removed with a call to `PageContext.removeAttribute(java.lang.String name)`. On the other hand, if you do specify a scope attribute, the `PageContext.removeAttribute(java.lang.String name, int scope)` method is used instead.

The JSP in Listing 5.7 sets a session-scoped attribute called `username`.

Listing 5.7 **A JSP That Sets a Session-Scoped Attribute** (`setAttribute.jsp`)

```
<%@ taglib uri="http://java.sun.com/jstl-el/core" prefix="c" %>

<c:set var="userName" value="Mark" scope="session" />

<html>
  <head>
    <title>Chapter 5 - Set a scoped attribute</title>
  </head>
  <body>
    This page sets a session-scoped attribute that is removed
    by <a href="removeAttribute.jsp">this</a> page.
  </body>
</html>
```

The JSP in Listing 5.8 displays the value of the `username` attribute, but then removes it before attempting to display its value again.

Listing 5.8 **A JSP That Displays and Removes a Session-Scoped Attribute (`removeAttribute.jsp`)**

```
<%@ taglib uri="http://java.sun.com/jstl-el/core" prefix="c" %>

<html>
  <head>
    <title>Chapter 5 - Remove a scoped attribute</title>
  </head>
  <body>
    The session-scoped attribute called <b>userName</b> had a value
    of <b> <c:out value="${sessionScope.userName}" /> </b>, but it is about
    to be removed!<p/>

    <c:remove var="userName" scope="session" />

    The value is now <c:out value="${sessionScope.userName}" /> - NYA ha ha!
  </body>
</html>
```

When the JSP attempts to display the value of the removed attribute, the value of the expression is simply an empty string:

```
${sessionScope.userName}
```

Thus, the output is

```
The value is now  - NYA ha ha!
```

The `c:catch` *Action*

The JSP error page mechanism is covered in Chapter 2. If you have any actions that are of primary importance to a JSP, and that must be forwarded to an error-handling page, you should use that mechanism to deal with them.

A second error-handling mechanism is available for you to use. This one is provided by JSTL in the form of the `c:catch` action. You can wrap actions that are of secondary importance to a JSP inside `c:catch` actions. Any exceptions that are thrown from the nested actions are caught by the parent `c:catch` action and are not handled by the error-page mechanism.

The syntax of the `c:catch` action is simple because it has but one attribute, and even that is optional. The syntax is

```
<c:catch [var="exception_name"]>
  nested actions
</c:catch>
```

The body content of the c:catch action is any valid JSP code.

If you specify a value for the var attribute, the c:catch action exports any exceptions because page-scoped attributes can be accessed by other actions in the JSP. In the case where the nested actions within the c:catch action execute without generating an exception, the c:catch action removes any existing page-scoped attribute with the name that you specified.

If you omit the var attribute, any generated exceptions are still caught by the c:catch action and are not forwarded to an error page if one is specified by the JSP. The only difference when you omit the var attribute is that the exception is not stored in a page-scoped attribute.

The JSP in Listing 5.9 revisits the cell phone example from Chapter 2.

Listing 5.9 **A JSP That Uses the** c:catch **Action** (catch.jsp)

```
<%@ taglib uri="http://java.sun.com/jstl-el/core" prefix="c" %>

<html>
  <head>
    <title>Chapter 5 - The jsp:useBean action</title>
  </head>
  <body>
    <h1>So you want to make a call from your cell phone?!</h1>
    <h2>Checking the signal strength....</h2>
    <c:catch var="signalException">
      <%
        int i= (int) (Math.random() * 10);

        if (i < 5 )
          throw new NullPointerException(); %>
    </c:catch>

    <c:choose>
      <c:when test="${not empty signalException}">
        Oh dear! There is an inadequate signal to make a call!
        Refresh the page in your web browser to try again.
      </c:when>
      <c:otherwise>
        The signal strength is OK! Go ahead with your call.
      </c:otherwise>
    </c:choose>
  </body>
</html>
```

The c:catch action looks like this:

```
<c:catch var="signalException">
  <%
```

```
    int i= (int) (Math.random() * 10);

    if (i < 5 )
      throw new NullPointerException(); %>
</c:catch>
```

Its body content is simply a scriptlet that generates a random number in the range 0 to 10. If the value of the random number (or cell-phone signal strength, if you prefer) is less than 5, the scriptlet throws an exception. The actual exception thrown in the listing is a `NullPointerException`, for convenience. In reality, you would obviously use a more suitable exception for your needs.

The `c:catch` action stores the generated exception in a page-scoped attribute called `signalException`. If an exception was not thrown, any existing page-scoped attribute with the name `signalException` is removed.

The rest of the listing uses a `c:choose` action with nested `c:when` and `c:otherwise` actions, which are described later in this chapter. A quick word on this line of code:

```
<c:when test="${not empty signalException}">
```

This uses the `empty` operator, which is a prefix operator that can be used to test if a variable has the value `null` or is empty. The `not` operator simply performs a Boolean inversion of the result. So, the test is essentially the same as this:

```
<c:when test="${signalException != null}">
```

Conditional Core Actions

JSTL conditional actions are designed to make it easy to perform conditional programming on a JSP. The alternative is to resort to using scriptlets, but this means embedding code for a scripting language (usually Java). This can be error-prone for those page authors who are unfamiliar with scripting languages.

The conditional core actions provided by JSTL are `c:if`, `c:choose`, `c:when`, and `c:otherwise`. They enable you to perform two different kinds of processing: simple and mutually exclusive conditional processing.

The `c:if` *Action*

The `c:if` action enables you to perform simple conditional processing. That is, you can provide a test condition that is evaluated to a boolean value. If the condition evaluates to a value of `true`, the body content of the `c:if` action is processed. Otherwise, the body content is ignored. Again, as with most of the core tags, the body content can be any valid JSP code.

The syntax of the `c:if` action can take two forms. One has body content and one does not. The form without body content looks like this:

```
<c:if test="test_condition"
      var="variable_name"
      [scope="{page | request | session | application}"] />
```

This first form might look odd because you specify a condition through the `test` attribute, but do not specify any kind of action to take if the condition evaluates to `true`. You use this form of the `c:if` action when you want the result to be stored in a scoped attribute for use later in the JSP. The name of the scoped attribute is given by the `var` attribute, and its scope by the `scope` attribute. If you omit the `scope` attribute, its value defaults to `page`. The type of the scoped attribute is `java.lang.Boolean`.

The form with body content looks like this:

```
<c:if test="test_condition"
      [var="variable_name"]
      [scope="{page | request | session | application}"]>
    body content
</c:if>
```

This second form enables you to dictate whether the body content is rendered based on the test condition you provide. The test condition can be a dynamically computed value, unlike the values for the `var` and `scope` attributes. If the test condition evaluates to `true`, the body content is evaluated and the result is placed into the output that the client sees.

The `if` action is provided by both versions of JSTL—the version that supports the EL as well as the one that supports expressions that are RT-based. For the EL-based library, the `test` attribute must have an expression that evaluates to either a primitive `boolean` or `java.lang.Boolean` value. The RT-based library, on the other hand, only accepts expressions that evaluate to `boolean` type.

An alternative version of the example in Listing 5.9 is shown in Listing 5.10.

Listing 5.10 **A JSP That Uses `c:if` Actions (`catchWithIf.jsp`)**

```
<%@ taglib uri="http://java.sun.com/jstl-el/core" prefix="c" %>

<%
  int i= (int) (Math.random() * 10);
  pageContext.setAttribute("signalStrength",
                           new Integer(i),
                           PageContext.PAGE_SCOPE);
%>

<html>
  <head>
    <title>Chapter 5 - The c:catch action</title>
  </head>
  <body>
    <h1>So you want to make a call from your cell phone?!</h1>
    <h2>Checking the signal strength...</h2>
```

Listing 5.10 **Continued**

```
    <c:if test="${pageScope.signalStrength < 5}">
      <c:set var="signalFailure" value="true" scope="page" />
    </c:if>

    <c:choose>
      <c:when test="${pageScope.signalFailure == true}">
        <h3>Oh dear! There is an inadequate signal to make a call!</h3>
        Refresh the page in your web browser to try again.
      </c:when>
      <c:otherwise>
        <h3>The signal strength is OK! Go ahead with your call.</h3>
        Refresh the page in your web browser to make another call.
      </c:otherwise>
    </c:choose>
  </body>
</html>
```

This version again starts with a scriptlet, but it stores the generated signal strength in a page-scoped attribute called `signalStrength`. The following code tests the value of this `signalStrength` attribute, and if it has the value `true`, it sets another page-scoped attribute (`signalFailure`) to show that the signal strength is insufficient to place a call:

```
<c:if test="${pageScope.signalStrength < 5}">
  <c:set var="signalFailure" value="true" scope="page" />
</c:if>
```

However, there is no if-then-else functionality provided by the `if` action. In very simple cases, you might want to use a small number of mutually exclusive `c:if` actions to cover the different cases you are interested in. However, it is a better idea to use the `choose` action instead. The rest of the code in Listings 5.9 and 5.10 is explained in the following sections on the `c:choose`, `c:when`, and `c:otherwise` actions.

The `c:choose` *Action*

The `c:choose` action enables you to perform mutually exclusive condition processing, where only one of many options is processed. The syntax of the `c:choose` action is

```
<c:choose>
    body content
</c:choose>
```

The body content of the `c:choose` action can contain:

- One or many `c:when` actions.
- Zero or one `c:otherwise` action. This action must appear after all `c:when` actions.
- Whitespace characters between the `c:when` and `c:otherwise` actions.

You can think of the `c:choose` action as an `if/else if/else if/else` in Java. For example, the pseudo-code in Table 5.2 illustrates how Java code maps to the `c:choose` action.

Table 5.2 **Pseudo-Code Mapping Java to the `c:choose` Action**

Java pseudoPseudo-codeCode	JSTL actions

if (condition_1)
   // path 1
	<c:choose>
	   <c:when test="condition_1">
	      // path 1
	   </c:when>

else
if (condition_2)
   // path 2
else
   // path 3
	<c:when test="condition_2">
	      // path 2
	   </c:when>
	   <c:otherwise>
	      // path 3
	   </c:otherwise>
	</c:choose>

The `c:choose` action processes at most *one* of its nested actions. The rule is that the `c:choose` action processes the *first* `c:when` action whose test condition evaluates to `true`. However, if none of the `c:when` actions is applicable, the `c:otherwise` action is processed, if it is present. If you provide a `c:otherwise` action, you must make sure that it is the *last* action within its parent `c:choose` action.

The `c:when` and `c:otherwise` actions are described next.

The `c:when` *Action*

You use the `when` action when you want to specify a path of execution within a `c:choose` action. The syntax of the `when` action is

```
<c:when test="test_condition">
   body content
</c:when>
```

As with most of the tags that you have seen thus far, the body content can be any valid JSP code. Just make sure that the `c:when` action is a child element of a `c:choose` action. Also, be careful to make sure that all your `c:when` actions appear *before* the `c:otherwise` action (if you have one).

The `c:when` action used earlier in Listing 5.10 looks like this:

```
<c:when test="${pageScope.signalFailure == true}">
    <h3>Oh dear! There is an inadequate signal to make a call!</h3>
    Refresh the page in your web browser to try again.
</c:when>
```

It tests to see if there is a signal failure preventing the phone call from proceeding by comparing the value of the page-scoped `signalFailure` attribute with the literal value `true`. If the condition evaluates to `true`, the two lines of nested text are inserted into the output that the client sees.

Both forms of the JSTL libraries provide the `when` action. Just use the correct tag library descriptor URI in the `taglib` directive. The only difference between the two implementations is that the RT-based library only accepts test conditions that evaluate to a primitive `boolean` value. The EL-based library accepts `boolean` or `java.lang.Boolean` values.

The `c:otherwise` *Action*

You can specify a `c:otherwise` action that the JSP container should evaluate if none of its sibling `c:when` actions evaluates to `true`, although in this case there is only one. It must be the last action within a `c:choose` action, and its syntax is

```
<c:otherwise>
    body content
</c:otherwise>
```

The body content is any valid JSP code.

Listing 5.10 uses a `c:otherwise` action that is evaluated if its sibling `c:when` action is not processed:

```
<c:otherwise>
    <h3>The signal strength is OK! Go ahead with your call.</h3>
    Refresh the page in your web browser to make another call.
</c:otherwise>
```

Iterator Core Actions

There are many situations that you encounter while writing JSPs where you need to iterate through a collection of objects. For example, you might have executed a database query and need to process each returned result to display it in a table on the page.

It is, of course, possible to perform such processing by embedding a scriptlet into a JSP. This is problematical for those page authors who are unfamiliar with the scripting language used on the page. When using Java as the scripting language, apart from the actual syntax, another problem is that you must have knowledge of the collection classes that are used. For example, the collection classes provided as part of the Java libraries store and retrieve objects of type `java.lang.Object`. The implication of this is that you must cast a retrieved object to the correct type before invoking any class-specific methods on it. Also, you must know details of how the iteration process is utilized for a given collection. Although this is relatively simple for arrays, for most of the Java 2 collection classes you must know about the `java.util.Iterator` interface.

The iterator actions are designed to alleviate many of these concerns. They make it easy to iterate over numerous different types of collection.

The `c:forEach` *Action*

The `c:forEach` action supports all the J2SE collection types. Arrays of primitives, classes that implement the `java.util.List`, `java.util.Set`, and `java.util.Map` are therefore supported. You can also iterate over a `java.lang.String` object. The string must contain comma-separated values for this to do anything useful, or you just get back the whole string. For example, the string `"Mark, Tracy"` returns the two elements `"Mark"` and `"Tracy"`, whereas `"Mark Tracy"` is returned as a single element.

> **Caution**
>
> The `c:forEach` action supports classes that implement the `java.util.Iterator` and `java.util.Enumeration` interfaces. However, you should take care when using these because neither interface provides methods to reset the cursor back to the beginning of the collection. Therefore, you can only safely use such objects within *one* `c:forEach` action.

There are several ways that you can use the `c:forEach` action, whose syntax is

```
<c:forEach items="collection"
           [var="variable_name"]
           [varStatus="varStatus_name"]
           [begin="begin_value"]
           [end="end_value"]
           [step="step_value"]>
    body content
</c:forEach>
```

The first way is to iterate over the entire collection. You specify the collection to iterate using the `items` attribute. Then, for each element within the collection, the body content of the action is processed and any output is written for the client to see.

> **Note**
>
> The `c:forEach` action does not support iteration of a `java.sql.ResultSet` object (see section 6.1.1, Collections of objects to iterate over, of the JSTL specification for more details). If you want to perform database access from a JSP, you should either use the SQL actions that are provided by JSTL, or encapsulate the logic in your own custom action or JavaBean.

If you specify a value for the optional `var` attribute, the current element in the collection is exported for use within the action. The exported variable is said to have *nested visibility* because it can only be used within the body of the action.

The second way that you can use the `c:forEach` action is to iterate over a subset of the collection. In this case, you specify values for the `begin` and `end` attributes. A collection's elements are indexed from zero, and the values of both the `begin` and `end` attributes are inclusive. You can also specify a value for the `step` attribute to skip over the specified number of elements between iterations. The JSP in Listing 5.11 shows an example JSP that displays every other item in a collection of strings.

Listing 5.11 **A JSP That Uses the `c:forEach` Action (`forEach.jsp`)**

```
<%@ taglib prefix="c"    uri="http://java.sun.com/jstl-el/core" %>

<c:set var="names"
       value="Peter, Pat, Mark, Tracy"
       scope="page" />

<html>
  <head>
    <title>Chapter 5 - forEach and status</title>
  </head>

  <body>
    <h1>The forEach tag exposes a scoped variable called 'count', which
    is the position of the current iteration of the collection.</h1>

    <h2>(Note, it is <i>not</i> the position of the element in the
        underlying collection)</h2>

    <c:forEach items="${pageScope.names}"
               var="currentName"
               varStatus="status"
               begin="0"
               end="3"
               step="2"
    >
      Family member #<c:out value="${status.count}" /> is
        <c:out value="${currentName}" /> <br />
    </c:forEach>
  </body>
</html>
```

The code that sets up the comma-separated values that are iterated over is

```
<c:set var="names"
       value="Peter, Pat, Mark, Tracy"
       scope="page" />
```

The `c:forEach` action then iterates over this collection because it has an `items` attribute with the value `${pageScope.names}`.

Each item in the collection is exported with the loop with a name of `currentName` (through the `var` attribute). However, note that it is not *every* item in the collection that appears in the output. This is because it is a subset of the collection that is processed. The `begin` and `end` attributes specify the bounds of the subset. Both of their values are inclusive.

The first item to be processed is specified by the `begin` attribute, which has a value of zero (inclusive). The last item has an index of 3 (inclusive). However, there is also a value for the `step` attribute. It has the value 2, meaning to only process every second item in the collection, after the first. Thus, the elements that are returned are `Peter` (item 0) and `Mark` (item 2).

There are two `c:out` actions within the JSP. The first displays the number of the current iteration, starting at 1, by using the variable specified through the `varStatus` attribute:

```
<c:out value="${status.count}" />
```

The second displays the current item from the collection, specified through the `var` attribute:

```
<c:out value="${currentName}" />
```

The output from the JSP in Listing 5.11 is shown in Figure 5.1.

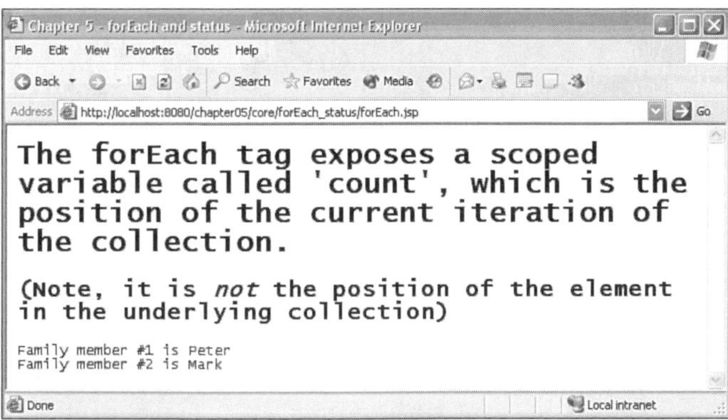

Figure 5.1 Screenshot of the JSP in Listing 5.11.

The optional `varStatus` attribute enables you to specify a name for a nested visibility object that implements the `javax.servlet.jsp.jstl.core.LoopTagStatus` interface. This interface provides the methods shown in Table 5.3.

Table 5.3 **Method of the `javax.servlet.jsp.jstl.core.LoopTagStatus` Interface**

Method	Description
public java.lang.Object getCurrent()	Returns a reference to the current element in the iteration.
public int getIndex()	Returns the index of the current item in the iteration of the collection. The index begins at a value of 0.
public int getCount()	Returns the count of the number of elements that have been iterated over. Thus, when used in an iteration with begin=0, end=5, and the step attribute set to a value of 2, the count goes 1, 2, 3. The count begins at a value of 1.
public boolean isFirst()	This method takes subsetting of a collection into account. Returns a value of true if the current iteration is the first one. Returns false otherwise. This method always returns a value of true when getCount() returns a value of 1.
public boolean isLast()	This method takes subsetting of a collection into account. Returns a value of true if the current iteration is the last one in the iteration. Returns false otherwise.
public int getBegin()	Returns the value of the begin attribute of the forEach action. null is returned if the begin attribute is not specified.
public int getEnd()	Returns the value of the end attribute of the forEach action. Null is returned if the end attribute is not specified.
public int getStep()	Returns the value of the step attribute of the forEach action. Null is returned if the step attribute is not specified.

When you use a `forEach` action to iterate over the contents of a `java.util.Map`, the current item for each iteration is actually a utility object of type `java.util.Map.Entry`. This object has two properties, `key` and `value`. The `key` property exposes the key that is used to store each object in the map, whereas the `value` property is the actual object that corresponds to the key. The sort of code you would write to iterate over the contents of a `Map` would be

```
<c:forEach items="${someHashMap}"
           var="currentItem">
    The current item from the hashmap is <c:out value="${currentItem.value}" />
</c:forEach>
```

The `c:forTokens` *Action*

Very similar to the `c:forEach` action is the `c:forTokens` action. The `c:forTokens` action enables you to iterate over a string of tokens. Its syntax is

```
<c:forTokens items="string_of_tokens"
           delims="set_of_delimiters"
           [var="variable_name"]
           [varStatus="varStatus_name"]
           [begin="begin_value"]
           [end="end_value"]
           [step="step_value"]>
    body content
</c:forTokens>
```

If you have used the `java.util.StringTokenizer` class before, the `c:forTokens` action will seem very familiar. In fact, the action uses the `StringTokenizer` class in its implementation. The `StringTokenizer` constructor that takes two `java.lang.String` arguments is the one that is used:

```
public StringTokenizer(String stringToParse, String delimiters)
```

When you use the `c:forTokens` action, the string that you want to iterate through is set using the `items` attribute. You must separate the actual tokens within the string with one of the characters specified in the value of the `delims` attribute. The other attributes are the same as for the `c:forEach` action.

The JSP in Listing 5.12 shows a JSP that illustrates how to use the `c:forTokens` action.

Listing 5.12 **A JSP That Uses the `c:forTokens` Action**

```
<%@ taglib prefix="c" uri="http://java.sun.com/jstl-el/core" %>

<c:set var="names" value="Peter:Pat;Mark|Tracy" scope="page" />

<html>
  <head>
    <title>Chapter 5 - forTokens action</title>
  </head>

  <body>
    <c:forTokens items="${pageScope.names}"
                 delims=":;|"
                 var="currentName"
                 varStatus="status"
      >
      Family member #<c:out value="${status.count}" /> is
        <c:out value="${currentName}" /> <br />
    </c:forTokens>
  </body>
</html>
```

The string that is used is set using the following line of code:

```
<c:set var="names" value="Peter:Pat;Mark|Tracy" scope="page" />
```

Notice that the individual names are separated by a variety of delimiters: `:`, `;`, and `|` characters. The string to be iterated over, and the three delimiters, are set on the `forTokens` action through the `items` and `delims` attributes, respectively:

```
<c:forTokens items="${pageScope.names}"
             delims=":;|"
             ...
</c:forTokens>
```

The output for the JSP contains the text:

```
Family member #1 is Peter
Family member #2 is Pat
Family member #3 is Mark
Family member #4 is Tracy
```

URL-Related Core Actions

As a page author, you often need to deal with resources that are URL-based. For example, you might want to include the content of a file that is located elsewhere on the Web. Working with URLs can be complex, especially when query strings must be encoded, or when cookies are unavailable, and therefore, session IDs must be appended to URLs. JSTL provides a set of actions that make such situations much easier to deal with.

The `c:import` *Action*

In Chapter 2, you saw the `<jsp:include>` directive that enables you to embed content from other parts of the Web application into the current JSP. However, there are two limitations that you encounter when using this directive.

The first limitation is that you can only specify a *relative* URL. You cannot use content from other Web applications, or from an absolute URL. The second limitation is that the unnecessary buffering occurs when the directive is a child element of a tag that processes the included content. This is because of the fact that the `jsp:include` directive reads the included content, and writes it as the body content of the enclosing tag. The enclosing tag then reads in the same content before processing it.

The `c:import` action was designed to provide a mechanism that did not have these two limitations. You can use it in three ways, as listed in Table 5.4. The syntax of the `c:import` action for embedding content inline, or exporting the content as a string if you use the `var` and `scope` attributes, is

```
<c:import url="url_of_resource"
          [context="context"]
          [var="variable_name"]
          [scope="{page | request | session | application}"]
```

```
        [charEncoding="character_encoding"]>
    optional c:param actions
</c:import>
```

See Table 5.5 for a description of the `url` and `context` attributes. The other attributes are explained shortly.

Table 5.4 **The `c:import` Action**

Form	Description
`<c:import url="absolute_url" />`	Imports the resource that is specified by the absolute URL.
`<c:import url="/relative_url" />` or `<c:import url="relative_url" />`	Imports the resource that is specified by the relative URL. The resource belongs to the same context (Web application). If the relative URL begins with a forward slash character, the resource is relative to the Web application. If the URL does not begin with a forward slash character, the resource is relative to the current JSP.
`<c:import url="/relative_url" context="/otherContext" />`	Imports the resource that is specified by the relative URL. The `context` attribute enables you to specify a *foreign context* (another Web application). Both the URL and the context must begin with a forward slash character.

Instead of embedding the external resource within the JSP, you can also store the content in a variable. This is useful when you have custom tags that process the stored content. A benefit of doing this is that the stored content is reusable. The general form of this approach is

```
<c:import url="/newsfeed/newsItem01.xml" var="currentNewsItem" />
<myPrefix:myCustomTag in="$currentNewsItem" />
```

You can set the variable's name and scope with the `var` and `scope` attributes. The `charEncoding` attribute is used to specify the character encoding of the external resource. If you do not specify it, the JSP container attempts to determine the character encoding from the `URLConnection` object that is used to acquire the resource. If that information is not available, the character encoding defaults to `ISO-8859-1`.

Alternatively, instead of exporting the external resource as a string, you can export it as a `java.io.Reader` object by specifying a `varReader` attribute using this syntax:

```
<c:import url = "url_of_resource"
        varReader = "variable_name"
        [context = "context"]
        [charEncoding = "character_encoding"]>
    body content
</c:import>
```

Depending on the implementation, this can be beneficial when the external resource is large because there is no buffering. This means that the content of the external resource can be accessed directly. A disadvantage of this approach is that the `varReader` is only accessible from within the `c:import` action itself. Note the lack of a `scope` attribute using this syntax. The implication of this is that any custom actions that need to process the content must be child elements of the `c:import` action. For example:

```
<c:import url = "http://www.myNewsSite.com/newsfeed/newsItem01.xml"
        varReader = "currentNewsItem">
    <myPrefix:myCustomTag in="$currentNewsItem" />
</c:import>
```

> **Note**
> The reason that you cannot assign a scope to the exported reader is that the tag handler implementation of the `c:import` action must ensure that the exported reader is closed by the time that the JSP ends.

The `c:param` *Action*

You can use the `c:param` action when you want to create request parameters for the URLs that are used by the `c:import`, `c:url`, and `c:redirect` actions.

The syntax for the `c:param` action is simple. You can specify the value for a parameter using either an attribute

```
<c:param name="parameter_name"
        value="parameter_value" />
```

or in body content of the action:

```
<c:param name="parameter_name">
    body_content
</c:param>
```

Both the name and the value of a parameter can be dynamic values. If the dynamic value for a name is the empty string or `null`, you would probably expect it to be an error. However, the parameter is simply ignored. If the value is `null`, the parameter has a value that is the empty string.

The `c:url` *Action*

The `c:url` action is useful when you need to rewrite a URL with the client's session ID in case cookies are not available on the client's machine. It is also helpful when you want to URL-encode parameters and their values to form a query string for use with a URL.

You must be careful to only use relative URLs with the `c:url` action if session tracking is important to you. For security reasons, absolute URLs are *not* rewritten. This is because if such processing did occur, it would be possible that an external URL could expose a user's session ID.

> **Caution**
>
> You are responsible for encoding the URL itself, if necessary. Space characters must be converted to + characters, and other characters to a % sign and a hashcode. You can use the `java.net.URLEncoder` class's `encode()` method to encode the relevant parts of the URL.

The syntax that you use to create a URL is

```
<c:url value="url_value"
       [var="variable_name"]
       [scope="{page | request | session | application}]
       [context="context"]
>
   optional c:param actions
</c:url>
```

The `value` attribute is the URL that you want to process. If you specify a `var` attribute, that is the exported variable that contains the processed URL. As usual, you can set the scope of the exported variable through the `scope` attribute. The `context` attribute is used when you want to use a relative URL for the `value` attribute, but the resource belongs to a foreign context (another Web application). As with the `c:import` action, a foreign context must begin with a forward slash character.

You can place `c:param` actions within the body content of the `c:url` action to generate query string arguments on the URL. The three JSPs in Listings 5.13, 5.14, and 5.15 show how to use the `c:url` action.

Listing 5.13 **A JSP That Prompts for Information** (`prompt.jsp`)

```
<%@ taglib uri="http://java.sun.com/jstl-el/core" prefix="c" %>

<c:set var="originalURL"
       value="http://localhost:8080/chapter05/core/url/url.jsp" />

<html>
  <head>
    <title>Chapter 5 - the c:url action (1)</title>
  </head>
  <body>
    This page takes 3 values that you specify, and forwards them to another JSP.
    That JSP will create a URL to another page, that then extracts the
    parameters and displays them.
    <p />
```

Listing 5.13 **Continued**

```
      <form action="createURL.jsp" method="post">
        <table>
          <tr><td>Enter name:</td>
              <td><input type="text" name="name"   /></td></tr>
          <tr><td>Enter age:</td>
              <td><input type="text" name="age"    /></td></tr>
          <tr><td>Enter gender:</td >
              <td><input type="text" name="gender" /></td></tr>
        </table>
        <input type="submit" value="Submit details" />
      </form>
  </body>
</html>
```

The JSP in Listing 5.13 contains a simple HTML form that prompts the user for her name, age, and gender, and then forwards these parameters to the JSP in Listing 5.14.

Listing 5.14 **A JSP That Creates a URL from Parameters (`createURL.jsp`)**

```
<%@ taglib uri="http://java.sun.com/jstl-el/core" prefix="c" %>

<c:url value="displayValues.jsp" var="displayURL">
  <c:param name="nameParam"   value="${param.name}" />
  <c:param name="ageParam"    value="${param.age}" />
  <c:param name="genderParam" value="${param.gender}" />
</c:url>

<html>
  <head>
    <title>Chapter 5 - the c:url action (2)</title>
  </head>
  <body>
    This page receives the values you specified, and creates a URL that contains
    them.
    <p />
    The generated URL is <c:out value="${displayURL}" />. <p/>
    Click <a href='<c:out value="${displayURL}" />'>here</a> to view the it.
  </body>
</html>
```

This JSP starts with the code:

```
<c:url value="displayValues.jsp" var="displayURL">
  <c:param name="nameParam"   value="${param.name}" />
  <c:param name="ageParam"    value="${param.age}" />
```

```
  <c:param name="genderParam" value="${param.gender}" />
</c:url>
```

This creates a rewritten (if necessary) URL with three URL-encoded paramet URL is displayed later in the page, along with a hyperlink to another page tha the encoded parameters:

```
The generated URL is <c:out value="${displayURL}" />. <p/>
Click <a href='<c:out value="${displayURL}" />'>here</a> to view the it.
```

For example, if you had specified a name of `Samuel Greenhough`, an age of `1`, and a gender of `male`, the generated URL would be something like

```
/chapter05/core/url/displayValues.jsp?nameParam=Samuel+Greenhough
&ageParam=1&genderParam=male
```

The JSP that this URL references is shown in Listing 5.15.

Listing 5.15 **A JSP That Processes the Encoded URL (`displayValues.jsp`)**

```
<%@ taglib uri="http://java.sun.com/jstl-el/core" prefix="c" %>

<html>
  <head>
    <title>Chapter 5 - the c:url action (3)</title>
  </head>
  <body>
    <h3>List of query string parameters:</h3>
    <ul>
      <c:forEach items="${param}" var="currentParam">
        <li><c:out value="${currentParam.key}" />
            = <c:out value="${currentParam.value}" /></li>
      </c:forEach>
    </ul>
  </body>
</html>
```

This page uses a simple `c:forEach` action to process the `param` map of request parameters, and display them in a list.

The `c:redirect` *Action*

You can use the `c:redirect` action when you want to abort processing the current JSP, and instruct the client Web browser to redirect to a different URL.

You can optionally nest `c:param` actions to specify parameters to the redirect URL. The rules for rewriting the URL, and its parameters are exactly the same as for the `c:url` action.

The syntax of the c:redirect action is

```
<c:redirect url="url_value"
         [context="context"]>
   optional_c:param_actions
</c:redirect>
```

The url attribute contains the URL that you want to redirect to. If the URL belongs to a foreign context, you specify it using the context attribute. As with the c:url and c:import actions, the value for the context attribute must begin with a forward slash character.

You often use the c:redirect action when you want to deal with errors. For example, consider a page with a form. If the user fills in the form incorrectly, you can redirect them to a page that asks for more information before posting the information back to the handler page. Similarly, consider the case when a user uses a Web application and visits a page that requires them to be logged in. In that case, the c:redirect action enables you to redirect the user to a page that asks them for their username and password. The Shopping Cart mini case study in Chapter 8 uses exactly this approach in Listing 8.14 (doLogin.jsp), so look there for a worked example.

The XML actions

JSTL provides you with a tag library for performing XML-related activities. This tag library is logically separated into three distinct areas: core, flow control, and transformation. These three areas are discussed briefly in this part of the chapter. You can find examples of these actions in use later in this book in Chapters 10 and 11.

XML Core Actions

The XML core actions use the XPath language as their expression language. However, the designers of the XML actions identified that there is a requirement to somehow extend XPath so that it can access the scoped attributes that are available to a JSP. For example, there is no way in standard XPath to access a parameter on the query string. You access JSP variables from the custom tags using XPath as follows:

```
$scope:variable
```

The JSTL XPath engine supports the scopes listed in Table 5.5.

Table 5.5 **JSTL XPath Scopes**

Scope Example	Description
`$variable`	Looks for an attribute called `variable` in the page context. Equivalent to `pageContext.findAttribute("variable")`
`$applicationScope:variable`	Looks for an application-scoped attibute with the name variable. Equivalent to `pageContext.getAttribute("variable", PageContext.APPLICATION_SCOPE)`

Table 5.5 **Continued**

Scope Example	Description
`$cookie:variable`	Looks for a cookie with the name variable.
`$header:variable`	Looks for a header with the name variable. Equivalent to `request.getHeader("variable")`
`$initParam:variable`	Looks for an initialization parameter with the name variable. Equivalent to application.getInitParameter ("variable")
`$pageScope:variable`	Looks for a page-scoped attribute called variable. Equivalent to `pageContext.getAttribute("variable", PageContext.PAGE_SCOPE)`
`$param:variable`	Looks for a request parameter called `variable`. Equivalent to `request.getParameter("variable")`
`$requestScope:variable`	Looks for a request-scoped attribute called `variable`. Equivalent to `pageContext.getAttribute("variable", PageContext.REQUEST_SCOPE)`
`$sessionScope:variable`	Looks for a session-scoped attribute called `variable`. Equivalent to `pageContext.getAttribute("variable", PageContext.SESSION_SCOPE)`

For example, if you want to access a session-scoped attribute called `shoppingCart`, you would use the expression:

$sessionScope:shoppingCartNotice that the scope names are the same as for the JSTL core tags. For a brief introduction to XPath, see Chapter 11. Alternatively, you can find the XPath home page at the W3C on `http://www.w3.org/TR/xpath`.

The XML core actions are very similar to the core tags `c:out` and `c:set` that you saw earlier in this chapter. The difference is that the XML core actions use XPath, rather than the JSTL EL.

The `x:parse` *Action*

You can use the `x:parse` action to parse an XML document. However, this action does not perform any validation of the source document. That is, any DTD or Schema that the source document specifies is ignored.

The basic syntax of the `x:parse` action is

```
<x:parse xml="source_XML_document"
        var="variable_name"
        scope="{page | request | session | application}" />
```

The source XML document that you want to parse is set through the `xml` attribute, and the parsed document is exported by the `var` attribute. The type of the exported variable is implementation-dependent. The scope of the exported attribute is set with the `scope` attribute.

You can use the `c:set` action mentioned earlier in this chapter in conjunction with the `x:parse` action. For example, the following code fragment causes the specified XML to be parsed using these two actions:

```
<c:set var="someXML">
  <person>
    <name>Ruth</name>
    <age>29</age>
  </person>
</c:set>
<x:parse var="parsedDocument" xml="${someXML}" />
```

You can also use the `c:import` action to read an XML document from a URL into a scoped attribute, and then specify this attribute to the `x:parse` action. The general form that your code would take in this case is

```
<c:import url="http://someHost/someResource" var="theXML" />
<x:parse var="parsedDocument" xml="${theXML}" />
```

Rather than use the implementation-dependent type for the exported `var` document, you can instead export an object in the form of the well-known W3C DOM. You do this by specifying a `varDom` attribute to export a parsed document of type `org.w3c.dom.Document`. You can control the scope of this exported document with the `scopeDom` attribute. For example, the previous example can be modified to this:

```
<c:import url="http://someHost/someResource" var="theXML" />
<x:parse varDom="parsedDocument" scopeDom="page" xml="${theXML}" />
```

The `x:out` *Action*

After you have a parsed XML document, you can then apply XPath expressions against it to extract subsets of the document. You can insert the result of applying the XPath expression into the output of the JSP by using the `x:out` action, which has this syntax:

```
<x:out select="xpath_expression" [escapeXML="{true | false}"] />
```

The `x:out` action is thus very similar to the standard JSP expression tag (`<%= ... %>`). Taking the example code fragment cited in the earlier section on the `x:parse` action, you can use the `x:out` action to extract the person's name as follows:

```
<c:set var="someXML">
  <person>
    <name>Ruth</name>
    <age>29</age>
  </person>
</c:set>
<x:parse var="parsedDocument" xml="${someXML}" />

The person's name is <x:out select="$parsedDocument//name" />
```

When XML is sent back to the client by way of the `x:out` action, any of following XML characters are by default converted to their character entity code: `<`, `>`, `&`, `'`, and `"`. If you want the XML to be sent "as is," just use the `escapeXML` attribute with a value of `false`.

The `x:set` *Action*

If you want to execute an XPath expression and store the result for later use, you would use the `x:set` action. It is a simple action, which has the following syntax:

```
<x:set var="variable_name"
       select="xpath_expression"
       [scope="{page | request | session | application}"] />
```

The three attributes have the meanings that you would expect: `select` is the XPath expression you want to evaluate; and `var` is the name of the variable that holds the result. Its scope is set by the value of the optional `scope` attribute. If you omit the `scope` attribute, then the variable holding the result defaults to `page` scope.

The XML Flow-Control Actions

There are five XML flow-control actions: `x:if`, `x:choose`, `x:when`, `x:otherwise`, and `x:forEach`. They are much the same as the similarly named actions from the Core tag library. The only difference is that they use XPath expressions rather than EL-based expressions.

For example, the following code fragment extracts the names of people from the embedded XML document, and creates an HTML unordered list from them:

```
<c:set var="someXML">
  <people>
    <person>
      <name>Mark</name>
      <age>30</age>
    </person>
    <person>
      <name>Ruth</name>
      <age>29</age>
    </person>
  </people>
</c:set>
<x:parse var="parsedDocument" xml="${someXML}" />

Here is a list of people:
<ul>
  <x:forEach select="$parsedDocument/people/person">
    <li> <x:out select="name" /> </li>
  </x:forEach>
</ul>
```

The syntax for each of the XML actions is given when they are used later in the book in Chapters 11 and 12, as well as in Appendix C.

The XML Transform Actions

There are two XML transform actions that enable you to take an XML document and transform it according to an XSLT stylesheet. The main action is `x:transform`, which allows you to specify the XML and XSLT documents. Within the body content of the `x:transform` action you can embed `x:param` actions to pass parameters to the XSLT stylesheet.

See Chapter 11 and Appendix C for more details.

The SQL Actions

It is recommended that you put any kind of business logic that requires database access within JavaBeans or Enterprise JavaBeans (EJB). However, JSTL provides a set of SQL actions for very simple applications and prototypes. JSTL provides SQL actions for querying and updating a relational database (`sql:query` and `sql:update`), as well as transaction support (through the `sql:transaction` action).

You can find examples of using the SQL actions in Chapter 14 and a summary of their syntax in Appendix C.

The Internationalization and Formatting Actions

When writing Web applications today, you can no longer assume that English is the only language in which users want to view your Web site. It is becoming increasingly common that Web applications must support more than one language. *Internationalization* is the name given to the procedure of designing an application that works in such a way.

> **Note**
>
> Internationalization is also known as *I18N* because there are 18 letters between the first and last!
>
> You can find a tutorial about I18N on Sun's Web site at this URL:
>
> `http://java.sun.com/docs/books/tutorial/i18n/index.html`.

J2SE supports the internationalization of applications through the use of *resource bundles*, which are just text files. Rather than hard-coding the textual output of an application, such as a Web browser title, you instead put the various translations into separate resource bundles, one for each language.

Actually, the correct term, rather than *language*, is *locale*. A locale is a particular cultural, geographical, or political region. Locales are specified using two pieces of information: a language code and an optional country code. For example, `en_US` denotes the English as spoken in the USA, whereas `fr_CA` is French Canadian.

Resource bundle files contain name/value pairs, where the name is a *key* used by the JSP to access the language-specific value for a message. You configure a Web application's resource bundles through its `web.xml` file. Resource bundles are named in this way:

```
MyMessagesBundle_en_US.properties
MyMessagesBundle_fr_CA.properties
```

and so on. The contents of a resource bundle for an English locale might look something like this:

```
greeting = Hello and welcome!
farewell = Goodbye and take care!
```

JSTL makes it very easy for you to internationalize a JSP through the use of the `fmt:message` action. At the relevant point in the JSP, you could insert a greeting for the locale of the user by simply inserting this action:

```
<fmt:message key="greeting" />
```

The JSP container inspects the user's locale, loads the correct resource bundle, extracts the value for the specified key, and then embeds it into the output.

JSTL also provides actions for formatting dates and numbers. These actions include `fmt:formatNumber` and `fmt:formatDate`. When you use the formatting actions, you can allow them to use their built-in default formatting rules, or you can specify your own custom patterns. See Appendix C for a summary of the syntax of the I18N actions.

Backwards Compatibility and Migrating from JSTL 1.0 to JSTL 1.1

JSTL 1.0 was not a JSP 2.0 development. JSTL 1.0 requires a J2EE 1.3 platform, as required by JSP 1.2. Some of JSTL 1.0, for example the EL, was leveraged into JSP 2.0. This is in fact the main difference between JSTL 1.0 and JSTL 1.1. JSTL 1.1 is a maintenance release to go hand-in-hand with JSP 2.0, and as such JSTL 1.1 requires a JSP 2.0 platform, as per J2EE 1.4.

You might be wondering why the JSTL 1.1 URIs have the string "el" in them, if JSTL 1.1 does not perform EL processing in a JSP 2.0 environment! The reason is to indicate the JSTL 1.1 is JSTL 1.0 *minus* EL. For example:

```
http://java.sun.com/jstl-el/core
```

If you are running an environment that supports JSTL 1.1, then you are encouraged to migrate any JSTL 1.0 applications to JSTL 1.1 so that you can take advantage of the extra capabilities that are available to you. Having said that, you can run JSTL 1.0 applications in a JSTL 1.1 container without having to make any changes.

A JSP 2.0 container supports the evaluation of EL expressions. In order to provide support for JSP 1.2 web applications, the container disables EL expression evaluation. It can do this by inspecting the `web.xml` file, and seeing if it is a Servlet 2.3 (for JSP 1.2) descriptor. In this case, EL expressions are ignored by the container, and the JSTL 1.0 libraries deal with them.

JSTL 1.0 has the following URIs for EL-based actions:

```
http://java.sun.com/jstl/core
http://java.sun.com/jstl/xml
http://java.sun.com/jstl/fmt
http://java.sun.com/jstl/sql
```

You can see that they are very similar to JSTL 1.1's URIs used already in this chapter. However, JSTL 1.0 has a separate set of URIs for RT-based libraries:

```
http://java.sun.com/jstl/core_rt
http://java.sun.com/jstl/xml_rt
http://java.sun.com/jstl/fmt_rt
http://java.sun.com/jstl/sql_rt
```

In order to migrate a JSTL 1.0 web application to JSTL 1.1, you need to perform the following steps:

- Use JSTL 1.1 URIs instead of JSTL 1.0's EL and RT URIs.
- Escape all occurrences of "{" in template text and RT actions, as per the JSP 2.0 Specification, section 1.6.
- Migrate the web application deployment descriptor (`web.xml`) from Servlet 2.3 to Servlet 2.4, as per the Servlet 2.4 Specification.

Third-Party Tag Libraries

Many tag libraries are available for free or for a fee. For example, the Apache Software Foundation (`http://www.apache.org/`) is an organization that produces free software that you can use for personal or commercial ends. Volunteers run it, so anybody can get involved and contribute to the source code of the projects that it hosts. One of the projects that Apache hosts is the Jakarta project, which consists of server-side software for the Java platform. Jakarta's subprojects include

- Ant: an XML- and Java-based build tool.
- Struts: a framework for writing Model 2 architecture Web applications.
- Tomcat: the reference implementation (RI) for the Java Servlet and JSP specifications.

Another project that you will no doubt come across is the Jakarta Taglibs project.

The Jakarta Taglibs Project

The Jakarta Taglibs project was set up to produce Web publishing tool extensions and JSP custom tag libraries. All the software that makes up the project is freely available as open source. The project's home page is at this URL: `http://jakarta.apache.org/taglibs/index.html`.

As with any tag library, the custom tags within it are reusable pieces of functionality that help to separate the presentation within the JSP from its actual implementation. Some of the older custom tags written for the Taglibs project are JSP 1.1–compliant, and the rest are for later versions. Fortunately, the JSP 1.1 custom tags can be used in a JSP 1.2+ container. Table 5.6 lists some of the tag libraries that you can download from `http://jakarta.apache.org/taglibs/index.html`.

Table 5.6 **Jakarta Taglibs Subprojects**

Jakarta Sub-project	JSP Version	Status	Description
Standard taglib	1.2	Released	The JSTL RI
Cache taglib	1.2	Prerelease	Provides tags for caching JSP fragments
Mailer taglib	1.1	Released	Contains tags for sending email from a JSP
Regexp taglib	1.1	Released	Provides tags that enable you to use Perl regular expressions from with a JSP
UltraDev CTLX	N/A	Prerelease	A Custom Tag Library extension (CLTX) that enables Dreamweaver UltraDev 4.0 to use JSP custom tag libraries in its JSPs

As you can see from Table 5.7, the Jakarta Taglibs Project hosts the JSTL reference implementation; its URL is `http://jakarta.apache.org/taglibs/doc/standard-doc/intro.html`. You can download the latest nightly build of JSTL from `http://cvs.apache.org/builds/jakarta.taglibs/nightly/projects/standard/`.

Summary

This chapter has shown you that although the ability to embed scripting code into a page is very powerful, it can quickly lead to unmaintainable Web applications. Similarly, it is inadvisable to hard-code HTML with Java servlets. Tag libraries were designed to be a solution to the problem of separating the roles of page authors and Java developers.

JSP 2.0 provides JSTL, which is a collection of reusable custom actions that enable you to perform often-needed operations. JSTL is actually composed of four tag libraries that provide actions that cover Core, XML, SQL, and I18N areas of functionality.

You can find information on how to write your own custom actions in Chapter 9. It covers the lifecycle of a custom tag, the syntax of the tag library descriptor file, as well as the deployment of custom tag libraries.

In the next chapter, you will learn about JavaBeans and how best to utilize them from a Web application.

6

JSP and JavaBeans

THE COMPONENT-ORIENTED BENEFITS OF JAVABEANS can be utilized from JSP technology. In this chapter, you will learn how JavaBeans can be used from JSP, and also how JavaBeans can be populated from HTML form data. This chapter also investigates how best to use JavaBeans as a container of your Web application business logic.

This chapter begins with a basic introduction to JavaBean technology, and then moves on to introduce the special elements that can be included in a JSP to set and get JavaBean properties. You will also learn how to invoke JavaBean methods.

Chapter 1, "JSP, J2EE, and the Role of the Servlet," covers the concept of scope. This chapter describes how JavaBeans can be globally scoped, session scoped, request scoped, or page scoped. You will be told when each level of scope is useful and given examples of typical JavaBeans that are used at that level.

All the sample code from this chapter is available on the book Web site at `http://www.samspublishing.com`. Enter this book's full ISBN (0672324385) in the Search window to reach a page with links to the source code and updates about the book.

What Is a JavaBean?

For the last ten years or so, Visual Basic has probably been the best-known rapid-application development (RAD) environment for writing computer software, at least for Microsoft operating systems. Visual Basic uses software components such as buttons and check boxes that have a set of properties and methods. For a button, these properties are the text label, the foreground and background colors, the size, position, and so on. A Visual Basic button uses an `onClick` method that is invoked when the button is clicked with a mouse. These properties and methods are easily accessible using the mouse in the design phase. You can drag and drop components onto forms and edit their properties through property sheets. Whole applications can be assembled from prebuilt components that are connected by the developer. Components can be either visual or nonvisual at runtime, although nonvisual components must have some kind of onscreen representation while the application is being developed. The Visual Basic *timer* is an example of a component that is not seen on the user interface while the application is running, but is seen on the design-time form inside the Visual Basic IDE.

Sun Microsystems released version 1.1 of the Java Development Kit (JDK) in February 1997, which included a new API known as *JavaBeans*. The JavaBeans API describes a software component model for the Java programming language. JavaBean components are Java classes that can be reused and linked to form new applications. Any Java class that follows certain design conventions can be a JavaBean component.

Originally, the JavaBeans specification was targeted towards integrated development environments (IDE) such as JBuilder. The controls can thus be used in any IDE that supports the JavaBeans specification. Having said that, the JavaBeans specification is also applicable when writing server-side components. You can think of server-side JavaBeans as providing a service. Such services could be for database access, writing to log files, and so on. Another term that you might have heard for describing JavaBeans is that they *encapsulate business logic*.

The Benefit of Component-Based Development

A software component in the software world is equivalent to an integrated circuit (IC) in the hardware world. For example, as a poor student I used to make cash by selling "fake" car alarms to other students. These devices were built around a 555 timer chip that caused a red LED to flash until a battery went flat.

If one of my devices had a burnt-out 555 timer chip, I could go to a hardware store and pick up a new 555. The new chip would conform to the same specification, and I could switch the components without affecting the rest of the circuit.

The important benefit that components give you is that they provide specific, reusable functionality. The 555 timer chip is used in a great many different circuits. In terms of using software components to write application software, you make gains in the areas of faster development, fewer bugs, and reduced cost.

Software components can vary in size from a single class to a full-blown application. Examples of such components are

- Spell checker
- Graphical user interface controls (such as buttons)
- Database connector

A framework is necessary for components to interoperate. Such a framework must provide mechanisms for the components to control each other, and to exchange data. Three mechanisms are commonly used:

- Properties: Hold the state of a component. For example, its color, display language, database to connect to, and so forth.
- Methods: These can be invoked to request the component perform some service. For example, to save some data, or to perform a database query.

- Events: A component generates these to indicate that something important has occurred. An event could be that a button is clicked, a file error occurred, or that a database update has succeeded, for example.

The diagram in Figure 6.1 shows a simple component-based system.

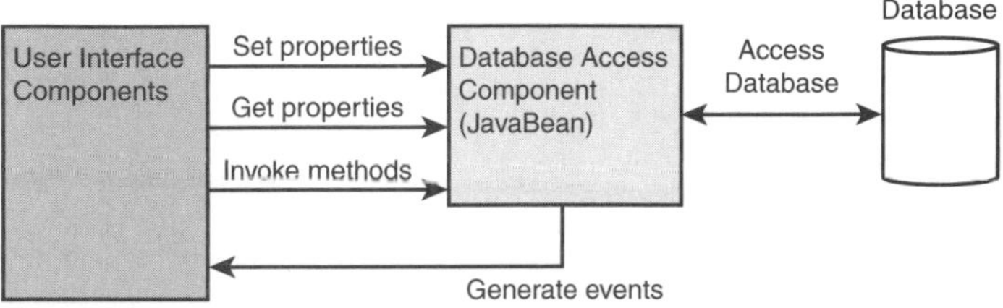

Figure 6.1 A simple component-based system.

Figure 6.1 has a user interface that has a reference to the database access component. Properties, such as the database URL, can be set on the component that is to be accessed. For instance, say the user interface has a menu option or button that, when selected or clicked, causes a database query method to be invoked on the database access component. When the database completes the query, the component can pass back the requested information by generating an event that is fired at the user interface.

The Role of the Bean in Component-Based Development

JavaBeans take on the role of the *model* in the Model-View-Controller architecture, and are used in Web applications in several common areas.

Note

The Model-View-Controller architecture is discussed in Chapter 1.

For example, JavaBeans are useful for

- Accessing data from various data sources, such as SQL databases and LDAP servers
- Performing validation of data that users enter into HTML forms
- Separating the presentation code from the controlling logic within a JSP

Web applications that are built together from a series of Java method calls quickly become very difficult, if not impossible, to manage. It is much easier to understand and modify Web applications that are built from JavaBeans.

An often-asked question is, "What is the difference between a Java class and a JavaBean?" The answer is that a JavaBean is usually a class (could be more than one class), but a class is not necessarily a JavaBean. The JavaBeans specification (`http://java.sun.com/beans/spec.html/`) details what a class must do to be considered a JavaBean.

There are many parts to the JavaBeans specification, including sections covering

- Events that are used to communicate with other JavaBeans.
- Properties that define a JavaBean's behavior and appearance.
- Persistence so that JavaBeans can save and subsequently restore their state.
- Methods that can be invoked, in the same way as any other Java method.
- The dynamic discovery of a JavaBean's features when software executes.

These points are further discussed in the following sections.

Events

The JavaBean specification defines a mechanism that is used to enable JavaBeans to notify other objects in the system that important events have occurred. For example, a JavaBean might receive data over a network connection that other entities in the system need to know about. JavaBeans use the delegation event model introduced in Java 1.1. The delegation event model uses the concept of event sources and event listeners. You can find more information in the Java Tutorial at `http://java.sun.com/tutorial/javabeans/index.html`.

Properties

Extensive coverage of the properties of a JavaBean are provided later in this chapter.

Persistence

Persistence is the process of saving the important parts of the state of an object so that the state can subsequently be restored. There are two streams that are generally used when a JavaBean is read from, or written to, a stream: `java.io.ObjectInputStream` and `java.io.ObjectOutputStream`. You can chain these streams together with other streams, just as you do when using any of the other streams supplied by the Java platform. Common streams that you connect the `java.io.ObjectInputStream` and `java.io.ObjectOutputStream` to are file and network streams. You might use a file stream to save an object's state to disk for subsequent restoration, and a network stream to copy an object to another process.

The JavaBeans specification states that all JavaBeans should implement the `java.io.Serializable` interface if you want to be able to save and restore beans and their state. The `Serializable` interface is a *marker* interface and as such contains no method signatures. If you need absolute control over the stream format, you can instead implement a subinterface of `java.io.Serializable`, called `java.io.Externalizable`. If an object implements neither of these interfaces, an exception is thrown at runtime when an attempt is made to serialize the object. All the object's instance fields (that is, non-`static`) are written out, except for any fields that are declared with the `transient` keyword.

Note

The `java.io.Externalizable` interface is a subinterface of `java.io.Serializable`. Thus, you only need to implement one of the two interfaces, not both.

Java objects are not `Serializable` by default because the designers of the language wanted to force developers to think about the issues involved when an object is serialized. Certain objects do not make sense to serialize. A common example is if you were to serialize an instance of the `java.lang.Thread` class. A thread object has certain information that would not make sense to serialize from one Java Virtual Machine (JVM) to another; for example, all the stack-based information. File objects are another example of objects that you would not serialize because the underlying operating system allocates file handles. If the file object is serialized on one machine and deserialized on another, the file handle will almost certainly be invalid. In practice, you mark such fields as files and threads within the object with the `transient` keyword, and generate new instances when the object is deserialized. In fact, you tend to mark anything that is not `Serializable` as `transient`. Examples include JDBC objects such as `Connection` and `Statement`.

For simple JavaBeans, all you need to do is declare that the class implement the `java.io.Serializable` interface, and that is it. If and when the Web container needs to serialize and deserialize the JavaBean, everything happens automatically. The Java serialization process writes out not just the object in question, but also any objects that it references. In this way, it is possible to write out the entire application if you are not careful! Also, you need to consider sensitive data within an object; for example, credit-card details and passwords. There are two steps that you can take to protect such data.

The first thing that you do is mark the fields within the object with the `transient` keyword. This causes the Java serialization mechanism to ignore the fields when serializing the object to the stream. That is but half the story because you probably still want the data to be stored in some form. Therefore, the second thing you do is provide a pair of `readObject` and `writeObject` methods. These two methods enable you to hook into the serialization and deserialization processes. The signatures for these methods are

```
private void readObject(java.io.ObjectInputStream ois)
➥    throws java.io.IOException

private void writeObject(java.io.ObjectOutputStream oos)
➥    throws java.io.IOException
```

Note

You will not find these two methods in any interface, so if you use them, you must take care to get the method signature exactly right or they will not be invoked by the Java runtime.

methods are called automatically by the Java runtime when an object is read from, or written to, a stream. Thus, when the object is written to a stream, you can put code into the `writeObject` method to encrypt the sensitive data. Similarly, you can put code into the `readObject` method to decrypt the sensitive data when it is read back in its encrypted form. For more information on this process, consult `http://java.sun.com/docs/books/tutorial/essential/io/serialization.html`.

The serialization of JavaBeans becomes useful in the context of using JSPs when session failover is supported by the Web container, and the JavaBeans need to be migrated from one Web container to another. The concept of session failover is covered in Chapter 8, "Session Tracking Using JSP." However, many JavaBeans do not implement the `java.io.Serializable` interface, either because they were not designed to be saved and restored, or simply because the developer forgot! This is perfectly valid, but bear in mind that if anybody ever tries to serialize your JavaBean, an exception will be thrown.

Dynamic Discovery

Dynamic discovery is especially useful for integrated development environments (IDEs). This is because you can purchase, or write, a component that you want to use in an IDE. The question is, how does the IDE know what properties, events, and methods the JavaBean has? How should the IDE display these features on a property sheet so that you can edit them? How does the IDE display your JavaBean on a form? Consider the case where you write a new JFC (Java Foundation Class or Swing) visual component that you want to use in a graphical Java application. The IDE, or *builder tool*, uses a technique called *introspection* to determine the features of the JavaBean.

Points to Remember

The JavaBeans specification covers a lot of ground, but as far as using JavaBeans in a JSP is concerned, there are really only two important points that you need to know:

- A no-argument constructor must be defined.
- Properties should be accessed using `get` and `set` methods.

These points are covered further in the next two sections.

The No-Argument Constructor

The class that is used to implement the JavaBean must have a no-argument constructor. When a JavaBean is created from a JSP, it is this constructor that is invoked. The no-argument constructor usually has some initialization code, although it is not mandatory for the constructor to perform any processing.

There is no way to pass additional parameters to have a different constructor called. However, there is nothing to stop you from having other constructors that are called in other situations or applications.

> **Note**
>
> It is a good idea to declare the no-argument constructor as `public`, or your Web container might be unable to access it.

If you already have access to the source code for a JavaBean, you might have seen an *empty*, `public` no-argument constructor declared even if there are no other constructors in the class, as follows:

```
public class MyJavaBean {
    public MyJavaBean() {}
    ...
}
```

This is purely defensive programming: Consider what would happen if the constructor on line 2 were omitted. The JavaBean would work fine in a JSP, but if at a later date another constructor were added, problems would arise.

This is due to the fact that the Java programming language specification states that if *no* constructors are defined for a class, a default constructor that takes no arguments is provided. However, as soon as *any* constructor is provided, the default no-argument constructor is no longer available. This is a good thing, generally, because it forces the client of the Java class to provide initialization data when an object is instantiated.

When a user tries to view the JSP in her Web browser, an error occurs stating that the JavaBean could not be instantiated. To safeguard against this kind of problem, the no-argument constructor is often explicitly declared in the first case, even if it does nothing.

The `set` and `get` Methods

Encapsulation is one of the key principles in object-oriented design and because JavaBeans are implemented using Java class definitions, it is no less important. You write `set` and `get` methods when you want to expose a JavaBean's properties for read-and-write access by a client.

If you make the instance data of an object private to the object, you protect both the object and its client. The reasons for this are

- The client is protected against the effects of change. Because the client cannot access the internal, private parts of the object in the first place, you are free to change the internal implementation of the object without any changes being necessary to the client(s).
- The state of the object is protected against the client making any invalid changes. Instead, the client must use *accessor* methods to store and retrieve the object's state. The accessor methods can have logic that normalizes data into sensible values or throws an error back to the client instead.

The Java code in Listing 6.1 shows a simple implementation of a `Book` JavaBean. You will see this JavaBean used again in the mini case study in Chapter 8.

Listing 6.1 **A JavaBean for a Book (**`Book.java`**)**

```
package com.conygre.jspdevhandbook.chapter6;

public class Book {
    // Instance variables
    private String author, id, title;
    private double price;

    // Methods
    public String getId() {
        return id;
    }
    public String getTitle() {
        return title;
    }
    public double getPrice() {
        return price;
    }
    public String getAuthor() {
        return author;
    }

    // Constructors
    public Book(){
        System.out.println("No-arg constructor");
    }

    public Book(String t, double p, String a, String i) {
        title  = t;
        price  = p;
        author = a;
        id     = i;
        System.out.println("Book c'tor with args");
    }
}
```

At the beginning of the `Book` class are the implementations of the four properties of the JavaBean. The properties are implemented using instance variables, one for each property. The four instance variables are followed by the `get` methods that provide read-only access to these properties. If read/write access were required, an additional group of `set` methods would be necessary, too. It is possible, although slightly odd, to have a property that is exposed only for write access, by providing a `set` method, but not a `get` method.

The `Book` class ends by declaring two constructors. One is the public, no-argument constructor that is required when a JavaBean is instantiated using this class from a JSP.

Another constructor that takes four parameters can be used by Java code. This second constructor is used in the mini case study in Chapter 8.

There are different kinds of property that a JavaBean can expose. A *simple* property holds a single value. The signatures for read/write methods for a simple property of a JavaBean follow a *design pattern*, and are as follows:

```
public <DATATYPE> getXyz() {
    /// return the current value of the property called xyz
}
```

and

```
public void setXyz(<DATATYPE> newValue) {
    // store new value in the property called xyz
}
```

Notice that although the `get` and `set` method names use a capital `X` character, the comments inside the method bodies imply that the property is called `xyz`. Note the lowercase letter at the beginning of the property name. This is simply the naming convention that is used when working with JavaBeans. You can see that this convention is used in Listing 6.1 for the four properties of the `Book` JavaBean.

The only time that you do not follow these rules for naming the accessor methods of a property is when the property is of type `boolean`. In that case, you can either use the `get/set` pair of methods or an `is/set` pair instead. For example, what if the `Book` class needs an extra property to indicate whether the book has a hardback covering or not? The accessor methods could look like this:

```
public boolean isHardback() { ... }
public void setHardback(boolean value) { ... }
```

Properties of a JavaBean that hold multiple values are known as *indexed* properties, and could be implemented using an array, for example.

Other types of property do exist, such as *constrained* and *bound* properties. Bound properties generate events when they are changed, and a property is known to be constrained when any change to that property can be vetoed. The JavaBean can veto a property change, but it is usually an outside object that vetoes a change.

So far, the properties of a JavaBean have been discussed as if each property is implemented as an instance variable. However, there is nothing in the JavaBeans specification that says this must be the case. This means that you are free to expose a property via a pair of `get` and `set` methods, but you can implement the property any way you see fit.

For more information about JavaBeans, consult one of the many books on the subject. You can also find useful JavaBeans documentation on Sun's Web site at `http://java.sun.com/docs/books/tutorial/javabeans/index.html` and `http://java.sun.com/products/javabeans/`.

The Importance of Scope in a Web Application

Later in this chapter, you will see how JavaBeans can be used in a JSP. However, it is first useful to understand that there are several distinct *scopes* in which the JavaBean can be stored. The answer to the question, "What is a scope?" is found in Chapter 1. This chapter answers the question, "What values can I specify when I declare a JavaBean?"

The Role of Scope

In Chapter 1, you saw an example that stored objects in the `ServletContext` object. The example referred to these stored objects as having as *application scope*. The other three scopes are known as *session*, *page*, and *request*.

JavaBeans can be stored in these four different scopes. The scope of a JavaBean indicates how long the JavaBean exists after it has been created. The lifetime of a JavaBean has a direct correlation with the JSPs that can access it. The four distinct scopes range from the entire lifetime of the Web container down to the lifetime of the individual page that declares the JavaBean.

Later in this chapter, you will see that the `jsp:useBean` tag is used to define a JavaBean for use on a page. The JavaBean can be initialized when it is created, by embedding `jsp:setProperty` tags within the body of the `useBean` tag. The JavaBean instance is given a name through the `id` attribute, which maps to a local variable inside the generated servlet's `jspService` method. In addition, the JavaBean instance is also stored in one of the four scopes that are accessible through the predefined JSP variables (see Chapter 2, "The Basic Syntax of JSP," for a discussion of these). Objects that are stored in a particular level of scope are referred to as *attributes* of the scope.

The diagram in Figure 6.2 shows the different scopes within an application running in a Web container. Figure 6.2 shows a client Web browser that makes a request for a page called `requestedPage.jsp`. This page includes a JSP called `includedPage.jsp`. The arrows that emanate from the two pages show which scopes are accessible to the pages. The next four subsections discuss the different scopes.

The `page` Scope

The default scope level is `page`. When a JavaBean is declared within this scope, the JavaBean instance is stored in the predefined `pageContext` object. However, the JavaBean is stored in the `pageContext` object only while the current request is executing. At the end of the current page request, the JavaBean instance is removed from the `pageContext` object and is eligible for garbage collection. This means that the JavaBean is not available to included JSPs.

There are two ways you can write JSPs that access JavaBeans that are declared with `page` scope. One way is to use the `pageContext` object's `getAttribute()` method from a scriptlet or expression tag. After the JavaBean is retrieved, you can then invoke its accessor methods directly. This technique is not particularly common because the JavaBeans are simply local variables in the generated `_jspService` method and, as such, are accessible by name within the JSP.

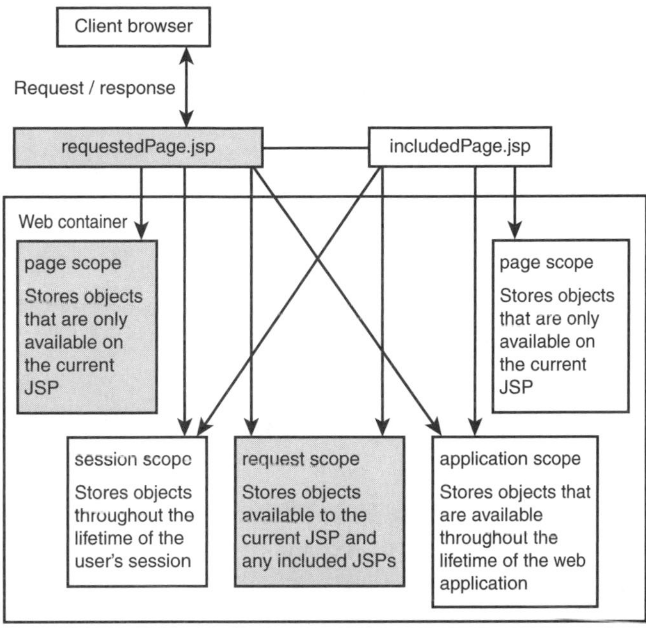

Figure 6.2 Scopes in a Web application.

The other, more common, way to access the JavaBean's properties is to use the `jsp:getProperty` and `jsp:setProperty` methods described later in this chapter.

The `request` Scope

The `ServletRequest` object stores any JavaBeans that are declared to use the `request` scope. The `ServletRequest` object is available through the predefined `request` object that is available to JSPs.

The `request` scope is similar to the `page` scope in that the stored JavaBean instance is discarded at the end of the page request. However, unlike the `page` scope, the stored JavaBean *is* available to any included JSPs.

Again, you can access the stored JavaBean either by using the standard action elements described in this chapter, or by using the `request` object's `getAttribute()` and `setAttribute()` methods. Their signatures are

```
java.lang.Object getAttribute(java.lang.String attribute_name)
void setAttribute(java.lang.String attribute_name,
                  java.lang.Object object_to_store)
```

The `session` Scope

JavaBeans that have a scope of `session` are stored in the `HttpSession` object that is available to JSPs through the predefined `session` object. The effect that this has is that the JavaBean is available throughout the entire user's session. An example of a session-scoped object is the shopping cart that you commonly see in web applications.

You can access a session-scoped JavaBean either using the `jsp:setProperty` and `jsp:getProperty` tags, or by invoking the `session` object's `getValue()` method that takes the JavaBean's name as a parameter. Another way is to use the `session` object's `getAttribute()` and `setAttribute()` methods. Their signatures are

```
java.lang.Object getAttribute(java.lang.String attribute_name)
void setAttribute(java.lang.String attribute_name,
                  java.lang.Object object_to_store)
```

Do not use the `session` scope on a JSP that uses a `page` directive that has its `session` attribute set to `false`. For example:

```
<%@ page session="false" %>
<jsp:useBean id="user" class="com.conygre.Person" scope="session" />
...
```

If you attempt to do this, the Web container generates an error along the lines of

```
org.apache.jasper.compiler.CompileException: /chapter06/scope/ses
sionDisabled.jsp(1,0) Cant use as session bean {0} since it is prohibited by
jsp directive defined earlier
```

The `application` Scope

If a JavaBean has been declared to use the `application` scope, the JavaBean instance is stored in the `ServletContext` object. The `ServletContext` object is available to JSPs through the predefined `application` object.

The `application` object is shared by all JSPs that are running in a given Web container. The effect that this has is to make the JavaBean object available to any other JSP or servlet (through the `ServletContext`) that is running in the Web container. This is true until the Web container is shut down. After a restart, the JavaBean would have to be created again before it could be accessed.

The shared JavaBean can be accessed by using the `application` object's `getAttribute()` and `setAttribute()` methods. Their signatures are

```
java.lang.Object getAttribute(java.lang.String attribute_name)
void setAttribute(java.lang.String attribute_name,
                  java.lang.Object object_to_store)
```

When to Use the Different Scopes

The `page` scope means that JavaBean components are only available on the current page, not even on any JSPs that the current JSP includes. You generally want to use `page`-scoped JavaBeans for storing information in the short term for the current JSP.

The `request` scope is basically the same as the `page` scope, except that the JavaBean components are accessible to any included JSPs. As such, `request`-scoped JavaBeans are only useful for storing information in the short term. If a JSP declares a `request`-scoped JavaBean, two simultaneous requests see two different instances of the JavaBean. This is true even if the two requests come in at exactly the same time, which is possible when frames are used.

A common use of `request`-scoped JavaBeans is for validation of form data. When a form is submitted, the data values can be stored in the JavaBean. If the user enters invalid data, the JavaBean can be used to highlight the problems on the form; for example, a missing email address or credit-card number. When the JavaBean is populated with satisfactory values, the user can be shown the next JSP in the application. This is a technique that uses the ATG Dynamo application server with its `GenericFormHandler` component.

If a JavaBean is declared on a page as being of `session` scope, each client of the application gets his own copy. Typical examples of `session`-scoped components are shopping carts and objects that represent the users. A `session`-scoped JavaBean can be used on any page that the user visits in the Web application. `Session`-scoped JavaBeans are also useful when information needs to be shared between JSPs and servlets on a per-user basis.

An `application`-scoped JavaBean is shared by all servlets and JSPs in the Web application. You typically use `application`-scoped JavaBeans when you want to store global information about a Web application. Common examples are the number of users browsing the site and also the number of visits to the site.

Using JavaBeans from a JSP

You can use JavaBean components in a JSP by using JSP language elements. For example, there are tags that enable you to create and initialize a JavaBean from a JSP. There are also JSP tags for getting and setting the properties of a JavaBean.

Because a JSP can create and use an object of *any* valid Java type from inside a JSP declaration tag or a JSP scriptlet tag, you might question why you would need a separate set of tags to use JavaBean from the JSP. The answer is that the JSP tags lend themselves to creating much more readable, concise JSPs than using declarations and scriptlets. Another benefit is that it leads to a separation of content from code.

Using JavaBeans from JSP with Standard Action Elements

The standard action elements that are predefined for use in a JSP are `jsp:useBean`, `jsp:setProperty`, and `jsp:getProperty`. These tags are defined in the following two subsections: "Instantiating JavaBeans from a JSP" and "Accessing and Setting JavaBean Properties from a JSP."

Instantiating JavaBeans from a JSP

The `jsp:useBean` tag exists to enable you to write JSPs that make use of JavaBean classes. The tag enables you to instantiate JavaBeans, use JavaBeans, and assign names to them. The syntax of the `jsp:useBean` tag can take several slightly different forms. The simplest of these is

```
<jsp:useBean id="bean_name" class="fully_qualified_Classname" />
```

The JavaBean is only instantiated if it does not already exist. This is covered in detail later in this chapter.

One thing to be aware of is that the syntax of the jsp:useBean tag follows the production rules of elements and attributes in XML. That is, the element and attribute names are case sensitive, and the attribute values must be enclosed in either single or double quotes. Also, do not forget to close the jsp:useBean tag using either the shorthand XML form (<... />) or the longhand form that uses a separate close tag (</jsp:useBean>). Note that you do not need to specify an XML namespace declaration that binds the jsp prefix to a URI.

The forms that the jsp:useBean can take are shown in Table 6.1. For each form, the scope attribute is optional, and it defaults to page scope if omitted. As you will see later, the jsp:useBean tag has an optional body.

Table 6.1 **Forms of the jsp:useBean Tag**

Syntax	Description
<jsp:useBean id="bean_name" scope="scope_level" class="qualified_class_name" />	The JavaBean is instantiated with the specified name, in the specified scope, from the specified class definition. This is the form that is used the most.
<jsp:useBean id="bean_name" scope="scope_level" class="qualified_class_name" type="Java_type" />	The JavaBean is instantiated with the specified name, in the specified scope, from the specified class definition. The JavaBean is assigned to a reference that is of a type that is a parent class, or implemented interface, of the specified class. This is the standard polymorphic ability that you have in normal Java code. It is useful when you want to use different subtypes of the specified type, at different points in the JSP. For example, you might wish to have a generic reference of type Person that points to different subtypes such as Administrator, Guest, RegisteredUser and so on at different times.
<jsp:useBean id="bean_name" scope="scope_level" beanName="bean_name" type="Java_type" />	The JavaBean is instantiated using the java.beans.Bean.instantiate() method, with the beanName as its parameter. The beanName attribute's value must be a fully qualified class name. The type of the reference is specified with the type attribute. This form is similar to the previous form, except that the value for the beanName attribute can have a dynamic value. You can use an expression tag as the value.

Table 6.1 **Continued**

Syntax	Description
`<jsp:useBean id="bean_name" scope="scope_level" type="Java_type" />`	This form is effectively a cast to the specified type. It looks up a JavaBean with the specified id in the specified scope, and assigns the JavaBean to a reference of the specified type. You can then access methods and properties that are specific to the new type. For example, the new type can be a subclass that has extra functionality. A `java.lang.InstantiationException` is thrown if the specified JavaBean is not found.

The `jsp:useBean` tag instantiates the named class using the no-argument constructor. If this constructor is not available, the Web container will be unable to generate the servlet for the JSP.

To see the predefined tags in action, you will now see a simple example that uses two JSPs: one JSP to instantiate the `Book` class from earlier in this chapter, and the other JSP to access its properties. The example will begin by using scriptlets to instantiate the JavaBean, and expression tags to retrieve the values of properties. The example pages are then converted to use the predefined tags, and you will be shown the important parts of the generated servlets.

Consider the JSP in Listing 6.2. There are three parts to the JSP: a `page` directive, a scriptlet, and some HTML code. It starts by using the `page` directive to import the `Book` class. After the `page` directive, the JSP uses a scriptlet that checks to see if there is a JavaBean bound to the name `myBook` already instantiated in the session. If not, it creates one and stores it in the user's session. In this example, the fact that the `Book` JavaBean is `session`-scoped means that it can be accessed from other JSPs that are visited by the client. The third part of the JSP is the HTML code that sets up a hyperlink to a second JSP that accesses the JavaBean that was instantiated.

Listing 6.2 **A JSP That Uses Embedded Java Code (1)** (`useBean1_scriptlet.jsp`)

```
<%@ page import="com.conygre.jspdevhandbook.chapter6.Book" %>

<%
  Book myBook = (Book) session.getAttribute("myBookBean");

  if ( myBook == null )
  {
    myBook = new Book();
    session.setAttribute("myBookBean", myBook);
  } // end of if ()
%>

<html>
```

Listing 6.2 **Continued**

```
  <head>
    <title>JavaBean usage with scriptlets (1)
    </title>
  </head>
  <body>
    This page creates a JavaBean if you don't already have one.<P></P>
    Click <a href="useBean2_scriptlet.jsp">here</a> to go to a page that
    retrieves it.
  </body>
</html>
```

The second JSP in this example is shown in Listing 6.3. The content of the JSP is fairly self-explanatory. Again, there are three parts: a `page` directive, a scriptlet, and the HTML code. The JSP begins with the `page` directive that imports that class for the `Book`. The `page` directive is followed by a scriptlet that obtains a reference to the JavaBean that was instantiated on the first page.

Listing 6.3 **A JSP That Uses Embedded Java Code (2)** (`useBean2_scriptlet.jsp`)

```
<%@ page import="com.conygre.jspdevhandbook.chapter6.Book" %>
<%
  Book myBook = (Book) session.getAttribute("myBookBean");
%>

<html>
  <head>
    <title>JavaBean usage with scriptlets (2)
    </title>
  </head>
  <body>
    This page retrieves a JavaBean, and its properties.<P>

    <table border="1">
      <th>JavaBean property</th><th>Value</th>
      <tr><td>id</td>     <td><%= myBook.getId()     %></td></tr>
      <tr><td>title</td> <td><%= myBook.getTitle()  %></td></tr>
      <tr><td>author</td><td><%= myBook.getAuthor() %></td></tr>
      <tr><td>price</td> <td><%= myBook.getPrice()  %></td></tr>
    </table>
  </body>
</html>
```

Error checking has been omitted for the sake of clarity. In practice, you would normally perform a check at this point to make sure that a value of `null` has not been returned by the `session.getAttribute()` method; otherwise, the page will fail further down when the reference is used to access properties of the JavaBean.

You can invoke the methods of a JavaBean directly by using either a scriptlet or an expression tag. The syntax is exactly the same as for invoking a method on any other Java object, even the predefined page variables such as `page` and `session`. All you need is a reference to the JavaBean, and the name of the method that you want to invoke. For example, using a scriptlet you might write something like

```
<% shoppingCartBean.displayContents(); %>
```

When the reference to the shared JavaBean has been acquired, the expression tags within the HTML code access the four properties `id`, `title`, `author`, and `price`.

The output from the JSP in Listing 6.3 is shown in Figure 6.3. Due to the fact that the no-argument constructor for the `Book` class is empty, the properties displayed are the initial values for any constructed Java object. That is, zero for numeric types, `null` for object references, `false` for `boolean` variables, and the `null` character for variables of datatype `char`.

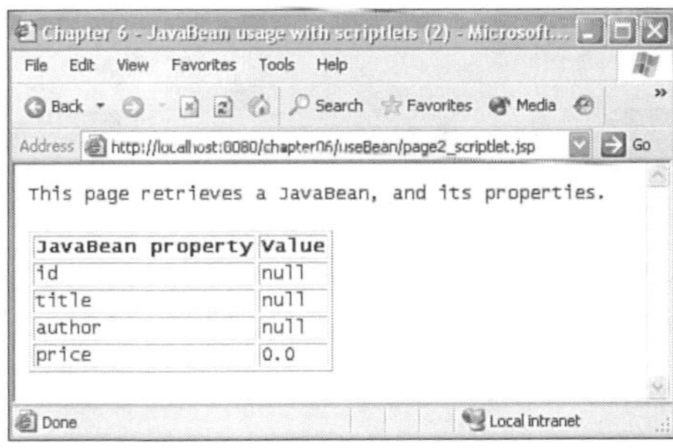

Figure 6.3 A JSP that uses embedded Java code.

The problem with the JSPs in Listings 6.2 and 6.3 is that they require knowledge of the Java programming language to write the scriptlets and expression tags.

The example JSP in Listing 6.2 is rewritten in Listing 6.4 to use the `useBean` tag. The JSP begins with the `useBean` tag and its attributes. The `id` attribute's value is the name of the reference to the JavaBean. In this case, the name of the reference is `myBookBean`. The class that is used to instantiate the JavaBean is `com.conygre.jspdevhandbook.chapter6.Book`, and the JavaBean's scope is set to `session`. The `scope` attribute has been added so that the declared JavaBean is visible on other JSPs that the user visits.

Listing 6.4 **A JSP That Uses the `useBean` Tag (1) (`useBean1.jsp`)**

```
<jsp:useBean id    = "myBookBean"
             class = "com.conygre.jspdevhandbook.chapter6.Book"
             scope = "session" />

<html>
  <head>
    <title>JavaBean usage - useBean and setProperty
           tags
    </title>
  </head>
  <body>
    This page creates a JavaBean if you don't already have one.<P></P>
    Click <a href="useBean2.jsp">here</a> to go to a page that retrieves it.
  </body>
</html>
```

The `useBean` tag in Listing 6.4 is equivalent to the following lines of Listing 6.2:

```
<%@ page import="com.conygre.jspdevhandbook.chapter6.Book" %>

<%
  Book myBook = (Book) session.getAttribute("myBookBean");

  if ( myBook == null )
  {
    myBook = new Book();
    session.setAttribute("myBookBean", myBook);
  } // end of if ()
%>
```

Not only is the `useBean` tag more readable, but it is less work and there is no Java code in sight!

When it has been translated into a servlet, the important lines of code look something like those shown in Listing 6.5.

Listing 6.5 **The Generated Servlet for Listing 6.4**

```
public void _jspService(...) {
    com.conygre.jspdevhandbook.chapter6.Book myBookBean = null;
    boolean _jspx_specialmyBookBean  = false;
    synchronized (session) {
        myBookBean= (com.conygre.jspdevhandbook.chapter6.Book)
                    pageContext.getAttribute("myBookBean",
                                                 PageContext.SESSION_SCOPE);
        if ( myBookBean == null ) {
           _jspx_specialmyBookBean = true;
```

Listing 6.5 **Continued**

```
            try {
                myBookBean = (com.conygre.jspdevhandbook.chapter6.Book)
                             java.beans.Beans.instantiate(
                                     this.getClass().getClassLoader(),
                                     "com.conygre.jspdevhandbook.chapter6.Book");
            } catch (ClassNotFoundException exc) {
               throw new InstantiationException(exc.getMessage());
            } catch (Exception exc) {
               throw new ServletException
                   (" Cannot create bean of class "
                    + "com.conygre.jspdevhandbook.chapter6.Book", exc);
            }
            pageContext.setAttribute("myBookBean", myBookBean,
                                     PageContext.SESSION_SCOPE);
          }
        }
}
```

The code that queries the pageContext object for a session-scoped object bound to the name myBookBean is

```
myBookBean= (com.conygre.jspdevhandbook.chapter6.Book)
            pageContext.getAttribute("myBookBean",
                                     PageContext.SESSION_SCOPE);
```

If the object cannot be located, then a new one is created with this code:

```
myBookBean = (com.conygre.jspdevhandbook.chapter6.Book)
             java.beans.Beans.instantiate(
                 this.getClass().getClassLoader(),
                 "com.conygre.jspdevhandbook.chapter6.Book");
```

Any problems encountered at runtime, when the Web container tries to instantiate the JavaBean, are handled by the two catch blocks. If the JavaBean class cannot be located when the application is running, a ClassNotFoundException is thrown by the Java runtime and handled by the first catch block. If there is any other problem instantiating the JavaBean, for example, when a no-argument constructor cannot be found, the second catch block deals with that.

The new object is bound into the user's session by the final line of code:

```
pageContext.setAttribute("myBookBean", myBookBean,
                         PageContext.SESSION_SCOPE);
```

Accessing and Setting JavaBean Properties from a JSP

There are two predefined tags that are available to access and manipulate the properties of a JavaBean: jsp:getProperty and jsp:setProperty.

The `jsp:getProperty` *Tag*

The `jsp:getProperty` tag enables you to retrieve the value of a property in a JavaBean, and embed it into the output. Its syntax is

```
<jsp:getProperty name="bean_name" property="property_name" />
```

With this knowledge, the second JSP (Listing 6.3) in the example can be rewritten. The new version is shown in Listing 6.6.

Listing 6.6 **A JSP That Uses the `getProperty` Tag (`useBean2.jsp`)**

```
<html>
  <head>
    <title>JavaBean usage - getProperty tag (2)
    </title>
  </head>
  <body>
    This page retrieves a JavaBean, and its properties.<P>

    <table border="1">
      <th>JavaBean property</th><th>Value</th>
      <tr><td>id</td>     <td><jsp:getProperty name="myBookBean"
                                             property="id"      /></td>
      </tr>
      <tr><td>title</td> <td><jsp:getProperty name="myBookBean"
                                             property="title"   /></td>
      </tr>
      <tr><td>author</td><td><jsp:getProperty name="myBookBean"
                                             property="author"  /></td>
      </tr>
      <tr><td>price</td> <td><jsp:getProperty name="myBookBean"
                                             property="price"   /></td>
      </tr>
    </table>
  </body>
</html>
```

If you refer back to Listing 6.3, you will see that the `page` directive to import the `Book` class and scriptlet that retrieved the JavaBean instance from the user's session, have both been omitted from Listing 6.6. They are both rendered unnecessary by the `jsp:getProperty` tag.

The code that is inside the HTML `table` tag in Listing 6.3 accesses the four properties of the JavaBean. Behind the scenes, the `jsp:getProperty` tag is implemented using the standard Java Reflection API. That is, for a property whose name is `id`, the Web container translates the `jsp:getProperty` tag into Java code that looks for an accessor method called `getId()`. If you try to access a property that is not defined, the JSP is translated into a servlet, but the Web container generates an error when the servlet is executed.

The important lines from the generated servlet's `_jspService` method are shown in Listing 6.7.

Listing 6.7 **The Generated Servlet for the JSP in Listing 6.6**

```
...
out.print(JspRuntimeLibrary.toString(JspRuntimeLibrary.handleGetProperty(
    pageContext.findAttribute("myBookBean"), "id")));
...
out.print(JspRuntimeLibrary.toString(JspRuntimeLibrary.handleGetProperty(
    pageContext.findAttribute("myBookBean"), "title")));
...
out.print(JspRuntimeLibrary.toString(JspRuntimeLibrary.handleGetProperty(
    pageContext.findAttribute("myBookBean"), "author")));
...
out.print(JspRuntimeLibrary.toString(JspRuntimeLibrary.handleGetProperty(
    pageContext.findAttribute("myBookBean"), "price")));
...
```

A few things are happening for each `out.print` method invocation:

- The JavaBean is located using the `pageContext.findAttribute()` method.
- The `JspRuntimeLibrary.handleGetProperty()` method takes two parameters. The first is the JavaBean located in the previous step, and the second is the property of interest. This is where the Java Reflection API is used to locate and invoke the correct accessor method.
- The retrieved property value is then converted to a `String` by the `JspRuntimeLibrary.toString()` method.

When viewed in a Web browser, the output from Listing 6.6 looks like that shown in Figure 6.4. Notice that the three `String` values for the `id`, `author`, and `price` properties appear to be missing from the table. This is because of the way that the `JspRuntimeLibrary.toString()` method works. Rather than pass back a value of `null`, the `JspRuntimeLibrary.toString()` instead returns an empty string.

The `jsp:setProperty` *Tag*

To finish off the example, it would be nice if we could set values for the properties of the `Book` JavaBean. You can use the `jsp:setProperty` tag to do this, the basic syntax is

```
<jsp:setProperty name="bean_name"
                 property="property_name"
                 value="new_property_value" />
```

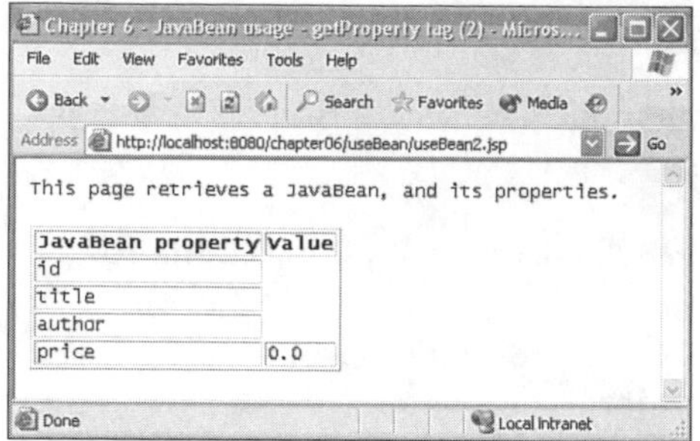

Figure 6.4 A JSP that uses the `getProperty` tag.

By the time that you have read this chapter, you will have seen all the different forms that the `jsp:setProperty` tag can take. The `name` attribute is mandatory, but can be accompanied by a variety of other attributes, which are listed in Table 6.2.

Table 6.2 **Forms of the `jsp:setProperty` Tag**

Syntax	Description
<jsp:setProperty name="bean_name" property="property_name" />	Sets the specified JavaBean property from an equivalently named request parameter.
<jsp:setProperty name="bean_name" property="*" />	Sets all the specified JavaBean properties that have names matching those of the request parameters.
<jsp:setProperty name="bean_name" property="property_name" param="param_name" />	Sets the specified property of the specified JavaBean. The value set is from the specified request parameter.
<jsp:setProperty name="bean_name" property="property_name" value="new_value" />	Sets the specified property of the JavaBean to the specified value.

You can use the `jsp:setProperty` tag anywhere in a JSP, but here it is embedded inside the `jsp:useBean` tag where it can be used to provide initial values for the JavaBean. This idea is revisited later in this chapter when the concept of scope has been discussed.Consider the JSP in Listing 6.8.

Listing 6.8 **A JSP That Uses the `useBean` and `setProperty` Tags (`useAndSet1.jsp`)**

```
<jsp:useBean id="myBookBean"
             class="com.conygre.jspdevhandbook.chapter6.Book"
             scope="session">
    <jsp:setProperty name="myBookBean"
                     property="id"
                     value="42" />
    <jsp:setProperty name="myBookBean"
                     property="author"
                     value="Ruth" />
    <jsp:setProperty name="myBookBean"
                     property="title"
                     value="Cookery for accountants" />
    <jsp:setProperty name="myBookBean"
                     property="price"
                     value="29.99" />
</jsp:useBean>

<html>
  <head>
    <title>JavaBean usage - useBean and setProperty
            tags
    </title>
  </head>
  <body>
    This page creates a JavaBean if you don't already have one.<P></P>
    Click <a href="useAndSet2.jsp">here</a> to go to a page that retrieves it.
  </body>
</html>
```

Even though the `setProperty` tags are child elements of the `useBean` tag in this example, don't be confused into thinking that they somehow cause the Web container to search for a *constructor* that takes arguments matching the specified values. The no-argument constructor is still called, and then the correct `set` method is called for each property. This becomes obvious if you do not nest the `setProperty` tags inside the `useBean` tag—you still get the same result.

The JSP from Listing 6.8 translates to a servlet whose `_jspService` method contains code similar to that shown in Listing 6.9.

Listing 6.9 **`_jspService` Method for the JSP in Listing 6.8**

```
com.conygre.jspdevhandbook.chapter6.Book myBookBean = null;
boolean _jspx_specialmyBookBean  = false;
synchronized (session) {
```

Listing 6.9 **Continued**

```
    myBookBean= (com.conygre.jspdevhandbook.chapter6.Book)
    pageContext.getAttribute("myBookBean",PageContext.SESSION_SCOPE);
    if ( myBookBean == null ) {
        _jspx_specialmyBookBean = true;
        try {
            myBookBean = (com.conygre.jspdevhandbook.chapter6.Book)
                          java.beans.Beans.instantiate(
                              this.getClass().getClassLoader(),
                              "com.conygre.jspdevhandbook.chapter6.Book");
        } catch (ClassNotFoundException exc) {
            throw new InstantiationException(exc.getMessage());
        } catch (Exception exc) {
            throw new ServletException (
                " Cannot create bean of class "
                +"com.conygre.jspdevhandbook.chapter6.Book", exc);
        }
        pageContext.setAttribute("myBookBean", myBookBean,
                                 PageContext.SESSION_SCOPE);
    }
}
if(_jspx_specialmyBookBean == true) {
    JspRuntimeLibrary.introspecthelper(pageContext.findAttribute("myBookBean"),
                                       "id",
                                       "42",
                                       null,
                                       null,
                                       false);
    JspRuntimeLibrary.introspecthelper(pageContext.findAttribute("myBookBean"),
                                       "author",
                                       "Ruth",
                                       null,
                                       null,
                                       false);
    JspRuntimeLibrary.introspecthelper(pageContext.findAttribute("myBookBean"),
                                       "title",
                                       "Cookery for accountants",
                                       null,
                                       null,
                                       false);
    JspRuntimeLibrary.introspecthelper(pageContext.findAttribute("myBookBean"),
                                       "price",
                                       "29.99",
                                       null,
                                       null,
                                       false);
}
```

Listing 6.9 **Continued**

```
        out.write("\r\n\r\n<html>\r\n  <head><title>"
                  + "JavaBean usage - useBean and setProperty tags"
                  + "</title></head>\r\n  <body>\r\n    This page creates a
                  + "JavaBean if you don't already have one.<P></P>\r\n    "
                  + "Click <a href=\"page2.jsp\">here</a> to go to a page that"
                  + " retrieves it.\r\n  </body>\r\n</html>");
```

The lines of code in the `synchronized` block are similar to the example in Listing 6.5. However, the new lines are the ones that follow. The `_jspx_specialmyBookBean` variable is used to indicate whether the `myBookBean` JavaBean has been created (or whether it already existed in the user's session).

If the JavaBean has just been created (inside the `if` statement in the `synchronized` block), and the `_jspx_specialmyBookBean` variable has a value of `true`, the contents of the `if` statement after the `synchronized` block are executed.

The `JspRuntimeLibrary.introspecthelper()` method is used by the generated servlet to set the properties of a JavaBean; it takes six parameters. The first three are of interest and are a reference to the JavaBean, the property name, and the new property value. The latter three parameters are the servlet request, response, and a boolean that indicates whether to throw an error if a `set` method cannot be located for the specified property. You can see this method used to set values for the four properties of the `Book` JavaBean. These lines of Java code that use the `JspRuntimeLibrary.introspectHelper()` method correspond to the `jsp:setProperty` tags of Listing 6.8.

You might be wondering how a string value is converted into the correct type for a given property. The JSP container uses the `valueOf` method from the relevant wrapper class for each of the following datatypes: `boolean`, `byte`, `short`, `int`, `long`, `float`, and `double`. For example, the `java.lang.Double.valueOf(string s)` method is used to convert a string to a `double`. This value can then be passed as an argument to the relevant setter method. The other two datatypes that are supported for conversion purposes are `java.lang.Object` and `char`. For `Object`, a new `String` object is instantiated that contains the value specified in the `jsp:setProperty` action. For `char`, the `String.charAt(0)` method is used.

The JSTL `c:set` *and* `c:out` *Actions*

As you saw in Chapter 5, "The JSP Standard Tag Library," you can use the JSTL `c:set` action in order to set the value for a target object's property. Here is the syntax:

```
<c:set  target="object_name"  property="property_name"  value="some_value" />
```

and

```
<c:set  target="object_name"  property="property_name" >
    body_content
</c:set>
```

The value of the `target` attribute must evaluate to a JavaBean that has a setter method for the specified property name and value. For example,

```
<c:set  target   = "${sessionScope.myShoppingCart}"
        property = "numberOfItems"
        value    = "0"        />
```

Alternatively, you can specify a `java.util.Map` object as the target, rather than a JavaBean.

You also saw the `c:out` action in Chapter 5. You can use it instead of the `jsp:getProperty` action in order to output the value of a JavaBean's property. For example,

```
<c:out value="${sessionScope.myShoppingCart.numberOfItems}" />
```

The `jsp:useBean` Tag and Existing JavaBeans

Now that you have seen the `jsp:useBean`, `jsp:getProperty`, and `jsp:setProperty` tags, it is time to consider what happens when your Web application has multiple JSPs that declare the same JavaBean. When a JSP that contains a `useBean` tag is viewed, it is possible that the JavaBean in question already exists. For a `useBean` tag such as

```
<jsp:useBean id="myBook"
             class="com.conygre.jspunleased.chapter6.Book"
             scope="session" />
```

the following happens. First, the Web container searches for a JavaBean with the id `myBook` that is stored in the predefined `session` object. If the JavaBean is found, the new `id` is simply initialized to point to the existing JavaBean. Remember that the new `id` is a local variable of the generated `_jspService()` method. The code that performs the lookup in `_jspService()` looks like this:

```
...
com.conygre.jspdevhandbook.chapter6.Book myBook = null;
...
myBook = (com.conygre.jspdevhandbook.chapter6.Book) pageContext.getAttribute(
➥          "myBook", PageContext.SESSION_SCOPE);
...
```

Thus, there is no problem if an application needs to instantiate more than one JavaBean of a particular type to different `id`s.

If such a JavaBean cannot be located, the Web container makes an attempt to load the `com.conygre.jspdevhandbook.chapter6.Book` class and instantiate a JavaBean from it. The JavaBean is then bound to the specified `id` and stored in the appropriate scope. The important part of the `jspService()` method looks like this:

```
...
if (myBook == null){
    try {
```

```
        myBook = (com.conygre.jspdevhandbook.chapter6.Book)
                  java.beans.Beans.instantiate(this.getClass().getClassLoader(),
                                     "com.conygre.jspdevhandbook.chapter6.Book");
...
```

If the JavaBean has been created, the body of the `jsp:useBean` tag is then processed. Note that if the JavaBean already exists and is located, that the body of the `jsp:useBean` tag is *not* executed. Earlier in this chapter, it was noted that the `jsp:useBean` tag always uses the default constructor when instantiating a JavaBean. From a certain point of view, you can imagine the `jsp:useBean` tag and any `jsp:setProperty` tags within it as combining to *simulate* a constructor that takes arguments. This is because the body of the `jsp:useBean` tag is only executed the first time, when the JavaBean is created.

This can be seen from the examples in Listings 6.10 and 6.11. Listing 6.10 defines the first JSP in this example. It creates a `session`-scoped JavaBean, and gives a hyperlink to a second JSP (Listing 6.11) that redeclares the JavaBean.

> **Note**
>
> If you have been running the examples as you read through this chapter, then you will need to restart your Web container before you run this example. This is so that a new `Book` JavaBean is instantiated with its properties set to new values.

Listing 6.10 **A JSP That Declares a `session`-scoped JavaBean (`beanAlreadyExists.jsp`)**

```
<jsp:useBean id="myBookBean"
             class="com.conygre.jspdevhandbook.chapter6.Book"
             scope="session">
  <%-- The setProperty tag is only executed when a JavaBean is created --%>
  <jsp:setProperty name="myBookBean" property="author" value="Mark" />
</jsp:useBean>

<html>
  <head>
    <title>When a JavaBean already exists...</title>
  </head>
  <body>
    The author of your book is <jsp:getProperty name="myBookBean"
                                                 property="author" /><P>

    Click <a href="beanAlreadyExists2.jsp">here</a> to see another page that
    declares a JavaBean that uses the same name and scope.
  </body>
</html>
```

Listing 6.10 declares an instance of the `com.conygre.jspdevhandbook.chapter6.Book` class, and assigns it the name `myBookBean`. Because this is the first page in the example, the JavaBean does not yet exist, therefore, the Web container will not be able to locate it. The `Book` class is loaded, the JavaBean instantiated, then the `author` property is set to the value `Mark`. This is all done with the following lines of code:

```
<jsp:useBean id="myBookBean"   class="com.conygre.jspdevhandbook.chapter6.Book"
             scope="session">
  <jsp:setProperty name="myBookBean" property="author" value="Mark" />
</jsp:useBean>
```

When the user clicks the hyperlink, he is redirected to the JSP in Listing 6.11.

Listing 6.11 **A JSP That Redeclares a JavaBean (`beanAlreadyExists2.jsp`)**

```
<jsp:useBean id="myBookBean"
             class="com.conygre.jspdevhandbook.chapter6.Book"
             scope="session" />

<html>
  <head>
    <title>When a JavaBean already exists...</title>
  </head>
  <body>
    This page redeclares the JavaBean, but does not set any of its properties.
    The same name and scope were used for the JavaBean, so the original bean
    is used.
    <P>
    The author of your book is <jsp:getProperty name="myBookBean"
                                                 property="author" /><P>
  </body>
</html>
```

Listing 6.11 starts by declaring a JavaBean with the same name and scope, so the Web container simply locates the existing JavaBean instance. The important lines of code from the generated servlet's `_jspService` method are

```
myBookBean = (com.conygre.jspdevhandbook.chapter6.Book)
              pageContext.getAttribute("myBookBean",PageContext.SESSION_SCOPE);
if ( myBookBean == null ) {
    // create new JavaBean
}
...
```

The first line looks up the existing JavaBean, which succeeds, so the `if` statement is ignored. The rest of the `_jspService` method for Listing 6.11 contains

```
out.write("<html><head><title>When a JavaBean");
out.write(" already exists...</title></head><body>This page redeclares the");
out.write(" JavaBean, but does not set any of its properties. The same name");
out.write(" and scope were used for the JavaBean, so the original bean is");
out.write(" used.<P>The author of your book is ");

out.print(JspRuntimeLibrary.toString((((com.conygre.jspdevhandbook.chapter6.Book)
                    pageContext.findAttribute("myBookBean")).getAuthor())));

out.write("<P>\r\n  </body>\r\n</html>");
```

The `out.print` statement is due to the `jsp:getProperty` tag in the JSP.

If the JSP in Listing 6.11 had `jsp:setProperty` tags within the `jsp:useBean` tag, they would be ignored. For example, this would happen if you tried to change the author's name with the following lines:

```
<jsp:useBean id="myBookBean"   class="com.conygre.jspdevhandbook.chapter6.Book"
             scope="session">
  <%-- This jsp:setProperty tag is not executed if the myBookBean is
       already found in the session --%>
  <jsp:setProperty name="myBookBean" property="author" value="Ruth" />
</jsp:useBean>
...
```

Remember that the body of a `jsp:useBean` tag is only executed when a JavaBean is created.

JavaBeans and HTML Forms

JSPs can use HTML forms to allow the user to enter information that is to be processed. In Web applications, users typically enter data such as usernames, passwords, credit-card numbers, and so on.

This section shows an example that starts by passing the information that the user supplies as page parameters between two JSPs, and progresses to using a JavaBean to store the information.

Consider the JSP in Listing 6.12, that displays a simple form for a user to enter details of a book.

Listing 6.12 **A Form for Entering Book Details** (`bookEntryForm.jsp`)

```
<html>
  <head>
    <title>Book entry form</title>
  </head>
  <body>
    <h1>Please enter the details of the book</h1>
    <form action="bookProcess.jsp" method="get">
      <table>
```

Listing 6.12 **Continued**

```
        <tr><td>ID:</td> <td><input type="text" name="id" size="10"></td></tr>
        <tr><td>Author:</td> <td><input type="text" name="author"
                                    size="30"></td></tr>
        <tr><td>Title:</td>  <td><input type="text" name="title"
                                    size="40"></td></tr>
        <tr><td>Price:</td>  <td><input type="text" name="price"
                                    size="10"></td></tr>
      </table> <p>
      <input type="submit" value="Submit book details" >
    </form>
  </body>
</html>
```

When the user has entered the information and clicks the submit button, the form forwards the information to the `bookProcess.jsp` page (see the `form` tag's `action` attribute).

The user can enter the values into the form by way of the four HTML form `input` fields. Even though the four form fields all have their type specified as `text`, it is the value of their `name` attributes that gives each parameter its name and, thus, distinguishes them. Whatever the user types into the field on the form is the value of the parameter.

The input fields from the form are supplied to the `action` page as name/value pairs. The correct terminology is that form fields are passed as *parameters* to the next page. When the submit button is clicked, it creates a query string that is then appended to the URL that is declared in the form's `action` attribute. The reason that the parameters are appended to the query string in this way is because the form's `method` attribute has a value of `get`.

If the `method` attribute for the `form` tag had a value of `post` instead of `get`, you would not see the form parameters appended to the query string. Instead, the parameters would be passed as name/value pairs in the HTTP header of a request to the second page.

For the example in Listing 6.12, if the user entered information as in the screenshot in Figure 6.5, the query string that is generated is

```
http://localhost:8080/chapter06/beans_and_forms/bookProcess.js
?id=3&author=Joshua+Greenhough&title=Got+a+right+job+on%21&price=9.99
```

You can see that the URL that the form redirects the browser to is `http://localhost:8080/chapter06/beans_and_forms/bookProcess.jsp`, and appended to this is a `?` character followed by the name/value pairs for the parameters. The individual parameters are separated by the `&` character:

```
id=3&author=Joshua+Greenhough&title=Got+a+right+job+on%21&price=9.99
```

You can also see that any space characters in the parameter values are encoded using the `+` character, and that the exclamation mark character is encoded using its Unicode value (21 in hexadecimal).

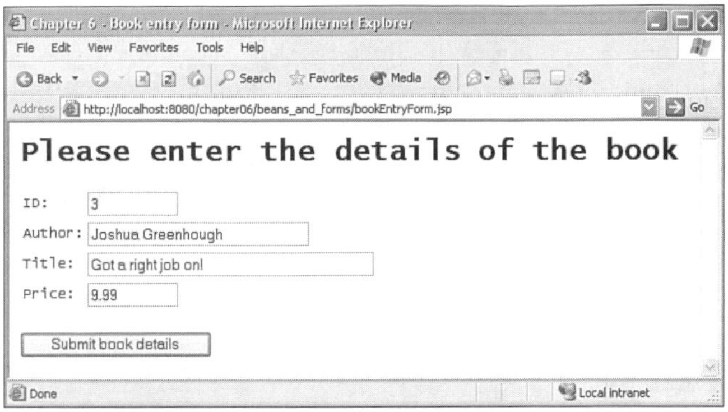

Figure 6.5 A JSP that uses an HTML form.

When the user submits values for the form fields, the values can be retrieved on a JSP by accessing the `request` object. See Listing 6.13, that simply displays the supplied parameters in a list.

Listing 6.13 **A JSP That Displays the Form Parameters (`bookProcess.jsp`)**

```
<html>
  <head>
    <title>Book details</title>
  </head>
  <body>
    <h1>You entered the following details for the book</h1>
    <ul>
      <li>ID is     '<%= request.getParameter("id")     %>'</li>
      <li>Author is '<%= request.getParameter("author") %>'</li>
      <li>Title is  '<%= request.getParameter("title")  %>'</li>
      <li>Price is  '<%= request.getParameter("price")  %>'</li>
    </ul>
  </body>
</html>
```

When using the `get` method with HTML forms, there is a limit imposed by the HTTP specification on the type of data that can be sent. As you have just seen, the `get` method of sending data appends form parameters to the query string. Because the query string is exactly that, a *string*, any data that you send must conform to the rules for URL strings. Any invalid characters must be escaped or encoded, such as the exclamation character in the previous example.

There is no limit on the amount of data that can be sent using the `post` method. Although there is nothing in the HTTP 1.1 specification about the limit of data that can be sent using the `get` method, in practice most Web servers tend to have a limit of something in the region of 1KB or 2KB.

HTML forms are a useful tool for acquiring data, but it can quickly become tedious to write code that processes the form parameters. An alternative is to use JavaBeans that store the form parameters. Form parameters are sets of unrelated name/value pairs, but they can be logically grouped by using one or more JavaBeans.

This can be achieved for the current example by using the same form page as Listing 6.12, but with the `action` attribute changed so that it points to the JSP in Listing 6.14. You can find the modified file in the Web application from the book Web site as `bookEntryForm2.jsp`.

Listing 6.14 **A JSP That Uses a JavaBean to Hold Parameter Values (`bookProcessBean.jsp`)**

```
<jsp:useBean id="myBookBean"
             class="com.conygre.jspdevhandbook.chapter6.Book"
             scope="session">
  <jsp:setProperty name="myBookBean"
                   property="id"
                   value='<%= request.getParameter("id") %>' />
  <jsp:setProperty name="myBookBean"
                   property="author"
                   value='<%= request.getParameter("author") %>' />
  <jsp:setProperty name="myBookBean"
                   property="title"
                   value='<%= request.getParameter("title") %>' />
  <jsp:setProperty name="myBookBean"
                   property="price"
                   value='<%= Double.parseDouble(
                               request.getParameter("price")) %>' />
</jsp:useBean>

<html>
  <head><title>Book details</title></head>
  <body>
    <h1>You entered the following details for the book</h1>
    <ul>
      <li>ID is     '<jsp:getProperty name="myBookBean"
                                       property="id"     />'</li>
      <li>Author is '<jsp:getProperty name="myBookBean"
                                       property="author" />'</li>
      <li>Title is  '<jsp:getProperty name="myBookBean"
                                       property="title"  />'</li>
      <li>Price is  '<jsp:getProperty name="myBookBean"
                                       property="price"  />'</li>
    </ul>
  </body>
</html>
```

There are two parts to Listing 6.14: a `jsp:useBean` tag, and the HTML code. The `jsp:useBean` tag and its nested `jsp:setProperty` tags instantiate a JavaBean and set its properties to the values of the form fields that are passed as parameters on the `request` object. So far, the values that have been set for a JavaBean property using the `jsp:setProperty` tag have been fixed values. However, the four `jsp:setProperty` tags in this example use a runtime expression to compute the value that is to be set. Also, note that single quotes were used to delimit the `value` attribute's value. This is because the JSP expression tag itself uses double quotes in the `request.getParameter()` method call. Thus, the single quotes were used to conform with the XML production rules for attribute values.

Notice the code used for setting the `price` property:

```
<jsp:setProperty name="myBookBean"
                 property="price"
                 value='<%= Double.parseDouble(
                           request.getParameter("price")) %>' />
```

The `Double.parseDouble` method was used to convert the string value for the `price` parameter to a `double`. This is so that the `jsp:setProperty` tag can look for a method of the JavaBean called `setPrice` that takes an argument of primitive type `double`. If this conversion is not performed, the Web container is unable to find an accessor method, and displays an error to that effect.

> **Note**
>
> There is a wrapper class for each of the eight primitive Java datatypes. The wrapper classes provide useful constants (such as minimum and maximum values), as well as conversion methods from strings to the corresponding primitive datatype. For example, the `java.lang.Integer` class provides a `parseInt()` method that takes a `java.lang.String` and returns an `int`. Each wrapper class except for `Character` provides a `valueOf()` method that converts a `java.lang.String` to an instance of the wrapper class.

There is an alternative form of the `jsp:setProperty` tag that enables you to associate a JavaBean property with a named form parameter:

```
<jsp:setProperty name="bean_name"
                 property="property_name"
                 param="form_parameter_name" />
```

Instead of specifying a `value` attribute, you can instead specify a `param` attribute whose value is the name of the form parameter. An advantage to using this form of the tag is that it automatically performs a conversion from a string to a Java primitive datatype (`boolean`, `byte`, `char`, `short`, `int`, `long`, `float`, and `double`). The JSP in Listing 6.14 can be rewritten using this alternative form shown in Listing 6.15.

Listing 6.15 **Example of Associating JavaBean Properties with Request Parameters (`bookProcessBeanNamedParams.jsp`)**

```
<jsp:useBean id="myBookBean"
             class="com.conygre.jspdevhandbook.chapter6.Book"
             scope="session">
  <jsp:setProperty name="myBookBean" property="id"     param="id"     />
  <jsp:setProperty name="myBookBean" property="author" param="author" />
  <jsp:setProperty name="myBookBean" property="title"  param="title"  />
  <jsp:setProperty name="myBookBean" property="price"  param="price"  />
</jsp:useBean>

<html>
  <head><title>Book details</title></head>
  <body>
    <h1>You entered the following details for the book</h1>
    <ul>
      <li>ID is     '<jsp:getProperty name="myBookBean"
                                     property="id"     />'</li>
      <li>Author is '<jsp:getProperty name="myBookBean"
                                     property="author" />'</li>
      <li>Title is  '<jsp:getProperty name="myBookBean"
                                     property="title"  />'</li>
      <li>Price is  '<jsp:getProperty name="myBookBean"
                                     property="price"  />'</li>
    </ul>
  </body>
</html>
```

In fact, if you are setting each property individually, and the JavaBean property names match the parameter names, you can use a shorthand syntax:

```
<jsp:setProperty name="bean_name" property="property_name" />
```

The downside to setting each of the properties separately becomes apparent when there are many JavaBean properties. The problem becomes even more pronounced when the form parameters on the query string do not match the property names of the JavaBean. The pages become difficult to maintain because of the added complexity.

The `jsp:setProperty` tag can take an alternative form of syntax. The following syntax enables you to set *all* properties of a JavaBean that have a matching form parameter:

```
<jsp:setProperty name="bean_name" property="*" />
```

It is the value of `*` for the value of the `property` attribute that is the important part. The `jsp:setProperty` tag inspects the form parameters, and looks for a matching `set` method in the JavaBean. For example, if there is a form parameter called `author`, a search is made for a method called `setAuthor()`.

There are a couple of important points that apply to these last two forms of the `jsp:setProperty` tag (that is, associating a JavaBean property with a form parameter, or matching all JavaBean properties with form parameters). The first is that if a match cannot be found between a form parameter and a `set` method, the form parameter is ignored and no action is taken. If it is not possible, as part of the page and JavaBean design, to make the form parameters and JavaBean properties match, you must set the JavaBean properties explicitly as shown in Listing 6.15.

The second important point to note pertains to JavaBean properties that are not of type `java.lang.String`. Again, consider the conversion that had to be made when setting the `price` property in Listing 6.14, from a string to a `double`. An automatic conversion is made from a string to a Java primitive type when you map JavaBean properties to either all, or named, form parameters. The implementation of the conversions is in terms of the wrapper classes that are provided as part of the `java.lang` package.

Because the example for this section of the book has form parameters with the same names as the JavaBean properties, then the JSP in Listing 6.15 can be rewritten as shown in Listing 6.16.

Listing 6.16 **A JSP That Associates All Form Parameters with JavaBean Properties (bookProcessBeanAllParams.jsp)**

```
<jsp:useBean id="myBookBean"
             class="com.conygre.jspdevhandbook.chapter6.Book"
             scope="session">
  <jsp:setProperty name="myBookBean" property="*"     />
</jsp:useBean>

<html>
  <head><title>Book details</title></head>
  <body>
    <h1>You entered the following details for the book</h1>
    <ul>
      <li>ID is     '<jsp:getProperty name="myBookBean"
                                     property="id"     />'</li>
      <li>Author is '<jsp:getProperty name="myBookBean"
                                     property="author" />'</li>
      <li>Title is  '<jsp:getProperty name="myBookBean"
                                     property="title"  />'</li>
      <li>Price is  '<jsp:getProperty name="myBookBean"
                                     property="price"  />'</li>
    </ul>
  </body>
</html>
```

Finally, a word about the limitations of the `jsp:getProperty` and `jsp:setProperty` tags. It is possible from a scriptlet or expression tag to access a JavaBean property directly, either by name or by accessor method (assuming of course that the property or accessor method is not inaccessible, for example, if it is declared as `private`). However, the `jsp:getProperty` and `jsp:setProperty` tags only enable you to access JavaBean properties that follow the naming conventions set out in the JavaBeans specification. That is, for a property called *foo*, the accessor methods must be of the form `isFoo()/setFoo()` for `boolean` types, and `getFoo()/setFoo()` for other data types.

Summary

JavaBeans were originally designed with a view of making it easy to write new user interface components that could be integrated into existing development environments. However, JavaBeans are useful in the context of writing JSPs because they can encapsulate business logic.

A JavaBean in its simplest form can be a Java class definition that follows a set of rules for naming its methods. This allows JavaBeans to have properties and methods that can be accessed from a JSP. There are several ways, such as scriptlets, to access these, but JSP provides tags for creating and manipulating JavaBean instances. These tags enable you to eliminate Java code from your JSPs.

You also saw in this chapter that there are four scopes that are available to JSPs. A JavaBean's lifetime is dictated by which scope it is associated with.

7

JSP Application Architecture

IN THIS CHAPTER, THE VARIOUS ARCHITECTURE options for JSP applications will be explored. As JSP technology has matured, there have been a number of initiatives to help with the design of JSP applications. This chapter explores the various architectures that can be employed in the building of Java Web applications.

The key issues are the roles and relationships surrounding the JSPs, servlets, tag libraries, and JavaBeans. What is the role of servlets, for example? As you have seen so far in the book, JavaServer Pages become servlets, are easier to write, and do not require manual compiling. So, do we need servlets? Surely it can all be done with JSP, with the Beans and tags doing the business logic. This question and others will be addressed in this chapter.

The Model 1 Architecture

The first architecture model to be discussed in this chapter is the simplest. It is referred to as the Model 1 architecture. It is the most intuitive architecture, and Figure 7.1 shows how it works.

The Model 1 architecture involves the client requesting specific JSPs via a URL, and the server delivering the output from the JSP. The JSP might employ tag libraries to minimize the use of scriptlets, and it might also use JavaBeans to contain the business logic for the application. These Beans are created and used from the JSPs. The Model 1 architecture is said to be decentralized because the next page to be displayed is determined by the previous one. There is no need for servlets in this architecture.

The alternative to the Model 1 architecture is the imaginatively named Model 2 architecture.

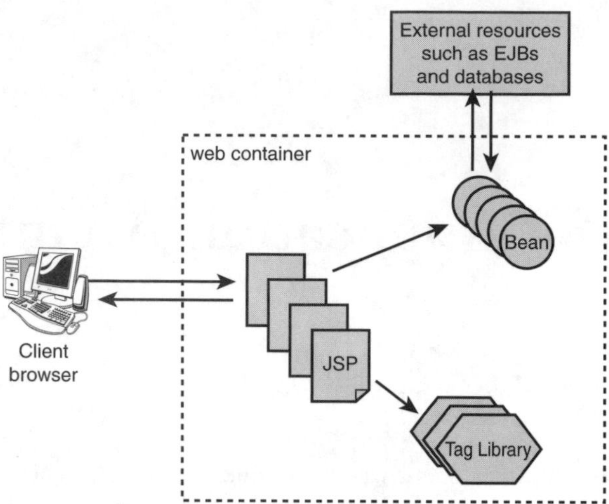

Figure 7.1 The Model 1 architecture.

> **Note**
>
> You might be wondering where the names Model 1 and Model 2 came from. The names are historical and are from some of the earlier drafts of the JSP specification. These terms are no longer used within specification documents, but are still widely used in the literature.

The Model 2 Architecture

The Model 2 architecture involves a more centralized Web application, with what is referred to as a *controller servlet* directing requests to specific JSPs, with the appropriate JSP being determined from the parameters within the query string. This can be seen in Figure 7.2.

As you can see from Figure 7.2, this architecture is not as simple as the Model 1 architecture. In fact, the architecture largely follows the Model View Controller (MVC) design pattern.

The MVC pattern has three component parts:

- The model. This is the functionality of your application. It can be complex business logic or simple Beans with `get` and `set` methods.
- The view. This is the presentation of the application. In a Java application, this could be a Swing interface, a Web interface, or a command-line interface. It reads its data from the model, although it does not change the model. It is also informed about any changes that take place in the model. In Web applications, this would be the JSP.

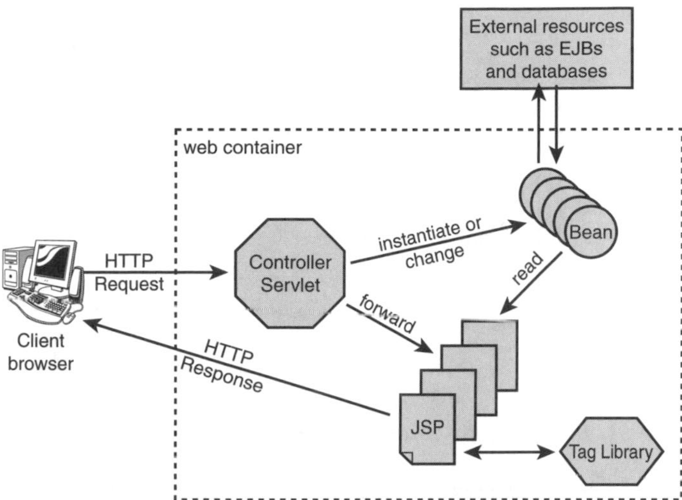

Figure 7.2 The Model 2 architecture.

> **Note**
>
> The Swing classes referred to here are used to build feature-rich user interfaces using the Java programming language. More information can be found in the online Java tutorial at `www.java.sun.com/tutorial`.

- The controller. This sits between the view and the model, and depending on what the user does, it will create and modify the model.

So, how is this applied to a Web application? The key features of the Model 2 architecture are as follows:

1. Every request goes through a controller servlet. This is the equivalent of the controller in the MVC pattern.
2. The controller servlet will instantiate any required JavaBeans and pass them into the Web application environment so that they can be accessed from the JSPs, typically via JSP elements, such as the `<jsp:useBean>` standard action. The Beans become the model in the MVC pattern. The controller can change any of the Beans, if required.
3. After any relevant Beans are instantiated or modified, the request is forwarded to the appropriate JSP, which then sends a response to the client. The JSPs are the view in the MVC pattern.

The main difference between this compared to the MVC approach is that the view has no way of being informed by the model of any changes that have occurred. The view in our case is presented in a Web browser that is disconnected between requests. This means that if the model changes, the view will not be informed. This is why the Model 2 architecture is not, strictly speaking, an MVC implementation.

To fully understand how this Model 2 architecture works, you'll now see an example site that is built with this approach. The example is of a site that shows product information concerning DVDs, CDs, and books. The user will have two views of the product information, one for browsing and one for purchasing.

Figure 7.3 shows a picture of what the site looks like. It is part of the download from the book Web site called `chapter07.zip`. Figure 7.3 is the Web application within it called `chapter07Model2.war`. You can access the book download from the Sams Web site, `www.samspublishing.com`. Simply enter the ISBN number (0672324385) in the search window, and that will guide you to the book home page.

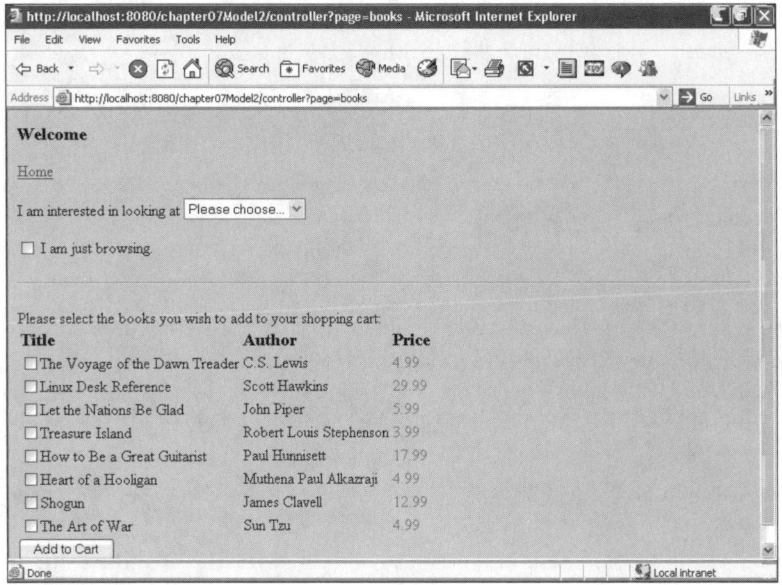

Figure 7.3 The Model 2 architecture demonstration Web site.

The model in this application is the Stock Bean, which comprises three basic arrays of CDs, DVDs, and Books. The Stock Bean is shown in Listing 7.1.

Listing 7.1 `Stock.java`

```
package com.conygre;
public class Stock{
  private Book[] books;
```

Listing 7.1 **Continued**

```
  private CompactDisc[] cds;
  private DVD[] dvds;

  public Stock() {
    Initialiser init = new Initialiser();
    books = init.books();
    cds = init.cds();
    dvds = init.dvds();
  }

  public Book[] getBooks(){
    return books;
  }

  public CompactDisc[] getCds(){
    return cds;
  }

  public DVD[] getDvds(){
    return dvds;
  }
  // inner class to initialise the products for the stock
  class Initialiser {
    public Book[] books(){
      Book[] bookArray = {
        new Book("The Voyage of the Dawn Treader",4.99,"C.S. Lewis","1"),
        new Book("Linux Desk Reference",29.99,"Scott Hawkins","2"),
        new Book("Let the Nations Be Glad",5.99,"John Piper","3"),
        new Book("Treasure Island",3.99,"Robert Louis Stevenson","4"),
        new Book("How to Be a Great Guitarist",17.99,"Paul Hunnisett","5"),
        new Book("Heart of a Hooligan",4.99,"Muthena Paul Alkazraji","6"),
        new Book("Shogun",12.99,"James Clavell","7"),
        new Book("The Art of War",4.99,"Sun Tzu","8")
      };
      return bookArray;
    }

    public CompactDisc[] cds(){
      CompactDisc[] discArray = {
        new CompactDisc("Is This It",13.99,"The Strokes",11,"9"),
        new CompactDisc("Just Enough Education to Perform",10.99,
                                    "Stereophonics",11,"0"),
        new CompactDisc("Parachutes",11.99,"Coldplay",10,"a"),
        new CompactDisc("White Ladder",9.99,"David Gray",10,"b"),
        new CompactDisc("Greatest Hits",14.99,"Penelope",14,"c"),
```

Listing 7.1 **Continued**

```
        new CompactDisc("Echo Park",13.99,"Feeder",12,"d"),
        new CompactDisc("Mezzanine",12.99,"Massive Attack",11,"e")
        };
      return discArray;
    }

    public DVD[] dvds(){
      DVD[] filmArray = {
        new DVD("It's a Wonderful Life",7.99,"Frank Capra","f"),
        new DVD("Crouching Tiger, Hidden Dragon",15.99,"Ang Lee","g"),
        new DVD("Breakfast at Tiffany's",14.99,"Blake Edwards","h"),
        new DVD("Romeo Must Die",10.99,"Andrzej Bartkowiak","i"),
        new DVD("Scent of a Woman",17.99,"Martin Brest","j"),
        new DVD("Snatch",18.99,"Guy Ritchie","k"),
        new DVD("Scarface",16.99,"Brian De Palma","l")
      };
      return filmArray;
    }
  }
}
```

The types referred to in the Stock Bean for `CompactDisc`, `DVD`, and `Book` are all basic JavaBeans with `get` and `set` methods, as discussed in the previous two chapters. `Book.java` can be seen in Listing 6.1. `CompactDisc.java` and `DVD.java` are very similar so are not shown. In Chapter 14, "Databases and JSP," you will see how this data could be extracted from a database as opposed to being set up in an array.

There are six views for this application, two for each type of data. One view for each contains a form, which enables people to purchase products. The alternative view is a simple list, which is shown when people select a Just Browsing box, which is shown in the home page in Figure 7.3. Listing 7.2 shows the CD JSP containing the form, and Listing 7.3 shows the CD JSP for those users who are simply browsing.

Listing 7.2 `cd.jsp`

```
<html>
<%@ taglib uri="http://java.sun.com/jstl-el/core" prefix="c" %>
  <head>
    <title>Welcome to Ashdown.com -
     The best deals for Books, CDs and DVDs!</title>
  </head>
  <body bgcolor="#FFCC99">
    <c:import url="header.jsp" />
    <form method="post" action="addToCart.jsp">
      Please select the CDs you wish to add to your shopping cart:<br>
      <table>
```

Listing 7.2 **Continued**

```
        <tr>
          <td><b><font size="4">Title </font></b></td>
          <td><b><font size="4">Artist</font></b></td>
          <td><b><font size="4">Number of Tracks</font></b></td>
          <td><b><font size="4">Price</font></b></td>
        </tr>
        <c:forEach var="item" items="${stock.cds}">
          <tr>
            <td><input type="checkbox" name="id"
                 value="<c:out value='${item.id}' />">
             <c:out value="${item.title}"/></td>
            <td><c:out value="${item.artist}"/></td>
            <td><c:out value="${item.tracks}"/></td>
            <td><font color="red"><c:out value="${item.price}"/></font></td>
         </tr>
        </c:forEach>
      </table>
     <input type="submit" value="Add to Cart">
    <form>
  </body>
</html>
```

Listing 7.3 `cdBrowse.jsp`

```
<html>
<%@ taglib uri="http://java.sun.com/jstl-el/core" prefix="c" %>
  <head>
    <title>Welcome to Ashdown.com - The best deals for Books,
            CDs and DVDs!</title>
  </head>
  <body bgcolor="#FFCC99">
    <c:import url="header.jsp" />
      Here are the available CDs:<br>
      <table>
        <tr>
          <td><b><font size="4">Title </font></b></td>
          <td><b><font size="4">Artist</font></b></td>
          <td><b><font size="4">Number of Tracks</font></b></td>
          <td><b><font size="4">Price</font></b></td>
        </tr>
        <c:forEach var="item" items="${stock.cds}">
          <tr>
            <td><c:out value="${item.title}"/></td>
            <td><c:out value="${item.artist}"/></td>
            <td><c:out value="${item.tracks}"/></td>
```

Listing 7.3 **Continued**

```
            <td><font color="red"><c:out value="${item.price}"/></font></td>
         </tr>
        </c:forEach>
      </table>
    <form>
  </body>
</html>
```

The difference between Listings 7.2 and 7.3 is that Listing 7.2 contains an HTML form, whereas 7.3 does not. They both, however, share an included file called `header.jsp`. The included file contains a basic drop-down list to enable users to browse to the different views of the data. This include file is shown in Listing 7.4.

Listing 7.4 `header.jsp`

```
<%@ taglib uri="http://java.sun.com/jstl-el/core" prefix="c" %>
      <h3>Welcome</h3>

<a href="controller">Home</a>
<p>
<form action="controller" method="get">
I am interested in looking at
<%-- use the client side onChange event to submit this form
     when the user selects a category --%>
<select name="page" onChange="document.forms[0].submit()">
  <option SELECTED>Please choose...</option>
  <option value="books">Books</option>
  <option value="cds">CDs</option>
  <option value="dvds">DVDs</option>
</select>
<p><input type="checkbox" name="browsing"> I am just browsing.
</form>
<hr>
```

The file `header.jsp` contains a basic drop-down list that submits a form when an item is selected from it. The relevant view is selected based on the possible values `books`, `dvds`, or `cds`. The form is submitted using a basic snippet of client-side JavaScript. Notice that the form also contains the check box to specify whether the user chooses to simply browse or wants to potentially purchase. Finally, notice the `action` attribute of the form. It is pointing to something called `controller`. This is the controller servlet as defined in the `web.xml` deployment descriptor. The controller servlet is shown in Listing 7.5.

Listing 7.5 ShoppingCartController.java

```
package com.conygre;
import java.io.*;
import javax.servlet.*;
import javax.servlet.http.*;

public class ShoppingCartController extends HttpServlet {

  // initialise the stock bean
  // note that it is done from the controller not a JSP
  public void init(ServletConfig config) throws ServletException {
    super.init(config);
    ServletContext application = getServletContext();
    application.setAttribute("stock",new Stock());
  }

  // this is where the controller allocates the appropriate redirection
  public void doGet(HttpServletRequest req, HttpServletResponse res)
          throws ServletException, IOException {
    ServletContext application = getServletContext();
    if (req.getParameter("page") != null) {
        boolean browsing = (req.getParameter("browsing")) != null;
        String page = req.getParameter("page");
        String nextURL = "";
        // the logic here could be factored out
        // into separate request handler classes
        if (page.equals("books") && browsing)
            nextURL="/booksBrowse.jsp";
        else if (page.equals("books") && !browsing)
            nextURL="/books.jsp";
        else if (page.equals("cds") && browsing)
            nextURL="/cdBrowse.jsp";
        else if (page.equals("cds") && !browsing)
            nextURL="/cd.jsp";
        else if (page.equals("dvds") && browsing)
            nextURL="/dvdBrowse.jsp";
        else if (page.equals("dvds") && !browsing)
            nextURL="/dvd.jsp";
        else
            nextURL="/errorPage.jsp";
        // now forward the request to the appropriate page
        RequestDispatcher dispatcher =
                application.getRequestDispatcher(nextURL);
        dispatcher.forward(req,res);
    }
    else {
```

Listing 7.5 **Continued**

```
        RequestDispatcher dispatcher =
                application.getRequestDispatcher("/welcome.jsp");
        dispatcher.forward(req,res);
    }
  }
}
```

This controller has two main features that we need to point out at this stage:

- Notice the `init()` method. It sets up the Stock Bean for use in the JSP pages. This is part of the role of any controller that is to instantiate any required Beans for use in the JSP views.
- In the `doGet()` method, the controller is carrying out the appropriate forwarding to the various JSPs based on the values of the two request parameters, `page` and `browsing`. If page is not set, it defaults to a `welcome.jsp` home page shown in Listing 7.6.

> **Note**
>
> The controller servlet does not have to be a servlet. The controller could also be a JSP that uses `<jsp:forward>` actions to forward requests. This is not ideal because you are using a presentation medium (JSP) to contain business logic. Nevertheless, you will sometimes see controllers implemented this way.

Listing 7.6 `welcome.jsp`

```
<html>
<%@ taglib uri="http://java.sun.com/jstl-el/core" prefix="c" %>
  <head>
    <title>Welcome to Ashdown.com - The best deals for Books,
           CDs and DVDs!</title>
  </head>
  <body bgcolor="#FFCC99">
    <c:import url="header.jsp" />
    At the moment we have many very exiting items
    for sale at amazing prices including:
    <font color="blue">
    <p><c:out value="${stock.books[0].title}" /> -
    <c:out value="${stock.books[0].author}" /> @
    <c:out value="${stock.books[0].price}" />
    <p><c:out value="${stock.cds[0].title}" /> -
    <c:out value="${stock.cds[0].artist}" /> @
    <c:out value="${stock.cds[0].price}" />
    <p><c:out value="${stock.dvds[0].title}" /> -
```

Listing 7.6 **Continued**

```
    <c:out value="${stock.dvds[0].director}" /> @
    <c:out value="${stock.dvds[0].price}" />
    </font>
    <p><b>If you wish to add items to your shopping cart, then please select
    the type of product you are interested in from the drop down above.
    <p>If you only wish to browse, then please tick the browse box first.</b>
</body>
</html>
```

This welcome page displays a single book, CD, and DVD product. It also incorporates `header.jsp`, enabling users to select which page of products they want to view.

To help visualize the application, the flow is shown in Figure 7.4.

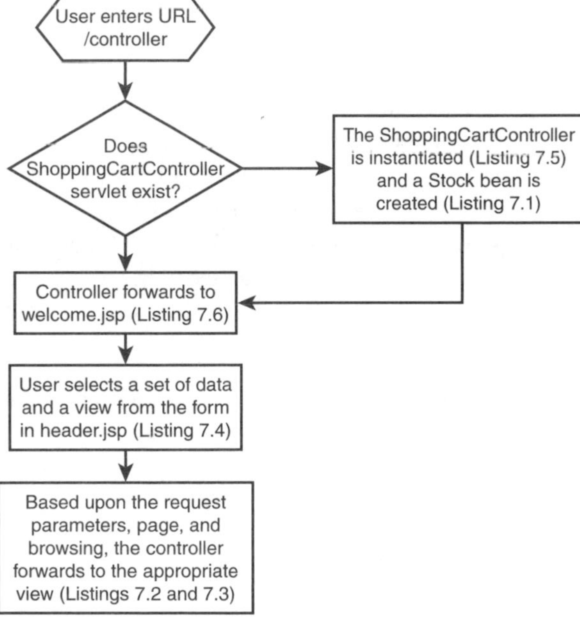

Figure 7.4 Application flow for a Model 2 example.

> **Note**
>
> The listings for the shopping cart functionality are discussed in the next chapter on session tracking.

Which Architecture to Use?

Now that you have seen an overview of the two architectures, how do you decide which approach to take? If you read some articles, you get the impression that the Model 1 architecture is the old or obsolete way, and that Model 2 is the new, better way. This is not the case, and the J2EE BluePrints back that up.

> **Note**
>
> The J2EE BluePrints are written to help Java developers with best practice guidelines for the development of J2EE applications. More information can be found at the BluePrints home page, which is `http://java.sun.com/blueprints`.

The Model 1 architecture is appropriate for Web applications that have the following characteristics:

- Small applications in particular will benefit from this architecture. There is no need to go to the complexity of a controller servlet when there are only a handful of JSPs!
- Applications that have a basic linking structure also lend themselves to the Model 1 architecture. If there is not much in the way of processing that needs to be done as the user navigates between pages, you might not benefit a great deal from having a controller. It can make it unnecessarily complex.
- Applications that do not require security control can also be built using the Model 1 architecture. A controller can help manage security, but if there is no security to manage, this is irrelevant! The security of Web applications is discussed in more detail in Chapter 16, "Security and JSP."

The main drawback of the Model 1 architecture is that as sites built on this architecture grow and evolve, they can become very difficult to manage. Various pages are created with business logic within them, and debugging can become harder and harder as you end up with scriptlets in various locations containing small fragments of business logic.

It is in these larger applications that the Model 2 architecture can really help. The main benefits of using the Model 2 architecture are as follows:

- Having a controller makes the maintenance of larger sites more straightforward because you can manage the navigation centrally through the use of the controller servlet.
- You can also manage security more easily with the Model 2 architecture because every request goes through the central controller servlet, which can check the user credentials against any requested resource.
- Internationalization, although never straightforward, can be implemented more easily when using the Model 2 architecture. Presentation in different languages can be forwarded depending on the locale of the client. This will be discussed again

later in this chapter when frameworks are discussed. For basic internationalization, you can use the i18n tags discussed in Chapter 5, in the section entitled, 'The Internationalization and Formatting Actions.'

- Multiclient device sites can be built more easily using the Model 2 approach because different views of the data can be presented depending on the client device type. So, a mobile device can be presented with one view, a browser with another, and so on.
- It is easier to build the site in a modular way, and then unit-test the site in discrete functional blocks. This is not so easy with the Model 1 architecture because the various Beans are created and set up from different JSPs, and in a large site, it becomes increasingly difficult to modularize the application, and identify from which pages Beans are created and modified.

Although the Model 2 architecture has been introduced already with the sample shopping cart application, there are a number of substantial improvements that could be made. Take this section of the controller servlet for example:

```
if (page.equals("books") && browsing)
    nextURL="/booksBrowse.jsp";
else if (page.equals("books") && !browsing)
    nextURL="/books.jsp";
else if (page.equals("cds") && browsing)
    nextURL="/cdBrowse.jsp";
else if (page.equals("cds") && !browsing)
    nextURL="/cd.jsp";
else if (page.equals("dvds") && browsing)
    nextURL="/dvdBrowse.jsp";
else if (page.equals("dvds") && !browsing)
    nextURL="/dvd.jsp";
else
    nextURL="/errorPage.jsp";
```

This is only a simplistic example application. Imagine a real application with potentially hundreds of different views. I wouldn't want to be the person maintaining an `if/else` block for that! Also, there is no business logic associated with each view, but if there was, where would it go? In this example, it would need to be invoked somehow from the `if/else` block.

There has now emerged a number of architectural frameworks that add substantially to the basic Model 2 architecture that you have seen in the previous example. These frameworks will be discussed in the remaining pages of this chapter.

Introducing Frameworks

Many frameworks are around to help with the building of Web applications using the Model 2 architecture. These include

- Jakarta Struts
- JavaServer Faces
- Web Application Framework (WAF) from the J2EE BluePrints

So, what exactly are these frameworks, and why should you be interested in using one? In summary, these frameworks provide the following:

- A controller servlet.
- An 'action' class of some description that can be subclassed, providing classes that invoke your business logic.
- Tag libraries to help with the building of HTML forms and Web page templates.
- Various utility classes to enable you to put much of the configuration of your application into external XML files rather than hard-coded into your application.

The benefits you get from using one of these frameworks are as follows:

- The infrastructure for your Web application is ready-made, thus reducing your development time.
- Various framework-specific modules that have been developed by third parties can be used within your Web applications.
- A framework will help you to use a good design for your application; for some frameworks, there is strong community support available.
- There is also increasing interest from the tool community in these frameworks. Tool support should also reduce your development time.
- It should reduce your costs in training staff because individuals who have learned a framework can reuse the skills in multiple projects.

These benefits are over and above those already listed for using a Model 2 architecture approach.

In this chapter, we will focus mainly on the Struts framework from Jakarta. This framework is very popular within the developer community and is already being used in real-world applications, a list of which is available at `http://jakarta.apache.org/struts/resources/powered.html`.

Jakarta Struts

The Struts framework was developed by Craig McClanahan and donated to the Apache Foundation in May 2000. Craig is also the lead developer on the Apache Tomcat project, which is one of the reasons for its prominence.

An Overview of Struts

The Struts framework is shown in Figure 7.5.

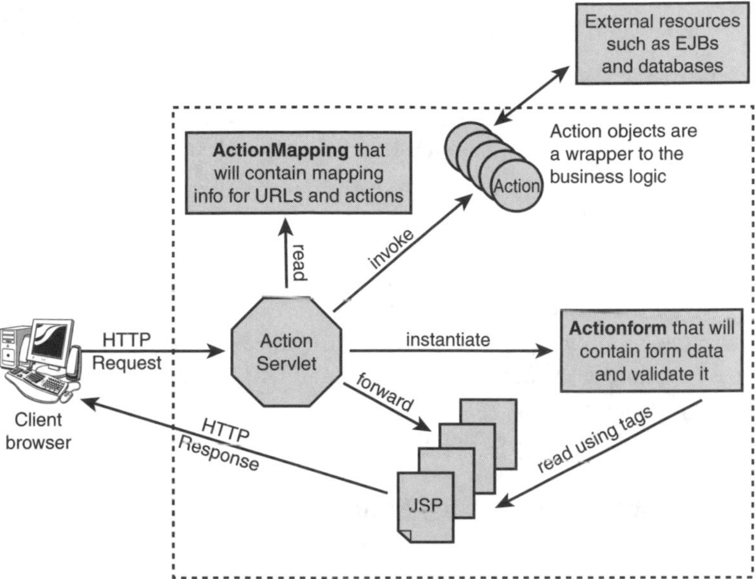

Figure 7.5 The Struts framework.

The core components of this architecture are all found in a package called `org.apache.struts.action`, and are as follows:

- `ActionServlet`—The `org.apache.struts.action.ActionServlet` is the controller in the Struts framework. It is responsible for creating and interacting with the `Action` objects. This class can also be extended, although this is not always necessary.
- `ActionForm`—The `org.apache.struts.action.ActionForm` class can be described as a form handler. It always needs to be extended and instances are pre-populated with the form data, and then validated (if required) by the invocation of a user-defined `validate()` method. This takes place before an associated `Action` object is invoked.
- `Action`—The `org.apache.struts.action.Action` class is also extended and is used as a wrapper for any business logic. Typically, the business logic will be elsewhere and will be invoked from an `Action` object. This is to maintain reusability of any business components.
- `ActionMapping`—The `org.apache.struts.action.ActionMapping` class is used by the controller to map specific requests to specific `Action` objects. The mapping for which requests go with which action is all contained in an XML file called `struts-config.xml`. You'll see an example of this later in the chapter. It is from this XML file that the `ActionMapping` objects are created. `ActionMapping` objects are stored in a container of type `org.apache.struts.action.ActionMappings`.

You will see how to create objects of these types later, but how do you install Struts?

Installing the Struts Framework

The Struts framework is relatively straightforward to install. You can access the latest binaries from the Struts home page, which is `http://jakarta.apache.org/struts/index.html`.

The version used in this book is 1.0.2. After you have downloaded the `INSTALL` file for your platform, you can extract it to a suitable location on your hard drive. Within the subfolder called `webapps`, there are a number of WAR files. These include sample sites, the documentation, and a blank application that you can use as a starter for your own projects. To set these up in a Web container such as Tomcat, simply deploy the WAR. In Tomcat, this is as simple as dropping the appropriate WAR file into your `<tomcat-home>\webapps` folder. The `INSTALL` file in the Struts root directory has further instructions specific to a number of different Web containers.

Building an Application Using Struts

> **Note**
>
> The application discussed here is available as part of the book download, which you can get by visiting `www.samspublishing.com` and entering the book ISBN in the search field. This application is available as `chapter07struts.war`.

By far the easiest way to build a Struts application is to use the blank Struts application WAR as a starter. The WAR is called `struts-blank.war`. So, to get started, you will need to deploy this WAR in your container, and get it into an extracted state that can be modified. In Tomcat, dropping it into `<tomcat-home>\webapps`, and then restarting Tomcat will achieve this for you, and it will be in the right place for you to start working on the application and testing your changes.

> **Tip**
>
> Depending on how you are going to deploy the blank application, you might want to rename `struts-blank.war` before you deploy it so that you have a Web application with a sensible name.

To help put Struts into context, you'll now see a Web application that has been built using the Struts framework. We used the `struts-blank.war` as our starter. The example application consists of two basic HTML forms that will ask for some personal information, which will be used to provide a car purchase recommendation.

Figures 7.6, 7.7, and 7.8 show the three pages involved in the application.

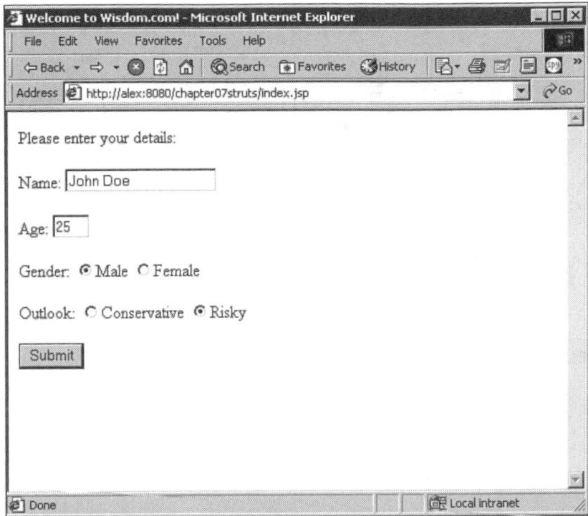

Figure 7.6 Struts example first form.

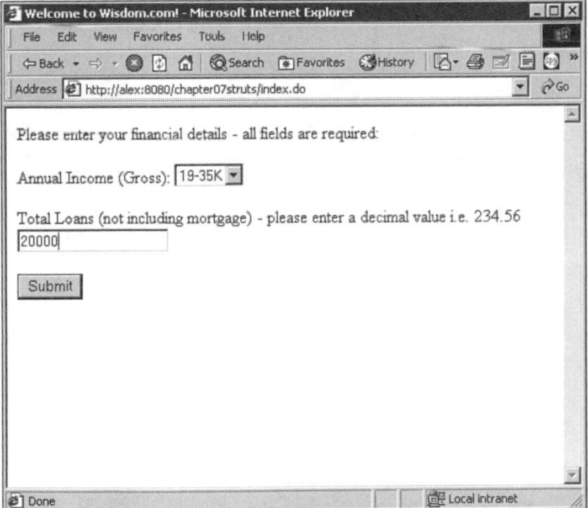

Figure 7.7 Struts example second form.

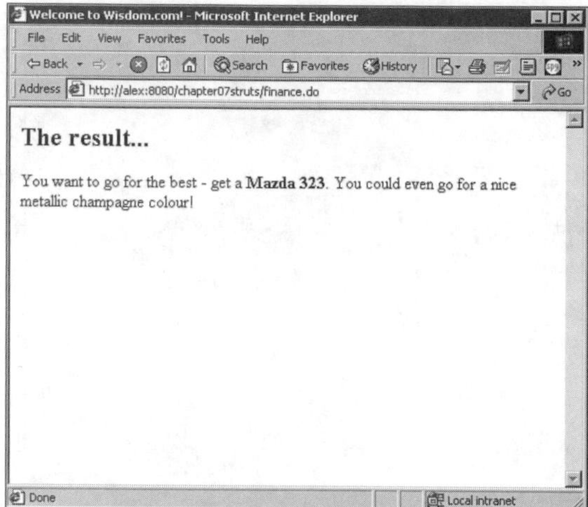

Figure 7.8 Struts example result page.

As you can see, it consists of two basic forms that when completed and submitted recommend a car. Remember, in a Struts application, there is a clear division of labor. `Action` objects contain the code that invokes the business logic, `ActionForm` objects process the form data, and there will also need to be an `ActionMapping` to map the various URLs to the forms. Finally, there will be the JSPs that represent the forms and response page.

Figure 7.9 shows the files that are being used in the sample application.

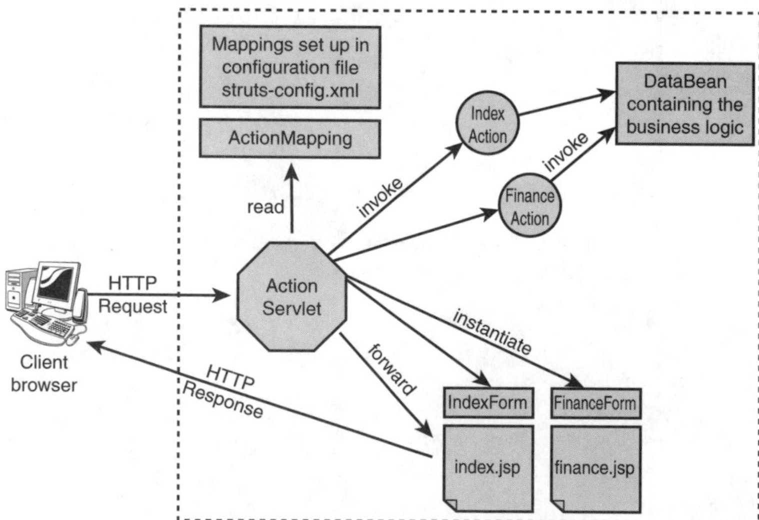

Figure 7.9 Sample application architecture.

Setting Up the Mappings

We'll start with the mapping for the various URLs to two actions, `index` and `finance`. The `index` action is the name given to the first submission (the form in Figure 7.6), and `finance` is the name given to the second submission (the form in Figure 7.7). To set up this mapping, when using the `struts-blank.war` application, it is a simple matter of modifying the main Struts configuration file. This file is called `struts-config.xml`, and it is shown along with the modifications in Listing 7.7.

Listing 7.7 `struts-config.xml`

```
<?xml version="1.0" encoding="ISO-8859-1"?>
<!DOCTYPE struts-config
    PUBLIC "-//Apache Software Foundation//DTD Struts Configuration 1.0//EN"
    "http://jakarta.apache.org/struts/dtds/struts-config_1_0.dtd">
<struts-config>
  <form-beans>
    <form-bean name="indexForm" type="com.conygre.ch07.IndexForm"/>
    <form-bean name="financeForm" type="com.conygre.ch07.FinanceForm"/>
  </form-beans>
  <global-forwards>
  </global-forwards>
  <action-mappings>
    <action path="/index" type="com.conygre.ch07.IndexAction"
       name="indexForm" scope="request" input="/index.jsp">
      <forward name="success" path="/finances.jsp"/>
      <forward name="failure" path="/index.jsp"/>
    </action>
    <action path="/finance" type="com.conygre.ch07.FinanceAction"
        name="financeForm" scope="request" input="/finances.jsp">
      <forward name="success" path="/result.jsp"/>
      <forward name="failure" path="/finances.jsp"/>
    </action>
    <action path="/admin/addFormBean"
        type="org.apache.struts.actions.AddFormBeanAction"/>
    <action path="/admin/addForward"
        type="org.apache.struts.actions.AddForwardAction"/>
    <action path="/admin/addMapping"
        type="org.apache.struts.actions.AddMappingAction"/>
    <action path="/admin/reload"
        type="org.apache.struts.actions.ReloadAction"/>
    <action path="/admin/removeFormBean"
        type="org.apache.struts.actions.RemoveFormBeanAction"/>
    <action path="/admin/removeForward"
        type="org.apache.struts.actions.RemoveForwardAction"/>
    <action path="/admin/removeMapping"
        type="org.apache.struts.actions.RemoveMappingAction"/>
```

Listing 7.7 **Continued**

```
  </action-mappings>
</struts-config>
```

As you can see, this file adheres to a specific DTD. It has the root element of <struts-config>, and there are two child elements from the root that you need to pay special attention to. One is the `<form-beans>` element, and the other is the `<action-mappings>` element.

The `<form-beans>` element contains individual `<form-bean>` elements. Each `<form-bean>` element maps a form bean class to a logical name which is used later in the configuration file.

```
<form-beans>
  <form-bean name="indexForm" type="com.conygre.ch07.IndexForm"/>
  <form-bean name="financeForm" type="com.conygre.ch07.FinanceForm"/>
</form-beans>
```

The classes specified here used to create the objects that will be populated with the form data upon submission, and will also validate the data before it is passed to the appropriate action object, defined in the `<action-mapping>` element discussed next. The use of these logical names enables you to avoid hard coding the class names into your application logic.

The `<action-mappings>` element contains individual `<action>` elements. These elements are responsible for mapping the form bean named in the <form-bean> element to an actual form, to an action URL, and to a specific action bean.

```
<action path="/finance" type="com.conygre.ch07.FinanceAction"
    name="financeForm" scope="request" input="/finances.jsp">
  <forward name="success" path="/result.jsp"/>
  <forward name="failure" path="/finances.jsp"/>
</action>
```

The `<action>` element shown here links the form bean called `financeForm` with the specific JSP `/finances.jsp`. It also specifies that the form on this page with an action attribute with the path `/finance` will invoke this particular action.

The `<forward>` child elements contains paths called `success` and `failure`. These are used to determine the next page following the success or failure of the processing of this form by the action objects.

A bit like natural history programs that follow various creepy crawlies through their daily lives, what we'll do now is follow the path of the data from when it is first filled in on the form, to its eventual resting place in what we have called the `DataBean`.

The data is first entered into Web pages, and this is where we'll start.

The Pages

The HTML forms are built using Struts-specific tag libraries. Listing 7.8 shows the `index.jsp` form that appears in the browser as Figure 7.6.

Listing 7.8 `index.jsp`

```
<%@ taglib uri="/WEB-INF/struts-html.tld" prefix="html" %>
<%@ taglib uri="/WEB-INF/struts-bean.tld" prefix="bean" %>
<html>
<head>
<title>Welcome to Wisdom.com!</title>
</head>
<body>
<!-- puts error messages in if there is a problem
       these messages come from ApplicationResources.properties -->
<html:errors />
Please enter your details:<br>
<!-- the form -->
<html:form action="index.do">
   <p><bean:message key="prompt.name"/>:
          <html:text property="name"/>
   <p><bean:message key="prompt.age"/>:
         <html:text property="age" size="2"/>
   <p><bean:message key="prompt.gender"/>:
         <html:radio property="gender" value="male"/>Male
         <html:radio property="gender" value="female"/>Female
   <p><bean:message key="prompt.outlook"/>:
          <html:radio property="outlook" value="con"/>Conservative
          <html:radio property="outlook" value="risk"/>Risky
   <p><html:submit/>
</html:form>

</body>
</html>
```

> **Tip**
> If you use the `struts-blank.war` as a starter, the tag libraries are already set up for you in `web.xml`.

Two tag libraries are in use on this page. One is the `form` tag library and the other is the `bean` tag library.

The `html` *Library*

The HTML tag library provides tags associated with HTML markup. So, in Listing 7.8, it has been used for all the various form elements, plus tags for presenting error messages. Depending on how familiar you are with HTML forms, you can probably identify what most of the tags in Listing 7.8 are for. A selection of the HTML tags involved in creating these forms is shown in Table 7.1.

Table 7.1 **The Struts HTML Forms Tags**

Name	Description
`<html:form>`	This tag is used to begin the form. It inserts an HTML `form` tag. The `action` attribute here specifies a somewhat unusual URL, `index.do`. If you look in `web.xml`, you will see that any URL with the postfix `.do` is mapped to the action servlet, which is the struts controller. <html:form action="index.do">
`<html:text>`	This is a straightforward HTML text field. The `property` attribute becomes the `name` of the form field. <html:text property="name"/>
`<html:radio>`	The radio button. The `property` attribute is the name of the button, and the `value` attribute is the value that is sent to the server. <html:radio property="gender" value="female"/>
`<html:checkbox>`	This tag creates a check box with the name specified by the `property` attribute. <html:checkbox property="married"/>
`<html:submit>`	This tag puts a Submit button on the form.
`<html:select>`	This tag creates an HTML `select` tag. The attribute called `property` sets the `name`. The options elements are created using the `option` tag, discussed next. <html:select property="income">
`<html:option>`	This tag is used within the `select` tag to specify the various options available for the client to use. The `value` attribute specifies the option value to be returned to the server. <html:select property="income"> <html:option value="low">0-18K</html:option> <html:option value="medium">19-35K</html:option> <html:option value="high">36k+</html:option> </html:select>

The `<html:errors>` tag is slightly different in that it is not used in the context of the form, but it will automatically cause the insertion of any error messages. Figure 7.10 shows what happens if the form on `index.jsp` is submitted incorrectly by forgetting to provide a name.

The error message at the top of the page shown in Figure 7.10 is there because of the presence of the `<html:errors>` tag. This tag processes error messages that you set up in another of the Struts configuration files, this time a properties file. The file is `ApplicationResources.properties`, and is located in the `WEB-INF\classes` folder. Listing 7.9 shows our modified version `ApplicationResources.properties`.

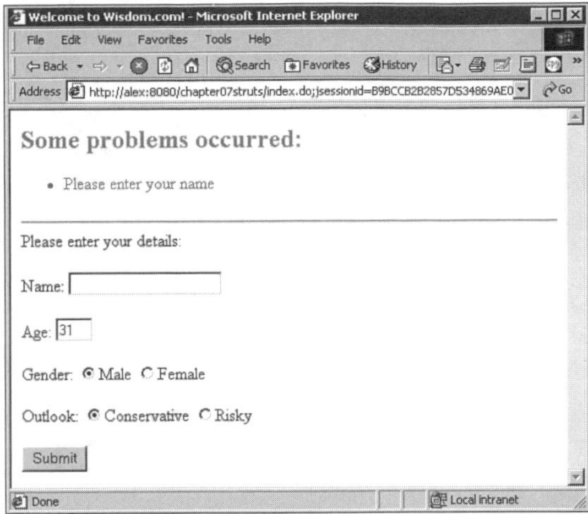

Figure 7.10 Struts error message.

Listing 7.9 ApplicationResources.properties

```
index.title=Struts Starter Application
index.heading=Hello World!
index.message=To get started on your own application ...

errors.header=<font color=red><h2>Some problems occurred: </h2><ul>
errors.footer=</ul></font><hr>

errors.name=<li>Please enter your name
errors.age=<li>Please enter your age
errors.gender=<li>Please specify your gender
errors.outlook=<li>What is your outlook?

errors.income=<li>Please specify your income
errors.loans=<li>Please enter total amount of your loans, excluding mortgage
errors.number=<li>The value you entered for loans is not a valid number

prompt.name=Name
prompt.age=Age
prompt.gender=Gender
prompt.outlook=Outlook

prompt.income=Annual Income (Gross)
prompt.loans=Total Loans (not including mortgage)
          - please enter a decimal value i.e. 234.56
```

This properties file is central to a Struts application because it contains the messages that will be used within the application.

> **Tip**
>
> If you are interested in how this property file is processed, you can download the source code for Apache Struts. Locate the source code for the `org.apache.struts.action.ActionServlet` class, and locate the method `initApplication()`. This method processes this file.

The errors are listed with each error having a name and a message containing any relevant HTML formatting. There is also an `error.header` and an `error.footer` value. These values are displayed at the beginning and end of any errors within the browser.

The `prompt.xxx` entries, which you can see in Listing 7.9, are used by the Bean tag library that is used on `index.jsp`. This library will be discussed next.

The `bean` *Library*

The `bean` library is used for the manipulation of JavaBeans within pages that are using the Struts framework. These tags can be used to create and modify JavaBean instances from pages. The tag that we are interested in, however, for the benefit of our application is the `message` tag because this tag enables us to use messages defined in `ApplicationResources.properties`:

```
<bean:message key="prompt.age"/>
```

The use of the `message` tag will result in the insertion of the text with the property name `prompt.age` from `ApplicationResources.properties` as shown here:

```
prompt.age=Age
```

There are a number of benefits when setting these values in property files like this. One is internationalization. You can have multiple property files set up for various Locales that your application needs to support. Another benefit is that all your messages and textual fragments such as form field labels are in one convenient location, and can be changed with relative ease.

For further information on the `bean` tags, visit `http://jakarta.apache.org/struts/struts-bean.html`.

You have now seen the HTML forms that have been built using tags from the struts tag libraries `html` and `bean`. After a form has been filled in and submitted, what happens next?

The `ActionForm` objects

The `action` attribute of the form is the clue to what happens next:

```
<html:form action="index.do">
```

The `action` attribute has the extension `.do`, which results in the `ActionServlet` being invoked. This is because of the following entry in `web.xml`:

```
<servlet>
  <servlet-name>action</servlet-name>
  <servlet-class>org.apache.struts.action.ActionServlet</servlet-class>
  <!--a few parameters are also set here>
</servlet>
<servlet-mapping>
  <servlet-name>action</servlet-name>
  <url-pattern>*.do</url-pattern>
</servlet-mapping>
```

As you can see, the servlet referred to as `action` in the `web.xml` is in fact the `ActionServlet`.

The `ActionServlet` will now instantiate an `ActionForm` object of the appropriate type for the form that has been submitted. This information will have come from the mapping in `struts-config.xml` discussed earlier. In this example, it will be an instance of `IndexForm.java`. `ActionForm` classes are typically named `xxxForm.java`, where `xxx` is the name of the `Action`. So, in this example, the name of the `Action` will be `Index`. `IndexForm.java` is shown in Listing 7.10.

Listing 7.10 IndexForm.java

```
package com.conygre.ch07;

import javax.servlet.http.HttpServletRequest;
import org.apache.struts.action.*;

public class IndexForm extends ActionForm {
  private String name;
  private String age;
  private String gender;
  private String outlook;

  // a whole bunch of get/set methods for the above properties
  // would go here

  // here is the optional validation method
  // it will be invoked automatically
  public ActionErrors validate(ActionMapping map, HttpServletRequest req){
    ActionErrors errors = new ActionErrors();

    // check that the name has a value
    if ((name == null)||(name.equals(""))){
      errors.add("Name",new ActionError("errors.name"));
    }
    // check that the age is a valid number, if not,
    // this conversion to a double will throw an exception
    // and an ActionError will be added to the list
```

Listing 7.10 **Continued**

```
    try {
      Double d = new Double(age);
      d.doubleValue();
    }
    catch(Exception e){
      errors.add("Age", new ActionError("errors.age"));
    }
    // check the gender is set. There are only two possible values
    // so only check for null
    if (gender == null){
      errors.add("Gender",new ActionError("errors.gender"));
    }
    // check that the outlook has a value
    if ((outlook == null) ||(outlook.equals(""))){
      errors.add("Outlook",new ActionError("errors.outlook"));
    }
    return errors;
  }
}
```

After the `IndexForm` object has been created, the controller will populate all its properties with the request parameters from the form, in a similar way to how the `<jsp:setProperty>` standard action is used (see Chapter 6, "JSP and JavaBeans"). For this to work, the names of the request parameters must match the names of the `IndexForm` properties.

Validation

The Struts framework provides a simple mechanism to allow for the validation of your data. To incorporate validation into your `ActionForm` Bean, you will also need to provide a `validate()` method to validate the data. The `validate()` method of the superclass `org.apache.struts.action.ActionForm` is basically a `stub` method and is as follows:

```
public ActionErrors validate(ActionMapping mapping, HttpServletRequest request){
  return (null);
}
```

This method (or your overridden method) is invoked before the `Action` Bean itself is invoked. The `validate()` method returns an `ActionErrors` object, which is essentially a collection of individual `ActionError` objects found in the form. If an empty `ActionErrors` object is returned, or if `null` is returned, it is assumed that the form data is valid, and the `Action` object is invoked. If the `ActionErrors` object contains any individual `ActionError` objects, the form data is assumed to be invalid, and control is passed back to the form again for resubmission. Figure 7.11 shows a summary of the validation process.

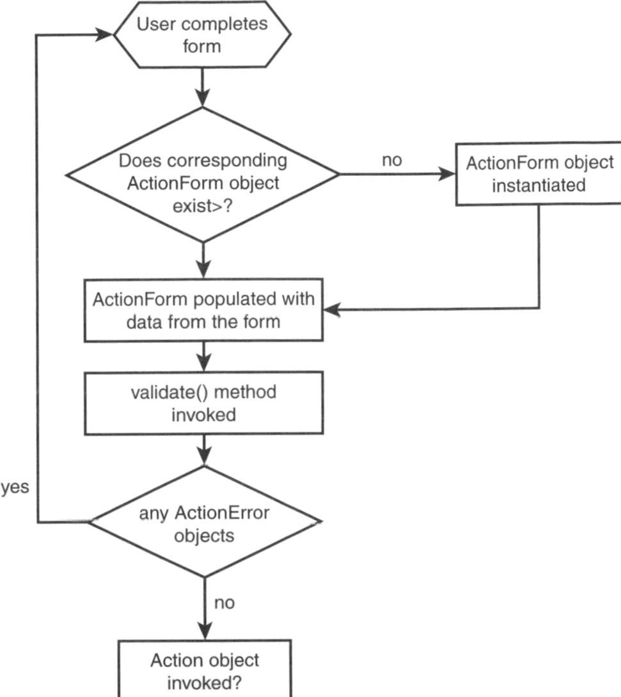

Figure 7.11 Validation using struts.

If control is passed back to the form, the `<html:errors>` element discussed in the earlier section will use the `ActionErrors` collection to add the appropriate error messages on the form (see Figure 7.10).

The `Action` Objects

The `Action` objects are responsible for causing the appropriate response to take place to the submission of the form. These `Action` classes subclass `org.apache.struts.action.Action`, and override a single method called `perform()`. The signature is shown here:

```
public ActionForward perform(ActionMapping map, ActionForm reqForm,
                             HttpServletRequest req, HttpServletResponse res)
```

This method takes the `ActionMapping` object, which contains all the mapping information from `struts-config.xml`; it takes in the form data as the `ActionForm` object; and it takes the `request` and `response` objects.

The `Action` object then invokes the appropriate business method, typically located in a `JavaBean`. It is important to stress that the `Action` object does *not* necessarily contain the business method itself. Action classes are typically given the name *xxx*`Action`, where *xxx* is the name of the specific action. So, in the example, the action class is called `IndexAction`. `IndexAction.java` is shown in Listing 7.11.

Listing 7.11 `IndexAction.java`

```
package com.conygre.ch07;

import javax.servlet.http.*;
import org.apache.struts.action.*;

public class IndexAction extends Action{

  public ActionForward perform(ActionMapping map, ActionForm reqForm,
                               HttpServletRequest req, HttpServletResponse res){
    HttpSession session = req.getSession();
    DataBean data = (DataBean)session.getAttribute("data");
    if(data == null){
      data = new DataBean();
    }
    IndexForm form = (IndexForm)reqForm;
    data.setName(form.getName());
    data.setAge(form.getAge());
    data.setGender(form.getGender());
    data.setOutlook(form.getOutlook());

    session.setAttribute("data",data);
    return(map.findForward("success"));
  }
}
```

The `IndexAction` object instantiates a basic Bean called `DataBean` and populates it with the data from the form. Notice that the `DataBean` is an object that is to be within the `session` object. The `DataBean` is shown in Listing 7.12.

Listing 7.12 `DataBean.java`

```
package com.conygre.ch07;

import javax.servlet.http.HttpServletRequest;
import org.apache.struts.action.*;

public class DataBean {

  private String name = null;
  private int age = 0;
  private String gender = null;
  private String outlook = null;
```

Listing 7.12 **Continued**

```
  private String income = null;
  private double loans = 0;
  private String result = null;

  // here would be a series of get/set methods for the
  // above properties


  // here is the method that decides what you should have
  public void calculate(){
    if((age<20)&&(income.equals("low"))){
      result = "Best go for something less expensive and reliable";
    }
    else if((age<20)&&(income.equals("medium"))){
      result = "Perhaps a nice new <b>Merccdes Smart</b>";
    }
    else if((age>20)&&(age<30)){
      result = "You want to go for the best - get a <b>Mazda 323</b>. ";
    }
    else if((age>30)&&(income.equals("medium"))){
      result = "I would go for something stylish, not too flash";
    }
    else if((age>30)&&(income.equals("high"))){
      result = "What about a more 'mature' person's car - like a <b>BMW</b>";
    }
    else if(loans>10000){
      result = "I should pay off my debts if I were you";
    }
    else{
      result = "hard to say... perhaps a <b>Ford</b>?";
    }
  }
}
```

As you can see from Listing 7.12, this is a regular Bean. There is no Struts-specific content in this listing. The `calculate()` method is used by the results page.

The last thing we need to discuss regarding `IndexAction.java` is the last line of the `perform()` method. After the `DataBean` is set up, the following line of code is reached:

```
return(map.findForward("success"));
```

The map variable is the `ActionMapping` object, which has all the mapping information from `struts-config.xml`. This method call to `findForward()` relates to the following entry in `struts-config.xml`:

```
<action path="/index" type="com.conygre.ch07.IndexAction"
 name="indexForm" scope="request" input="/index.jsp">
    <forward name="success" path="/finances.jsp"/>
    <forward name="failure" path="/index.jsp"/>
</action>
```

As you can see, for the action called `indexForm`, which is this one, there is a `forward` element with the `name` attribute set to `success`, which has a path specified to the next JSP form, `finances.jsp`.

What happens is that the `perform` method returns the path for the next page to be displayed to the user. The action could potentially have several different `forward` elements specified for it.

You have now seen how the data gets from the form to the business logic within the JavaBean. The Struts framework is not simple, but it enables you to clearly separate the different roles within an application to different components.

This is not an exhaustive discussion of Struts, but at the time of writing, a number of books specifically on the subject are being published if you want to explore Struts in more detail. Of course, with none yet available it is hard to make a concrete recommendation! The Jakarta Struts Web site is also a good source of further information:

`http://jakarta.apache.org/struts/`

JavaServer Faces

Struts is not the only framework for building Web applications. Another framework that is emerging at the time of writing is JavaServer Faces (JSF). Craig McClanahan, the creator of Struts, is developing this framework, and the intention is that JSF will eventually supercede Struts. Here is a quote from the Struts FAQ:

> At some point, we would not be surprised to see Faces become the preferred UI implementation technology once it is standardized and available. You can be assured that any future migration will be made as painless as possible, and maximize your investment in Struts.

It is currently part of the Java Community Process as JSR-127. At the time of writing, it was in the Community Review Stage (for an overview of the JCP, read Appendix F, "The Java Community Process"). One of the main benefits of this technology will be that tool vendors will be able to build tools that will enable the Web developer to be able to build Web applications in a drag-and-drop way. This is a similar style to how ASP.NET applications can be built using the Microsoft Visual Studio product.

General Guidelines

You have now seen the various architecture options available to you as a Web application developer. There are, however, a number of general guidelines that apply regardless of the architecture that you have chosen to use, and I will finish the chapter with these. I have adapted these from some very helpful guidelines written by Michael Fasosin and Alan Peng of ATG.

Separating HTML and Java

Although it is tempting and technically valid to place both HTML and Java code in a single JSP, there are several reasons architecturally why this should not be done:

- Combining HTML and Java code will clutter the page, which will make the code significantly harder to read.
- Separation of HTML and Java code enables the page developers and the Java developers to work concurrently.
- Separation of Java code into Beans and Tag Libraries enables better reuse and decreases duplication.

Encapsulating the Business Logic in Beans

The encapsulation of business logic in Beans or `Action` objects of some kind will enable modularization of the code and allow reuse of business logic by multiple pages or clients. The decoupling of business logic and presentation logic will allow changes to either without causing side effects to both. Common sense needs to be applied here if performance considerations are an issue.

Finally, it is also sensible to generalize common behavior to custom tags.

Using the Most Appropriate Inclusion Mechanism

Duplication of code on the JSP level can be reduced by using JSP includes, directives, and actions. This technique requires the development of small, reusable JSP fragments that can then be shared by other pages. Currently, two methods can be used to include these fragments.

The JSP `<%@ include>` directive includes the content of the specified file during the translation phase and merges it with the parent page. This means that scripting variables declared in the parent file are visible in all files and must, therefore, have unique names.

The JSP `<jsp:include>` action includes the response generated by executing the specified page. Because it's the response generated by the page that is included, and not the content of the page itself, scripting variables declared in one file are not available to the other files. To share an object between the pages you must instead place it in one of the following JSP scopes: request, session, or application.

The general guidelines for when to use the different mechanisms are

- Use the `<% @include>` directive if the file changes rarely. It's the fastest mechanism and allows the reuse of environment and scripting variables.
- Use the `<jsp:include>` for all other cases.

Stylesheets

Stylesheets enable designers to place appearance control in a single location. Cascading Style Sheets (CSS) are used to control such items as font families, font sizes, and table characteristics. Stylesheets enable the designer to make changes in one location; those changes immediately reflect on all appropriate pages, resulting in increased maintainability and consistent appearance to users.

Comments, Style, and Structure

Although a simple, efficient, and elegant design goes a long way in simplifying maintenance, code that is well-documented, well-structured, and consistent will also greatly improve the maintainability of the application.

To make your pages easier to understand:

- Use indentation to clearly signify scope and coding blocks
- Use XML-compliant HTML tag constructs
- Comment your pages
- Use HTML comments when you want the comment to appear in the HTML page source: `<!-- -->`
- Use Java comments when you want the comment to appear in the Java source: `<% /* */ %>`
- Use JSP comments when you want the comment to only appear in the JSP page source: `<%-- --%>`

Exception Handling

Simply writing good, defensive code can prevent many exceptions. This style of coding leaves little to assumption and cuts out the meticulous checks and validation of all input and results. But, of course, in the real world this is not always possible. First, the developer does not always have total control; an example of this is the use of third-party software or frameworks that do not function as expected or as documented. Second, project constraints such as time and resources sometimes also inhibit this style of coding, and the level of testing. So, no matter how meticulous and diligent you are, exceptions will always occur.

JSPs enable developers to catch and handle exceptions in the code, resulting in more robust and aesthetically pleasing exception handling. This can be done using the `catch` tag from the JSTL, as discussed in Chapter 5, "The JSP Standard Tag Library."

To handle runtime exceptions thrown in a JSP page, the `errorPage` attribute can be added to your page directive. Any runtime exceptions encountered while displaying the page will be available to this page in the exception object:

```
<%@ page errorPage="errorPage.jsp" %>
```

If you follow these guidelines as far as possible given the constraints that you have, this will help you to build scalable, reliable, and maintainable Web applications.

You can therefore use the catch tag for exceptions that should not prevent the page from displaying and use error pages for the primary exceptions that would prevent the page from displaying correctly. It is worth noting also that you can specify specific error pages for specific types of exceptions from within the `web.xml` deployment descriptor using the simple syntax shown below:

```
<error-page>
  <exception-type>com.conygre.CustomException</exception-type>
  <location>/customExceptionPage.html</location>
</error-page>
```

Summary

In this chapter, you have seen the architectural options available to the Web developer. The basic Model 1 architecture was discussed first; in this architecture, pages are accessed directly by clients, and the pages use Beans when they need them. The Model 2 architecture was discussed next; this architecture lets you create a controller servlet that instantiates any required Beans and forwards requests to the appropriate JSPs.

Finally, we looked at the concept of a framework for Web applications. We discussed the Jakarta Struts framework from Apache and briefly mentioned the up-and-coming JavaServer Faces framework that is being developed at the time of writing. It is worth noting that these are not the only frameworks available today; for example, the RealMethods framework, which is proven, is commercially available from `http://j2eeframework.com`. Some application servers also ship with built-in proprietary frameworks. A good example of this is the ATG Dynamo Framework (`www.atg.com`), which is another tried-and-tested model for building Web applications.

8

Session Tracking Using JSP

SESSION TRACKING IS VITAL TO NEARLY EVERY Web application. Put simply, session tracking is identifying individual users as they navigate through your site. If you have ever read anything on session tracking, you will most probably have read about a shopping cart. The shopping cart is an ideal example of session tracking.

HTTP as a protocol is stateless, which means that for every request/response pair, a separate connection is used.

This poses a fundamental problem for Web applications. Suppose a user fills out an online form with all his delivery information for a purchase. Then, he gets presented with another page, but the connection used when he submitted his data is closed. When he submits the next form that asks him for his credit-card number, the server has to somehow identify that these two form submissions have come from the same person. This is session tracking.

Using Cookies to Track Sessions

The most popular way to track sessions is through the use of session cookies. There is another kind of cookie called a persistent cookie, which will be discussed later. Cookies are identifiers that are passed with responses to the client machine in the HTTP header.

Figure 8.1 shows how cookies work.

The following list of steps outlines what is going on in Figure 8.1:

1. The client makes an initial request to your server:

   `www.yourserver.com/colors/index.jsp.`

2. The server receives the request and creates a cookie for the client machine and also a corresponding session object for the server.
3. The server responds to client with the page plus the cookie information in the HTTP header.

4. The client makes a subsequent request for another page, and the browser places the cookie information in the request header.
5. The server recognizes the client has returned because of the cookie that has come back, and the server locates the appropriate session object based on the information stored in the cookie.

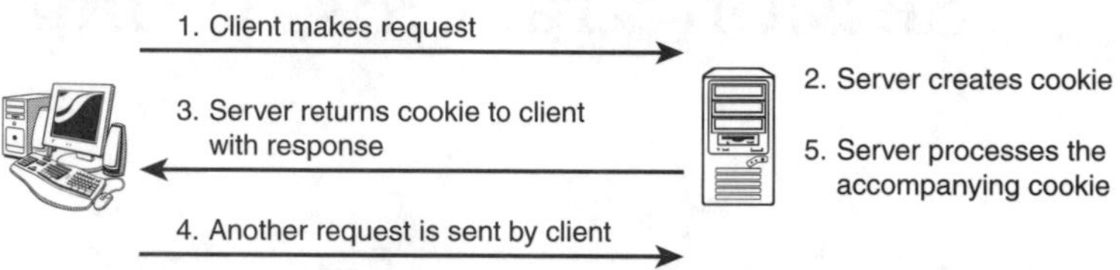

Figure 8.1 This is how cookies work.

A server adding the following to the HTTP header could leave a session cookie on a client machine:

```
Set-Cookie: favoriteColor=red; path=/colors; domain=www.contentmaster.com;
expires=Wednesday, 05-Feb-04 00:00:01 GMT
```

The previous header contains the following information:

- `favoriteColor=red`—This defines the cookie name and value as `favoriteColor` and `red`, respectively.
- `path=/colors`—This defines the relative path that this cookie applies to. In this case, the client returns the cookie to the server when the client requests resources within the colors folder on the server.
- `domain=www.contentmaster.com`—This is the domain that set the cookie. An important point to note is that cookies can only be read by the domain that set them. Products from companies such as Netegrity enable you to use cookies across domains if you have more than one. Say `www.mydomain.com` and `www.mydomain.co.uk`. This is important for applications requiring single-point sign on.
- `expires=Wednesday, 05-Feb-04 00:00:01 GMT`—This is the time that the cookie will expire.

Interacting with Cookies from JSP

JSP technology does enable you to interact with cookies. There is a `javax.servlet.http.Cookie` class that can be instantiated. Instances can then be used to leave cookies on the client with the `addCookie(Cookie cookie)` method of the `HttpServletResponse`.

Listing 8.1 provides an example of a basic JSP that will store a cookie on the client machine.

Listing 8.1 `cookies.jsp`

```
<%@ page import="javax.servlet.http.Cookie" %>
<html>
<head>
<title>This page leaves a cookie</title>
</head>

<body>
<h1>Cookies</h1>

<%
  Cookie[] allCookies = request.getCookies();
  Cookie ourCookie = null;
  if (allCookies!=null)
  {
    for (int i=0; i<allCookies.length; i++)
    {
      if (allCookies[i].getName().equals("TestCookie"))
        {
          ourCookie = allCookies[i];
        }
    }
  }

  if (ourCookie == null)
  {
    Cookie cookie = new Cookie("TestCookie", "hello from cookie");
    response.addCookie(cookie);
%>
    A cookie has been added to your machine!
    <br>Select refresh to see the details of this cookie.

<%
  }
  else
  {
%>
    The following cookie was added earlier to your machine:
    <br>Version: <%=ourCookie.getVersion() %>
    <br>Name: <%=ourCookie.getName() %>
    <br>Value: <%=ourCookie.getValue() %>
    <br>MaxAge: <%=ourCookie.getMaxAge() %>
<%
```

Listing 8.1 **Continued**

```
  }
%>

</body>
</html>
```

> **Note**
>
> The listings found in the first part of this chapter are available at the book's Web site. Go to `www.samspublishing.com` and enter the book's ISBN number (0672324385). The code is part of the Web application `chapter08.war`.

The first scriptlet in this example is used to obtain the current cookie information. This is done with a call to the `getCookies()` on the `HttpServletRequest` object. This array is then queried to obtain our test cookie if it exists.

The example JSP then creates the new cookie object, providing both a name and a value for the cookie. This block is only invoked when the cookie does not already exist.

At the foot of the page, the cookie information is displayed. This is only invoked when the cookie exists.

Thus, when you first visit this page in a browser, the output states that a cookie has been added to your machine. However, when a subsequent visit is made, the cookie information is displayed. See Figure 8.2 to see the output.

> **Note**
>
> The lifetime for this cookie ends when the browser is closed. The `maxAge` value of -1, which is seen in Figure 8.2, denotes this. Persistent cookies, which will be discussed later, must be used to enable cookies to persist beyond this.

Cookie Versions

Both Internet Explorer and Netscape browsers understand cookies. There are, however, two different versions of cookies: version 0, which is the original Netscape specification, and also a more recent version referred to as RFC 2109. The standards are defined at the following URLs:

- RFC 2109: `http://www.ietf.org/rfc/rfc2109.txt`
- Version 0: `http://www.netscape.com/newsref/std/cookie_spec.html`

You can also find information on cookies at

`http://www.cookiecentral.com`

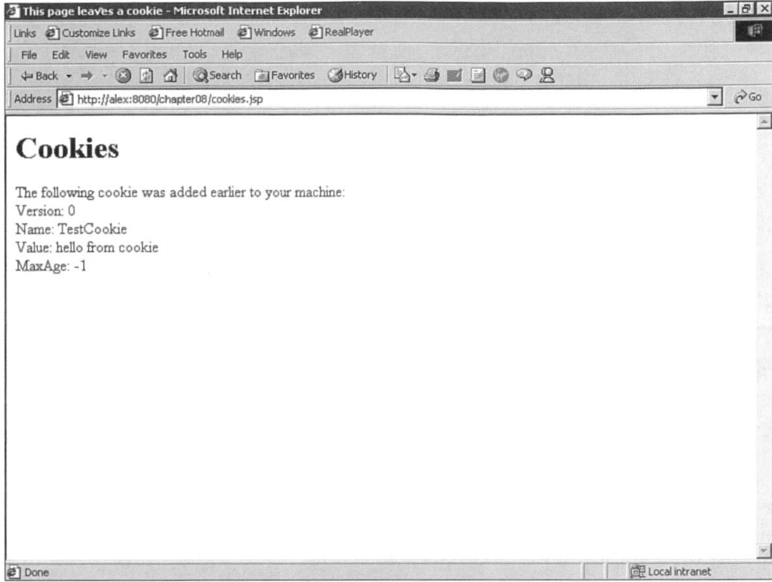

Figure 8.2 The output from Listing 8.1 after a cookie has been created.

You have control over the version of your cookie with the following two methods:

```
void setVersion (int version)
int getVersion()
```

The accepted version numbers are 0 for the original Netscape specification, and 1 for the new RFC 2109. Currently, 2109 is not widely in use, but it may well become more popular in the future. The default is version 0.

Cookie Comments and Cookie Security

Cookies can also have comments set for them, which are typically used to describe the purpose of the cookie. Cookie comments are set and retrieved with the following methods:

```
void setComment (String comment)
String getComment()
```

It is also possible to specify that a cookie be sent using a secure protocol. HTTP on its own is not a secure protocol, and it might be that your cookie must only be sent over a secure protocol. To ensure that a cookie is only sent over a secure protocol such as HTTPS, you can use the method:

```
void setSecure (boolean bool)
```

To query a cookie to identify whether it is only to be sent over a secure protocol you can use the following:

```
boolean getSecure()
```

A more detailed discussion on Web security can be found in Chapter 16, "Security and JSP."

Persistent Cookies

Cookies can be created to live beyond the lifetime of a browser session. Sites such as `http://www.amazon.com` use these cookies. Sites that use these cookies remember users even after the browser has been shut down.

To create a persistent cookie using JSP, you will need to set the `maxAge` property. This property is an `int`, specifying the number of seconds that this cookie should last. The following line of code could be added to Listing 8.1 at the point where our cookie is created.

```
cookie.setMaxAge(1800);
```

If you add this line and load the page again, it should result in the same output. The difference will be when you restart the browser. When you restart, it should still display a page similar to Figure 8.2. The cookie has survived. In fact, it will survive for 1,800 seconds! You might notice that the `maxAge` value shown in the Web page remains on –1. This is an issue with the implementation not returning the `maxAge` correctly.

When cookies are persistent, they have to be saved somewhere as a text file. Internet Explorer 6 on Windows XP, for example, saves the cookie file as a text file with the name as follows:

```
<user name>@<domain specific identifier>.txt.
```

This file will be placed into the `Cookies` folder under your user folder within the `Documents and Settings` folder.

So for this example, it would be as follows:

```
C:\Documents and Settings\Nick Todd\Cookies\nick todd@chapter08[1].txt
```

The saved persistent cookie from my computer referred to previously looked like this:

```
TestCookie
hello+from+cookie
localhost/chapter08/
1024
332579840
29481335
3808816320
29481330
*
```

Cookie Limitations

Cookies are not the only way to track user interactions. In fact, a significant number of Web users have cookies disabled within their browsers. Some large corporate organizations, for example, disable cookies in the browsers of all their staff. Depending on which surveys you believe, anywhere between 10% and 40% of browser users have cookies disabled. It is also worth noting that not all handheld devices support the use of cookies.

The main reasons for people deliberately disabling cookies are concerns about privacy. Some companies use cookies to provide targeted banner advertising. Practices such as these, combined with misinformation about what cookies actually are, have contributed to many individuals and organizations disabling cookies. There are reasons to be concerned though. Both Netscape and Internet Explorer have needed patches to be installed to prevent the malicious stealing of cookies from client machines. The following URLs from news sites contain articles about the vulnerabilities of both IE and Netscape:

- IE—`http://www.idg.net/go.cgi?id=633629`
- Netscape—`http://www.cnn.com/2002/TECH/internet/01/30/netscape.flaw.idg/index.html`

The problem facing developers is this: What do I do if some of my clients have disabled cookies? There is an alternative mechanism, called URL rewriting, which can be used to track users in your site.

URL Rewriting

URL rewriting is essentially the rewriting of every URL contained within a Web page being delivered by your server. Take the following basic HTML examples.

Here is `page1.htm`:

```
<html>
<head>
<title>Page 1</title>
</head>
<body>
<h1>URL Re-writing Demo</h1>
<a href="page2.htm">Click here</a> to visit page 2.
</body>
</html>
```

This page contains a hyperlink to `page2.htm`, which looks like the following:

```
<html>
<head>
<title>Page 2</title>
</head>
<body>
```

```
<h1>URL Re-writing Demo</h1>
<a href="page1.htm">Click here</a> to visit page 1.
</body>
</html>
```

Assuming cookies are disabled in the browsers, as users click through each of these pages, there is no way of differentiating one user from another. If, however, these pages were dynamically modified for each user with all URLs now containing a unique identifier, then whenever a user clicks a link, this unique identifier can be extracted to identify the user when the request reaches the server.

To encode a URL with the session identifier, there is a method in the `HttpServletResponse` object called `encodeURL(String url)`. This method takes in a String to represent the URL to be encoded, and then adds the session identifier to the end of the URL. Here is `page1.htm` rewritten as a JSP with the URL encoded:

```
<html>
<head>
<title>Page 1</title>
</head>
<body>
<h1>URL Re-writing Demo</h1>
<a href="<%=response.encodeURL("page2.htm")%>">Click here</a> to visit page 2.
</body>
</html>
```

When this page is viewed in a browser, selecting View/Source from the menu reveals what has happened to the URL:

```
<html>
<head>
<title>Page 1</title>
</head>
<body>
<h1>URL Re-writing Demo</h1>
<a href="page2.htm;jsessionid=4FC337A8E5579635B11D4E09BE0AEF74">
               Click here</a> to visit page 2.
</body>
</html>
```

Note that the URL now has the session ID on the end. This can be used to identify the current session on the server. URL rewriting is not as sophisticated as using cookies. Here are some of the limitations of using URL rewriting:

- It does not support storing name/value pairs on the client like cookies can.
- It does not support the persistence of a session after a browser shutdown like persistent cookies can.
- You lose the session if only one URL has failed to be rewritten, or if the user manually enters a URL to one of your pages.

The key benefit of URL rewriting is that it works in every browser! The rewriting of the URLs happens on the server, so any client application can be used.

So, given these two alternative approaches to session tracking, which should you use? In summary, the best approach is to use cookies if possible, but default to URL rewriting if cookies are not supported. If you are using an application server, this may well be taken care of for you. You will need to modify a configuration somewhere.

The Session Object

The JSP specification provides a higher-level object that you can interact with that maintains information about the current session. This is the `session` object (an implicit object that can be accessed from within a JSP). This means that for the developer, you can avoid having to interact with cookies directly. The Web container maintains the session objects for you, and the container uses either cookies or URL rewriting to do this.

Web containers provide a class to represent a session with a client. This is very similar to the session object provided with ASP and ASP.NET, for those of you familiar with those technologies.

The session object is of type `jaxax.servlet.http.HttpSession`. The container vendor implements this interface, and each user within a site can be assigned a session object on the server. The session object has two key roles:

- It stores information about the creation time and last accessed time for a particular session, along with a unique ID for the session.
- It also enables other objects to be tied to the session, such as shopping carts, and so on.

When a session is created, typically by way of a user visiting a Web site, a session object is created on the server, which can then be used to track the user through the site.

If you have read Chapter 6, "JSP and JavaBeans," you will recall the session-scoped beans. These are maintained using the session object being discussed here. Let's look at how you interact with session objects.

A basic JSP (`SessionObject.jsp`) is shown below that displays information about the session object to the user. Note that the session object is one of the predefined variables that you have access to directly from a JSP page:

```
<html>
<head>
<title>The Session Object</title>
</head>
<body>
<h1>The Session Object</h1>
Here are some properties of your session object.
<br>The session was created at <%= session.getCreationTime() %>
<br>The session has an inactive interval of
```

```
                <%= session.getMaxInactiveInterval() %>
<br>The session id is <%= session.getId() %>
</body>
</html>
```

This page displays information about the session object, but you can do a great deal more than that!

Consider Listings 8.2, 8.3, and 8.4. The scenario is a training company enabling users to ask for further information regarding their courses. The first page is an HTML form that the user will complete to request further information, and the second is the page that will create a session-scoped object containing that data and bind it to the session object. The third listing is the bean that is being used to store the data.

Listing 8.2 `moreCourseInfo.htm`

```
<html>
<head>
<title>Request More Information</title>
</head>
<body>
<h1>More Information</h1>
Please use this basic form to select the course
that you would like further information on.

<form method="get" action="moreInformationRequest.jsp">
<br>
<input type="radio" name="courses" value="Java Programming"> Java Programming
<br>
<input type="radio" name="courses" value="Java Web Development">
                   Java Web Development
<br>
<input type="radio" name="courses" value="J2EE Development"> J2EE Development
<br>
<input type="radio" name="courses" value="XML Introduction"> XML Introduction
<br><input type="radio" name="courses" value="XML Schema"> XML Schema
<br><input type="radio" name="courses" value="Web Services"> Web Services

  <p>First name: <input type="text" name="firstName">
  <br>Last name: <input type="text" name="lastName">
  <br>Email: <input type="text" name="email">

  <p><input type="submit" name="Submit">
</form>
</body>
</html>
```

Listing 8.3 moreInformationRequest.jsp

```
<%@ page import="com.conygre.courses.*"%>
<html>
<head>
<title>Thankyou for your request</title>
</head>
<body>
<h1>Thankyou for your request</h1>
Thankyou for your request for more information.
It will be sent to you shortly.
<%
  MoreInfoRequest infoRequest = new MoreInfoRequest();
  infoRequest.setCourses(request.getParameter("courses"));
  infoRequest.setFirstName(request.getParameter("firstName"));
  infoRequest.setLastName(request.getParameter("lastName"));
  infoRequest.setEmail(request.getParameter("email"));

  // this is the method that will bind an object to a session
  session.setAttribute("infoRequest", infoRequest);
%>
<p>Click <a href="displayYourRequest.jsp">here</a> to view your request.
</body>
</body>
</html>
```

Listing 8.4 MoreInfoRequest.java

```
package com.conygre.courses;

public class MoreInfoRequest
{
  public String getFirstName() {
    return firstName;
  }
  public void setFirstName(String firstName) {
    this.firstName = firstName;
  }

  public String getLastName() {
    return lastName;
  }
  public void setLastName(String lastName) {
    this.lastName = lastName;
  }
```

Listing 8.4 **Continued**

```
  public String getCourses() {
    return courses;
  }
  public void setCourses(String courses) {
    this.courses = courses;
  }

  public String getEmail() {
    return email;
  }
    public void setEmail(String email) {
    this.email = email;
  }

  private String firstName;
  private String lastName;
  private String email;
  private String courses;
}
```

The JSP in Listing 8.3 has two functions. First, it creates a `MoreInfoRequest` object, which is a simple JavaBean with `get` and `set` properties for the `course`, `firstName`, `lastName`, and `email`. This bean is shown in Listing 8.4. The page then associates the new object with the session object using the `setAttribute(String name, Object value)` method. The two parameters are a String for the name of the object, and the other parameter is the object reference that you want to bind.

> **Note**
> In earlier versions of JSP, the method `setValue()` was used with a corresponding `getValue()` for binding and retrieving objects from the `session` object. These methods have been deprecated in favor of `getAttribute()` and `setAttribute()`.

Listing 8.5 shows a JSP that now retrieves the object from the session and displays the properties.

Listing 8.5 `displayYourRequest.jsp`

```
<%@ page import="com.conygre.courses.*"%>
<html>
<head>
<title>Your request</title>
</head>
<body>
<h1>Your Request</h1>
```

Listing 8.5 **Continued**

```
Here is the information that you submitted to us for processing.
<%
  MoreInfoRequest infoRequest =
            (MoreInfoRequest) session.getAttribute("infoRequest");
%>
<br>Course name:<b> <%=infoRequest.getCourses()%></b>
<br>Your name: <b><%=infoRequest.getFirstName()%>
<%=infoRequest.getLastName()%></b>
<br>Your email: <b><%=infoRequest.getEmail()%></b>
</body>
</html>
```

Note that in the previous listing the bound object is retrieved using the `getAttribute()` method.

If you recall from the earlier chapter on using JavaBeans, you saw the standard action tags that can be used to interact with JavaBeans. Listing 8.6 is a JSP that does exactly the same as Listing 8.3, but uses standard action tags instead of directly interacting with the session object. If you wish to try Listing 8.6, you will need to modify the `action` attribute of the form in Listing 8.2. Having now seen how the session object works, you should now understand what is going on when session-scoped beans are accessed using the standard actions.

Listing 8.6 `moreInformationRequestWithBean.jsp`

```
<%@ page import="com.conygre.courses.*"%>
<jsp:useBean id="infoRequest" scope="session"
type="MoreInfoRequest"/>
<jsp:setProperty name="infoRequest" property="*"/>
<html>
<head>
<title>Thankyou for your request</title>
</head>
<body>
<h1>Thankyou for your request</h1>
Thankyou for your request for more information.
It will be sent to you shortly.
<p>Click <a href="displayYourRequest.jsp">here</a> to view your request.
</body>
</html>
```

In the previous example, the properties of the bean are set using the `setProperty` standard action, with the property set to be `*`. This results in the request parameters with names identical to the bean property names passed directly to the bean instance.

Terminating a Session

Sessions will always have a timeout allocated to them as discussed previously. This defaults to half an hour, or 1,800 seconds. However, you might want to explicitly terminate a session, typically when a user hits a logout button. This can be done using the `invalidate()` method on a session object.

This `invalidate()` method will terminate the session, and also unbind any session-scoped objects. Listing 8.7 is a JSP that can be used to invalidate a session.

Listing 8.7 `logout.jsp`

```
<html>
<head>
<title>Log out</title>
</head>
<body>
<h1>Log Out Page</h1>
<%
if (session != null) {
  session.invalidate();
}
%>
You are now logged out. Bye
</body>
</html>
```

This is a very straightforward page, and to enable users to log out you would simply provide links to this page

Sessions and Events

There might be things that you want to happen within your application when sessions start and finish. Consider the concept of a wish list, which many online stores have. They are one of the cleverest bits of marketing on the Internet. The customer thinks the site is doing them a favor by enabling her to make a list of all the things that she wants to buy, but for the site owners, it is invaluable marketing information!

The problem the site developer has, however, is when to save the wish list. The business development team will not want to lose the information contained within the wish list, but the developers will not want to have every entry to the wish list saved to a database each time an entry is added. Although you will want to save it, to do it every time it changes will not be good for performance reasons. So when do you save it? The answer might be when the session is finished or expired. This is where session-based events can come in very useful.

It is possible with JSP to initiate callbacks to session-bound objects when a session is terminated; in other words, cause a method to be invoked when sessions end.

There is an interface in the Servlet API:

```
javax.servlet.http.HttpSessionBindingListener
```

This interface can be implemented by objects that need to be informed of the binding and unbinding of objects to sessions. The interface has only two methods:

```
void valueBound (HttpSessionBindingEvent evt)
void valueUnbound(HttpSessionBindingEvent evt)
```

These methods are invoked when objects are bound and unbound, respectively.

Here is an example of what we're discussing. Listing 8.8 is a basic JSP form that adds items to a wish list.

Listing 8.8 `wishListForm.jsp`

```
<html>
  <head>
    <title>WishList</title>
    <jsp:useBean class="com.conygre.WishList" id="wishList" scope="session"/>
    <jsp:useBean class="com.conygre.WishListItems" id="wishListItems"
      scope="application" />
  </head>
  <body>
    Please Select items for your WishList:<br>
    <form method="post" action="wishList.jsp">
      <input type="checkbox" name="<%=wishListItems.getItem(0).getId()%>"/>
      <%=wishListItems.getItem(0).getName()%>
      <br>
      <input type="checkbox" name="<%=wishListItems.getItem(1).getId()%>"/>
      <%=wishListItems.getItem(1).getName()%>
      <br>
      <input type="checkbox" name="<%=wishListItems.getItem(2).getId()%>"/>
      <%=wishListItems.getItem(2).getName()%>
      <br>
      <input type="checkbox"
name="<%=wishListItems.getItem(3).getId()%>"/><%=wishListItems.getItem(3).getName(
)%>
      <br>
      <input type="checkbox"
name="<%=wishListItems.getItem(4).getId()%>"/><%=wishListItems.getItem(4).getName(
)%>
      <br>
      <input type="submit" value="Add to My WishList">
    </form>
    <p><a href="wishList.jsp">Show me my wishlist</a>
    <p><a href="logout.jsp">Log Out</a>
  </body>
</html>
```

Note that in the code there are two beans being used: one is a wish list, and the other is a basic bean containing a number of individual wish list items.

The form submits the data to another JSP called `wishlist.jsp` shown in Listing 8.9. You will note here that the wish list itself is implemented as a `java.util.Set`. A `Set` is an unordered list without duplicates, which is ideal for a wish list!

Listing 8.9 `wishList.jsp`

```
<%@ page import="java.util.*" %>
<html>
  <head>
    <title>WishList</title>
    <jsp:useBean class="com.conygre.WishList" id="wishList" scope="session"/>
    <jsp:useBean class="com.conygre.WishListItems"
     id="wishListItems" scope="application" />
  </head>
  <body>
    <% Enumeration e = request.getParameterNames(); %>
    <% Set map = wishList.getMap(); %>
    <% while(e.hasMoreElements()){
      String key = (String)e.nextElement();
        if(key.equals(wishListItems.getItem(0).getId())){
          map.add(wishListItems.getItem(0));
        }
        if(key.equals(wishListItems.getItem(1).getId())){
          map.add(wishListItems.getItem(1));
        }
        if(key.equals(wishListItems.getItem(2).getId())){
          map.add(wishListItems.getItem(2));
        }
        if(key.equals(wishListItems.getItem(3).getId())){
          map.add(wishListItems.getItem(3));
        }
        if(key.equals(wishListItems.getItem(4).getId())){
          map.add(wishListItems.getItem(4));
        }
      } %>
      Items currently In your Wish List:<br>
      <% if(map.size()==0){ %>
           There are no items in your Wish List<br>
 <%        }
      else {
        Set set = map; %>
        <% if (set!=null){
            com.conygre.Item[] keys = new com.conygre.Item[0];
            keys = (com.conygre.Item[])set.toArray(keys);
```

Listing 8.9 **Continued**

```
            for (int i=0;i<keys.length;i++){ %>
              <%=keys[i].getName()%><%="<br>"%>
    <%        }
            }
        }%>
    <br><a href="wishListForm.jsp">Add another Item</a>
  </body>
</html>
```

This JSP sets up the wish list object. The use of the `HttpSessionBindingListener` is in the class, `WishList.java`, shown in Listing 8.10.

Listing 8.10 `WishList.java`

```
package com.conygre;
import javax.servlet.http.HttpSessionBindingListener;
import javax.servlet.http.HttpSessionBindingEvent;
import java.util.Set;
import java.util.HashSet;
import java.util.Iterator;

public class WishList implements HttpSessionBindingListener {
  private Set map = new HashSet();
  public Set getMap(){
    return map;
  }

  //Session binding methods
  public void valueBound(HttpSessionBindingEvent e){
    System.out.println("The WishList has been Bound!");
  }

  public void valueUnbound(HttpSessionBindingEvent e){
    Item[] keys = new Item[0];
    System.out.println("Getting values...");
    Iterator it = map.iterator();
    while(it.hasNext()){
      Item item = (Item)it.next();
      System.out.println(item.getName());
    }
  }
}
```

The two methods, `valueBound()` and `valueUnbound()`, will be invoked now by the container when objects of type `WishList` are bound and unbound from the session. You can see in this example that the binding and unbinding of objects results in the wish list being written out to the console, but you could be doing a variety of things from these methods, such as persisting and retrieving the wish list to and from a database. The complete wish list demonstration is available through the book's Web site at `www.samspublishing.com`.

`HttpSession` Object Summary

Now you have seen how the session object works, Table 8.1 presents a summary of the session object methods.

Table 8.1 **Core Methods of the `javax.servlet.http.HttpSession` Interface**

Method Name	Description
Object getAttribute(String name)	Returns the object bound to the session with this specific name. Returns null if no object is bound with that name.
void setAttribute(String name, Object value)	Binds the object passed as a parameter to the session with the name defined by the String parameter.
Enumeration getAttributeNames()	Returns all bound attribute names as an array of Strings.
void removeAttribute(String name)	Unbinds an object from the session object.
long getCreationTime()	Returns the time the session was created in milliseconds since 1 January 1970 GMT.
String getId()	Returns the session identifier as a String.
long getLastAccessedTime()	Returns the time the session was last accessed in milliseconds since 1 January 1970 GMT.
int getMaxInactiveInterval()	Returns how long in seconds this session will remain active while the user remains inactive.
void setMaxInactiveInterval(int interval)	Sets how long in seconds this session will remain active while the user remains inactive.
void invalidate()	Terminates the session and unbinds any objects that are bound to it.
ServletContext getServletContext()	Returns the current ServletContext for this session.
boolean isNew()	Returns true if the current session is not being used by the client

We need to mention one last thing about the `HttpSession` object. What if you want your sessions to persist after the browser has been shut down? What modifications do you need to make to your Web application? To make your sessions persist, you must set the maximum timeout for the cookie. The problem is that if you are only working with the session object, you do not have direct access to the cookie's `maxAge` property. However, there is a workaround, which is to create a cookie using the following code:

```
<% Cookie sessionCookie = new Cookie("JSESSIONID", session.getId());
sessionCookie.setMaxAge(3600);
sessionCookie.setPath("/shoppingCart");
response.addCookie(sessionCookie);
%>
```

This will create a cookie with exactly the same name and value as Tomcat does under the covers. It essentially overwrites the Tomcat cookie with the `maxAge` value set in the code. A very useful tip if you are a Tomcat user!

Keeping Track of Your Session Objects

Web applications need to provide live information, such as how many sessions are currently running, and so on, to the people who manage a Web site. This is important for things such as maintenance, where servers need to be taken down for whatever reason, and also to enable the business team to view information like how many users are currently accessing the site at any given time.

To do this, you need to provide a mechanism to track and possibly identify the current live sessions on your server.

First, you'll see how to create and define a class that will inform you how many live sessions currently exist on your server.

> **Note**
>
> If you are using an application server such as Web Logic, or SunOne, there will be facilities that do this for you already, so check the documentation. If you are using Tomcat, however, you will need to implement your own solution as shown later.

Earlier in the chapter you were introduced to the `HttpSessionBindingListener`. Listeners of this type listened for objects being bound and unbound from sessions. You will now be introduced to another listener type, the `javax.servlet.http.SessionListener` interface.

Using a `SessionListener`

A session listener has two methods:

```
void sessionCreated (HttpSessionEvent evt)
void sessionDestroyed(HttpSessionEvent evt)
```

Listing 8.11 is an example of a basic `SessionListener` implementation that will keep track of how many sessions are currently active.

Listing 8.11 `SessionCount.java`

```
package com.conygre;

import javax.servlet.http.*;

public class SessionCount implements HttpSessionListener
{
  private static int numberOfSessions = 0;

  public void sessionCreated (HttpSessionEvent evt)
  {
    numberOfSessions++;
  }

  public void sessionDestroyed (HttpSessionEvent evt)
  {
    numberOfSessions--;
  }

  // here is our own method to return the number of current sessions
  public static int getNumberOfSessions()
  {
    return numberOfSessions;
  }
}
```

In this code example, note that the class implements the `HttpSessionListener` interface, and contains the two methods. Note the static variable `numberOfSessions`. This variable is incremented and decremented as sessions are created and destroyed. The class provides a basic accessor method to return this variable.

The question to be addressed now is how to set this listener class up within our Web application. The solution is to define this class as a listener in the `web.xml` file for this application.

Various listeners can be defined in `web.xml` within the `<listeners>` elements. Each listener is specified within `<listener-class>` elements. A complete example of a suitable `web.xml` file for the listener in Listing 8.11 is as follows:

```
<?xml version="1.0" encoding="UTF-8"?>
<web-app xmlns="http://java.sun.com/xml/ns/j2ee"
   xmlns:xsi="http://www.w3.org/2001/XMLSchema-instance"
   xsi:schemaLocation="http://java.sun.com/xml/ns/j2ee
   http://java.sun.com/xml/ns/j2ee/web-app_2_4.xsd" version="2.4">
  <listener>
    <listener-class>com.conygre.SessionCount</listener-class>
  </listener>
</web-app>
```

The listener class then needs to be in the `classes` folder for your Web application.

The listener can now be used from within our JSPs. A `sessionCounter.jsp` follows that informs you how many current sessions are active within the server:

```
<html>
<head>
<title>Session Counter</title>
</head>
<body>
<h1>Session Counter</h1>
On this server, there are currently
<%=com.conygre.SessionCount.getNumberOfSessions()%> active sessions.
</body>
</html>
```

Figure 8.3 shows the page in a browser.

Figure 8.3 Session counter.

You can do more with this information than simply keep track of the number of sessions. The `HttpSessionEvent` parameter that is passed in to the event handling methods has one method, `getSession()`. This returns the session object, which you can then use to extract additional information such as creation time. Logs can therefore be created to store information such as when sessions are starting and ending.

Application server vendors typically provide this kind of functionality. Figure 8.4 shows a screenshot of how one J2EE application server displays session information to administrators of a Web application. The server we are showing is the Dynamo application server from ATG.

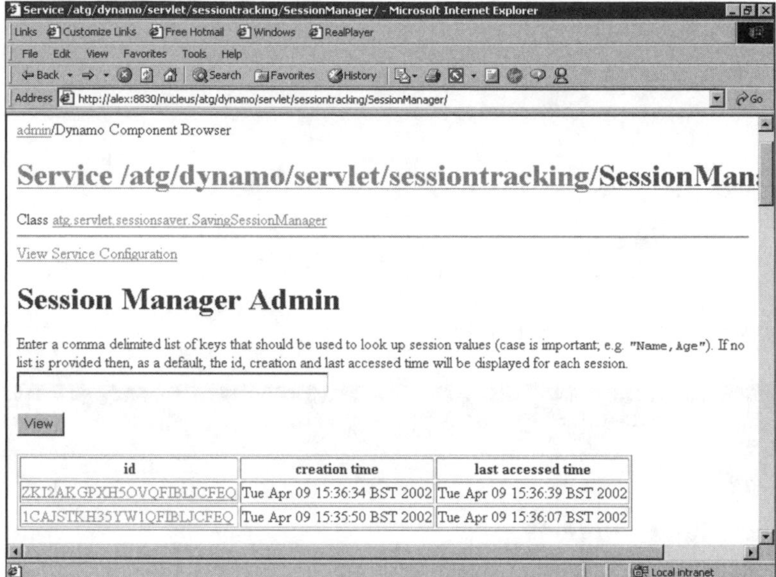

Figure 8.4 The Session Manager in the ATG Dynamo Application Server.

Session Failover

One issue that needs to be addressed is what happens if your server goes down while sessions are running. What happens to all the objects bound to the session? Imagine visiting your local grocery store with a full cart, and then someone from the store takes your cart away and tells you that you need to start again with an empty cart. You would not want to go back there in a hurry! This is what could happen to your online customers if you do not have a strategy for session failover.

Tomcat does not have any built in session failover support, which is a frustration to many developers (just take a look at some of the newsgroups!). However, if you are developing an application to run on one of the application servers such as Web Logic from BEA, Sun ONE, and so on, there is built in support for session failover.

To be able to have session failover, you really need at least two instances of your server running, ideally on different machines.

What the application servers provide for you is a mechanism by which the session information from one machine is backed up to the other machine throughout the duration of a session. If either machine goes down for some reason, the active sessions can be continued on the other machine using the backed-up data. Figure 8.5 shows the process.

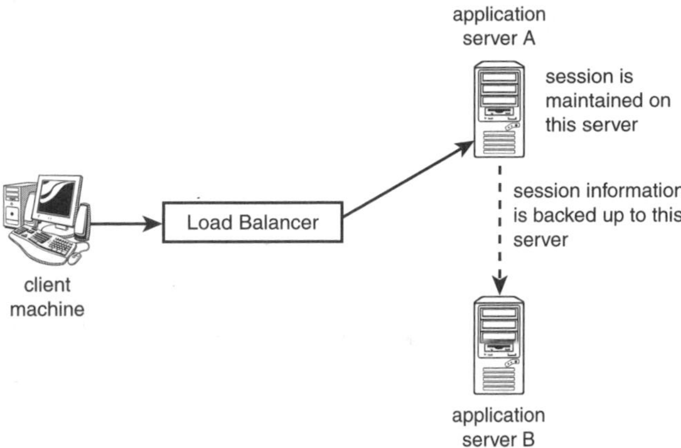

Figure 8.5 A typical session failover architecture.

In Figure 8.5 you will note the presence of a load balancer. The load balancer is there to spread the session load across all your servers. Application server vendors will typically provide this for you. In the diagram, the user has been assigned to application server A, and as they are navigating the site, maybe adding products to their shopping cart, that information is being backed up to application server B. If application server A goes down for some reason, application server B can pick up the sessions using the backed up data. This can be seen in Figure 8.6, which is based upon the same architecture as Figure 8.5.

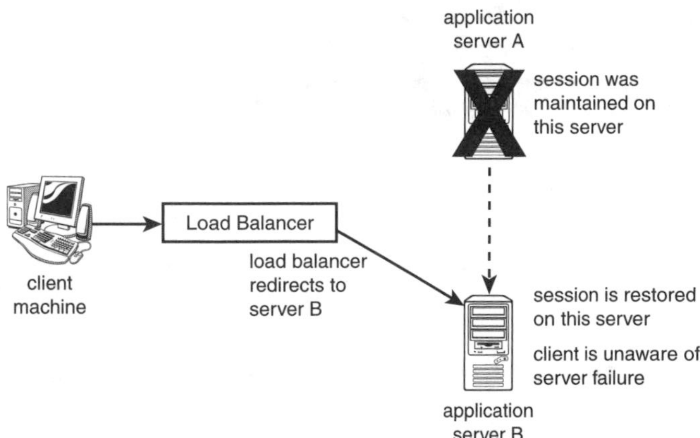

Figure 8.6 Resolving a server crash.

As you can see from the diagram, the load balancer automatically redirects the client to the appropriate available server, and then picks up the session from the backup information.

In terms of how this facility is achieved, the various application server vendors have adopted differing approaches. The following URLs provide further information for a selection of the server vendors:

- BEA Web Logic:

  `http://e-docs.bea.com/wls/docs61/cluster/servlet.html`
- Sun ONE:

  `http://docs.sun.com/source/816-7150-10/dwsessn.html#18285`
- ATG Dynamo:

  `http://www.atg.com/repositories/ContentCatalogRepository_en/manuals/ATG6.0.0/installdas/index.html`

When using a distributed session management solution, objects that are bound to sessions will need to be `Serializable` because they will need to be streamed to the other server VMs. This can also have performance implications if these objects are large, so you need to consider the size of objects that are going to be bound to sessions to avoid a negative impact on performance. This needs to be taken into account when planning the implementation of a site.

Configuring the distributed session management is done within most servers by either editing XML-based deployment files, or via a browser interface. Figure 8.7 shows the browser-based interface provided by the ATG Dynamo Application server.

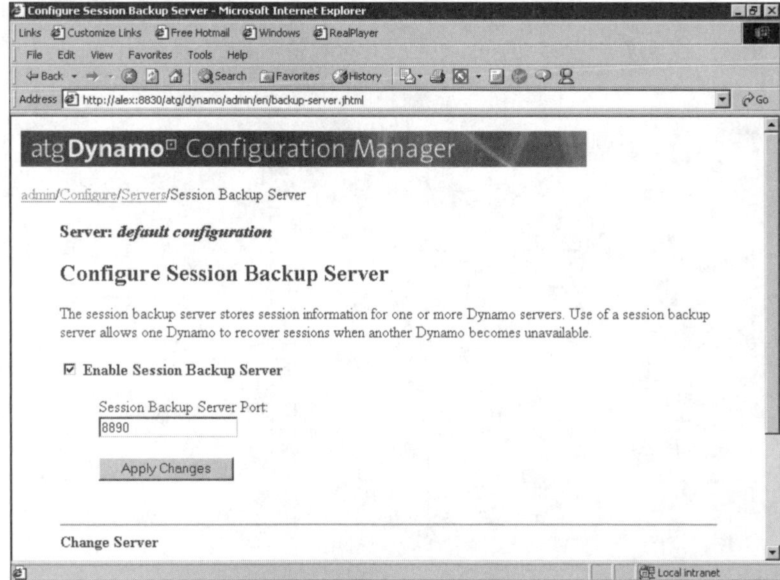

Figure 8.7 Configuring session backup in the ATG dynamo application server.

Shopping Cart Mini Case Study

For the remainder of this chapter, we'll walk through a shopping cart application, demonstrating how the information covered in this chapter can be applied to this specific scenario. Not every piece of code will be shown, but the complete example is available through the book's Web site at `www.samspublishing.com`. It is called `chapter08shoppingCart.war`. When deployed, visit the application on your server with the following URL:

```
http://localhost:8080/shoppingCart/
```

The application will consist of the following JSPs:

- A login page
- A number of product pages with the facility to make purchases
- A checkout page

There will also be a number of beans that will be used within the application:

- Beans to represent the items that are available—Books, Compact Discs, and DVDs
- A bean to represent the user
- A shopping cart bean and a bean to provide the capability to add items to the shopping cart
- A stock bean to contain the stock items

The site will use the model 2 architecture, so there is also a controller servlet to forward the requests to the appropriate JSPs.

The Beans

The individual product beans have basic properties with `get/set` methods as discussed in the beans chapter earlier in the book. The three product types `CompactDisc`, `DVD`, and `Book` all implement an interface, which is called `Item`:

```
package com.conygre;
public interface Item {
  String getTitle();
  double getPrice();
  String getId();
}
```

Normally, the actual products in a Web site such as this will come from a database. For simplicity, they are set up in a separate bean called `Stock.java`, which is shown in Listing 8.12. This bean is responsible for initializing all the product items.

Listing 8.12 `Stock.java`

```
package com.conygre;
public class Stock{
  private Book[] books;
  private CompactDisc[] cds;
  private DVD[] dvds;

  public Stock() {
    Initialiser init = new Initialiser();
    books = init.books();
    cds = init.cds();
    dvds = init.dvds();
  }

  public Book[] getBooks(){
    return books;
  }

  public CompactDisc[] getCds(){
    return cds;
  }

  public DVD[] getDvds(){
    return dvds;
  }
  // inner class to initialise the products for the stock
  class Initialiser {
    public Book[] books(){
      Book[] bookArray = {
        new Book("The Voyage of the Dawn Treader",4.99,"C.S. Lewis","1"),
        new Book("Linux Desk Reference",29.99,"Scott Hawkins","2"),
        new Book("Let the Nations Be Glad",5.99,"John Piper","3"),
        new Book("Treasure Island",3.99,"Robert Louis Stevenson","4"),
        new Book("How to Be a Great Guitarist",17.99,"Paul Hunnisett","5"),
        new Book("Heart of a Hooligan",4.99,"Muthena Paul Alkazraji","6"),
        new Book("Shogun",12.99,"James Clavell","7"),
        new Book("The Art of War",4.99,"Sun Tzu","8")
      };
      return bookArray;
    }

    public CompactDisc[] cds(){
      CompactDisc[] discArray = {
        new CompactDisc("Is This It",13.99,"The Strokes",11,"9"),
        new CompactDisc("Just Enough Education to Perform",10.99,
                                            "Stereophonics",11,"0"),
```

Listing 8.12 **Continued**

```
        new CompactDisc("Parachutes",11.99,"Coldplay",10,"a"),
        new CompactDisc("White Ladder",9.99,"David Gray",10,"b"),
        new CompactDisc("Greatest Hits",14.99,"Penelope",14,"c"),
        new CompactDisc("Echo Park",13.99,"Feeder",12,"d"),
        new CompactDisc("Mezzanine",12.99,"Massive Attack",11,"e")
        };
      return discArray;
    }

    public DVD[] dvds(){
      DVD[] filmArray = {
        new DVD("It's a Wonderful Life",7.99,"Frank Capra","f"),
        new DVD("Crouching Tiger, Hidden Dragon",15.99,"Ang Lee","g"),
        new DVD("Breakfast at Tiffany's",14.99,"Blake Edwards","h"),
        new DVD("Romeo Must Die",10.99,"Andrzej Bartowiak","i"),
        new DVD("Scent of a Woman",17.99,"Martin Brest","j"),
        new DVD("Snatch",18.99,"Guy Ritchie","k"),
        new DVD("Scarface",16.99,"Brian De Palma","l")
      };
      return filmArray;
    }
  }
}
```

This bean will be used to set up a series of products that can now be purchased.

The user is set up in a simple bean called `Person.java`. This bean has two simple properties called `name` and `password`, and it has `get` and `set` methods for these properties.

The cart is another bean that is also used from the pages. Listing 8.13 contains our `Cart` bean.

Listing 8.13 `Cart.java`

```
package com.conygre;
import java.util.Vector;
public class Cart {
  private Item[] items = new Item[0];
  public Item[] getItems(){
    return items;
  }

  public void setItems(Item item){
    Vector v = new Vector(1);
    for (int i=0;i<items.length;i++){
```

Listing 8.13 **Continued**

```
      v.add(items[i]);
    }
    v.add(item);
    items = (Item[])v.toArray(items);
  }

  public void setReset(){
    items = new Item[0];
  }

  public double getTotal(){
    double total = 0;
    for (int i=0;i<items.length;i++){
      total+=items[i].getPrice();
    }
    return total;
  }
}
```

You will notice that in this class there is an array property called `items` of type `Item`, which is the interface that all the product item types implement. An array has been used for simplicity; in a real scenario a `List` or `Vector` can be used instead. The three methods are described in Table 8.2.

Table 8.2 **The Methods of the `com.conygre.Cart` Class**

Method Name	Description
`void setItems()`	Puts a new item into the items array.
`void setReset()`	Empties the cart.
`double getTotal()`	Calculates, and then returns the total price of the cart.

The Controller Servlet

You have seen the beans containing the business logic. Our architecture also contains a controller servlet as described in the earlier architecture chapter. This servlet is shown in Listing 8.14.

Listing 8.14 `ShoppingCartController.java`

```
package com.conygre;
import java.io.*;
import javax.servlet.*;
import javax.servlet.http.*;
```

Listing 8.14 **Continued**

```
public class ShoppingCartController extends HttpServlet {

  public void init(ServletConfig config) throws ServletException {
    super.init(config);
    ServletContext application = getServletContext();
    Person user = new Person();
    user.setName(config.getInitParameter("username"));
    user.setPassword(config.getInitParameter("password"));
    application.setAttribute("user",user);
    Person person = new Person();
    person.setName("Guest");
    application.setAttribute("guest",person);
    application.setAttribute("stock",new Stock());
  }
  public void doGet(HttpServletRequest req, HttpServletResponse res)
            throws ServletException, IOException {
    doPost(req, res);
  }

  public void doPost(HttpServletRequest req, HttpServletResponse res)
            throws ServletException, IOException {
    HttpSession session = req.getSession();
    ServletContext application = getServletContext();
    if (session.getAttribute("currentUser") == null){
      session.setAttribute("currentUser", application.getAttribute("guest"));
      session.setAttribute("cart", new com.conygre.Cart());
    }
    String forward = req.getParameter("page");
    if (forward == null){
      RequestDispatcher rd = application.getRequestDispatcher("/welcome.jsp");
      rd.forward(req, res);
    }
    else {
      RequestDispatcher rd = application.getRequestDispatcher(forward);
      rd.forward(req, res);
    }
  }
}
```

This controller servlet has two main functions. It is forwarding requests to the appropriate JSPs, and it is initializing several attributes. Three are application-scoped, and two are session-scoped.

The three application-scoped components will be discussed first. Note the `void init(ServletConfig config)` method of the servlet. This method is invoked when the servlet is loaded, and it sets up three application-scoped components. One is a Stock bean for all the products, whereas the other two are Person objects. The reason for this is simply because databases are not being used in this application, and when users come to the site, they will need to be assigned to a particular user. Two users are set up; one is a Guest account, and the other is an actual account. The user will begin as a guest, but can log in as the user specified with the username and password, as shown here. Notice for the actual account, the user information is being extracted from what are called initialization parameters. These can be set in `web.xml` as shown here:

```
<servlet>
    <servlet-name>
        controller
    </servlet-name>
    <servlet-class>
        com.conygre.ShoppingCartController
    </servlet-class>
    <init-param>
        <param-name>username</param-name>
        <param-value>John</param-value>
    </init-param>
    <init-param>
        <param-name>password</param-name>
        <param-value>password</param-value>
    </init-param>
</servlet>
```

This enables the passing in of values to servlets through the deployment descriptor. In the next chapter, you'll see how users can be set up within a database.

Note

If you want to explore servlets in more detail, an excellent resource for learning more about how servlets work is *Developing Java Servlets* by James Goodwill and Brian Morgan from Sams Publishing.

In the `doPost()` method, you can see the session object being retrieved using the `getSession()` method of the `Request` object. It is then being checked for an attribute called `currentUser`. If this session attribute is `null`, this session must be a brand-new session, so it is assigned the guest account. This is then set as the attribute value for `currentUser`.

The other session-scoped object that is set up by the controller is the shopping cart for the user.

Table 8.3 summarizes the attributes set up by the controller and their respective scopes.

Table 8.3 **The Attributes Set Up by the `com.conygre.ShoppingCartController` Class**

Attribute Name	Scope and Description
`CurrentUser`	Session-scoped. Represents the current user in the application.
`Cart`	Session-scoped. Is an instance of the shopping cart.
`Stock`	Application-scoped. This object is the stock within the store. It is set as an application scoped attribute, so the user can access it from any page.
`User`	Application-scoped. This object represents the registered user account.
`Guest`	Application-scoped. This object represents the guest account.

The other role of the controller servlet is to forward requests on to the appropriate JSPs, which will be discussed next.

The JSPs

The JSPs in this application have been designed to include as little Java code as possible. They make extensive use of both the standard tag library and JavaBeans.

Figure 8.8 shows how the site looks when you visit the home page.

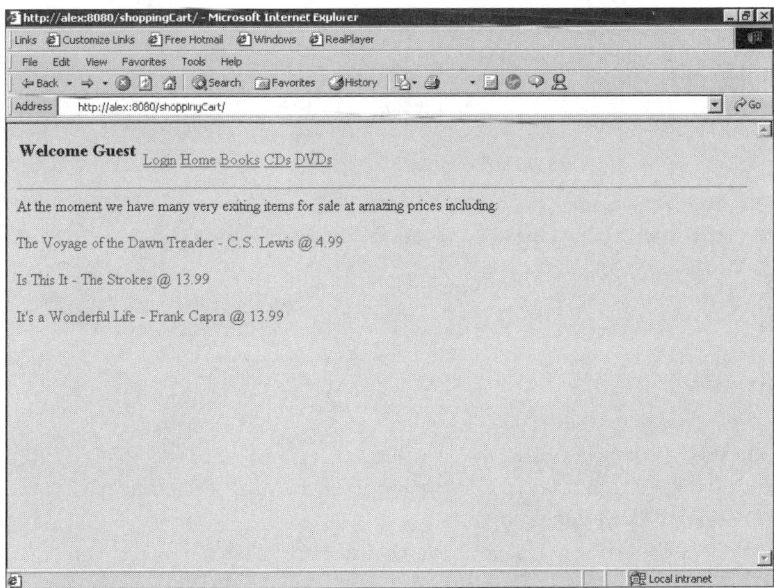

Figure 8.8 A screenshot showing the home page of the shopping site.

The top navigation part of this page is also visible on all pages, so it has been done as a page fragment, as shown in Listing 8.15.

Listing 8.15 `header.jsp`

```
<%@ taglib uri="http://java.sun.com/jstl-el/core" prefix="c" %>
<table>
  <tr>
    <td>
      <h3>Welcome <c:out value="${currentUser.name}"/></h3>
    </td>
    <td></td>
    <td>
      <c:if test="${currentUser.name == 'Guest'}">
        <a href="controller?page=/login.jsp">Login</a>
      </c:if>
    </td>
    <td>
      <a href="controller?page=/welcome.jsp">Home</a>
    </td>
    <td>
      <a href="controller?page=/books.jsp">Books</a>
    </td>
    <td>
      <a href="controller?page=/cd.jsp">CDs</a>
    </td>
    <td>
      <a href="controller?page=/dvd.jsp">DVDs</a>
    </td>
    <td>
      <c:if test="${currentUser.name != 'Guest'}">
        <a href="controller?page=/logout.jsp">Logout</a>
      </c:if>
    </td>
  </tr>
</table>
<hr>
```

Note in the listing that there is no Java in this header, and note too that all the links are to the controller servlet, but with a page parameter defining which page that the servlet is meant to forward the request to.

Listing 8.16 is the welcome page. Note that it incorporates `header.jsp`.

Listing 8.16 `welcome.jsp`

```
<html>
<%@ taglib uri="http://java.sun.com/jstl-el/core" prefix="c" %>
  <head>
    <title>Welcome to Ashdown.com - The best deals for Books, CDs and DVDs!
    </title>
```

Listing 8.16 **Continued**

```
  </head>
  <body bgcolor="#FFCC99">
    <c:import url="header.jsp" />
    At the moment we have many very exiting items
   for sale at amazing prices including:
    <font color="blue">
    <p><c:out value="${ stock.books[0].title}" /> -
    <c:out value="${ stock.books[0].author}" /> @
    <c:out value="${ stock.books[0].price}" />
    <p><c:out value="${ stock.cds[0].title}" /> -
    <c:out value="${ stock.cds[0].artist}" /> @
    <c:out value="${ stock.cds[0].price}" />
    <p><c:out value="${ stock.dvds[0].title}" /> -
    <c:out value="${ stock.dvds[0].director}" /> @
    <c:out value="${ stock.dvds[0].price}" />
</body>
</html>
```

You can also see from Listing 8.16 that the JSP Standard Tag Library is used here to display a selection of values from the application-scoped object called `stock`.

Listing 8.17 shows the JSP for the compact discs called `cd.jsp`. There would be a similar JSP (not shown) for DVDs and books.

Listing 8.17 `cd.jsp`

```
<html>
<%@ taglib uri="http://java.sun.com/jstl-el/core" prefix="c" %>
  <head>
    <title>Welcome to Ashdown.com - The best deals for Books, CDs and DVDs!
    </title>
  </head>
  <body bgcolor="#FFCC99">
    <c:import url="header.jsp" />
    <form method="post" action="controller?page=/addToCart.jsp">
      Please select the CDs you wish to add to your shopping cart:<br>
      <table>
        <tr>
          <td><b><font size="4">Title </font></b></td>
          <td><b><font size="4">Artist</font></b></td>
          <td><b><font size="4">Number of Tracks</font></b></td>
          <td><b><font size="4">Price</font></b></td>
        </tr>
        <c:forEach var="item" items="${stock.cds}">
          <tr>
            <td><input type="checkbox" name="id"
```

Listing 8.17 **Continued**

```
                value="<c:out value='${item.id}' />">
             <c:out value="${item.title}"/></td>
             <td><c:out value="${item.artist}"/></td>
             <td><c:out value="${item.tracks}"/></td>
             <td><font color="red"><c:out value="${item.price}"/></font></td>
          </tr>
         </c:forEach>
       </table>
      <input type="submit" value="Add to Cart">
     <form>
   </body>
</html>
```

This page creates a list of check boxes from which the users will select their purchases. The check boxes are part of an HTML form, which when submitted goes to `addToCart.jsp`. Figure 8.9 shows what `cd.jsp` looks like when shown in the browser.

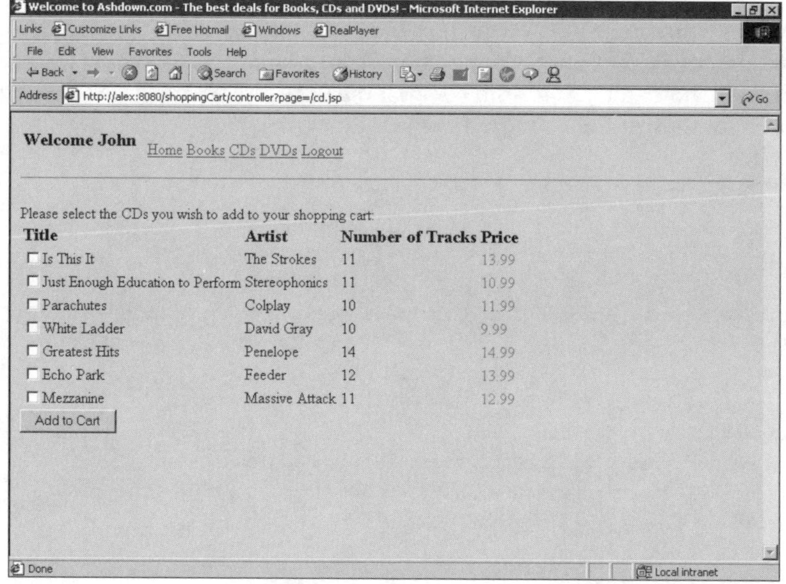

Figure 8.9 The product page `cd.jsp`, shown in a Web browser.

The `addToCart.jsp` (Listing 8.18) then lists the products that are currently in the shopping cart.

Listing 8.18 `addToCart.jsp`

```
<html>
  <head>
    <title>Welcome to Ashdown.com -
           The best deals for Books, CDs and DVDs!</title>
    <%@ taglib uri="http://java.sun.com/jstl-el/core" prefix="c" %>
    <jsp:useBean id="cart" class="com.conygre.Cart" scope="session"/>
    <jsp:useBean id="stock" class="com.conygre.Stock" scope="application" />
    <jsp:useBean id="add" class="com.conygre.AddToCart" scope="page"/>
  </head>
  <body bgcolor="#FFCC99">
    <c:import url="header.jsp" />
    <%
      String[] ids = request.getParameterValues("id");
      add.add(ids, cart, stock);
    %>
    The Items currently in your basket:<br>
    <ul>
      <c:forEach var="item" items="${cart.items}">
        <li><c:out value="${item.title}" /> @ <c:out value="${item.price}" /><br>
      </c:forEach>
    </ul>
    <p><b>Total</b> £<font color="red"><c:out value="${cart.total}"/>
     </font><br>
    <c:choose>
      <c:when test="${currentUser.name == 'Guest'}">
        <c:set var="currentPage" value="checkout" scope="session"/>
        You must be <a href="controller?page=/login.jsp">logged</a>
        in to purchase these items.
      </c:when>
      <c:otherwise>
        <c:set var="currentPage" value="checkout" scope="session"/>
        <a href="controller?page=/checkout.jsp">Proceed to checkout</a>
      </c:otherwise>
    </c:choose>
  </body>
</html>
```

This page is the most complex of all the pages. It is here that products are added to the cart. Note the `useBean` tags at the top of the page. The `cart` and `stock` beans are the ones created by the controller servlet. The bean with the `id` of `add` is a utility bean called `AddToCart.java` that we have created, which will invoke the `setItems()` method of the `Cart` bean (Listing 8.13). The source for `AddToCart.java` is shown in Listing 8.19.

The way that `addToCart.jsp` works is to create a `String` array of all the parameter values with the name `id`. The `add` method of the `AddToCart.java` utility bean, which contains the logic to actually populate the `cart` bean, is then invoked.

Notice too that it checks to see if users are logged in before giving the user the option to proceed to the checkout.

Listing 8.19 `AddToCart.java`

```
package com.conygre;
public class AddToCart {
  public void add(String[] ids, Cart cart, Stock stock){
    com.conygre.Book[] books = stock.getBooks();
    com.conygre.CompactDisc[] cds = stock.getCds();
    com.conygre.DVD[] dvds = stock.getDvds();
    for (int a=0;a<ids.length;a++){
      for (int b=0;b<stock.getBooks().length;b++){
        if (ids[a].equals(books[b].getId())){
          cart.setItems(books[b]);
        }
      }
      for (int b=0;b<stock.getCds().length;b++){
        if (ids[a].equals(cds[b].getId())){
          cart.setItems(cds[b]);
        }
      }
      for (int b=0;b<stock.getDvds().length;b++){
        if (ids[a].equals(dvds[b].getId())){
          cart.setItems(dvds[b]);
        }
      }
    }
  }
}
```

The checkout page lists the products that have been purchased, and then empties the cart. Listing 8.20 shows `checkout.jsp`.

Listing 8.20 `checkout.jsp`

```
<html>
  <head>
    <title>Welcome to Ashdown.com - The best deals for Books, CDs and DVDs!
    </title>
    <jsp:useBean id="cart" class="com.conygre.Cart" scope="session"/>
    <%@ taglib uri="http://java.sun.com/jstl-el/core" prefix="c" %>
  </head>
  <body bgcolor="#FFCC99">
```

Listing 8.20 **Continued**

```
    <c:import url="header.jsp" />
    <h1> Congratulations on your purchases!</h1>
    You have bought the following items:<p>
    <ul>
      <c:forEach var="item" items="${cart.items}">
        <li><c:out value="${item.title}" /> @ <c:out value="${item.price}" /><br>
      </c:forEach>
    </ul>
    <p><b>Total</b> £<font color="red"><c:out value="${cart.total}"/></font><br>
    <% cart.setReset();%>
  </body>
</html>
```

We have nearly seen the entire application now. The only part that has not been discussed yet is the logging in and logging out functionality. This is provided by three JSPs: one containing a login form, one is the page that the login form directs to, and the other is a logout page.

They are shown in Listings 8.21 to 8.23, respectively.

Listing 8.21 `login.jsp`

```
<html>
  <head>
    <title>Welcome to Ashdown.com - The best deals for Books, CDs and DVDs!
    </title>
  </head>
  <body bgcolor="#FFCC99">
    <form method="post" action="controller?page=/doLogin.jsp">
      User Name: <input type="text" name="user">
      Password: <input type="password" name="password">
      <input type="submit" value="login">
    </form>
  </body>
</html>
```

Listing 8.22 `doLogin.jsp`

```
<%@ taglib uri="http://java.sun.com/jstl-el/core" prefix="c" %>
<c:choose>
  <c:when test="${param.user == 'John' and param.password == 'password'}">
    <c:set var="currentUser" value="${user}" scope="session" />
    <c:choose>
      <c:when test="${currentPage == 'checkout'}">
        <c:set var="currentPage" value="none" scope="session"/>
        <c:redirect url="checkout.jsp"/>
```

Listing 8.22 **Continued**

```
      </c:when>
      <c:otherwise>
        <c:redirect url="controller"/>
      </c:otherwise>
    </c:choose>
  </c:when>
  <c:otherwise>
    Login failed please try <a href="controller?page=/login.jsp">again</a>
  </c:otherwise>
</c:choose>
```

Listing 8.23 `logout.jsp`

```
<%@ taglib uri="http://java.sun.com/jstl-el/core" prefix="c" %>
<c:set var="currentUser" value="${guest}" scope="session" />
<jsp:forward page="welcome.jsp"/>
```

You have now seen all the pages that make up our shopping cart application. Remember that the entire application is available through the book's Web site at `www.samspublishing.com` if you want to try it without typing it all.

Summary

Session tracking is a vital part of any Web application. In this chapter, you have learned the various strategies used to track sessions, namely cookies and URL rewriting. You have also learned how to use the session object to bind and unbind session-based objects. You have seen the shopping cart application that takes full advantage of the session object.

If you are using an application server, you will find that much of the hard work is done for you, but even then it is important that you understand the principles involved in tracking sessions.

9

Developing Custom Tag Libraries

HAVING COVERED HOW TO USE TAG LIBRARIES within a JSP in Chapter 5, "The JSP Standard Tag Library," this chapter will focus on how to develop your own custom tag libraries.

The lifecycle of the tag will be examined and also the syntax of the tag library descriptor file. The deployment of tag libraries and where they fit into a Web application will also be looked at.

> **Note**
>
> The examples contained in this chapter are all available as part of `chapter09.war`, which is part of the book download available from the book Web site. You can locate this by visiting `www.samspublishing.com` and entering the ISBN number (0672324385) in the search box.

Tag Extensions

The JSP specification has a section entitled *Tag Extensions* that describes a mechanism for creating new actions that can be used in a JSP. The mechanism consists of two parts: custom tags and custom tag libraries. A custom tag is an individual action, and a custom tag library is a collection of such actions. In this chapter, you will see how various components come together to provide a custom tag.

There are several design goals that the writers of the specification had for tag extensions, including

- The tags must be simple enough that nonprogrammers can use them.
- It must be possible to use the tags in any JSP-compliant container.
- The tag extension mechanism must be flexible enough to support a wide variety of custom actions. For example, actions that expose or use scripting variables, actions that have nested actions, and those actions that have scripting elements within their bodies.

In Chapter 5, you saw that to use a custom tag, you need to do just two things. The first is to use the `taglib` directive to tell the JSP which custom tag library you are using. The second thing you must do is use the custom tag itself. This part of the chapter begins by describing how to build some simple custom tags, and progresses to more complicated tags.

Writing a Custom Tag

Several steps must be taken to build and use a custom tag. For now, these steps can be limited to

1. Implementing a tag handler for the custom tag.
2. Writing a Tag Library Descriptor (TLD) document that describes the custom tag, for example its name, attributes, and body content.
3. Using the custom tag from a JSP.

Depending on how the tag behaves, you can have the tag handler implement one of three interfaces: `Tag`, `IterationTag`, or `BodyTag`. The `IterationTag` interface is a subinterface of `Tag`, and the `BodyTag` interface is a subinterface of the `IterationTag` interface.

To make it easier to write custom tag implementations, there are two utility classes that provide default implementations of the methods in these interfaces: `TagSupport` and `BodyTagSupport`. `TagSupport` implements both the `Tag` and `IterationTag` interfaces, whereas the `BodyTagSupport` class is a subclass of `TagSupport` that additionally implements the `BodyTag` interface.

Rather than describe each of these interfaces and classes at this point, each will be described as the different examples progress throughout the chapter. However, see Figure 9.1 for a simplified UML diagram that shows the relationship between these classes and interfaces.

The simplest type of custom action is a tag that has neither attributes nor body content. As with all actions, such a custom action is used to perform some kind of processing and maybe generate some output that is to be sent back to the client.

Expression Language Functions

Chapter 3 introduced the notion of functions that are available to the Expression Language in JSP 2.0. Such functions must be implemented as `public static` methods in the handler class. Before you see the other kinds of custom actions available to you, here is an example of how to write such a function.

It is actually rather simple; you only need to do two things:

- Describe the function in the TLD file.
- Implement the function using a `public static` Java method.

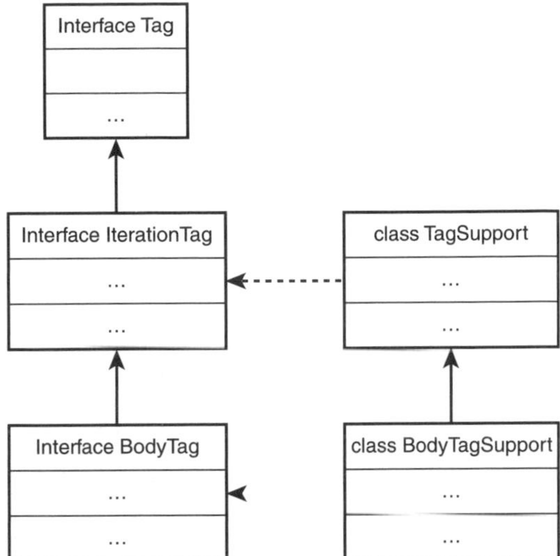

Figure 9.1 Simplified UML diagram for tag interfaces and support classes.

Look at the simple `ELFunctions` class in Listing 9.1, which defines a `reverse()` method that reverses a `String` that is passed to it, and passes back the result.

Listing 9.1 **A Class That Implements a `public static` Method (`ELFunctions.java`)**

```
package com.conygre.jspdevhandbook.chapter9;

public class ELFunctions
{
  public static String reverse(String param)
  {
    return new StringBuffer(param).reverse().toString();
  }
}
```

Note that the `reverse()` method is both `public` and `static`.

To describe this method in the TLD file, you need to add these lines of code to the TLD file:

```
<taglib ...>
    ...
    <function>
      <name>ReverseString</name>
      <function-class>com.conygre.jspdevhandbook.chapter9.ELFunctions</function-
class>
```

```
    <function-signature>String reverse(String)</function-signature>
  </function>
</taglib>
```

The `name` element is used to give a name to the actual tag that you will use in your JSPs. In this example, the tag name is `ReverseString`. The class that implements the method is named using the `function-class` element, and the method that implements the tag is named through the `function-signature` element.

Look at the JSP in Listing 9.2 to see how to use the function from the JSP Expression Language.

Listing 9.2 **A JSP that uses an EL Function (`elFunctions.jsp`)**

```
<%@ taglib uri="/chapter09TagLib" prefix="chapter09" %>

<html>
  <head>
    <title>Chapter 9 - An Expression Language Tag</title>
  </head>
  <body>
    This page uses an expression language tag that reverses a string passed to
    it. The handler function is a public static Java method. <br />
    Here is its output:
    <h1>${chapter09:ReverseString("!dlrow olleH")}</h1>
  </body>
</html>
```

An Empty Custom Action

For an empty tag that does not want to process any body content, the `Tag` interface is the one of interest. The `Tag` interface enables you to write a custom tag that performs processing for its start and end tags. If you need to process body content or iterate a number of times, you would implement one of the other two interfaces instead. For an empty custom tag such as the one discussed here, it is possible in the TLD to specify that the custom tag must have no body content. This will be shown after the tag handler has been written.

Consider the JSP in Listing 9.3, which uses a custom tag called `emptyTag`.

Listing 9.3 **A JSP That Uses an Empty Custom Tag (`emptyTag.jsp`)**

```
<%@ taglib uri="/chapter09TagLib" prefix="chapter09" %>

<html>
  <head>
    <title>Chapter 9 - A custom tag that is empty</title>
  </head>
```

Listing 9.3 **Continued**

```
  <body>
    This page uses a custom tag that has neither attributes nor body content.
    Here is its output:
    <h1><chapter09:emptyTag /></h1>
  </body>
</html>
```

The tag handler for this custom tag (`emptyTag`) will simply place some text into the output stream, that is displayed instead of the custom tag itself. When viewed, the JSP looks like the screenshot in Figure 9.2.

Figure 9.2 A JSP that uses the `emptyTag` custom tag.

The first line of Listing 9.3 references a tag library that is identified with the URI string `/chapter09TagLib`:

```
<%@ taglib uri="/chapter09TagLib" prefix="chapter09" %>
```

The JSP uses a custom tag from this library with the line of code that looks like this:

```
<h1><chapter09:emptyTag /></h1>
```

The `chapter09` prefix used by both the `taglib` directive and this line of code is arbitrary. This is because of the fact that if the custom tag library's author fixed the prefix, it would be possible to have a clash with other custom tag libraries that chose the same prefix. Thus, it is up to the page author to pick a prefix that does not clash with any other prefixes used on the page.

It should also be noted at this point that it is perfectly legal to use either XML closing-tag syntax. That is, the shorthand syntax for an empty element used in Listing 9.3 could have been replaced with the longhand form without affecting the result:

```
<h1><chapter09:emptyTag></chapter09:emptyTag></h1>
```

When you implement a custom tag, there is always one tag handler implementation per custom tag. The code for the tag handler for the `emptyTag` custom tag is shown in Listing 9.4. As stated earlier, all that the tag handler will do is place some text into the output stream, which replaces the custom tag in the JSP. In this case, the text is `in EmptyTag.doStartTag()`.

Listing 9.4 **The Tag Handler Code for the `emptyTag` Custom Tag (`EmptyTag.java`)**

```
package com.conygre.jspdevhandbook.chapter9;

import java.io.IOException;
import javax.servlet.jsp.JspException;
import javax.servlet.jsp.tagext.TagSupport;

public class EmptyTag extends TagSupport
{
  public int doStartTag() throws JspException
  {
    try
    {
      pageContext.getOut().print("in EmptyTag.doStartTag()");
    }
    catch (IOException e)
    {
      System.out.println("Error in EmptyTag.doStartTag()");
      e.printStackTrace();
      throw new JspException(e); // throw the error to the error page (if set)
    } // end of try-catch

    return SKIP_BODY;
  }
}
```

The `EmptyTag` class extends the utility `TagSupport` class, and overrides the inherited `doStartTag()` method. The `TagSupport` class is a utility class in the `javax.servlet.jsp.tagext` package. You subclass `TagSupport` whenever you want to write a tag handler for a tag that does not want to process any body content. In this example, the `doStartTag()` method simply returns `SKIP_BODY` to indicate that any body content should be ignored by the container. In the later examples of this chapter, you will see that you can include any body content "as is" by instead returning `EVAL_BODY_INCLUDE`.

Within the `doStartTag()` method, note that the `pageContext` variable is used even though you cannot see a declaration of it anywhere in the class. This is perfectly legal because the `TagSupport` superclass defines a `protected` member thus:

```
protected PageContext pageContext
```

This means that any subclasses of `TagSupport` (such as the `EmptyTag` class) can use the `pageContext` variable to access any data available to the current JSP that uses the custom tag. For example, the tag handler can access data in the user's session or data in the request object. In fact, because the `pageContext` object is exactly the same one that you can access from a scriptlet on a JSP, you can access the `out`, `page`, `request`, `response`, `servletConfig`, `ServletContext`, and `session` objects by calling the appropriate `get()` method. For example, you could use the `getOut()` method to retrieve a reference to the `out` object. See Chapter 2, "The Basic Syntax of JSP," for more information on the `pageContext` object.

Table 9.1 lists the methods that the `Tag` interface declares, and Table 9.2 shows its fields.

Table 9.1 **The Methods in the `javax.servlet.jsp.tagext.Tag` Interface**

Method name	Description
public int doEndTag() throws JspException	The generated servlet invokes this method to process the end tag for this instance. This method is only ever called after a matching call to doStartTag(). This method can return EVAL_PAGE to cause the generated servlet to process the rest of the page. Alternatively, the method can return SKIP_PAGE to indicate that the request is complete and that the rest of the page should not be evaluated.
public int doStartTag() throws JspException	The generated servlet invokes this method on the tag handler when a start tag is encountered in the page. If the method returns SKIP_BODY, any body content is ignored. You should return EVAL_BODY_INCLUDE from this method if you want the body content to be processed in the usual way and placed into the output stream.
public Tag getParent()	This method returns a reference to the closest enclosing tag handler for the current tag handler. The returned reference is of type javax.servlet.jsp.tagext.Tag
public void release()	The generated servlet invokes this method on a tag handler, so the handler can release any resources it has references to. However, note that the JSP specification states that there could be multiple calls to the doStartTag() and doEndTag() methods before this happens. This is so that tag handlers can be reused if there are multiple occurrences of a custom tag on the JSP.
public void setPageContext(PageContext p)	The generated servlet calls this method to set the current page context before it calls doStartTag().
public void setParent(Tag t)	The generated servlet calls this method to set the closest enclosing tag handler of the current tag handler. A value of null can be passed for the outermost tag handler, and a value is passed otherwise.

Table 9.2 lists the fields that are defined in the `Tag` interface.

Table 9.2 **The Fields in the `javax.servlet.jsp.tagext.Tag` Interface**

Field name	Description
public static final int EVAL_BODY_INCLUDE	The doStartTag() method can return this value to indicate that the body content should be evaluated and placed into the output stream.
public static final int EVAL_PAGE	The doEndTag() method can return this value to indicate that the rest of the JSP should be processed.
public static final int SKIP_BODY	The doStartTag() and doAfterBody() (from the IterationTag interface) methods can return this method to indicate that any body content should be skipped.
public static final int SKIP_PAGE	The doEndTag() method can return this value to cause the rest of the page to be skipped.

So far in this example, the JSP and the tag handler exist. The question now is, "How does the JSP container map the custom tag to its tag handler?" As discussed in Chapter 5, a TLD file is simply an XML document that describes a custom tag library and the custom actions that it contains. The `taglib` directive on the JSP specifies the URI for the custom tag library, and there must be an entry in the Web application's `web.xml` file that maps this URI to a TLD file. So, for the JSP in Listing 9.3 to work, you must add the following lines to your Web application's `web.xml` file:

```
<taglib>
    <taglib-uri>/chapter09TagLib</taglib-uri>
    <taglib-location>/WEB-INF/lib/emptyTags.tld</taglib-location>
</taglib>
```

This assumes that the TLD file is in the `WEB-INF/lib` directory of the current Web application. Note that although your Web container might allow you to place your TLD files in any directory of the Web application, the JSP 2.0 specification states that TLD files must be located in the `/WEB-INF` directory of the WAR file, or one of its subdirectories.

It is useful at this point to summarize which files are stored in which directories within the Web application structure (see Table 9.3).

Table 9.3 **Directory Structure for a Web Application**

Directory	Contents	Description
/WEB-INF	web.xml	The deployment descriptor for the Web application.
	*.tld	TLD files for the various custom tag libraries used by the Web application. Examples: c.tld x.tld
/WEB-INF/lib	*.jar	Java archive (JAR) files that contain tag handler implementations. Examples: jstl.jar Standard.jar
/WEB-INF/classes	*.class, *.jar	Java classes that are needed by the Web application.
<TOMCAT_HOME>/common/lib	*.jar	JAR files for tag libraries that are used by multiple Web applications.

The contents of the TLD for this example are shown in Listing 9.5.

Listing 9.5 **The TLD for the Empty Custom Tag (`emptyTags.tld`)**

```
<taglib xmlns="http://java.sun.com/xml/ns/j2ee"
  xmlns:xsi="http://www.w3.org/2001/XMLSchema-instance"
  xsi:schemaLocation="http://java.sun.com/xml/ns/j2ee/web-jsptaglibrary_2_0.xsd"
  version="2.0">
  <tlib-version>1.0</tlib-version>
  <jsp-version>2.0</jsp-version>
  <short-name>Empty Tags</short-name>
  <description>Some custom tags that do not process body content</description>

  <!-- this tag just outputs some text -->
  <tag>
    <name>emptyTag</name>
    <tag-class>com.conygre.jspdevhandbook.chapter9.EmptyTag</tag-class>
    <body-content>empty</body-content>
  </tag>
</taglib>
```

Note

JSP 2.0 requires that you use an XML Schema to describe a TLD file. However, web containers must support JSP applications that conform to earlier JSP versions which used DTDs instead of Schemas. See Section JSP.D.1 of the JSP 2.0 Specification for more information.

The first part of this TLD is a reference to the DTD that is used to describe the TLD document. This is followed by a `taglib` element that has two main sections. The first is a description of the tag library itself:

```
<tlib-version>1.0</tlib-version>
<jsp-version>2.0</jsp-version>
<short-name>Empty Tags</short-name>
<description>Some custom tags that do not process body content</description>
```

The `tlib-version` element describes the version of the tag library, whereas the `jsp-version` element dictates which version of the JSP specification on which this tag library depends. The `short-name` element is intended for use with authoring tools (such as for providing a default prefix in the `taglib` directive), whereas the `description` element is a string that expresses what the tag library is for.

The second part of the `taglib` content is used to describe the different custom tags that form the library:

```
<tag>
  <name>emptyTag</name>
  <tag-class>com.conygre.jspdevhandbook.chapter9.EmptyTag</tag-class>
  <body-content>empty</body-content>
</tag>
```

The text content of the `name` element shows the name of the custom tag, as used in any JSP that makes use of it. The `tag-class` element identifies the corresponding tag handler class that the generated servlet needs to use to process the custom tag. In this example that uses an empty tag, the `body-content` element has a value of `empty` to show that the custom tag is not allowed to have any body content. This is useful for debugging JSPs at translation-time when the generated servlet is created.

Other possible values for the `body-content` attribute are `JSP` and `tagdependent`. `JSP` is the default value, used to indicate that the body content of the custom tag is simply any valid JSP code. The `tagdependent` value is used to pass any body content directly to the tag handler "as is." This is useful in cases where you want the tag handler to interpret the body content, for example if you want to pass in expressions from another language such as XPath or SQL.

You might be wondering why you specify a value of `JSP` or `tagdependent` in the TLD, but return either `EVAL_BODY_INCLUDE` or `SKIP_BODY` from the tag handler class. The reason is that the TLD is used at compile time when the JSP is converted into a servlet, whereas the tag handler is used at runtime when the client requests the page.

So, all the pieces of the puzzle are now in place:

1. The JSP uses the `taglib` directive to identify the custom tag library through a URI.
2. The Web application's `web.xml` file maps the URI to a TLD file.

3. The TLD file identifies the tag handler class for a given tag.
4. The generated servlet uses the appropriate tag handler class to process custom tags in the JSP.

The example is now expanded to include attributes on the custom tag.

An Empty Custom Action with Attributes

It is common to modify the way that a tag works by providing attributes, which are simply name/value pairs. For the next example, consider a simple custom tag that is nested within a pair of HTML `<ul>...</ul>` tags to create the content of an unordered list. The content that this new custom tag generates is a set of random numbers, and the page author can set how many are required by specifying a value for an attribute called `howMany`. See Figure 9.3 for an example of the output that will be generated when this example is finished.

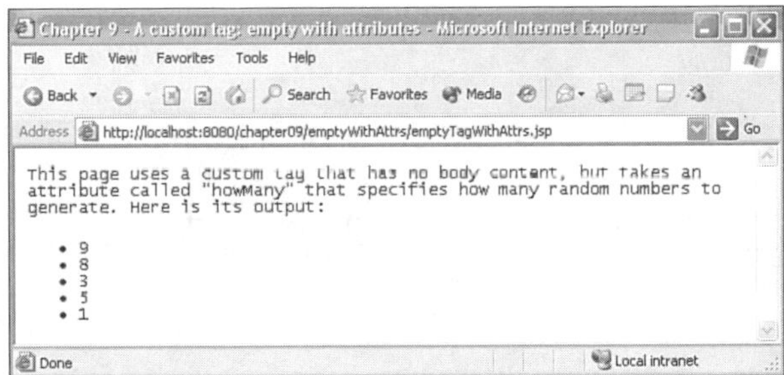

Figure 9.3 A JSP that uses the `emptyTagWithAttrs` custom tag.

The JSP that this example uses is shown in Listing 9.6. Note that the `taglib` directive is exactly the same as in the previous example. This is because the new tag handler belongs to the same custom tag library as the previous custom tag.

Listing 9.6 **A JSP That Uses an Empty Custom Tag That Has Attributes (`emptyTagWithAttrs.jsp`)**

```
<%@ taglib uri="/chapter09TagLib" prefix="chapter09" %>

<html>
  <head>
    <title>Chapter 9 - A custom tag: empty with attributes</title>
  </head>
  <body>
    This page uses a custom tag that has no body content, but takes
    an attribute called "howMany" that specifies how many random
    numbers to generate. Here is its output:
    <ul>
```

Listing 9.6 **Continued**

```
      <chapter09:emptyTagWithAttrs howMany="5" />
    </ul>
  </body>
</html>
```

The important line from this listing is

```
<chapter09:emptyTagWithAttrs howMany="5" />
```

The `howMany` attribute in this example tells the custom tag to output five random numbers to the JSP. The way that the attributes are dealt with by the tag extension mechanism is very simple. All that you need to do is expose a property of the tag handler, as described in Chapter 6, "JSP and JavaBeans." That is, for an attribute called `howMany` of type `int`, you would provide the following methods in your tag handler class:

```
public void setHowMany(int i) { ... }
public int getHowMany() { ...}
```

The Java code in Listing 9.7 is for the custom tag handler in this example.

Listing 9.7 **A Tag Handler Class That Implements an Attribute (EmptyTagWithAttrs.java)**

```
package com.conygre.jspdevhandbook.chapter9;

import java.io.IOException;
import javax.servlet.jsp.JspException;
import javax.servlet.jsp.JspWriter;
import javax.servlet.jsp.tagext.TagSupport;

/* This tag handler generates the random numbers. The "howMany" attribute
   specifies how many numbers to generate and display.
 */

public class EmptyTagWithAttrs extends TagSupport
{
  // Code to implement the "howMany" attribute

  private int howMany;
  public int getHowMany()
  {
    return howMany;
  }
  public void setHowMany(int i)
  {
    howMany = i;
```

Listing 9.7 **Continued**

```
  }

  public int doStartTag() throws JspException
  {
    try
    {
      JspWriter out = pageContext.getOut();

      for ( int i=0; i<this.howMany; i++ )
      {
        int nextNumber = (int) (Math.random() * 10);
        out.println("<li>" + nextNumber + "</li>");
      } // end of for ()
    }
    catch (IOException e)
    {
      System.out.println("Error in EmptyTagWithAttrs.doStartTag()");
      e.printStackTrace();
      throw new JspException(e); // throw the error to the error page (if set)
    } // end of try-catch

    return SKIP_BODY;
  }
}
```

The order in which events occur is

1. A tag handler object is instantiated, if required, by the container.
2. The `parent` and `pageContext` properties are set on the tag handler.
3. Any attributes (the attribute `howMany` in this case) are then set.
4. Finally, the `doStartTag()` method is invoked by the generated servlet.

Later in this chapter you can find a custom tag that outputs messages as each of its methods are called.

For now, the important lines from the tag handler class are

```
JspWriter out = pageContext.getOut();

for ( int i=0; i<this.howMany; i++ )
{
    int nextNumber = (int) (Math.random() * 10);
    out.println("<li>" + nextNumber + "</li>");
} // end of for ()
```

These cause the requisite number of random numbers to be generated and placed into the output stream. Because this tag is designed to be used inside a pair of `<ul>...</ul>` tags, each random number is placed inside a pair of `<li>...</li>` tags.

One problem with the way that the tag handler has been written is that there is some HTML hard-coded into it (the `<li>` and `</li>` tags). Later in this chapter, you will see examples that use scripting variables and nested scoping. By using these techniques, you can separate logic from presentation.

The only other addition that must be made is to modify the custom tag library's TLD file to include the new custom tag. You must, therefore, add the following lines to it:

```
<tag>
    <name>emptyTagWithAttrs</name>
    <tag-class>com.conygre.jspdevhandbook.chapter9.EmptyTagWithAttrs</tag-class>
    <body-content>empty</body-content>
    <attribute>
        <name>howMany</name>
    </attribute>
</tag>
```

JSP Fragments

The simple attributes that you have seen so far are evaluated by the container. It is also possible to pass *JSP Fragments* that are evaluated by the tag handler. The tag handler can use the fragment as many times as is required. JSP fragments are also known as *fragment attributes*.

You specify a JSP fragment as the body content of a `jsp:attribute`. Note that the body content is allowed to contain JSP code, but not scripting elements such as scriptlets, declarations and expressions (see Chapter 2 for details). Thus, you can only use standard actions, custom actions, and template text in a JSP fragment.

Here is a simple example a tag called `emptyTagWithFragment` that takes a JSP fragment called `message`:

```
<emptyTagWithFragment>
    <jsp:attribute name="message">
        Hello world
    </jsp:attribute>
</emptyTagWithFragment>
```

In the TLD file for this custom tag, you must also specify that the `jsp:attribute` is a JSP fragment by using a `fragment` element like this:

```
<tag>
    <name>emptyTagWithFragment</name>
    <tag-class>...</tag-class>
    <body-content>JSP</body-content>
    <attribute>
```

```
        <name>message</name>
        <required>true</required>
        <fragment>true</fragment>
    </attribute>
</tag>
```

If you omit the `fragment` element, then the JSP container assumes a default value of `false` which means that the attribute value is evaluated before it is passed to the tag handler. A value of `true` means that the content is passed to the tag handler as is.

More on Attributes

If you need to specify more than one attribute for a custom tag, all you need to do is provide another `attribute` section in your TLD file. For example, if you wanted to modify the tag you have just seen so that it generated random numbers in a certain range, you might expect the JSP to look like this:

```
<chapter09:emptyWithAttrs howMany="10" lowerBound="50" upperBound="100" />
```

and the TLD would need to look like this:

```
<tag>
    <name>emptyTagWithAttrs</name>
    <tag-class>com.conygre.jspdevhandbook.chapter9.EmptyTagWithAttrs</tag-class>
    <body-content>empty</body-content>
    <attribute>
        <name>howMany</name>
    </attribute>
    <attribute>
        <name>lowerBound</name>
    </attribute>
    <attribute>
        <name>upperBound</name>
    </attribute>
</tag>
```

Actually, there are three other elements that you can nest within an `attribute` element, in addition to the `name` element. These are defined in the DTD for TLD documents as

```
<!ELEMENT attribute (name, required?,rtexprvalue?, type?, description?) >
```

See Table 9.4 for a description of all five fields.

Table 9.4 **The Child Elements of** `attribute`

Element name	Description
Name (this element is required)	This is the name that is used in a JSP to set a value for an attribute. Because all attributes must have a name, you must specify a value for this element.
Required (this element is optional)	You can use this element to indicate whether an attribute must appear on an element. If you mark an attribute as required, but the page author omits it, that leads to a translation-time error, which is useful for debugging JSPs. There is a choice for the values that you can give: true (or yes) to mark an attribute as required, or false (or no) to mark it as optional. Default value: false (meaning that the named attribute is not required).
Rtexprvalue (this element is optional)	This element is used to indicate whether the value of the attribute should be dynamically processed when the page is requested. If so, the dynamic value can be specified using a scriptlet. Otherwise, the attribute value is static and decided at translation-time. You can use the same values as for the required element: true (or yes), or false (or no). Default value: false (means that the attribute value is not processed when the page is requested).
Type (this element is optional)	Used to set the type of the attribute's value. The type is always java.lang.String when rtexprvalue has a value of false. When you use scriptlets to dynamically compute a value, you specify the fully qualified class name of the result of the expression. You should make sure that the type you specify matches the type used by the JavaBean property accessor methods in the tag handler class. Default value: java.lang.String
Description (this element is optional)	You can use this element to provide a textual description of the attribute.

If you do not use the `type` element in the TLD file, the generated servlet uses a `set()` method that takes an argument of type `java.lang.String`. When setting attribute values from a JSP, be careful that the values that are passed from the JSP are of the type used by the `set()` method in the handler class. If you don't, the JSP can fail at translation time.

Also, if you use a scriptlet as an attribute value, make sure that you set use the `rtexprvalue` with a value of either `true` or `yes`. If you do not, the generated servlet attempts to pass the scriptlet text straight through to the handler without processing it! In fact, it is a good idea to set `rtexprvalue` to `true` unless you explicitly want it to be disabled. Do not assume that it is enabled by default!

Lifecycle of the Tag Interface

The order in which the methods of the `Tag` interface are invoked was briefly mentioned earlier in the chapter. The order in which the different methods are called in an implementation of the `Tag` interface can be found by examining the tag handler in Listing 9.8.

Listing 9.8 **A Simple Implementation of the `Tag` Interface (`TagLifecycle.java`)**

```
package com.conygre.jspdevhandbook.chapter9;

import java.io.IOException;
import javax.servlet.jsp.JspException;
import javax.servlet.jsp.JspWriter;
import javax.servlet.jsp.PageContext;
import javax.servlet.jsp.tagext.Tag;
import javax.servlet.jsp.tagext.TagSupport;

/* This tag handler outputs information about when different methods
   are called in the Tag interface.
 */

public class TagLifecycle extends TagSupport
{
  // Constructor

  public TagLifecycle()
  {
    System.out.println("TagLifecycle constructor called");
  }

  // Methods inherited from TagSupport

  public void setPageContext(PageContext p)
  {
    super.setPageContext(p);
    System.out.println("setPageContext() called. PageContext = " + p);
  }

  public void setParent(Tag t)
  {
    super.setParent(t);
    System.out.println("setParent() called. Parent = " + t);
  }

  public Tag getParent()
  {
```

Listing 9.8 **Continued**

```
    System.out.println("getParent() called");
    return super.getParent();
  }

  public void release()
  {
    System.out.println("release() called");
  }

  // Code to implement the "attr1" attribute

  private String attr1;
  public String getAttr1()
  {
    return attr1;
  }
  public void setAttr1(String s)
  {
    System.out.println("setAttr1() called with value " + s);
    attr1 = s;
  }

  // Code to implement the "attr2" attribute

  private String attr2;
  public String getAttr2()
  {
    return attr2;
  }
  public void setAttr2(String s)
  {
    System.out.println("setAttr2() called with value " + s);
    attr2 = s;
  }

  public int doStartTag() throws JspException
  {
    System.out.println("doStartTag() called");

    return SKIP_BODY;
  }

  public int doEndTag() throws JspException
  {
```

Listing 9.8 **Continued**

```
    System.out.println("doEndTag() called");
    return super.doEndTag();
  }
}
```

The code simply implements each of the methods in the `Tag` interface by first of all subclassing `TagSupport`, and overriding the default implementations that that class provides. A simple textual message is printed out for each method. In addition, the tag handler also implements two properties for attributes of the custom tag. The custom tag is defined with this fragment of the TLD file:

```
<tag>
  <name>tagLifecycle</name>
  <tag-class>com.conygre.jspdevhandbook.chapter9.TagLifecycle</tag-class>
  <body-content>empty</body-content>
  <attribute>
    <name>attr1</name>
  </attribute>
  <attribute>
    <name>attr2</name>
  </attribute>
</tag>
```

The JSP in this example uses two instances of the custom tag (`tagLifecycle`) so that you can see if the tag handler object is reused or not. Here is the JSP:

```
<%@ taglib uri="/chapter09TagLib" prefix="chapter09" %>

<html>
  <head>
    <title>Chapter 9 - The lifecycle of the Tag interface</title>
  </head>
  <body>
    <chapter09:tagLifecycle attr1="Samuel" attr2="Greenhough" />
    <chapter09:tagLifecycle attr1="Joshua" attr2="Greenhough" />
  </body>
</html>
```

As you can see, it is a very simple JSP that uses the `tagLifecycle` custom action twice, with different values for the `attr1` attribute each time (but the same value for `attr2`). Here is the output that you see on the JSP container's console window when you view the JSP:

```
TagLifecycle constructor called
setPageContext() called (org.apache.jasper.runtime.PageContextImpl@1ef443)
setParent() called (null)
```

```
setAttr1() called with value Samuel
setAttr2() called with value Greenhough
doStartTag() called
doEndTag() called
release() called
TagLifecycle constructor called
setPageContext() called (org.apache.jasper.runtime.PageContextImpl@1ef443)
setParent() called (null)
setAttr1() called with value Joshua
setAttr2() called with value Greenhough
doStartTag() called
doEndTag() called
release() called
```

The sequence of steps for the first occurrence of the custom tag is

1. A new handler object is instantiated (the constructor is called).
2. The `pageContext` object is stored.
3. The parent tag handler is set.
4. The two attribute values are stored.
5. The `doStartTag()` and `doEndTag()` methods are called.
6. The `release` method is called.

Perhaps surprisingly, the same process occurs for the second occurrence of the custom tag. Although the JSP specification enables a page to reuse an object, there is no way for you to force the issue one way or the other. Depending on your JSP container, you could be given a new instance of the tag handler each time, or the same one.

So, if you ran the example you have just seen in a different container you could see different behavior. For example, after invoking `doEndTag()` for the first tag, the server could simply set values for the attributes of the second tag that are different from the first. Then, it could call `doStartTag()`, `doEndTag()`, and `release()` as before.

Repeated Processing of Body Content

Before you see how to read body content and perform manipulations on it, let's first examine how to simply iterate over body content a number of times. In such situations you can use the `IterationTag` interface. If you refer back to Figure 9.1, you will see that the `IterationTag` interface is a subinterface of the `Tag` interface that has been used in the examples so far.

The `IterationTag` interface declares one property and one method. The method is invoked by the generated servlet to give the tag handler a chance to say whether it wants to process its body content again:

```
public int doAfterBody() throws JspException
```

If you output anything from the `doAfterBody()` method, it appears *after* any content that is specified in the body of the custom tag. The reason for this will become clear when you see an example in a moment.

The following field that is declared in the `IterationTag` interface can be returned from the `doAfterBody()` method to indicate that further evaluations are required:

```
public static final int EVAL_BODY_AGAIN
```

If you do not want the body to be evaluated again, simply return `SKIP_BODY`, as defined in the parent `Tag` interface.

In the example that you are about to see, there is a custom action that displays its body content a number of times, as specified by an attribute called `howMany`.

The JSP that is used for this example looks like that in Listing 9.9.

Listing 9.9 **A JSP That Uses a Custom Iteration Action (`iterationTag.jsp`)**

```
<%@ taglib uri="/chapter09TagLib" prefix="chapter09" %>

<html>
  <head>
    <title>Chapter 9 - A custom tag: iteration</title>
  </head>
  <body>
    <p>
    This page uses a custom tag that has body content that is processed
    a number of times. The attribute called "howMany" specifies how many
    times to iterate. Here is its output: </p>

    <chapter09:iterationTag howMany="5">
      Here is a random number:
    </chapter09:iterationTag>
  </body>
</html>
```

As before, the `iterationTag` belongs to the same custom tag library as the other examples in this chapter, so the `taglib` directive is unchanged and looks like this:

```
<%@ taglib uri="/chapter09TagLib" prefix="chapter09" %>
```

The important part of the JSP contains the following lines:

```
<chapter09:iterationTag howMany="5">
    Here is a random number:
</chapter09:iterationTag>
```

The flow of control when the JSP container processes this tag is as follows:

1. The tag handler object is instantiated.
2. Its setter methods are called (for the `pageContext` and `parent` objects, as well as the `howMany` attribute).
3. The tag handler's `doStartTag()` method is called by the generated servlet.
4. The container evaluates the body content of the tag, and here is the important bit: The generated servlet invokes the tag handler's `doAfterBody()` method. If the `doAfterBody()` method returns `EVAL_BODY_AGAIN`, this same step repeats. That is, the body is evaluated, and the `doAfterBody()` method is invoked.
5. After the `doAfterBody()` method returns `SKIP_BODY`, the `doEndTag()` method is invoked. If the container does not want to reuse the tag handler instance, it invokes the `release()` method on the tag handler.

For this example, these steps mean that the output for the JSP in Listing 9.9 looks like that in Figure 9.4. In a moment, you will see the tag handler code that generates this output, and the changes that are necessary to the custom tag library's TLD file.

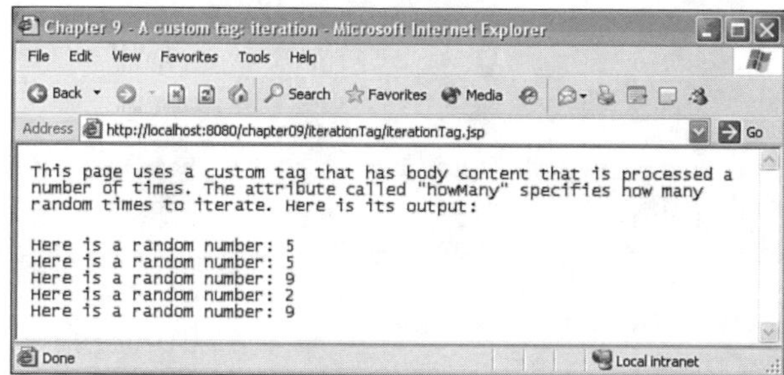

Figure 9.4 Screenshot of a JSP that uses a custom iteration action.

The Java code in Listing 9.10 is the implementation of the custom iteration action.

Listing 9.10 **The Implementation of the Custom Iteration Action (`IterationTag.java`)**

```
package com.conygre.jspdevhandbook.chapter9;

import java.io.IOException;
import javax.servlet.jsp.JspException;
import javax.servlet.jsp.JspWriter;
import javax.servlet.jsp.tagext.TagSupport;

/* This tag iterates a number of times, as specified by
   its "howMany" attribute.
 */
```

Listing 9.10 **Continued**

```
public class IterationTag extends TagSupport
{
  // Code to implement the "howMany" attribute

  private int howMany;
  public int getHowMany()
  {
    return howMany;
  }
  public void setHowMany(int i)
  {
    howMany = i;
  }

  public int doStartTag() throws JspException
  {
    return EVAL_BODY_INCLUDE;
  }

  private int countIterations = 0;
  public int doAfterBody() throws JspException
  {
    int retValue = (countIterations >= (howMany - 1)) ? SKIP_BODY
➥                                                  : EVAL_BODY_AGAIN;

    try
    {
      JspWriter out = pageContext.getOut();

      if ( countIterations < howMany)
      {
        int nextNumber = (int) (Math.random() * 10);
        out.println(nextNumber + "<br />");
      }
    }
    catch (IOException e)
    {
      System.out.println("Error in IterateTag.doAfterBody()");
      e.printStackTrace();
      throw new JspException(e); // throw the error to the error page (if set)
    } // end of try-catch

    countIterations++;
    return retValue;
  } // end of doAfterBody()
} // end of class IterationTag
```

Notice that the class used is declared as a subclass of `TagSupport`:

```
public class IterationTag extends TagSupport
```

If you refer back to Figure 9.1, you will see that the utility `TagSupport` class implements the `IterationTag` interface, which is a subinterface of `Tag`. Thus, the example can use the same superclass as the rest of the example tag handlers that you have seen thus far.

The custom action's `howMany` attribute is implemented the same way as before, but the inherited `doStartTag()` method is overridden to look like this:

```
public int doStartTag() throws JspException
{
    return EVAL_BODY_INCLUDE;
}
```

This is because the default implementation of the `doStartTag()` method returns `SKIP_BODY`, which is not what is required in this case!

> **Note**
>
> You do not always have to return `SKIP_BODY` or `EVAL_BODY_INCLUDE` from the `doStartTag()` method. You can of course dynamically decide which to return, perhaps based on values retrieved from one of the implicit objects that are available through the `pageContext` object.

An instance variable is then declared before the `doAfterBody()` method to keep track of the number of iterations that have been carried out:

```
private int countIterations;
```

If you have worked with servlets, you might be worried by the fact that this example uses an instance variable. However, a JSP container ensures that there is only ever one thread executing the code inside a tag handler. Although this makes the tag handler thread-safe, you must still be careful, if you write code in the tag handler that accesses any shared objects, such as those in the user's session.

The `doAfterBody()` uses the `countIterations` variable when deciding what to pass as a return value. If the number of iterations that has occurred is greater than or equal to the number of iterations—1, no more iterations are required after the current one. Otherwise, more iterations are necessary. Here is the code that determines which of the two options is the case:

```
int retValue = (countIterations >= (howMany - 1)) ? SKIP_BODY
➥                                                 : EVAL_BODY_AGAIN;
```

Remember that the `doAfterBody()` method is invoked after the body content has been processed. This means that the text `Here is a random number:` is already in the output stream, and any content that is output from the `doAfterBody()` method appears after it (refer back to Figure 9.4 if you need to remind yourself what the output looks like).

Thus, these lines of code execute and print out a random number followed by a line-break sequence:

```
if ( countIterations < howMany )
{
    int nextNumber = (int) (Math.random() * 10);
    out.println(nextNumber + "<br />");
}
```

The count of the number of iterations is then incremented, and the precomputed return value is passed back:

```
countIterations++;
return retValue;
```

Once again, you must add some lines to the custom tag library's TLD file, and here they are

```
<tag>
    <name>iterationTag</name>
    <tag-class>com.conygre.jspdevhandbook.chapter9.IterationTag</tag-class>
    <body-content>JSP</body-content>
    <attribute>
      <name>howMany</name>
    </attribute>
</tag>
```

Custom Actions with Body Content

You saw in Listing 9.10 that the `doStartTag()` method of the `IterationTag` class returned a value of `EVAL_BODY_INCLUDE` to have the generated servlet evaluate the body content of the custom tag. Although the body content of a tag can be any valid JSP code, it is not possible to modify it in any way from the tag handler. If that is what you need to do, use the third interface from Figure 9.1: `BodyTag`.

If you want to *manipulate* the body content of an action, there is a need to prevent the server from writing it straight to the output stream. This is achieved by having the body content written to a buffer first, which you can manipulate before having its content written to the output. The actual body content of the custom tag is represented by an instance of a subclass of the `javax.servlet.jsp.tagext.BodySupport` abstract class, which is itself a subclass of `JspWriter`. The `BodySupport` class declares these methods:

- `public void clearBody()`: this empties the contents of the buffer. It does not throw an exception.
- `public void flush()`: this method is overridden so as to throw an `IOException`. You cannot flush a `BodyContent` object because there is no stream that sits behind it.

- `public JspWriter getEnclosingWriter()`: returns a reference to the `JspWriter` that was passed to the constructor of this `BodyContent` object.
- `public abstract java.io.Reader getReader()`: returns the value of the `BodyContent` object as a `Reader`.
- `public abstract java.lang.String getString()`: returns the value of the `BodyContent` object as a `String`.
- `public abstract void writeOut(java.io.Writer w)`: enables you to write the contents of the `BodyContent` object to the specified `Writer` object.

You write a tag handler that implements the `BodyTag` interface when you need a custom tag that manipulates its body content. There are two methods declared in the `BodyTag` interface, as described in Table 9.5. Normally, you simply extend the `javax.servlet.jsp.tagext.BodyTagSupport` class rather than implement the interface yourself.

Table 9.5 **The Methods in the** `javax.servlet.jsp.tagext.BodyTag` **Interface**

Method name	Description
public void setBodyContent(BodyContent b)	This method is invoked by the generated servlet to set the body content for the custom action (but at most just once for a given action). It is not invoked if there is no body content, nor is it invoked if the doStartTag() method returns EVAL_BODY_INCLUDE or SKIP_BODY.
public int doInitBody() throws JspException	If there is any body content for the custom action, this method is invoked after the body content is set and before the first time that the body content is to be evaluated. Otherwise, this method is not invoked. This method is not invoked for empty tags, nor for nonempty tags whose doStartTag() method returns either EVAL_BODY_INCLUDE or SKIP_BODY.

> **Note**
>
> The `EVAL_BODY_INCLUDE` variable mentioned in the description of the `doInitBody()` method in Table 9.5 is defined in the `Tag` interface, and can be returned from a `doStartTag()` method to indicate that the body content should be evaluated into the output stream.

The `BodyTag` interface declares a field called `EVAL_BODY_BUFFERED`:

```
public static final int EVAL_BODY_BUFFERED
```

If you want the container to evaluate the body content and place the result into a buffer for you to manipulate, you should return this value from the tag handler's `doStartTag()` method. The container subsequently passes a buffer of type `BodyContent` into the tag handler's `setBodyContent()` method (see Table 9.4).

Here is the sequence of events that occurs when a custom tag that implements the `BodyTag` interface is encountered on a JSP:

1. The tag handler object is instantiated.
2. The `parent` and `pageContext` objects are set, along with any attributes.
3. The `doStartTag()` is invoked. If the method returns `EVAL_BODY_BUFFERED`, a new `BodyContent` object is created and passed to `setBodyContent()` in the next step.
4. The `setBodyContent()` and `doInitBody()` methods are called.
5. The body content of the tag is evaluated by the server.
6. The generated servlet then invokes the `doAfterBody()` method, where you can manipulate the result of the body content's evaluation. The method returns a value to indicate whether the body must be evaluated again. If so, the process starts again from step 5. If not, go to step 7.
7. The `doEndTag()` is invoked. If the server is going to reuse the tag handler object, subsequent occurrences of the tag on the JSP start at step 4 of this list. If not, the `release()` method is invoked on the tag handler object.

This process should become a little clearer if you take a look at the following example. All that it does is use a custom tag that iterates over its body content a number of times, and alternately converts the body content to all uppercase, and then all lowercase. Here is the JSP:

```
<%@ taglib uri="/chapter09TagLib" prefix="chapter09" %>

<html>
  <head>
    <title>Chapter 9 - A custom tag: body content</title>
  </head>
  <body>
    This page uses a custom tag manipulates its body content.
    Here is its output:
    <ol>
      <chapter09:bodyContentTag howMany="3">
        <li>PrIvYeT MiR!</li>
      </chapter09:bodyContentTag>
    </ol>
  </body>
</html>
```

The important lines are the following ones:

```
<ol>
  <chapter09:bodyContentTag howMany="3">
    <li>PrIvYeT MiR!</li>
  </chapter09:bodyContentTag>
</ol>
```

The custom tag is called `bodyContentTag`. It belongs to the same custom tag library that has been used throughout the chapter, hence the `taglib` directive at the top of the JSP is the same as usual. Also, the tag has a `howMany` attribute that is used to specify how many times the body content should be processed.

Before you see the Java code for the tag handler, take a look at the output that is generated in Figure 9.5.

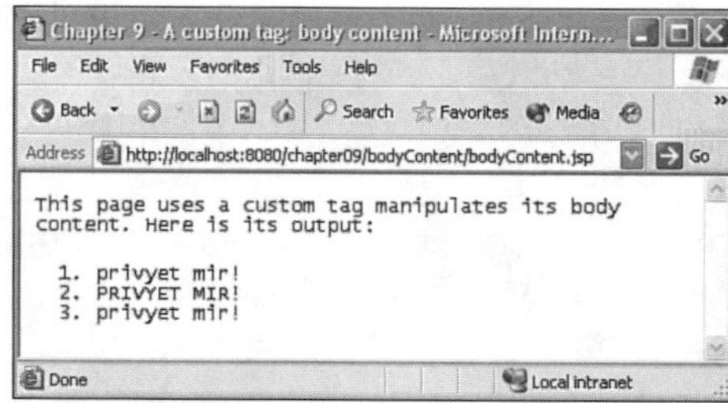

Figure 9.5 A JSP that uses a custom tag that manipulates its body content.

The `bodyContentTag` used in the JSP is mapped to a tag handler class by this fragment of the TLD file:

```
<tag>
    <name>bodyContentTag</name>
    <tag-class>com.conygre.jspdevhandbook.chapter9.BodyContentTag</tag-class>
    <body-content>JSP</body-content>
    <attribute>
      <name>howMany</name>
    </attribute>
  </tag>
```

You can see that the `body-content` element specifies `JSP` as the content for the custom tag, and the handler class is `BodyContentTag`. Here is the source code for the tag handler:

```
package com.conygre.jspdevhandbook.chapter9;

import java.io.IOException;
import javax.servlet.jsp.JspWriter;
import javax.servlet.jsp.tagext.BodyContent;
import javax.servlet.jsp.tagext.BodyTagSupport;
```

```
public class BodyContentTag extends BodyTagSupport
{
  private int iterations, howMany;

  public void setHowMany(int i)
  {
    this.howMany = i;
  }

  public int doAfterBody()
  {
    try
    {
      BodyContent bodyContent = super.getBodyContent();
      String      bodyString  = bodyContent.getString();
      JspWriter   out         = bodyContent.getEnclosingWriter();

      if ( iterations % 2 == 0 )
        out.print(bodyString.toLowerCase());
      else
        out.print(bodyString.toUpperCase());

      iterations++;
      bodyContent.clear(); // empty buffer for next evaluation
    }
    catch (IOException e)
    {
      System.out.println("Error in BodyContentTag.doAfterBody()"
                         + e.getMessage());
      e.printStackTrace();
    } // end of catch

    int retValue = SKIP_BODY;

    if ( iterations < howMany )
    {
      retValue = EVAL_BODY_AGAIN;
    }

    return retValue;
  }
}
```

The bulk of the work is performed in the `doAfterBody()` method. If you refer back to the steps earlier in this section that list the lifecycle of a tag handler such as this one, you will recall that the following has already occurred by the time that the `doAfterBody()` method is invoked:

1. The tag handler was instantiated, and its properties and attributes set.
2. Its `doStartTag()` method was invoked, and returned `EVAL_BODY_BUFFERED`.
3. Its `setBodyContent()` method was passed a reference to a `BodyContent` buffer object, and then the `doInitBody()` method was called to give you a chance to prepare for evaluation of the body content.

The JSP container then evaluates the body content of the custom tag, and places it into the `BodyContent` object before calling the tag handler's `doAfterBody()` method. So, the first thing that this method does in the example tag handler is to retrieve the body content as a `String`:

```
BodyContent bodyContent = super.getBodyContent();
String      bodyString  = bodyContent.getString();
```

Then, a local reference is stored to the enclosing JSP Writer object so that the output can be written out later in the method:

```
JspWriter   out         = bodyContent.getEnclosingWriter();
```

The next four lines decide whether to convert the body content to uppercase or lowercase. This is where the `iterations` instance variable is used: an even number for the iteration gives lowercase. The converted string is written out, and the variable is then incremented for the next time around:

```
if ( iterations % 2 == 0 )
    out.print(bodyString.toLowerCase());
else
    out.print(bodyString.toUpperCase());

iterations++;
```

Importantly, in this example the body content buffer must be cleared. This is because of the fact that when the JSP container evaluates the body content the next time around, the result is simply appended to the buffer. If the buffer were not cleared, this example would have the string `"privyet mir"` appear once in lowercase, then twice in uppercase, and then finally three times in lowercase! The buffer is cleared like this:

```
bodyContent.clear();
```

The rest of the code simply dictates whether the body content needs to be re-evaluated by the container. If so, the value `EVAL_BODY_AGAIN` is returned, otherwise `SKIP_BODY` is passed back instead:

```
    int retValue = SKIP_BODY;

    if ( iterations < howMany )
      retValue = EVAL_BODY_AGAIN;

    return retValue;
```

Remember that after the `doAfterBody()` method returns `SKIP_BODY` (which could even be the first time), the next method to be invoked is `doEndTag()`. It is common practice to open tags in the `doStartTag()`method, iterate over the body while manipulating and outputting the results, and then finally use the `doEndTag()` method to close any open tags that are still open.

Tags That Interact

Tags that share data are referred to in the JSP specification as *cooperating actions*. There are several different ways that tags can communicate with each other, although the general idea is that a custom action can create an object, such as a JavaBean, for use by another action. For example, you might want to cache a result-set from a database query and have another action process it. One way would be for the first action to store the object as an attribute in the `pageContext` by using the `setAttribute()` method. When you do this you must be very careful that the name that you bound the object to is not already in use, or you will erase the reference to the existing object. Such a shared object is visible to scriptlet code through the `pageContext.getAttribute()` method as long as you know the name to which the object is bound, and the type to which you want to cast the retrieved reference.

Earlier in this chapter, in the example that used an empty tag with attributes (Listing 9.5), the tag handler implementation contained some hard-coded HTML. This can be avoided by instead using a tag that exposes data so that the page author can display it with other tags in any way that she sees fit. For example, the handler in Listing 9.5 could have exposed an array of values. Then, the page author could iterate through the array with a `c:forEach` action, displaying each element with any formatting she chooses.

Two main approaches can be taken to help tags cooperate: scripting variables and nested scope.

Scripting Variables

One way that you can share objects between actions is with the use of scripting variables. A tag handler can export a JavaBean, or any other object, with the `pageContext.setAttribute()` method. Another tag can then access the JavaBean through the `pageContext.getAttribute()` method.

You can describe the exported object by writing a subclass of `TagExtraInfo`, although for simple variables you can use a block within the TLD file. For example, consider the JSP in Listing 9.11. It uses a custom action called `defineObjects`, which is the action name recommended by the JSP specification for an action that creates objects for use on the page. In this case, the `defineObjects` action exports an array of random numbers. The size of the array is set by the value of the `howMany` attribute.

Listing 9.11 **A JSP That Uses an Action That Exports a Scripting Variable (`emptyTagWithAttrsExport.jsp`)**

```
<%@ taglib uri="/chapter09TagLib" prefix="chapter09" %>
<%@ taglib uri="http://java.sun.com/jstl-el/core" prefix="c" %>

<html>
  <head>
    <title>Chapter 9 - A custom tag: scripting variable</title>
  </head>
  <body>
    This page uses a custom tag that has no body content, but takes
    an attribute called "howMany" that specifies how many random
    numbers to generate. The random numbers are exported through
    an array whose name is set by the "name" attribute. Here is its
    output:

    <chapter09:defineObjects howMany="5" name="numbers" />
    <ul>
      <c:forEach items="${numbers}" var="currentNumber">
        <li>
          <c:out value="${currentNumber}" />
        </li>
      </c:forEach>
    </ul>
  </body>
</html>
```

The line that generates the array of random numbers and exports it under the name `numbers` is

```
<chapter09:defineObjects howMany="5" name="numbers" />
```

If you have read the rest of the listing already, you will have seen that the JSTL `c:forEach` action uses the `numbers` scripting variable and exposes each element of the array as a variable called `currentNumber`:

```
<c:forEach items="${numbers}" var="currentNumber">
```

Each number from the array is then displayed in a list with the JSTL `c:out` action:

```
<li>
    <c:out value="${currentNumber}" />
</li>
```

Before you see the Java code, and the TLD file, take a look at the screenshot in Figure 9.6.

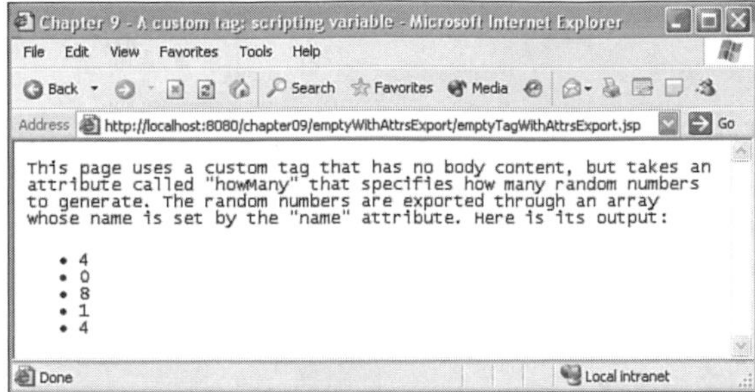

Figure 9.6 A JSP that uses a custom action that exports a scripting variable.

The Java code that implements the tag handler for the custom action is in Listing 9.12.

Listing 9.12 **Tag Handler Code for the `defineObjects` Custom Action (`EmptyTagWithAttrsExport.java`)**

```
package com.conygre.jspdevhandbook.chapter9;

import javax.servlet.jsp.*;
import javax.servlet.jsp.tagext.*;

public class EmptyTagWithAttrsExport extends BodyTagSupport
{
  /* Code to implement the "howMany" attribute
   */
  private int howMany;
  public int getHowMany()
  {
    return howMany;
  }
  public void setHowMany(int i)
  {
    howMany = i;
  }

  /* Code to implement the "name" attribute
   */
  private String exportedArrayName;
  public String getName()
  {
    return exportedArrayName;
  }
  public void setName(String s)
  {
```

Listing 9.12 **Continued**

```
    exportedArrayName = s;
  }

  public int doStartTag() throws JspException
  {
    int[] outputArray = new int[howMany];

    for ( int i=0; i<howMany; i++ )
      outputArray[i] = (int) (Math.random() * 10);

    pageContext.setAttribute(exportedArrayName, outputArray);
    return SKIP_BODY;
  }
}
```

The `name` attribute of the `defineObjects` action is implemented in the usual way, except the value is stored in an instance variable called `exportedArrayName`. This is just to show that the attribute name of the custom action does not have to match the name of a field in the tag handler implementation.

The important part is at the end of the `doStartTag()` method:

```
pageContext.setAttribute(exportedArrayName, outputArray);
```

The question is, "So what is different between manually exporting a variable by using `pageContext.setAttribute()` from a scriptlet, and this approach?" The answer is that you can make an addition to the tag library's TLD that saves the page author from having to call `pageContext.getAttribute()` to access the exported variable. That is, the variable is implicitly available. The requisite changes look like this:

```
<tag>
    <name>defineObjects</name>
    <tag-class>com.conygre.jspdevhandbook.chapter9.EmptyTagWithAttrsExport</
tag-class>
    <body-content>empty</body-content>
    <variable>
      <name-from-attribute>name</name-from-attribute>
      <variable-class>int []</variable-class>
      <declare>TRUE</declare>
      <scope>AT_END</scope>
    </variable>
     <attribute>
      <name>howMany</name>
    </attribute>
    <attribute>
      <name>name</name>
    </attribute>
  </tag>
```

The only part that is new is the `variable` element. See Table 9.6 for a description of its contents.

Table 9.6 **Child Elements of the `variable` Element**

Child element name	Description
name-from-attribute	Enables you to specify which attribute of the custom action gives the exported variable its name. Alternatively, you can hard-code a name into the TLD by using the name-given element instead of name-from-attribute. Using both is not allowed.
variable-class	Specifies the type of the exported variable. Examples: int, String[], com.foo.BarClass
Declare	Whether the variable should be declared (depends on the scripting language). Possible values are true and false.
Scope	Specifies the scope of the exported variable. Permissible values are AT_END (visible after the custom action's close tag), AT_BEGIN (visible just after the end of the opening tag), and NESTED (visible just after the end of the opening tag and before the start of the closing tag).

Note

An example is available on the book Web site that converts this latest example to use the `TagExtraInfo` class.

Hierarchical Tag Structures

Apart from using scripting variables, yet another way that actions can communicate is through the use of *nested scoping*. The way that it works is that an enclosing, or *parent*, action can make data and JavaBeans available to nested, or *child*, actions. For page authors, this is a logical approach to sharing data because they tend to be familiar with using certain tags within other tags. For example, `<li>` is used within `<ul>` to create an unordered list of items. Even for software developers, the `switch` statement in Java has `case` and `default` constructs, which is mirrored in JSTL's `c:choose`, `c:when`, and `c:otherwise` actions.

The data that is exposed by the enclosing action is made available when the enclosing action's `doStartTag()` method is called, and removed when the `doEndTag()` method is invoked. To understand how the nested action accesses the exposed data, remember that a tag handler has its `setParent()` method invoked early in its lifecycle to allow it to store a reference to its enclosing tag. The `getParent()` method is used by the following method that is declared by the `TagSupport` class:

```
public static final Tag findAncestorWithClass(Tag from, java.lang.Class class)
```

You can use this method to find an enclosing tag handler of a certain type. The first parameter is the tag to begin searching from, and the second parameter is the tag handler type.

Let's put all this together with an example. This example uses an enclosing action that computes the average of two numbers supplied through attributes, and exposes the result as a nested scoped variable. A nested action retrieves the average value and displays it. The JSP for this example is in Listing 9.13.

Listing 9.13 **A JSP That Uses Nested Actions** (`averager.jsp`)

```
<%@ taglib uri="/chapter09TagLib" prefix="chapter09" %>

<html>
  <head>
    <title>Chapter 9 - Nested tags: averager</title>
  </head>
  <body>
    This page uses a tag that exposes data for its lifetime, for use
    by nested actions. Here is its output:
    <h1>
      <chapter09:averager number1="32" number2="5">
        <chapter09:displayResult />
      </chapter09:averager>
    </h1>
  </body>
</html>
```

The important lines are

```
<chapter09:averager number1="32" number2="5">
    <chapter09:displayResult />
</chapter09:averager>
```

The enclosing action is called `averager`, and the two numbers to compute the average of are set by the `number1` and `number2` attributes. The nested action is `displayResult`, and is the tag responsible for retrieving the average value from its enclosing action and displaying it. The Java code for the tag handler for the enclosing action is in Listing 9.14.

Listing 9.14 **The Tag Handler for the** `averager` **Action** (`Averager.java`)

```
package com.conygre.jspdevhandbook.chapter9;

import java.io.IOException;
import javax.servlet.jsp.JspWriter;
import javax.servlet.jsp.JspException;
import javax.servlet.jsp.tagext.TagSupport;
```

Listing 9.14 **Continued**

```
public class Averager extends TagSupport
{
  private int number1, number2;
  private double averageValue;

  public void setNumber1(int i)
  {
    this.number1 = i;
  }
  public int getNumber1()
  {
    return number1;
  }

  public void setNumber2(int i)
  {
    this.number2 = i;
  }
  public int getNumber2()
  {
    return number2;
  }

  public double getAverageValue()
  {
    return averageValue;
  }

  public int doStartTag() throws JspException
  {
    // Do a cast before dividing, or we could lost the fractional part

    averageValue = ((double) number1 + number2) / 2;
    return EVAL_BODY_INCLUDE;
  }
}
```

The vast majority of this tag handler is for storing the two attributes (`number1` and `number2`) and the computed average value (`averageValue`). The average value is calculated in the `doStartTag()` method, which returns `EVAL_BODY_INCLUDE` so that the body content is evaluated and passed to the output. The `doEndTag()` method is not overridden because the inherited version from the parent `TagSupport` class returns `EVAL_PAGE` to indicate that the rest of the page should be evaluated, which is exactly what we want.

The tag handler for the nested action, `displayResult`, can be found in Listing 9.15.

Listing 9.15 **The Tag Handler Implementation for the `displayResult` Action (`DisplayResult.java`)**

```
package com.conygre.jspdevhandbook.chapter9;

import java.io.IOException;
import javax.servlet.jsp.JspException;
import javax.servlet.jsp.tagext.Tag;
import javax.servlet.jsp.tagext.TagSupport;

public class DisplayResult extends TagSupport
{
  public int doStartTag() throws JspException
  {
    Averager parentTag = (Averager) findAncestorWithClass(this, Averager.class);
    double averageValue = parentTag.getAverageValue();

    try
    {
      pageContext.getOut().print("The average value is " + averageValue);
    }
    catch (IOException e)
    {
      System.out.println("Error displaying the average value");
      throw new JspException(e);
    }

    return SKIP_BODY;
  }
}
```

There are three important lines of code in Listing 9.15, the first being the most important of all:

```
Averager parentTag = (Averager) findAncestorWithClass(this, Averager.class);
```

This line of code is the one that uses the `getParent()` method to find the enclosing tag that is of type `Averager`. In this example, it is the immediately enclosing action. However, in more complex examples, the `findAncestorWithClass()` method searches all the way up to the top-level action until the required action is found. If the specified action cannot be located, a value of `null` is returned instead.

After the correct enclosing action has been located, the other two important lines of code are

```
double averageValue = parentTag.getAverageValue();
```

which retrieves the average value, and:

```
pageContext.getOut().print("The average value is " + averageValue);
```

which writes it out.

For completeness, here are the lines that must be added to the TLD file:

```
<tag>
    <name>averager</name>
    <tag-class>com.conygre.jspdevhandbook.chapter9.Averager</tag-class>
    <body-content>JSP</body-content>
    <attribute>
      <name>number1</name>
    </attribute>
    <attribute>
      <name>number2</name>
    </attribute>
</tag>

<tag>
    <name>displayResult</name>
    <tag-class>com.conygre.jspdevhandbook.chapter9.DisplayResult</tag-class>
    <body-content>empty</body-content>
</tag>
```

Summary

In this chapter you learned that the tag extension mechanism provides a way for you to introduce new actions into a JSP. The main focus of this chapter was to show that you can write your own custom actions, ranging from simple actions with neither body content nor attributes, all the way up to actions that cooperate with each other through the sharing of objects and data.

You were shown that to implement a custom action, you must write a tag handler class and a tag library descriptor (TLD) file. You also saw the common ways to deploy and use a tag library in a Web application.

In the next chapter, you will learn to use various editors and development environments, which you can use to write JSP, to their best effect.

II

XML, Web Services, and Enterprise JSP

10 Utilizing XML from JSP

11 Transforming XML Using XSLT and XSLFO

12 Invoking Web Services from JSP

13 Locating Resources Using JNDI

14 Databases and JSP

15 JSP and EJB Interaction

16 Security and JSP

17 Personalization and Web Applications

18 Case Study

10

Utilizing XML from JSP

THIS CHAPTER BEGINS WITH AN INTRODUCTION to XML and introduces the importance of XML as a technology before explaining the syntax of XML documents. The chapter also explains the role of the Document Type Definition (DTD) and Schema, but does not cover the syntax of these files. You can find an introduction to both of these in Appendix B, "An Overview of XML Schema."

The chapter then discusses how you can extract XML data so that it can be presented using JSP technology. The SAX and DOM APIs as implemented in JAXP 1.1 are explained, but with a clear focus on how they can be used within JSP. The chapter finishes by exploring the JDOM API as an alternative to DOM.

To learn more about XML than is presented in this chapter, you might want to read *Sams Teach Yourself XML in 21 Days* in which you can find everything that you need to know about XML, plus related standards.

> **Note**
>
> If you want to run the demonstration applications for this chapter, you will need the `chapter10.war` file by visiting the book's Web site (`www.samspublishing.com`), and entering the ISBN number (0672324385) in the search box.

Introduction to XML

Before you see some XML, it is worth briefly discussing where XML originated, and why it is of such importance in today's Web applications.

XML Is Portable Data

You can broadly dissect any application into two main parts: code and data. The code is, of course, the functionality provided by the program, whereas the data is the information that the code manipulates. The way that the data is stored and managed in a computer's memory is a fundamental aspect of any programming language and operating system. When a programmer works on an application, he is generally free to decide on whatever representation he likes for the application's data. The headaches come when an application needs to exchange data with another application.

One approach to solving the problem of data interchange is to use a shared storage medium such as a relational database. You can then use SQL and JDBC to access and manipulate the shared data.

However, the two applications might not both have access to the shared database. Another scenario might be when two applications have a requirement to interface with each other directly. In these situations, you must decide on some data-encoding format upon which both applications agree. Before the advent of XML, this type of situation often resulted in application-specific data formats that programs store data within. For example, you might have come across binary `.dat` files and textual `.conf` files.

Such application-specific formats tend to lack flexibility in the representation of data, which leads to problems when you want to change versions of the communicating applications, or send the data to a different application altogether.

The World Wide Web Consortium (W3C) developed the Extensible Markup Language (XML) to address these issues. XML provides a data format that has the following characteristics:

- Simple syntax
- Human-readable (text format)
- Flexible
- Portable
- Extensible (you can make up your own tags and attributes)
- Generic (you can model any data using it)
- Free!

The W3C is responsible for maintaining the XML specification. You can find the latest version of the specification, along with useful tools and information, on the W3C Web site at `http://www.w3.org`.

XML gives you a way to model structured data in a textual format. Structured data is simply data that conforms to a particular format, such as invoices, text documents, address books, and configuration parameters. One great point in the favor of XML is that it is both machine-readable and human-readable. Having said that, it is easily possible to write XML that is not readable by choosing cryptic element and attribute names. When data is passed between different parts of an application, it is not particularly important that the data is human-readable. However, it makes debugging much easier when things go wrong.

Features of XML

The XML 1.0 specification consists of a set of rules for creating text formats to represent the structure of the data in your applications. XML is *not* a programming language, which makes it easy for nonprogrammers to learn.

Here is a list of design goals that the authors of the XML 1.0 specification had when they devised XML:

- It should be easy to use XML over the Internet.
- XML documents should be human-readable and relatively clear.
- It should be easy to create XML documents.
- The number of optional features in XML should be kept to the minimum possible—ideally, there should be none.
- XML should support a wide variety of applications.
- XML should be compatible with the Standard Generalized Markup Language (SGML).
- Terseness in XML was of minimal importance.

You might have noticed in the previous list that XML was designed to be compatible with SGML. SGML is a powerful, but complex meta-language that describes languages for document management, document publishing, and electronic document interchange. The best-known markup language is probably HTML, which is itself an example of an SGML application.

> **Note**
>
> Many people are frightened when they hear the term *meta-language*. A meta-language, such as XML, enables you to create new vocabularies for particular business domains. All this really means when you use XML is that you can invent your own element and attribute names!

SGML provides a very rich syntax, but its complexity means that it is not used as widely as you might think. The main use of SGML today is in the field of technical documentation.

The W3C designed XML to have the flexibility and power of SGML, with most of the complexity removed. As such, XML has all the best parts of SGML and its commonly used features, but has a more regular structure and is easier to use.

XML's Syntax and Structure

If you follow the rules laid out in the XML 1.0 Specification while creating an XML document, you end up with a *well-formed* document. Before you see the actual rules that an XML document must conform to, take a look at the simple XML document in Listing 10.1.

Listing 10.1 **A Simple XML Document (`people.xml`).**

```
<people>
  <person>
    <name>Mark</name>
    <age>30</age>
  </person>
  <person>
    <name>Ruth</name>
    <age>29</age>
  </person>
</people>
```

The best way to familiarize yourself with XML is to write an XML document such as the one in Listing 10.1. A simple way to check that a document that you have typed in is well formed is to open it inside a Web browser such as Microsoft Internet Explorer. When you do this, you take advantage of the fact that an XML browser includes an XML parser. If the document is well formed, the browser displays the document in a structured format with indentation, as in Figure 10.1.

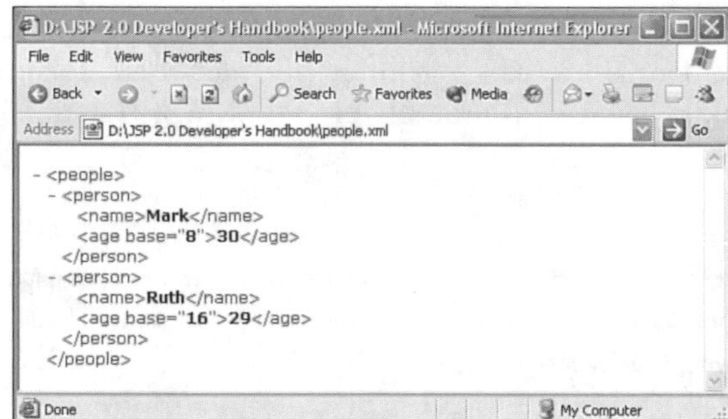

Figure 10.1 A well-formed document viewed in Microsoft Internet Explorer.

If you make a mistake when typing in the XML document, you see an error displayed in the Web browser when you try to view it. For example, if you omit the closing `</people>` tag from the XML document, you see output as shown in Figure 10.2.

Note

You might be wondering why you can expand and collapse the tags when viewing an XML document in Microsoft Internet Explorer (IE). This is because IE has a built-in stylesheet that it uses to generate Dynamic HTML (DHTML) from the XML input document that you supply. You will learn more about stylesheets in Chapter 11, "Transforming XML Using XSLT and XSLFO."

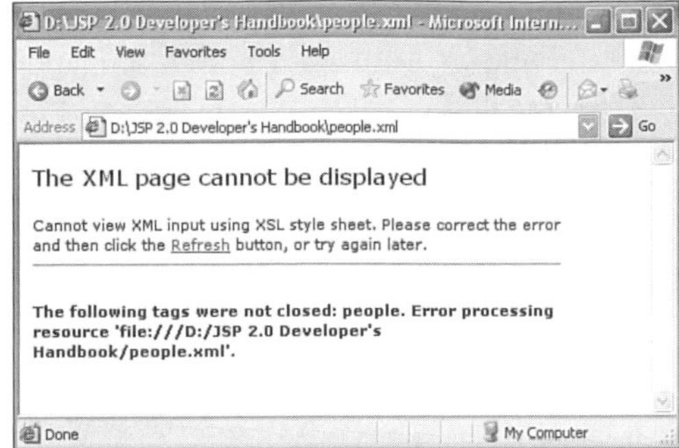

Figure 10.2 A malformed document viewed in Microsoft Internet Explorer.

The XML document in Listing 10.1 might look similar to HTML and JSP documents, and you are right if you are thinking that! Just like HTML, an XML document has elements that consist of a start tag and an end tag. The document in Listing 10.2 is both well-formed XML and HTML.

Listing 10.2 **An Example XML and HTML File** (`xmlExample.html`)

```
<html>
  <head>
    <title>Example XML and HTML File</title>
  </head>
  <body>
    <h1>Utilizing XML from JSP</h1>
    <p>This page is both well-formed XML and well-formed HTML.</p>
  </body>
</html>
```

If you have worked with HTML documents, you are no doubt aware of the fact that most Web browsers have a fairly relaxed attitude towards poorly formed HTML documents. For example, browsers often ignore missing end tags that go unnoticed until you try to display the page in a stricter browser that then displays an error. When you write an XML document, it is *illegal* to miss an end tag. There are other rules that you must follow, which are covered next.

The Structure of an XML Document

You can only have *one* element at the top level within an XML document. People refer to this element by several names, including the *root element*, and the *top-level element*.

However, the W3C has defined a specification called the *XML Information Set (InfoSet)*, which names the topmost element in your XML document the *document element information item*. The InfoSet is a completely abstract specification that defines a tree-like data model for representing the information in an XML document. As well as element information items, the InfoSet defines attribute information items, character information items, plus others for all the XML constructs that can appear in your documents.

All the higher-level XML technologies such as SAX, DOM, XPath, and XSLT are based on the InfoSet, so it is worth knowing at least a little about it.

For the XML document in Listing 10.1, the corresponding InfoSet looks like that shown in Figure 10.3.

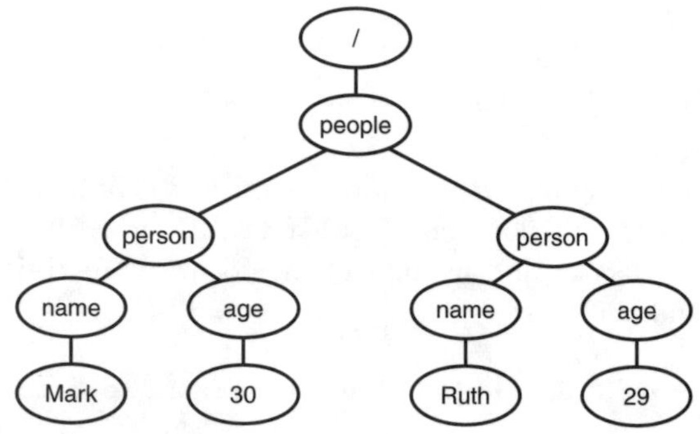

Figure 10.3 The InfoSet for the document in Listing 10.1.

Notice in Figure 10.3 that at the very top of the tree there is a node with the character / in it. This is the root of the InfoSet tree, known as the *document* information item. It is common to wonder how this maps to anything within the XML document, and the answer is that it does not! The reason that it exists in the InfoSet is in case any comments or processing instructions occur before the document element information item. The document information item gives them all a single place to live.

> **Note**
>
> A processing instruction (PI) is out-of-band information for the application that is processing the XML. It takes the form `<?target data?>`. However, PIs are not used overly much because they do not support XML namespaces. Web services and SOAP do not use PIs.

XML Declarations

The only other thing that can appear before the document element information item is an XML prolog that contains an XML declaration. If your XML document is encoded using UTF-8 or UTF-16, you do not need to use an XML declaration.

Even though it is not required, it is a good idea to put the XML prolog at the top of the file so that the version of XML, and the document's encoding, are explicitly stated. The next version of XML (version 1.1) will make the prolog mandatory.

This is because all XML parsers must support at least these two encodings. You will have to consult the documentation for whichever parser you are using to see if it supports any other encodings. The only reason you would want to do this, however, is if you already have documents that are stored in those encodings. For all new documents, you should use either UTF-8 or UTF-16.

For an XML document that is encoded using UTF-8 or UTF-16, you can optionally put an XML declaration at the top of your file that looks like this:

```
<?xml version="1.0"?>
```

This tells the XML parser that this XML document conforms to the XML version 1.0 specification (which the W3C finalized and made into a Recommendation on February 10, 1998).

If you want to make the encoding explicit for a document that uses UTF-8, you would put in this declaration:

```
<?xml version="1.0" encoding="UTF-8"?>
```

For a UTF-16 file you would use this:

```
<?xml version="1.0" encoding="UTF-16"?>
```

If the XML document is encoded in a character-encoding scheme other than UTF-8 or UTF-16, you *must* specify the encoding using a valid identifier such as `Shift_JIS` or `ISO-8859-1`.

Hang on a minute! If the document is encoded in a scheme other than UTF-8 or UTF-16, how can a parser know how to read the XML declaration to know which *other* encoding to switch to? The answer is that the XML team at the W3C used an elegant hack. The only characters that are valid for use within the *names* of character encoding are those defined in US-ASCII, which is a subset of UTF-8. Whether those characters are encoded using `UTF-8`, `Shift_JIS`, or `EBCDIC` is unimportant.

So, if the encoding scheme is neither UTF-8 or UTF-16, the first line is read in as if it were UTF-8 and an alternative coding is searched for. If not found or not supported, the XML parser throws an error and stops.

> **Note**
>
> For a full description of the algorithm that is used, see Appendix F, "Autodetection of Character Encodings," in the Extensible Markup Language specification on the W3C Web site (`http://www.w3.org/TR/2000/REC-xml-20001006`).

Elements

As mentioned earlier, XML does not define any element names. The authors of the document can come up with their own names for the elements that are used.

An element always has start and end tags that are enclosed in < and > characters. One of the things that can catch you out is that XML is entirely case sensitive, including the names of elements, so make sure the text you use in the start and end tags is exactly the same. The start and end tags look the same, except that the end tag has a / character at the beginning. For example, `<tag>. . .</tag>` is a valid combination, but `<tag>. . .</TaG>` is not.

In addition, the only characters that you can use in an element name are digits, letters, periods (.), colons (:), underscores (_), and hyphens (-). However, digits, hyphens, and periods cannot *begin* an element name.

The children of an element occur between the start and end tags of their parent. For example, if you refer back to Listing 10.1, you can see that the top-level `people` element has two children called `person`. Each `person` element has two children, `name` and `age`, that have textual child content.

If an element is empty (because it has no child elements or text), you have a choice about the syntax you use. For example,

```
<salary></salary>
```

can also be written using a shorthand, thus:

```
<salary />
```

Some characters you should *not* use in the name of an element are `<`, `>`, and `&`. The first two characters are fairly obvious because they delimit start and end tags. The third character is used to introduce an *entity*. You can define your own entities in a Document Type Definition (DTD, but more on this later), and there are several that are built-in to XML parsers. If you need to use any of these three characters in the body content of an element between the start and end tags, you should use the appropriate symbolic form from Table 10.1. Strictly speaking, the `>` entity in the table is not necessary, but is provided to give symmetry with the `<` entity.

Table 10.1 **Special XML Characters**

Character	Name	Symbolic Form
<	Open angle bracket	<
>	Close angle bracket	>
&	Ampersand	&

When you nest elements, you must make sure that the elements are not interleaved. For example, the following is correct nesting:

```
<i><u>underlined and italicized</u></i>
```

but this is not:

```
<i><u>underlined and italicized</i></u>
```

Attributes

You can annotate elements with attributes, which are name/value pairs. Here are the rules for using attributes:

- Attributes always appear on an element's start tag, never the end tag.
- Attribute names are case sensitive and are limited in the same way that element names are with respect to letters, underscores, periods, and so forth.
- Attribute names must be unique on a given element. Therefore, it is legal to use the same attribute name on a different element.
- Attribute values are textual and must always be delimited by either single (') or double (") quotes. It is a syntax error not to delimit an attribute value.

When you specify an attribute value, you cannot use the < character within it. Instead, you should use the < entity from Table 10.1. Also, if you need to use the same character as the delimiter, there are two other built-in entities that are useful: ' for the ' character, and " for ". For example, this is invalid:

```
<quote text="I said, "Hello!"" />
```

Whereas this is legal:

```
<quote text="I said, &quot;Hello!&quot;" />
```

Many people ask, "When should I use an attribute, and when should I use an element?" There is no right or wrong answer to this question—you just need to be aware of the issues:

- Elements can model structured content (that is, child elements), textual content, or both (known as mixed content). A disadvantage of choosing an element is that it takes up more space than an attribute (start tag and end tag versus just an attribute name/value pair).
- A disadvantage of choosing an attribute is that it can only model textual content, never structured content. This means that you must think ahead to decide whether the content will ever need to be structured in the future. An advantage of choosing an attribute is that it takes up less space than an element that models textual content.

Listing 10.3 shows a simple rewrite of the XML document from Listing 10.1. The document now includes a base attribute on the person's age, in order to specify what numerical base is used to represent the age. For example, octal, decimal, hexadecimal and so on.

Listing 10.3 **An XML Document with Elements and Attributes** (peopleAttrs.xml).

```
<people>
  <person>
    <name>Mark</name>
    <age base="8">30</age>
  </person>
  <person>
    <name>Ruth</name>
```

Listing 10.3 **Continued**

```
    <age base="16">29</age>
  </person>
</people>
```

Comments

Comments are used in many places such as code, JSPs, HTML files, and XML documents. Comments should always be useful, correct, and make whatever they are commenting easier to read.

XML comments have the same form as HTML comments. For example,

```
<!-- Here is a comment -->
```

You can place a comment almost anywhere in an XML document. You cannot put a comment in certain places such as within a start tag or end tag or inside attribute values.

Any character can occur within a comment, except you cannot nest comments, nor can you use the `--` character sequence. This latter condition is one imposed by compatibility with SGML.

DTDs and Schemas

You will hear people talk about the well-formed documents that this chapter has discussed so far, but you will also hear people mention *valid* documents. They are not the same thing.

A well-formed document might have no syntax errors in it, but can still have semantic errors. For example, a `person` element in Listing 10.3 is only valid if you provide both `name` and `age` child elements, with a `base` attribute on the `age` element. However, the question is, "How can you force the XML document author to provide these values?"

A Document Type Definition (DTD) provides a template that defines which elements can appear, in which order, and which attributes those elements can have. You can then instruct a parser to run in validating mode, to check that the XML document conforms to the DTD template. This simplifies your application because you can assume certain things about the document, such as which elements and attributes appear and where.

When you use a DTD, you can define:

- Element ordering and hierarchy.
- An element's attributes.
- Enumeration values and default values for attributes.
- Entity references that the document uses. An entity is a unit of storage. For example, you can use an entity to include a file from disk, or the contents of a URL.

A disadvantage of DTDs is that they are not defined in XML, meaning that you must learn yet another syntax to write them. This is because DTDs originated from SGML. There are several other issues, which are beyond the scope of this chapter:

- DTDs do not work easily with XML Namespaces.
- It is not easy to extend a DTD.
- You cannot define type information other than text in a DTD.
- There can be only one DTD per XML document, so you cannot have different definitions of an element in a single document and still have the document be valid against a DTD.

To address these issues, the W3C wrote the XML Schema specification, which is a more flexible and powerful mechanism than DTD. XML Schemas are written in XML, and allow you to

- Specify the structure and constraints of an XML document.
- Define new data types.

You can find more information on XML Schema at the W3C Web site (`http://www.w3.org`).

Parsing XML

J2EE includes the Java API for XML Processing (JAXP), which makes it easy for Java applications to process XML data. JAXP covers three main standards:

- The Document Object Model (DOM), which builds a tree in memory that represents the XML document.
- The Simple API for XML (SAX) for parsing XML into a stream.
- The XML Stylesheet Language Transformations (XSLT) for converting XML into a different format. You will see more about XSLT in Chapter 11, "Transforming XML Using XSLT and XSLFO."

JAXP provides a common interface for creating and using SAX and DOM parsers from different vendors. You can find the JAXP APIs in the `javax.xml.parsers` package. Different vendors provide their own implementations of SAX and DOM parsers, but JAXP hides the differences in a layer of abstraction provided by two important factory classes in this package: `DocumentBuilderFactory` and `SAXParserFactory`.

You use the two factory classes to obtain an instance of a SAX or DOM parser, identified by the `SAXParser` and `DocumentBuilder` classes. The reason that this layer of abstraction is useful is that it enables you to change the XML parser implementation that you use without changing your code.

If you want to use a different parser implementation, all that you need to do is set a system property. You set the `javax.xml.parsers.SAXParserFactory` property when you want to use a different factory for creating SAX parsers. Similarly, you set the `javax.xml.parsers.DocumentBuilderFactory` property when you want to specify a different factory for creating DOM documents. Unless you override these properties at runtime, the default values point to the reference implementation provided as part of JAXP. Crimson is the parser pointed to by the default values, originally known as Sun's Project X.

So far in this chapter, you have seen an example that used Microsoft Internet Explorer to parse and display an XML document. Now, you will see three APIs (two from JAXP) that enable you to access and manipulate the information that is stored in an XML document. DOM and SAX are the first two, the Java Document Object Model (JDOM) is the third.

The DOM API

When you use the DOM API to parse an XML document, the parser builds a tree structure in memory that represents the information in the XML document. When you use the DOM, a benefit is that you get a simple mapping of the structure of the XML, but for documents that approach more than a few megabytes in size, you will notice a drain on your system resources. You tend to use the DOM when the document is relatively small, or when you want to process most or all the information in the document.

The mechanism for instantiating a DOM parser is simple. All you need to do is instantiate a `DocumentBuilderFactory` from the JAXP API, and use this to create a new `DocumentBuilderObject`, which is the parser.

A `DocumentBuilderObject` provides a `parse()` method that returns an object that represents the XML document tree. This returned object implements the `org.w3c.dom.Document` interface. For example, the following three lines of Java code build a tree in memory:

```
DocumentBuilderFactory factory = DocumentBuilderFactory.newInstance();
DocumentBuilder        builder = factory.newDocumentBuilder();
Document               doc     = builder.parse(new java.io.File("foo.xml"));
```

This code snippet parses a file `foo.xml`, but you can also specify a URL or a `java.io.InputStream` as a parameter to the `parse()` method.

After the `parse()` method has executed, the DOM parser has built an in-memory representation of the document that looks like that shown in Figure 10.4.

After you have an object that implements the `Document` interface, you can access the nodes in the tree through the methods in the interface (see Table 10.2). All the methods except for `getDocumentElement()` and `getElementsByTagNames()` are inherited from the `Document` interface's parent interface, `org.w3c.dom.Node`. The methods all return either a `NodeList` (an ordered collection of nodes) or a single `Node`.

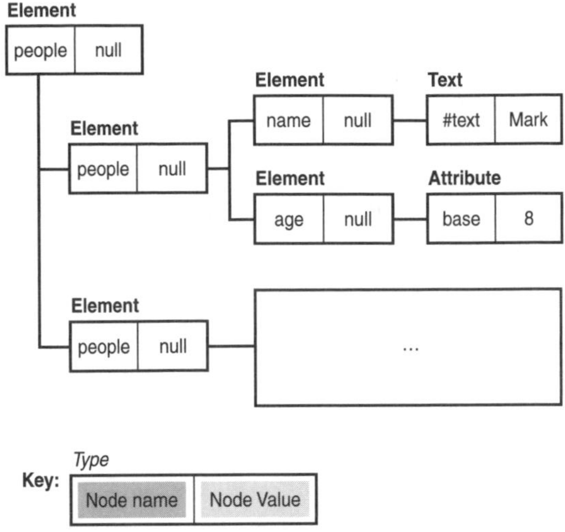

Figure 10.4 The DOM tree for the XML document in Listing 10.3.

Table 10.2 **DOM Methods to Traverse a Tree**

Method	Description
getChildNodes()	Returns a NodeList that contains all the children of this node
getFirstChild()	Returns the first child of this node
getLastChild()	Returns the last child of this node
getParentNode()	Returns the parent of this node
getPreviousSibling()	Returns the node that immediately precedes this node
getNextSibling()	Returns the node that immediately follows this node
getDocumentElement()	Returns the top-level node in this document
getElementsByTagNames(String)	Returns a NodeList of all the elements with the specified tag name under this node in the order they occur in the tree

Going back to the code snippet, you can gain access to the document element (the top-level element in the XML document) through the `getDocumentElement()` method like this:

```
Element peopleElement = doc.getDocumentElement();
```

An `org.w3c.dom.Element` is just a node in the tree that can have attributes. Elements have a hierarchical relationship with other elements.

You will now see an example that processes the document in Listing 10.1, and displays a table of people's names and ages. The first run through this example uses scriptlets to show you the Java code that is necessary to process an XML document. Then, you will see the example rewritten to use JSTL actions.

Take a look at the JSP in Listing 10.4.

Listing 10.4 **A JSP that Processes the XML Document from Listing 10.1 (`parseDoc.jsp`)**

```
<%@page import="org.w3c.dom.Node, org.w3c.dom.Element, org.w3c.dom.Document,
➥    org.w3c.dom.NodeList, javax.xml.parsers.DocumentBuilder,
➥    javax.xml.parsers.DocumentBuilderFactory" %>

<%!
  public boolean isTextNode(Node n)
  {
    return n.getNodeName().equals("#text");
  }
%>

<html>
  <head><title>Parsing using the DOM</title></head>
  <body>
    <%
      DocumentBuilderFactory factory = DocumentBuilderFactory.newInstance();
      DocumentBuilder        builder = factory.newDocumentBuilder();
      Document               doc     = builder.parse("http://localhost:8080/"
➥                                        + "chapter10/people.xml");
    %>

    <h1>List of people</h1>
    <table border="1">
      <tr><th>Name</th><th>Age</th></tr>

    <%
      Element  root        = doc.getDocumentElement(); // "people" node
      NodeList personNodes = root.getChildNodes();     // 2 "person" nodes

      for (int i=0; i<personNodes.getLength(); i++)
      {
        Node currentPerson = personNodes.item(i);

        if (isTextNode(currentPerson)) // skip whitespace node
          continue;

        // get the "name" and "age" nodes
        NodeList nameAndAge = currentPerson.getChildNodes();
```

Listing 10.4 **Continued**

```
    %>

    <tr>

    <%
        for (int j=0; j<nameAndAge.getLength(); j++ )
        {
          Node currentItem = nameAndAge.item(j);

          if ( isTextNode(currentItem))
            continue;
    %>
      <td><%= currentItem.getFirstChild().getNodeValue() %></td>
    <%
        } // end of name & age loop
    %>
    </tr>

    <%
      } // end person loop
    %>

    </table>
  </body>
</html>
```

This JSP begins by importing the classes and interfaces that are used in the scriptlets:

```
<%@page import="org.w3c.dom.Node, org.w3c.dom.Element, org.w3c.dom.Document,
➥     org.w3c.dom.NodeList, javax.xml.parsers.DocumentBuilder,
➥     javax.xml.parsers.DocumentBuilderFactory" %>
```

The next thing that you see is the declaration of a utility method called `isTextNode()` that the scriptlet uses later.

Within the body tag, you see the first piece of scriptlet code, which creates a DOM parser and processes an XML file that is identified by a URL:

```
DocumentBuilderFactory factory = DocumentBuilderFactory.newInstance();
DocumentBuilder        builder = factory.newDocumentBuilder();
Document               doc     = builder.parse("http://localhost:8080/"
➥                                              +"chapter10/people.xml");
```

You then see some HTML tags that start the table, with column headings `Name` and `Age`. This is immediately followed by another scriptlet that drills down into the XML and finds the `name` and `age` elements for each `person`:

```
Element  root        = doc.getDocumentElement(); // "people" node
NodeList personNodes = root.getChildNodes();     // 2 "person" nodes
                                                 // + whitespace nodes
```

These two lines of code first get hold of the document element (`people`), and retrieve a collection of all its child nodes. This collection contains the two `person` nodes.

Then, for each `person`, we want to find their name and age and display this information in a row in the table. However, if we simply assume that there are only *two* nodes in the `personNodes` collection, we would be wrong! This is because the DOM models whitespace-only text nodes as nodes in the tree. Thus, there are actually five nodes in the `personNodes` collection:

- One for the whitespace after the opening `people` tag
- One for the first `person` tag
- One for whitespace between the end tag for the first `person` and the start tag for the second `person`
- One for the second `person` tag
- One for the whitespace between the closing tag for the second `person` and the end `people` tag

Thus, the scriptlet uses the utility `isTextNode()` method from earlier in the page, and skips any text nodes. The utility method makes use of the fact that any text node has a name of `#text` when you query using the `getNodeType()` method:

```
for (int i=0; i<personNodes.getLength(); i++)
{
    Node currentPerson = personNodes.item(i);

    if (isTextNode(currentPerson)) // skip whitespace node
      continue;

    // Find "name" and "age" nodes
    NodeList nameAndAge = currentPerson.getChildNodes();
    . . .
```

Therefore, after skipping any whitespace text nodes, the page gets a list of the child nodes for each person and stores them in the `nameAndAge` collection. The information from this collection will form another row in the table. Again, any whitespace nodes from the input document (this time between the `name` and `age` tags) are skipped:

```
<tr>
<%
    for (int j=0; j<nameAndAge.getLength(); j++ )
    {
      Node currentItem = nameAndAge.item(j);
```

```
        if ( isTextNode(currentItem))
          continue;
%>
    <td><%= currentItem.getFirstChild().getNodeValue() %></td>
    <%
    } // end of name & age loop
    %>
</tr>
```

Perhaps the only other thing worthy of note from this example is the piece of code that inserts the text for the name and age:

```
<td><%= currentItem.getFirstChild().getNodeValue() %></td>
```

Because the `currentItem` is a reference to either a `name` or an `age` element in the tree, why do you need to call `getFirstChild()` before you can extract the node value? Well, the DOM does not only represent whitespace-only text in the tree! If you refer back to Figure 10.4, you can see that all text between elements in the input document has its own node in the tree. Thus, `getFirstChild()` returns a reference to the text node, which is then queried using `getNodeValue()` for the text in question.

If you run the example, you see output like that shown in Figure 10.5.

Figure 10.5 Output for the JSP in Listing 10.4.

After all that, you might be thinking that it sounds like a lot of work, and you would be right! Fortunately, JSTL provides a set of actions that simplify the processing of XML. You can achieve the same result in a lot less time by writing the JSP using these tags, as in Listing 10.5. The JSTL XML actions are very similar to the Core actions that you saw in Chapter 5, "The JSP Standard Tag Library," except that they use XPath expressions rather than runtime expressions or the Expression Language.

> **Note**
> You can find a quick reference to the XML tags that JSTL provides in Appendix C, "A Checklist of the Tags in the JSP Standard Tag Library."

Listing 10.5 **A JSP that Uses JSTL XML Actions (`parseDoc_JSTL.jsp`)**

```
<%@ taglib uri="http://java.sun.com/jstl-el/xml"  prefix="x" %>
<%@ taglib uri="http://java.sun.com/jstl-el/core" prefix="c" %>

<html>
  <head>
    <title>Parsing using the DOM and JSTL</title>
  </head>
  <body>
    <c:import url="http://localhost:8080/chapter10/people.xml"
              var="personXml" />
    <x:parse doc="${personXml}" varDom="parsedXml" />

    <h1>List of people</h1>
    <table border="1">
      <tr><th>Name</th><th>Age</th></tr>

      <x:forEach select="$parsedXml/people/person" var="currentPerson">
      <tr>
        <x:forEach select="*">
          <td><x:out select="." /></td>
        </x:forEach>
      </tr>
      </x:forEach>
    </table>
  </body>
</html>
```

To parse the document using the DOM, and to expose the result in a page-scoped variable of type `org.w3c.dom.Document`, all you need to do is use the `c:import` and `x:parse` actions:

```
<c:import url="http://localhost:8080/chapter10/people.xml"
          var="personXml" />
<x:parse doc="${personXml}" varDom="parsedXml" />
```

You saw the `c:import` action in Chapter 5. The contents of the `url` are exported as a string, stored in the `personXml` variable. The `x:parse` action processes this content and exposes the DOM tree through the `parsedXml` variable (set by the `varDom` attribute).

Inside the HTML table, the `x:forEach` action is used. This action is similar to the `c:forEach` action, except that it uses XPath expressions to identify what it loops over. In this case, the code iterates over each `/people/person` node, storing the current node in the `currentPerson` variable:

```
<x:forEach select="$parsedXml/people/person" var="currentPerson">
```

Note

You can find an introduction to XPath in Chapter 11, "Transforming XML Using XSLT and XSLFO." That chapter also contains examples that use the other JSTL XML actions.

Within this `x:forEach`, you can see that there is a nested `x:forEach` that selects all child nodes of the current `person` node by specifying an XPath expression of `*`. This selects the `name` and `age` nodes, for each of which a separate cell in the table is displayed that contains the node's value. The JSP uses the `x:out` action for this:

```
<tr>
    <x:forEach select="*">
        <td><x:out select="." /></td>
    </x:forEach>
</tr>
```

The Simple API for XML (SAX)

The members of the XML-DEV mailing list (`http://www.xml.org`) cooperatively developed SAX, and David Brownell coordinates its development (`http://www.saxproject.org`). JAXP 1.1 supports the current version of SAX, which is version 2.0, as released in May 2000. The designers of SAX originally wrote it for Java, although there are implementations available for most other languages too, including Visual Basic, C++, Python, and Perl.

SAX takes a different approach to parsing XML than DOM. DOM is a tree-based API, whereas SAX is stream-based and decomposes the information in an XML document into a sequence of method calls.

The choice to use SAX is a good one

- If the document is large
- When processing speed is important
- If you only want to search for a small number of tags within an XML document

When you want to parse an XML document using SAX through JAXP, you must instantiate a `javax.xml.parsers.SAXParseFactory` object, and use it to create a SAX-based parser. You can then use this parser to read the XML document, one character at a time. This idea is illustrated in Figure 10.6, which shows the steps you need to perform:

1. After you have the parser, register the object (known as the *handler*) that needs to know the contents of the XML. The diagram shows a fictitious handler called `MyHandler`.
2. Call `parse()` on the SAX parser, specifying the document to parse.
3. The SAX parser reads the input document.
4. The SAX parser calls back into the registered handler object as it encounters information in the XML document.

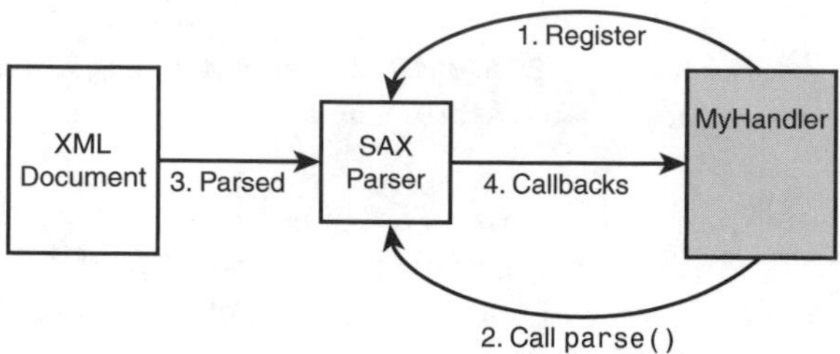

Figure 10.6 Parsing an XML document with SAX.

The following code fragment shows you the basic approach that you take when you want to parse a document using SAX:

```
SAXParserFactory factory = SAXParserFactory.newInstance();
SAXParser        parser  = factory.newSAXParser();
DefaultHandler   handler = new MyHandler();
parser.parse( new File(xmlDoc), handler);
```

To write your handler object, you write a subclass of the `org.xml.sax.helpers.DefaultHandler` class as signified in Figure 10.6 by the `MyHandler` object. The `DefaultHandler` class defines a set of empty, stub methods that do nothing. The idea is that you subclass `DefaultHandler` and provide your own implementations of the methods in which you are interested. For example, the `startElement()` method is invoked by the SAX parser when a new element is encountered in the XML document. The parser passes in the element's name and attributes to the `startElement()` method.

The component's of an element's qualified name are passed to the `startElement()` method in its first three parameters (see Table 10.3). Exactly what you get in these parameters depends on whether the XML document uses namespaces. The signature of the `startElement()` method is

```
public void startElement(String namespaceURI, String localName,
➥                        String qName, Attributes attrs)
```

Table 10.3 **Parameters to the `startElement()` Methods in the `org.xml.sax.helpers.DefaultHandler` Interface**

Parameter	Description
namespaceURI	This is the namespace URI associated with the element. If there is no namespace, or namespace processing is not being performed, this parameter is the empty string.
localName	This is the element name, without a prefix. Example: out for an element <c:out>.
qName	This is the element name, with a prefix. Example: c:out for an element <c:out>.
attrs	A collection of the element's attributes.

Table 10.4 lists all the methods that you can override when you write a subclass of `DefaultHandler`. Consult the JAXP documentation for a description of the parameters to these methods.

Table 10.4 **Methods in the `org.xml.sax.helpers.DefaultHandler` Interface**

Method	Receives Notification Of
void startDocument()	The beginning of the document
void endDocument()	The end of the document
void startElement(String namespaceURI, String localName, String qName, Attributes attrs)	The start of an element
void endElement(String namespaceURI, String localName, String qName)	The end of an element
void characters(char[] ch, int start, int length)	Character data within an element
void ignorableWhitespace(char[] ch, int start,	Whitespace in the element contents int length)
void processingInstruction(String target, String data)	A processing instruction
void startPrefixMapping(String prefix, String namespaceURI)	Start of a namespace mapping
void endPrefixMapping(String prefix)	End of a namespace mapping
void setDocumentLocator(...)	An object that can locate the origin of SAX events (that is line and column number from the input XML document)
void notationDecl(String name, String publicID, String systemID)	Notation declaration
void error(SAXParseException e)	A recoverable parser error. For example, a validity problem between the XML document and its DTD or schema
void fatalError(SAXParseException e)	A fatal XML parsing error. For example, a document that is not well formed
void warning(SAXParseException e)	A parser warning
void resolveEntity(String publicID, String systemID)	For resolving an external entity. You can override to provide special translations, such as caching and URL redirection
void skippedEntity(String name)	A skipped entity (SAX parsers can skip entities if they have not seen the entity declaration)

Here is an example that processes the XML document in Listing 10.3. It displays messages whenever the parser invokes a method in the handler, and displays the total for the ages that are present in the input document. The JSP for the example is shown in Listing 10.6.

Listing 10.6 **A JSP that Uses SAX** (`MyHandler.jsp`)

```
<%@ page import="javax.xml.parsers.SAXParserFactory,
                 javax.xml.parsers.SAXParser,
                 com.conygre.jspdevhandbook.chapter10.MyHandler"%>

<html>
  <head><title>JSP and SAX</title></head>
  <body>
    <%
      SAXParserFactory factory   = SAXParserFactory.newInstance();
      SAXParser        parser    = factory.newSAXParser();
      MyHandler        myHandler = new MyHandler(out);

      parser.parse("http://localhost:8080/chapter10/peopleAttrs.xml",
                   myHandler);
    %>
  </body>
</html>
```

The JSP begins by importing the `SAXParserFactory` and `SAXParser` classes, as well as the custom handler class that you will see in a moment (`MyHandler`).

A scriptlet performs the main work in these examples to keep the size of the examples as small as possible so that you can more easily follow what's happening. In practice, you would normally embed the parsing functionality inside a JavaBean or a custom action. You can see that the scriptlet uses a `SAXParserFactory` to create a new `SAXParser`. Also, a `MyHandler` object is instantiated and passed a reference to the implicit `out` object. Finally, the scriptlet calls the parser's `parse()` method to instruct the parser to parse the `peopleAttrs.xml` document, and to invoke the appropriate methods on the `myHandler` object.

Listing 10.7 shows the implementation of the `MyHandler` class.

Listing 10.7 **The `MyHandler` Class** (`MyHandler.java`).

```
package com.conygre.jspdevhandbook.chapter10;

import java.io.IOException;
import javax.servlet.jsp.JspWriter;
import org.xml.sax.Attributes;
import org.xml.sax.SAXException;
import org.xml.sax.helpers.DefaultHandler;

public class MyHandler extends DefaultHandler
{
  private int       stepCount, totalAge;
  private JspWriter out;
```

Listing 10.7 **Continued**

```
private boolean   insideAgeElement;

public MyHandler(JspWriter out)
{
  this.out = out;
}

public void startDocument() throws SAXException
{
  try
  {
    out.write(++stepCount + ". Start of document<br>");
  }
  catch (IOException e)
  {
    throw new SAXException(e);
  }
} // end of startDocument()

public void endDocument() throws SAXException
{
  try
  {
    out.write(++stepCount + ". End of document<p>");
    out.write("The total of all ages in the XML document is <b><i>"
              + totalAge + "</i></b>");
  }
  catch (IOException e)
  {
    throw new SAXException(e);
  }
} // end of endDocument()

public void startElement(String namespaceURI, String localName,
                         String qName, Attributes attrs)
    throws SAXException
{
  if ( qName.equals("age"))
  {
    insideAgeElement = true;
  }

  try
  {
    out.write(++stepCount + ". Start of element: <b>" + qName + "</b>");
```

Listing 10.7 **Continued**

```
      int numberOfAttributes = attrs.getLength();

      if ( numberOfAttributes > 0 )
      {
        out.write(". Attributes: <ul>");
      } // end of if ()
      else
        out.write("<br>");

      for ( int i=0; i<numberOfAttributes; i++)
      {
        out.write("<li>" + attrs.getQName(i) + " = "
                  + attrs.getValue(i) + "</li>");
      } // end of for ()

      if ( numberOfAttributes > 0 )
      {
        out.write("</ul>");
      }
    }
    catch (IOException e)
    {
      throw new SAXException(e);
    }
  } // end of startElement()

  public void endElement(String namespaceURI, String localName, String qName)
      throws SAXException
  {
    if ( qName.equals("age") )
    {
      insideAgeElement = false;
    }

    try
    {
      out.write(++stepCount + ". End of element <b>" + qName + "</b><br>");
    }
    catch (IOException e)
    {
      throw new SAXException(e);
    } // end of try-catch

  } // end of endElement()
```

Listing 10.7 **Continued**

```
  public void characters(char[] chars, int start, int length) throws SAXException
  {
    String content = new String(chars, start, length);

    if ( insideAgeElement )
    {
      int age  =  Integer.parseInt(content);
      totalAge += age;
    }

    try
    {
      out.write(++stepCount + ". Character content = ");

      if ( length > 0 )
        out.write("<b>" + content + "</b><br>");
    }
    catch (IOException e)
    {
      throw new SAXException(e);
    } // end of try-catch

  } // end of characters()
} // end of class MyHandler
```

The code in Listing 10.7 might look complicated at first glance, but it is really quite simple. The first two methods are

- A constructor that stores a reference to the implicit JSP `out` variable.
- The `startDocument()` method that prints a message when the document begins.

Notice that the `MyHandler` class declares two instance variables of type `int`. One is `stepCount` and the other is `totalAge`. The former variable keeps a count of how many methods the parser has invoked in the handler, and the latter stores the sum of the ages in the XML document.

All the methods use the `stepCount` variable to generate a numbered list in the output.

One of the trickiest things about writing SAX applications is that you need to maintain your own context. That is, when a SAX parser calls your handler's `characters()` method with the string `42`, you need to decide whether that is somebody's age, a price in dollars, or whatever. One way to do this is to have a set of `boolean` flags that you set to indicate which element you are currently inside. Another technique that you might find easier to work with is to have a state variable and a set of `private static int` values that enumerate the possible states. This makes it possible to use `switch` statements in your methods.

In this example, the `startElement()` method performs a few tasks. First, it makes a check to see if the parser has just encountered an `age` element in the input document. If so, a `boolean` variable called `insideAgeElement` is set to `true`. This is so that when a subsequent call is made to the `characters()` method, a check can be made inside that method to see whether the current text should be converted to an integer and added to the sum of the ages:

```
if ( insideAgeElement )
{
  int age  =  Integer.parseInt(content);
  totalAge += age;
}
```

The `endElement()` method makes a check to see if an `age` element has just ended so that the `boolean` variable `insideAgeElement` can be reset to `false`.

The other thing that the `startElement()` method does is access and display any attributes that belong to an element, by way of the `getLength()`, `getQName()` and `getValue()` methods of the `Attributes` collection.

The `endDocument()` method displays a message when the parser finishes processing the document and outputs the total value for the ages that occurred in the document.

You can see the output from running the JSP in Listing 10.6 in Figure 10.7. Actually, the document that is parsed to generate the output in Figure 10.7 is the same as the document in Listing 10.3, but with all the carriage return and tab characters removed. This was simply to remove from the output the corresponding calls to the `characters()` method.

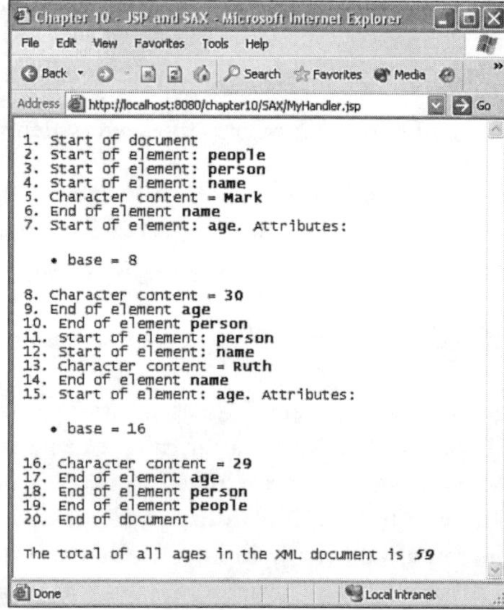

Figure 10.7 Output of the JSP in Listing 10.6.

JDOM

Thus far in this chapter, you have seen the DOM and SAX APIs for accessing XML documents, and now you are about to see JDOM (JDOM is not an acronym). Jason Hunter and Brett McLaughlin created JDOM in the Spring of 2000 as an open-source API that is similar to DOM, but not built on it or modeled after it. JDOM is an open-source library for Java-optimized XML operations, released under the Apache license. Basically, this means that you can do pretty much anything you like with JDOM except use its name in a work derived from it.

> **Note**
>
> The JDOM homepage is at `http://www.jdom.org`. You can download the JDOM source code, binaries, and documentation from there. At the time of writing (August 2002), JDOM is currently at Beta 8. It is also a Java Specification Request (JSR-102), opening the door to JDOM eventually becoming a part of the core Java platform. This chapter's examples from the book web site contain the required `jdom.jar` file.

After seeing SAX and DOM, you might be wondering why there is a need for yet another XML API. What JDOM attempts to do is to take the best from SAX and DOM, and create a lightweight, Java-based, API that has low memory and processing overheads. JDOM has two key philosophies:

- The loading and manipulation of XML documents should be quick, with a low memory overhead.
- To make the programmer's life as simple as possible.

JDOM was created because its inventors found that DOM and SAX were not capable enough for their needs. For example, when you use SAX you cannot modify the original XML document or jump around in the stream. When you write a SAX application, you often need to create your own finite state machine or custom object model to keep track of whereabouts in the XML document you are currently up to.

With respect to the DOM, you find a tree-based API very useful in situations where you want to keep the whole tree in memory and access parts of it in a random fashion. Unfortunately, the DOM has some limitations inherent in its design. This is because the DOM was designed to be compatible with the different object models that were available in Web browsers at the time, which inevitably led to a solution that can be clunky at best and infuriating at its worst. In addition, the DOM API is defined in IDL, which means that it is a lowest common denominator API, therefore, limited to only those features that are present in all the programming languages that have an IDL mapping. Similarly to the DOM, but unlike SAX, JDOM presents a view of the full XML document as a tree that is available at all times.

JDOM's creators wrote the JDOM API from scratch, with the express intent of writing an API that is invoked from Java to process XML. In fact, the stated mission goal on the JDOM home page is "to build a complete, Java-based solution for accessing, manipulating, and outputting XML data from Java code." This means that it is a more elegant API than DOM, which was designed to be a cross-language technology.

As a Java-based API, JDOM takes full advantage of the features of the Java programming language and libraries. For example, the Java Collections API and method overloading are used extensively. In addition, JDOM represents the XML document in an object-oriented way that is familiar to Java programmers. You often find that the first and simplest way to do something is the way that JDOM actually lets you do it! For example, if you want to create an element to insert into an existing JDOM tree, that looked like this:

```
<age base="8">30</age>
```

you could use this code:

```
Element age = new Element("age");
age.setText("30");
age.setAttribute("base", 8);
```

And, if you then wanted to add this `age` element to a `person` element, you could do this:

```
Element person = new Element("person");
person.addContent(age);
```

giving this result:

```
<person>
    <age base="8">30</age>
</person>
```

As another example, recall that towards the end of Listing 10.4 you saw this expression to extract the text content of a `name` element from the XML document in Listing 10.1:

```
<%= currentItem.getFirstChild().getNodeValue() %>
```

The `currentItem` in this case is a reference to a node in the DOM tree. The call to `getFirstChild()` was necessary to first retrieve the text node under the `name` element, which could then be queried for its textual content through the `getNodeValue()` method.

JDOM makes this example much more intuitive to work with, because JDOM makes the text content of an element available through a call to `getText()`. Listing 10.8 shows how you can rewrite the example from Listing 10.4 so that it uses the JDOM API rather than the DOM.

Listing 10.8 **A JSP that Parses Listing 10.1 Using JDOM (`parseJDOM.jsp`).**

```
<%@ page import="org.jdom.Element,
                 org.jdom.Document,
                 org.jdom.input.SAXBuilder,
```

Listing 10.8 **Continued**

```
                 java.util.List,
                 java.util.Iterator"
%>

<%
  SAXBuilder builder  = new SAXBuilder();
  Document   doc      = builder.build("http://localhost:8080"
                                      + "/chapter10/people.xml");
  List       children = doc.getRootElement().getChildren(); // 2 person nodes
  Iterator   iter     = children.iterator();
%>

<html>
  <head><title>Parsing using JDOM</title></head>
  <body>
    <h1>List of people</h1>

    <table border="1">
      <tr><th>Name</th><th>Age</th></tr>

      <%
        while (iter.hasNext()) // for each "person" node
        {
          Element  currentItem = (Element) iter.next();     // each "person"
          List     nameAndAge  = currentItem.getChildren();
          Iterator nameAgeIter = nameAndAge.iterator();
      %>
      <tr>
      <%
          while ( nameAgeIter.hasNext() )
          {
            Element child = (Element) nameAgeIter.next(); // "name" or "age"
      %>
        <td><%= child.getText() %></td>
      <%
          }
        }
      %>
      </tr>
    </table>
  </body>
</html>
```

To be able to view this page, you must have the various imported classes and interfaces on your Web application's classpath. The `org.jdom.Element`, `org.jdom.Document`, and org.jdom.input.SAXBuilder classes are part of the jdom.jar file that you can download from http://www.jdom.org/downloads/index.html. The java.util.Iterator and java.util.List interfaces are a standard part of the Java 2 Collections API.

> **Note**
> JDOM does not include a parser, although Xerces is shipped with it. You can use any SAX2-compliant parser instead if you want.

After the page directive that imports these classes and interfaces, a short scriptlet loads the XML document:

```
SAXBuilder builder  = new SAXBuilder();
Document   doc = builder.build("http://localhost:8080"
➥                               + "/chapter10/people.xml");
```

JDOM provides two builders that you can use to load XML: SAXBuilder and DOMBuilder. Normally, you use the SAXBuilder class because it is quicker. In addition, you would not usually require the additional overhead of the DOM tree model because you have the JDOM model instead.

The scriptlet then continues with:

```
List        children = doc.getRootElement().getChildren(); // 2 person nodes
Iterator    iter     = children.iterator();
```

As the comment indicates, the first line retrieves a collection of the two person elements. The second line of code here then acquires a standard Java iterator that can be used to step through the contents of the collection.

Within the HTML table later in the page, another scriptlet uses this iterator to obtain a collection of name and age elements for each person element:

```
<%
while (iter.hasNext()) // for each "person" node
{
    Element  currentItem = (Element) iter.next();     // each "person"
    List     nameAndAge  = currentItem.getChildren();
```

The scriptlet then uses a second iterator, nameAgeIter, to display these names and ages in the table:

```
    Iterator nameAgeIter = nameAndAge.iterator();
%>
    <tr>
<%
    while ( nameAgeIter.hasNext() )
    {
        Element child = (Element) nameAgeIter.next(); // "name" or "age"
%>
```

```
        <td><%= child.getText() %></td>
<%
    }
}
%>
```

Finally, it is worth listing a few things that should enable you to decide whether you want to use SAX or DOM instead of JDOM:

- JDOM cannot provide you with type information from a DTD or a schema.
- For large documents, you will still want to use SAX. This is because JDOM loads the whole tree into memory and keeps it there. Depending on the particular DOM you use, JDOM might take up more or less memory.
- If you want to traverse a tree, it is easier to use the DOM through the properties defined in its `Node` interface (for example, `parentNode` and `childNodes`).

Summary

This chapter introduced XML, including its structure and syntax. XML is a human-readable, structured data-encoding format that is generic, simple, extensible, flexible, and free to use.

You saw that one of the most important features of XML is that it enables you to create flexible data structures that are inherently portable. In fact, a common term that is applied to XML is that it is *portable data*.

Although not covered in detail in this chapter, you can use DTD and Schema to validate the data that is in an XML document. The difference between well-formed XML and valid XML is that the former is XML that is structurally and syntactically correct, whereas the latter means that the XML is well formed *and* conforms to the constraints specified by a DTD or schema.

You can parse an XML document in several different ways. You saw the DOM, SAX, and JDOM APIs, and you should now recognize the advantages and disadvantages of each. There is no single API that you will use in all situations, and you must make a decision as to which of these APIs, or others, you will use in any given situation. For example, SAX is generally faster than any other API, whereas DOM and JDOM can make heavy use of memory.

In the next chapter, you will see how to use XSLT and XSLTFO from your Web applications in order to transform XML into a presentation format such as HTML, XHTML, WML, or PDF.

11

Transforming XML Using XSLT and XSLFO

THIS CHAPTER INTRODUCES XSLT AS A TECHNOLOGY that can be used from JSP to transform XML into a presentation format such as HTML, XHTML, or WML. It discusses the basic syntax of XSLT, introducing the role of templates and XPath.

The chapter then demonstrates how you can use XSLT in conjunction with JSP to present XML data to a variety of presentation devices using HTML, CHTML, and WML. You will see worked examples for each data format. You will see Xalan used as the Java implementation for transforming XML. There are also references made to the XSLT compiler (XSLTC) from Sun.

The chapter then moves on to discuss the role of XSLFO, and introduces how XML data can be converted into a format such as PDF. The cocoon framework from Apache is introduced at this point as an example of how both XSLT transformation and XSLFO technology can be harnessed by Web containers such as Tomcat.

> **Note**
>
> If you want to run the demonstration applications for this chapter, you will need the `chapter11.war` file from the book Web site (`www.samspublishing.com`).

Introduction to XSLT

XSLT (eXtensible Stylesheet Language: Transformations) is all about transforming an XML document into something else. According to the XSLT specification, the original purpose of XSLT was to transform one XML document into another one. However, you can use XSLT to generate any other text format.

You might as well ask why you would ever want to transform XML in the first place. One reason is that you often want to separate data from the way in which it is presented to users, to allow for flexibility in the way that the data is rendered. For example, most users use a Web browser to view data over the Internet, so you might want to convert the XML into HTML. It is also becoming more common for users to use other display devices such as WAP-enabled cell phones, so you might need to render the XML as WML too.

Another reason that you might want to transform XML is evident when you want to send data between applications. If the recipient software expects the document to conform to a different version of a DTD or XML Schema than the one you are using, you could go about achieving interoperability between your software and the recipient software in several ways. For example, you might need to convert some elements into attributes, or modify the namespace that is used to qualify the elements and attributes. One approach would be to write a utility in a standard programming language such as Perl or Java that would perform the transformation. But, you have seen that processing a document using DOM or SAX can become tricky and fortunately, there is an alternative: You can use XSLT to transform the original document.

Yet another situation in which you might want to use XSLT is when you want to have a programming-language neutral class definition written in XML Schema. You could then have an XSLT program that could generate a class definition specific to Visual Basic, C++, or Java (or whatever), depending on an input parameter.

XSLT Input and Output

It was mentioned earlier in this chapter that you could write a utility program in a language such as Java that could transform an XML document. The problem with doing this is that you usually end up writing each custom utility from the very beginning. One of the main reasons that you would want to use XSLT instead is that it works at a higher level than a custom utility. When you write an XSLT program, you define a set of rules that tell the XSLT processor how to transform the input document into the output document.

XSLT is a programming language in which you write the programs XML. This means that an XSLT processor must have some kind of XML parser, although the XSLT specification says nothing about what kind of XML parser an XSLT processor should use. You can find the XSLT specification at `http://www.w3.org/TR/xslt`.

Figure 11.1 shows a block diagram of the XSLT process, with the input document and the XSLT program both written in XML. The XSLT processor reads the program and the input document, and generates the output text document.

There are many XSLT processors available, including

- Michael Kay's Saxon (`http://users.iclway.co.uk/mhkay/saxon`)
- Microsoft's MSXML (`http://msdn.microsoft.com/xml`)
- Apache's Xalan (`http://xml.apache.org/xalan-j/index.html`)

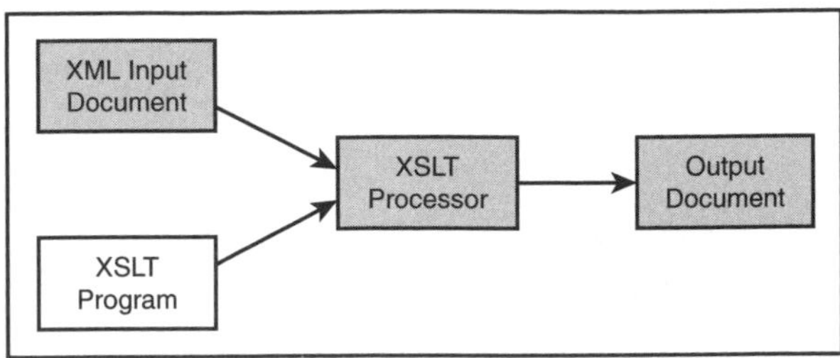

Figure 11.1 The XSLT process.

Later in the chapter you will be exposed to the Xalan processor, which is built into the J2SDK 1.4 platform.

Three different ways can be used to write an XSLT program. You can write a single template, multiple templates, or write procedural programs. These approaches are all explained later in this chapter.

XPath

Before you see any of the ways that you can write an XSLT program, you first need to know about *XPath*. XPath is an intradocument addressing language that enables you to select a subset of a document based on selection criteria. You need to know how to write XPath patterns that select subsets of the input document to write XSLT programs. You can find the XPath specification at `http://www.w3.org/TR/xpath`.

The basic format for an XPath location path is

```
/GrandParentElement/ParentElement/ChildElement
```

The XPath location path shown previously is an *absolute* location path because it begins with the / character. Thus, the search always begins at the root of the input document and evaluates to a *nodeset*. To illustrate what happens, look at the XML document in Listing 11.1.

Listing 11.1 **An XML Document**

```
<people>
  <person>
    <name>Joshua</name>
    <age>4</age>
  </person>
  <person>
    <name>Samuel</name>
    <age>1</age>
  </person>
</people>
```

When an XSLT processor evaluates an XPath location path, it breaks the location path up into *location steps* and interprets each against a *context* to give a *result node set*. Thus, an absolute location path such as

```
/people/person/name
```

is evaluated in the following way:

1. Against the context of the root (/) of the input document, select all `people` nodes, to give the first result node set.
2. The result node set then becomes the context for the next location step. Thus, for each node in the context, apply the next location step (`person`) to give another result node set.
3. The result node set from step 2 then becomes the context node set. The next location step (`name`) is then applied to each node in the context node set to give the final result node set. This node set contains the two `name` elements.

See Figure 11.2 for a diagram of this process.

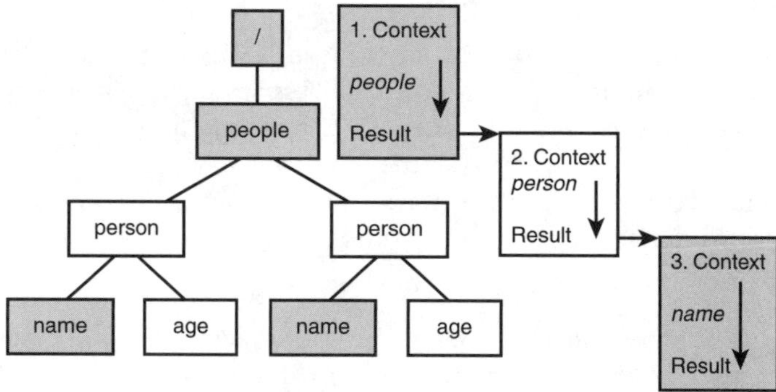

Figure 11.2 XPath Evaluation of `/people/person/name`.

So, what if you tried to evaluate a location path such as `/people/name` against the XML document in Listing 11.1? The same process occurs. First, the `people` location step is applied to the root of the input document to give a result node set that contains the single `person` element. This node set then becomes the context for the next location step. Remember, the rule is that the XPath applies the next location step to each node in the context node set. In this case, this says, "Under the current node, find a child node called `name`." Because there is not a `name` node under `people`, the result of executing this location path (`/person/name`) is an empty node set.

As mentioned earlier, relative location paths work in pretty much the same way as absolute expressions except that they do not begin with a forward slash. For example, a relative location path is

```
person/name
```

If you applied this location path to the people node in the example, you would obtain the same result. That is, the two name nodes from the input document. If you were to apply this location path to any other node in the input document, you would get back an empty node set.

You can evaluate a relative location path against any context node. You usually do this in application software, by applying an XPath location path to a node in the tree. For example, Xalan2 provides the XPathAPI class with this method:

```
public static XObject eval(Node contextNode, String s)
```

XPath is the addressing language used by XSLT to search for nodes within the input document. However, one thing that you should be wary of is the fact that XPath knows nothing of XML's default namespace mechanism. That is, if you are processing an input document that uses default namespaces and you want to search it, you must take extra steps first. You must define prefix/namespace mappings to the XSLT processor, and use those prefixes in the XPath expressions. For simplicity, the examples in this chapter assume that there are no namespaces in scope, default, or explicit.

Axis Identifiers

In the XPath section, from the path examples you have seen so far in this chapter, it has been implicit that the nodes in the result node set are one level down in the tree from the context node that the location step is applied to. A valid question to ask is, "Can I select nodes that are in a *different* direction than one level down?" The answer is yes, but you need to explicitly state the direction.

In fact, the location path you saw earlier

```
/people/person/name
```

is a shorthand for

```
/child::people/child::person/child::name
```

The child part is known as an axis identifier. An axis identifier enables you to search in different directions from a context node.

There is never a situation where you *must* use the child axis, but if you want to search in a direction other than child, you must specify one of the axes in Table 11.1.

Table 11.1 **XPath Axis Identifiers**

Axis	Description
Child	It selects nodes that are children of the context node. This is the default axis, and can be omitted.
Self	The current node (the context node). Can be abbreviated to .
Parent	Finds the parent node of the context node. Can be abbreviated to ..

Table 11.1 **Continued**

Axis	Description
Attribute	Finds the attributes of the context node. Can be abbreviated to @
Namespace	Finds the namespace declarations of the context node.
Ancestor	Finds the ancestors of the context node, from the parent up to the root of the input tree.
Ancestor-or-self	Does the same as the ancestor axis, except it also includes the context node in the result.
Descendant	Finds the descendant nodes of the context node.
Descendant-or-self	Does the same as the descendant axis, except it also includes the context node in the result.
Preceding	Finds all nodes whose end tag comes before the context node's start tag.
Preceding-sibling	Does the same as the preceding axis, except it only locates nodes that are siblings of the context node (that is, have the same parent node).
Following	Finds all nodes whose start tag comes after the context node's end tag.
Following-sibling	Does the same as the following axis, except it only locates nodes that are siblings of the context node (that is, have the same parent node).

For the XML document in Listing 11.2, you can see the results in Table 11.2 of applying the different axes to the context node that is the first `name` element. The location paths in Table 11.2 all use a node test of `*`, which selects all elements in the specified axis.

Listing 11.2 **XML Document**

```
<people>
  <person>
    <age>4</age>
    <name>                                      <!-- context node -->
      <firstName>Joshua</firstName>
      <lastName>Greenhough</lastName>
    </name>
    <eyeColor>blue</eyeColor>
  </person>
  <person>
    <age>1</age>
    <name>
      <firstName>Samuel</firstName>
      <lastName>Greenhough</lastName>
    </name>
    <eyeColor>green</eyeColor>
  </person>
</people>
```

Table 11.2 **XPath Axis Identifiers**

Location path	Result node set contents
Child::*	
Equivalent to *	firstName, lastName
Self::*	
Equivalent to .	name
Parent::*	
Equivalent to ..	The first of the two person elements in the document.
Attribute::*	
Equivalent to @*	Empty result node set because there are no attributes on the context node.
Namespace::*	Empty result node set because there are no namespace declarations on the context node.
Ancestor::*	person, people, / Notice that axes have a direction associated with them. Hence, this node set is ordered in reverse because the location path is evaluated going back up the tree.
Ancestor-or-self	name, person, people, /
Descendant	firstName, lastName
Descendant-or-self	name, firstName, lastName
Preceding	The first age element in the document (with text content 4).
Preceding-sibling	The first age element in the document (with text content 4).
Following	eyeColor (with content blue), the second person element, along with its child elements age, name, firstName, lastName, and eyeColor (with content green).
Following-sibling	The first eyeColor element (with content blue).

A useful shorthand that is not shown in Table 11.2 is the // axis. This axis is a shorthand for `/descendant-or-self::node()/child::`. The XPath `node()` function selects all structured nodes (elements, comments, processing instructions, and text) in a document. Thus, if you searched a document using this absolute location path

```
//name
```

you would be returned all `name` elements, regardless of where they occur in the tree.

Caution

Try to avoid using the `descendant`, `descendant-or-self`, `following`, and `preceding` axes where possible. They lead to performance degradation because the XPath processor must search large parts of the document to satisfy the query. The `child` axis is the one to use where possible.

Predicates

The location paths that you have seen so far have consisted of two parts: an axis and a node test. The node tests that you have seen have been by name (for example, `/child::people`) and by wildcard (for example, `/child::people/child::*`).

In fact, there are *three* parts to a location path. Along with the first two parts, you can also specify an optional predicate list:

```
axis_identifier::node_test[predicate_A][predicate_B]...
```

Predicates always appear after a node test, and enable you to filter a result node set to give another node set. The way it works is that the predicate is applied for each node in the result node set, and the node only makes it into the new node set if the predicate evaluates to `true`.

For example, say that you want to find the name of a person who has blue eyes and a surname of Greenhough from the document in Listing 11.1. In that case you could use this location path:

```
//firstName[../following-sibling::eyeColor='blue']
```

This says to find all `firstName` elements in the XML document, but then to filter them so that only those `firstNames` are left that have a parent with a following sibling `eyeColor` element with a text value of `blue`.

When you combine predicates as a list of square brackets, the conditions are effectively `AND`'ed together. You can explicitly `AND` conditions like this:

```
axis_identifier::node_test[predicate_A and predicate_B]
```

You can also `OR` conditions like this:

```
axis_identifier::node_test[predicate_A or predicate_B]
```

The XPath `not()` function enables you to invert logical conditions. If you want more details on XPath, see *Essential XML Quick Reference* by Aaron Skonnard and Martin Gudgin (ISBN 0-201-74095-8), or *XML and Web Services Unleashed* by Ron Schmelzer, et al (ISBN 0-672-32341-9).

Single Template Programming (Exemplar Approach)

It is possible to write XSLT programs that look like JavaServer Pages. That is, you can run a template program against different input to provide different output. An XSLT program written in this style is known as an *exemplar*. The single template approach was designed so that HTML designers could write XSLT programs without necessarily being a software developer.

An XSLT program contains a mixture of static text and XSLT instructions. The way that the XSLT processor distinguishes between the two is by inspecting the namespace that is associated with elements. The XSLT namespace is `http://www.w3.org/1999/XSL/Transform`.

> **Caution**
> Namespaces in XML are case sensitive. Make sure you type the XSLT namespace exactly as it is shown here. Also, notice that there is no trailing / character. This is unlike the SOAP namespace that you will see later in this book!

Any elements/attributes in the exemplar that are not associated with the XSLT namespace are copied directly to the output document. Elements or attributes that *are* associated with the XSLT namespace are treated as XSLT programming instructions. Unrecognized instructions cause an error when the transformation is executed.

Consider the code in Listing 11.3 that shows an XML document that is about to be transformed into HTML.

Listing 11.3 **XML Input Document (`people.xml`)**

```
<people>
  <person>
    <name>Peter</name>
    <age>54</age>
  </person>
  <person>
    <name>Patricia</name>
    <age>50</age>
  </person>
</people>
```

In this simple example, assume that an output document is required that looks like the HTML document in Listing 11.4.

Listing 11.4 **The Required Output Document**

```
<html>
  <head><title>Single Template Output</title></head>
  <body>
    <h1>List of people in the XML document</h1>
    <table border="1">
      <th>Name</th><th>Age</th>
      <tr><td>Peter</td><td>54</td></tr>
      <tr><td>Patricia</td><td>50</td></tr>
    </table>
  </body>
</html>
```

The XSLT program in Listing 11.5 shows how you could write a single template that uses these instructions to transform Listing 11.3 to Listing 11.4. Two of the most common XSLT instructions are `value-of` and `for-each`.

Listing 11.5 **An XSLT Single Template** (`people.xslt`)

```
<html xmlns:xsl="http://www.w3.org/1999/XSL/Transform" xsl:version="1.0">
  <head><title>Single Template Output</title></head>
  <body>
    <h1>List of people in the XML document</h1>
    <table border="1">
      <th>Name</th><th>Age</th>
      <xsl:for-each select="/people/person">
        <tr>
            <td><xsl:value-of select="name/text()" /></td>
            <td><xsl:value-of select="age/text()" /></td>
        </tr>
      </xsl:for-each>
    </table>
  </body>
</html>
```

Points to note about Listing 11.5 are that the top-level `html` tag contains an XML namespace declaration for the XSLT namespace, as well as an `xsl:version` attribute. Both the namespace declaration and the attribute are dropped from the output, but they are necessary to indicate to the XSLT processor that this is an XSLT program.

> **Caution**
>
> Take care when you write an XSLT stylesheet using any of the forms in this chapter. An XSLT stylesheet must *always* be well-formed XML, even when you want to output HTML. This means that you must always close tags, enclose attributes in quotes, and so on.

Both the `for-each` and `value-of` instructions have a `select` attribute whose value is an XPath expression.

The `for-each` tag has a `select` attribute that specifies which nodes from the input document to iterate over. In this case, the two `person` nodes are selected from the input document:

```
<xsl:for-each select="/people/person">
```

When inside the `for-each` tag, the context becomes each `person` node that has been selected from the input document.

For each `person` element in the input document, a new row is emitted in the table in the output document. Two things are emitted within each row: the current person's name, followed by that person's age:

```
<tr>
    <td><xsl:value-of select="name/text()" /></td>
    <td><xsl:value-of select="age/text()" /></td>
</tr>
```

You have now been introduced to the basics of XSLT. Some of the more common instructions used in XSLT programs are described in Table 11.3. You can find details of each instruction in *Essential XML Quick Reference*.

Table 11.3 **Common XSLT Instructions**

Instruction name	Description
value-of	Used to generate text in the output.
Element	Used to create an element in the output document. The name and the value can be dynamically assigned.
Attribute	Used to create an attribute in the output document. The name and the value can be dynamically assigned.
Processing-instruction	Processing instructions in the XSLT program are ignored. This instruction is used to generate an XML processing instruction in the output document.
Comment	Comments in the XSLT program are ignored. This instruction is used to generate an XML comment in the output document.
copy, copy-of	These instructions copy nodes from the input document to the output document. The copy instruction copies the context node, but does not copy its attributes or descendant elements. The copy-of instruction copies a set of nodes specified using a select attribute.
if, choose	Used to perform conditional processing.
`for-each`	Used to loop through a specified input node set. XPath node sets are 1-based (that is, index of first node is 1, not 0).

Using the Xalan XSLT Processor

The XSLT processor used for the previous example was Xalan, and was invoked like this:

```
D:\> set classpath=D:\xerces-j\xerces.jar;D:\xalan\xalan.jar;%CLASSPATH%
D:\> java org.apache.xalan.xslt.Process -in people.xml
➥ -xsl people.xslt -out people.html
========= Parsing file:D:/people.xsl ==========
Parse of file:D:/people.xsl took 188 milliseconds
========= Parsing file:D:/people.xml ==========
Parse of file:D:/people.xml took 31 milliseconds
=============================
Transforming...
transform took 16 milliseconds
XSLProcessor: done
```

When you view the output of the transformation in a Web browser, you see something like that shown in Figure 11.3.

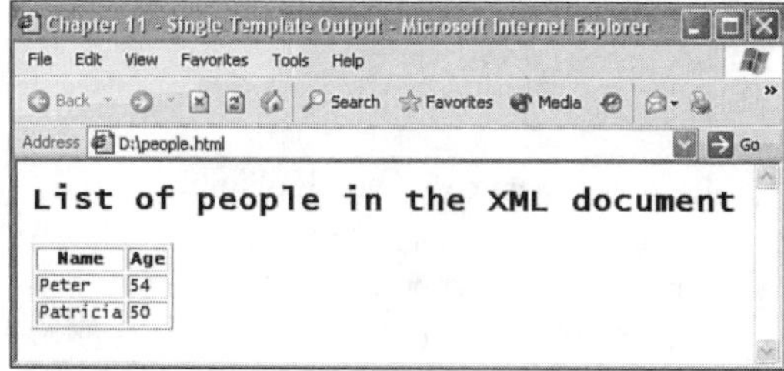

Figure 11.3 Result of the XSLT transformation.

> **Note**
>
> It is also possible to compile stylesheets into Java classes called *translets*. This is done using the XSLT Compiler (XSLTC), and it can improve performance when reusing stylesheets because the stylesheet is not being parsed multiple times. More information on XSLTC can be found at `http://xml.apache.org/xalan-j/xsltc_usage.html`.

Using XSLT from a JSP with Xalan

You have been introduced to Xalan, which is a Java-based XSLT processor. If you are using a Java 2 SE version of 1.4 or higher, you will have this as part of your Java Runtime. It was incorporated into the Java APIs for XML Processing (JAXP), which was originally a separate download. If you are using a version of Java prior to 1.4, you will need to download and set up the JAXP on your machine. It is available from `http://www.java.sun.com` as part of the JAX-PACK. The easiest way to to install the JAXP is to put the relevant Jar files in your `<JRE-HOME>/lib/ext` folder.

Assuming you have it on your machine in one form or another, you can use it from your JSPs; the next section will demonstrate how.

Take look at Listing 11.6.

Listing 11.6 `usingXalan.jsp`

```
<%@ page import="javax.xml.transform.*,
➥ javax.xml.transform.stream.*, java.io.*" %>
<%
try
{
  TransformerFactory tFactory = TransformerFactory.newInstance();
  Transformer transformer = tFactory.newTransformer(
```

Listing 11.6 **Continued**

```
       new StreamSource("http://localhost:8080/chapter11/people.xslt"));
       transformer.transform(
              new StreamSource("http://localhost:8080/chapter11/people.xml"),
              new StreamResult(response.getOutputStream()));
}
catch (TransformerException e) {
  System.out.println("Transformer exception " + e);
}
catch (IOException e) {
  System.out.println("IOException " + c);
}
%>
```

Listing 11.6 shows a JSP that will transform `people.xml` shown in Listing 11.3. This will be done using `people.xslt` shown in Listing 11.5, to produce the HTML output shown in Listing 11.5. Most of the page is error handling. If you remove that, there are actually only three lines of code required to complete a transformation from a JSP in this way:

```
TransformerFactory tFactory = TransformerFactory.newInstance();
Transformer transformer = tFactory.newTransformer(
  new StreamSource("http://localhost:8080/chapter11/people.xslt"));
transformer.transform(
     new StreamSource("http://localhost:8080/chapter11/people.xml"),
     new StreamResult(response.getOutputStream()));
```

1. First, a `javax.xml.transform.TransformerFactory` is created using the `newInstance()` method. This is used in the next step.
2. Then, a `javax.xml.transform.Transformer` is created from the factory with the appropriate XSLT passed in as a parameter wrapped in a `javax.xml.transform.stream.StreamSource`.
3. Finally, a transformation can be carried out with a call to the `transform()` method. This essentially takes in two parameters, the XML source, also wrapped as a `StreamSource`, and a `StreamResult`, which encapsulates the result of the transformation. Because this is a JSP, the `ServletOutputStream` is where we want the output to go.

A Word On `StreamSource` and `StreamResult`

The `SreamSource` and `StreamResult` classes enable the `transform()` and `newTransformer()` methods to take a variety of XML sources and results as their arguments. So, for example, for transformation you can pass an XML file or some kind of XML stream. The result can similarly go to a `java.io.OutputStream`, a `java.io.File`, or a `java.io.Writer`.

Clearly, it could be argued that this code would be better placed in a servlet because it contains no presentation markup at all because it is all coming from the stylesheet. I have used a JSP for clarity.

Declarative Template Programming

Simple template programs are most useful when the structure of the input document is known and fixed. However, for more complex and open content models, a more sophisticated approach becomes necessary. This is for many of the same reasons that you do not put all code inside the `main` method when writing a Java application.

When writing XSLT programs that consist of multiple templates, the templates can be called either by the XSLT processor or by the template itself. The former approach is covered now, and the latter approach in the section "Procedural Programming."

In either case, however, the top-level element looks the same. See Listing 11.7 for an example. The top-level element can be called either `transform` or `stylesheet`. Note that the `version` attribute is unqualified, unlike the case when using an exemplar.

Listing 11.7 **The Framework for a Multitemplate XSLT Program**

```
<xsl:transform xmlns:xsl="http://www.w3.org/1999/XSL/Transform" version="1.0">
    …
</xsl:transform>
```

Within the top-level element, you write *templates*. A template has the following syntax:

```
<xsl:template match="…">
    …
</xsl:template>
```

The value of the `match` attribute is an XPath expression, although there are certain limitations that apply. For example, not all XPath axes are available. The XSLT processor runs the matching template as it encounters nodes in the input document.

Listing 11.8 shows how the exemplar from Listing 11.5 could be rewritten using the multitemplate approach. This example is a JSP that loads a piece of XML, applies a transform to it, and outputs the result. The great thing about this example is that you only need three tags to do it, and JSTL provides them all! The XML document that is transformed is shown in Listing 11.3.

Listing 11.8 **A Multitemplate XSLT Program (`multiTemplate.jsp`)**

```
<%@ taglib uri="http://java.sun.com/jstl-el/xml"  prefix="x" %>
<%@ taglib uri="http://java.sun.com/jstl-el/core" prefix="c" %>

<html>
  <head>
    <title> Multi-template Programming</title>
  </head>
```

Listing 11.8 **Continued**

```
  <body>
    <c:import url="http://localhost:8080/chapter11/people.xml"
              var="inputDoc" />

    <c:import url="http://localhost:8080/chapter11/transform.xsl"
              var="stylesheet" />

    <x:transform doc="${inputDoc}"
                 xslt="${stylesheet}" />
  </body>
</html>
```

The first `c:import` action loads the XML document into a variable called `inputDoc`, and the second loads the XSLT stylesheet into a variable called `stylesheet`. The important work is then performed by the `x:transform` action that applies the stylesheet to the input document and renders the result on the page.

Listing 11.9 shows the XSLT stylesheet for this example.

Listing 11.9 **The Multitemplate XSLT Stylesheet (`transform.xsl`)**

```
<xsl:transform xmlns:xsl="http://www.w3.org/1999/XSL/Transform" version="1.0">

  <xsl:template match="people">
    <h1>List of people in the XML document</h1>
    <table border="1">
      <th>Name</th><th>Age</th>
      <xsl:apply-templates />
    </table>
  </xsl:template>

  <xsl:template match="person">
    <tr>
      <td><xsl:value-of select="name/text()" /></td>
      <td><xsl:value-of select="age/text()"  /></td>
    </tr>
  </xsl:template>

</xsl:transform>
```

This XSLT is simpler than previous ones because the JSP has already output the `html`, `head`, `title`, and `body` tags. All that the XSLT needs to do is apply transformations to the `people` and `person` elements from the input document.

The body of the first template (for `people` elements) contains mainly static HTML that is copied to the output stream. However, there is one very important XSLT instruction that you must be aware of: `apply-templates`. The `apply-templates` instruction causes the XSLT processor to carry on processing the input document. It selects the child elements of the context node, and the XSLT processor then calls other templates in the XSLT program when it finds matches between input nodes and templates.

Therefore, when the XSLT processor encounters `person` nodes in the input document, it calls the second template in the XSLT program (that is, the one that has a `match` attribute with a value of `person`).

An important point to grasp about the XSLT program in Listing 11.7 is that the XSLT processor invokes the second template for *any* `person` nodes, no matter where they occur in the input document.

> **Tip**
>
> When writing multitemplate XSLT programs, it is often useful to know when the different templates are being invoked. The Xalan processor accepts a `-tt` (trace templates) switch that causes trace information to be output to the console.

What if the XSLT processor finds more than one template that matches the input node? The XSLT specification defines a set of rules that assign priorities to the XPath expressions used in a template's match attribute. The XSLT processor invokes the template with the highest priority. The XSLT specification considers it an error if there is still a clash after assigning these priorities. However, most XSLT processors today call the last matching template in the XSLT program.

Built-in Templates

Notice that the XSLT stylesheet in Listing 11.8 does not have a match for the root node of the InfoSet, and yet it works. This is because all XSLT processors have built-in templates for the following nodes:

- The root of the InfoSet (/) and any element (*)
- Comments and processing instructions
- Text nodes within elements, and attribute values

The three built-in templates look like this:

```
<xsl:template match="/ | *">
   <xsl:apply-templates />
</xsl:template>
```

This is the important template that matches the root of the Infoset (that is, the root of the logical XML tree, rather than the top-level element in the input document) of the input document. It also matches elements for which there is not a more specific match. For either the Infoset root or any element, the XSLT will by default simply carry on and process the rest of the tree. This is because of the nested `apply-templates` instruction.

The second built-in template is

```
<xsl:template match="comment() | processing-instruction()" />
```

This template simply causes the XSLT processor to ignore any processing-instructions and comments. XSLT provides instructions to generate required comments and processing-instructions in the output document.

The third built-in template is

```
<xsl:template match="text() | @*">
   <xsl:value-of select=".">
</xsl:template>
```

This template simply copies the value of any text nodes from the input document to the output. You might also expect it to copy attribute node values as well, but it does not. This is because, according to the XML Infoset, attributes are not child nodes, so when the tree is processed this built-in template will never select on attributes.

Therefore, if you ever try to run an XSLT program that does not actually declare any templates of its own, the output simply contains a concatenation of all text nodes in document order.

You can override any of these built-in templates by specifying your own template with the same `match`, or a more specific match for elements and attributes (for example, match by name).

> **Tip**
>
> Many people override a built-in template for an element, but forget to call `xsl:apply-templates` when they do so. If you forget, the XSLT stylesheet stops executing because you have not told the XSLT processor to continue.

Working with Subsets

You do not need to transform or display an entire document or its transformation. Here are some examples of transforming and displaying subsets of a document.

Displaying a Subset

You can use the `x:out` action to evaluate an XPath expression, and display the result in a JSP. The `x:forEach` action is useful when you need to display the contents of an XPath result set that has more than one node. For example, the JSP in Listing 11.10 does not use an XSLT, but uses the JSTL `x:forEach` and `x:out` actions to display a list of people over the age of 45.

Listing 11.10 **Display a Subset of an XML Document** (`displaySubset.jsp`)

```
<%@ taglib uri="http://java.sun.com/jstl-el/xml"  prefix="x" %>
<%@ taglib uri="http://java.sun.com/jstl-el/core" prefix="c" %>
```

Listing 11.10 **Continued**

```
<html >
  <head>
    <title> Displaying a Subset</title>
  </head>

  <body>
    <c:import url="http://localhost:8080/chapter11/people.xml"
              var="inputDoc" />

    <x:parse  doc = "${inputDoc}"
              var = "parsedDoc" />

    Here is a list of people over the age of 45:
    <ul>
      <x:forEach select="$parsedDoc/people/person/name[../age > 45]"
                 var="currentName" >
        <li><x:out select="." />
      </x:forEach>
    </ul>
  </body>
</html>
```

The `c:import` and `x:parse` actions are the same as before. The `x:forEach` action finds a list of names for people over the age of 45, and the nested `x:out` action displays each name. The body content of an `x:forEach` action is executed once per result node. Also, the context is the current node in the iteration, which is why the example uses an XPath expression of `.` for the `x:out` action.

Transforming a Subset of an XML Document

Consider the case when you want to apply an XSLT transformation to the output from an XPath expression. In that case, all you need to do is

1. Load the XML
2. Use an XPath expression to extract the subset
3. Apply the transformation

For example, imagine that you want to run through the previous example again, except this time you are looking for the name of the person who is older than 50. In that case, you could write a JSP like that in Listing 11.11.

Listing 11.11 **Transforming the Result of an XPath Expression** (`transformSubset.jsp`)

```
<%@ taglib uri="http://java.sun.com/jstl-el/xml"  prefix="x" %>
<%@ taglib uri="http://java.sun.com/jstl-el/core" prefix="c" %>
```

Listing 11.11 **Continued**

```
<html>
  <head>
    <title> Transforming with XPath</title>
  </head>

  <body>
    <c:import url="http://localhost:8080/chapter11/people.xml"
              var="inputDoc" />

    <c:import url="http://localhost:8080/chapter11/transform.xsl"
              var="stylesheet" />

    <x:parse  doc="${inputDoc}"  var="parsedDoc" />

    <x:set select="$parsedDoc/people/person/name[../age > 50]"
           var="subset" />

    <x:transform doc="${subset}"  xslt="${stylesheet}" />

  </body>
</html>
```

The XPath location path that finds the name element for the person older than 50 is

```
$parsedDoc/people/person/name[../age > 50]
```

This location path is evaluated against the root of the Information Set of the parsed document (see Chapter 10, "Utilizing XML from JSP," for more details). Note that the result of evaluating this location path against the parsed document (`parsedDoc`) is exported using the `x:set` action. This result is then transformed using the `x:transform` action as before. The output is simply the string `Peter`, despite the fact that there is no template written that matches on `name` elements. In this case, the built-in template for unmatched elements is invoked, which calls `apply-templates`. This selects the child text node `Peter`, and the built-in template for text displays this string.

A word of warning here: If you use the `x:set` action to export the result of evaluating an XPath expression, the result must be well-formed XML if you are going to pass it to the `x:transform` action. For example, you cannot export a partial document with more than one top-level element. In this example, it would have been nice to find all names with an expression like this:

```
$parsedDoc/people/person/name
```

Unfortunately, this leads to an error because the result node set has two top-level elements called `name`.

Procedural Programming

The templates described in the earlier section "Declarative Template Programming" have a `match` attribute, and are called by the XSLT processor when necessary. Alternatively, you can write a template that has a `name` attribute instead of a `match` attribute. You can invoke such templates by name, similarly to methods in a procedural programming language.

You can make use of both styles of template with your stylesheet. For example, you can write declarative templates that are invoked by the XSLT processor. Then, you can partition the required logic into several named templates that the declared template invokes when necessary.

The syntax for a named template is

```
<xsl:template name="someName">
    ...
</xsl:template>
```

You invoke a named template with the `call-template` instruction:

```
<xsl:call-template name="someName" />
```

The XSLT program from Listing 11.5 can be rewritten to partition the logic so that it looks something like Listing 11.12.

Listing 11.12 **namedTemplate.xsl.**

```
<xsl:transform xmlns:xsl="http://www.w3.org/1999/XSL/Transform" version="1.0">
  <xsl:template match="/">
    <h1>List of people in the XML document</h1>
    <table border="1">
      <th>Name</th><th>Age</th>
      <xsl:for-each select="/people/person">
        <xsl:call-template name="processPerson" />
      </xsl:for-each>
    </table>
  </xsl:template>

  <xsl:template name="processPerson">
    <tr>
      <td><xsl:value-of select="name/text()" /></td>
      <td><xsl:value-of select="age/text()" /></td>
    </tr>
  </xsl:template>
</xsl:transform>
```

If you wish to view the result of this transformation, then you can use the example JSP `namedTemplate.jsp` from the demonstration application. You can pass parameters between named functions, similar to the way that you can pass parameters between methods in Java code. The JSP in Listing 11.11 searched for people over the age of 50. The XSLT stylesheet in Listing 11.13 shows how you can pass a parameter containing the age for which to search.

Listing 11.13 **Named Templates and Parameters (`param.xsl`)**

```
<xsl:transform xmlns:xsl="http://www.w3.org/1999/XSL/Transform" version="1.0">

  <xsl:template match="people">
    <h1>List of people in the XML document</h1>
    <table border="1">
      <th>Name</th><th>Age</th>
      <xsl:apply-templates />
    </table>
  </xsl:template>

  <xsl:template match="person">
    <xsl:call-template name="processPerson">
      <xsl:with-param name="ageParam">
        50
      </xsl:with-param>
    </xsl:call-template>
  </xsl:template>

  <xsl:template name="processPerson">
    <xsl:param name="ageParam" />

    <tr>
      <td>
        <xsl:value-of select="name/text()" />
      </td>
      <td>
        <xsl:value-of select="age/text()"  />
        <xsl:if test="age/text() > $ageParam">
            (old!)
        </xsl:if>
      </td>
    </tr>
  </xsl:template>
</xsl:transform>
```

The important work starts in the `person` template, which calls the `processPerson` template with an embedded `with-param` instruction. The parameter is called `ageParam`, and is assigned a value of 50.

> **Caution**
>
> Unlike most programming languages, you must make sure that the parameter names used by the caller and the called template match each other in XSLT.

The `processPerson` template declares the `ageParam` parameter that it expects, and references it with a `$` character:

```
<xsl:if test="age/text() > $ageParam">
```

The `xsl:if` instruction is used here to print the string `(old!)` if the person's age is greater than the value passed in the parameter. The output looks like that in Figure 11.4.

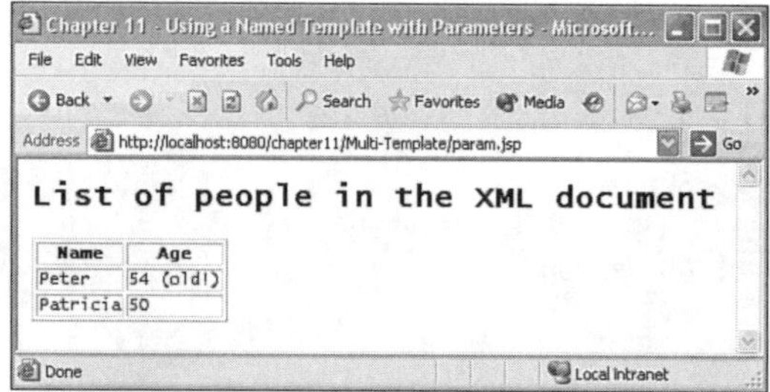

Figure 11.4 Output from Listing 11.12.

You can also have global parameters available to a stylesheet, with values that are passed in from an external source. For example, say that you want to modify the stylesheet in Listing 11.12 so that you can pass in a value for the age from the JSP. In Listing 11.14 you can see how to do this by nesting a `x:param` action within the `x:transform` action.

Listing 11.14 **Passing a Parameter to a Stylesheet** (`globalParam.jsp`)

```
<%@ taglib uri="http://java.sun.com/jstl-el/xml"  prefix="x" %>
<%@ taglib uri="http://java.sun.com/jstl-el/core" prefix="c" %>

<html >
  <head>
    <title> Using a Named Template
           with Global Parameters
    </title>
  </head>

  <body>
    <c:import url="http://localhost:8080/chapter11/people.xml"
              var="inputDoc" />
```

Listing 11.14 **Continued**

```
    <c:import url="http://localhost:8080/chapter11/
➥                 globalParam.xsl"
              var="stylesheet" />

    <x:transform doc  = "${inputDoc}"
                 xslt = "${stylesheet}">
      <x:param name="ageParam"  value="49" />
    </x:transform>
  </body>
</html>
```

The modified stylesheet is shown in Listing 11.15.

Listing 11.15 **A Stylesheet with a Global Parameter (`globalParam.xsl`)**

```
<xsl:transform xmlns:xsl="http://www.w3.org/1999/XSL/Transform" version="1.0">
  <xsl:param name="ageParam">60</xsl:param>

  <xsl:template match="people">
    <h1>List of people in the XML document</h1>
    <table border="1">
      <th>Name</th><th>Age</th>
      <xsl:apply-templates />
    </table>
  </xsl:template>

  <xsl:template match="person">
    <xsl:call-template name="processPerson">
      <xsl:with-param name="ageParam">
        51
      </xsl:with-param>
    </xsl:call-template>
  </xsl:template>

  <xsl:template name="processPerson">
    <tr>
      <td>
        <xsl:value-of select="name/text()" />
      </td>
      <td>
        <xsl:value-of select="age/text()"  />
        <xsl:if test="age/text() > $ageParam">
            (old!)
          </xsl:if>
```

Listing 11.15 **Continued**

```
      </td>
    </tr>
  </xsl:template>
</xsl:transform>
```

Notice that this latest stylesheet declares a parameter at the top-level, outside of any templates. This makes the parameter available to all templates. Also notice that the parameter declares a default value of `60` in case the JSP does not pass a value.

Applying Browser-Specific Transformations

Consider the following scenario. A mobile telephone company wants to advertise their charging tariffs online to customers and potential customers. There are many different tariffs catering for business users, teenage users, children, occasional users, and so on. This information needs to be available in the following media:

- Traditional browsers such as Netscape Communicator and Microsoft Internet Explorer
- WAP-enabled mobile phones
- PDAs
- XML format for retailers who sell their handsets
- Printed format

In this kind of scenario, XSLT comes into its own. If the data can be obtained in an XML format, it can be transformed according to the presentation device being used. To demonstrate this, we will use a simple XML file to represent a mobile-phone tariff, two stylesheets, one for Wireless Markup Language (WML) and one for HTML. We will then have a JSP that identifies the browser and applies the appropriate transformation.

Listing 11.16 shows our XML data file.

Listing 11.16 `tariffs.xml`

```
<?xml version="1.0" encoding="UTF-8"?>
<tariffs>
  <tariff id="a0">
    <talkPlan>Talk 60</talkPlan>
    <offPeak>5</offPeak>
    <peak>15</peak>
    <weekend>5</weekend>
    <otherNetworkCalls>30</otherNetworkCalls>
    <wap>5</wap>
    <text>5</text>
    <freeMinutes>60</freeMinutes>
  </tariff>
```

Listing 11.16 **Continued**

```
  <tariff id="a1">
    <talkPlan>Talk 100</talkPlan>
    <offPeak>5</offPeak>
    <peak>10</peak>
    <weekend>5</weekend>
    <otherNetworkCalls>30</otherNetworkCalls>
    <wap>5</wap>
    <text>5</text>
    <freeMinutes>100</freeMinutes>
  </tariff>
  <tariff id="a2">
    <talkPlan>Talk 400</talkPlan>
    <offPeak>5</offPeak>
    <peak>5</peak>
    <weekend>5</weekend>
    <otherNetworkCalls>20</otherNetworkCalls>
    <wap>5</wap>
    <text>5</text>
    <freeMinutes>400</freeMinutes>
  </tariff>
</tariffs>
```

This XML file contains the XML data for three fictitious mobile-phone tariffs. Two stylesheets will then perform the transformation, shown in Listings 11.17 and 11.18.

Listing 11.17 `tariffsHTML.xslt`

```
<?xml version="1.0" encoding="UTF-8"?>
<xsl:stylesheet version="1.0" xmlns:xsl="http://www.w3.org/1999/XSL/Transform">
  <xsl:template match="/tariffs">
    <html>
      <head>
        <title>Tariff Information</title>
      </head>
      <body>
        <h1>Current Tariff information</h1>
        <table width="400" border="1">
          <tr>
            <th>Plan</th>
            <th>On Peak</th>
            <th>Off Peak</th>
            <th>Weekend</th>
            <th>Other Networks</th>
            <th>WAP</th>
            <th>Text</th>
            <th>Free Minutes</th>
```

Listing 11.17 **Continued**

```
        </tr>
        <xsl:apply-templates select="tariff"/>
      </table>
    </body>
  </html>
</xsl:template>
<xsl:template match="tariff">
  <tr>
    <td>
      <xsl:value-of select="talkPlan"/>
    </td>
    <td>
      <xsl:value-of select="peak"/>
    </td>
    <td>
      <xsl:value-of select="offPeak"/>
    </td>
    <td>
      <xsl:value-of select="weekend"/>
    </td>
    <td>
      <xsl:value-of select="otherNetworkCalls"/>
    </td>
    <td>
      <xsl:value-of select="wap"/>
    </td>
    <td>
      <xsl:value-of select="text"/>
    </td>
    <td>
      <xsl:value-of select="freeMinutes"/>
    </td>
  </tr>
</xsl:template>
</xsl:stylesheet>
```

Listing 11.18 `tariffsWML.xslt`

```
<xsl:stylesheet xmlns:xsl="http://www.w3.org/1999/XSL/Transform" version="1.0">
  <xsl:output method="xml"
      doctype-public="-//WAPFORUM//DTD WML 1.1//EN"
      doctype-system="http://www.wapforum.org/DTD/wml_1.1.xml"/>
  <xsl:template match="/">
    <wml>
```

Listing 11.18 **Continued**

```
      <xsl:apply-templates/>
    </wml>
  </xsl:template>
  <xsl:template match="tariffs">
    <xsl:apply-templates/>
  </xsl:template>
  <xsl:template match="tariff">
    <card id="{@id}" title="{talkPlan}">
      <p> Off Peak calls <xsl:value-of select="offPeak"/>
      </p>
      <p> On Peak calls <xsl:value-of select="peak"/>
      </p>
      <p> Weekend calls <xsl:value-of select="weekend"/>
      </p>
      <p> Other networks <xsl:value-of select="otherNetworkCalls"/>
      </p>
      <p> WAP Calls <xsl:value-of select="wap"/>
      </p>
      <p> Text Messages <xsl:value-of select="text"/>
      </p>
      <p> Free Minutes <xsl:value-of select="freeMinutes"/>
      </p>
      <xsl:if test="following-sibling::tariff">
        <p>
          <a href="#{following-sibling::tariff/@id}">Next</a>
        </p>
      </xsl:if>
      <xsl:if test="preceding-sibling::tariff">
        <p>
          <a href="#{preceding-sibling::tariff/@id}">Previous</a>
        </p>
      </xsl:if>
    </card>
  </xsl:template>
  <xsl:template match="*"/>
</xsl:stylesheet>
```

If you are not familiar with WML markup, it is not important to our discussion. Just be aware that we have two possible stylesheets that can be applied to the XML file of Listing 11.16. What we will use is a servlet that will identify the browser, and then apply the appropriate transformation based on the browser. This servlet is shown in Listing 11.19.

Listing 11.19 BrowserDependentServlet.java

```
package com.conygre;

import javax.xml.transform.*;
import javax.xml.transform.stream.*;
import java.io.*;
import javax.servlet.http.*;
import javax.servlet.*;

public class BrowserDependentServlet extends HttpServlet {

  public void doGet(HttpServletRequest request, HttpServletResponse response)
                           throws IOException {
    String styleSheet = setStyleSheet(request, response);
    transform(styleSheet, response.getOutputStream());
  }

  private String setStyleSheet(HttpServletRequest request,
                             HttpServletResponse response) {
    String xslFile = "";
    // identify browser
    String browser = request.getHeader("User-Agent");
    // if it's a Nokia, then change the stylesheet to the WML stylesheet
    // and set the content type
    if (browser.startsWith("Noki")) {
      xslFile = "http://localhost:8080/chapter11/phone/tariffsWML.xslt";
      response.setContentType("text/vnd.wap.wml");
    }
    // if it isn't a Nokia in other words, IE or Netscape
    else if (browser.startsWith("Mozi")) {
        // could be set in web.xml
        xslFile = "http://localhost:8080/chapter11/phone/tariffsHTML.xslt";
    }
    else {
      // could be set in web.xml
      xslFile = "http://localhost:8080/chapter11/phone/tariffsHTML.xslt";
    }
    return xslFile;
  }

  private void transform(String stylesheet, ServletOutputStream out) {
    try {
      TransformerFactory tFactory = TransformerFactory.newInstance();
      Transformer transformer =
              tFactory.newTransformer(new StreamSource(stylesheet));
       transformer.transform(
```

Listing 11.19 **Continued**

```
        new StreamSource("http://localhost:8080/chapter11/phone/tariffs.xml"),
        new StreamResult(out));
    }
    catch (TransformerException e) {
      System.out.println("Transformer exception " + e);
    }
  }
}
```

In the servlet, two methods have been defined, one to set the stylesheet to be used, `setStylesheet()`, and the other to carry out the transformation, `transform()`. The one that sets the stylesheet identifies the browser by using the `User-Agent` header value. If it starts with the text *Noki*, it will be a Nokia phone, so the stylesheet is set to `tariffsWML.xslt`. If the `User-Agent` starts with the text *Mozi*, it must be a Netscape browser or Microsoft Internet Explorer (`Mozilla` is the codename of these browsers). We could test for other browsers as well if we wanted. The `transform()` method contains nothing new, it has the same three lines of code to complete the transformation that you saw in the JSP using the Xalan processor in Listing 11.6.

So what is the result? The URL for the page is

```
http://localhost:8080/chapter11/browserDependent
```

The name `browserDependent` is mapped in the `web.xml` file for the servlet.

If you visit the servlet in Netscape 6.2, the result appears as shown in Figure 11.5.

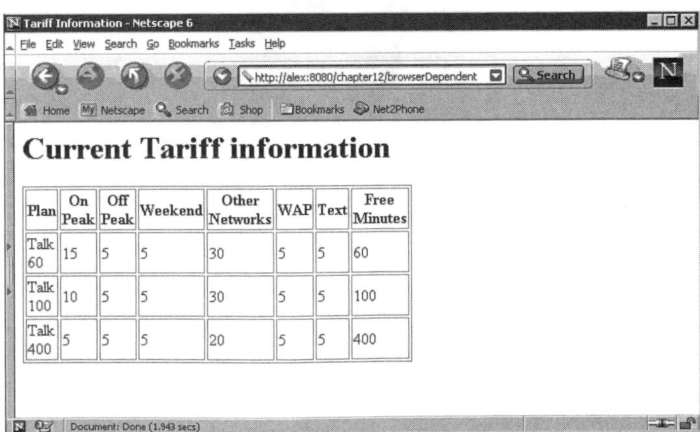

Plan	On Peak	Off Peak	Weekend	Other Networks	WAP	Text	Free Minutes
Talk 60	15	5	5	30	5	5	60
Talk 100	10	5	5	30	5	5	100
Talk 400	5	5	5	20	5	5	400

Figure 11.5 Browser-specific transformation in Netscape 6.2.

To test the site using a WAP browser, I have chosen to use the Nokia WAP Toolkit available from the Nokia Web site at `http://www.nokia.com`. This tool provides emulators for various Nokia handsets. I will use the emulator for the Nokia 7110, one of the first WAP-enabled handsets.

Caution

If you want to use the Nokia WAP Toolkit, you need to be aware that it does not work with J2SDK 1.4. You have to be using either J2SDK 1.2.x or J2SDK 1.3.x. This is because of the presence of the JAXP APIs in J2SDK 1.4. These APIs are required, however, for the servlet to work in Tomcat, so either the Nokia Toolkit will need to be installed on a different machine, or you will need to have two versions of the J2SDK on your machine. This demo was done using two machines.

Figure 11.6 shows the result of visiting exactly the same URL, but with the Nokia WAP Toolkit with the 7110 emulator.

Figure 11.6 The Nokia 7110 emulator.

Transformation Using XSLFO

In the last section on transforming for specific browsers, the need to transform to print formats was also mentioned. HTML and WML are not the only media.

A technology closely related to XSLT is called XSLFO, or XSL. It involves two stages:

1. The transformation of an XML document using XSLT into an XML vocabulary called *formatting objects*.
2. The formatting of these formatting objects into a suitable presentation medium (often Portable Document Format or PDF). Although the formatting objects could

be delivered to a printer to be printed out, assuming the printer understands formatting objects.

This is illustrated in Figure 11.7.

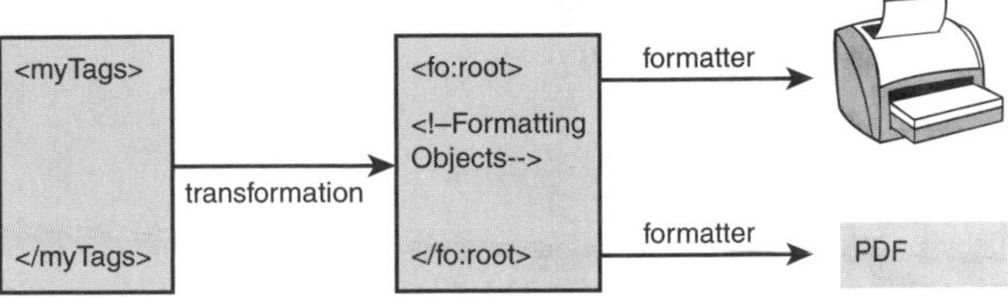

Figure 11.7 The XSLFO Processing Model.

This technology is vital for Web applications that need to create PDF-based documents as opposed to HTML or even WML-based documents. PDF provides the following benefits:

- Content cannot be easily modified by users.
- It allows for absolute and precise formatting of content.
- It is a widely supported and widely used format with the freely available Acrobat Viewer from Adobe.
- Created content can be printed with less problems than HTML pages, which print with page breaks in unhelpful places, with sections of text missing at times, and so on.

XSLFO is more to do with creating this kind of media than Web pages. So, what exactly are these formatting objects that can be formatted to create dynamic PDF documents?

Formatting Objects

Listing 11.20 shows a basic example of how the `tariffs.xml` data structure could be rendered as formatting objects. This would have been obtained using a transformation using XSLT technology already discussed.

Listing 11.20 `tariffs.fo`

```
<?xml version="1.0" encoding="UTF-8"?>
<fo:root xmlns:fo="http://www.w3.org/1999/XSL/Format">
  <fo:layout-master-set>
    <fo:simple-page-master master-name="A4" page-width="297mm"
      page-height="210mm" margin-top="0.5in" margin-bottom="0.5in"
     margin-left="0.5in" margin-right="0.5in">
      <fo:region-body/>
    </fo:simple-page-master>
```

Listing 11.20 **Continued**

```
  </fo:layout-master-set>
  <fo:page-sequence master-reference="A4">
    <fo:flow flow-name="xsl-region-body">
      <fo:block font="Arial">Tariff Information</fo:block>
      <fo:block> -  </fo:block>
      <fo:block>
        <fo:block font-weight="bold">Talk Plan:Talk 60</fo:block>
        <fo:block>Offpeak price: 5</fo:block>
        <fo:block>Peak 15</fo:block>
        <fo:block>Weekend Price 5</fo:block>
        <fo:block>Other networks: 30</fo:block>
        <fo:block>WAP: 5</fo:block>
        <fo:block>Text Messages: 5</fo:block>
        <fo:block>Free minutes: 60</fo:block>
      </fo:block>
    </fo:flow>
  </fo:page-sequence>
</fo:root>
```

The output of Listing 11.20 when viewed as PDF is shown in Figure 11.8.

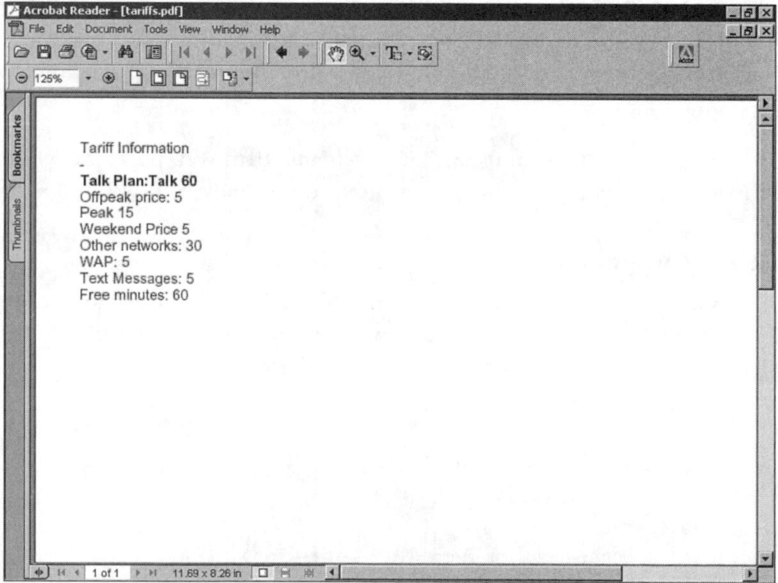

Figure 11.8 The conversion of `tariffs.fo` into a PDF format.

The elements and attributes that are used in formatting objects are all from the http://www.w3.org/1999/XSL/Format namespace. The generally used prefix is fo. The example in Listing 11.20 has been kept straightforward to enable you to clearly see what is going on. The outer element is <fo:root>, and within it there are two child elements, a <layout-master-set> defining how the content is to be arranged, and then there is the <page-sequence> defining the output:

```
<fo:root>
  <fo:layout-master-set/>
  <fo:page-sequence/>
</fo:root>
```

The <layout-master-set> in our example contains the information required to set up A4 pages, which is the most common page format in the UK, slightly larger than the regular US paper size. The margins and sizes are all set up as what is effectively a page template:

```
<fo:simple-page-master master-name="A4" page-width="297mm"
   page-height="210mm" margin-top="0.5in" margin-bottom="0.5in"
   margin-left="0.5in" margin-right="0.5in">
```

This page template is then used within the <fo:page-sequence> element:

```
<fo:page-sequence master-reference="A4">
```

Within the page-sequence, you can then define the style and content and layout for the output. In the example, <fo:block> elements have been used to specify sections of text:

```
<fo:block font-weight="bold">Talk Plan:Talk 60</fo:block>
```

Each block effectively becomes a separate rectangle on the page, so in some ways it is a bit like a <div> element in HTML, except that a block can contain child block elements, as in our example.

Many formatting options exist for these elements defined within attributes, so for example, the block element has more than 100 possible attributes! In the example, just two have been used.

To generate the FO output shown in Listing 11.20, an XSLT file such as that shown in Listing 11.21 could be used.

Listing 11.21 tariffsFO.xslt

```
<?xml version="1.0" encoding="UTF-8"?>
<xsl:stylesheet version="1.0" xmlns:xsl="http://www.w3.org/1999/XSL/Transform">
  <!-- generate PDF page stable-rowucture -->
  <xsl:template match="/">
    <fo:root>
      <fo:layout-master-set>
        <fo:simple-page-master master-name="page" page-height="29.7cm"
```

Listing 11.21 **Continued**

```
      page-widtable-cell="21cm" margin-top="1cm" margin-bottom="2cm"
      margin-left="2.5cm" margin-right="2.5cm">
       <fo:region-before extent="3cm"/>
       <fo:region-body margin-top="3cm"/>
       <fo:region-after extent="1.5cm"/>
      </fo:simple-page-master>
      <fo:page-sequence-master master-name="all">
        <fo:repeatable-page-master-alternatives>
          <fo:conditional-page-master-reference
           master-reference="page" page-position="first"/>
        </fo:repeatable-page-master-alternatives>
      </fo:page-sequence-master>
    </fo:layout-master-set>
    <fo:page-sequence master-reference="all">
      <fo:flow flow-name="xsl-region-body">
        <fo:block>
          <fo:table>
            <fo:table-body>
              <fo:table-row>
                <fo:table-cell>Plan</fo:table-cell>
                <fo:table-cell>On Peak</fo:table-cell>
                <fo:table-cell>Off Peak</fo:table-cell>
                <fo:table-cell>Weekend</fo:table-cell>
                <fo:table-cell>Other Networks</fo:table-cell>
                <fo:table-cell>WAP</fo:table-cell>
                <fo:table-cell>Text</fo:table-cell>
                <fo:table-cell>Free Minutes</fo:table-cell>
              </fo:table-row>
              <xsl:apply-templates/>
            </fo:table-body>
          </fo:table>
        </fo:block>
      </fo:flow>
    </fo:page-sequence>
  </fo:root>
</xsl:template>
<xsl:template match="tariff">
  <fo:table-row>
    <fo:table-cell>
      <xsl:value-of select="talkPlan"/>
    </fo:table-cell>
    <fo:table-cell>
      <xsl:value-of select="peak"/>
    </fo:table-cell>
    <fo:table-cell>
      <xsl:value-of select="offPeak"/>
```

Listing 11.21 **Continued**

```
      </fo:table-cell>
      <fo:table-cell>
        <xsl:value-of select="weekend"/>
      </fo:table-cell>
      <fo:table-cell>
        <xsl:value-of select="otherNetworkCalls"/>
      </fo:table-cell>
      <fo:table-cell>
        <xsl:value-of select="wap"/>
      </fo:table-cell>
      <fo:table-cell>
        <xsl:value-of select="text"/>
      </fo:table-cell>
      <fo:table-cell>
        <xsl:value-of select="freeMinutes"/>
      </fo:table-cell>
    </fo:table-row>
  </xsl:template>
</xsl:stylesheet>
```

> **Note**
> For more information on the syntax of formatting objects, you can read Chapter 18 of the *XML Bible*, Second Edition, which is available online at `http://www.ibiblio.org/xml/books/bible2/chapters/ch18.html`. Another source of information is the home page for XSLFO, which is found at `http://www.w3.org/TR/xsl/`. This page at the W3C site is well worth a visit. It is one of the better-explained standards.

As you can see from Figure 11.7, to get to the FO file, an XSLT transformation is used. This is done using an XSLT processor, which uses a stylesheet that instead of creating HTML as our examples have done up until now, it will create FO markup.

To then process the resultant formatting objects, a formatter that can process them is required. One example would be the Formatting Objects Processor (FOP) from the Apache Project. This is available from `http://xml.apache.org/fop`.

This can understand formatting objects and process them, but as Web developers we need more than this. We need to publish the processed formatting objects on the Web somehow, and this is where a tool that incorporates FOP comes in. It is also from the Apache project, and is called Cocoon.

Cocoon

Cocoon enables the processing of XML files using XSLFO to create an FO stream, which it can then convert into a variety of formats, including HTML, WML, and the popular PDF format among others. Cocoon is available from `http://xml.apache.org/cocoon`.

The benefits of using a framework such as Cocoon include the fact that it uses SAX instead of DOM as its model for processing the XML documents, and it also has built-in caching of your output. Not only that, it also facilitates the separation of roles in terms of the logic, the content, the style and the management of the application. Below is a brief introduction to Cocoon, for more information visit the cocoon Web site referred to above.

Cocoon is essentially a WAR file that can be deployed in your Web container, and then it can host your XML data and transformation (XSLT) files, allowing for the conversion to your chosen format. The Web application is packaged as `cocoon.war`. This can be deployed within your Web container, and in Tomcat, once deployed, you can visit it at `http://localhost:8080/cocoon`.

The local home page is shown in Figure 11.9.

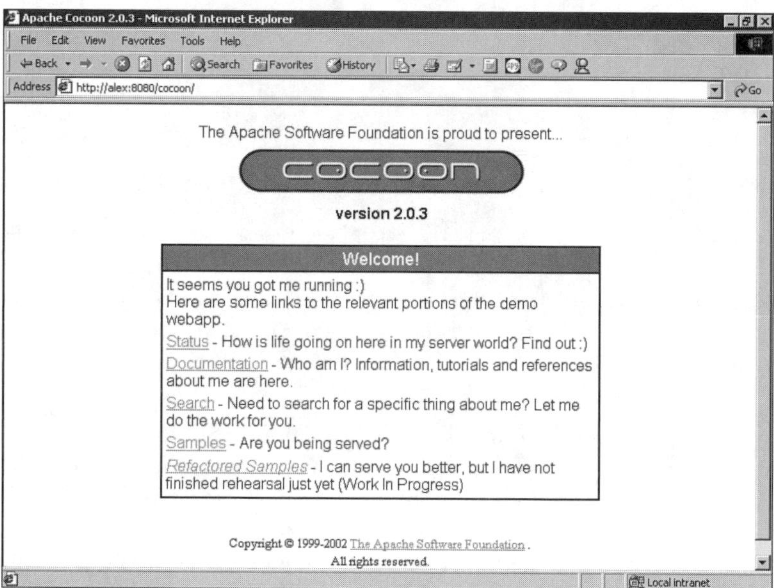

Figure 11.9 The Cocoon home page.

The Cocoon Architecture

Cocoon is actually a framework in the same way that Struts, which was discussed in Chapter 7, "JSP Application Architecture," is a framework. It is a framework for Web applications that require XML publishing and transformations. We will explore the basics of how Cocoon works here.

How does Cocoon take an XML file such as `tariffs.xml`, and create output in the form of PDF or HTML? The basic architecture of Cocoon is shown in Figure 11.10.

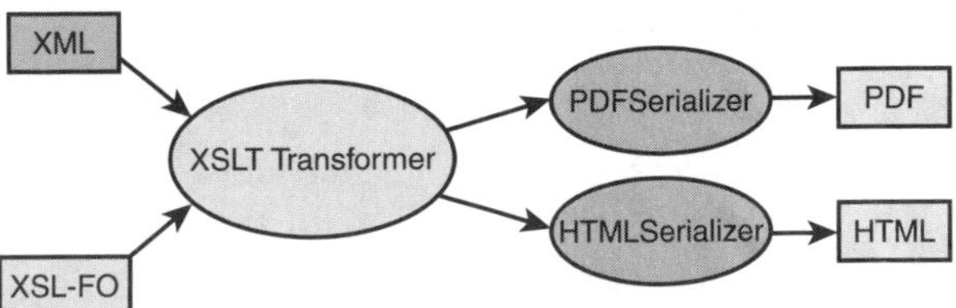

Figure 11.10 The architecture of Cocoon.

The Cocoon architecture involves several core components that process the XML using SAX.

> **Note**
> Version 1 of Cocoon used DOM to represent the XML data passed in, but clearly this restricted the size of the XML documents that could be processed. From version 2, SAX is now used.

Within Cocoon, the core components that actually transform the XML data into something usable by the client are referred to as *transformers*. The most common of which is the *XSLT transformer*. The XML data is transformed using the XSLT transformer into formatting objects discussed earlier for PDF and typically into XHTML for traditional Web content.

After the transformation has been carried out by a transformer, the output from the XSLT processor needs to be converted into the required end format (PDF or HTML4 for example). This is the role of the *serializer*. The two serializers important for our discussion are

- `HTMLSerialize` —Converts XHTML to HTML4
- `PDFSerializer`—Processes FO to generate PDF output

> **Note**
> XHTML is XML compliant HTML, so tags like `<br>` in HTML are `<br/>` in XHTML. Not all browsers can understand XHTML, so the `HTMLSerializer` converts this XHTML markup to HTML 4, which can be displayed by all the current Web browsers.

These components are all provided with Cocoon, and you configure them in what is called a `sitemap.xmap` XML file. More information can be found in the Cocoon documentation that is part of the installed Cocoon Web application. If you want to try building a simple Cocoon application, there is a basic walkthrough in the Cocoon documentation that will enable you to quickly get an example up and running. This is found at `http://xml.apache.org/cocoon/howto/howto-html-pdf-publishing.html`.

Summary

In this chapter, you have been exposed to how JSP technology can incorporate the transforming capabilities of XSLT. As you have seen, this can be through the use of tags, or through the direct use of XSLT processor APIs such as Xalan.

You have also been introduced to the role of XSL-FO, and how XML data can be transformed to PDF, using XSLFO processors such as FOP and within the Web application Cocoon.

In this chapter, you have seen how XML data can be presented to users. Although XML is used extensively in the presentation technologies discussed in this chapter, there are other uses of XML in relation to the Internet that might significantly change the way that the Internet is used—Web services. Web services involve XML being used as a means to invoke method calls remotely, typically over HTTP. Web services are the subject of the next chapter.

12

Invoking Web Services from JSP

WEB SERVICES ARE AN INCREASINGLY IMPORTANT TECHNOLOGY, now available to the Java developer, and more importantly, the JSP developer. All of the major technology vendors are offering support for Web services. In this chapter, you will be exposed to what Web services are, and then some of the implementations will be discussed. You will see the various Java APIs for web services, and learn how to build and deploy a basic Web service using the Axis implementation from Apache. Finally, after you have learned what Web services are, you will discover how they can be accessed from your Web applications.

Web Services Fundamentals

> **Note**
> This chapter assumes that you have read the preceding two chapters on XML processing, or that you are familiar with the various technologies surrounding XML.

So, what is a Web service? Unfortunately, the term does not have a universally agreed on definition. But essentially, a Web service is a software component that can be invoked over a network (typically, though not exclusively, an HTTP network). This invocation is done using XML technology, and the platform and language of the software component should be transparent to the invoker of the component.

There are three core technologies surrounding Web services:

- Simple Object Access Protocol (SOAP)
- Web Services Description Language (WSDL)
- Universal Description, Discovery, and Integration (UDDI)

These technologies will be explored as you progress through the chapter.

Let's take a simple example and see how it could be turned into a Web service. Consider an online bookstore. Currently, the bookstore can be searched by author, book title, publisher, and so on with the results appearing in your browser as a dynamically built Web page. The store is a Java Web application running within a popular application server. Sites like this are hugely successful as we all know, but the search results are only available in one form, and that is HTML delivered to a browser. What if this information was wanted in a more generic form for a client application? Maybe the search results were to be used within a completely different user interface, or maybe the results were to be used internally by a company to make recommendations to its employees. Maybe prices for bulk purchases are needed, and then fed into client applications, or maybe there are partners of the bookshop who need to access the bookshop database remotely for some reason.

If you have read the previous two chapters, you are probably thinking XML! XML would be an ideal medium for this kind of functionality. The request to the online bookshop could be sent in XML, and the results also returned as XML. This process is outlined in Figure 12.1.

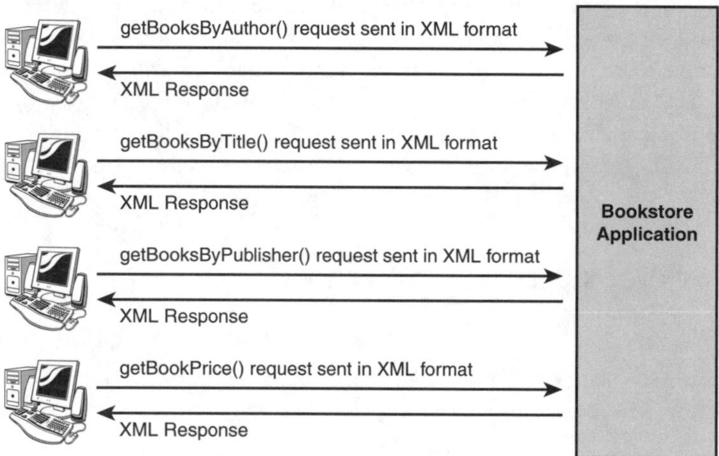

Figure 12.1 Using XML to send and receive messages.

Here are three issues that Figure 12.1 raises:

- What grammar should be used for this XML?
- How would the client applications know what functions are available from the Web service? How would clients know what parameters to pass, and what responses should be expected from the service?
- How did the client locate the service in the first place? If it were locating the regular Web site, a search engine would be used, but what about Web services?

These three issues are all addressed by the technologies SOAP, WSDL, and UDDI. The grammar that is used in Web services for this XML that is going backwards and forwards is Simple Object Access Protocol, or SOAP. One of the key benefits of using SOAP is that it does make your service available in a platform-independent manner. To identify what services are available from a Web service, Web Services Description Language (WSDL) is used. This describes to the client the various methods available, and the requests and responses expected for each of these methods. Finally, how is the Web service located? That is the role of the last technology mentioned, Universal Description, Discovery, and Integration, or UDDI. UDDI can be used to build a registry of Web services that services can be registered with, and clients can look up services from. The role of SOAP, WSDL, and UDDI is summarized in Figure 12.2.

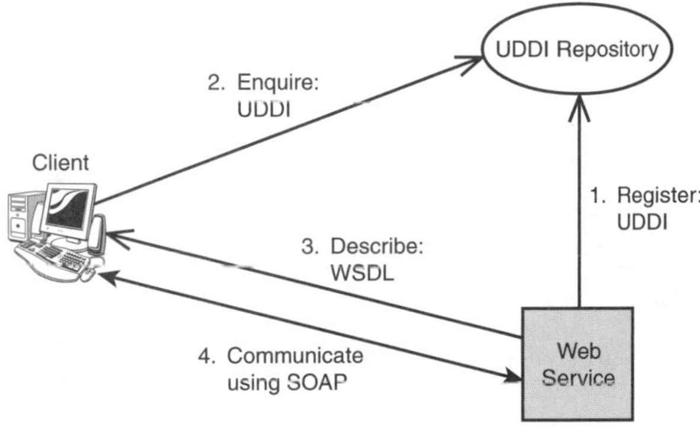

Figure 12.2 The roles of SOAP, WSDL, and UDDI.

The process can be summarized as follows:

1. Register—The service provider registers its services with a UDDI registry (the equivalent of the search engine).
2. Enquire—The client then looks up the service from the UDDI registry.
3. Describe—The client obtains a description of the various methods and parameter types from the service provider in the form of WSDL.
4. Communicate—The client then invokes the Web service using SOAP, and the service sends a SOAP response back to the client.

Note

It is worth noting that you do not have to have a UDDI registry to invoke a Web service. Just as you do not need a search engine to use a Web site, assuming that you know where it is!

Java APIs for Web Services

There are a number of APIs that are part of J2EE 1.4 that are specifically related to the technologies used within web services. These APIs are

- `SAAJ`—SOAP with Attachments API for Java. The SAAJ API provides functionality to process the SOAP messages that are involved in the invocations of web services. This API is used extensively within Java based implementations of web services such as Axis which will be introduced later in the chapter. The core package of the API is `javax.xml.soap`.
- `JAX-RPC`—Java API for XML-based RPC. The JAX-RPC API provides the ability for Java applications to make remote procedure calls using XML messaging protocols such as SOAP. You will see it used when we come to discuss how web service clients can be written using Java. One of the benefits of this API is that there is no specific requirement for the remote procedure being invoked to be a Java based remote procedure. This could be implemented on a completely different platform such as Microsoft .NET.
- `JAXR`—Java API for XML Registries. The JAXR API provides the ability to interact with registries such as UDDI registries mentioned earlier. You can query registries for service providers and also use the API to programmatically register your own services.

Now you have a basic understanding of what a Web service is and the related Java APIs, you will now see how the functionality of a Java class can be made available as a Web service, and you will see where SOAP, WSDL, and UDDI and the APIs SAAJ, JAX-RPC and JAXR fit in. You will also be introduced to the Apache Axis project.

The class that will be made available as a Web service is shown in Listing 12.1.

Listing 12.1 `Averager.java`

```
// this basic class is to be made available as a web service
// using Apache Axis
package com.conygre.webservices;

public class Averager
{
    public double getAverage (int a, int b) {
        return ((double)(a+b)/2);
    }

    public double getAverage(int[] numbers) {
        int total = 0;
        for (int i=0; i<numbers.length; i++) {
            total +=numbers[i];
        }
```

Listing 12.1 **Continued**

```
        return (double)total/numbers.length;
    }

    public int getLowest(int[] numbers) {
        int lowest = numbers[0];
        for (int i=0; i<numbers.length; i++) {
            if (numbers[i] < lowest) lowest = numbers[i];
        }
        return lowest;
    }

    public int getHighest(int[] numbers) {
        int highest = numbers[0];
        for (int i=0; i<numbers.length; i++) {
            if (numbers[i] > highest) highest = numbers[i];
        }
        return highest;
    }
}
```

The class shown in Listing 12.1 is a mathematical class that contains methods to provide average numbers, and also returns the highest and lowest numbers for an array of numbers.

> **Note**
>
> The class in Listing 12.1 is part of the download for this chapter called `chapter12.zip` (available from `www.samspublishing.com`, where you can enter the book ISBN number). Within this ZIP file are all the demos that you encounter in this chapter. You will find this file in `services\com\conygre\webservices\Averager.java`.

Notice that there is nothing unusual about this class. If you are familiar with Java technologies, such as remote method invocation (RMI) or CORBA, you will be familiar with all the RMI- or CORBA-specific code that is to be accessed remotely and needs to go into this class. But, with Web services, you do not need to do anything specific to the class. So, how can an ordinary class such as this be turned into a Web service? This is where Apache Axis is introduced.

Introducing Apache Axis

The Apache project initially had a project called Apache SOAP, which was its first project to enable the Java developer to deploy Web services. Apache Axis has since superceded it, and the home page is `http://xml.apache.org/axis/index.html`.

Note

The name Axis apparently stands for Apache eXtensible Interaction System. This doesn't seem to mean much to me, but many of the Apache names are somewhat obscure: Xalan, Xerces, Jakarta, just to mention three!

Apache Axis is essentially a SOAP engine that runs as a Java Web application that can host Web services. It can, therefore, be deployed within a Web container such as Tomcat. You can download an installation of Apache Axis from the site referred to previously, and when you install it, you get a Web application in the installation directory that can be successfully deployed within Tomcat.

Installing Apache Axis

Caution

When this book was written, the 1.0 version of Axis was used. Therefore, some details might be different if you have a later version.

You need to do two things to successfully deploy Axis in the Tomcat Web container:

1. Copy the Axis Web application from the Axis installation folder to the `<tomcat-home>\webapps` folder.
2. Copy the JAR files from the `<tomcat-home>\webapps\axis\WEB-INF\lib\` to the `<tomcat-home>\server\lib folder.` This is because some of the classes are in packages starting `javax`, and Tomcat will not load classes from packages prefixed with that name from JARS in `WEB-INF\lib` folders.

After you have done this, you can test your Axis and Tomcat set up by starting Tomcat and visiting the following URL:

```
http://localhost:8080/axis/
```

Depending on your version of Axis, you should see something like Figure 12.3:

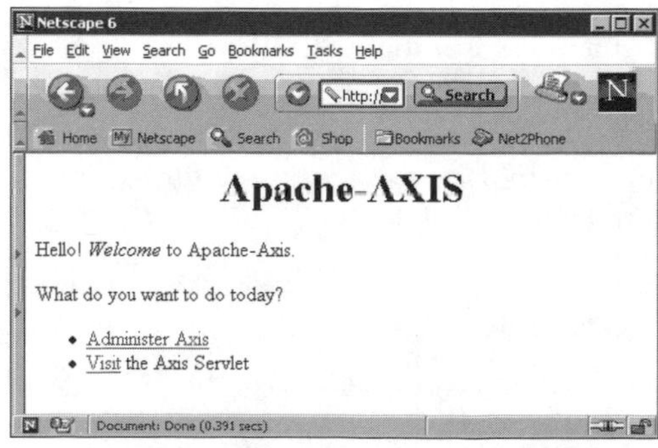

Figure 12.3 The Axis home page.

Deploying a Web Service to Axis

> **Note**
> If you want to deploy this example, download the `chapter12.zip` file from the book Web site (`www.samspublishing.com`). There you will find all the code referred to in this chapter.

You have two choices if you want to deploy a Web service to Apache Axis. The easiest way is to take the Java source, rename the extension to `jws`, and save it in the `webapps\axis` folder. This makes every public method within a class available to remote clients as a Web service. Also, to deploy a class in this way, you have to have access to the source file.

A more controlled way to deploy a Web service is to write an Axis Web Services Deployment Descriptor (WSDD) that Axis can use to set up a particular Web service. This file is an XML file that specifies the class and the methods that are to be made available to client applications.

The typical structure of a WSDD file is as follows:

```
<deployment>
 <service>
   <parameter . . ./>
   <parameter . . ./>
 </service>
</deployment>
```

The root element is `<deployment>`, and within this element, `<service>` elements are then used to specify each service to be deployed. The service to be deployed is then configured using individual `<parameter>` elements.

A complete WSDD deployment example is shown in Listing 12.2.

Listing 12.2 `AveragerDeploymentDescriptor.wsdd`

```
<deployment xmlns="http://xml.apache.org/Axis/wsdd/"
xmlns:java="http://xml.apache.org/Axis/wsdd/providers/java">
 <service name="averager" provider="java:RPC">
  <parameter name="className" value="com.conygre.webservices.Averager"/>
  <parameter name="allowedMethods" value="getAverage getLowest getHighest"/>
 </service>
</deployment>
```

This deployment file is specific to Apache Axis, and it enables you to specify the following:

- The name of the service using the `name` attribute of the `<service>` element.
- The type of the service (`java:RPC` in this case). RPC based services will have this value specified as shown in the `provider` attribute of the `<service>` element.

- The class containing the methods is defined as a `<parameter>` element. The attribute `name` has the value `className`, and the attribute called `value` has the value of the actual class, which in our case is `com.conygre.webservices.Averager`.
- The names of the methods to be made available separated by spaces, and this is done in a further `<parameter>` element as can be seen in Listing 12.2. In this case, the attribute called `name` has the value `allowedMethods`.

You will see where these elements are used for a deployed service as the example progresses.

So, you have now seen an XML WSDD file and you have a class, but how do you use them to deploy the service? Axis comes with a command-line tool called the `AdminClient` that can be used to deploy your service. The class is

```
org.apache.axis.client.AdminClient
```

The tool takes in two parameters, the URL of the Web service host and the deployment descriptor file. An example of how to run it is

```
java org.apache.axis.client.AdminClient
        -lhttp://localhost:8080/axis/services/AdminService
        AveragerDeploymentDescriptor.wsdd
```

The argument specifying the server is actually optional, since it will default to the URL shown if it is not specified. If you simply want to specify a different port, you can use a -p flag.

```
java org.apache.axis.client.AdminClient
        -p8000 AveragerDeploymentDescriptor.wsdd
```

If you want to try this particular example, it is found in the `chapter12.zip` file within a folder called `services`. To run this, you will need to ensure that the Axis libraries are in the classpath. We have provided a batch file to make this process easier for you. All you will need to do is set an environment variable called `AXIS_HOME`, and point it to the Axis install directory. You will need a command prompt or shell in the services directory as well. Unix users can create a shell script to do what the batch file does. Figure 12.4 shows a command prompt on a Windows machine that has successfully deployed the application.

You will also need to copy the folder containing the `Averager` class into the Axis web application so that it can be accessed by the Axis web application. This means copying the `com` folder from the `services` folder of the `chapter12.zip` file, into the `<tomcat-home>\webapps\axis\WEB-INF\classes`.

After the application is successfully deployed, you can make sure by visiting the following URL in a browser:

```
http://localhost:8080/axis/servlet/AxisServlet
```

You should see the `averager` service listed with all its methods, as shown in Figure 12.5.

```
C:\WINDOWS\System32\cmd.exe
Microsoft Windows XP [Version 5.1.2600]
(C) Copyright 1985-2001 Microsoft Corp.

C:\JSPHandbookWebServices\services>setpaths

C:\JSPHandbookWebServices\services>set classpath=c:\Java\xml-axis-10\lib\axis.ja
r;c:\Java\xml-axis-10\lib\jaxrpc.jar;c:\Java\xml-axis-10\lib\commons-logging.jar
;c:\Java\xml-axis-10\lib\log4j-1.2.4.jar;c:\Java\xml-axis-10\lib\saaj.jar;c:\Jav
a\xml-axis-10\lib\wsdl4j.jar;c:\Java\xml-axis-10\lib\axis-ant.jar;c:\Java\xml-ax
is-10\lib\commons-discovery.jar;;.;C:\Java\Tomcat 4.1\common\lib\servlet.jar
C:\JSPHandbookWebServices\services>java org.apache.axis.client.AdminClient -lhtt
p://localhost:8080/axis/services/AdminService AveragerDeploymentDescriptor.wsdd
- Processing file AveragerDeploymentDescriptor.wsdd
- <Admin>Done processing</Admin>

C:\JSPHandbookWebServices\services>
```

Figure 12.4 Deploying the averager service to Axis.

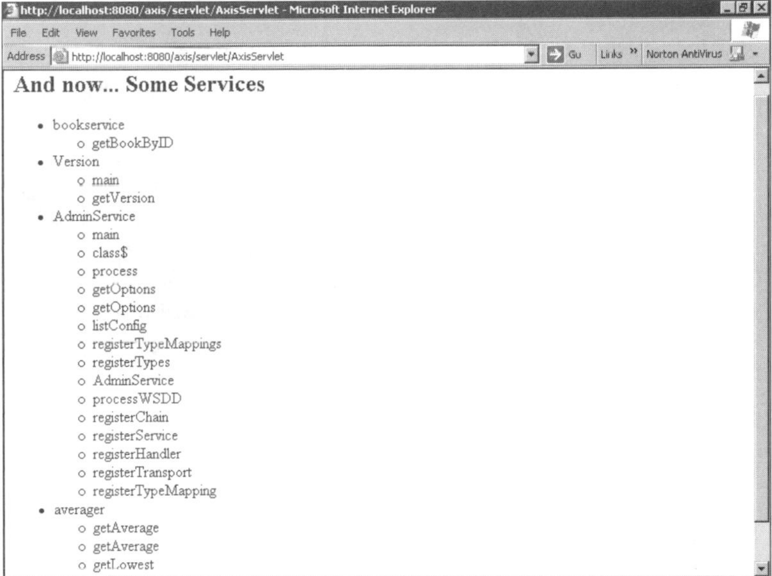

Figure 12.5 The Axis servlet listing the deployed services.

Now the service is successfully deployed, the next logical question is how do you interact with the Web service?

SOAP—Interacting with Web Services

Shortly, you will see how a Java client can be written to interact with our `averager` service, but first we'll look at SOAP, and the structure of the XML messages that go back and forth between the service and the client, as seen in Figure 12.1.

Essentially, SOAP messages are very simple, and at their simplest comprising of two XML elements, `<envelope>` and `<body>`. A basic example of a SOAP message is shown in Listing 12.3.

Listing 12.3 **A Basic SOAP Request**

```
<SOAP-ENV:Envelope
xmlns:SOAP-ENV="http://schemas.xmlsoap.org/soap/envelope/"
xmlns:SOAP-ENC="http://schemas.xmlsoap.org/soap/encoding/"
xmlns:xsi="http://www.w3.org/2001/XMLSchema-instance"
xmlns:xsd="http://www.w3.org/2001/XMLSchema"
SOAP-ENV:encodingStyle="http://schemas.xmlsoap.org/soap/encoding/">
  <SOAP-ENV:Body>
    <m:averager xmlns:m="getAverage">
      <in0 xsi:type="xsd:int">0</in0>
      <in1 xsi:type="xsd:int">0</in1>
    </m:averager>
  </SOAP-ENV:Body>
</SOAP-ENV:Envelope>
```

Notice that in this basic example, there is an `<envelope>` tag and a `<body>` tag. Within the `<body>` tag is some XML, which will be used to invoke a remote method. In this case, the remote method provides the average of two numbers of type `int`. This SOAP message can be used to invoke the `getAverage` method of the `averager` Web service. If you look carefully at the contents of the `<body>` element, you will see that this is what is represented. Two integers passed in to the `getAverage` method, which is part of the `averager` service:

```
<m:averager xmlns:m="getAverage">
  <in0 xsi:type="xsd:int">0</in0>
  <in1 xsi:type="xsd:int">0</in1>
</m:averager>
```

Notice also, the use of namespaces in the SOAP XML. Table 12.1 lists the main namespaces used in SOAP messages along with their function.

Table 12.1 **The Namespaces Used in SOAP**

Namespace	Description
http://schemas.xmlsoap.org/soap/envelope	This namespace defines the basic SOAP elements such as envelope, header, and body.
http://schemas.xmlsoap.org/soap/encoding	This namespace defines the encoding to be used in the SOAP messages. This is particularly useful for passing array objects. This namespace is not always necessary if all the types are defined using XML Schema.

Table 12.1 **Continued**

Namespace	Description
http://www.w3.org/2001/XMLSchema-instance	This namespace is the schema namespace used for instance documents. It is often used for the xsi:type attribute.
http://www.w3.org/2001/XMLSchema	This is the schema namespace. It can be used to define datatypes being passed. For example, <age xsi:type="xsd:int">12</age>.

Using XML Spy as a Client

One simple way to access and create these XML messages is to use the XML-editing software XML Spy. You do not have to try this, but we recommend it because it is a convenient visual way to see how these XML messages are created and used. To do this, you will need XML Spy 4.4 or XML Spy 5. A trial version is available from `www.xmlspy.com`.

To test out your Web service using XML Spy, follow these simple steps. Note that you will need to be connected to the Internet whilst completing this so that XML Schemas can be located

1. Launch XML Spy and go the SOAP menu. Select the `Create New SOAP Request` menu option.
2. Now enter the following URL:

   ```
   http://localhost:8080/axis/services/averager?wsdl
   ```

3. You should now be prompted with a box asking you which Web service method you want to invoke. This is shown in Figure 12.6. Select one of the `getAverage()` methods. They are overloaded in the Java class (see Listing 12.1), and in this case it does not matter which one, as you will edit the XML SOAP request in the next stage.

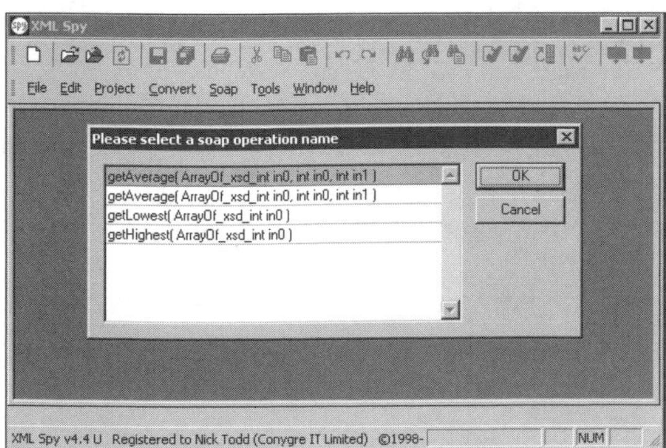

Figure 12.6 XML Spy interface for Web services.

4. Now you should be prompted with a SOAP message similar to that shown in Listing 12.3. Within the `<body>` element, modify the parameter list so that there are two parameters of type `int` as they are in Listing 12.3.
5. Finally, submit the request using the SOAP menu item, `Send Request to Server`.
6. You will now be presented with the SOAP response, as shown in Listing 12.4.

Listing 12.4 **SOAP Response from the Averager Web Service**

```
<?xml version="1.0" encoding="UTF-8"?>
<SOAP-ENV:Envelope
xmlns:SOAP-ENV="http://schemas.xmlsoap.org/soap/envelope/"
xmlns:xsd="http://www.w3.org/2001/XMLSchema"
xmlns:xsi="http://www.w3.org/2001/XMLSchema-instance">
  <SOAP-ENV:Body>
    <ns1:getAverageResponse
     SOAP-ENV:encodingStyle="http://schemas.xmlsoap.org/soap/encoding/"
     xmlns:ns1="getAverage">
       <getAverageReturn xsi:type="xsd:double">3.0</getAverageReturn>
    </ns1:getAverageResponse>
  </SOAP-ENV:Body>
</SOAP-ENV:Envelope>
```

When using Web services, although this is the XML that is going back and forth between the client and the service, in the normal run of things, this would be transparent to the client application and also the service deployer.

> **Note**
> You may also wish to try invoking some other services available on the Internet. If you visit `www.xmethods.com`, you will see a whole raft of services. Simply click on one that interests you, and use the WSDL URL specified for the service on the XMethods site in XML Spy with the `Create New SOAP Request` menu option.

Building Your Own Java Client

You have seen how XML Spy can be used to interact with your Web service. Now, let's see how a Java client can be written to also interact with your Web service. This is where we will introduce the Java APIs related to web services. The web service itself did not have any Web service specific code! Take a look at Listing 12.5.

Listing 12.5 `AveragerClient.java`

```
// This class acts as a client to the getAverage(int, int) method in the
// web service averager
import org.apache.axis.client.Call;
```

Listing 12.5 **Continued**

```
import org.apache.axis.client.Service;
import javax.xml.namespace.QName;

public class AveragerClient {
  public static void main(String[] args)  {
    try {
      // set a string to contain the target URL for the service
      String target = "http://localhost:8080/axis/services/averager";

      // create a service object
      Service service = new Service();

      // now create the call to the service object
      Call call  = (Call)service.createCall();

      // set the URL of the service for your call object
      call.setTargetEndpointAddress(new java.net.URL(target));

      // specify the method that you wish to invoke
      call.setOperationName(new QName("getAverage"));

      // now create an array containing the two parameters
      Object[] paramArray = new Object[2];
      paramArray[0] = new Integer(2);
      paramArray[1] = new Integer(4);

      Double averageNumber = (Double) call.invoke(paramArray);
      System.out.println("The web service says that the average number is "
                          + averageNumber);
    }
    catch (Exception e){
      System.out.println("A problem occured with the RPC: " + e);
    }
  }
}
```

To invoke web services using the Java programming language, we can use the JAX-RPC API that is part of J2EE 1.4. This API has been implemented within Axis so we don't need any further downloads. To invoke a Web service from a Java application using the JAX-RPC, you need to go through a number of steps. These are summarized here:

1. Create a `Service` object.
2. Create a `Call` object.
3. Set the URL for the `Call` object.

4. Set the method or operation name for the `Call` object.
5. Set up the method parameters as an array of objects.
6. Invoke the method, passing in the array of parameters, and process the response.

Notice that there is nothing here to do with manually creating or interacting with SOAP messages; they are transparent and it is done for us by Axis using the SAAJ API discussed earlier. In fact, if you run the `AveragerClient` application, you will find that you do not see any SOAP messages at all—you just get the result.

Note

`AveragerClient` is found within the `chapter12.zip` file in a folder called `clients`. There is also a batch file called `setpaths.bat`, which you can use to put the required classes into the classpath.

Three classes are used in Listing 12.5 that require some attention:

- `Service`—The `org.apache.axis.client.Service` class represents the starting point for a client's access into Web services when using SOAP. It is the Axis implementation of the JAX-RPC interface `javax.xml.rpc.Service`.
- `Call`—The `org.apache.axis.client.Call` class is used to represent the actual method call to the service. It is the Axis implementation of the `javax.xml.rpc.Call` interface from JAX-RPC.
- `QName`—The `javax.xml.namespace.QName` class represents a qualified XML name. A qualified XML name is a name that contains the namespace prefix. The alternative to a qualified name in XML is the local name, which is the XML name without the prefix. In our example, a `QName` object is used to specify which method is being invoked. The constructor being used only specifies the local name, `getAverage`.

As you can see, invoking a service is a little more involved than deploying the service. You'll see a way of simplifying your client application when we look at WSDL.

Error Handling with SOAP—the SOAP Fault

In the `AveragerClient` class in Listing 12.5, the error handling is simply, `catch (Exception e)`—hardly a comprehensive strategy! Let's look at a more appropriate approach.

There is a specific format for what is returned from a server when an error occurs. This could be because the SOAP request is not valid, for example, so the server cannot process it. Listing 12.6 shows an invalid SOAP request to our `averager` service. It is very similar to the correct version in Listing 12.3, but it is passing values of the wrong types—a `xsd:string` is passed in as the first parameter instead of an `xsd:int`.

Listing 12.6 **An Invalid SOAP Request**

```
<SOAP-ENV:Envelope xmlns:SOAP-ENV="http://schemas.xmlsoap.org/soap/envelope/"
xmlns:SOAP-ENC="http://schemas.xmlsoap.org/soap/encoding/"
xmlns:xsi="http://www.w3.org/2001/XMLSchema-instance"
xmlns:xsd="http://www.w3.org/2001/XMLSchema"
SOAP-ENV:encodingStyle="http://schemas.xmlsoap.org/soap/encoding/"
xmlns:m0="http://schemas.xmlsoap.org/soap/encoding/">
  <SOAP-ENV:Body>
    <m:getAverage xmlns:m="getAverage">
      <in0 xsi:type="xsd:string">2</in0>
      <in1 xsi:type="xsd:int">4</in1>
    </m:getAverage>
  </SOAP-ENV:Body>
</SOAP-ENV:Envelope>
```

You can simulate this by passing this XML in as a request using XML Spy if you want. The response that comes back is shown in Listing 12.7.

Listing 12.7 **The SOAP Response to an Invalid SOAP Request**

```
<?xml version="1.0" encoding="UTF 8"?>
<SOAP-ENV:Envelope
xmlns:SOAP-ENV="http://schemas.xmlsoap.org/soap/envelope/"
xmlns:SOAP-ENC="http://schemas.xmlsoap.org/soap/encoding/"
xmlns:xsi="http://www.w3.org/2001/XMLSchema-instance"
xmlns:xsd="http://www.w3.org/2001/XMLSchema"
xmlns:m0="http://schemas.xmlsoap.org/soap/encoding/">
  <SOAP-ENV:Body>
    <SOAP-ENV:Fault>
      <faultcode xmlns:ns1="http://xml.apache.org/Axis/">
          ns1:Server.userException
      </faultcode>
      <faultstring>
        org.xml.sax.SAXException: Bad types (class java.lang.String -&gt; int)
      </faultstring>
      <detail>
        <ns2:stackTrace xmlns:ns2="http://xml.apache.org/axis/">
           org.xml.sax.SAXException:
           Bad types (class java.lang.String -&gt; int)&#xd;
           at org.apache.axis.message.RPCHandler.onStartChild
           (RPCHandler.java:205)&#xd;
       ...
        </ns2:stackTrace>
      </detail>
    </SOAP-ENV:Fault>
  </SOAP-ENV:Body>
</SOAP-ENV:Envelope>
```

Some of the stack trace has been removed for clarity, but you should be able to see the basic structure of what is called a SOAP *fault*. Within the `<body>` element, there is a `<Fault>` element. The structure of a fault is shown here:

```
<SOAP-ENV:Fault>
  <faultcode>The code for the fault</faultcode>
  <faultstring>Text describing the fault</faultstring>
  <detail>The details of the fault</detail>
</SOAP-ENV:Fault>
```

This fault XML can be accessed from a client application as shown in Listing 12.8.

Listing 12.8 `AveragerFaultHandler.java`

```
import org.apache.axis.client.Call;
import org.apache.axis.client.Service;
import javax.xml.namespace.QName;
import org.apache.axis.AxisFault;
import org.w3c.dom.Element;
import org.w3c.dom.Node;
import javax.xml.rpc.ServiceException;
public class AveragerFaultHandler {
  public static void main(String[] args)  {
    try {
      String target = "http://localhost:8080/axis/services/averager";
      Service service = new Service();
      Call call  = (Call)service.createCall();
      call.setTargetEndpointAddress(new java.net.URL(target));
      call.setOperationName(new QName("getAverage"));
      Object[] paramArray = new Object[2];
      paramArray[0] = new String("oops");
      paramArray[1] = new Integer(4);

      Double averageNumber = (Double) call.invoke(paramArray);
      System.out.println("The web service says that the average number is "
                        + averageNumber);
    }
    // process the axis fault
    catch (AxisFault fault){
      System.out.println("The fault code is " + fault.getFaultCode());
      System.out.println("The fault string is " + fault.getFaultString());
      // the fault details are returned as a org.w3c.dom.Element object
      Element[] e = fault.getFaultDetails();
      // get the text node containing the stack trace
      Node details = e[0].getFirstChild();
      // print out the stack trace, which is the
      // value of the retrieved text node
      System.out.println("The fault detail is\n " + details.getNodeValue());
```

Listing 12.8 **Continued**

```
      }
      catch (ServiceException e) {
          System.out.println("A service exception has occurred " + e);
      }
      catch (java.rmi.RemoteException e) {
          System.out.println("A remote exception has occurred " + e);
      }
      catch (java.net.MalformedURLException e) {
              System.out.println("A malformed URL exception has occurred " + e);
      }
    }
}
```

Note the first catch block. Here the fault is being processed. Axis provides a class called `org.apache.axis.AxisFault` to encapsulate the `<fault>` element and its contents. In Listing 12.8, a fault is deliberately created by the passing of a `String` instead of an `int` as one of the two parameters.

There are two other exception classes that deserve noting here. One is the `javax.xml.rpc.ServiceException`, and the other is the `java.rmi.RemoteException`, both of which are being handled in Listing 12.8.

The `RemoteException` will be familiar to readers who have worked with CORBA or RMI before. This exception type is thrown when the `invoke()` method is called on the `Call` object, and either the call is configured incorrectly or there is an error within the remote call itself.

The `ServiceException` is thrown when there is a problem with the service itself. In Listing 12.8, the `ServiceException` is thrown when the Call object is instantiated.

Intercepting the XML—`tcpmon`

One challenge with the examples so far is that you cannot see the SOAP requests and responses that are being sent back and forth. To enable you to intercept and view the SOAP messages, Axis comes with a basic utility that will intercept all the SOAP XML and present it in a Java user interface. It is called the `tcpmon` tool. To launch the tool, make sure that the Axis classes are in the classpath, and then enter the following at a console:

```
java org.apache.axis.utils.tcpmon [listenPort] [targetHost] [targetPort]
```

The *`listenPort`* is where you want `tcpmon` to listen for requests, the *`targetHost`* is where the requests are to be forwarded to, and *`targetPort`* is the port number of where the requests are to be forwarded.

An example might be

```
java org.apache.axis.utils.tcpmon 8830 localhost 8080
```

To then run the `AveragerClient` from Listing 12.5, you would modify the target URL variable to incorporate the different port number of 8830, as shown:

```
String target = "http://localhost:8830/axis/services/averager";
```

When the `tcpmon` tool and Tomcat are both running, you can now invoke the client application `AveragerClient` as before. This will result in `tcpmon` appearing with the following request and response XML, as shown in Figure 12.7.

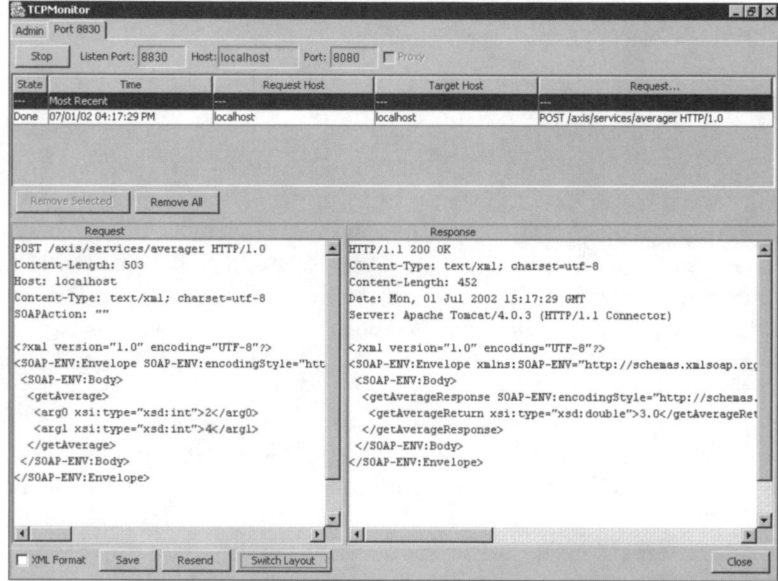

Figure 12.7 The `tcpmon` tool.

Passing Custom Objects

So far, in our examples, only primitive data types have been passed back and forth across using SOAP. You can also pass your own custom data types. Consider the basic `Book` type used in Chapter 6, "JSP and JavaBeans." It has been modified slightly, and is shown in Listing 12.9. It is a basic Bean with properties for `id`, `title`, `price`, and `author`. The challenge for the SOAP environment is to know how to encode objects of these types in XML. The primitives are straightforward because there are schema data types that can be used for those. For object types, a process of serialization and deserialization needs to take place. Axis comes with classes that can convert objects to and from XML.

Listing 12.9 `Book.java`

```
package com.conygre.webservices;

public class Book {
    // Instance variables
    private int id;
    private String author, title;
    private double price;

    // Methods
    public int getId() {
        return id;
    }
    public String getTitle() {
        return title;
    }
    public double getPrice() {
        return price;
    }
    public String getAuthor() {
        return author;
    }

    public void setId(int id) {
        this.id = id;
    }
    public void setTitle(String title) {
        this.title = title;
    }
    public void setPrice(double price) {
        this.price = price;
    }
    public void setAuthor(String author) {
        this.author = author;
    }

    // Constructors
    public Book(){}

    public Book(String t, double p, String a, int i) {
        title  = t;
        price  = p;
        author = a;
        id     = i;
    }
}
```

> **Note**
> In the sample application, Listings 12.8 and 12.9 are both located in the `services\com\conygre\webservices` directory.

The Web service that will be passing objects of this type is shown in Listing 12.10. It is called `BookRetriever.java`. It creates a number of books, and then returns them to clients based upon their ID values.

Listing 12.10 `BookRetriever.java`

```
package com.conygre.webservices;

public class BookRetriever {
    Book[] bookshelf;
    public BookRetriever() {
      // set up an array of books using an array initializer
      Book[] bookArray = {
        new Book("The Voyage of the Dawn Treader",4.99,"C.S. Lewis",1),
        new Book("Linux Desk Reference",29.99,"Scott Hawkins",2),
        new Book("Let the Nations Be Glad",5.99,"John Piper",3),
        new Book("Treasure Island",3.99,"Robert Louis Stevenson",4),
        new Book("How to Be a Great Guitarist",17.99,"Paul Hunnisett",5),
        new Book("Heart of a Hooligan",4.99,"Muthena Paul Alkazraji",6),
        new Book("Shogun",12.99,"James Clavell",7),
        new Book("The Art of War",4.99,"Sun Tzu",8)
      };
      // assign the instance variable be the array of books
      bookshelf = bookArray;
  }

  public Book getBookByID(int id) {
      // we will keep this simple
      if (id<=8)
        return bookshelf[id-1];
      else return null;

  }
  // other methods could go here for book retrieval as well
}
```

In Listings 12.9 and 12.10, there are no clues as to how the `Book` objects will be converted to XML. They are, if you look, regular classes. Listing 12.11 shows the WSDD for this book service.

Listing 12.11 `BookSearchDeploymentDescriptor.wsdd`

```
<deployment xmlns="http://xml.apache.org/axis/wsdd/"
   xmlns:java="http://xml.apache.org/axis/wsdd/providers/java">
  <service name="bookservice" provider="java:RPC">
    <parameter name="className" value="com.conygre.webservices.BookRetriever"/>
    <parameter name="allowedMethods" value="getBookByID"/>
    <beanMapping qname="ns:Book" xmlns:ns="bookns"
     languageSpecificType="java:com.conygre.webservices.Book"/>
  </service>
</deployment>
```

> **Note**
>
> If you want to try this example, the files are all in the ZIP file for this chapter. Instructions are within the `readme.txt` file in the top level of the ZIP file.

The deployment descriptor is similar to the `averager` example, except that it has the additional `<beanMapping>` element. What this element is specifying is how the `Book` object should be passed in the SOAP messages. It is stating the following:

- The namespace for the passed book object XML is `bookns`.
- The type of the object to be passed is `com.conygre.webservices.Book`.
- The root element for the passed object is of type `Book`, which will be part of the `bookns` namespace.

If this service is deployed, it can be accessed using XML Spy in exactly the same way as the `averager` example. The XML requests and responses are as shown in Listings 12.12 and 12.13. Pay special attention to Listing 12.13, the response.

Listing 12.12 **A SOAP Request for the** `BookService`

```
<SOAP-ENV:Envelope
  xmlns:SOAP-ENV="http://schemas.xmlsoap.org/soap/envelope/"
  xmlns:SOAP-ENC="http://schemas.xmlsoap.org/soap/encoding/"
  xmlns:xsi="http://www.w3.org/2001/XMLSchema-instance"
  xmlns:xsd="http://www.w3.org/2001/XMLSchema"
  SOAP-ENV:encodingStyle="http://schemas.xmlsoap.org/soap/encoding/">

  <SOAP-ENV:Body>
    <m:getBookByID xmlns:m="getBookByID">
      <in0 xsi:type="xsd:int">1</in0>
    </m:getBookByID>
  </SOAP-ENV:Body>
</SOAP-ENV:Envelope>
```

Listing 12.13 **A SOAP Response from the** `BookService`.

```
<?xml version="1.0" encoding="UTF-8"?>
<SOAP-ENV:Envelope
 xmlns:SOAP-ENV="http://schemas.xmlsoap.org/soap/envelope/"
 xmlns:xsd="http://www.w3.org/2001/XMLSchema"
 xmlns:xsi="http://www.w3.org/2001/XMLSchema-instance">
  <SOAP-ENV:Body>
    <ns1:getBookByIDResponse
      SOAP-ENV:encodingStyle="http://schemas.xmlsoap.org/soap/encoding/"
      xmlns:ns1="getBookByID">
      <getBookByIDReturn href="#id0"/>
    </ns1:getBookByIDResponse>
    <multiRef id="id0"
    SOAP-ENC:root="0"
    encodingStyle="http://schemas.xmlsoap.org/soap/encoding/"
    xsi:type="ns3:Book"
    xmlns:SOAP-ENC="http://schemas.xmlsoap.org/soap/encoding/"
    xmlns:ns2="http://schemas.xmlsoap.org/soap/envelope/:encodingStyle"
    xmlns:ns3="bookns">
      <id xsi:type="xsd:int">1</id>
      <title xsi:type="xsd:string">The Voyage of the Dawn Treader</title>
      <price xsi:type="xsd:double">4.99</price>
      <author xsi:type="xsd:string">C.S. Lewis</author>
    </multiRef>
  </SOAP-ENV:Body>
</SOAP-ENV:Envelope>
```

The response has a very interesting body. Notice the type of the element `<multiRef>`. The type is specified as `xsi:type="ns3:Book"`. The namespace for the prefix `ns3` is set to `bookns`. This is the namespace specified within the deployment descriptor shown in Listing 12.11. Within the `multiRef` element, there are elements containing the id, title, author, and price.

> **Note**
>
> The definition of the book type will be discussed again in the section entitled "The Web Service Description Language (WSDL)," as it is within the WSDL file that the types are explicitly defined.

Finally, Listing 12.14 shows a Java client that can be used to interact with the Web service. The listing introduces you to the Axis classes used for serializing and deserializing the passed objects.

Listing 12.14 `BookClient.java`

```
import org.apache.axis.client.Call;
import org.apache.axis.client.Service;
import javax.xml.namespace.QName;
import com.conygre.webservices.Book;

public class BookClient {
  public static void main(String[] args)  {
    try {
      // set a string to contain the target URL for the service
      String target = "http://localhost:8080/axis/services/bookservice";
      // create a service object
      Service service = new Service();
      // now create the call to the service object
      Call call  = (Call)service.createCall();
      // set the URL of the service for your call object
      call.setTargetEndpointAddress(new java.net.URL(target));
      // specify the method that you wish to invoke
      call.setOperationName(new QName("getBookByID"));
      // now create an array containing the parameter for the book id to look up
      Object[] paramArray = new Object[1];
      paramArray[0] = new Integer(3);
      // set up the deserializer for the returned book
      QName qn  = new QName( "bookns", "Book" );
      call.registerTypeMapping(com.conygre.webservices.Book.class, qn,
        new org.apache.axis.encoding.ser.BeanSerializerFactory
               (com.conygre.webservices.Book.class, qn),
        new org.apache.axis.encoding.ser.BeanDeserializerFactory
               (com.conygre.webservices.Book.class, qn));

      Book result = (Book) call.invoke(paramArray);
      System.out.println("The returned book is called " + result.getTitle());
    }
    catch (Exception e){
      System.out.println("A problem occured with the RPC: " + e);
    }
  }
}
```

The part of Listing 12.14 most crucial to the discussion is the following excerpt:

```
QName qn  = new QName( "bookns", "Book" );
call.registerTypeMapping(com.conygre.webservices.Book.class, qn,
        new org.apache.axis.encoding.ser.BeanSerializerFactory
           (com.conygre.webservices.Book.class, qn),
```

```
        new org.apache.axis.encoding.ser.BeanDeserializerFactory
                (com.conygre.webservices.Book.class, qn));
```

The `QName` class was seen in our earlier `averager` example, but in this case, note the namespace and type. The namespace is the book namespace `bookns`, and the local part is `Book`.

Axis comes with classes that can be used to serialize and deserialize objects that are JavaBeans. The classes are respectively:

```
org.apache.axis.encoding.ser.BeanSerializerFactory
org.apache.axis.encoding.ser.BeanDeserializerFactory
```

These classes are being used in the call to the `registerTypeMapping()` method of the `Call` object. This method takes in four parameters:

- The class being mapped
- The qualified name of the XML type it is to be mapped to
- The serializer
- The deserializer

Note too the constructor for the serializer and deserializer. Both take in the class that they are to be used with and the qualified name of the XML type that they are to be mapped to:

```
new org.apache.axis.encoding.ser.BeanDeserializerFactory
                (com.conygre.webservices.Book.class, qn)
new org.apache.axis.encoding.ser.BeanSerializerFactory
                (com.conygre.webservices.Book.class, qn)
```

After the serialization has been set up, the remote method can be invoked in exactly the same way as in the `averager` example. The code at the end of Listing 12.14 demonstrates this.

SOAP and JSP

The role of SOAP in Web applications is of increasing significance. As more and more Web applications take advantage of available Web services, Web applications will need to interact with Web services. This is after all one of the core benefits Microsoft talks about in the discussion about ASP.NET and the traditional ASP. ASP.NET can be used to invoke Web services in a straightforward manner. How can JavaServer pages be used to interact with Web services?

Particularly with the emergence of portal technology, Web services will become more and more critical to Web applications. Portals provide feature-rich Web front ends, enabling users to interact with stock prices, weather forecasts, discussion groups, flight times, or whatever, all from one main home page. Figure 12.8 shows an example of a portal home page, taken from one of the ATG Dynamo Portal Server demonstration portal.

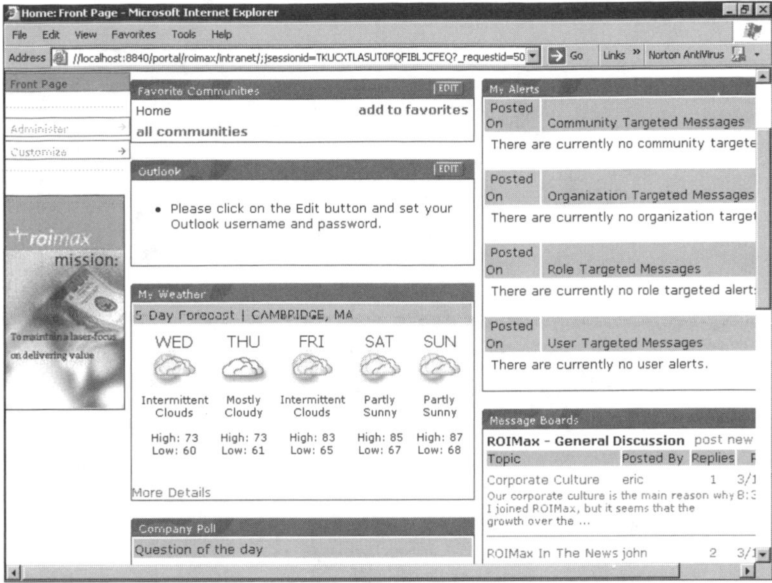

Figure 12.8 A portal home page.

Figure 12.8 shows a portal page built using JSP page fragments. Those fragments are the front end to components of application logic, and they could easily be implemented as Web services. For example, if you consider the weather component in the page shown in Figure 12.8, the weather information could easily come from a Web service.

Now you'll see how a Web application could act as a client to a Web service. A Web application client will take advantage of the `bookservice` previously discussed.

> **Caution**
>
> Do not confuse Web applications acting as *clients* to Web services with Axis, which is a Web application that *hosts* Web services.

A new Web application will be used to access the Web service. If you are using the book download for this chapter, you will find the Web application in the `clients\serviceClient` folder. The Web application has been kept simple. There is a JSP containing a form, and a servlet that actually invokes the service. Listing 12.15 shows the JSP.

Listing 12.15 `index.jsp`

```
<html>
<head>
<title>Web Service Client JSP</title>
</head>
<body>
<jsp:useBean class="com.conygre.webservices.Book" id="book" scope="session"/>
<h1>Web Service Client</h1>
<p>This basic form is submitted to a servlet called <i>BookClientServlet.</i>
This then accesses the <i>
bookservice</i> web service and creates a session scoped component called book.
The servlet finally forwards back to this page. The properties of the session
scoped book are displayed below.</p>
<form method="POST" action="bookClientServlet">
  Please enter the book ID you wish to search for:
 <input type="text" name="id" size="4"><input type="submit" value="Search"></p>
</form>
<p>The results of your last search are:</p>
<p><b>Title:</b> <jsp:getProperty name="book" property="title"/> </p>
<p><b>Author:</b> <jsp:getProperty name="book" property="author"/> </p>
<p><b>Price: </b> <jsp:getProperty name="book" property="price"/> </p>
</body>
</html>
```

The JSP uses a JavaBean, which is of type `Book`. This is the type used in Listing 12.9. The form within the JSP has one field, which is for the `id` of the book to be searched for. The action attribute points to an instance of the servlet shown in Listing 12.16.

Listing 12.16 `BookClientServlet.java`

```
package com.conygre.webservices;

import org.apache.axis.client.Call;
import org.apache.axis.client.Service;
import javax.xml.namespace.QName;
import javax.servlet.http.*;
import javax.servlet.*;

public class BookClientServlet extends HttpServlet{
   private String url;
   private ServletContext context;

   public void init(ServletConfig config) throws ServletException {
       super.init(config);
       // get the service URL from the init parameter in web.xml
       url = config.getInitParameter("url");
```

Listing 12.6 **Continued**

```
      context = getServletContext();
   }

   public void doPost(HttpServletRequest request, HttpServletResponse response) {
     try {
       // invoke the web service
       Service service = new Service();
       Call call  = (Call)service.createCall();
       call.setTargetEndpointAddress(new java.net.URL(url));
       call.setOperationName(new QName("getBookByID"));
       Object[] paramArray = new Object[1];
       paramArray[0] = new Integer(request.getParameter("id"));
       QName qn  = new QName( "bookns", "Book" );
       call.registerTypeMapping(com.conygre.webservices.Book.class, qn,
         new org.apache.axis.encoding.ser.BeanSerializerFactory
                                 (com.conygre.webservices.Book.class, qn),
         new org.apache.axis.encoding.ser.BeanDeserializerFactory
                                 (com.conygre.webservices.Book.class, qn));

       Book result = (Book) call.invoke(paramArray);
       // assign the current book to the
       // session object as a session scoped object
       HttpSession session = request.getSession();
       session.setAttribute("book", result);
       // now forward the request to index.jsp
       RequestDispatcher rd = context.getRequestDispatcher("/index.jsp");
       rd.forward(request,response);
     }
     catch (Exception e){
       try {
        // redirect to an error message page if there is a problem
        RequestDispatcher rd = context.getRequestDispatcher("/errorPage.html");
        rd.forward(request,response);
       } catch (Exception se) {}
     }
   }
}
```

The servlet is initialized, taking the URL for the Web service from `web.xml` (Listing 12.17). This way, you can deploy the service and client on different machines, and simply change this deployment descriptor to specify where the service actually is.

The servlet will take in the `POST` request from the client, and then invoke the Web service using the `id` value from the form. The servlet then sets up the session object to have a book attribute containing a copy of the book object returned from the service.

Listing 12.17 web.xml

```
<?xml version="1.0" encoding="UTF-8"?>
<web-app xmlns="http://java.sun.com/xml/ns/j2ee"
   xmlns:xsi="http://www.w3.org/2001/XMLSchema-instance"
   xsi:schemaLocation="http://java.sun.com/xml/ns/j2ee
   http://java.sun.com/xml/ns/j2ee/web-app_2_4.xsd" version="2.4">
  <servlet>
    <servlet-name>BookClientServlet</servlet-name>
    <servlet-class>com.conygre.webservices.BookClientServlet</servlet-class>
    <init-param>
     <param-name>url</param-name>
     <param-value>http://localhost:8080/axis/services/bookservice</param-value>
    </init-param>
  </servlet>
  <servlet-mapping>
    <servlet-name>BookClientServlet</servlet-name>
    <url-pattern>/bookClientServlet</url-pattern>
  </servlet-mapping>
</web-app>
```

Finally, the servlet redirects back to the index.jsp page as shown in Listing 12.15. This now shows the requested book. Figure 12.9 shows how index.jsp appears in a Web browser.

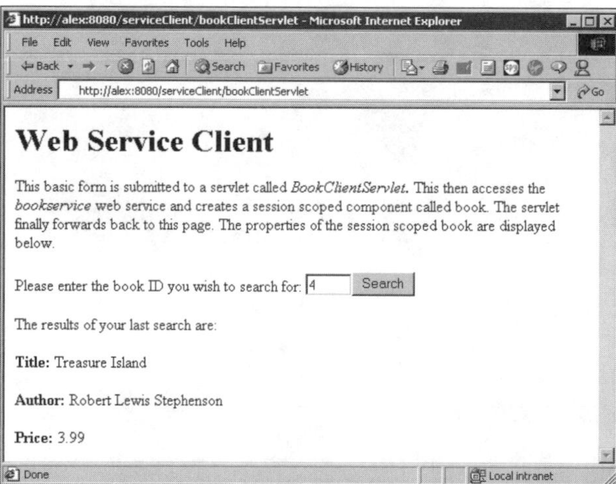

Figure 12.9 index.jsp as it appears in a browser.

You have now seen much of the workings of SOAP. Web service clients can interact with these Web services, but only if they know the methods available and the types being used. What if a client wants to invoke a Web service, but doesn't know anything about the service? How can a client interact with a Web service that it is not familiar with? The answer is found in the Web Service Description Language (WSDL).

The Web Service Description Language (WSDL)

WSDL is an XML format that describes a Web service for clients. Listing 12.18 shows the WSDL file for the `BookService` discussed in the section on SOAP.

Listing 12.18 `bookservice.wsdl`

```
<?xml version="1.0" encoding="UTF-8"?>
<wsdl:definitions
  targetNamespace="http://localhost:8080/axis/services/bookservice"
  xmlns:wsdlsoap="http://schemas.xmlsoap.org/wsdl/soap/"
  xmlns:xsd="http://www.w3.org/2001/XMLSchema"
  xmlns:tns1="bookns"
  xmlns:SOAP-ENC="http://schemas.xmlsoap.org/soap/encoding/"
  xmlns:intf="http://localhost:8080/Axis/services/bookservice"
  xmlns:wsdl="http://schemas.xmlsoap.org/wsdl/"
  xmlns:impl="http://localhost:8080/Axis/services/bookservice-impl"
  xmlns="http://schemas.xmlsoap.org/wsdl/">
  <types>
    <schema xmlns="http://www.w3.org/2001/XMLSchema" targetNamespace="bookns">
      <complexType name="Book">
        <sequence>
          <element name="id" type="xsd:int"/>
          <element name="author" nillable="true" type="xsd:string"/>
          <element name="title" nillable="true" type="xsd:string"/>
          <element name="price" type="xsd:double"/>
        </sequence>
      </complexType>
      <element name="Book" nillable="true" type="tns1:Book"/>
    </schema>
  </types>
  <wsdl:message name="getBookByIDResponse">
    <wsdl:part name="return" type="tns1:Book"/>
  </wsdl:message>
  <wsdl:message name="getBookByIDRequest">
    <wsdl:part name="in0" type="xsd:int"/>
  </wsdl:message>
  <wsdl:portType name="BookRetriever">
    <wsdl:operation name="getBookByID" parameterOrder="in0">
      <wsdl:input message="intf:getBookByIDRequest"/>
      <wsdl:output message="intf:getBookByIDResponse"/>
    </wsdl:operation>
```

Listing 12.8 **Continued**

```
  </wsdl:portType>
  <wsdl:binding name="bookserviceSoapBinding" type="intf:BookRetriever">
    <wsdlsoap:binding style="rpc"
            transport="http://schemas.xmlsoap.org/soap/http"/>
    <wsdl:operation name="getBookByID">
      <wsdlsoap:operation soapAction=""/>
      <wsdl:input>
        <wsdlsoap:body use="encoded"
          encodingStyle="http://schemas.xmlsoap.org/soap/encoding/"
          namespace="getBookByID"/>
      </wsdl:input>
      <wsdl:output>
        <wsdlsoap:body use="encoded"
           encodingStyle="http://schemas.xmlsoap.org/soap/encoding/"
           namespace="http://localhost:8080/Axis/services/bookservice"/>
      </wsdl:output>
    </wsdl:operation>
  </wsdl:binding>
  <wsdl:service name="BookRetrieverService">
    <wsdl:port name="bookservice" binding="intf:bookserviceSoapBinding">
      <wsdlsoap:address
         location="http://localhost:8080/Axis/services/bookservice"/>
    </wsdl:port>
  </wsdl:service>
</wsdl:definitions>
```

One of the first things that you will notice about this XML document is the namespaces. There are six namespaces used in this document. Table 12.2 shows these namespaces and what they are used for.

Table 12.2 **The Namespaces used in** `bookservice.wsdl`

Standard Namespaces Used in WSDL	Description
http://schemas.xmlsoap.org/wsdl/	The WSDL descriptions namespace.
http://schemas.xmlsoap.org/wsdl/soap/	The SOAP binding for WSDL. Web services can also be accessed by other protocols, and the bindings for those can be seen at the bottom of this table, namely http and mime.
http://www.w3.org/2001/XMLSchema	The XML Schema namespace. This is used to define the types that are to be passed in the messages.
http://schemas.xmlsoap.org/soap/encoding/	The standard SOAP encoding namespace.

Table 12.2 **Continued**

Standard Namespaces Used in WSDL	Description
NAMESPACES SPECIFIC TO THE BOOKSERVICE APPLICATION	
Bookns	This is the namespace defined for the bookservice. It is used as the namespace for the service specific datatypes.
http://localhost:8080/axis/services/bookservice	This is the interface namespace for the book service. It contains the definitions for the methods that are to be made available. It is different from the bookns namespace, as that defines the actual custom datatypes.
OTHER NAMESPACES SOMETIMES USED IN WSDL	
http://schemas.xmlsoap.org/wsdl/http/	The HTTP binding for WSDL.
http://schemas.xmlsoap.org/wsdl/mime/	The MIME binding for WSDL.

A WSDL document consists of five core structures:

- `<types>`
- `<message>`
- `<portType>`
- `<binding>`
- `<service>`

The `<types>` Element

The `<types>` element contains the definitions of any data types that are to be passed back and forth to and from the Web service. Here is the `<types>` element from `bookservice.wsdl`:

```
<types>
    <schema xmlns="http://www.w3.org/2001/XMLSchema" targetNamespace="bookns">
      <complexType name="Book">
        <sequence>
          <element name="id" type="xsd:int"/>
          <element name="author" nillable="true" type="xsd:string"/>
          <element name="title" nillable="true" type="xsd:string"/>
          <element name="price" type="xsd:double"/>
        </sequence>
      </complexType>
      <element name="Book" nillable="true" type="tns1:Book"/>
    </schema>
  </types>
```

The first thing to note is that the types are defined using the W3C XML Schema language. The type defined here is called a `Book`. There is a nillable element called `Book`, which is of the `Book` type.

> **Note**
> If you are not familiar with the XML Schema Language, then please look at Appendix B, "An Overview of XML Schema."

The `<types>` element can also import and include schemas from external sources if necessary. This is especially useful when the types are already defined elsewhere in existing schemas.

The `<message>` Element

What the `<types>` element does not define is how the types are used. It simply states what they are. The types are used in the context of parameters and return types to the Web service. The parameters and return types are defined within the WSDL file as `<message>` elements. Here are the message elements for `bookservice.wsdl`:

```
<wsdl:message name="getBookByIDResponse">
    <wsdl:part name="return" type="tns1:Book"/>
  </wsdl:message>
  <wsdl:message name="getBookByIDRequest">
    <wsdl:part name="in0" type="xsd:int"/>
  </wsdl:message>
```

There are two messages defined the `bookservice` Web service. One is for the request, and the other is for the response. The request parameter is an `int`, and the response is a `Book`. The `Book` was defined in the `<types>` element previously discussed.

The `<portType>` Element

The `<portType>` element is analogous to a Java class. It defines the various methods that are available to client applications. Here is the `<portType>` element from the `bookservice.wsdl`:

```
<wsdl:portType name="BookRetriever">
    <wsdl:operation name="getBookByID" parameterOrder="in0">
      <wsdl:input message="intf:getBookByIDRequest"/>
      <wsdl:output message="intf:getBookByIDResponse"/>
    </wsdl:operation>
  </wsdl:portType>
```

As you can see, this is almost a class definition, with the `<operation>` element defining the available methods, and then for each `<operation>`, appropriate `<input>` and `<output>` messages. The message types here correspond to the `<message>` elements discussed earlier.

The <operation> Element

In WSDL, it is possible to have four distinct types of operation:

- One-way—The service receives a message, but does not respond.
- Request-Response—The service receives a message, and then sends a reply (as in our example—this is the most common for remote procedure calls).
- Solicit-Response—The service sends a message, and receives a reply message, the opposite of Request-Response.
- Notification—The service sends a message. It does not receive messages.

These different operation types have different sequences of `<input>` and `<output>` elements. Examples of these can be seen at the WSDL page at the W3C site `http://www.w3.org/TR/wsdl`.

The <binding> Element

The `<binding>` element contains the protocol-specific content for the Web service. If you look again at Table 12.2 showing the namespaces used in WSDL, you will note that there are three namespaces that are associated Web service bindings. These are

```
http://schemas.xmlsoap.org/wsdl/soap/
http://schemas.xmlsoap.org/wsdl/http/
http://schemas.xmlsoap.org/wsdl/mime/
```

The `<binding>` element is required because what has been seen up until now does not say anything about how the messages should be sent. Although the messages themselves have been defined, there is nothing specific to SOAP, for example, or any other possible protocol. At least one `<binding>` element is required. If your service is made available via the SOAP protocol, as the `bookservice` is for example, then elements from the SOAP binding namespace are used to define how the various `portTypes` are to be accessed. Here is the `<binding>` element from the `bookservice.wsdl` file:

```
<wsdl:binding name="bookserviceSoapBinding" type="intf:BookRetriever">
  <wsdlsoap:binding style="rpc"
           transport="http://schemas.xmlsoap.org/soap/http"/>
  <wsdl:operation name="getBookByID">
    <wsdlsoap:operation soapAction=""/>
    <wsdl:input>
      <wsdlsoap:body use="encoded"
        encodingStyle="http://schemas.xmlsoap.org/soap/encoding/"
        namespace="getBookByID"/>
    </wsdl:input>
    <wsdl:output>
      <wsdlsoap:body use="encoded"
         encodingStyle="http://schemas.xmlsoap.org/soap/encoding/"
         namespace="http://localhost:8080/axis/services/bookservice"/>
```

```
      </wsdl:output>
    </wsdl:operation>
  </wsdl:binding>
```

This <wsdl:binding> contains a child <soap:binding> element. The SOAP binding element is from the SOAP binding namespace.

```
<wsdlsoap:binding style="rpc"
              transport="http://schemas.xmlsoap.org/soap/http"/>
```

The style attribute defines whether the SOAP message will be for RPC or messaging. The alternative value for the style attribute is document. The transport specified is SOAP over HTTP. It could also have been SOAP over FTP or SOAP over SMTP, which would have been specified as follows:

```
http://schemas.xmlsoap.org/soap/ftp/
http://schemas.xmlsoap.org/soap/smtp/
```

Within the <soap:binding> element, there is a set of elements defining the various operations along with their corresponding <input> and <output> elements. This section closely resembles the <portType> element. The purpose of these elements is to specify how the various messages are to appear in the SOAP body. In our example, this is relatively straightforward:

```
      <wsdl:output>
        <wsdlsoap:body use="encoded"
           encodingStyle="http://schemas.xmlsoap.org/soap/encoding/"
           namespace="http://localhost:8080/axis/services/bookservice"/>
      </wsdl:output>
```

Here, the output from the operation (which, if you recall, returns a book object) is encoded using the standard SOAP encoding.

The <service> Element

The last element in the WSDL file is the <service> element. This element defines the actual URL of the Web service being accessed:

```
  <wsdl:service name="BookRetrieverService">
    <wsdl:port name="bookservice" binding="intf:bookserviceSoapBinding">
      <wsdlsoap:address
         location="http://localhost:8080/axis/services/bookservice"/>
    </wsdl:port>
  </wsdl:service>
```

If you look at this element, it states that for the bookServiceSoapBinding, the URL is http://localhost:8080/axis/services/bookservice.

The bookServiceSoapBinding is the name given to the binding element discussed previously.

Generating WSDL

If you are using Apache Axis, you will be pleased to know that the WSDL file can be created dynamically for you. In fact, if you successfully deployed the Web services that have been discussed so far, namely `averager` and `bookservice`, you will be able to view the WSDL file by simply visiting the following URLs in a browser:

```
http://localhost:8080/axis/services/averager?wsdl
http://localhost:8080/axis/services/bookservice?wsdl
```

In fact, these are the URLs that you would have used when accessing the services through XML Spy. It is these dynamically generated WSDL files that XML Spy uses to give you the dialog box that you can see in Figure 12.6.

You can also create the WSDL file from the command line by using the `Java2WSDL` command-line tool that comes with Axis.

Generating Java from the WSDL

It is also possible to create the Java code from the WSDL! The tool is called `WSDL2Java`. This can be especially useful when developing Web applications that access Web services. If you consider the example Web application that accesses the `bookservice`, it consisted of a servlet (Listing 12.16), and a JSP (Listing 12.15). Within the Web application code, all the code to interact with the Web service also had to be written. `WSDL2Java` can be used to not only create Web services themselves, but it can be used to create client stubs to simplify the code you would need to write to access the Web service. Figure 12.10 demonstrates this.

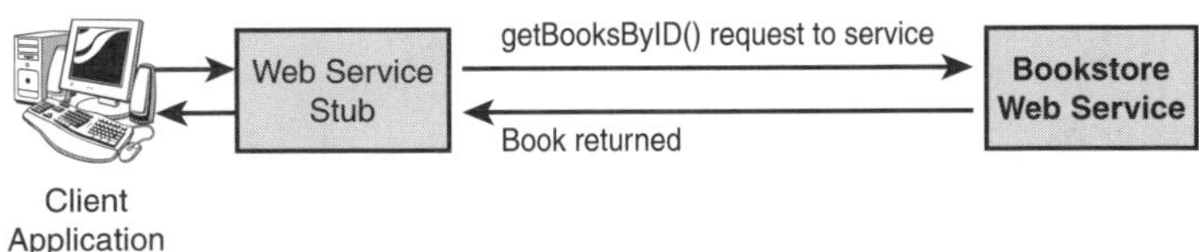

Figure 12.10 Accessing Web services using stubs.

The benefit of using a stub is that the client application no longer needs to concern itself with interacting with the Web service directly. It can simply interact with the dynamically generated stub.

To create the stub and associated classes for the `bookservice`, you will need to bring up a command prompt in the folder containing the WSDL file (it has been saved for you in `\services\bookservice.wsdl`). Then, set the classpath to include the Axis classes, and enter the following at the prompt:

```
java org.apache.axis.wsdl.WSDL2Java -v bookservice.wsdl
```

The `-v` flag means `verbose`, so you get feedback on what is going on when you run the program. The WSDL file is then passed in as an argument.

Running this creates a number of classes, interfaces, and also a deployment and undeployment descriptor for the Web service. In this section, the focus will be on the generated classes that will help in the building of a Web application that accesses Web services.

There are several classes that require our attention because they could be used within a Web application. The most important of the generated classes is the stub (Listing 12.19). It has been placed in a package called localhost in our example because that is the domain being used in the WSDL file.

Listing 12.19 `BookserviceSoapBindingStub.java`

```
/**
 * BookserviceSoapBindingStub.java
 *
 * This file was auto-generated from WSDL
 * by the Apache Axis WSDL2Java emitter.
 */

package localhost;

public class BookserviceSoapBindingStub extends org.apache.axis.client.Stub
                                         implements localhost.BookRetriever
{
  . . .

  public bookns.Book getBookByID(int in0) throws java.rmi.RemoteException {
    if (super.cachedEndpoint == null) {
        throw new org.apache.axis.NoEndPointException();
    }
    org.apache.axis.client.Call _call = createCall();
    _call.addParameter(new javax.xml.namespace.QName("", "in0"),
                       new javax.xml.namespace.QName
                          ("http://www.w3.org/2001/XMLSchema", "int"),
                       int.class,
                       javax.xml.rpc.ParameterMode.IN);
    _call.setReturnType(new javax.xml.namespace.QName("bookns", "Book"),
                                                   bookns.Book.class);
    _call.setUseSOAPAction(true);
    _call.setSOAPActionURI("");
    _call.setOperationStyle("rpc");
    _call.setOperationName(new javax.xml.namespace.QName("getBookByID",
                                                      "getBookByID"))

    java.lang.Object _resp =
           _call.invoke(new java.lang.Object[] {new java.lang.Integer(in0)})

    if (_resp instanceof java.rmi.RemoteException) {
```

Listing 12.19 **Continued**

```
      throw (java.rmi.RemoteException)_resp;
    }
    else {
      try {
          return (bookns.Book) _resp;
      } catch (java.lang.Exception _exception) {
          return (bookns.Book)
            org.apache.axis.utils.JavaUtils.convert(_resp, bookns.Book.class);
      }
    }
  }
}
```

Not all of the code from the class has been shown because it is fairly large, but the core method has been left in. The method shown is the method that accesses the Web service, and our Web client can use the class. Note the `Book` type referred to is from a different package (`bookns`). That is because a `Book` class has also been created by the WSDL2Java utility. It is very similar to the `Book.java` from Listing 12.9.

The class also implements an interface called `localhost.BookRetriever`. This interface contains the remote methods. It is shown in Listing 12.20.

Listing 12.20 `localhost.BookRetriever.java`

```
package localhost;
public interface BookRetriever extends java.rmi.Remote {
 public bookns.Book getBookByID(int in0) throws java.rmi.RemoteException;
}
```

Notice the use of the `java.rmi.RemoteException` class. This has been used as the type of exception that is thrown if there is a problem invoking the remote procedure.

To locate the service, an additional class is also created. This is called the `BookRetrieverServiceLocator`. The listing for this is not shown, but it is part of the demonstration application mentioned in the next paragraph.

Finally, here is a Web application that takes advantage of these automatically generated classes. The servlet can be seen in Listing 12.21. It can be found in the `clientWithStub.war` web application in the chapter12.zip file.

Listing 12.21 `BookClientServlet.java`

```
// this servlet invokes a stub generated from WSDL2Java
// the stub then invokes the web service
package com.conygre.webservices;
import javax.servlet.http.*;
import javax.servlet.*;
```

Listing 12.21 **Continued**

```
public class BookClientServlet extends HttpServlet{
   public void doPost(HttpServletRequest request,HttpServletResponse response){
        localhost.BookRetriever binding;
        try {
          // use the service locator class to find the service
          binding=new localhost.BookRetrieverServiceLocator().getbookservice();
          bookns.Book result = null;
          int id = Integer.parseInt(request.getParameter("id"));
          // now use the returned stub to invoke a service
          result = binding.getBookByID(id);
          HttpSession session = request.getSession();
          session.setAttribute("book", result);
          // now forward the request to index.jsp
          RequestDispatcher rd =
                 getServletContext().getRequestDispatcher("/index.jsp");
          rd.forward(request,response);
       }
       // there are two possible exceptions, a javax.xml.rpc.ServiceException
       // and a java.rmi.RemoteException
       // we will simply redirect regardless
     catch (Exception e){
       try {
        RequestDispatcher rd =
              getServletContext().getRequestDispatcher("/errorPage.html");
        rd.forward(request,response);
       } catch (Exception se) {}
     }
   }
}
```

The Web application within which the servlet resides is exactly the same as the one used for the earlier `bookservice` example. The only difference is that the JSP `useBean` element for the `Book` is now of type `bookns.Book` as opposed to `com.conygre.webservices.Book`. The compiled classes generated by `WSDL2Java` also need to be in the `classes` folder of the Web application.

The main thing to notice about the servlet code in Listing 12.21 is that it has no Axis- or Web service–specific code in it any longer. It has all been hidden within the stub class, which was generated automatically. The benefits are substantial. Client developers no longer need to concern themselves with the details of SOAP or WSDL. They do not need to consider serialization issues at all because it is all taken care of. You can even generate stubs for services that are not written using the Java programming language. Web services hosted on the .NET platform, for example, can also be accessed via stubs created in this way. All that is required is a WSDL file.

Finally, it is worth pointing out that there is also a Java class called Java2WSDL. This class can be used to generate WSDL bindings for your application based upon a WSDL file created from nothing more than a Java interface. It creates the class for the web service with the required methods as defined by the Java interface. You can then provide the appropriate implementation code within these methods. See the Axis documentation for more details on Java2WSDL.

Accessing WSDL Programmatically

As you would expect, it is also possible to access WSDL, programmatically. There is an API called WSDL4J that you can use, and there is also an API called the Web Service Invocation Framework, or WSIF. At the time of writing, the WSDL4J API is in the Community Review stage of the Java Community Process. It is JSR 110.

> **Note**
> If you are not familiar with the Java Community Process, you might want to take a look at Appendix F, which explains how the Java Community Process works.

WSIF is an API from the IBM AlphaWorks. It enables you to interact with Web services using SOAP based on the contents of the WSDL file. This API relies on the precursor to Apache Axis, however, which is Apache SOAP 2.2, so if you wanted to test it, you will need to download and install Apache SOAP, and place the relevant classes for Apache SOAP into the classpath. These are *not* compliant with Apache Axis. For more information on WSIF, visit `http://www.alphaworks.ibm.com/tech/wsif`.

Universal Description, Discovery, and Integration (UDDI)

You have seen now how to interact with a Web service using SOAP; you have also seen how to find out about what the service offers using WSDL. The final question that we will discuss here is this. How do you find the Web service in the first place?

If you want to find a Web site that offers something you have never looked for before, the easiest way to find what you are after is to visit a search engine. The equivalent for a Web service is a UDDI Registry. Service providers register with the registry, and then clients can locate the services by querying the registry.

UDDI registries enable you to locate businesses and services in a number of different ways:

- Yellow Pages—Locate businesses by business type.
- White Pages—Locate businesses by names, addresses, and so on.
- Green Pages—Locate information about the services that a business offers.

The information that enables the data to be accessed in this way is stored in an XML structure. This structure is part of the UDDI specification. The UDDI specification covers more than this data structure, however.

UDDI defines a number of standards surrounding these registries of Web services:

- An XML Schema defining a UDDI entry
- A UDDI API covering methods for publishing services and methods for accessing services
- A specification for the replication of service information between registries
- A specification for registry operators covering issues such as security

The details of the UDDI specification are available from the UDDI home page `www.uddi.org`.

In this section, we will focus on the interaction with UDDI registries to locate Web services and find out about them. The technology is still emerging and evolving surrounding UDDI, but you can still try some of these techniques out.

There are a number of registries available that you can register your Web services with. IBM and Microsoft both have UDDI registries. The URLs for them are `http://uddi.microsoft.com/default.aspx` and `http://www.ibm.com/services/uddi/`.

These URLs provide a browser front end to the UDDI registries. It can be helpful to have a browse around these sites because it helps to crystallize what sort of information is stored about a specific business entity.

The UDDI XML

Every new entry in a UDDI registry is available as an XML document. If you notice in the earlier list of what UDDI defines. One is the schema defining a UDDI entry. Listing 12.22 shows a UDDI XML file for a company offering the `averager` service that we entered into the IBM UDDI registry. This can be found at the IBM Web Services Test Area at `http://demo.alphaworks.ibm.com/browser/`.

Listing 12.22 **UDDI Entry in the IBM Test Registry**

```
<?xml version="1.0" encoding="utf-8"?>
<businessDetail generic="1.0"
   xmlns="urn:uddi-org:api"
   operator="www.ibm.com/services/uddi" truncated="false">
  <businessEntity authorizedName="1000008Y3V"
                operator="www.ibm.com/services/uddi"
                businessKey="BFB0ED70-7499-11D6-ACB4-000C0E00ACDD">
    <discoveryURLs>
      <discoveryURL useType="businessEntity">
   http://www-3.ibm.com/services/uddi/testregistry/uddiget
   ?businessKey=BFB0ED70-7499-11D6-ACB4-000C0E00ACDD</discoveryURL>
```

Listing 12.22 **Continued**

```
    </discoveryURLs>
    <name>Conygre IT Limited</name>
    <description xml:lang="en">Java and XML Training and Consultancy Provider
     </description>
    <contacts>
      <contact useType="Director">
        <personName>Nick Todd</personName>
      </contact>
    </contacts>
    <businessServices>
      <businessService serviceKey="4C648700-7A2A-11D6-AC1C-000C0E00ACDD"
                       businessKey="BFB0ED70-7499-11D6-ACB4-000C0E00ACDD">
        <name>Averager</name>
        <description xml:lang="en">This service returns the average of two
                                    supplied numbers</description>
        <bindingTemplates>
          <bindingTemplate bindingKey="4C657160-7A2A-11D6-AC1C-000C0E00ACDD"
                           serviceKey="4C648700-7A2A-11D6-AC1C-000C0E00ACDD">
            <accessPoint URLType="http">
      http://localhost:8080/Axis/services/averager?wsdl</accessPoint>
            <tModelInstanceDetails>
              <tModelInstanceInfo
            tModelKey="UUID:68DE9E80-AD09-469D-8A37-088422BFBC36"/>
            </tModelInstanceDetails>
          </bindingTemplate>
        </bindingTemplates>
        <categoryBag>
          <keyedReference
          tModelKey="UUID:C0B9FE13-179F-413D-8A5B-5004DB8E5BB2"
          keyName="Computer Training" keyValue="61142"/>
        </categoryBag>
      </businessService>
    </businessServices>
  </businessEntity>
</businessDetail>
```

This entry was submitted through a series of HTML forms. I did not have to submit the XML file itself. The XML contains information about the company, along with the services provided. Note the access point in the XML referring to the Web service WSDL file. This is only a test area, so the fact that it is pointing to `localhost` does not matter.

The UDDI XML contains the following core elements:

- `<businessEntity>`
- `<tModel>`
- `<businessService>`

- <categoryBag>
- <bindingTemplate>
- <publisherAssertion>

The <businessEntity> Element

The <businessEntity> element defines the business itself. It contains child elements and attributes defining the contact information, the business name, and any services that are available to clients. The information stored includes the equivalent of a yellow and white pages entry.

The <businessService> Element

The <businessService> element defines a service that is available from a business. Each <businessService> is a child of a <businessServices> element. Notice the use of various unique identifiers throughout this element:

```
<businessService serviceKey="4C648700-7A2A-11D6-AC1C-000C0E00ACDD"
                businessKey="BFB0ED70-7499-11D6-ACB4-000C0E00ACDD">
<name>Averager</name>
<description xml:lang="en">This service returns the average of two
                              supplied numbers</description>
<bindingTemplates>
    <bindingTemplate bindingKey="4C657160-7A2A-11D6-AC1C-000C0E00ACDD"
                    serviceKey="4C648700-7A2A-11D6-AC1C-000C0E00ACDD">
    <accessPoint URLType="http">
http://localhost:8080/axis/services/averager?wsdl</accessPoint>
    <tModelInstanceDetails>
        <tModelInstanceInfo
    tModelKey="UUID:68DE9E80-AD09-469D-8A37-088422BFBC36"/>
    </tModelInstanceDetails>
    </bindingTemplate>
</bindingTemplates>
<categoryBag>
    <keyedReference
    tModelKey="UUID:C0B9FE13-179F-413D-8A5B-5004DB8E5BB2"
    keyName="Computer Training" keyValue="61142"/>
</categoryBag>
</businessService>
```

The <businessService> element consists of a name, description, a bindingTemplate, and a categoryBag. The name and description are self explanatory, but the other two are not so obvious.

The <categoryBag> Element

The <categoryBag> element contains categorization information for the service. There are already a number of ways to categorize companies and organizations, and UDDI rather sensibly does not try to define another one, but use the pre-existing mechanisms.

The supported categorization standards are currently:

- UNSPSC—Universal Standard and Products Classification
- NAICS—North American Industry Classification System
- ISO 3166—Geographic Classification System
- Other—General keywords

Each of these has a unique identifier to specify which classification mechanism is being used. In the example shown, the tModelKey refers to the classification system.

```
<categoryBag>
    <keyedReference
    tModelKey="UUID:C0B9FE13-179F-413D-8A5B-5004DB8E5BB2"
    keyName="Computer Training" keyValue="61142"/>
</categoryBag>
```

The key value UUID:C0B9FE13-179F 413D-8A5B-5004DB8E5BB2 specifies that the classification in use here is the NAICS classification. The keyName and keyValue both have values from the NAICS classification system.

The <bindingTemplate> Element

Notice the use of more unique identifiers in this section of the UDDI XML file. The business and the service have both been assigned unique identifiers.

The role of the <bindingTemplate> element is to hold the specific information about the actual service. It contains two child elements, the <accessPoint> and the <tModelInstance>.

The accessPoint is the location of the service itself:

```
<accessPoint URLType="http">
   http://localhost:8080/axis/services/averager?wsdl
</accessPoint>
```

The <tModelInstance> requires some further explanation.

The <tModelInstance> and the <tModel> Elements

What exactly is a tModel? The name doesn't exactly give it away! The tModel represents a technical specification within the context of a UDDI registry, and this specification will have a unique ID. A good example would be a tModel referring to a WSDL file. The WSDL is the specification document for the Web service.

In Listing 12.22, the tModelInstance is a reference to a pre-existing tModel:

```
<tModelInstanceDetails>
```

```
  <tModelInstanceInfo tModelKey="UUID:68DE9E80-AD09-469D-8A37-088422BFBC36"/>
</tModelInstanceDetails>
```

This `tModel` key identifies the resource being referred to. This key value refers to any browser or HTTP-based Web service. In the context of the UDDI XML file in Listing 12.22, this informs any clients of the kind of service that is being referenced here.

You have now seen the basics of the UDDI XML file. The question is, how can this information be accessed from clients who want to invoke locate the Web service?

The UDDI API

From a Web application perspective, you might well want to query a UDDI registry to locate appropriate Web services. This can be achieved using the UDDI API. This API is also part of the UDDI specification, and there is an implementation written with the Java Programming Language called UDDI4J. It can be obtained from `http://uddi4j.org`.

Using this API, service providers can modify and publish services and information about themselves, and clients can query this information. Essentially, the API enables service providers to programmatically modify their UDDI XML entry, and clients can query the UDDI XML entries.

Listing 12.23 is an example of a JSP that queries the IBM UDDI registry for a specific service and displays the information about that service. The code has been kept in one JSP to make it clear as to how it works.

Listing 12.23 `uddiClient.jsp`

```
<%@ page import="java.util.Vector, org.uddi4j.UDDIException,
                 org.uddi4j.response.*, org.uddi4j.client.*,
                 org.uddi4j.request.*" %>
<html>
<head><title>UDDI Looking up a Service</title></head>
<body>
<h1>Looking up a Web Service Using UDDI</h1>
<h2>Using UDDI4J</h2>
<%
  try {
    System.setProperty("org.uddi4j.TransportClassName",
                       "org.uddi4j.transport.ApacheAxisTransport");
    UDDIProxy uddi = new UDDIProxy();
    uddi.setInquiryURL
         ("http://www-3.ibm.com/services/uddi/testregistry/inquiryapi");
    ServiceList serviceList = uddi.find_service
         ("BFB0ED70-7499-11D6-ACB4-000C0E00ACDD", null, null, null, null, 5);
    Vector serviceInfoVector =
             serviceList.getServiceInfos().getServiceInfoVector();
    for (int i = 0; i < serviceInfoVector.size(); i++) {
```

Listing 12.23 **Continued**

```
      ServiceInfo serviceInfo = (ServiceInfo)serviceInfoVector.elementAt(i);
      // Print name for each service
      out.println("Name of Service : " + serviceInfo.getNameString() + "<br>");
      out.println("Service key     : " + serviceInfo.getServiceKey() + "<br>");
      out.println("Business key     : " + serviceInfo.getBusinessKey() + "<br>");
     }
  }
  catch(UDDIException e){
    out.println("UDDI lookup problem: " + e);
   }
%>
</body>
</html>
```

This JSP will look up the services based on a specific business ID, and then display its name, key, and the business key. If you are trying this out, it is located within the `clientStub` Web application within the `chapter12.zip` file.

> **Caution**
> You might have thought it more intuitive to do a search based on a company name. Unfortunately, there can be a problem with using the UDDI4J `find_business` method, in that the XML returned contains an attribute `xml:lang`. Not all parsers understand this, so the application fails.

The system property being set is used by the UDDI4J API to determine what kind of transport it should be using to interact with the UDDI registry. The alternatives are Apache SOAP, and HP SOAP. The property values are

```
TransportClassName=org.uddi4j.transport.ApacheSOAPTransport
TransportClassName=org.uddi4j.transport.ApacheAxisTransport
TransportClassName=org.uddi4j.transport.HPSOAPTransport
```

The `org.uddi4j.client.UDDIProxy` class represents the UDDI server, so all actions that you want to do are against this object. There are two URLs associated with this object. One is the inquiry URL, and the other is the publish URL. The UDDI registry publishes these URLs. If you are a service provider and want to change the services you provide, you would use the publish URL. If you are a client, you use the inquiry URL. To set these URLs, there are two methods of the `UDDIProxy` class:

```
void setInquiryURL (String url)
void setPublishURL (String url)
```

In Listing 12.23, the `setInquiryURL` method is being used. The URL is for the IBM Web Services test area.

The `find_service` method is then used to locate services for a specific business ID. The various arguments can be used to specify details such as filter criteria. This returns a `ServiceList` object, which contains a vector of `ServiceInfo` objects, one for each provided service. The `ServiceInfo` object can then be queried for the service name and id.

Figure 12.11 shows the result in a browser, and Figure 12.12 shows the screen from which the two returned services were set up.

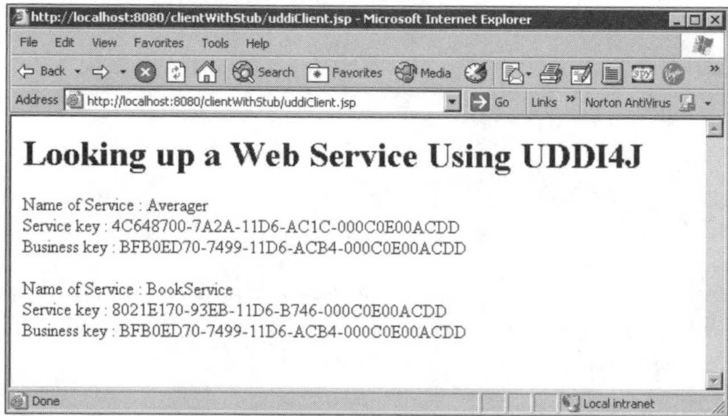

Figure 12.11 `uddiClient.jsp` in a Web browser.

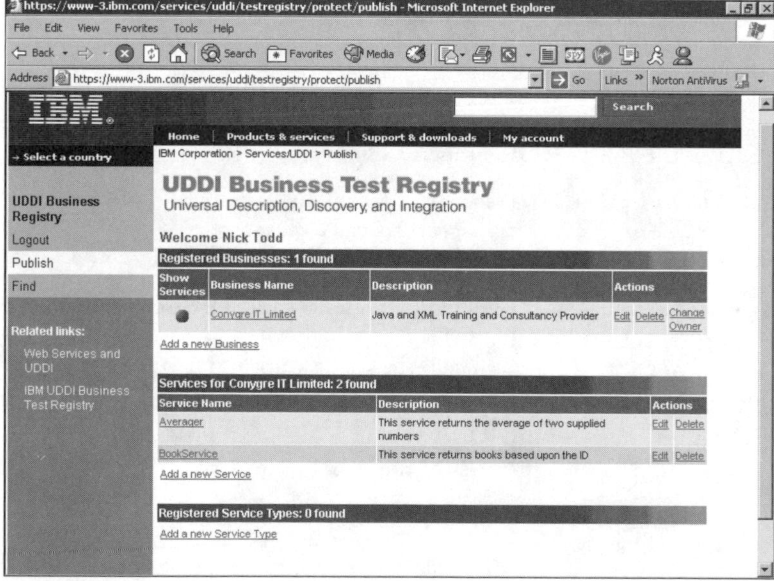

Figure 12.12 Setting up information in a UDDI registry.

There is a related API that can be used with UDDI called the Java API for XML Registries (JAXR) which was introduced earlier in the chapter along with the SAAJ API for SOAP, and the JAX-RPC API for invoking web services. JAXR is part of J2EE 1.4, and is specifically for the purpose of interacting with registries - they do not have to be UDDI. The benefits of JAXR over UDDI4J are that it not restricted to UDDI registries only, and it is also a J2EE standard. Listing 12.24 shows a JAXR application that queries the IBM UDDI test registry.

Listing 12.24 **JAXRQueryExample.java**

```
import javax.xml.registry.*;
import javax.xml.registry.infomodel.*;
import java.net.*;
import java.util.*;

public class JAXRQueryExample {
  public static void main(String[] args){
    Connection conn = null;
    String query = args[0];
    Properties props = new Properties();
    props.setProperty("javax.xml.registry.queryManagerURL",
     "http://www-3.ibm.com/services/uddi/testregistry/inquiryapi");
    props.setProperty("javax.xml.registry.factoryClass",
     "com.sun.xml.registry.uddi.ConnectionFactoryImpl");
    try {
      ConnectionFactory factory = ConnectionFactory.newInstance();
      factory.setProperties(props);
      conn = factory.createConnection();
      System.out.println("Successfully connected to the registry");
      RegistryService service = conn.getRegistryService();
      BusinessQueryManager manager = service.getBusinessQueryManager();
      Collection qualifiers = new ArrayList();
      qualifiers.add(FindQualifier.SORT_BY_NAME_DESC);
      Collection patterns = new ArrayList();
      patterns.add(query);
      BulkResponse response = manager.findOrganizations(
         qualifiers, patterns, null, null, null, null);
      Collection results = response.getCollection();
      if(results.size() == 0){
        System.out.println("No results were returned from this query");
      }
      else {
        System.out.println("There are " + results.size()
                           + " results from this query:");
        System.out.println("");
      }
```

Listing 12.24 **Continued**

```
      Iterator iter = results.iterator();
      while (iter.hasNext()){
        Organization org = (Organization)iter.next();
        System.out.println("Name: " + org.getName().getValue());
        System.out.println("Description: " +
                           org.getDescription().getValue());
        displayServices(org);
        System.out.println("");
      }
    }
    catch(Exception e){
      System.out.println("An error has occurred: " + e);
    }
  }

  public static void displayServices(Organization org){
    try {
      Collection services = org.getServices();
      Iterator iter = services.iterator();
      while(iter.hasNext()){
        Service service = (Service)iter.next();
        System.out.println("Service name: " +
                           service.getName().getValue());
        Collection bindings = service.getServiceBindings();
        Iterator iterTwo = bindings.iterator();
        while(iterTwo.hasNext()){
          ServiceBinding binding = (ServiceBinding)iterTwo.next();
          System.out.println("Service binding: " +
                             binding.getAccessURI());
        }
      }
    }
    catch(JAXRException e){
      System.out.println("A problem occured whilst obtaining services: " + e);
    }
  }
}
```

If you wish to try this example, it is found in the zip file download for this chapter in the folder `clients\jaxr`, and to run it you will require the JARs from the `common\lib` folder within the Java Web Services Developers Pack (JWSDP) from Sun to be in the classpath. This can be downloaded from the Sun site at `http://java.sun.com/webservices/webservicespack.html`. There is a batch file called `setclasspath.bat` provided with the example that assumes an environment variable has been set called `JWSDP_HOME` which points to your JWSDP installation folder.

The code in Listing 12.24 when run requires an argument which is a search string. You can use any company name that may have a web service registered with the IBM UDDI Test registry.

We will now unpack the code in Listing 12.24 and explain what is going on. It is similar to the UDDI4J API. First, a `Connection` is obtained to the IBM Test Registry. This is done by configuring a `ConnectionFactory` via properties, and then using it to obtain a connection to the registry. Once a connection to the registry is established, you can then obtain a reference to a `BusinessQueryManager` which can be used to execute a query against the registry. The query is carried out using the `findOrganizations` method. This method takes in six arguments, the first two of which are of interest in our example:

```
BulkResponse response = manager.findOrganizations(
        qualifiers, patterns, null, null, null, null);
```

The `qualifiers` argument is a collection that specifies how the results from any queries are to be returned. The `patterns` argument specifies what is being searched for. In our case, the `patterns` argument contains the query argument provided at the command line.

The response from the registry is encapsulated in a `BulkResponse` object, which can be queried for the data. There are various methods that can then be used to extract information about the organization and the services that it provides. For example, to extract the collection of returned UDDI entries as a `Collection`, you use the `getCollection` method of the `BulkResponse` object. You can then iterate through the collection as demonstrated. Note that the collection contains `Organization` objects.

```
Organization org = (Organization)iter.next();
```

You can then access the `name` and `description` of the organization, and any services that it has.

```
System.out.println("Name: " + org.getName().getValue());
System.out.println("Description: " + org.getDescription().getValue());
```

For more information on JAXR, visit `http://www.jcp.org/jsr/detail/93.jsp`. Another good resource is the J2EE Tutorial, which has a whole section devoted to JAXR. This can be found at `http://java.sun.com/j2ee/1.4/docs/tutorial/index.html`.

Summary

You have seen in this chapter the basic building blocks of Web services, namely SOAP, WSDL, and UDDI. Web services are still in their infancy, and technologies surrounding Web services are evolving fairly quickly at this time.

The vision for Web services is that you will be able to dynamically locate the services using UDDI, dynamically find out what they offer using WSDL, and then invoke them using SOAP. That is not really possible right now, and there are also other issues such as security that are still being addressed. However, there is no question that Web services will become increasingly important to businesses and organizations.

This concludes our section covering XML technologies in conjunction with JSP. The remainder of the book will now look at JSP specifically within the context of J2EE enterprise applications.

13

Locating Resources Using JNDI

THIS CHAPTER INTRODUCES THE CONCEPTS SURROUNDING the Java Naming and Directory Interface (JNDI). It discusses the need for naming services, and the purposes for which Web applications use them. Directory services are also described, and by the time you have read this chapter you will be able to distinguish between the two types of service.

You will then be introduced to JNDI and its architecture before seeing the specifics of using JNDI in a Web application. In the next chapter (Chapter 14, "Databases and JSP") there are examples of using JNDI to locate JDBC datasources. In Chapter 15, "JSP and EJB Interaction," you will see Web applications that use JNDI to locate Enterprise JavaBeans (EJBs).

> **Note**
>
> If you want to run the demonstration applications for this chapter, you will need the `chapter13.ear` and `chapter13.jar` files from the book Web site (`www.samspublishing.com`). The source code for the standalone examples is in the file `chapter13.jar` in the `CommandLineJNDI` folder.

Naming and Directory Services

This part of the chapter discusses naming services, and then directory services. After you have read them you will know what each is, as well as the differences between them. You have probably already come across several such services, such as DNS and NDS.

Overview of Naming Services

A naming service is quite simply a software application that associates a *name* with the location of information or services. This means that the software you write can utilize objects without any knowledge of where those objects are located. The objects need not even reside on your local machine, but can live on any machine that is accessible on the network.

Another benefit to using a naming service is that for most people it is much easier to remember a logical name rather than a URL or some other object reference. For example, you can associate a logical name with a JDBC datasource. It is much easier to remember a name like `CUSTOMER_ADDRESSES` than a JDBC URL such as `jdbc:mysql://localhost:3306/ADDRESS`!

This really is not that much different from many examples in day-to-day life. For example, if you want to make a telephone call to somebody whose number you don't know, you normally look that number up in a telephone book. Conversely, you can register your own telephone number with the producers of the telephone book so that other people can look you up.

The only tricky part about looking up somebody's number in a telephone book (assuming that they are listed) is making sure that you are looking in the *correct* telephone book. You have a similar problem to overcome when writing computer software that uses a naming service, in that you can only lookup an object if you search the correct naming service. The term given to this is that you must *obtain a context.*

When you then use a context to retrieve information from a naming service, you are said to perform a *lookup*. The act of storing the name/resource pair in the naming service in the first place is known as *binding*. However, when people use the term *a binding*, they are referring to the association between an object and its name. After an object has been registered by name in the naming service, a client can retrieve a reference to the object by specifying the same name.

Figure 13.1 shows the basic architecture involved with using a naming service. The diagram depicts a client that retrieves an object by specifying a name that was previously used to bind an object into the naming service. You can see that the naming service associates a name with an object (a binding).

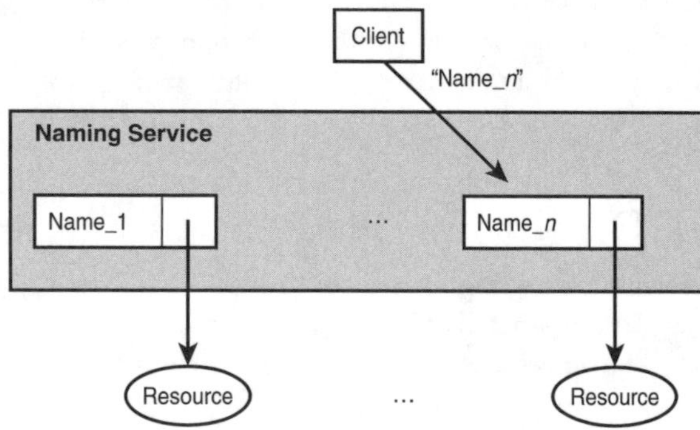

Figure 13.1 The architecture of a naming service.

You have just read that a context is a set of name/resource pairs. A `naming system` contains a set of related contexts that have the same naming convention. It is this naming system that provides the naming service to clients. The set of names in a naming system is known as a `namespace`.

Several common naming services are

- The CORBA Common Object Services (COS) Naming Service provides a hierarchical directory in which you can store object references, in a way that is comparable to directories in file systems. The COS Naming Service is widely used in Java-based distributed environments as a way of storing information about the location of remote objects. You can find further information on the COS Naming Service at `http://www.omg.org`.
- Domain Name Service (DNS) is the Internet naming service that identifies hosts on a network by performing a translation between host names and Internet addresses. All Internet clients use DNS, for example, Web browsers. More information on DNS can be found online at `http://www.dns.net/dnsrd/rfc/`.
- Network Information Service (NIS) from Sun Microsystems provides system-wide information about users, files, printers, machines, and networks. You will normally encounter NIS when working with systems that use the Solaris operating system. There are, however, other systems such as Linux and other Unix operating systems that support NIS.
- Novell Directory Services (NDS) provides information about network services such as printers and files. NDS is mainly found in environments where Novell provides the main networking software.
- File systems in general. File and directory objects are bound to names and are generally stored in a hierarchical form.
- The RMI registry is a simple server-side bootstrap naming facility that enables remote clients to obtain a reference to a remote object.

One example of a binding is a file that is bound to its filename. Another is an IP address that is bound to a hostname in DNS or WINS.

At the very least, a naming service must provide the capability to bind objects to a name and support the retrieval of those objects by name. However, the way in which the naming service can store the objects can differ. For example, the actual resource might be stored inside or outside the naming service. A naming service that does not store the resource directly is DNS. DNS simply maps a logical name such as `www.samspublishing.com` to an IP address (`165.193.123.117`), but does not store the remote host itself. This situation also arises when the object that is associated with the name is large, and you do not want to store it in the naming service. In this case you can store a reference to the object instead.

An example of a naming service that can store objects internally is the file system provided by Microsoft Windows NT. For efficiency, NTFS stores files that are smaller than about 1KB in the Master File Table (MFT). Anything larger than this is stored externally.

It is possible to overwrite an existing binding by specifying the same name, but a different resource. This is known as *rebinding*. In the previous telephone number example, this is analogous to moving and being allocated a new number by the telephone company. Other things that you can do with a naming service include renaming a bound object, and unbinding it completely so that it is no longer available to clients.JNDI also supports the notion of `federated namespaces`.This is when a resource is identified by a name that spans multiple naming systems. For example, consider the name `myhost.somedomain.com/documents/manual.txt`.The first part of this name (`myhost.somedomain.com`) is a host name that must be resolved via DNS, and the rest of the name (`documents/manual.txt`) is a file system name. For details of how this works, see the JNDI tutorial at `http://java.sun.com/products/jndi/tutorial/beyond/fed/index.html`.

Overview of Directory Services

A directory service is similar to a naming service in that it enables you to associate names with objects. However, a major distinction between the two is that a directory service enables you to store information *about* the object (these pieces of information are known as *attributes*), in addition to providing mechanisms for searching for objects based on that information. For example, if you need to print out a color photograph, you could use a directory service to find the locations of color printers in your office building. See Figure 13.2 for a diagram of a generic directory service.

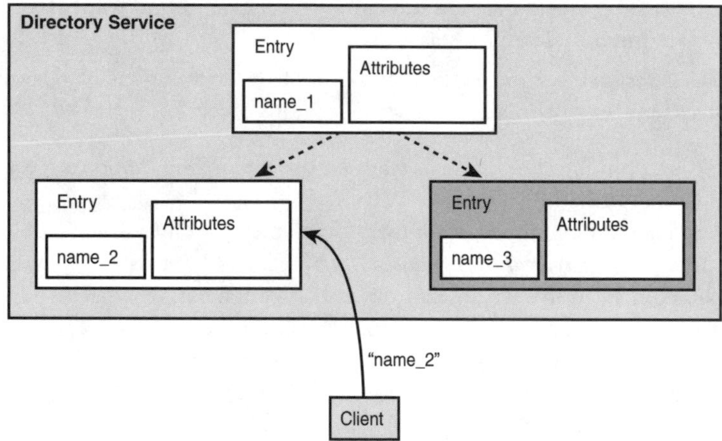

Figure 13.2 The architecture of a directory naming service.

Going back to the real-world telephone book example, using a directory service is similar to using the Yellow Pages phone directory. Instead of simply listing the name of a business along with a contact telephone number, the Yellow Pages directory often includes advertisements that contain additional information that add value to the entry. For example, a business might list location maps, professional qualifications, and even affiliated organizations. The fact that a directory service enables you to search for objects based on the values of these attributes means that you can, for example, search for all plumbers who operate a 24-hour emergency service in your neighborhood.

A popular protocol for accessing directory services is the Lightweight Directory and Access Protocol (LDAP). LDAP is a protocol that defines how client applications can manipulate data on a directory server, but says nothing about how the data should be stored. Generally speaking though, directory services usually allow you to store objects in a hierarchical fashion. LDAP servers, for example, arrange all objects in a tree known as the *Directory Information Tree* (DIT). The categorization of entries can simplify the search for particular objects. For example, a Yellow Pages directory might have categories for lawyers and carpet fitters. The categorized entries are a form of subcontext within the directory context of the Yellow Pages directory.

In essence, a directory service is really just a simple database that enables you to search for data, and to narrow that search by specifying search criteria. When you perform a search of a directory service, there are three pieces of information that you need to specify:

- A *search filter* with the values of the attributes. For example, you could search for all employees whose `gender` attribute has the value `male`.
- A *search base* that identifies the node in the tree that you want the search to begin from.
- A *scope* that limits the depth of the tree that is searched.

Relational Database Management Systems (RDBMS) is another technology that might spring to mind while reading this discussion of directory services. An RDBMS enables you to create, update, retrieve, and remove entries that are stored within it, as does a directory service. One difference is that the internal data tends to be stored differently. This is because an RDBMS generally uses a relational information model that involves the use of tables. An RDBMS usually also supports transactions that allow a group of operations to be rolled back if a particular step fails for some reason. Directory services are designed more to be very quick at reading and searching for data, and use a hierarchical data model as mentioned earlier.

Naming Conventions

Note that the syntax for specifying names varies between naming services. For example, the Microsoft Windows operating system allows you to use the \ character to separate the components in a path such as `c:\winnt\system32\drivers\etc\hosts`. When you use the DNS naming convention, you specify a name, such as `www.samspublishing.com`, where each component in the path is separated by the . character.

LDAP servers use names that are based on the X.500 standard. Such names (known as *distinguished* names) have the following general form:

```
cn=Peter Szolkowski, ou=Bikers, o=MANX_RACERS, c=uk
```

This form might also be familiar to you if you have used Microsoft's Active Directory service, which also uses names based on the X.500 standard. The difference is that it uses the / character rather than commas to delimit the name components:

```
cn=Peter Szolkowski/ou=Bikers/o=MANX_RACERS/c=uk
```

Both LDAP and Active Directory use hierarchical names. When the names are read from left to right, the most specific part of the name occurs first and the least specific part occurs last.

> **Tip**
>
> Some JNDI naming service implementations (also known as JNDI Service Providers) use case-sensitive names, and some do not. However, to maintain the portability of your applications you should avoid names that only differ by case. It is also a good idea to make sure that names are always spelled in a consistent fashion.

When you use JNDI, most of the time you simply specify a string that JNDI passes on to the underlying naming service with a minimum of interpretation. You should be aware that JNDI also provides support for creating and manipulating structured names.

Why Use a Naming Service?

One reason to use a naming service is that it enables you to decouple the provider of a service from its consumer. This is because the name that the supplier of the service uses to register the service is the only thing that the consumer needs to know.

Another reason to use a naming service is that it can provide an application with a single repository of information in which it can find all of its required resources.

When you use a naming service, you have a consistent way of publishing services that is independent of any particular platform and, therefore, is portable. In addition, you are free to migrate a service from one host to another. All that you would need to do is update the entry in the naming service to point to the new location of the service. The beauty of this is that the client needs to know nothing about the fact that the service has moved.

If you did not use JNDI to access a naming service, life would be a lot more difficult when you have to provide services such as those that are implemented using J2EE objects such as message queues, EJBs, and data sources. Every vendor would have to implement a proprietary mechanism that defined how client code gains access to J2EE objects. For example, one vendor might use TCP/IP broadcast network packets, whereas another could use textual configuration files.

What Is JNDI?

JNDI is a Java API that has been available since J2SE 1.2, and is also a part of J2EE 1.3.1. If you are using older versions of the SDKs, you should be aware that JNDI is also included in J2EE 1.2 and is available as a standard Java extension for JDK 1.2 and earlier releases.

The JNDI API defines an interface that Java programs can use to access a variety of naming and directory services in a uniform way. JNDI was designed specifically for the Java platform, and uses Java's object model. Therefore, you can use JNDI to store and retrieve Java objects of any type.

It is perhaps helpful to also state what JNDI is *not*: It is not a naming and directory service implementation, only an API. Thus, to use JNDI, you must also have available an implementation of a naming and directory service.

Without JNDI, it is necessary to learn the specific APIs that are implemented by the naming and directory service that you are using. This makes life a lot more difficult for application developers because they need to know all the APIs for the different naming and directory services used in their enterprise, thus leading to harder-to-maintain code. Figure 13.3 shows the architecture of a client and multiple services that each provides its own API.

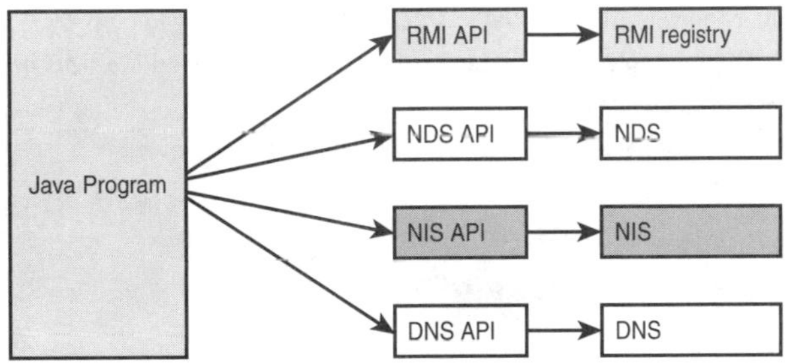

Figure 13.3 The architecture of a system that does not use JNDI.

In fact, JNDI consists of both an Application Programmer's Interface (API) and a Service Provider's Interface (SPI). Figure 13.4 shows the architecture of how your application, the JNDI API, SPI, and the naming service implementations fit together. Because the JNDI API is defined in a way that is independent of any individual directory service implementation, it is possible to use additional naming services as long as they implement the SPI for JNDI. A service provider is basically a driver that your application can use to communicate with a directory service.

The JNDI architecture's layered design was constructed to help insulate client code from naming service provider code.

The JNDI classes and interfaces are divided into five main packages: `javax.naming`, `javax.naming.directory`, `javax.naming.event`, `javax.naming.ldap`, and `javax.naming.spi`. These packages are covered in the next five subsections of this chapter.

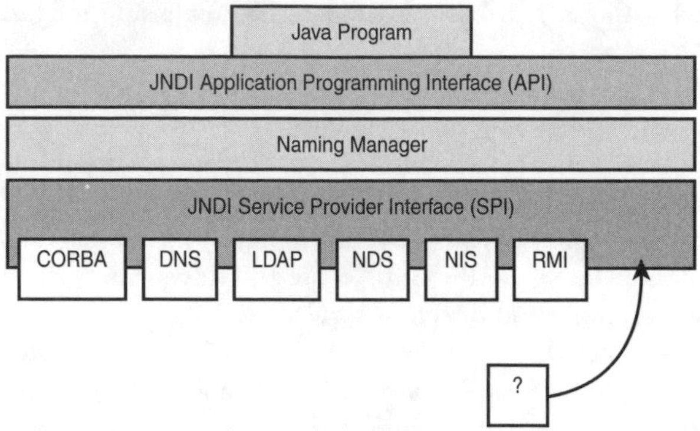

Figure 13.4 The JNDI architecture.

> **Note**
>
> You might be wondering why JNDI is so large. If all that you ever want to do is look up J2EE objects, Sun could have made JNDI as simple as a name to an object mapping service. Most of the time, this is exactly what you want. However, Sun designed JNDI to interoperate with many existing naming and directory services so that it would not be used as a proprietary product with J2EE servers.

The `javax.naming` Package

The `javax.naming` package contains the classes and interfaces that your application can use to access naming services. The `Context` and `Name` interfaces are part of this package, as well as the `Reference` and `Binding` classes.

The `javax.naming.Binding` Class

A binding is a set of information that contains an object's name, the name of the class used to instantiate the object as well as the actual object itself.

The `javax.naming.Context` Interface

Within a naming service, a set of bindings is referred to as a *context*. The `javax.naming.Context` interface is the principal interface in JNDI because it defines methods that enable you to

- Bind objects to, and unbind objects from, names.
- Rename objects.
- Retrieve objects with the `lookup` method.

You can also use the `list` and `listBindings` methods to retrieve an enumeration of name-to-object bindings. The `listBindings` method returns an enumeration of type javax.naming.NamingEnumeration, where each element in the enumeration is of type javax.naming.Binding, as described later.

The list method is more lightweight, in that it also returns an enumeration, but this time each element is of type javax.naming.NameClassPair. An instance of this class contains an object's name and the name of the class that was used to instantiate the object. The list method is useful when an application needs information about the object, but not the object itself. For example, you might be writing some kind of browser that displays a list of objects in the naming service.

The javax.naming.Name Interface

This interface symbolizes a generic name of an object that is bound into a naming service. There can be many different implementations of a name, such as URLs or host names, but the Name interface provides methods for accessing the name that are independent of the underlying naming service. A name typically consists of a string or a group of name components.

In general, applications that need to manipulate individual components in a name would use the Name interface to build a name or compare with another name, for instance. Simple applications generally use a java.lang.String to perform a lookup operation.

The javax.naming.Reference Class

Depending on the naming and directory service that you use, you might or might not be able to store a serialized Java object directly within the service. Even if your service is capable of storing the object, you might decide not to do so. For example, the object might be very large, or there could be applications written in languages other than Java that access the object in which case a serialized Java object would be of no use.

JNDI defines the javax.naming.Reference class that represents a reference to an object. A reference contains information that enables you to access an object. JNDI maintains the illusion that what the client looks up in the naming service (a reference) is in fact an object.

The javax.naming.directory Package

The javax.naming.directory package contains classes and interfaces that you can use to access directory services. For example, you can retrieve the attributes that are associated with an object. You can also perform searches for objects whose attributes match certain search criteria that you specify.

The two most important interfaces in the javax.naming.directory package are Attribute and DirContext.

The javax.naming.directory.Attribute Interface

This interface represents an attribute of a named object in the directory service. The actual forms that an attribute's name and value can take are dictated by the directory service. Some directory services allow you to specify a schema that sets the forms for the name and value.

An attribute has zero or many values associated with it. It is perfectly legal for a particular attribute value to be `null`. You can use the `get` and `getAll` methods to obtain the attribute values; the `set` method allows you to set a value at a specified index; and the `remove` method deletes an attribute at a specified index.

The `javax.naming.directory.DirContext` Interface

This interface represents a directory context, and defines methods that enable you to write software that examines (`getAttributes`) and updates (`modifyAttributes`) the attributes of a named object in the directory service.

There is also a set of overloaded `search` methods that enable you to search the directory service based on the name of a context (or object) and attribute values.

The `DirContext` interface extends the `javax.naming.Context` interface, and thus you can also use it as a naming context. This means that any object in the directory service can act as a naming context. For example, there could be an object in the directory service that represents an employee in your company. The employee object can have attributes associated with it as well as act as a naming context so that you could locate objects that belong to the employee such as their PCs, mobile telephones, and PDAs.

The `javax.naming.event` Package

The `javax.naming.event` package defines classes and interfaces that support event notification mechanisms in naming and directory services.

If you have used the Java Event Model (as used in GUIs and by JavaBeans) that has been available since JDK 1.1, the mechanism described here will sound familiar. The basic idea is that an *event source* generates events that are sent to registered *event listeners*. The event mechanism is of an asynchronous nature, and means that applications can register an interest in changes to the directory service without having to poll the directory service for changes.

The `NamingEvent` class and the `NamingListener` interface described later are part of the `javax.naming.event` package.

The `javax.naming.event.NamingEvent` Class

The `javax.naming.event.NamingEvent` class represents an event object that is generated when something changes in a naming or directory service. The object contains information about the event that occurred, such as the source of the event, as well as a *type* that indicates the form that the event took. Events are classified into those that affect the namespace, and those that do not. An example of the former category would be when an object is added, whereas an example of the latter category is when an object is changed.

Other information about the change, such as information before and after the change, is also stored in the `NamingEvent` object.

An event source creates an instance of the `NamingEvent` class, and passes it to the registered listeners who can then use the instance methods of the object to extract information about the event.

The `javax.naming.event.NamingListener` Interface

You can implement the `javax.naming.event.NamingListener` interface to listen for `NamingEvents`. However, there are several subinterfaces of `NamingListener` that correspond to the different categories of event that can occur.

For example, there is a `NamespaceChangeListener` for events that change the namespace, such as the addition, removal, or renaming of an object. There is also the `ObjectChangeListener` for notification of modifications to objects in the namespace, which covers when an object's binding is replaced with another and when an object's attributes are replaced or removed.

Typically, you implement a subinterface rather than directly implement `NamingListener`.

The `javax.naming.ldap` Package

You can find classes and interfaces in the `javax.naming.ldap` package that enable you to access features specific to LDAP v3 that are not already covered by the classes and interfaces in the `javax.naming.directory` package.

Most JNDI applications will not need to use the `javax.naming.ldap` package. The only time that you will is if you are writing software that needs access to LDAP functions such as Controls, Extended Operations, and Unsolicited Notifications. You can find more information about these in the LDAP RFC at `http://www.ietf.org/rfc/rfc2251.txt`.

The `javax.naming.spi` Package

The classes and interfaces defined in the `javax.naming.spi` package are primarily for use by developers of naming/directory service providers.

Using JNDI

As mentioned earlier in this chapter, JNDI is a standard component of JDK 1.3 and higher, and as such, is also shipped as part of J2EE 1.2 and above. If you want to run JNDI applications under JDK 1.2 then you can download a standard extension from Sun's Web site at `http://java.sun.com/products/jndi`.

While you are developing an application, you must ensure that the `CLASSPATH` contains the location of the JNDI libraries so that the Java compiler has access to them. This will be the case as long as the `JAVA_HOME` environment variable has been set to correctly point to the installation directory of a compatible JDK.

When you run a JNDI-aware application, whether it is a simple command-line client or a Web application, there must be a JNDI service running, and the classes for that service must be available to the program. Again, this means setting the `CLASSPATH` correctly, usually by placing one or more vendor-supplied JAR files on the `CLASSPATH`. For specifics, you should consult the documentation supplied by either the JNDI provider or J2EE server vendor.

When you start a J2EE server, the default behavior is that a naming service is automatically started, too. If this default behavior is not required, for example, if you want to use an existing JNDI server, you need to change the J2EE server configuration appropriately.

In this part of the chapter you will see a command-line example that uses Sun's J2EE Reference Implementation (RI) to bind and look up an object. Later in the chapter you can find an example that uses BEA's WebLogic J2EE server to publish an Enterprise JavaBean (EJB) that a JSP uses.

JNDI and Sun's J2EE Reference Implementation

It is straightforward to set up your machine so that you can use JNDI with Sun's J2EE RI. All you must do is ensure that

- The `J2EE_HOME` environment variable is set to the directory in which the J2EE SDK is installed. You can download the J2EE SDK from `http://java.sun.com/products/j2ee`.
- The `CLASSPATH` environment variable contains the `j2ee.jar` file that is in the `lib` directory under the J2EE home directory, for use by JNDI clients.

The way that I tend to set up my development machines is to set a system-wide environment variable for `J2EE_HOME`, and then have a command-line script that I can run from a command prompt to set up the `CLASSPATH` when I need it. This prevents unnecessary clutter, and means that I know exactly what is on the `CLASSPATH` at any given point! Setting the `CLASSPATH` as a system-wide variable can lead to all sorts of confusion when you have multiple JAR files from different vendors, especially when they ship different versions of the same JARs.

The batch file on my Windows XP machine looks like this:

```
set path=%J2EE_HOME%\bin;%PATH%
set classpath=%J2EE_HOME%\lib\j2ee.jar;%CLASSPATH%;.
```

Under Unix or Linux, you could use a line like this:

```
CLASSPATH=$J2EE_HOME/lib/j2ee.jar:$CLASSPATH
```

To start the J2EE server, all you need to do is issue the following command at a command prompt:

```
j2ee -verbose
```

The J2EE server runs until you either close its window, or issue the following command at another command prompt:

```
j2ee -stop
```

Obtaining an Initial Context

The first thing you must do when you use a JNDI naming service is to obtain a context in which you can add and find names. The context that represents the entire namespace is known as the *initial context*. You need to have an initial context, since all of the operations that you can perform on naming and directory services are performed relative to a context.

In Java code, you represent the initial context with an instance of the `javax.naming.InitialContext` class. As mentioned earlier in this chapter, this class implements the `javax.naming.Context` interface that defines methods for examining and updating bindings within a naming service.

The way that you retrieve a reference to an initial context is very simple and can be performed with this line of code:

```
Context initialContext = new InitialContext();
```

However, there are several things that can go wrong when this code is executed. In any of these cases, an instance of the `javax.naming.NamingException` class is thrown. The four most common errors and their reasons are as follows.

First of all, you get the following exception if the JNDI server is not running or if the JNDI properties for the server are not set correctly:

```
javax.naming.CommunicationException: Can't find SerialContextProvider
```

Second, if the `InitialContext` class has neither default properties for the JNDI service provider nor explicitly configured server properties, you will see the following exception:

```
javax.naming.NoInitialContextException:
➥Need to specify class name in environment or system property, or as an applet
➥parameter, or in an application resource file: java.naming.factory.initial
```

Third, if the classpath for the JNDI program does not contain the JNDI server classes, you see this exception:

```
javax.naming.NoInitialContextException: Cannot instantiate class: XXX
  [Root exception is java.lang.ClassNotFoundException: XXX]
```

Fourth, if the JNDI properties for the program do not match the JNDI Service Provider, you see this exception:

```
javax.naming.ServiceUnavailableException:
➥ Connection refused: no further information
[Root exception is java.net.ConnectionException:
➥ Connection refused: no further information]
```

The next section, "Configuring the JNDI Service Provider," details how to avoid all four of these exceptions.

Configuring the JNDI Service Provider

Although you are developing an application on your personal development machine, it is perfectly reasonable for you to use a JNDI service that is running on your local machine. For example, you could use the default service provider shipped with your J2EE server. However, when you deploy the application you need to use the naming service used by your organization. This means that you must configure your application to use a specific naming service rather than the one that is running on your personal development J2EE server.

Some implementations from vendors might require additional parameters, but the core information that you need to provide to define a JNDI service is

- The server's DNS host name
- The socket port number on the server
- The JNDI service class name

There are several ways to provide this information to an application, but all you need to do is choose one of these options:

- Add the properties to a JNDI Properties file in the Java runtime home directory.
- Provide an application resource file for the program.
- Set command-line parameters that are passed to the application. You can do this using the Java interpreter's `-D` option. The downside to using this approach is that the command lines tend to become unwieldy, although you could always use a script that contains the properties that you set.
- In the case of an applet, you can specify parameters that are passed to it by using the `<param>` tags that can be nested in `<applet>` tags.
- Hard-code the values into the application. This is not a preferred approach because it restricts the application to the naming service on the host that you specify.

The use of hard-coded properties is the least desirable because you have to edit, recompile, and redeploy an application if you change the service provider or if the naming server moves to a different host. However, if you want to try it out, perhaps in a test environment, you simply set the properties using a hashtable, with code like this:

```
Hashtable env = new Hashtable();
env.put(Context.INITIAL_CONTEXT_FACTORY,
    "com.sun.enterprise.naming.SerialInitContextFactory");
env.put(Context.PROVIDER_URL,
    "localhost:1099");
Context initialContext = new InitialContext(env);
```

Notice that the code does not use the property names such as `java.naming.factory.initial`, but instead uses `Context.INITIAL_CONTEXT_FACTORY` and `Context.PROVIDER_URL`. This is because the `javax.naming.Context` interface defines a set of constants for the names of the properties that you need to set. Thus, you do not have to remember strings such as `java.naming.factory.initial`. This also makes your code more flexible because it is independent of any changes that might be made to the property names in future versions of JNDI. You will see more on the different properties and their names shortly.

Although it is possible to hard code the JNDI properties, it is the first two approaches that are the most suitable for production environments. For both, all that you need to do is distribute a text file with the application.

When you create an `InitialContext`, JNDI searches for any application resource files called `jndi.properties` on the classpath. JNDI also looks in the Java runtime home directory (which is the `jre` subdirectory in the Java JDK home directory) for a file called `lib\jndi.properties`. All the properties that you define in these files are placed into the environment that belongs to the initial context.

For example, the `j2ee.jar` file in the `lib` directory of the J2EE RI contains these lines::

```
java.naming.factory.initial=com.sun.enterprise.naming.SerialInitContextFactory
java.naming.factory.url.pkgs=com.sun.enterprise.naming
```

These are a set of *properties*, which are simply name/value pairs. In practice, as long as the `j2ee.jar` file is on the classpath, you should be all set. The first of these two properties, `java.naming.factory.initial`, enables you to set the fully qualified class name of the Initial Context Factory for the JNDI Service Provider. That is, you use this property to specify which JNDI Service Provider you want to use.

If you want to use the default naming service supplied with the J2EE RI (and the `j2ee.jar` file is not on your classpath), you would use the following line in your `jndi.properties` file:

```
java.naming.factory.initial=com.sun.enterprise.naming.SerialInitContextFactory
```

Sun Microsystems provides several free reference implementations that are mentioned in the Table 14.1. You can specify the values from the table for the `Context.INITIAL_CONTEXT_FACTORY` environment property. Sun Microsystems maintains a list of service providers for JNDI on its Web site at `http://java.sun.com/products/jndi/serviceproviders.html`.

Table 13.1 **Values of** `Context.INITIAL_CONTEXT_FACTORY` **(**`java.naming.factory.initial`**)**

Value	Naming Service
`com.sun.jndi.cosnaming.CNCtxFactory`	CORBA Naming Service (COS)
`com.sun.jndi.fscontext.RefFSContextFactory`	File System
`com.sun.jndi.dnc.DnsContextFactory`	DNS
`com.sun.jndi.ldap.LdapCtxFactory`	LDAP
`com.sun.jndi.rmi.registry.RegistryContextFactory`	RMI Registry

You can find more information on these properties in the documentation for the `javax.naming.Context` and Sun's JNDI Tutorial (`http://java.sun.com/products/jndi/tutorial/index.html`).

How about if you need to access a JNDI service on a remote machine? If you needed to reference a JNDI service on a machine called `nameserver.samspublishing.com` on port 4242, you would set this property in the `jndi.properties` file:

```
java.naming.provider.url=nameserver.samspublishing.com:4242
```

The `java.naming.provider.url` property specifies the DNS host name and service port number of the machine that is running the JNDI service. This is the only property that the network administrator needs to modify, but JNDI uses port 1099 on the localhost by default, and most sites do not need to change this value.

Binding JNDI Objects

After you have obtained an initial context, you can use it to bind new objects into the naming service and look up objects that are bound to a name.

In J2EE applications, when working with EJBs, for example, the main use of JNDI is to look up objects that have already been bound. The J2EE server usually performs the actual binding of objects.

To bind an object to a name within a J2EE naming service, you use code similar to that shown in Listing 13.1. The code simply binds a `java.lang.String` object (`Some_String`) to the name `sams/book`.

Listing 13.1 **Binding an Object to a Name (`BindObject.java`)**

```
package com.conygre.jspdevhandbook.chapter13;

import javax.naming.Context;
import javax.naming.InitialContext;
import javax.naming.NamingException;

public class BindObject
{
  public static final String TITLE = "sams/book";

  public static void main (String[] args)
  {
     Object object = "Some_String";

     try
     {
       Context initialContext = new InitialContext();

       initialContext.bind(TITLE, object);
       System.out.println("Bound object to name: " + TITLE);
```

Listing 13.1 **Continued**

```
      }
      catch (NamingException e)
      {
        System.err.println("An error occurred while binding the object ("
                          + object + ") to the name '" + TITLE + "'");
        e.printStackTrace();
      }
   }
}
```

A couple of common errors can occur when you attempt to bind an object to a name. First, you must make sure that the object implements the `Serializable` interface so that the server can store a copy of the object.

Second, the `Context.bind()` method fails if an object is already bound to the name that you specify. In this case, a subclass of `NamingException` is thrown: `NameAlreadyBoundException`.

Note that the code in Listing 13.1 does not set values for any of the properties mentioned earlier in this chapter for specifying the service provider. This is because this example uses the J2EE RI, and the `j2ee.jar` file contains a `jndi.properties` file that is identical to the one mentioned earlier.

Name Persistence

You might have noticed that if you run the program from Listing 13.1 twice in succession, you get an error of the form:

```
An error occurred while binding the object (Some_String)
to the name 'sams/book'

javax.naming.NameAlreadyBoundException: Use rebind to override
```

However, if you restart the J2EE RI, then you do *not* get an error. This is due to the fact that the default naming service for the J2EE RI is a *transient service*. This means that any objects that are bound through configuration files in the SDK home directory are rebound when the server starts up, but any objects bound programmatically through the `Context.bind()` method are not.

Rebinding Objects

You have two options if you want to avoid the `javax.naming.NameAlreadyBoundException` mentioned earlier. The first is to unbind an existing object, and then bind the new one. The next section, "Unbinding Objects," describes this process.

The second option is to do what the `NameAlreadyBoundExcpetion` recommends: You can use the `Context.rebind()` method that unbinds the old object and binds the new one for you. In this case, the code from Listing 13.1 would use this method call rather than a call to `bind()`:

```
initialContext.rebind(TITLE, object);
```

Unbinding Objects

The `Context.unbind()` method removes an object from a namespace. Generally this method is used when an application is closing down and you want to remove the object from the naming service so that other applications do not attempt to make use of the bound object. This is necessary because bindings are not automatically removed when an application that uses a naming service is shut down.

Another time that you commonly use the `unbind()` method is when you want to bind an object into a naming service under a name, but you first want to see if there is already an object bound under the name you are going to use. The advantage of using a combination of `unbind()/bind()` over just a call to `rebind()` is that you can add logic to see whether you should perform the `bind()` operation. For example, you might only want to bind the new object if it is of the same type (or a subclass) of the existing bound type:

```
String JNDI_NAME = "sams/book";
try
{
    Object o = initialContext.lookup(JNDI_NAME);
    if (o instanceof String)
        initialContext.unbind(JNDI_NAME);
}
catch (NameNotFoundException e)
{
    // ignore: means that the lookup failed, so there is no existing object
}

initialContext.bind(JNDI_NAME, "some other string");
```

There are three things that could happen with this code fragment when the `lookup()` method is invoked:

- The lookup fails because there is no object bound to the name `sams/book`, in which case the `NameNotFoundException` is ignored and the new object is bound in under the name `sams/book`.
- The lookup returns an object that is not of type `java.lang.String`, so the `unbind()` operation is not performed. In this case, the `bind()` method would throw a `javax.naming.NameAlreadyBoundException`.
- The lookup returns an object that is of type `java.lang.String`, and so the existing object is unbound and the new string is bound in its place.

Renaming Objects

It is a simple matter to change the name under which an object is already bound into the naming service. You simply use the `Context.rename()` method, which takes the old and new names as parameters:

```
initialContext.rename("the_old_name", "the_new_name");
```

There are only two things to be aware of; the first is that the new name must be in the same context as the old name. The second is that the old name must be bound to an object, and the new name must not. A `javax.naming.NamingException` is thrown if these conditions are not met.

JNDI Name Lookup

By far the most common use of JNDI in Web applications is to look up objects that have been bound to names. To perform the lookup, you need two pieces of information:

- The JNDI name that the object is bound to
- The class of the bound object

After you know this information, all you need to do is use the `Context.lookup()` method to return a reference to the object, and then cast the reference to the correct type. The code in Listing 13.2 shows how to retrieve a bound object from a naming service. If you are running the code samples as you work through this chapter, make sure that you run the code in Listing 13.1 first. Then again, you might prefer not to so that you can see the code in the `catch` block executed.

Listing 13.2 **Code That Looks Up a Bound Object (**`LookupObject.java`**)**

```
package com.conygre.jspdevhandbook.chapter13;

import javax.naming.Context;
import javax.naming.InitialContext;
import javax.naming.NamingException;

public class LookupObject
{
  public static void main (String[] args)
  {
     try
     {
       Context initialContext = new InitialContext();
       Object object = initialContext.lookup(BindObject.TITLE);

       if ( object instanceof java.lang.String)
       {
         String s = (String) object;
         System.out.println("Looked up this object: " + s);
```

Listing 13.2 **Continued**

```
      }
      else
      {
        System.err.println("Error: The looked up object is not of type "
                          + "java.lang.String");
      }
    }
    catch (NamingException e)
    {
      System.err.println("Couldn't find an object bound to the name "
                        + BindObject.TITLE);
    }
  }
}
```

The `if` statement is simply a sanity check because the code from Listing 13.1 binds a `java.lang.String` object under the name `sams/book`. The code in the else statement is executed if the object returned from the `lookup()` method is not a `String`.

Contexts

Contexts provide a hierarchical structure to JNDI names, and composite names group together related items. You have no doubt seen this same idea when using a file system where you might have a `/usr` directory for all the home directories of the users of a machine, such as `/usr/mark` and `/usr/ruth`.

The name used in Listings 14.1 and 14.2 (`sams/book`) is an example of a *composite name*. If you are looking up just one or two objects, you might want to use the full name each time. However, if you are looking up objects that are in the same context of a composite name, it is simpler to change to a subcontext and look up a simple name within that context. For example, if you wanted to look up two objects, `sams/book` and `sams/book_cd`, you can change to the `sams` context and perform two lookups, one for `book` and one for `book_cd`.

The subcontext is a name entry in the same way as any other name, and you look it up in exactly the same way as before. The return type of the object passed back from the `lookup()` method is `javax.naming.Context`. The code in Listing 13.3 is similar to Listing 13.2, and retrieves a name from a subcontext. Note that this example assumes that you have already run the code in Listing 13.1.

Listing 13.3 **Looking Up Objects from a Subcontext (`LookupObjectSubContext.java`)**

```
package com.conygre.jspdevhandbook.chapter13;

import javax.naming.Context;
import javax.naming.InitialContext;
```

Listing 13.3 **Continued**

```
import javax.naming.NamingException;

public class LookupObjectSubContext
{
  public static void main (String[] args)
  {
     try
     {
       Context initialContext = new InitialContext();
       Context samsContext    = (Context) initialContext.lookup("sams");
       String  stringObject   = (String) samsContext.lookup("book");
       System.out.println("Looked up: " + stringObject);
     }
     catch (NamingException e)
     {
       System.err.println("Couldn't find an object bound to the name "
                          + BindObject.TITLE);
     }
  }
}
```

For a given context you can also programmatically:

- List its subcontexts by invoking its `listBindings()` method.
- Create new subcontexts through its `createSubcontext()` method.
- Destroy subcontexts with its `destroySubcontext()` method.

JNDI and JSP

To give you a taste of things to come in later chapters, here is a simple JSP that obtains a reference to an EJB through JNDI. This example does not run through how to deploy the example because this is detailed in Chapter 17. However, if you are familiar with deploying an Enterprise Archive (an `.ear` file) in an application server, or if you have read Chapter 17 already, to run the example you will need the `chapter13.ear` file from the book Web site.

What you will see here are screenshots of the example running in the WebLogic application server from BEA, but of course you can run it equally well under Sun's free RI server if you do not have an application server available.

The code in Listing 13.4 is for the EJB in this example. Don't worry too much about most of the code for now. For the purposes of this chapter, the important thing to realize is that the EJB implements a `getHello()` method that returns the nauseatingly familiar string `Hello World!`.

Listing 13.4 **The EJB That Provides a `getHello()` Method (`HelloWorldBean.java`)**

```
package com.conygre.jspdevhandbook.chapter13;

import java.rmi.RemoteException;
import javax.ejb.SessionBean;
import javax.ejb.SessionContext;

public class HelloWorldBean implements SessionBean
{
  public String getHello()
  {
     return "Hello World!";
  }

  public void ejbCreate() {}
  public void ejbRemove() {}
  public void ejbActivate() {}
  public void ejbPassivate() {}
  public void setSessionContext(SessionContext sc) {}
}
```

The JSP in Listing 13.5 uses a simple scriptlet to lookup a reference to the EJB, which in this example is bound to the name `MyHelloWorld`.

> **Note**
> The use of scriptlets in JSPs is now discouraged. However, this example uses one to keep things simple. In practice, you would use a JavaBean rather than a scriptlet.

Listing 13.5 **The JSP That Looks Up the `MyHelloWorld` EJB (`HelloWorld.jsp`)**

```
<%-- The EJB's remote interface is "HelloWorld"; the JNDI name is "MyHelloWorld"

     Access this page through http://localhost:8000/HelloJNDI/Hello
                      or      http://localhost:8000/HelloJNDI/HelloWorld.jsp
--%>

<%@ page import="javax.naming.Context" %>
<%@ page import="javax.naming.InitialContext" %>
<%@ page import="javax.rmi.PortableRemoteObject"%>
<%@ page import="com.conygre.jspdevhandbook.chapter13.HelloWorld" %>
<%@ page import="com.conygre.jspdevhandbook.chapter13.HelloWorldHome" %>

<html>
  <head><title>HelloWorld, JNDI</title></head>
```

Listing 13.5 **Continued**

```
  <body>
    The EJB says,
    <%
      Context initCtx = new InitialContext();
      Object o = initCtx.lookup("MyHelloWorld");

      HelloWorldHome home = (HelloWorldHome) PortableRemoteObject.narrow(o,
                                                    HelloWorldHome.class);
      HelloWorld     hello       = home.create();
      String         theGreeting = hello.getHello();
      out.println(theGreeting);
    %>
  </body>
</html>
```

You can see from Listing 13.5 that the code to look up the EJB is practically the same as the examples you saw in Listing 13.2 and Listing 13.3:

```
Context initialContext = new InitialContext();
Object o = initialContext.lookup("MyHelloWorld");
```

The only difference is that when you look up an EJB, you must first look up something called the *home interface*, and then use that to create an instance of the EJB. When you get hold of the home interface, you must use the `PortableRemoteObject.narrow()` method rather than a simple programmatic cast. The reasons behind this are explained in Chapter 17.

After you have the EJB, invoke its methods as you would for any other Java object:

```
String theGreeting = hello.getHello();
```

When executed using the URL `http://localhost:7001/HelloJNDI/HelloWorld.jsp`, the output should be along the lines of what is shown in Figure 13.5.

Figure 13.5 The output from the HelloWorld JSP (`HelloWorld.jsp`).

You might be wondering how the mapping between the EJB and its name of `MyHelloWorld` is set up. Within the `chapter13.ear` file there is a JAR file called `ejb-jar-ic.jar` that contains an XML document called `weblogic-ejb-jar.xml`. This latest XML file is specific to the WebLogic application server and maps the EJB (`HelloWorldBean`) to its JNDI name (`MyHelloWorld`):

```
<?xml version="1.0"?>
<!DOCTYPE weblogic-ejb-jar PUBLIC "-//BEA Systems, Inc.//
➥DTD WebLogic 7.0.0 EJB//EN"
"http://www.bea.com/servers/wls700/dtd/weblogic-ejb-jar.dtd">
<weblogic-ejb-jar>
    <weblogic-enterprise-bean>
        <ejb-name>HelloWorldBean</ejb-name>
        <jndi-name>MyHelloWorld</jndi-name>
    </weblogic-enterprise-bean>
</weblogic-ejb-jar>
```

When the application is deployed in WebLogic, you can use the WebLogic Server Console to view this information as in Figure 13.6.

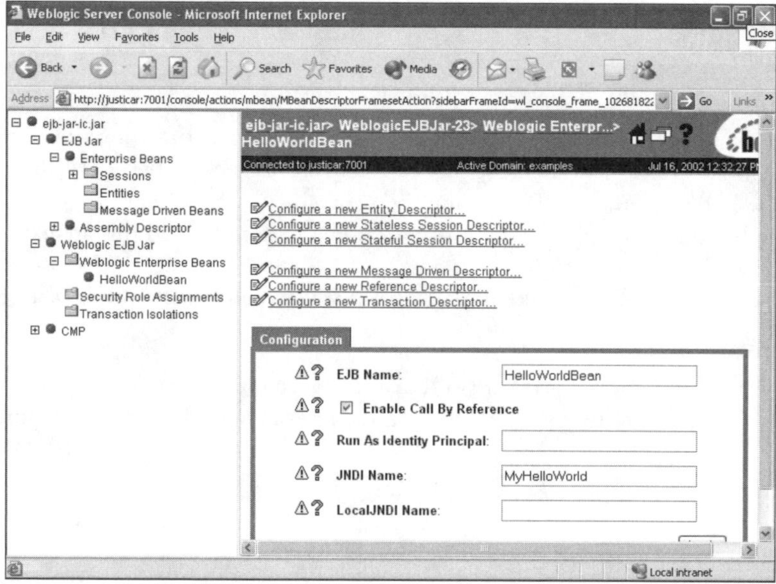

Figure 13.6 The WebLogic server console.

Summary

A *naming service* provides a means of storing simple information under a name, so that by specifying the registered name you can retrieve the information. A *directory service* is similar to a naming service except that it additionally allows attributes to be associated with the stored objects. Directory services use the attributes to categorize names, which means that powerful searching of the directory tree structure can be supported.

JNDI provides a uniform API into a naming or directory service. You can use any naming or directory service through JNDI as long as you have access to a Service Provider implementation for that service.

It is simple to use JNDI from any Java program, including Web applications.

The most common uses of JNDI in Web applications are to publish objects such as

- Databases (called *data sources*). You will see this in Chapter 14, "Databases and JSP."
- Enterprise JavaBeans (EJBs). See Chapter 15, "JSP and EJB interaction," for details.
- JMS message queues and topics.

14

Databases and JSP

DATA ACCESS IS OF CRITICAL IMPORTANCE for nearly all Web applications. In Web applications, databases are commonly used for all the following, and more:

- Storing product information for a commerce site
- Storing user information for a personalized site
- Storing site content to be used to build dynamic content
- Storing usage statistics

How does a Web application access these databases? Many issues need to be addressed as this subject is discussed—issues surrounding security, caching, performance, multi-threading, and transaction management, to name just a few.

Throughout this chapter there are various demonstration JSPs, which have been written to run against the MySQL database, available from `http://www.mysql.com`. This database has been selected for use with the book because it is freely available, readily accessible, and widely used in real-world applications. If you have never worked with MySQL before, Appendix I, "Installing MySQL and WebLogic Server," will be of particular interest to you because it explains how to install and set up the MySQL database. If you are already comfortable with JDBC, and want to use an alternative database, you should be able to modify the demo files without too much extra work.

> **Note**
> If you want to run the demonstration applications for this chapter, you will need `chapter14.war` and `chapter14shoppingCartDB.war` from the book Web site (`www.samspublishing.com`).

JDBC Fundamentals

Before launching into how JSP applications can be built to access databases, a brief tour of how Java database connectivity (also referred to as JDBC) would be helpful. If you are already familiar with JDBC, feel free to skip this section. This is not meant to be a complete discussion on JDBC. If you want to become more familiar with JDBC, the O'Reilly book *Database Programming with JDBC and Java, 2nd Edition* by George Reese, ISBN 1565926161, would be an ideal resource.

The JDBC API has been a part of Java since its inception with Java 1.0.2. It has gone through a few changes since then, however. The two key packages are

```
java.sql
javax.sql
```

Classes and interfaces from these packages will be discussed shortly. Both of these packages are part of J2SE1.4 and above. The basic architecture for JDBC is shown in Figure 14.1.

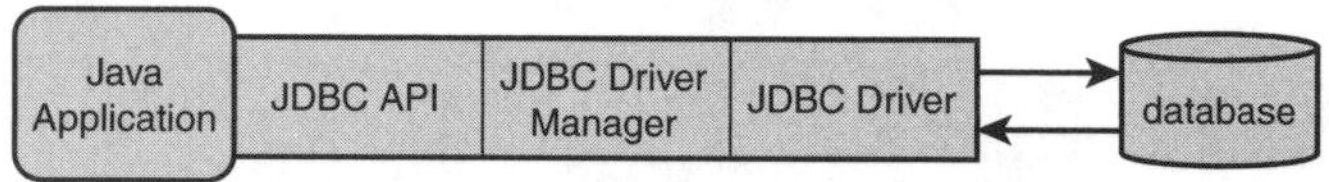

Figure 14.1 JDBC basic architecture.

As you can see from the diagram, there are a number of layers in a JDBC application.

The JDBC Driver

The JDBC driver is responsible for interacting with the database itself. There are several types of drivers, imaginatively named type 1 through to type 4.

Type 1 Drivers—the JDBC-ODBC Bridge

These drivers are those that map the JDBC API to the Open Database Connectivity (ODBC) API for data access. ODBC is a mechanism that Windows applications can use to access databases. Essentially, ODBC provides a uniform interface to various different database vendors for applications running on a Microsoft platform. The JDK ships with a JDBC-ODBC bridge driver, which basically means that your Java application interacts with ODBC, which in turn interacts with the database you are using. This requires native code on the client machine.

Type 2 Drivers—Native API, partly Java Driver

These hybrid drivers are partly written in Java, but still use native code often from the database vendor. In reality, they are often existing native drivers given a Java wrapper. These drivers negate the need to go through ODBC. These drivers are also less portable because of their reliance on native code, which will be required on the client. An example of this would be the Oracle OCI driver.

Type 3 Drivers—JDBC Net Pure Java Driver

These drivers provide the capability to make database calls across a network using a network protocol such as HTTP. Essentially, a Java client application would communicate with a middleware server over a network. The actual interaction with the database would be between the middleware server and the database server, but the client application would be pure Java.

Type 4 Drivers—Native Protocol Pure Java Driver

Most would regard this as the best solution where possible. These drivers are pure Java, so they are the most efficient and the most portable for the same reason. Pure Java drivers are available for nearly all the major database implementations, including Oracle and more recently, Microsoft SQL Server. They work by implementing the native database protocol in the Java programming language.

The Driver Manager

To use a JDBC driver, it needs to be registered, which is done by the `java.sql.DriverManager` class. There are two ways of loading a driver.

Loading a Driver Using Class.forName()

A JDBC driver registers itself when it is loaded. It does this because every JDBC driver must contain a static initializer as follows:

```
public class MyDriver implements java.sql.Driver {
  static {
    java.sql.DriverManager.registerDriver(new MyDriver());
  }
  // rest of driver implementation in here
}
```

> **Note**
>
> For those of you who have not come across static initializers before, they are sections of code that can be placed in a class that will be executed when a class is loaded by the virtual machine. A class can contain multiple static initializers.

This has caused confusion for many Java developers because to register a JDBC driver, it simply needs to be loaded by the class loader.

You will often, therefore, see early on in a JDBC application something like this:

```
try {
  Class.forName("sun.jdbc.odbc.JdbcOdbcDriver");
  }
catch (ClassNotFoundException e) {
  System.out.println("Could not locate class?");
}
```

This code is loading the driver into the VM, causing the static initializer within the driver class to run. The initializer contains the line of code to register the driver with the driver manager. The driver in the previous example is the JDBC-ODBC bridge driver that ships with the JSDK. If an application were using the MySQL database driver that is discussed in Appendix I, the driver class would be

```
com.mysql.jdbc.Driver
```

> **Caution**
> To load a driver, you will also sometimes see `Class.forName("driverClass").newInstance()` being used instead of `Class.forName("driverClass")`. This is because in a very small number of Java VM implementations, `Class.forName()` does not result in the invocation of the static initializers.

> **Note**
> Driver providers will always tell you what the name of the driver class is within their documentation. Any additional features of the drivers will also be discussed in documentation, so it is worth taking a look.

Loading a Driver Using the jdbc.drivers Property

An alternative way to specify the driver to be used, is to set the Java property called `jdbc.drivers`.

This property can be set using the following code:

```
Properties prop = System.getProperties();
prop.put("jdbc.drivers", "com.mysql.jdbc.Driver");
```

One of the benefits of using properties is that they can be set outside of the Java code, and read in from a properties file, allowing you to change the driver without changing the code. As you will see later in the chapter, there is now a more elegant mechanism for setting this information outside of the code with the use of a `DataSource`.

Obtaining a Connection

The role of the `DriverManager` is to obtain connections to databases and manage the loaded JDBC drivers. A connection is achieved using either of the following `DriverManager` methods:

```
public static java.sql.Connection getConnection
                                 (String url, String username, String password)
public static java.sql.Connection getConnection(String url)
```

An appropriate loaded driver for the database is selected to obtain the connection.

The `url` parameter is the URL of the database, and then the other two parameters, when used, are the username and password required to access the database.

JDBC URLs are of the following form:

```
jdbc:<subprotocol>:<subname>
```

The following code would obtain a connection to a database using the JDBC-ODBC bridge driver. The database in this example would be called `ADDRESS`:

```
Connection connection = DriverManager.getConnection("jdbc:odbc:ADDRESS");
```

Here is an example where the driver being used is a MySQL driver.

```
Connection connection =
           DriverManager.getConnection("jdbc:mysql://localhost:3306/ADDRESS");
```

> **Note**
> The driver documentation will contain details of how these JDBC URLs are formed for your particular database.

Connections and Statements

The `java.sql.Connection` interface represents a specific connection to a database. Within the context of this connection, statements can be executed against databases, and `ResultSets` can be returned.

Three broad kinds of statements are represented by three different interfaces:

```
java.sql.Statement
java.sql.CallableStatement
java.sql.PreparedStatement
```

The `Statement` interface represents an SQL query. This query will be expressed as a string. Two methods in the `Statement` interface are commonly used:

```
int executeUpdate (String sql)
java.sql.ResultSet executeQuery (String sql)
```

> **Note**
> SQL stands for Structured Query Language. It is used by relational databases as a language allowing the retrieval and modification of the database contents. It is an ISO and ANSI standard, but databases all have their own slight variations of SQL, and they will typically have a number of proprietary extensions.

To demonstrate how to use Connection and Statement objects, we will need a basic database. Following is a SQL Script that will create a database table called `AddressList` in a database called `ADDRESS`. This has been written for the MySQL database. It is fairly generic, so you should be able to run it, without too much modification, against an alternative database if you want:

```
CREATE DATABASE ADDRESS;
CREATE TABLE  ADDRESS.AddressList(
  id          INTEGER(2)     NOT NULL PRIMARY KEY AUTO_INCREMENT,
  name        varchar(254)  NOT NULL,
  street      varchar(254)  NULL,
  city        varchar(40)   NULL,
  zip         varchar(10)   NULL,
  country     varchar(40)   NULL,
  telephone   varchar(20)   NULL
);
INSERT INTO ADDRESS.AddressList
   (name, street, city, zip, country, telephone) VALUES
   ("Ella", "1 High Street", "London", "NW12", "UK", "020 1234");
INSERT INTO  ADDRESS.AddressList
   (name, street, city, zip, country) VALUES
   ("Sarah", "25 Redbrooke Street", "Canterbury", "CT3 9LJ", "UK");
INSERT INTO  ADDRESS.AddressList
   (name, street, city, zip, country, telephone) VALUES
   ("Alex", "10 Bella Way", "Boston", "MA123765", "USA", "617 23234");
INSERT INTO  ADDRESS.AddressList
   (name, street, city, zip, country, telephone) VALUES
   ("Abigail", "123 Dora Avenue", "Barcelona", "BARC", "Spain", "343 34321");
```

You will need to set up this table if you want to run the demos outlined in this chapter. Remember that Appendix I contains details of how to do this using MySQL if you have not worked with it before. You could also use a different database if you wish.

Assuming the database schema outlined previously has been created, Listing 14.1 is a complete example of how a connection could be obtained to the database, and then a statement executed using the `executeQuery()` method.

Listing 14.1 `jdbcConnection.jsp`

```
<%@page import="java.sql.*"%>
<html>
<head>
<title>Obtaining a Connection</title>
</head>
<body>
<h1>This Page Obtains a Connection to a Database</h1>
<%
    Connection conn = null;
    ResultSet result = null;
    Statement stmt = null;
    ResultSetMetaData rsmd = null;

    try {
      Class c = Class.forName("com.mysql.jdbc.Driver");
```

Listing 14.1 **Continued**

```
    }
    catch (Exception e) {
      System.out.println("Error occurred " + e);
     }
     try {
     conn = DriverManager.getConnection("jdbc:mysql://localhost:3306/ADDRESS");
     }
     catch (SQLException e) {
        System.out.println("Error occurred " + e);
     }
     try {
        stmt = conn.createStatement();
        result = stmt.executeQuery("SELECT * FROM AddressList");
        stmt.close();
        conn.close();
     }
     catch (SQLException e) {
         System.out.println("Error occurred " + e);
      }
      finally {
        try {
          if (stmt != null)
            stmt.close();
        }  catch (SQLException e) {}
        try {
          if (conn != null)
            conn.close();
        } catch (SQLException e) {}
      }
%>
</body>
</html>
```

Note that this JSP does not present any database content. That will come in the next section. One thing that you should note here is the closing of the database connection. It is very important when writing database applications that you remember to close connections and statements when you are finished with them. The `ResultSet` will be closed automatically when the statement is closed. Connections and Statements are closed using the `close()` method. Note too the presence of the `finally` block. This is important, because without it, if there were an exception, the connection and statement may not be closed, resulting in unused connections being maintained to the database.

Notice also the copious amount of error handling that is present in this example. An exception class, `java.sql.SQLException`, is used throughout JDBC applications. The example could have put all the code into one large try block, but then it is not always clear as to where exactly the exception occurred, so you will often see a significant number of `try/catch` blocks in JDBC code such as this, as shown.

In the previous example, the statement being used is of type `java.sql.Statement`. This is fine, but there is another kind of statement that can improve performance of your application. This is a `java.sql.PreparedStatement`. The `PreparedStatement` is a parameterized statement. These statements are precompiled, and the parameters are passed into the statement at runtime. Ideal for Web applications where the values of these parameters might be coming in from HTML forms for example.

The parameters are represented by a series of question marks in the SQL string that are replaced with parameter values when the code is executed.

Listing 14.2 is an example of how a prepared statement can be created and then used.

Listing 14.2 `preparedStatement.jsp`

```
<%@page import="java.sql.*"%>
<html>
<head>
<title>Obtaining a Connection</title>
</head>
<body>
<h1>This Page Obtains a Connection to a Database and executes a query</h1>
The query is based upon a PreparedStatement
<%
    Connection conn = null;
    ResultSet result = null;
    PreparedStatement stmt = null;
    ResultSetMetaData rsmd = null;

    try {
      Class c = Class.forName("com.mysql.jdbc.Driver");
    }
    catch (Exception e) {
      System.out.println("Error occurred " + e);
     }
     try {
     conn = DriverManager.getConnection("jdbc:mysql://localhost:3306/ADDRESS");
     }
     catch (SQLException e) {
        System.out.println("Error occurred " + e);
     }
     try {
      stmt = conn.prepareStatement("SELECT * FROM AddressList WHERE name= ?");
        stmt.setString(1, "Alex");
        result = stmt.executeQuery();
        stmt.close();
        conn.close();
```

Listing 14.2 **Continued**

```
      }
      catch (SQLException e) {
          System.out.println("Error occurred " + e);
       }
       finally {
         try {
           if (stmt != null)
             stmt.close();
         }  catch (SQLException e) {}
         try {
           if (conn != null)
             conn.close();
         } catch (SQLException e) {}
       }
%>
</body>
</html>
```

Pay special attention to the line containing the call to `prepareStatement()`. This is where the precompiled statement is set up. Note the use of the `?` in the SQL query. This denotes a parameter. The following line then sets a value for the parameter. In the example, the `setString` method has been used. There are other methods for the various other types. The parameters that this method takes are, first, a number indicating which SQL parameter you are setting, in this case, the first (and only) parameter is being set. The second parameter of the `setString` method is the value of the SQL parameter.

The last kind of statement is the `CallableStatement`. This would be used to invoke a stored procedure in the database.

The `ResultSet` and `ResultSetMetaData`

The `java.sql.ResultSet` interface represents the data that has been returned by the execution of a statement.

The `ResultSet` in this case is essentially a collection of rows. It also has a cursor, which can be scrolled throughout the records.

Table 14.1 shows the main methods for manipulating the `ResultSet` cursor.

Table 14.1 **The Cursor Manipulation Methods of the `java.sql.ResultSet` Interface**

Method Name	Description
`boolean next()`	Moves the cursor to the next row. Returns `false` if there are no more rows.
`boolean previous()`	Moves the cursor to the previous row. Returns `false` if there are no more rows.

Table 14.1 **Continued**

Method Name	Description
`boolean first()`	Moves the cursor to the first row. If there is not a valid first row, it returns `false`.
`boolean last()`	Moves the cursor to the last row. If there is not a valid last row, it returns `false`.
`void afterLast()`	Moves the cursor to just after the last row. If there is not a valid last row, it returns `false`.
`void beforeFirst()` beforeFirst	Moves the cursor to just before the first row. If there is not a valid first row, it returns `false`.
`boolean absolute (int row)`	Moves the cursor to a specific row. The `int` represents the number of the row to move to. If the number is negative, it regards it as a number from the end. The method returns `false` if no row exists at the location specified.
`boolean relative (int rows)`	Moves the cursor relative to its current position. If positive it will move forward the specified number of positions; if negative, it will move back the number of specified positions. The method returns `false` if no row exists at the specified location.

The `ResultSet` also has a number of methods for accessing the data within the individual records. The methods are all of the following form:

```
xxx getXXX (String columnName)
xxx getXXX (int columnNumber)
```

So for example, if column one was called `id` and contained an `int`, you could use either of the following method calls:

```
int myInt = resultSet.getInt("id"); or
int myInt = resultSet.getInt(1);
```

When obtaining data for display in a JSP, however, you can normally extract the data as a `String` because it is going to be displayed as a String anyway in the JSP:

```
String myId = resultSet.getString("id"); or
String myId = resultSet.getString(1);
```

To obtain information such as the column labels, there is an additional object that is returned with the `ResultSet`, and that is the `java.sql.ResultSetMetaData` interface. This provides meta information about the result set such as column names, the number of columns, and so forth.

To access the `ResultSetMetaData`, use the `getMetaData()` method of the `ResultSet`. The `ResultSetMetaData` then has a number of methods, such as

```
int getColumnCount()
String getColumnLabel(int columnNumber)
```

Listing 14.3 shows a JSP that will access the data in the database and present that information on the page by scrolling through the `ResultSet` and also accessing the meta data to provide column headings.

Listing 14.3 `resultSetDisplay.jsp`

```
<%@page import="java.sql.*"%>
<html>
<head>
<title>Presenting database content</title>
</head>
<body>
<h1>Address List</h1>
<%
    Connection conn = null;
    ResultSet result = null;
    Statement stmt = null;
    ResultSetMetaData rsmd = null;

    try {
      Class c = Class.forName("com.mysql.jdbc.Driver");
    }
    catch (Exception e) {
      System.out.println("Error occurred " + e);
     }
     try {
       conn =
         DriverManager.getConnection("jdbc:mysql://localhost:3306/ADDRESS");
     }
     catch (SQLException e) {
        System.out.println("Error occurred " + e);
     }
     try {
        stmt = conn.createStatement();
        result = stmt.executeQuery("SELECT * FROM AddressList");
     }
     catch (SQLException e) {
         System.out.println("Error occurred " + e);
      }

     int columns=0;
     try {
       rsmd = result.getMetaData();
       columns = rsmd.getColumnCount();
     }
```

Listing 14.3 **Continued**

```
     catch (SQLException e) {
        System.out.println("Error occurred " + e);
     }
%>
<table width="90%" border="1">
  <tr>
  <% // write out the header cells containing the column labels
     try {
        for (int i=1; i<=columns; i++) {
             out.write("<th>" + rsmd.getColumnLabel(i) + "</th>");
        }
  %>
  </tr>


  <% // now write out one row for each entry in the database table
        while (result.next()) {
           out.write("<tr>");
           for (int i=1; i<=columns; i++) {
             out.write("<td>" + result.getString(i) + "</td>");
           }
           out.write("</tr>");
        }

        // close the connection and the statement
        stmt.close();
        conn.close();
     } // end of the try block
     catch (SQLException e) {
        System.out.println("Error " + e);
     }
     // ensure everything is closed
   finally {
    try {
      if (stmt != null)
       stmt.close();
      }  catch (SQLException e) {}
      try {
       if (conn != null)
        conn.close();
       } catch (SQLException e) {}
   }
   %>
</table>
</body>
</html>
```

This page will provide the output shown in Figure 14.2 when viewed in a Web browser.

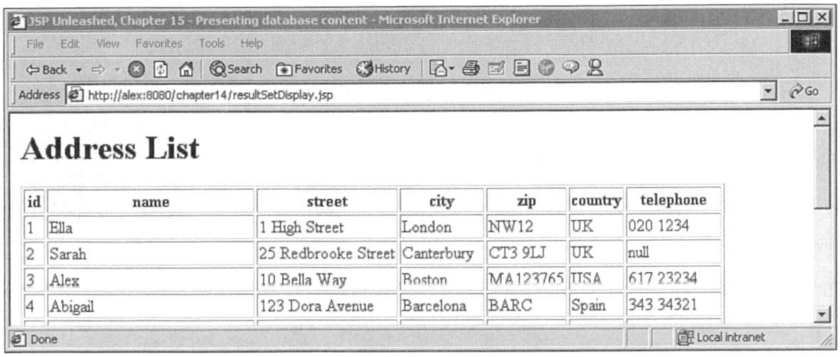
JSP Unleashed, Chapter 15 - Presenting database content - Microsoft Internet Explorer
File Edit View Favorites Tools Help
Back Search Favorites History
Address http://alex:8080/chapter14/resultSetDisplay.jsp
Go
Address List
id name street city zip country telephone
1 Ella 1 High Street London NW12 UK 020 1234
2 Sarah 25 Redbrooke Street Canterbury CT3 9LJ UK null
3 Alex 10 Bella Way Boston MA123765 USA 617 23234
4 Abigail 123 Dora Avenue Barcelona BARC Spain 343 34321
Done
Local intranet

Figure 14.2 Output from Listing 14.3, `resultSetDisplay.jsp`.

Modifying the Database

So far, the discussion has focused on how to read and display data. You can also modify database content from a JSP using JDBC. Instead of using `executeQuery()` on the `Statement`, you can use the `executeUpdate()` method to execute an SQL script that will modify the database content.

To add a new entry for example, the data from an HTML form could be processed. The following example demonstrates the use of the `executeUpdate()` method. First, there is the HTML form itself. This is shown in Listing 14.4. The JSP that is being used to update the database is shown in Listing 14.5. Note in Listing 14.5 the use of the `prepared` statement.

Listing 14.4 `newAddressForm.html`

```
<html>
<head>
<title>Add a new entry</title>
</head>
<body>
<h1>Please enter the new address information</h1>
<form method="POST" action="addNewAddress.jsp">
  Name: <input type="text" name="name" size="20"><br>
  Street: <input type="text" name="street" size="20"><br>
  City: <input type="text" name="city" size="20"><br>
  Zip Code: <input type="text" name="zip" size="20"><br>
  Country: <input type="text" name="country" size="20"><br>
  Telephone: <input type="text" name="tel" size="20">
  <p><input type="submit" value="Submit"></p>
```

Listing 14.4 **Continued**

```
</form>
</body>
</html>
```

Listing 14.5 `addNewAddress.jsp`

```
<%@page import="java.sql.*"%>
<html>
<head>
<title>Add a new Address</title>
</head>
<body>
<h1>New Address Creation using executeUpdate()</h1>
<%
    Connection conn = null;
    PreparedStatement stmt = null;
    try {
      Class c = Class.forName("com.mysql.jdbc.Driver");
    }
    catch (Exception e) {
      System.out.println("Error occurred " + e);
     }
     try {
       conn =
         DriverManager.getConnection("jdbc:mysql://localhost:3306/ADDRESS");
     }
     catch (SQLException e) {
        System.out.println("Error occurred " + e);
     }
     try {
        stmt = conn.prepareStatement("INSERT INTO AddressList ➥
                    (name, street, city, zip, country, telephone) ➥
                     VALUES (?, ?, ?,?, ?, ?)");
        stmt.setString(1, request.getParameter("name"));
        stmt.setString(2, request.getParameter("street"));
        stmt.setString(3, request.getParameter("city"));
        stmt.setString(4, request.getParameter("zip"));
        stmt.setString(5, request.getParameter("country"));
        stmt.setString(6, request.getParameter("tel"));
        stmt.executeUpdate();
        stmt.close();
        conn.close();
     }
     catch (SQLException e) {
```

Listing 14.5 **Continued**

```
        System.out.println("Error occurred " + e);
    }
    finally {
     try {
       if (stmt != null)
        stmt.close();
       } catch (SQLException e) {}
       try {
        if (conn != null)
        conn.close();
        } catch (SQLException e) {}
    }

%>
The new address has been created.
</body>
</html>
```

If you are trying out these examples, you can confirm that it has added a new row by visiting `resultSetDisplay.jsp` from Listing 14.1.

The `javax.sql.DataSource`

One challenge of the JSP pages you have seen so far is that the connection information for the database, such as the driver, the URL, and the username and password for the connection are all nested in the Java code. The `javax.sql.DataSource` interface enables this connection information to be separated out.

As discussed, the JDBC API is split into two packages, `java.sql` and `javax.sql`. The `javax.sql` package is the more recent JDBC 2.0 package that is bundled with J2SDK1.4 and higher. The `DataSource` interface within the optional extension package is the equivalent of the `DriverManager` of the "traditional" `java.sql` package.

When using a `DataSource`, drivers are not loaded explicitly within the client application; instead, all the connection information is contained within a `DataSource` object. Then, it is typically located using technologies such as the Java Naming and Directory Interface (JNDI) discussed in Chapter 13, "Locating Resources using JNDI."

One benefit of using `DataSources` is that the client application is decoupled from the JDBC connection information. The setting up of data sources should not really be the role of the developer, and using `DataSources` frees you from needing to concern yourself with the configuration of these data sources. Servers provide administrative interfaces to enable `DataSources` to be configured without entering any code at all.

Another benefit, and perhaps a more important benefit, is that of performance. Performance is greatly improved when using `DataSources` in conjunction with a concept called connection pooling, since the expensive process of creating connections is carried out in a more efficient manner. The example you are about to see uses connection pooling, and the concepts of connection pooling are discussed later in the chapter.

If you are using Tomcat, a `DataSource` can be set up within the configuration files `web.xml` or `server.xml`.

Within `server.xml` you can add the following elements shown in Listing 14.6:

Listing 14.6 **Datasource Configuration Extract from `server.xml`**

```
<Context path="/chapter14" docBase="chapter14" debug="0" reloadable="true">
  <ResourceParams name="jdbc/address">
    <parameter>
      <name>password</name>
      <value>admin</value>
    </parameter>
    <parameter>
      <name>url</name>
      <value>jdbc:mysql://localhost:3306/ADDRESS</value>
    </parameter>
    <parameter>
      <name>driverClassName</name>
      <value>com.mysql.jdbc.Driver</value>
    </parameter>
    <parameter>
      <name>username</name>
      <value>admin</value>
    </parameter>
  </ResourceParams>
</Context>
```

> **Caution**
>
> If you are trying out the various pages as we go through from the Web site download, be aware that this entry in `server.xml` is not part of the Web application download. You will need to modify `server.xml` manually. A good place to add this would be just before the closing `</host>` element close to the end of the file.

This entry will set up a data source for you with the JNDI name of `jdbc/address`. This will be of type `javax.sql.DataSource`, and will use the driver and JDBC URL as specified by the `<parameter>` elements in Listing 14.6.

> **Caution**
>
> Ensure that your MySQL user account has a password. If it does not, then Tomcat will not connect to it. The example has used an account with the username and password set to admin and admin.

With MySQL, you will also need to grant the appropriate privileges for Tomcat to be able to connect to it using the username and password. You can do this from a MySQL prompt by entering the following command:

```
mysql> grant all privileges on *.* to admin@localhost ➥
identified by 'admin' with grant option;
```

You can get a MySQL prompt by simply having a command console in the MySQL\bin folder, and entering the command `mysql`.

Depending upon which version of Tomcat you are using, you may also need to download two jar files that provide the facility to use `DataSources` in Tomcat. These jars are `commons-dbcp.jar`, and `commons-pool.jar`. You can obtain these respectively from

```
http://jakarta.apache.org/builds/jakarta-commons/release/commons-dbcp/v1.0/
http://jakarta.apache.org/builds/jakarta-commons/release/commons-pool/v1.0.1/
```

The jars can be extracted from the downloadable archives and placed in the `<TOMCAT_HOME>\common\lib` folder. You will also need to place the MySQL JDBC driver jar (`mysql-connector-java-3.x.x-stable-bin`) into `<TOMCAT_HOME>\common\lib`.

Once `server.xml` has been modified, the Web application can now configured to interact with the Database. A simple entry must also be added to `web.xml`, and this is shown here:

```
<resource-ref>
  <res-ref-name>jdbc/address</res-ref-name>
  <res-type>javax.sql.DataSource</res-type>
  <res-auth>Container</res-auth>
</resource-ref>
```

The important thing to note here is that the `<resource-ref-name>` element value must match the `name` attribute of the `<ResourceParams>` element in `server.xml`, shown in Listing 14.6.

We are now ready to see how a JSP will interact with the DataSource. This is shown in Listing 14.7:

Listing 14.7 `usingDataSource.jsp`

```
<%@page import="java.sql.*, javax.sql.*, javax.naming.*"%>
<html>
<head>
<title>Using a DataSource</title>
</head>
<body>
<h1>Using a DataSource</h1>
<%
    DataSource ds = null;
    Connection conn = null;
    ResultSet result = null;
```

Listing 14.7 **Continued**

```
    Statement stmt = null;
    ResultSetMetaData rsmd = null;
    try{
      Context context = new InitialContext();
      Context envCtx = (Context) context.lookup("java:comp/env");
      ds =  (DataSource)envCtx.lookup("jdbc/address");
      if (ds != null) {
        conn = ds.getConnection();
        stmt = conn.createStatement();
        result = stmt.executeQuery("SELECT * FROM AddressList");
       }
     }
     catch (SQLException e) {
        System.out.println("Error occurred " + e);
      }
      int columns=0;
      try {
        rsmd = result.getMetaData();
        columns = rsmd.getColumnCount();
      }
      catch (SQLException e) {
         System.out.println("Error occurred " + e);
      }
%>
<table width="90%" border="1">
  <tr>
  <% // write out the header cells containing the column labels
      try {
         for (int i=1; i<=columns; i++) {
              out.write("<th>" + rsmd.getColumnLabel(i) + "</th>");
         }
  %>
  </tr>
  <% // now write out one row for each entry in the database table
         while (result.next()) {
            out.write("<tr>");
            for (int i=1; i<=columns; i++) {
              out.write("<td>" + result.getString(i) + "</td>");
            }
            out.write("</tr>");
         }

         // close the connection, resultset, and the statement
         result.close();
         stmt.close();
         conn.close();
```

Listing 14.7 **Continued**

```
      } // end of the try block
      catch (SQLException e) {
         System.out.println("Error " + e);
      }
      // ensure everything is closed
    finally {
     try {
       if (stmt != null)
        stmt.close();
       } catch (SQLException e) {}
       try {
        if (conn != null)
         conn.close();
        } catch (SQLException e) {}
    }

    %>
</table>
</body>
</html>
```

The most important bit in Listing 14.7 is how the `DataSource` reference is obtained and how the connection is obtained.

```
Context context = new InitialContext();
Context envCtx = (Context) context.lookup("java:comp/env");
ds =  (DataSource)envCtx.lookup("jdbc/address");
if (ds != null) {
  conn = ds.getConnection();
```

If you have read the previous chapter, this should look familiar to you. It is an example of JNDI.

This section has introduced you to how JDBC code works, and JSPs were used to demonstrate this. However, it is unlikely that in reality you would want to write JSPs that were like the listings you have seen so far as the pages contain a mixture of JDBC code and presentation logic. One new development in JSP 2.0 is the standard tag library. Some of these tags are specific to database access, and these will be explored next.

Accessing Databases Using the JavaServer Pages Standard Tag Library

The first issue that will be addressed is how the database-specific tags of the standard tag library can be used to remove the Java code from the JSPs themselves.

The standard tag library has a number of tags (or actions) specifically written for database access within it. Using these tags can greatly simplify the JSP pages and also reduce the amount of code you need to write within your own classes because the tags already have much of the functionality to access databases and extract the contents for you.

In essence, the SQL tags within the standard tag library enable you to

- Query a database
- Access the results of the query
- Perform updates to a database
- Group a number of database interactions into a single transaction

Listing 14.8 shows the equivalent of Listing 14.4, but using the standard tag library. The difference is substantial!

Listing 14.8 `resultSetDisplayWithTagLibrary.jsp`

```
<%@ taglib prefix="sql" uri="http://java.sun.com/jstl-el/sql" %>
<%@ taglib prefix="c" uri="http://java.sun.com/jstl-el/core" %>
<html>
<head>
<title>Presenting database content using tags</title
<sql:setDataSource
  dataSource="jdbc/address"
  var="conn"
/> </head>
<body>
<h1>Address List</h1>
<sql:query dataSource="${conn}" var="addresses">
    SELECT * FROM AddressList
</sql:query>
<table width="90%" border="1">
<tr>
<!-- add the table column headings -->
<c:forEach var="columnName" items="${addresses.columnNames}">
  <th> <c:out value="${columnName}"/> </th>
</c:forEach>
</tr>
<!-- add the table rows from the result set -->
<c:forEach var="row" items="${addresses.rowsByIndex}">
  <tr>
    <c:forEach var="column" items="${row}">
      <td><c:out value="${column}"/></td>
    </c:forEach>
  </tr>
</c:forEach>
</table>
</body>
</html>
```

In fact, five SQL-specific actions are available to the JSP developer:

- `sql:setDataSource`
- `sql:query`
- `sql:update`
- `sql:param`
- `sql:transaction`

The `sql:setDataSource` and `sql:query` actions have been used in Listing 14.8. To use these actions from a page, they must be made available to the page using the by now familiar `taglib` directive. Although these actions are a part of the JSTL, they have their own specific URI:

```
<%@ taglib prefix="sql" uri="http://java.sun.com/jstl-el/sql" %>
```

The `sql:setDataSource` Action

Essentially, the `sql:setDataSource` action encapsulates the connection information to the database. Table 14.2 shows the possible attributes of the `sql:setDataSource` action. Under the covers, this action will create an object of type `javax.sql.DataSource`.

Table 14.2 **The Attributes of the `sql:setDataSource` Action**

Attribute Name	Dynamic	Type	Description
`dataSource`	`true`	`String` or `javax.sql.DataSource`	`DataSource`, either a JNDI lookup string, or a JDBC `String`. If not a `String`, it must be a reference to a `DataSource` object.
`driver`	`true`	`String`	This is the JDBC driver to be used to access the database, as discussed previously.
`url`	`true`	`String`	The JDBC URL of the database.
`user`	`true`	`String`	The username being used to access the database.
`password`	`true`	`String`	The password for accessing the database.
`var`	`false`	`String`	This is the name of the exported variable that can then be used by other actions. The exported variable will be of type `javax.sql.DataSource`.
`scope`	`false`	`String`	This is the scope of any exported variable. The options are page, request, session, or application. This attribute can only be used if the `var` attribute is present.

If you look again at Listing 14.8, you can see the use of this action. The code is shown here:

```
<sql:setDataSource
  dataSource="jdbc/address"
  var="conn"
/>
```

The `dataSouce` attribute can also contain the JDBC connection information as defined here:

```
url[,[driver][,[user][,password]]]
```

The following JSP extract shows the use of the JDBC syntax. It is synonymous with the earlier extract:

```
<sql:setDataSource
  var="conn"
  dataSource=" jdbc:mysql://localhost:3306/ADDRESS, com.mysql.jdbc.Driver, admin,
admin"
/>
```

The "cleanest" way to use this action is to use a JNDI lookup name as we have done. When used in this way, the JDBC connection information is decoupled completely from the page.

Note that in all the examples, the `scope` attribute is missing. This means that the scope will default to `page`. The exported variable is `conn`, so this can now be accessed from the rest of the page. Note also that there is no body content. This action does not have any processed body content.

The `sql:query` Action

The `sql:setDataSource` action can be used to provide a connection to a database, but how are queries made on that database? This is where the `sql:query` action can be used.

Here is how the action was used in Listing 14.8:

```
<sql:query dataSource="${conn}" var="addresses">
    SELECT * FROM AddressList
</sql:query>
```

Essentially, it is a very straightforward way of executing query type SQL scripts against a database. Table 14.3 shows the attributes of the `sql:query` action.

Table 14.3 **The Attributes of the `sql:query` Action**

Attribute Name	Dynamic	Type	Description
`sql`	`true`	`String`	This contains an SQL query statement of some description. The query can also be specified in the body of the action, as shown in the example.
`dataSource`	`true`	`String` or `javax.sql.DataSource`	This could be a reference to the `DataSource` itself. A `String` would be a JNDI resource or JDBC name as used in the `setDataSource` action.
`maxRows`	`true`	`Int`	Specifies the maximum number of rows to be returned and put into the result set. This can be useful to prevent overly large query results being returned.
`startRow`	`true`	`Int`	This specifies the first row of the result to be included in the returned result set. This can be especially useful when used in conjunction with `maxRows` for doing next 10/previous 10 type pages.
`var`	`false`	`String`	This is the name of the returned result variable. It is of type `javax.servlet.jsp.jstl.sql.Result`.
`scope`	`false`	`String`	This is the scope of any exported variable. The options are page, request, session, or application. This attribute can only used if the `var` attribute is present.

If you note the type of object that the `var` attribute refers to, it is not a straightforward `java.sql.ResultSet`, but a `javax.servlet.jsp.jstl.sql.Result`. This is an interface type that has been built into the tag library specification. The source can be seen in Listing 14.9.

Listing 14.9 `javax.servlet.jsp.jstl.sql.Result`

```
package javax.servlet.jsp.jstl.sql;
import java.util.SortedMap;
public interface Result {
  SortedMap[] getRows();
  Object[][] getRowsByIndex();
  String[] getColumnNames();
  int getRowCount();
  boolean isLimitedByMaxRows();
}
```

As you can see from Listing 14.9, the `Result` class provides methods to access not only the data, but also the column names that come from `ResultSetMetaData` objects when using conventional JDBC. Although it is not really necessary to show it here, if you look at the listing of the implementation of this interface from the Jakarta project, you will see that it is using under the covers, a `java.sql.ResultSet`, and a `java.sql.ResultSetMetaData`.

If you look at the `Result` interface in Listing 14.9, you will see that the output is an array of arrays. The return type is `Object[][]`. In Listing 14.10, this is being used by two nested `forEach` actions. The first array contains each row, and the second array contains the columns. The outer `forEach` loop is accessing each row. The inner loop is then accessing the individual columns within the rows.

Listing 14.10 `resultSetDisplayQueryTag.jsp`

```
<%@ taglib prefix="sql" uri="http://java.sun.com/jstl-el/sql" %>
<%@ taglib prefix="c" uri="http://java.sun.com/jstl-el/core" %>
<html>
<head>
<title>Using a Preconfigured DataSource</title>
</head>
<body>
<h1>Address List</h1>
<sql:query dataSource="jdbc/address" var="addresses">
    SELECT * FROM AddressList
</sql:query>
<table width="90%" border="1">
<tr>
<!-- add the table column headings -->
<c:forEach var="columnName" items="${addresses.columnNames}">
  <th> <c:out value="${columnName}"/> </th>
</c:forEach>
</tr>
<!-- add the table rows from the result set -->
<c:forEach var="row" items="${addresses.rowsByIndex}">
  <tr>
    <c:forEach var="column" items="${row}">
      <td><c:out value="${column}"/></td>
    </c:forEach>
  </tr>
</c:forEach>
</table>
</body>
</html>
```

There is an alternative way to access the data coming back from a query. The `Result` interface has an alternative method to access the data as an array of `SortedMap` objects. The method can be seen in Listing 14.9, and is shown here:

```
SortedMap[] getRows()
```

As an alternative to an array of array objects, the `SortedMap` array consists of key value pairs, where the key is the column name, and the value is the column value. The type of the column value object is defined by the column type to Java type mapping within the JDBC specification.

> **Note**
>
> In the JDBC specification, when column data is accessed, the type of object returned is dependent on the type in the database. There is a mapping defined within JDBC between SQL types and Java types. This mapping is outlined in the class `java.sql.Types`.

Listing 14.11 shows an alternative to Listing 14.10 using the `SortedMap` array property. Note that only the relevant fragment has been shown.

Listing 14.11 **Accessing the `SortedMap[]` property returned from `getRows()`**

```
<c:forEach var="row" items="${addresses.rows}">
  <tr>
    <c:forEach var="column" items="${row}">
      <td><c:out value="${column}"/></td>
    </c:forEach>
  </tr>
</c:forEach>
```

The output from this being used in a complete listing can be seen in Figure 14.3. This can be found in the sample application. Notice that the order of the columns is now alphabetic.

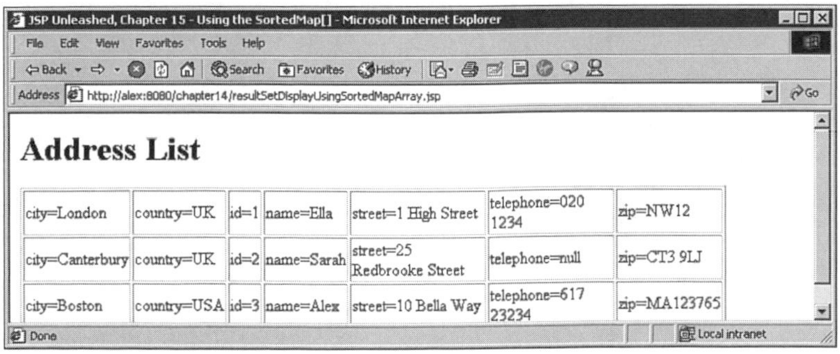
JSP Unleashed, Chapter 15 - Using the SortedMap[] - Microsoft Internet Explorer
File Edit View Favorites Tools Help
Back Search Favorites History
Address http://alex:8080/chapter14/resultSetDisplayUsingSortedMapArray.jsp
Go
Address List
city=London country=UK id=1 name=Ella street=1 High Street telephone=020 1234 zip=NW12
city=Canterbury country=UK id=2 name=Sarah street=25 Redbrooke Street telephone=null zip=CT3 9LJ
city=Boston country=USA id=3 name=Alex street=10 Bella Way telephone=617 23234 zip=MA123765
Done
Local intranet

Figure 14.3 `resultSetDisplayUsingSortedMapArray.jsp`.

The sql:update Action

The sql:query action can be used to execute straightforward queries against the database to return Result. To modify the database you use the sql:update action. The sql:update action supports a SQL INSERT, UPDATE, or DELETE, and indeed anything that a JDBC Statement.executeUpdate() method can be used for.

The sql:update action has the attributes listed in Table 14.4.

Table 14.4 **The Attributes of the sql:update Action**

Attribute Name	Dynamic	Type	Description
sql	True	String	This would contain a SQL update statement of some description. The query can also be specified in the body of the action.
dataSource	True	String or javax.sql.DataSource	This could be a reference to the DataSource itself. A String would be a JNDI resource. In the example shown, it is a DataSource object reference. Later you'll see how to use a JNDI name.
var	False	String	This is the name of the returned result variable. The type of this variable is java.lang.Integer, and it reflects the number of rows affected by the update.
scope	False	String	This is the scope of any exported variable. The options are page, request, session, or application. This attribute can only used if the var attribute is present.

Listing 14.12 shows a JSP performing a basic update using the sql:update action.

Listing 14.12 usingUpdateTag.jsp

```
<%@ taglib prefix="sql" uri="http://java.sun.com/jstl-el/sql" %>
<%@ taglib prefix="c" uri="http://java.sun.com/jstl-el/core" %>
<html>
<head>
<title> Updating a database using
       the sql:update tag</title>
<sql:setDataSource
  var="conn"
  dataSource="jdbc/address"
/> </head>
<body>
<h1>Modify Address List</h1>
<sql:update dataSource="${conn}" var="addresses">
    INSERT INTO AddressList (name, street, city, country, telephone) VALUES
➥                  ("Sarah", "Filton", "Bristol", "UK", "0117 915")
```

Listing 14.12 **Continued**

```
</sql:update>
</body>
</html>
```

This page as it stands is of limited use, however. If you recall when JDBC was discussed, the concept of a `PreparedStatement` was discussed. These were statements that were precompiled and had parameters supplied to them. An additional action can be used in conjunction with the `sql:update` action that enables the setting of SQL update parameters.

The `sql:param` Action

Parameters can be set for prepared statements using the `sql:param` action. This action has only one attribute, a `String` called `value`.

Here is the `sql:update` action from Listing 14.11, modified to use parameters:

```
<sql:update dataSource="${conn}" var="addresses">
    INSERT INTO AddressList (name, street, city, country, telephone)
➥                                           VALUES (?, ?, ?, ?, ?)
    <sql:param value="Fred"/>
    <sql:param value="High Street"/>
    <sql:param value="Boston"/>
    <sql:param value="USA"/>
    <sql:param value="617 829 2342 "/>
</sql:update>
```

The benefit of these parameters is that the values can now be set from HTML forms. In Listing 14.13, you can see a JSP that will cause an update to the database that will work in conjunction with the HTML form in Listing 14.4, with the form action attribute set to `usingParamTag.jsp`.

Listing 14.13 `usingParamTag.jsp`

```
<%@ taglib prefix="sql" uri="http://java.sun.com/jstl-el/sql" %>
<%@ taglib prefix="c" uri="http://java.sun.com/jstl-el/core" %>
<html>
<head>
<title>Updating a database
       using the sql:update tag</title>
<sql:setDataSource
  var="conn"
  dataSource="jdbc/address"
/>
</head>
<body>
```

Listing 14.13 **Continued**

```
<h1>Modify Address List</h1>
<sql:update dataSource="${conn}" var="addresses">
    INSERT INTO AddressList (name, street, city, country, telephone)
➥           VALUES (?, ?, ?, ?, ?)
    <sql:param value='${param["name"]}'/>
    <sql:param value='${param["street"]}'/>
    <sql:param value='${param["city"]}'/>
    <sql:param value='${param["country"]}'/>
    <sql:param value='${param["tel"]}'/>
</sql:update>
</body>
</html>
```

The `sql:transaction` Action

This is the last action that comes as a part of the SQL-specific actions. This action is used to group `sql:query` and `sql:update` actions together to form a transaction. Ordinarily, a JDBC connection will commit each statement automatically. This is not always what you want, though. Often, a series of SQL statements will need to be committed together as a single unit. This is where the `sql:transaction` action comes in. Essentially, it is a straightforward matter of enclosing the SQL queries and updates within these `sql:transaction` actions.

The `sql:transaction` action has two attributes. One is `dataSource`. This works the same way as the `dataSource` attributes that you have seen already. It is worth noting that the nested `sql:query` and `sql:update` actions cannot also have `dataSource` attributes. You will see this if you look at Listing 14.14.

Listing 14.14 `usingTransactions.jsp`

```
<%@ taglib prefix="sql" uri="http://java.sun.com/jstl-el/sql" %>
<%@ taglib prefix="c" uri="http://java.sun.com/jstl-el/core" %>
<html>
<head>
<title>Using Transactions</title>
<sql:setDataSource
  var="conn"
  dataSource="jdbc/address"
/>
</head>
<body>
<h1>Modify Address List</h1>
<!—at the time of writing, there was a disparity between the specification for
this tag and the tag library implementation used in the example. The isolation
attribute shows a different value to the specified possible values shown on the
facing page. -->
<sql:transaction dataSource="${conn}" isolation="TRANSACTION_SERIALIZABLE">
  <sql:update>
```

Listing 14.14 **Continued**

```
        INSERT INTO AddressList (name, street, city, country,
➥ telephone) VALUES (?, ?, ?, ?, ?)
        <sql:param value='${param["name"]}'/>
        <sql:param value='${param["street"]}'/>
        <sql:param value='${param["city"]}'/>
        <sql:param value='${param["country"]}'/>
        <sql:param value='${param["tel"]}'/>
    </sql:update>

    <sql:query var="addresses">
        SELECT * FROM AddressList
    </sql:query>
    <table width="90%" border="1">
    <tr>
    <!-- add the table column headings -->
    <c:forEach var="columnName" items="${addresses.columnNames}">
      <th> <c:out value="${columnName}"/> </th>
    </c:forEach>
    </tr>
    <!-- add the table rows from the result set -->
    <c:forEach var="row" items="${addresses.rowsByIndex}">
      <tr>
        <c:forEach var="column" items="${row}">
          <td><c:out value="${column}"/></td>
        </c:forEach>
      </tr>
    </c:forEach>
    </table>
</sql:transaction>
</body>
</html>
```

One big issue when working with databases is what to do about the fact that various interactions can be going on with the database at the same time. You might, for example, be reading some rows that are in the middle of being changed by another transaction. Which data do you want to read? The original data or the new data *before* it has been committed. There are four possible options, which are set using the `isolation` attribute in the `sql:transaction` action.

```
isolation= "read_committed" | "read_uncommitted" |
                      "repeatable_read" | "serializable"
```

Basically, three things can happen when reading from a database under high load that can affect the results that you get:

- Dirty reads—Data is read that is part of an uncommitted transaction. This means that if this transaction rolls back, you will have dirty data.
- Phantom reads—You might read some rows based on a where clause; subsequently, an additional row is added by another transaction. When your transaction rereads the data, a phantom row appears.
- Nonrepeatable read—You might read a row, which is then subsequently changed by a different transaction. When your transaction rereads the data, it has been changed.

Figure 14.4 shows how the four possible attribute values affect whether dirty reads, phantom reads, and nonrepeatable reads are permitted from your JSP.

	dirty reads	Non-repeatable reads	phantom reads
read_uncommitted	☑	☑	☑
read_committed	☒	☑	☑
repeatable_read	☒	☒	☑
serializable	☒	☒	☒

Figure 14.4 The four `isolation` attribute values.

Setting SQL Action Attributes Globally

There are two attributes from these actions that can be set globally with the use of initialization parameters being set within `web.xml`. The two values that can be set are shown in Table 14.5.

Table 14.5 **Action Parameters That Can Be Set from** `web.xml`

Action	Attribute Name	Parameter in web.xml
`sql:query` `sql:transaction,` `sql:update`	`dataSource`	`javax.servlet.jsp.jstl.sql.dataSource`
`sql:query`	`maxRows`	`javax.servlet.jsp.jstl.sql.maxRows`

This can be especially useful for setting the DataSource to be used for the entire Web application, so if the DataSource object to be used changes, you only change an initialization parameter in `web.xml`, rather than altering multiple pages. The main limitation of this, of course, is that it assumes that you are only working with one DataSource object, but then this is the case for many Web applications.

Here is an example of how these attributes can be set from within `web.xml`:

```
<web-app>
  <context-param>
    <param-name> javax.servlet.jsp.jstl.sql.dataSource</param-name>
    <param-value>jdbc/address</param-value>
  </context-param>
  …
</web-app>
```

To access the `DataSource` from a page, you would now simply have a `setDataSource` action used in the following way:

```
<sql:setDataSource var="conn" />
```

Note the lack of any `dataSource` attribute. This is because it has been set within the context-param elements in the `web.xml` instead.

As you have now seen, these SQL actions effectively enable you to interact with the JDBC API from a JSP without any Java code at all into your pages.

Connection Pools

When we discussed the use of `DataSources` in Tomcat, we mentioned that the mechanism used by Tomcat involved connection pooling. In this section, we will discuss how connection pooling works.

In our early examples using the `DriverManager` class, every request resulted in a new connection to the database being created and destroyed. This can be OK for very low-traffic sites, or sites with minimal database interaction, but this will very quickly become a performance bottleneck on high-traffic sites.

One very common solution to this problem is the concept of *connection pooling*. A connection pool is essentially a pool of active, connected database connections that can be used by your Web application when necessary. This would result in connections being taken from the pool when needed and then returned to the pool when they are finished with, avoiding the unnecessary process of constantly creating and destroying connections. Figure 14.5 shows the basic architecture of a connection pool.

In the diagram, some of the connections are in use, whereas others are free. Either way, they are all permanently connected to the database.

Application servers all provide connection pooling out of the box. You have also seen how it can be configured to work in Tomcat with the use of the DataSource.

In the J2EE architecture, connection pools work with `javax.sql.DataSource` objects, as shown in Figure 14.6.

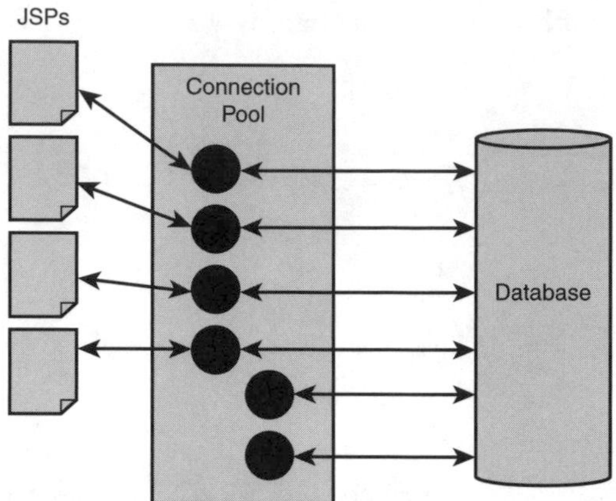

Figure 14.5 Connection pool architecture in a Web application.

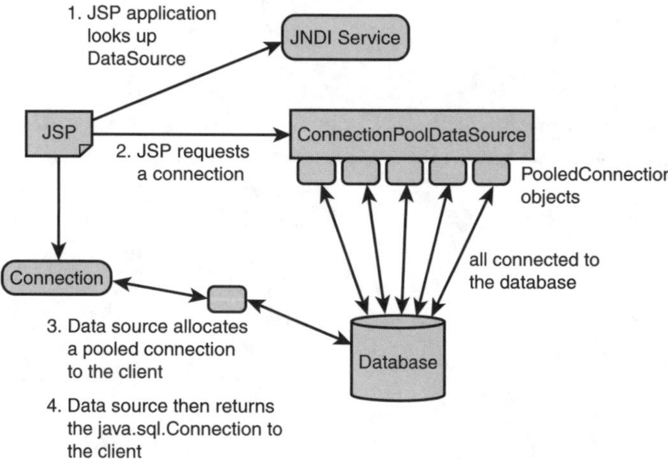

Figure 14.6 Connection pool architecture using DataSources.

To fully understand Figure 14.6, it is important to understand the various interfaces that are involved. Three unfamiliar interfaces are used to implement connection pooling:

```
javax.sql.ConnectionPoolDataSource
javax.sql.PooledConnection
javax.sql.ConnectionEventListener
```

The `ConnectionPoolDataSource` Interface

The `ConnectionPoolDataSource` in Figure 14.6 is very similar to a `javax.sql.DataSource`, except that it is used for pooled connections. It has an overloaded method:

```
public PooledConnection getConnection()
public PooledConnection getConnection(String user, String password)
```

When a connection is returned by a `ConnectionPoolDataSource`, it is a `PooledConnection`. This is the next important interface. The `PooledConnection` is a connection to the database. A `ConnectionPoolDataSource` will typically have a number of them live and ready, waiting to be used. They can be seen in Figure 14.6.

The `PooledConnection` Interface

The `javax.sql.PooledConnection` interface has the following methods:

```
java.sql.Connection getConnection()
void close()
void removeConnectionEventListener(ConnectionEventListener listener)
void addConnectionEventListener(ConnectionEventListener listener)
```

The method that might surprise you in this interface is the `getConnection()` method. You might be thinking that this *is* the connection, so why have a `getConnection()` method? If you notice, the method returns a `java.sql.Connection`. It is this object that actually gets returned to the client application.

This is what is happening: When the client requests a connection from the data source, a `PooledConnection` is retrieved from the connection pool by the `ConnectionPoolDataSource`. The `java.sql.Connection` reference is then obtained from the `PooledConnection` using the `getConnection()` method and sent to the client.

The client can then interact with this connection as they would any other connection. The important thing from the client point of view is that they can interact with a connection from a connection pool in exactly the same way as they would interact with a connection from a straightforward data source.

To access a connection from a connection pool using a JSP it will be exactly the same as if you were using any other data source. Assuming you are using the tag libraries, you would have something like the following in your page:

```
<sql:query dataSource="jdbc/address" var="addresses">
    SELECT * FROM AddressList
</sql:query>
```

The `dataSource` attribute above contains a JNDI lookup to a `DataSource` object as before. The fact that it might be implementing connection pooling is transparent to the client. As discussed, one of the key benefits of this architecture is that the client does not need to know how the connections are being implemented.

Application servers provide visual interfaces for setting up connection pools. Figure 14.7 shows the administration interface for WebLogic 7. The minimum and maximum numbers of connections are set up from here. You will revisit this in Chapter 15, "JPS and EJB Interaction."

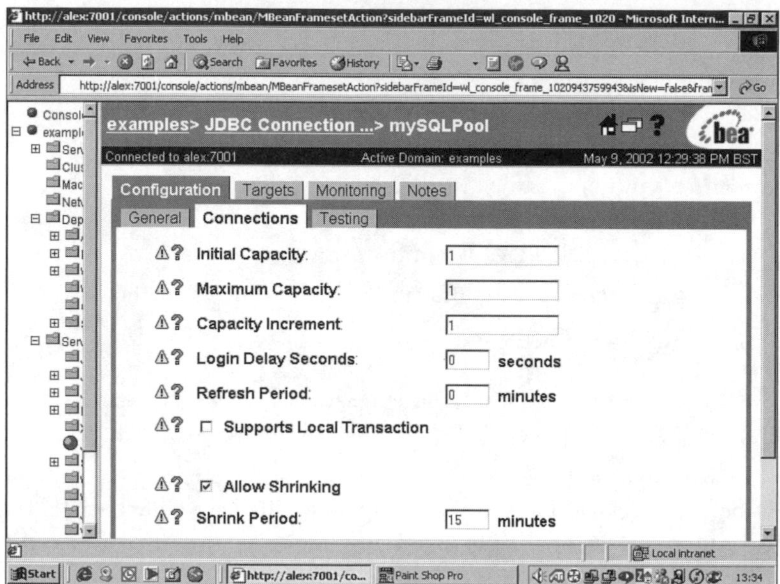

Figure 14.7 Web Logic connection pool management screen.

Other application servers provide a similar interface to enable these settings to be configured.

The `ConnectionEventListener` Interface

The last of the three interfaces that are involved in connection pooling is the `javax.sql.ConnectionEventListener`. This interface is used under the covers of the connection pool implementation to enable the application to keep track of which connections are checked back in.

The interface has two methods:

```
public void connectionClosed (ConnectionEvent evt)
public void connectionErrorOccurred (ConnectionEvent evt)
```

The client has the reference to a `java.sql.Connection` object. When `close()` is called on this object, the `connectionClosed (ConnectionEvent evt)` method is called on a `ConnectionEventListener`, and the `PooledConnection` is then returned to the pool to be used by other clients. Therefore, it is very important that connections are closed, otherwise you can end up with connection pools constantly running out of connections.

Content Caching

Consider the pages that you have seen that are doing select statements on your data source. They are pulling data out of the database, formatting it, and presenting it in a JSP. Every request for these JSPs will involve a hit on the database, even though the page created might be the same for multiple users. Also, after the data has been extracted once, it could be cached for use by other pages. The next section will explore the concept of content caching and how current JSP technology enables content caching to take place.

Caching JSP Output

One way of caching is to cache the output from the JSP servlets so that when the page is requested again, the content comes from a cache rather than being dynamically created over again.

As part of the Jakarta Taglibs project, there is a cache tag library being developed. In fact, only two tags are in the library: `cache` and `invalidate`. More information can be obtained from `http://jakarta.apache.org`.

This caching mechanism can be very attractive because not only are you reducing the load on the database, you are also reducing the processing load as the servlets will not always need to generate the output. However, this mechanism is not always sufficient. If you have any personalization in your site, as discussed in Chapter 17, pages will frequently be different for different people within your site. For sites where the output is fairly static for different users, and the database content does not change much, this can be of significant benefit.

Caching Database Content

An alternative to caching the JSP output is to cache the content of the database. This is a popular strategy because it reduces the hit on the database without restricting the dynamic content in any way. One of the easiest ways to do this is with the use of JavaBeans.

As you saw in Chapter 6, "JSP and JavaBeans," JavaBeans can be accessed relatively easily from pages using the JavaBean-specific standard actions:

```
<jsp:useBean>
<jsp:setProperty>
<jsp:getProperty>
```

If the data is cached within Beans, not only does it reduce the load on the database, but it is also a relatively straightforward process to access the data from your JavaServer Pages.

To demonstrate this, the shopping-cart application from Chapter 8, "Session Tracking Using JSP," will be modified. If you recall, the application is a basic shopping site that has the capability to log in and purchase products. In Chapter 8, the products were set up in JavaBeans and the users were defined in `web.xml`. We will now modify the application as follows:

- User information will be stored in a database
- Product information will be stored in a database
- Product information will be extracted and cached by the application as JavaBeans

The Shopping Cart Mini Case Study

Four tables will be required in our database: one for the users, one for the books, one for the DVDs, and one for the compact discs. The application will be built using the SQL tag library to access the database. What we will do though is cache the content of the book and DVD tables into JavaBeans. Listing 14.15 shows the SQL script for the database tables.

Listing 14.15 `shoppingCartTables.sql`

```
CREATE DATABASE IF NOT EXISTS jsphandbook;
use jsphandbook ; create table books
➥ (id int primary key,title varchar (50), author varchar(30),price double);
use jsphandbook ; insert into books values
➥ (1,'The Voyage of the Dawn Treader','C.S. Lewis',4.99);
use jsphandbook ; insert into books values
➥ (2,'Linux Desk Reference','Scott Hawkins',29.99);
use jsphandbook ; insert into books values
➥ (3,'Let the Nations Be Glad','John Piper',5.99);
use jsphandbook ; insert into books values
➥ (4,'Treasure Island','Robert Louis Stevenson',3.99);
use jsphandbook ; insert into books values
➥ (5,'How to Be a Great Guitarist','Paul Hunnisett',17.99);
use jsphandbook ; insert into books values
➥ (6,'Heart of a Hooligan','Muthena Paul Alkazraji',4.99);
use jsphandbook ; insert into books values
➥ (7,'Shogun','James Clavell',12.99);
use jsphandbook ; insert into books values
➥ (8,'The Art of War','Sun Tzu',4.99);
use jsphandbook ; create table compact_discs
➥ (id int primary key,title varchar (50),artist varchar(30),
➥                                   tracks int,price double);
```

Listing 14.15 **Continued**

```
use jsphandbook ; insert into compact_discs values
➥ (9,'Is This It','The Strokes',11,13.99);
use jsphandbook ; insert into compact_discs values
➥ (10,'Just Enough Education to Perform','Stereophonics',11,10.99);
use jsphandbook ; insert into compact_discs values
➥ (11,'Parachutes','Coldplay',10,11.99);
use jsphandbook ; insert into compact_discs values
➥ (12,'White Ladder','David Gray',10,15.99);
use jsphandbook ; insert into compact_discs values
➥ (13,'Greatest Hits','Penelope',14,14.99);
use jsphandbook ; insert into compact_discs values
➥ (14,'Echo Park','Feeder',12,13.99);
use jsphandbook ; insert into compact_discs values
➥ (15,'Mezzanine','Massive Attack',11,12.99);
use jsphandbook ; create table DVDs
➥ (id int primary key,title varchar (50),director varchar(30),price double);
use jsphandbook ; insert into DVDs values
➥ (16, "It's a Wonderful Life","Frank Capra",7.99);
use jsphandbook ; insert into DVDs values
➥ (17, 'Crouching Tiger, Hidden Dragon','Ang Lee',15.99);
use jsphandbook ; insert into DVDs values
➥ (18, "Breakfast at Tiffany's","Blake Edwards",14.99);
use jsphandbook ; insert into DVDs values
➥ (19, 'Romeo Must Die','Andrzej Bartkowiak',10.99);
use jsphandbook ; insert into DVDs values
➥ (20, 'Scent of a Woman','Martin Brest',17.99);
use jsphandbook ; insert into DVDs values
➥ (21, 'Snatch','Guy Ritchie',18.99);
use jsphandbook ; insert into DVDs values
➥ (22, 'Scarface','Brian De Palma',16.99);
use jsphandbook ; create table users
➥ (id int primary key, name varchar(50), password varchar(30));
use jsphandbook ; insert into users values(1,'John','password');
use jsphandbook ; insert into users values(2,'Janet','password') ;
```

The database is available using a DataSource within Tomcat, and it has been configured with the following entry in `server.xml`.

```
<Context path="/chapter14shoppingCartDB" docBase="chapter14shoppingCartDB"
      debug="0" reloadable="true">
  <ResourceParams name="jdbc/shopping">
    <parameter>
      <name>password</name>
      <value>admin</value>
    </parameter>
```

```
    <parameter>
      <name>url</name>
      <value>jdbc:mysql://localhost:3306/jsphandbook</value>
    </parameter>
    <parameter>
      <name>driverClassName</name>
      <value>com.mysql.jdbc.Driver</value>
    </parameter>
    <parameter>
      <name>username</name>
      <value>admin</value>
    </parameter>
  </ResourceParams>
</Context>
```

It has then been set up in the `web.xml` with the following entry:

```
<resource-ref>
  <res-ref-name>jdbc/shopping</res-ref-name>
  <res-type>javax.sql.DataSource</res-type>
  <res-auth>Container</res-auth>
</resource-ref>
```

The data from this `DataSource` is to be cached within JavaBeans. The Beans being used are similar to those used in Chapter 8. In summary, there is one for the stock called `Stock.class`, an interface for all the stock items called `Item.class`, and then implementations of `Item`, called `Book.class`, and `DVD.class`. The listing for `Stock.java` is shown in Listing 14.16. It contains array properties for books, CDs, and DVDs. The get methods are all standard, but let's look at the set methods.

Listing 14.16 `Stock.java`

```
package com.conygre;
import java.util.Vector;

public class Stock{

  private Book[] books = new Book[0];
  private CompactDisc[] cds = new CompactDisc[0];
  private DVD[] dvds = new DVD[0];

  public Stock() {
  }

  public Book[] getBooks(){
    return books;
  }
```

Listing 14.16 **Continued**

```
  public CompactDisc[] getCds(){
    return cds;
  }

  public DVD[] getDvds(){
    return dvds;
  }

  public void setBook(Book b){
    Book book = new Book();
    book.setId(b.getId());
    book.setTitle(b.getTitle());
    book.setAuthor(b.getAuthor());
    book.setPrice(b.getPrice());
    Vector v = new Vector(1);
    for (int i=0;i<books.length;i++){
      if(books[i] != null){
        v.add(books[i]);
      }
    }
  v.add(book);
  Book[] newBooks = new Book[0];
  newBooks = (Book[])v.toArray(newBooks) ;
  books = newBooks;
}

public void setCd(CompactDisc c){
  CompactDisc cd = new CompactDisc();
  cd.setId(c.getId());
  cd.setTitle(c.getTitle());
  cd.setArtist(c.getArtist());
  cd.setPrice(c.getPrice());
  cd.setTracks(c.getTracks());
  Vector v = new Vector();
  for (int i=0;i<cds.length;i++){
    if(cds[i] != null){
      v.add(cds[i]);
    }
   }
  v.add(cd);
  CompactDisc[] newCds = new CompactDisc[0];
  newCds = (CompactDisc[])v.toArray(newCds);
  cds = newCds;
}
```

Listing 14.16 **Continued**

```
public void setDvd(DVD d){
  DVD dvd = new DVD();
  dvd.setId(d.getId());
  dvd.setTitle(d.getTitle());
  dvd.setDirector(d.getDirector());
  dvd.setPrice(d.getPrice());
  Vector v = new Vector();
  for (int i=0;i<dvds.length;i++){
    if(dvds[i] != null){
      v.add(dvds[i]);
    }
  }
  v.add(dvd);
  DVD[] newDvds = new DVD[0];
  newDvds = (DVD[])v.toArray(newDvds);
  dvds = newDvds;
 }
}
```

Look at the set method for DVDs in Listing 14.16. Notice that it takes in an individual DVD object, effectively clones it, and then adds it to the array of DVDs by way of a `Vector`. The reason for this becomes apparent when we see how the data is cached.

The `Book`, `DVD` and `CompactDisc` classes are all regular JavaBeans with get and set methods for the `id`, `title`, and `price`. `Book.java` is shown in Listing 14.17.

Listing 14.17 `Book.java`

```
package com.conygre;

public class Book implements Item{

  //Instance variables
  private String title;
  private double price;
  private String author;
  private String id;

  //Methods
  public String getId(){
    return id;
  }

  public void setId(String s){
    id = s;
  }
```

Listing 14.17 **Continued**

```
  public String getTitle(){
    return title;
  }

  public void setTitle(String s){
    title = s;
  }

  public double getPrice(){
    return price;
  }

  public void setPrice(double d){
    price = d;
  }

  public String getAuthor(){
    return author;
  }

  public void setAuthor(String s) {
    author = s;
  }

  //constructors
  public Book(){}

  public Book(String t, double p,String a, String i){
    title=t;
    price=p;
    author=a;
    id=i;
  }
}
```

Now, we'll look at the JSP that is used to set up the cached DVD and book data. This is shown in Listing 14.18.

Listing 14.18 `cache.jsp`

```
<%@ taglib uri="http://java.sun.com/jstl-el/core" prefix="c" %>
<%@ taglib uri="http://java.sun.com/jstl-el/sql" prefix="sql" %>
<c:if test="${stock == null}">
<jsp:useBean id="stock" class="com.conygre.Stock" scope="application"/>
```

Listing 14.18 **Continued**

```
<sql:setDataSource var="handbookDb"
    dataSource="jdbc/shopping"/>

<sql:query var="books" dataSource="${handbookDb}" >
  select * from books
</sql:query>
<sql:query var="cds" dataSource="${handbookDb}" >
  select * from compact_discs
</sql:query>
<sql:query var="dvds" dataSource="${handbookDb}" >
  select * from DVDs
</sql:query>
<c:forEach var="bookRow" items="${books.rowsByIndex}" >
  <jsp:useBean id="bookRow" type="java.lang.Object[]" />
  <jsp:useBean id="newBook" class="com.conygre.Book" scope="page" />
  <jsp:setProperty name="newBook"
   value="<%= bookRow[0].toString()%>" property="id" />
  <jsp:setProperty name="newBook"
   value="<%= bookRow[1].toString()%>" property="title" />
  <jsp:setProperty name="newBook"
   value="<%= bookRow[2].toString()%>" property="author" />
  <jsp:setProperty name="newBook"
   value="<%= ((Double)bookRow[3]).doubleValue()%>" property="price" />
  <% stock.setBook(newBook);%>
</c:forEach>
<c:forEach var="cdRow" items="${cds.rowsByIndex}">
  <jsp:useBean id="cdRow" type="java.lang.Object[]" />
  <jsp:useBean id="newCd" class="com.conygre.CompactDisc" scope="page" />
  <jsp:setProperty name="newCd"
   value="<%=cdRow[0].toString()%>" property="id" />
  <jsp:setProperty name="newCd"
   value="<%=cdRow[1].toString()%>" property="title" />
  <jsp:setProperty name="newCd"
   value="<%=cdRow[2].toString()%>" property="artist" />
  <jsp:setProperty name="newCd"
   value="<%=((Integer)cdRow[3])%>" property="tracks" />
  <jsp:setProperty name="newCd"
   value="<%=((Double)cdRow[4]).doubleValue()%>" property="price" />
  <% stock.setCd(newCd);%>
</c:forEach>
<c:forEach var="dvdRow" items="${dvds.rowsByIndex}">
  <jsp:useBean id="dvdRow" type="java.lang.Object[]"  />
  <jsp:useBean id="newDvd" class="com.conygre.DVD" scope="page" />
  <jsp:setProperty name="newDvd"
   value="<%=dvdRow[0].toString()%>" property="id" />
```

Listing 14.18 **Continued**

```
  <jsp:setProperty name="newDvd"
   value="<%=dvdRow[1].toString()%>" property="title" />
  <jsp:setProperty name="newDvd"
   value="<%=dvdRow[2].toString()%>" property="director" />
  <jsp:setProperty name="newDvd"
   value="<%=((Double)dvdRow[3]).doubleValue()%>" property="price" />
  <% stock.setDvd(newDvd);%>
</c:forEach>
<jsp:useBean id="currentUser" class="com.conygre.Person" scope="session">
  <jsp:setProperty name="currentUser" property="name" value="Guest" />
</jsp:useBean>
</c:if>
```

There are some interesting things to point out in Listing 14.18. The listing takes advantage of both the standard tag library and JavaBeans. First of all, note the use of the application-scoped Bean with an `id` of `stock`. This Bean is an instance of `Stock.java` shown in Listing 14.16. This Bean will be populated by accessing the database using the `sql:query` action. The output from the `sql:query` action is then being used to populate Beans by looping sequentially through the rows with a `c:forEach` action. The easiest way to understand what is going on is to look carefully at just one of the `sql:query` and `c:forEach` elements. Study Listing 14.19, which is an extract from Listing 14.18.

Listing 14.19 **Populating the Stock Bean with Data**

```
<jsp:useBean id="stock" class="com.conygre.Stock" scope="application"/>
<sql:query var="books">
  select * from books
</sql:query>
. . .
<c:forEach var="bookRow" items="${books.rowsByIndex}" >
  <jsp:useBean id="bookRow" type="java.lang.Object[]" />
  <jsp:useBean id="newBook" class="com.conygre.Book" scope="page" />
  <jsp:setProperty name="newBook"
   value="<%= bookRow[0].toString()%>" property="id" />
  <jsp:setProperty name="newBook"
   value="<%= bookRow[1].toString()%>" property="title" />
  <jsp:setProperty name="newBook"
   value="<%= bookRow[2].toString()%>" property="author" />
  <jsp:setProperty name="newBook"
   value="<%= ((Double)bookRow[3]).doubleValue()%>" property="price" />
  <% stock.setBook(newBook);%>
</c:forEach>
. . .
```

The query is a basic `select` statement being executed on the books table in the database. The `forEach` is then looping around the `Object[][]` array returned by the `getRowsByIndex()` method of the `Result` interface.

> **Note**
> In the J2EE blueprints, it does say that tags should not be used for large significant portions of business logic, and that this should be done in a Java Servlet instead. We chose to use JSP with `cache.jsp` because it acts as a further demonstration of the use of the SQL tags.

The `cache.jsp` page also sets up the default user to be called `guest`:

```
<jsp:useBean id="currentUser" class="com.conygre.Person" scope="session">
  <jsp:setProperty name="currentUser" property="name" value="Guest" />
</jsp:useBean>
```

This Bean is then changed when the user logs in using the `doLogin.jsp` page, as shown in Listing 14.20.

Listing 14.20 `doLogin.jsp`

```
<%@ taglib uri="http://java.sun.com/jstl-el/core" prefix="c" %>
<jsp:include page="cache.jsp"/>
<%@ taglib uri="http://java.sun.com/jstl-el/sql" prefix="sql" %>

<sql:setDataSource var="handbookDb"
    dataSource="jdbc/shopping"/>

<sql:query var="login" dataSource="${handbookDb}">
  select * from users
</sql:query>
<c:forEach var="user" items="${login.rows}">
  <jsp:useBean id="user" type="java.util.TreeMap"/>
  <jsp:useBean id="currentUser" class="com.conygre.Person" scope="session"/>
  <c:choose>
     <c:when
      test="${param.user == user.name and param.password == user.password}">
        <jsp:setProperty name="currentUser" property="name"
          value="<%= user.get(\"name\").toString() %>"/>
        <jsp:setProperty name="currentUser" property="password"
          value="<%= user.get(\"password\").toString() %>"/>
        <c:choose>
          <c:when test="${session.currentPage == 'checkout'}">
            <c:set var="currentPage" value="none" scope="session"/>
            <c:redirect url="checkout.jsp"/>
          </c:when>
          <c:otherwise>
            <c:redirect url="welcome.jsp"/>
```

Listing 14.20 **Continued**

```
          </c:otherwise>
        </c:choose>
        </c:when>
      <c:otherwise>
    Login failed please try <a href="login.jsp">again</a>
   </c:otherwise>
 </c:choose>
</c:forEach>
```

This page does a simple check to ensure that the username matches one of the users within the database. If it does, the `currentUser` Bean is assigned the username and password from the database.

The pages used to display the products all have embedded in the top of them, `cache.jsp`. This results in a user being able to visit any page, and if the user happens to be the first user to visit a page in the application, the cache will be created. If you notice in Listing 14.15 containing `cache.jsp`, the populating of the Beans only happens if the `stock` Bean is `null`. In other words, the logic in `cache.jsp` has not run already. Listing 14.21 shows the page that displays the book products, `book.jsp`.

Listing 14.21 `books.jsp`

```
<%@ taglib uri="http://java.sun.com/jstl-el/core" prefix="c" %>
<jsp:include page="cache.jsp"/>
<html>
<head>
<title>
Welcome to Ashdown.com - The best deals for Books, CDs and DVDs!
</title>
</head>
<body bgcolor="#FFCC99">
<c:import url="header.jsp" />
<form method="post" action="addToCart.jsp">
Please select the books you wish to add to your shopping cart:<br>
<table>
<tr>
<td>
<b><font size="4">Title </font></b>
</td>
<td>
<b><font size="4">Author</font></b>
</td>
<td>
<b><font size="4">Price</font></b>
</td>
```

Listing 14.21 **Continued**

```
</tr>
<c:forEach var="item" items="${stock.books}">
  <tr>
  <td>
  <input type="checkbox" name="id"
     value="<c:out value='${item.id}'/>"><c:out value="${item.title}"/>
  </td>
  <td>
  <c:out value="${item.author}"/>
  </td>
  <td>
  <font color="red"><c:out value="${item.price}"/></font>
  </td>
  </tr>
</c:forEach>

</table>
<input type="submit" value="Add to Cart">
<form>
</body>
</html>
```

When this page is being displayed, the data will be coming from our cached Beans. The rest of the shopping site, such as the shopping cart and the checkout page, are the same as those listed in Chapter 8.

> **Note**
>
> Don't forget that this demonstration application is available as a download from the book Web site (`www.samspublishing.com`). If you set it up, you will see the site in its entirety. Once set up, visit `http://localhost:8080/chapter14shoppingCartDB/welcome.jsp`. Don't forget to add the <context> element to `server.xml`.

When you are working with an application server, you will most likely find that there are some very complex and effective caching strategies available to you. For example, in ATG Dynamo, you can cache data from databases specifically as we have done, so when it is interacted with from pages, the information is coming from the cache. When the data is changed however, the cache can be invalidated automatically across the servers in any cluster that you might have. If you are using WebLogic, there are some specific WebLogic custom tags that enable you to build caching into your JSPs. It is definitely worth investigating what is available to you in your application server in terms of caching support because this can significantly improve the performance of your Web application.

Enterprise JavaBeans and Database Access

Using the tag library provides the separation of Java and HTML. Using JavaBeans enables the caching of data. This is not always sufficient, however. Here are some limitations:

- What if your transactions span multiple data sources? The `sql:transaction` tag has no support for that.
- What if the data access logic is to be used by multiple applications, maybe not even Web applications? The data access code would have to be repeated in each application.
- What if there are a significant number of different data sources being used, with complex associated business logic with each? This would be difficult to maintain across many JSP pages.
- What if users are restricted in terms of data that can be accessed from pages? Not basic page or folder restrictions, but restrictions regarding certain business logic or restrictions against the ability to view certain pieces of data. I would not want to have to build that into a JSP application.

Enterprise JavaBeans can help in addressing all the above issues. They are not always the best solution, however. You have seen what is possible using a combination of tags and Beans, and if you think that your applications will work just fine with that, you should probably go for that. It is only in the more complex distributed applications that EJBs should be considered. I am convinced that many sites are built using EJBs when JSP and tags alone would have been perfectly sufficient.

We will talk in detail about when and how to use EJBs from JSP in Chapter 15, " JSP and EJB Interaction."

Summary

Database access is crucial to any Web application, and in this chapter, you have seen how to access databases manually using JDBC code, using the core tag library, and you have also seen how database content can be cached using JavaBeans. The benefits of connection pooling have also been discussed, and you have seen how application servers provide convenient interfaces to enable them to be set up and configured.

For many Web applications, using the core tag library will be sufficient, but you might want to consider using the caching strategies discussed to improve the performance of your Web application.

For large-scale distributed systems, an EJB tier might need to be introduced into your application. The next chapter will introduce you to Enterprise JavaBeans, and will show you how they can be used to improve the scalability and performance of large-scale, distributed applications. You will also see how the shopping-cart application from the end of this chapter can be extended to use EJBs instead of the SQL tags that were used here.

15

JSP and EJB Interaction

THIS CHAPTER WILL INTRODUCE YOU TO Enterprise JavaBeans (EJB). It contains everything you need to know about EJBs to interact with them effectively from a Web application, and, what's more, it will also show you the fundamentals of how EJBs work under the covers so that you can understand what you are dealing with from your Web application. The chapter will begin by introducing you to the concepts involved in EJB, and then move on to show the basic architecture of EJBs, and how EJBs are deployed in an EJB container. Then, the chapter will move on to how Web applications can interact with EJBs, and also how this should best be done according to the guidelines issued by Sun.

EJB Fundamentals

EJBs are a fundamental part of the Java 2 Enterprise Edition specification as introduced in Chapter 1, "JSP, J2EE, and the Role of the Servlet." The current version of EJB is EJB 2.0.

They are essentially middleware components that run within what is called an *EJB container*, and they take advantage of services provided by the EJB container in which they are deployed. It is these services that are the key to the success of EJB in distributed environments.

Figure 15.1, adapted from a diagram in Chapter 1, shows the EJB container with its related services. The different kinds of EJBs shown will be discussed as the chapter progresses.

If you cannot remember what all the services are, they are discussed in Chapter 1. So what does an EJB container do with a Bean that has been deployed in it?

> **Note**
>
> In case you are not familiar with what components are, an introduction to component-based architecture can be found at the start of Chapter 6, "JSP and JavaBeans."

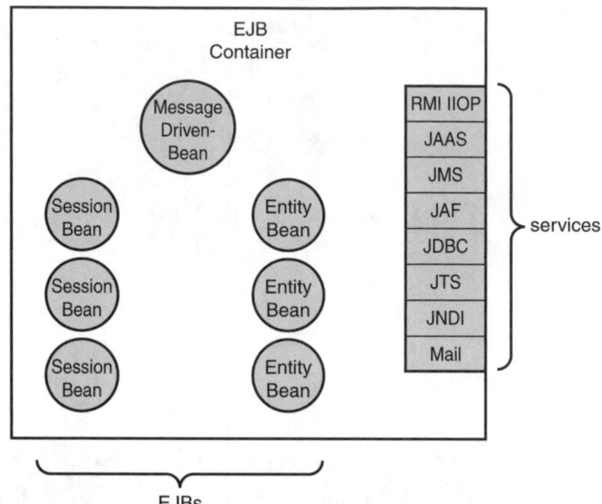

Figure 15.1 The EJB container and its services.

As well as the services shown in Figure 15.1, the container also provides the following functionality specific for the EJBs:

- Lifecycle management
- Transaction management
- Security management
- Resource pooling
- Instance swapping
- Activation and passivation of objects

When you think of the services provided by the container, and all this functionality specific for the EJBs, not much is left for the developer to do—and that is the whole point of EJB.

To quote the J2EE Blueprints available from Sun Microsystems:

> In a multi-tier J2EE application, the Enterprise JavaBeans (EJB) tier hosts application-specific business logic and provides system-level services such as transaction management, concurrency control, and security. Enterprise JavaBeans technology provides a distributed component model that enables developers to focus on solving business problems while relying on the J2EE platform to handle complex system level issues. This separation of concerns allows rapid development of scalable, accessible, robust, and highly secure applications.

Note

The J2EE Blueprints are a best-practice guide for building J2EE applications. Along with the guide, there is a J2EE application called the Java Petstore, which you can use as a best-practice application. You can find the Blueprints by visiting `http://www.java.sun.com/blueprints`.

Imagine that you needed to store some data in a database. You wouldn't write your own database. Most likely, you would use one that already exists. It has all the functionality for storing the data, for processing SQL statements, for handling multiple connections, and so forth. The EJB container is the same for your business objects. It does all the "bread and butter" work that is required in a distributed-application context. In EJB 2.1 (which is part of J2EE 1.4), you can also set up timers, which will invoke functionality within your beans at specific times or specific time intervals.

As you can see from Figure 15.1, there are three kinds of EJB: the entity Bean, the session Bean, and the message-driven Bean.

The entity Bean represents your business data. If you have data objects, for example, they would be entity Beans. These Beans are typically populated with data from relational databases, which is managed for you by the container. Session Beans, on the other hand, represent the business processes, or business logic—the processes that clients might want to use in conjunction with the business data. The container manages the client interactions with the session Beans. Figure 15.2 shows the relationship between entity Beans, session Beans, and the end client. Message-driven Beans enable asynchronous messages to be sent to your EJB container. They are not necessary for our discussion.

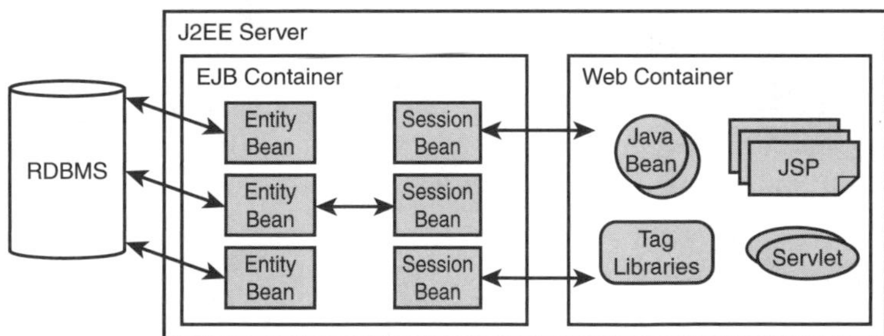

Figure 15.2 Entity Beans, Session Beans, and Clients.

In Figure 15.2, the client application is a Web application. Note the presence of all the core Web application components. Later, we'll discuss how a Web application should interact with an EJB container. The main thing to note in this diagram is that the Web container interacts with the session Beans, or business-logic components, which in turn interact with the entity Beans, or business data components. The session Beans are said to act as a façade to the entity Beans. This is not always necessary with basic entity Beans, but it can be beneficial, especially when the business logic involves more than one entity Bean type.

EJB Communication

EJBs are designed for distributed systems, which means that you can interact with EJBs remotely. In fact, in EJB 1.1 you could only interact with EJBs remotely! Even if two EJBs were side by side in the same container, the code would all be written as if they are accessing one another remotely.

Since EJB 2.0, EJBs can also access one another locally and be accessed locally by Web applications. This is discussed later in the chapter.

So what do we mean by accessing Beans remotely, and how does this work? If you are familiar with distributed programming, you might well have come across the idea of a stub and a skeleton. When accessing objects remotely, method calls (along with their parameters) have to get across a network, and get to the actual object on which the call is being made. The remote object then needs to get any return values back to the client. The process of getting the method call to work across the wire in this way is the responsibility of what are called *stub* and *skeleton* classes. These interfaces *marshall* and *unmarshall* the parameters over the network. The protocol used by EJB is RMI/IIOP. Figure 15.3 demonstrates the role of the stub and the skeleton classes.

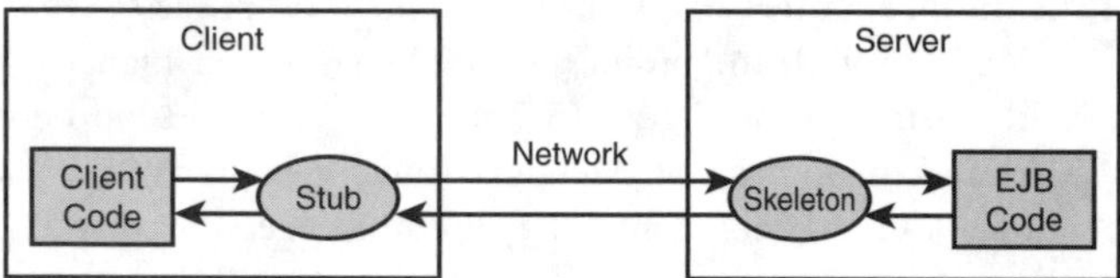

Figure 15.3 The role of the stub and the skeleton.

The stub and skeleton classes are created for you and are all used under the covers. From the developer and client point of view, the interfaces to an EJB are the *home* and *remote* interfaces. These will be discussed in the next section.

Anatomy of an EJB

To build a session or entity EJB, you must write three source files. They are called the *home* interface, the *remote* interface, and the *implementation* class.

Because EJBs need to be accessible remotely within a distributed system, interfaces are used to define the methods available to potential EJB clients. The methods that are available to be called by clients are found in both the remote and home interfaces. The methods are divided up as follows:

- The home interface contains the EJB lifecycle management methods for creating and removing beans and the methods for finding Bean instances.
- The remote interface contains the business methods.
- The implementation class contains the actual Bean code.

One important distinction to make is that home interface references are not tied to any specific Bean instances, whereas the references to the remote interfaces are. This will become clearer as we progress.

There is one other class used by some entity Beans, which is referred to as the *primary key* class. If you recall from Figure 15.2, entity Beans represent the business data, which typically comes from a relational database. The database uses primary keys to uniquely identify units of data, and this primary key can be represented by a class. This can be as simple as a `java.lang.Integer`, but for some EJBs, the primary key class is a class defined by the developer.

One criticism of EJB was that remote references were being used for interactions between EJBs residing in the same EJB container, and this was an unnecessary overhead, so in EJB 2.0, two additional interfaces were introduced, specifically for use by EJBs that are to be accessed locally. These two interfaces are the local home interface and the local interface.

This means that there can be quite a few class files for each EJB! The roles of the various class files are summarized in Table 15.1. The table also shows the naming conventions for each of these files.

Table 15.1 **The `.class` Files That Make Up a Session or Entity Bean**

.class file	Role
Home interface	Typically named *XXX*`Home.java`
Extends `javax.ejb.EJBHome`	Defines the lifecycle methods for the Bean—creating and removing methods, for example. In some cases, methods are also present to enable clients to find instances of the Bean. This interface is not tied to any specific EJB instances.
Remote interface	Typically named *XXX*`.java`
Extends `javax.ejb.EJBObject`	Defines the business methods of the Bean.
Local interface	Typically named `LocalXXX.java`
Extends `javax.ejb.EJBObjectLocal`	The equivalent of the `Remote` interface, this interface can be used locally, avoiding the need for remote method calls.
Local home interface	Typically named `LocalXXXHome.java`
Extends `javax.ejb.EJBHomeLocal`	The equivalent of the `Home` interface, this interface can be used locally, avoiding the need for remote method calls.
Implementation class	Typically named *XXX*`Bean.java` or *XXX*`EJB.java`. `XXXEJB is the convention.`
Implements `javax.ejb.EntityBean` or `javax.ejb.SessionBean`	Contains the actual Bean implementation, implementing many of the methods defined within the home and remote interfaces.
Primary Key class	Typically named *XXX*`PK.java`. For entity Beans. The primary key class represents the primary key of the data that the entity Bean contains.

Note in Table 15.1 that both the interfaces and the implementation extend other classes and interfaces. Figure 15.4 is a class diagram showing what extends what, and what implements what.

> **Note**
> Examples of the local home and remote interfaces are not shown in this book, but examples are in the example site that the chapter uses on the book Web site (`www.samspublishing.com`).

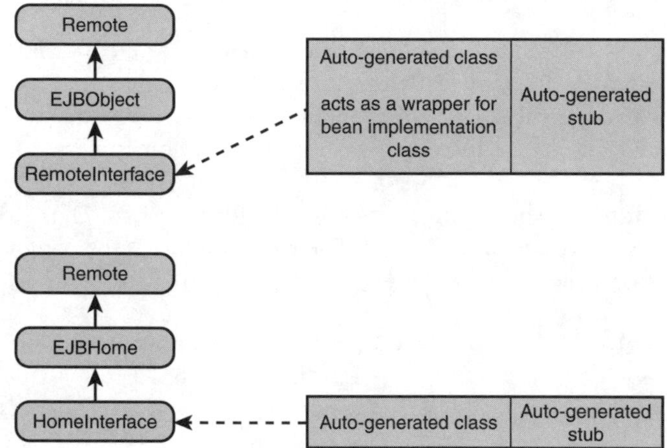

Figure 15.4 Class diagram showing the Home, Remote, and Implementation classes.

Accessing an EJB Remotely—What Goes On

At this point, it is worth a brief explanation of what goes on when an EJB method is invoked. We will focus on remote access in this section. You have seen how all methods are accessed remotely via stubs and skeletons, and you have also seen the role of the home and remote interfaces, so how does it all fit together? In Figure 15.4, you can see four auto-generated classes:

- A class that implements your home interface and, therefore, `javax.ejb.EJBHome`.
- A stub to enable clients to access the `EJBHome` implementation.
- A class that implements your remote interface and, therefore, `javax.ejb.EJBObject`—this class acts as a wrapper to your implementation Bean.
- A stub to enable clients to access the `EJBObject` implementation.

Figure 15.5 demonstrates how these auto-generated classes are used when a client accesses an EJB.

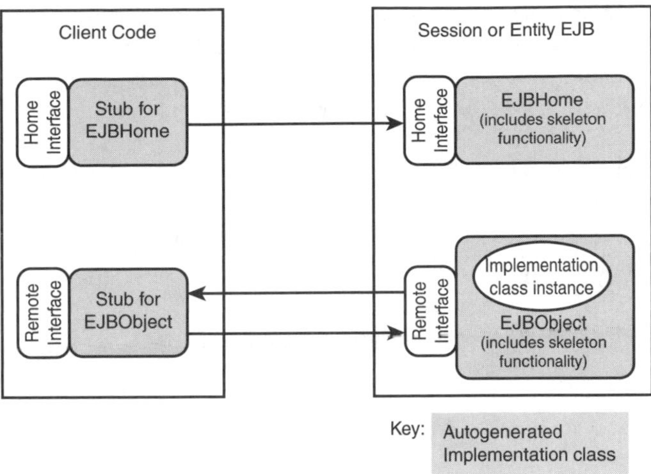

Figure 15.5 How home and remote interfaces work.

The skeleton functionality is contained within the `EJBObject` and `EJBHome` implementation classes, so separate skeleton classes are not required. You will probably be pleased to know that this is all transparent to client applications, but it does help to have some idea of what is going on when you invoke methods on an EJB!

The Client View of an EJB

Figure 15.6 demonstrates the client view of an EJB. This diagram hides much of the complexity shown in Figures 15.4 and 15.5. This is because the client does not have to get into that level of complexity to use an EJB.

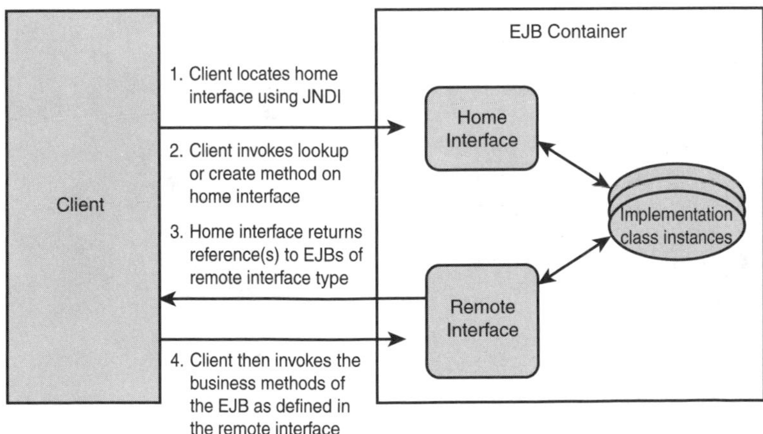

Figure 15.6 The client view of an EJB.

The client basically interacts with the home interface to find instances, and it then interacts with the returned remote interface references. It finds them using what is referred to as a *finder method*. The method used in the following example is called `findAll`, and has been defined by the developer of the Bean. You'll see it implemented later in the chapter.

Listing 15.1 shows a client JSP that interfaces to an entity EJB called `CompactDisc`. You'll see the internals of the Bean itself later, but first let's examine the client perspective on it. Notice that a scriptlet has been used instead of any tags or standard actions. This has been done so you can clearly see exactly what is going on.

Listing 15.1 `ejbClient.jsp`

```
<html>
<head>
<title>List of all Compact Discs Direct From Entity Bean</title>
</head>
<body>
<h1>All Available CDs Direct from the Entity Beans</h1>
The listing of compact discs on this page has been obtained by going direct
 to the entity beans.
<p>
<%@ page import="com.conygre.cd.*, javax.naming.*, java.rmi.*, javax.rmi.*" %>
<%
  // create the context
  Context context = new InitialContext();
  // look up the EJB using its JNDI name
  Object obj = context.lookup("java:comp/env/ejb/CompactDisc");
  // cast the returned remote reference to the home interface type
  // using the narrow() method
  CompactDiscHome home = (CompactDiscHome)
                 (PortableRemoteObject.narrow(obj, CompactDiscHome.class));

  // invoke a finder method
  Collection cds = (Collection) home.findAll();
  // convert the returned collection of remote references to an array
  Object[] array = cds.toArray();
  // cycle through the returned collection displaying the information
  for (int i=0;i<array.length; i++) {
    CompactDisc cd = (CompactDisc) array[i];
    out.println("CD " + cd.getId() + " is called "
             + cd.getTitle() + " and is by " + cd.getArtist() + ".<br>");
  }
%>
</body>
</html>
```

The most important part of Listing 15.1 is the first few lines of the scriptlet.

The client perspective of interacting with an EJB is as follows:

1. The client first locates the home interface using a JNDI lookup. JNDI was discussed in Chapter 13, "Locating Resources using JNDI." It has to cast the object returned to the appropriate type using the `PortableRemoteObject.narrow()` method:

   ```
   Context context = new InitialContext();
   Object obj = context.lookup("java:comp/env/ejb/CompactDisc");
   CompactDiscHome home = (CompactDiscHome)
     (PortableRemoteObject.narrow(obj, CompactDiscHome.class));
   ```

2. The client then invokes the appropriate method on the home interface to either create or locate EJB instances:

   ```
   Collection cds = (Collection) home.findAll();
   ```

3. References of the remote interface type are then returned to the client. This could be a single reference or some kind of collection of references. In this case, a finder method is being used, and a collection of remote references (of type `CompactDisc`) objects is returned. You will see the finder method implementation later. In this example, a `Collection` is returned, so we have converted it to an array of the appropriate type to loop through it:

   ```
   // convert the returned collection of remote references to an array
   Object[] array = cds.toArray();
   // cycle through the returned collection displaying the information
   for (int i=0;i<array.length; i++) {
     CompactDisc cd = (CompactDisc) array[i];
     . . .
   }
   ```

4. The client can then invoke the business methods on those returned remote references. Remember, the remote interface contains the business methods that can be accessed remotely by the client:

   ```
       out.println("CD " + cd.getId() + " is called "
         + cd.getTitle() + " and is by " + cd.getArtist() + ".<br>");
   ```

Writing EJBs

So far, you should have a feel for how EJBs work and also how a client JSP can access them. We'll now turn our attention to how EJBs are written. You will also get the chance to build and deploy your own EJBs if you want.

The main packages that you use when developing EJBs and interacting with EJBs are as follows:

```
javax.ejb
javax.naming
java.rmi
```

The `javax.ejb` package contains a number of interfaces and classes that are used by the EJBs themselves. As you have seen, the home and remote interfaces extend interfaces from this package, for example. The `javax.naming` is used for locating resources with JNDI, and the `java.rmi` package is used largely for the `RemoteException` class. This is the exception thrown by the remote methods.

To see exactly what is involved in building an application that uses EJB, we'll work through an example of using EJB. The example we'll use is the shopping-cart application that has been used as a case study in Chapter 14, "Databases and JSP." In that chapter, regular JavaBeans were created to contain the data from the database. If these JavaBeans were deployed as EJBs, the database access could be managed by the container. That would include all the database access code, and any transaction management that was required by the interactions with the database.

Remember, there are three types of EJB: entity Beans, session Beans, and message-driven Beans. We'll start with entity Beans, since the Bean that has been used in the example so far is an entity Bean.

Creating an Entity Bean

Entity Beans represent business data. There are two kinds of entity Bean: those that operate *container managed persistence*, and those that operate *Bean managed persistence*. The difference is as follows:

- Container Managed Persistence (CMP): The interaction with the database is managed by the container. No JDBC code is written by the developer. Transaction management is also managed by the container.
- Bean Managed Persistence (BMP): The Bean manages its own database access. These Beans are more complex because they need to include all their own database access code. It is generally best to avoid these Beans unless you have to use them. For example, you would use them when the data store being used is not supported by the EJB container, or the data for the Bean comes from multiple data sources.

The focus in this book is on CMP entity Beans. We will begin by looking at an entity Bean for the compact disc products within the shopping-cart application. If you recall, the `compact_discs` table was created with the following SQL:

```
create table compact_discs (id int primary key,
                            title varchar (50),
                            artist varchar(30),
                            tracks int,price double);
```

The entity Bean will require the home and remote interfaces and the implementation class.

> **Note**
> All the listings shown are for EJB 2.0, which is a part of the J2EE 1.3 standard. There is a version of all these listings on the book Web site (`www.samspublishing.com`).

The Entity Bean Remote Interface

First, you'll see the remote interface class. The remote interface can be seen in Listing 15.2.

Listing 15.2 `CompactDisc.java`

```
package com.conygre.cd;

public interface CompactDisc extends javax.ejb.EJBObject {
  Integer getId() throws java.rmi.RemoteException;
  String getTitle() throws java.rmi.RemoteException;
  void setTitle(String t) throws java.rmi.RemoteException;
  String getArtist() throws java.rmi.RemoteException;
  void setArtist(String a) throws java.rmi.RemoteException;
  double getPrice() throws java.rmi.RemoteException;
  void setPrice(double p) throws java.rmi.RemoteException;
  int getTracks() throws java.rmi.RemoteException;
  void setTracks(int i) throws java.rmi.RemoteException;
}
```

This remote interface contains the functional methods of the EJB that are to be available to clients. Notice the following about the remote interface:

- It extends `javax.ejb.EJBObject`.
- Every method throws a `java.rmi.RemoteException`.

The reason for the remote exceptions is that, if you recall, EJBs are accessed remotely over RMI/IIOP. The `EJBObject` interface is extended because this contains various methods that the auto-generated implementation class created by the container will have (see Figure 15.4 to remind you of the class diagram). The methods defined will all get and set the various properties of the compact disc entries in the database when implemented.

The Entity Bean Home Interface

The home interface contains the methods for creating and finding the EJBs. Listing 15.3 contains the home interface for the compact disc EJB.

Listing 15.3 `CompactDiscHome.java`

```
package com.conygre.cd;
import java.util.Collection;

public interface CompactDiscHome extends javax.ejb.EJBHome {
  // create method
  CompactDisc create(Integer id, String title, String artist,
                     double price, int tracks)
                   throws java.rmi.RemoteException, javax.ejb.CreateException;
  // finder methods
  CompactDisc findByPrimaryKey(Integer i)
                  throws java.rmi.RemoteException, javax.ejb.FinderException;
  Collection findAll()
                  throws java.rmi.RemoteException, javax.ejb.FinderException;
  Collection findByArtist(String art)
                 throws java.rmi.RemoteException, javax.ejb.FinderException;
  CompactDisc findByTitle(String title)
                throws java.rmi.RemoteException, javax.ejb.FinderException;
}
```

The home interface contains *create* methods and a number of what are referred to as *finder* methods, as well as *remove* methods:

- Create methods—These are used by the container to create instances of the entity Bean. You can have more than one create method, or if you do not want to allow users to create data, you cannot have any create methods. A vital point to note here is this: Because entity Beans represent the data, when an entity Bean is created, a new row in the database is also created. Similarly, when an entity Bean is destroyed, the entry is removed from the database.

  The create methods all throw `RemoteExceptions`, and they also throw `javax.ejb.CreateExceptions`. The `CreateException` is thrown when an entity Bean cannot be created using the `create()` method selected.

Caution

It is vital to appreciate what create methods do. You have to be very careful how you treat these entity Beans because creating them will directly affect your data source by creating new entries!

- Finder methods—If you consider the entity Beans as your data, you need to be able to search your data and locate specific entries. In Chapter 14, you saw how to do this using `sql:query` tags in your JSP pages. With EJB, you do not need to use these tags, as the finder methods return the data from the database as entity Beans. If you look again at Listing 15.3, you will see that the finder methods defined are as follows:

```
CompactDisc findByPrimaryKey(Integer i)
Collection findAll()
Collection findByArtist(String art)
CompactDisc findByTitle(String title)
```

These methods are the equivalent of SQL queries on the database. We'll see how they become SQL queries as we look at the deployment process.

Note

Since EJB 2.0, you can also have what are known as SELECT methods. These are very similar to finder methods, except that they are only available within the EJB class itself.

- Remove methods—Although we have not implemented any remove methods, they are used to remove entity Beans and, therefore, entries in the database.

In Listing 15.3, you can see that all the methods throw `RemoteExceptions` as you saw in the remote interface. What is different is the finder methods because these also throw `javax.ejb.FinderExceptions`. The `FinderException` is thrown when a find method fails.

The Entity Bean Implementation

You have seen both the home and the remote interface, so attention now turns to the implementation class for the entity Bean. There may be some things that surprise you in this Listing 15.4.

Listing 15.4 `CompactDiscBean.java`

```
package com.conygre.cd;
import javax.ejb.*;
import java.util.*;
import java.rmi.RemoteException;

public abstract class CompactDiscBean implements EntityBean {

  public Integer ejbCreate (Integer id, String title, String artist,
                            double price, int tracks)
                                    throws CreateException {
    setId(id);
    setTitle(title);
    setArtist(artist);
    setPrice(price);
    setTracks(tracks);
    return null;
  }
```

Listing 15.4 **Continued**

```
  public void ejbPostCreate (Integer id, String title,
                             String artist, double price, int tracks)
  {} // does nothing in this case, but is required


  // abstract get and sets from remote interface
  public abstract void setId(Integer id);
  public abstract Integer getId();
  public abstract String getTitle();
  public abstract void setTitle(String s);
  public abstract String getArtist();
  public abstract void setArtist(String s);
  public abstract void setPrice(double d);
  public abstract double getPrice();
  public abstract int getTracks();
  public abstract void setTracks(int t);

  // empty methods, in a BMP class or a more complex CMP class,
  // these would implement functionality
  public void setEntityContext (EntityContext pEntityContext)
            throws EJBException, RemoteException { }
  public void unsetEntityContext () throws EJBException, RemoteException { }
  public void ejbRemove () throws EJBException  { }
  public void ejbActivate () throws EJBException, RemoteException { }
  public void ejbPassivate () throws EJBException, RemoteException { }
  public void ejbLoad () throws EJBException, RemoteException { }
  public void ejbStore () throws EJBException, RemoteException {  }
}
```

There are a number of things in this listing that require explanation. For example, the implementation class does not implement the home and remote interface within its class declaration! I am sure that when you first learned Java, from a book or a course, you were taught when you learned about interfaces that implementation classes needed to implement the appropriate interfaces. The clue to why you do not implement the interfaces in this class is in Figure 15.5. Notice that your implementation class is wrapped in a class of type `EJBObject`. This wrapper class is dynamically generated by the container, and it is *this* class that implements the remote interface. A container-generated `EJBHome` object then implements the home interface. Here is the class declaration for the `EJBObject` created by the ATG Dynamo Application Server. Remember, you never write this, and you would normally never see it:

```
public class _CompactDisc_Impl  extends atg.dejb.RemoteImpl
                    implements com.conygre.cd.CompactDisc,
                               com.conygre.cd._CompactDisc_WCC
```

The RemoteImpl class here is an ATG Dynamo implementation of EJBObject.

Another thing that you might find surprising about Listing 15.4 is that there is nothing in here to actually access the database. This is because the container is going to interact with the database for us. If this entity Bean used BMP, you would see JDBC code in many of the methods.

We will now unpack this implementation Bean somewhat and look at what is present and why.

First, note the class declaration. It is an abstract class:

```
public abstract class CompactDiscBean implements EntityBean
```

This class will be extended by a container-generated class, which will implement the various abstract methods. If you look further down the listing, the abstract methods are the methods that were defined in your remote interface. Two of them are shown here:

```
public abstract String getTitle();
public abstract void setTitle(String s);
```

There are no declared properties in the implementation class. Instead, the get/set methods are provided, but in an abstract form. This frees the container to manage and store the actual properties how it wants in the container-generated class that will extend your implementation.

As well as the abstract get/set methods, there are methods used to create new instances. These are the create() methods, and they are next in Listing 15.4. They are shown here:

```
public Integer ejbCreate (Integer id, String title, String artist,
                          double price, int tracks)
                                   throws CreateException {
  setId(id);
  setTitle(title);
  setArtist(artist);
  setPrice(price);
  setTracks(tracks);
  return null;
  }

  public void ejbPostCreate (Integer id, String title,
                             String artist, double price, int tracks)
  {} // does nothing in this case, but is required
```

The ejbCreate() method is defined in the home interface. This method is called when an entity Bean of this type is created. This will set all the properties, and the container will then populate the database with the data for you. The return type is always the primary key. In a container-managed Bean such as this, you only need to return null, but in a BMP Bean, you would need to create a primary key object and return it because it will be needed later to persist the data. The ejbPostCreate() method is invoked immediately after the `create()` method. It is here because you do not have a reference to the newly created object until after `ejbCreate()` returns, and if you wanted to do something with it as soon as it was created, you would need to do it from within the `ejbPostCreate()` method. The `ejbPostCreate()` method has to be present, but it rarely contains anything. It always has the `void` return type and has the same arguments as `ejbCreate()`.

Last, in Listing 15.4 is a raft of empty methods. This also shows the exceptions that need to be thrown by each of these methods:

```
public void setEntityContext (EntityContext pEntityContext)
          throws EJBException, RemoteException { }
public void unsetEntityContext () throws EJBException, RemoteException { }
public void ejbRemove () throws EJBException  { }
public void ejbActivate () throws EJBException, RemoteException { }

public void ejbPassivate () throws EJBException, RemoteException { }
public void ejbLoad () throws EJBException, RemoteException { }
public void ejbStore () throws EJBException, RemoteException {  }
```

Many of the methods declared in the entity Bean are sometimes referred to as the *lifecycle methods*, and they are there to manage the lifecycle of the entity Bean instances. These methods, and also the create methods you have seen are regarded as the lifecycle methods. The lifecycle of an entity Bean will be discussed next.

The Entity Bean Lifecycle

Entity Bean instances exist within a container in one of two possible states: a *pooled* state or a *ready* state. Pooled entity Beans are not tied to a specific item of data from the data store, but are available. The Beans become ready when they are associated with an `EJBObject`. If you recall, this is the type that is created by the container. The state of an entity Bean is shown in Figure 15.7. The benefits of using this pool are performance related. When data is extracted from the data source, an object from the pool can be used to hold it, rather than having to create, and then garbage collect one each time.

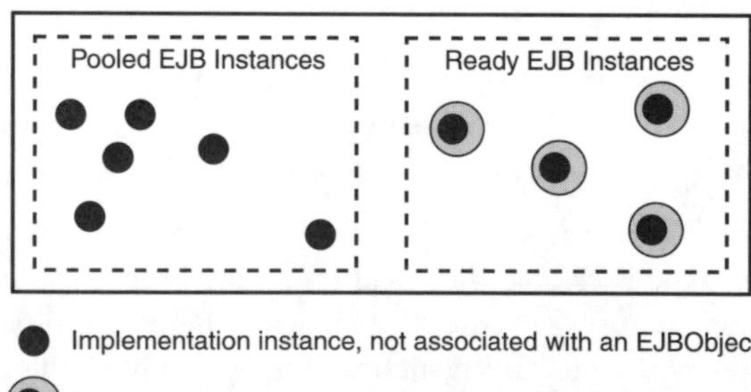

Figure 15.7 The state of an entity Bean.

So what does this mean for the lifecycle of an entity Bean? The lifecycle methods from Listing 15.4 are used when the Beans go from one state to the other. Figure 15.8 summarizes the entity Bean lifecycle, and shows when the different methods are invoked.

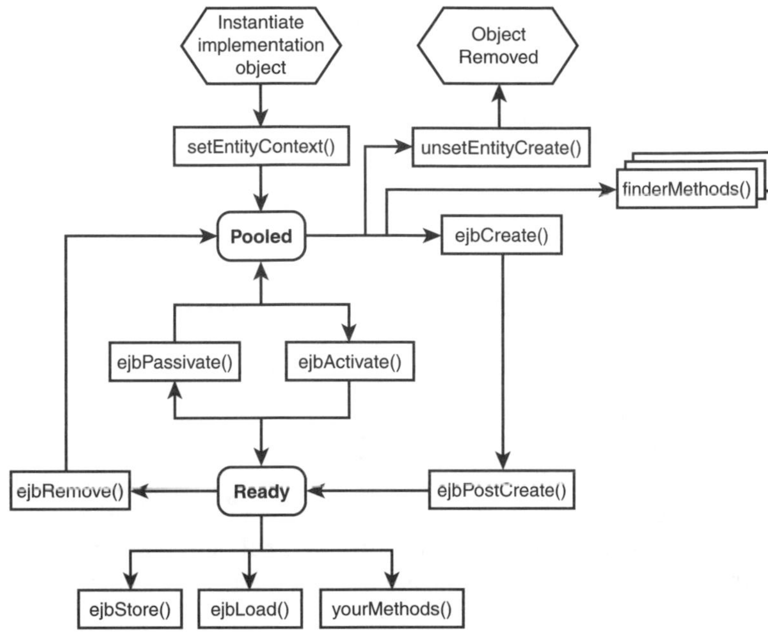

Figure 15.8 The lifecycle of an entity Bean.

The flow chart in Figure 15.8 shows how the various lifecycle methods are involved in the lifecycle of an entity Bean. To get a Bean from the pooled state to the ready state, for example, the `passivate` and `activate` methods are used. The roles of the other methods are listed in Table 15.2.

Table 15.2 **The EJB Lifecycle Methods**

Method	Role
ejbLoad()	This method is invoked by the container to synchronize the data in the Bean with the data in the underlying data source.
ejbStore()	This method causes the data in the Bean to be written to the underlying data store.
ejbPassivate()	Causes the Bean to go from the ready state to the pooled state.
ejbActivate()	Causes the Bean to go from the pooled state to the ready state.

Table 15.2 **Continued**

Method	Role
setEntityContext()	This method can be used to set an instance variable to point to the EntityContext. This is a reference to the EJB container. This method is called after the Bean is first created.
unsetEntityContext()	This method unsets the EntityContext set in the previous method. This is invoked when the Bean is to be destroyed.
ejbRemove()	This method is invoked immediately before an EJB object is removed. So, if you called remove on an entity Bean, this method would be invoked immediately before the record was removed from the data source by the container.

In CMP entity Beans, these methods are frequently left empty, as the container is doing all the hard work of managing all this for us. In BMP, however, these methods can become quite important.

Passivation and Activation

To help the container manage its resources effectively, these Beans can be passivated, which basically means that they can be serialized to disk if the container wants to conserve resources. When required the Bean can be *activated* so that it can be used again. This means that it is deserialized back to an object again. If there are certain things that need to happen just before passivation or just after activation, these can go into the `ejbPassivate()` and `ejbActivate()` methods, respectively.

Deploying an Entity Bean

If you recall from Chapter 1, when the concept of J2EE application development was introduced, you were introduced to deployment descriptors. Particular attention was paid to the familiar `web.xml` for Web applications. For EJBs, there is an additional deployment descriptor, `ejb-jar.xml`. This deployment descriptor is part of the J2EE specification. The deployment descriptor describes to the container how the entity Bean is to be handled.

When deploying however, there are some application server–dependent deployment descriptors as well. For our example, we'll use WebLogic 7 from BEA. An evaluation copy can be readily downloaded from `www.bea.com`. We selected this server for two main reasons:

- BEA WebLogic is one of the most popular application servers in use on the market today.
- WebLogic 7 has full support for EJB 2.0 which we need for this example.

There is no reason why you cannot deploy this application using an alternative application server; you will simply need to check the documentation for the vendor-specific aspects to deployment.

Listing 15.5 is the `ejb-jar.xml` deployment descriptor for the entity Bean used in the example for BEA WebLogic. This deployment descriptor would be the same, regardless of application server that supports J2EE 1.3 you choose to use. Note that in the sample application there is additional content in this file because it also contains references to the other EJBs discussed later in the chapter. The file `ejb-jarEntityOnly.xml` contains exactly what is shown in Listing 15.5.

Listing 15.5 `ejb-jar.xml`

```
<?xml version="1.0"?>
<!DOCTYPE ejb-jar PUBLIC
"-//Sun Microsystems, Inc.//DTD Enterprise JavaBeans 2.0//EN"
"http://java.sun.com/dtd/ejb-jar_2_0.dtd">
<ejb-jar>
  <enterprise-beans>
    <entity>
      <ejb-name>CompactDiscBean</ejb-name>
      <home>com.conygre.cd.CompactDiscHome</home>
      <remote>com.conygre.cd.CompactDisc</remote>
      <ejb-class>com.conygre.cd.CompactDiscBean</ejb-class>
      <persistence-type>Container</persistence-type>
      <prim-key-class>java.lang.Integer</prim-key-class>
      <reentrant>False</reentrant>
      <cmp-version>2.x</cmp-version>
      <abstract-schema-name>CompactDiscBean</abstract-schema-name>
      <cmp-field>
        <field-name>id</field-name>
      </cmp-field>
      <cmp-field>
        <field-name>price</field-name>
      </cmp-field>
      <cmp-field>
        <field-name>artist</field-name>
      </cmp-field>
      <cmp-field>
        <field-name>title</field-name>
      </cmp-field>
      <cmp-field>
        <field-name>tracks</field-name>
      </cmp-field>

      <primkey-field>id</primkey-field>

      <query>
        <query-method>
          <method-name>findAll</method-name>
          <method-params/>
```

Listing 15.5 **Continued**

```
        </query-method>
        <ejb-ql><![CDATA[SELECT OBJECT(a) FROM CompactDiscBean AS a]]></ejb-ql>
      </query>

      <query>
        <query-method>
          <method-name>findByTitle</method-name>
          <method-params>
            <method-param>java.lang.String</method-param>
          </method-params>
        </query-method>
        <ejb-ql>
     <![CDATA[SELECT OBJECT(a) FROM CompactDiscBean AS a WHERE a.title = ?1]]>
        </ejb-ql>
      </query>

      <query>
        <query-method>
          <method-name>findByArtist</method-name>
          <method-params>
            <method-param>java.lang.String</method-param>
          </method-params>
        </query-method>
        <ejb-ql>
     <![CDATA[SELECT OBJECT(a) FROM CompactDiscBean AS a WHERE a.artist = ?1]]>
        </ejb-ql>
      </query>
    </entity>
  </enterprise-beans>
  <assembly-descriptor>
    <container-transaction>
      <method>
        <ejb-name>CompactDiscBean</ejb-name>
        <method-name>*</method-name>
      </method>
      <trans-attribute>Required</trans-attribute>
    </container-transaction>
  </assembly-descriptor>
</ejb-jar>
```

Although it might appear a little daunting when you see the size of it, it is not as complex as you might think. Figure 15.9 shows a visual view of the XML, as shown by XML Spy 4.3. The diagram helps to show the structure of the document, and you might want to refer to this diagram as the roles of the various parts of the deployment descriptor are explained.

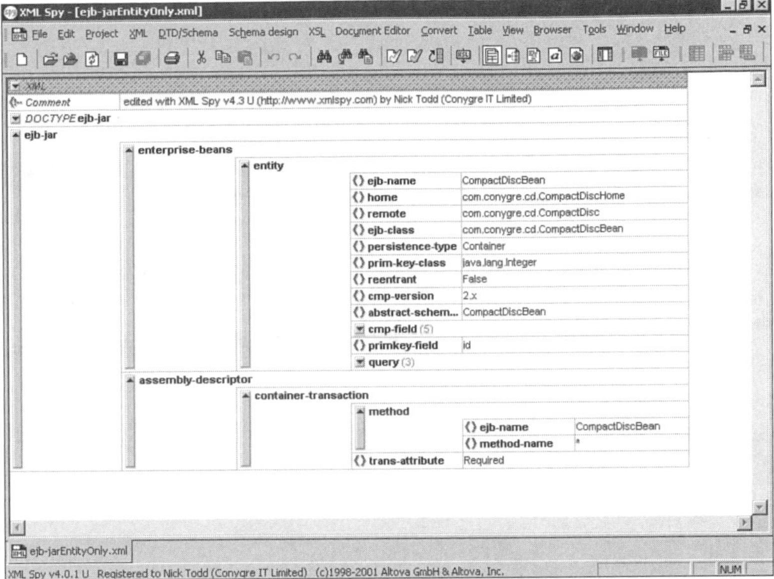

Figure 15.9 Structure of `ejb-jar.xml` as shown in XML Spy 4.3.

The deployment descriptor shown is in two discrete sections. One contains the EJBs themselves (enterprise-beans), and the other describes how transactions within the Beans are supposed to be handled (application-descriptor). We will look at the Bean definition first.

Describing the Entity Bean in the Deployment Descriptor

The Bean is defined using the `<entity>` element, and there will be one for each entity Bean that is deployed. The implementation class, and the two interfaces are described, and then the `<persistence-type>`. This is a CMP entity Bean so the value of this element is `Container`:

```
<entity>
  <ejb-name>CompactDiscBean</ejb-name>
  <home>com.conygre.cd.CompactDiscHome</home>
  <remote>com.conygre.cd.CompactDisc</remote>
  <ejb-class>com.conygre.cd.CompactDiscBean</ejb-class>
  <persistence-type>Container</persistence-type>
  <prim-key-class>java.lang.Integer</prim-key-class>
  <reentrant>False</reentrant>
  <cmp-version>2.x</cmp-version>
  <abstract-schema-name>CompactDiscBean</abstract-schema-name>
  . . .
</entity>
```

For the `<persistence-type>`, the alternative value is `Bean` for BMP entity Beans. No other value is valid. The primary key class is also defined using the `<prim-key-class>` element.

> **Note**
>
> When writing these deployment descriptors, class names must always be fully qualified—even the classes in `java.lang` such as `java.lang.String` or `java.lang.Integer`.

The reentrant should always be false, and the version is set to 2.x in our case. Lastly, we set what is called the abstract schema name. In EJB 2.0, relationships between entity Beans can be defined within the deployment descriptor, and this is the name of the schema. Our example does not require relationships because none are required for our application; however, the schema name will be used when we define the finder methods.

The container-managed fields are then defined using elements of the following construct:

```
<cmp-field>
  <field-name>id</field-name>
</cmp-field>
```

The mapping of these field names to the data source is then completed using an additional deployment descriptor that is application server vendor specific. We'll see this later. We'll now turn our attention to the finder methods.

If you recall, so far, the finder methods have had nothing but a method signature defined. The finder methods are defined here within the deployment descriptor. Remember, entity Beans basically represent your data, and this is coming from a database. If you were doing a query on the database, you would use SQL as you saw in Chapter 14. Because the container does all the database interaction when using CMP, you somehow need to inform the container what kind of query to execute. In EJB 1.1, this was done in a vendor-specific way. In EJB 2.0, there is a new query language called EJB QL. It is very similar to SQL.

Each finder method is defined within the deployment descriptor with the following format:

```
<query>
  <query-method>
    <method-name>findByTitle</method-name>
    <method-params>
      <method-param>java.lang.String</method-param>
    </method-params>
  </query-method>
  <ejb-ql>
<![CDATA[SELECT OBJECT(a) FROM CompactDiscBean AS a WHERE a.title = ?1]]>
  </ejb-ql>
</query>
```

Each finder method is defined within the XML using a `<query>` element. This element then consists of a `<query-method>` and an `<ejb-ql>` element. The `<query-method>` contains the name of the method from the home interface along with any parameters, and the `<ejb-ql>` element contains the query that the finder method corresponds to.

This query language does appear a little cryptic, but essentially the queries can contain three types of clause: `SELECT`, `WHERE`, and `FROM`. The `OBJECT` is the instance, and `(a)` is a variable declared that can be used to refer to the instance. The `?1` syntax should look familiar as it refers to the first parameter. It is also used in JDBC for prepared statements. The previous query states the following:

> Select all the `CompactDiscBean` instances where the title of the Bean is the value of the String parameter passed in.

A detailed description of EJB QL can be found as a part of the specifications for EJB2.0, at `http://jcp.org/aboutJava/communityprocess/final/jsr019/index.html`.

The second part of the deployment descriptor is the `<assembly-descriptor>`. This informs the container how transactions should be managed for the various methods involved. In the example we have, all the methods are set to `require` a transaction. The use of the `*` denotes all methods:

```
<assembly-descriptor>
  <container-transaction>
    <method>
      <ejb-name>CompactDiscBean</ejb-name>
      <method-name>*</method-name>
    </method>
    <trans-attribute>Required</trans-attribute>
  </container-transaction>
</assembly-descriptor>
```

> **Note**
>
> The value of the `trans-attribute` has to be one of five possible values denoting what is called the *transaction demarcation* mode. The modes determine whether a transaction is required, not required, can be a part of another transaction, and so on.

The Deployment Folder Structure

We have seen a number of classes, interfaces, and now, a deployment descriptor, but where do we put all these files?

There is a standard layout that J2EE applications often adhere to, just as we have seen for Web applications. An example J2EE folder structure is shown in Figure 15.10.

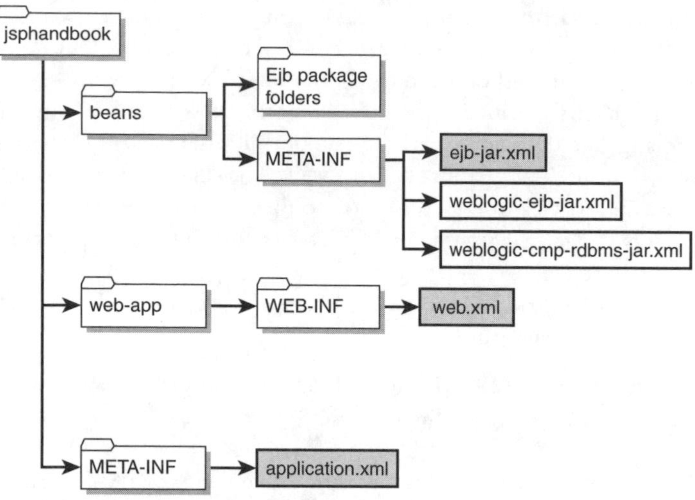

Figure 15.10 J2EE application folder structure.

The folder structure shown in Figure 15.10 is for a complete J2EE application. The top-level folder has been called `jsphandbook`. This will be the name of our application. The `beans` folder contains all the EJB deployment information and the EJB classes. The `web-app` folder will contain all the Web application structure, and the `META-INF` folder will contain another deployment descriptor, `application.xml`, which will be discussed later. For now, you only need to look at the top half of Figure 15.10, the folder structure underneath the `beans` folder.

> **Note**
>
> The names of the folders that do not end in the three letters *INF* can be called anything you want. Different server vendors tend to use different names, but it doesn't really matter; just avoid spaces.

Deployment in WebLogic

We now need to look at the vendor-specific deployment information. As stated earlier, we will be using BEA WebLogic 7. For WebLogic, we'll require two additional deployment descriptors, and we will need to configure WebLogic to work with our MySQL database because this contains the `compact_discs` table.

The two deployment descriptors for WebLogic are shown in Listing 15.6.

Listing 15.6 `weblogic-ejb-jar.xml`

```
<?xml version="1.0"?>
<!DOCTYPE weblogic-ejb-jar PUBLIC
        "-//BEA Systems, Inc.//DTD WebLogic 7.0.0 EJB//EN"
        "http://www.bea.com/servers/wls700/dtd/weblogic-ejb-jar.dtd">
<weblogic-ejb-jar>
  <weblogic-enterprise-bean>
    <ejb-name>CompactDiscBean</ejb-name>
    <entity-descriptor>
      <persistence>
        <persistence-use>
           <type-identifier>WebLogic_CMP_RDBMS</type-identifier>
           <type-version>6.0</type-version>
           <type-storage>META-INF/weblogic-cmp-rdbms-jar.xml</type-storage>
         </persistence-use>
      </persistence>
    </entity-descriptor>
  <jndi-name>CompactDiscHome</jndi-name>
  </weblogic-enterprise-bean>
</weblogic-ejb-jar>
```

This deployment descriptor describes the entity Bean to WebLogic. It informs WebLogic about the kind of persistence being used, and also has a `<type-storage>` element. This points to the other WebLogic-specific deployment descriptor, and this contains the mappings between the CMP fields of the Bean, and the actual datasource. This is shown in Listing 15.7.

Listing 15.7 `weblogic-cmp-rdbms-jar.xml`

```
<!DOCTYPE weblogic-rdbms-jar PUBLIC
'-//BEA Systems, Inc.//DTD WebLogic 7.0.0 EJB RDBMS Persistence//EN'
'http://www.bea.com/servers/wls700/dtd/weblogic-rdbms20-persistence-700.dtd'>
<weblogic-rdbms-jar>
  <weblogic-rdbms-bean>
    <ejb-name>CompactDiscBean</ejb-name>
    <data-source-name>jdbc/MySQL</data-source-name>
    <table-map>
      <table-name>Compact_Discs</table-name>
      <field-map>
        <cmp-field>id</cmp-field>
        <dbms-column>id</dbms-column>
      </field-map>
      <field-map>
         <cmp-field>price</cmp-field>
         <dbms-column>price</dbms-column>
      </field-map>
```

Listing 15.7 **Continued**

```
      <field-map>
         <cmp-field>tracks</cmp-field>
         <dbms-column>tracks</dbms-column>
      </field-map>
      <field-map>
        <cmp-field>title</cmp-field>
        <dbms-column>title</dbms-column>
      </field-map>
      <field-map>
        <cmp-field>artist</cmp-field>
        <dbms-column>artist</dbms-column>
      </field-map>
    </table-map>
  </weblogic-rdbms-bean>
  <create-default-dbms-tables>True</create-default-dbms-tables>
</weblogic-rdbms-jar>
```

This deployment descriptor maps all the entity Bean fields to individual columns in the database. In Chapter 14, we demonstrated how to set the data source up in WebLogic 7. In fact, Listing 15.7 relates directly to the data source that we described how to set up in Chapter 14.

As you can probably appreciate, the building and deployment of EJBs can be a very tedious process, and increasingly, tools exist to aid you in their completion. Tools such as JBuilder Enterprise Edition or IBM Visual Age for Java both have utilities to help in the creation of these deployment files. Even some application server vendors themselves provide visual tools to help you to create these XML files.

Deploying the EJBs with the Web Application

Listing 15.1 demonstrated how a JavaServer Page can be used to interact with an EJB, but we have not seen how to deploy a complete J2EE application with both the EJBs and the JSPs together. Revisit Figure 15.10, and remind yourself how a J2EE application fits together. You have seen how a Web application is deployed with the `web.xml` deployment descriptor. You have seen how an EJB is built and then deployed with the `ejb-jar.xml` deployment descriptor. You have also seen how the EJBs are deployed in WebLogic using the two WebLogic-specific deployment descriptors. To deploy them together as a J2EE application, the `web.xml` file is modified so that it knows about the EJBs, and one more deployment descriptor is created, `application.xml`.

The `web.xml` deployment descriptor for our J2EE application is shown in Listing 15.8. If you look at the solution, you will also see additional entries. Don't worry about those for now because they are discussed later.

Listing 15.8 `web.xml`

```
<?xml version="1.0"?>
<!DOCTYPE web-app PUBLIC
"-//Sun Microsystems, Inc.//DTD Web Application 2.2//EN"
"http://java.sun.com/j2ee/dtds/web-app_2_2.dtd">
<web-app>
  <welcome-file-list>
    <welcome-file>ejbClient.jsp</welcome-file>
  </welcome-file-list>
  <ejb-ref>
    <ejb-ref-name>ejb/CompactDisc</ejb-ref-name>
    <ejb-ref-type>Entity</ejb-ref-type>
    <home>com.conygre.cd.CompactDiscHome</home>
    <remote>com.conygre.cd.CompactDisc</remote>
    <ejb-link>CompactDiscBean</ejb-link>
  </ejb-ref>
</web-app>
```

You can see that the entity Bean is also referred to from `web.xml`. It has the `<ejb-ref>` element, which defines the EJB that is being used from our Web application. Most of it is self explanatory, but the `<ejb-ref-name>` and the `<ejb-link>` elements require some explanation. The `<ejb-ref-name>` element declares the JNDI name used by the JSP to locate the EJB, which it does if you look at the JSP line that locates the EJB, repeated here:

```
Object obj = context.lookup("java:comp/env/ejb/CompactDisc");
```

EJB lookups are always prefixed `java:comp/env/`. It is the last part of the lookup name that is determined by the `<ejb-ref-name>` element. The `<ejb-link>` element defines the name of the EJB that is being referred to, as defined in the `ejb-jar.xml` deployment descriptor. This `<ejb-link>` element is not mandatory however.

> **Note**
>
> If you are wondering how you can remember what all these elements are for in the various deployment descriptors, you can always visit their respective DTD files (XML schemas in J2EE1.4), which have very helpful comments regarding the uses of the various elements and attributes.

You can see where `application.xml` goes from Figure 15.10, and Listing 15.9 shows what it would look like for our J2EE application.

Listing 15.9 `application.xml`

```
<?xml version="1.0"?>
<!DOCTYPE application PUBLIC
'-//Sun Microsystems, Inc.//DTD J2EE Application 1.3//EN'
'http://java.sun.com/dtd/application_1_3.dtd'>
```

Listing 15.9 **Continued**

```
<application>
  <display-name>Compact Discs</display-name>
  <module>
    <ejb>beans</ejb>
  </module>
  <module>
    <web>
      <web-uri>web-app</web-uri>
      <context-root>jsphandbook</context-root>
    </web>
  </module>
</application>
```

As you can see, it is nowhere near as complex as the other deployment descriptors. It describes each part of the application as a module, and specifies the folder in which it lives. So the Web application is in a folder called `web-app`, since the `<web-uri>` element has that value. The EJBs are in a folder called `beans`, and this is specified by the `<ejb>` element. Note that both the `<web-uri>` element and the `<ejb>` element could also refer to war files or jar files respectively. The `<context-root>` specifies the root folder of the application when visited through a Web interface, so with this value of `jsphandbook`, the URL for the JSP in Listing 15.1 in WebLogic would be

```
http://<servername>:7001/jsphandbook/ejbClient.jsp
```

We are almost there. To see the application working in WebLogic, you will need to put all the listings together in the directory structure shown in Figure 15.10. I suggest that you put it directly under your `<bea-install>` directory for now, which is typically something such as `c:\bea`. Don't forget you can download the application from the book Web site (`www.samspublishing.com`) to save some typing.

Running the J2EE Application

First, we will need to set up the connection pool and data source in WebLogic 7 for our application. This process is as follows.

To set up WebLogic, you will need to complete the following steps:

1. Install WebLogic 7 from `www.bea.com`. A typical install will be sufficient because this will include a very comprehensive set of examples. Detailed instructions for installation for your platform will be available on the BEA Web site. If you are using a Windows platform, it is a straightforward executable.

> **Note**
>
> If you have never used WebLogic before, it is well worth installing the examples, which cover all sorts of aspects of the WebLogic server and J2EE. Basic installation instructions can also be found in Appendix I, "Installing MySQL and WebLogic Server."

2. Ensure that the .jar file containing the JDBC driver for MySQL is in the classpath for your machine. See the section called "Setting Up a JDBC Driver" in Appendix I, "Installing MySQL and WebLogic Server," for more information.
3. Start the WebLogic server with the examples. This can be done from the Start menu on Windows:

```
Start / Programs / BEA WebLogic Platform 7.x /
WebLogic Server 7 / Server Tour and Examples / Launch Examples Server
```

4. This should result in the server starting in a console window, and then a browser showing you the home page for the WebLogic examples. This can be seen in Figure 15.11. From this page, launch the Administration Console via the hyperlink. This will open a page asking for a username and password (precompleted with weblogic/weblogic). Submit this form. If the browser does not start for whatever reason, you can launch one separately and navigate to the following URL: http://<*servername*>:7001/examplesWebApp/index.jsp. You will need to put your server name in the placeholder. The value localhost should suffice if the browser is running on the same machine as WebLogic.

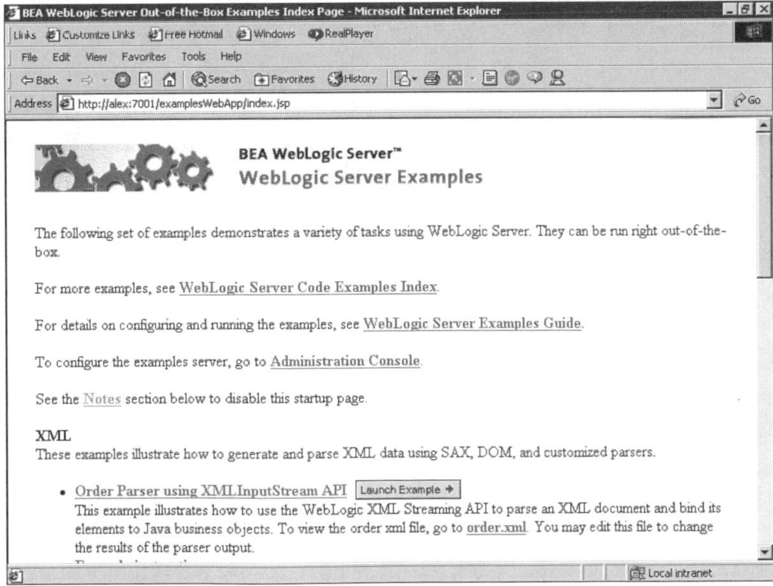

Figure 15.11 WebLogic examples server welcome page.

5. You should now be presented with the Administration Console for WebLogic, as shown in Figure 15.12. From here, select Connection Pools from the main screen, which is under the heading Services Configurations. It has been highlighted in Figure 15.12.

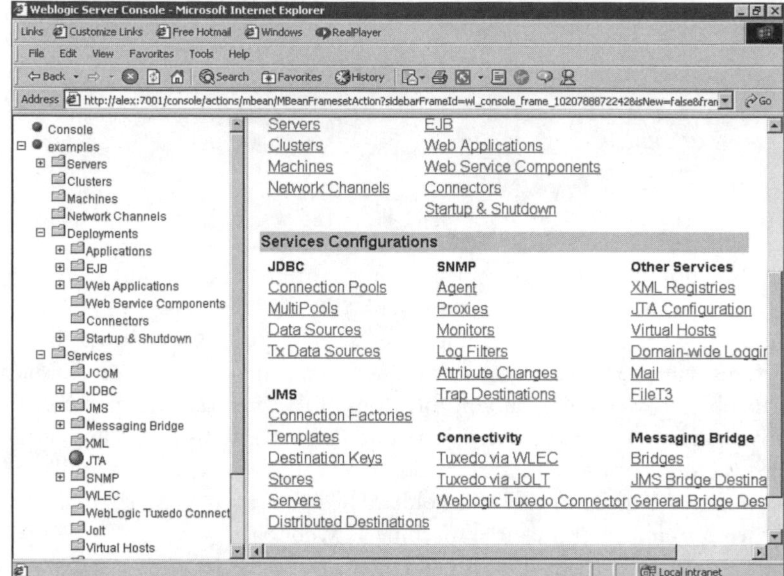

Figure 15.12 WebLogic 7 administration console.

6. Now you are in a position to create your own connection pool for the MySQL database. Select the option to Configure a New JDBC Connection Pool and a screen as shown in Figure 15.13 appears. The URL, driver, and username information all have to be completed on this page. The values are:

```
URL: jdbc:mysql://localhost:3306/jsphandbook
Driver Classname: com.mysql.jdbc.Driver
Properties: user=root
```

7. After the connection pool is set up, click the Targets tab, as shown in Figure 15.13, and select the `examplesServer` from the available list and move it over to the chosen server. This will make your connection pool available to the examples server. If any errors occur at this point, double-check that the MySQL driver classes are in the classpath. Also check that your URL and driver name are completed correctly.

8. You are nearly done! You can now create a DataSource that uses your new connection pool. Go back to the main page, which is shown in Figure 15.12, and select TX DataSources from the menu this time. You can also navigate to this from the left applet–based menu.

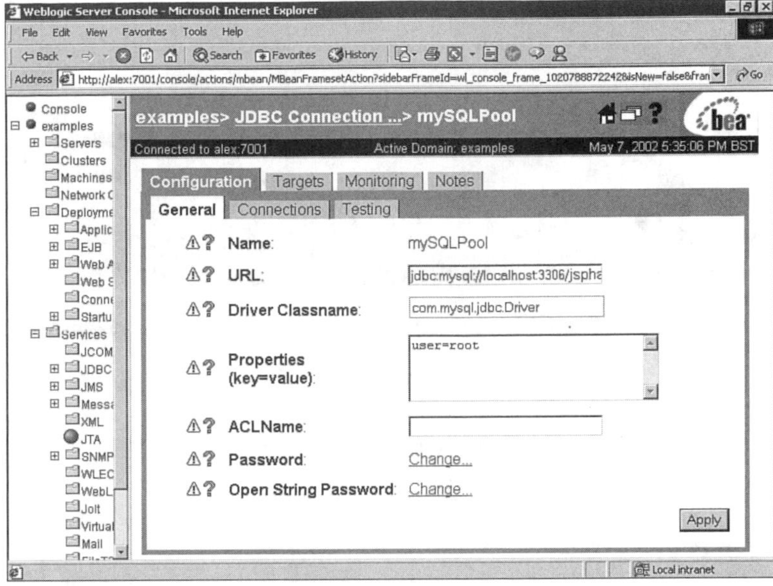

Figure 15.13 Configure a new JDBC connection pool.

> **Note**
>
> TX DataSources are those that have support for distributed transactions. Note that the MySQL driver does not in fact support XA transactions, so the driver 'fakes it'. Some application servers provide a specific DataSource type for these drivers called something like a FakeXADataSource. In WebLogic, you can simply use a normal XADataSource and connection pool.

9. From the page showing the XA DataSources, select that you want to Configure a New XA Datasource. Provide the name **`MySQLDataSource`**.
10. Now set up the data source, as shown in Figure 15.14. It is very important that the name you provide for the connection pool is the same as the name you provided when you created the connection pool.
11. Now click the Targets tab again, as you did for the Connection Pool, and choose the examplesServer. If this gives any errors, it's probably because the names are not completed correctly; most importantly the connection pool name must match.

After you have done that, it is time to run the application in WebLogic (at last)! Within the Administration Console, select the Applications link, which is under the heading Your Deployed Resources, and then choose the option to Configure a New Application.

Assuming that you created your J2EE application in a folder called `jsphandbook`, directly under your `<bea-install>` folder, then navigate to it, and click the [select] button next to it. This can be seen in Figure 15.15.

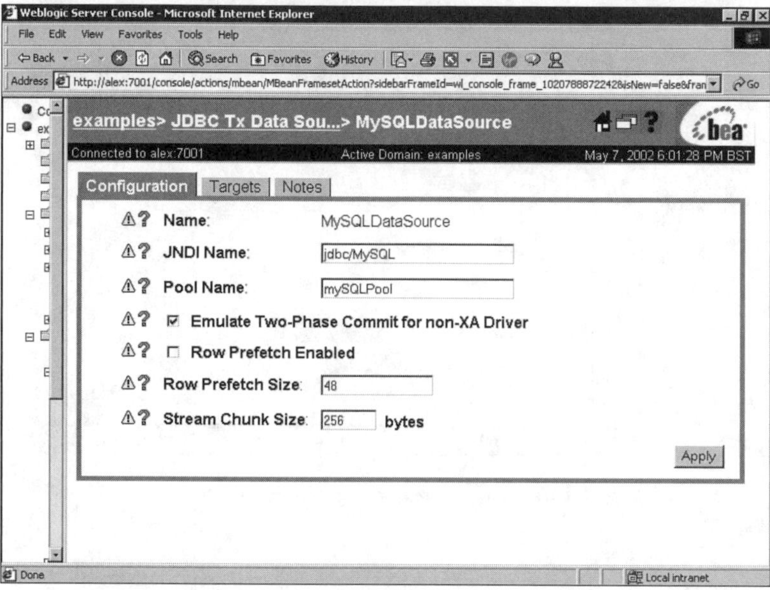

Figure 15.14 Configure a new XA DataSource.

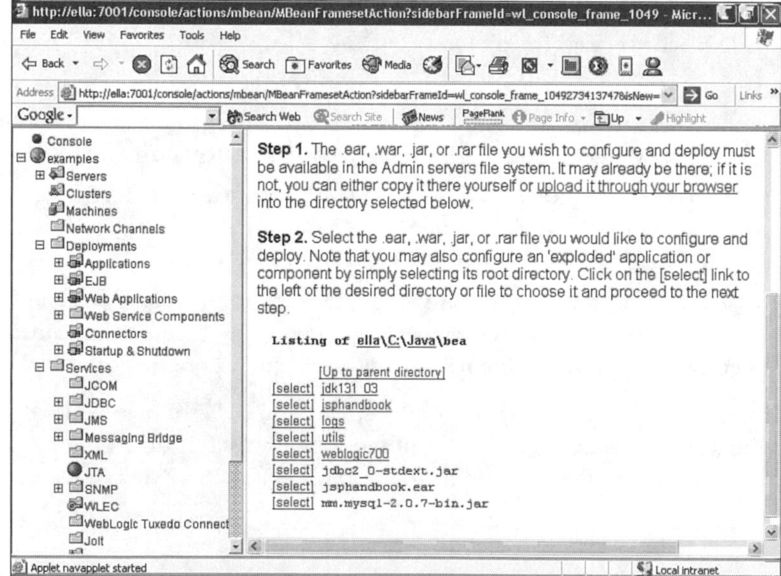

Figure 15.15 Deploying the J2EE application in WebLogic

After you have clicked [select] for the `jsphandbook` folder, you will be able to activate it on your target server, which is the `examplesServer`. Do this now, leaving the name in Step 4 unchanged, and then select the Configure and Deploy button in Step 5. See Figure 15.16.

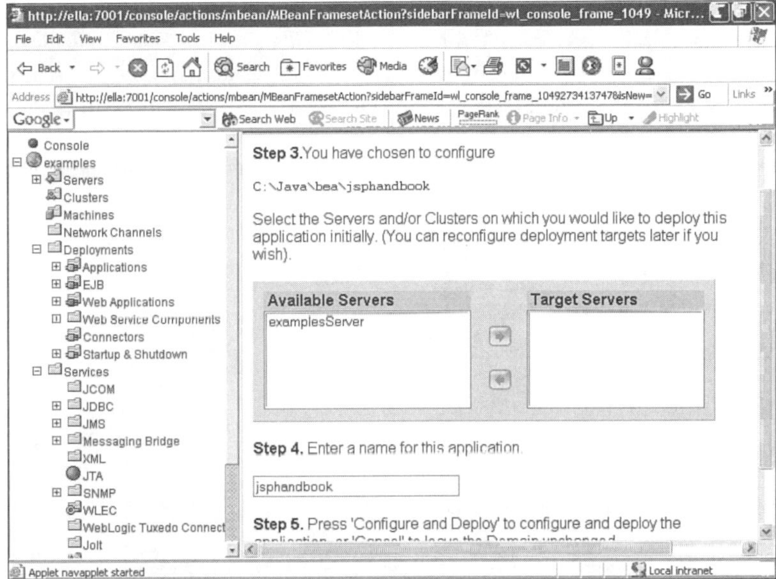

Figure 15.16 Configure and Deploy in WebLogic.

Figure 15.16 is a full screen browser view, and you can see the appropriate settings filled in already. You should now have a screen informing you that the application is deployed. The acid test is to visit the following URL:

```
http://<servername>:7001/jsphandbook/ejbClient.jsp
```

You should see a basic Web page showing all the CDs. If you are having problems, carefully revisit the steps above to ensure that you have done everything correctly. Any stack traces in the WebLogic console provide vital clues as to what you may have done incorrectly.

Session Beans

You have now seen the role of the entity Bean. It represents the business data, and using CMP, you can enable the container to manage the interaction with the data source. There is another key kind of EJB however: the session Bean.

Session Beans represent your business logic. If you look again at Figure 15.2, the clients (in our case, Web applications) normally interact with session Beans rather than entity Beans. One key reason for this is performance. Consider an application such as the shopping site with various tables containing product information such as CDs, DVDs, and books. Each of these could be represented by an entity Bean. The client would, therefore, need to interact with three different entity Bean types and, therefore, there will be three different sets of stubs on the client. A significant number of remote method calls will go to these three different EJB types (unless you are using local interfaces). Using a session Bean can significantly reduce this interaction. The session Bean provides the public interface to the functionality required by clients. The session Beans can then interface with the entity Beans on behalf of the client. The role of the session Bean is shown in Figure 15.17.

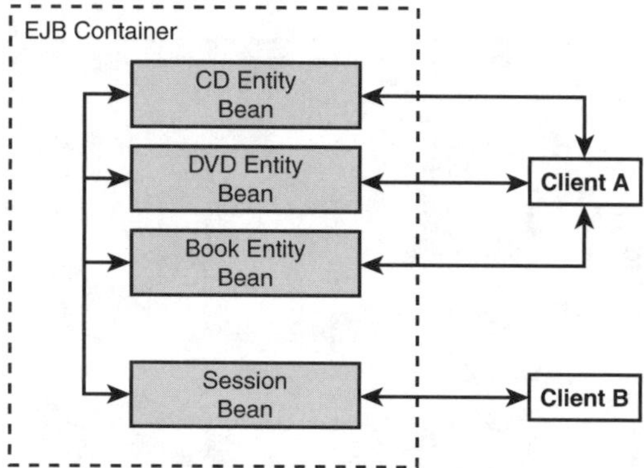

Figure 15.17 The role of the session Bean.

You can see from Figure 15.17 that there are fewer interactions between the client and the EJB container when session Beans are employed. To achieve this, the session Beans will need to populate the entity Bean data into a regular JavaBean class. Instances of this regular Java type can then be passed as parameters from the session Bean to the Web application. This is a very common way of reducing the amount of remote method calls that are required, which is important when the web application and the EJB are residing on different servers and local interfaces cannot be used.

> **Note**
>
> The J2EE Blueprints state that the exception to using session Beans is when the use of session Beans will not reduce the number of stubs in use, and remote calls carried out by the client application.

Session Beans are similar to entity Beans in that they have both the home and remote interface, and the implementation class. There are two kinds of session Bean:

- Stateful session Beans
- Stateless session Beans

The difference is in how the clients interact with the Bean. Imagine you had a session Bean containing the business logic for an online bank—the equivalent of the bank teller. If you had to do every transaction with the same bank teller, you would be dealing with a Stateful session Bean. In other words, each client would have his own session Bean that remembered the client state from one interaction to the next. If however, the bank teller is stateless, it would mean that for each interaction, any session Bean would do, you might never get the same one twice, and even if you did, they wouldn't remember you! They are stateless in other words. Stateless session Beans are the most efficient for performance reasons, as they can be pooled and managed by the container. Stateful session Beans are less efficient because each client will end up with their own instance, and the container has to manage all these instances.

It is also worth pointing out that in some situations, session beans can be used to interact with databases as well as entity beans. For more information on the design issues associated with when to use which type of EJB, take a look at the J2EE Blueprints referred to in the earlier note.

Creating a Session Bean

The session Bean also has the home and remote interface, plus an implementation class. It can also provide local interfaces, although they are not discussed here. We will create a session Bean that will interact with our `CompactDisc` entity Bean, allowing users to interact with the data from the `CompactDisc` entity Bean, but without interacting with the entity Bean directly. The application could easily be extended to include the data from the other tables in the database as well. The session Bean will be implemented as a stateless session Bean, and will be called `CompactDiscAccess`.

The Session Bean Home Interface

The home interface for the session Bean is relatively straightforward, as you can see from Listing 15.10.

Listing 15.10 `CompactDiscAccessHome.java`

```
package com.conygre.cd;

import javax.ejb.*;
import java.rmi.RemoteException;

public interface CompactDiscAccessHome extends EJBHome {
  CompactDiscAccess create() throws RemoteException, CreateException;
}
```

Only a create method is found in here, and it is used by clients to create instances of the session Bean so that it can be used. There is no concept of a finder method in session Beans because they do not represent any data.

The Session Bean Remote Interface

The remote interface contains the business methods of the EJB. This is shown in Listing 15.11.

Listing 15.11 `CompactDiscAccess.java`

```
package com.conygre.cd;

import javax.ejb.*;
import java.util.*;
import java.rmi.RemoteException;

public interface CompactDiscAccess extends EJBObject {
      Collection searchCatalog(String s) throws RemoteException;
      Collection getProducts() throws RemoteException;
      CompactDiscProduct getProductByTitle(String title) throws RemoteException;
      CompactDiscProduct getProductById(int n) throws RemoteException;
      Collection getProductByArtist (String s) throws RemoteException;
}
```

The business methods are all there to interact with products. As it stands, they are all compact discs, but it could be extended to include the other data types. If you look carefully, you will notice that the methods return either collections, or a type you have not yet seen, the `CompactDiscProduct`. This is our regular JavaBean type, which instances will be used to contain the data from the entity Bean, so they can be passed across to the Web application as serialized objects, thus reducing the remote method calling overhead. `CompactDiscProduct` can be seen in Listing 15.12. It is very similar to the `CompactDisc` Bean class used in the shopping-cart demonstration sites from Chapters 8 "Session Tracking Using JSP," and 14, "Databases and JSP."

Listing 15.12 `CompactDiscProduct.java`

```
package com.conygre.cd;

public class CompactDiscProduct implements java.io.Serializable {

  //Instance variables
  private String title;
  private double price;
  private String artist;
  private int tracks;
  private int id;

  //Methods
  public int getId(){
```

Listing 15.12 **Continued**

```
    return id;
  }

  public void setId(int s){
    id = s;
  }

  public void setTitle(String s){
    title = s;
  }

  public void setPrice(double d){
    price = d;
  }

  public void setArtist(String s){
    artist = s;
  }

  public void setTracks(int i){
    tracks = i;
  }

  public String getTitle(){
    return title;
  }

  public double getPrice(){
    return price;
  }

  public String getArtist(){
    return artist;
  }

  public int getTracks(){
    return tracks;
  }

  //constructors
  public CompactDiscProduct(){}

  public CompactDiscProduct(String t, double p,String a, int tr, int i){
    title=t;
    price=p;
    artist=a;
```

Listing 15.12 **Continued**

```
    tracks=tr;
    id = i;
  }
}
```

Remember, the class shown in Listing 15.12 is a regular JavaBean class, which will be used as a serialized Bean to get our entity Bean data to the Web application.

The Session Bean Implementation

The implementation class for the session Bean is fairly complex. Unlike the entity Bean where the container essentially does it all, with a session Bean, you do have to write your own business logic. That is one thing the container cannot do! The implementation is shown in Listing 15.13. Some of the methods have been omitted for brevity, but the version on the book Web site (`www.samspublishing.com`) has the whole thing.

Listing 15.13 `CompactDiscAccessBean.java`

```
package com.conygre.cd;

import javax.ejb.*;
import java.util.*;
import java.rmi.RemoteException;
import javax.naming.*;

public class CompactDiscAccessBean implements SessionBean {
  private CompactDiscHome home = null;

  public void ejbCreate() throws CreateException {}

  private void locateCDHomeInterface() {
    try {
      // get a reference to the JNDI context
      InitialContext context = new InitialContext();
      // lookup the CompactDiscHome interface
      Object obj = context.lookup("java:comp/env/ejb/CompactDiscHome");
      // casts reference to the right type
      home = (CompactDiscHome)
      javax.rmi.PortableRemoteObject.narrow(obj, CompactDiscHome.class);
    }
   catch (javax.naming.NamingException e) {
      System.out.println("Could not locate CompactDiscHome from CompactDiscAccess
" + e);
    }
  }
```

Listing 15.13 **Continued**

```
// methods as defined in remote interface
public Collection getProducts() {
 locateCDHomeInterface();
 if (home != null) {
  try {
   Collection entityCollection = home.findAll();
   return convertCollection(entityCollection);
  }
  catch (RemoteException e) {
    System.out.println("Remote Exception " +  e);
    return null;
  }
  catch (FinderException e) {
    System.out.println("Finder Exception " +  e);
    return null;
  }
 }
 else return null;
}

public CompactDiscProduct getProductByTitle(String s) {
 locateCDHomeInterface();
 if (home !-null) {
  try {
  // do a look up on the entity bean using the finder method
  // then convert the returned result to a regular JavaBean to be returned to
  // client application (in our case, a JSP)
  return convertBean (home.findByTitle(s));
  }
  catch (RemoteException e) {
    System.out.println("Remote Exception " +  e);
    return null;
  }
  catch (FinderException e) {
    System.out.println("Finder Exception " +  e);
    return null;
  }
 }
 else return null;
}

public CompactDiscProduct getProductById(int n) {
 locateCDHomeInterface();
 if (home != null) {
  try {
   // do a look up on the entity bean using the finder method
```

Listing 15.13 **Continued**

```
    // then convert the returned result to a regular JavaBean to be returned to
    // client application (in our case, a JSP)
     return convertBean (home.findByPrimaryKey(new Integer(n)));
   }
   catch (RemoteException e) {
     System.out.println("Remote Exception " +  e);
     return null;
   }
   catch (FinderException e) {
     System.out.println("Finder Exception " +  e);
     return null;
   }
  }
  else return null;
 }

 public Collection getProductByArtist (String s) {
  locateCDHomeInterface();
  if (home !=null) {
   try {
     Collection entityCollection = home.findByArtist(s);
     return convertCollection(entityCollection);
   }
   catch (RemoteException e) {
     System.out.println("Remote Exception " +  e);
     return null;
   }
   catch (FinderException e) {
     System.out.println("Finder Exception " +  e);
     return null;
   }
  }
  else return null;
 }

 public Collection searchCatalog(String s) {
  locateCDHomeInterface();
  if (home !=null) {
   // this list will contain the products that match the search
   LinkedList list = new LinkedList();
   try {
    // obtain all of the products
    Collection all = home.findAll();
    // loop through the products and search for the string provided
    Object[] array = all.toArray();
```

Listing 15.13 **Continued**

```
    for (int i=0;i<array.length; i++) {
    CompactDisc cd = (CompactDisc) array[i];
    if ( (s.equalsIgnoreCase(cd.getTitle() )  |
         (s.equalsIgnoreCase(cd.getArtist() ) )))
     list.add (convertBean((CompactDisc)array[i]));
       }
   }
    catch (RemoteException e) {
     System.out.println("Remote Exception " +  e);
     return null;
   }
   catch (FinderException e) {
     System.out.println("Finder Exception " +  e);
     return null;
   }
   return list;
  }
  else return null;
 }

 private CompactDiscProduct convertBean(CompactDisc entity) {
  CompactDiscProduct product = null;
  try {
   int id =entity.getId().intValue();
   product = new CompactDiscProduct(entity.getTitle(),
                                    entity.getPrice(),
                                    entity.getArtist(),
                                    entity.getTracks(),
                                    id);
  }
  catch (RemoteException e) {
   System.out.print(e);
  }
  return product;
 }

 private Vector convertCollection(Collection entityCollection) {
   Iterator iter = entityCollection.iterator();
   Vector vect = new Vector(1);
   while (iter.hasNext()) {
    CompactDiscProduct  localDisc =
                 convertBean((CompactDisc)iter.next());
    vect.add(localDisc);
  }
 return vect;
 }
```

Listing 15.13 **Continued**

```
// methods from session bean interface
public void setSessionContext (SessionContext context) {}
public void ejbActivate() {}
public void ejbPassivate() {}
public void ejbRemove() {}
}
```

There are three methods of special note in Listing 15.13:

- `locateCDHomeInterface()` —First we'll explain the private method, `locateCDHomeInterface()`. This utility method is used by the session Bean to locate the home interface of the entity Bean. It needs this so it can perform the appropriate finder methods on the entity Beans. Notice that it uses the same mechanism as the JSP seen earlier in Listing 15.1. It uses JNDI to do the lookup, and then the `PortableRemoteObject.narrow()` method to do the cast.
- `searchCatalog()` —The `searchCatalog()` method is our business method; it looks through both the titles and the artist names to see if they correspond. In the example, it is a basic String comparison, but obviously this could be extended to be checking Strings that contain values, and also, if we had other entity Beans, it could check through those as well. Notice that when it adds items to the `LinkedList`, it uses a further private utility method, `convertBean()`.
- `convertBean()` —This utility method is crucial to the performance of our application. Here, entity Beans returned by our search are converted into `CompactDiscProduct` instances. These are then added to the List, which can be serialized and sent back to the client Web application.

The final list of methods in the implementation are the lifecycle methods. They are very similar to the lifecycle methods of the entity Bean.

The Session Bean Lifecycle

The lifecycle of a stateless session Bean can be seen in Figure 15.18.

The lifecycle of a stateless session Bean is fairly straightforward, simply because these Beans are not tied to any particular client, so the EJB container can pool them. When a container requires additional Beans to be placed within the pool, it invokes the no argument constructor on the Bean, sets the session context which can be used by the business methods if required, and it then calls the `ejbCreate()` method. The Bean is now ready to accept client method calls.

When the container no longer requires the Bean to be in the pool, it will remove it by invoking the `ejbRemove()` method. Remember, with stateless session Beans, any client can access any Bean from the pool each time they use a stateless session Bean.

Stateful session Beans, however, are more complex. The lifecycle for a stateful session Bean is shown in Figure 15.19.

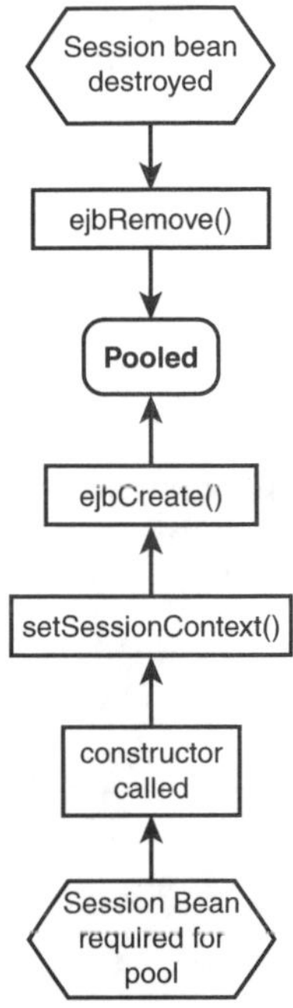

Figure 15.18 The stateless session Bean lifecycle.

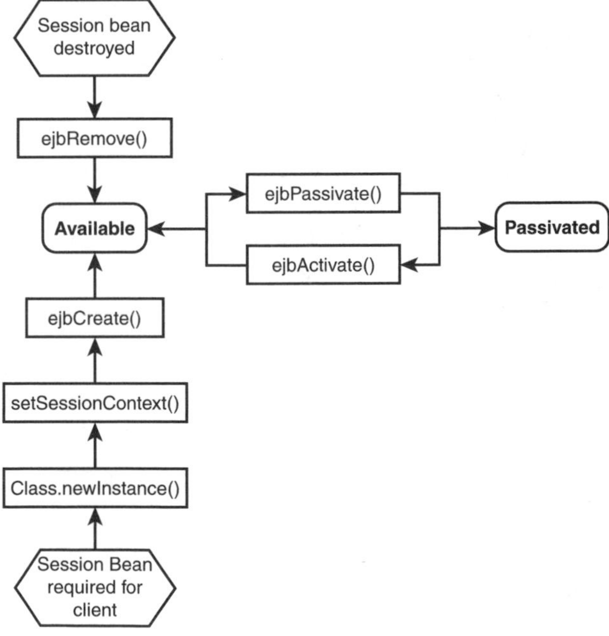

Figure 15.19 The stateful session Bean lifecycle.

The core difference is that the session Bean can now be *passivated*. Because stateful session Beans are not pooled, and because each client has their own instance of the session bean, there could potentially be a lot of resources taken up by these stateful session Beans whose clients are hardly ever using them. Therefore, the processes of passivation and activation discussed earlier in relation to entity Beans are employed here.

Deploying a Session Bean

To deploy a session Bean, the `ejb-jar.xml` file has some additional content. For WebLogic, additional content also needs to be added to `weblogic-ejb-jar.xml`. Because the session Bean will be used by our Web application, a modification will also need to be made here.

Listings 15.14 through 15.16 show these three deployment descriptors.

Listing 15.14 `ejb-jar.xml`

```
<?xml version="1.0"?>
<!DOCTYPE ejb-jar PUBLIC
         "-//Sun Microsystems, Inc.//DTD Enterprise JavaBeans 2.0//EN"
         "http://java.sun.com/dtd/ejb-jar_2_0.dtd">
<ejb-jar>
  <enterprise-beans>
    <entity>
      <!-- entity bean deployment information -->
    </entity>
    <session>
      <ejb-name>CompactDiscAccessBean</ejb-name>
      <home>com.conygre.cd.CompactDiscAccessHome</home>
      <remote>com.conygre.cd.CompactDiscAccess</remote>
      <ejb-class>com.conygre.cd.CompactDiscAccessBean</ejb-class>
      <session-type>Stateless</session-type>
      <transaction-type>Container</transaction-type>
      <ejb-ref>
        <ejb-ref-name>ejb/CompactDiscHome</ejb-ref-name>
        <ejb-ref-type>Entity</ejb-ref-type>
        <home>com.conygre.cd.CompactDiscHome</home>
        <remote>com.conygre.cd.CompactDisc</remote>
        <ejb-link>CompactDiscBean</ejb-link>
      </ejb-ref>
    </session>
  </enterprise-beans>
  <assembly-descriptor>
    <container-transaction>
      <method>
        <ejb-name>CompactDiscAccessBean</ejb-name>
        <method-name>*</method-name>
```

Listing 15.14 **Continued**

```
      </method>
      <trans-attribute>Required</trans-attribute>
    </container-transaction>
  </assembly-descriptor>
</ejb-jar>
```

Most of this should be self explanatory, and you have seen most of it before as well, except for the entity Bean. Notice that the session Bean deployment information contains a link to the entity Bean via an `<ejb-ref>` element. You have seen that before, in `web.xml`, where it was used to provide a JNDI lookup name for the JSP to locate the entity Bean. Here it is used to provide the JNDI lookup name for the entity Bean that the session Bean can use. You can see the lookup name in use in the private method of the session Bean.

The additional content in `weblogic-ejb-jar.xml` can be seen in Listing 15.15.

Listing 15.15 `weblogic-ejb-jar.xml`

```
<?xml version="1.0"?>
<!DOCTYPE weblogic-ejb-jar PUBLIC
         "-//BEA Systems, Inc.//DTD WebLogic 7.0.0 EJB//EN"
         "http://www.bea.com/servers/wls700/dtd/weblogic-ejb-jar.dtd">
<weblogic-ejb-jar>
  <!-- entity bean information was here -->
  <weblogic-enterprise-bean>
    <ejb-name>CompactDiscAccessBean</ejb-name>
    <jndi-name>CompactDiscAccessHome</jndi-name>
  </weblogic-enterprise-bean>
</weblogic-ejb-jar>
```

Finally, `web.xml` needs to be modified so that the Web application can access the session Bean. This can be seen in Listing 15.16.

Listing 15.16 `web.xml (for session bean)`

```
<?xml version="1.0"?>
<!DOCTYPE web-app PUBLIC
           "-//Sun Microsystems, Inc.//DTD Web Application 2.2//EN"
           "http://java .sun.com/j2ee/dtds/web-app_2_2.dtd">
<web-app>
  <welcome-file-list>
    <welcome-file>ejbClient.jsp</welcome-file>
  </welcome-file-list>
  <ejb-ref>
    <ejb-ref-name>ejb/CompactDiscAccess</ejb-ref-name>
    <ejb-ref-type>Session</ejb-ref-type>
    <home>com.conygre.cd.CompactDiscAccessHome</home>
```

Listing 15.16 **Continued**

```
    <remote>com.conygre.cd.CompactDiscAccess</remote>
    <ejb-link>CompactDiscAccessBean</ejb-link>
  </ejb-ref>
  <!-- ejb-ref for entity bean was here -->
</web-app>
```

As you can see, session Beans are very similar to entity Beans as far as the deployment process goes. We will finish this section with a JSP that interacts with the session Bean to complete a search using the `searchCatalog()` method defined in the session Bean; see Listing 15.17. We have not used tags or beans so you can clearly see what is going on in the Java code.

Listing 15.17 `productSearch.jsp`

```
<html>
<head>
<title>Find Compact Disc by Artist</title>
</head>
<body>
<h1>Product Search</h1>
<%@ page import="com.conygre.cd.*, javax.naming.*, java.rmi.*, javax.rmi.*" %>
<%
  // create the context
  Context context = new InitialContext();
  // look up the EJB using its JNDI name
  Object obj = context.lookup("java:comp/env/ejb/CompactDiscAccess");
  // cast the returned reference to the home interface type
  // using the narrow() method
  CompactDiscAccessHome home = (CompactDiscAccessHome)
            (PortableRemoteObject.narrow(obj,CompactDiscAccessHome.class));

  // call the create() method on the home interface referece
  // that returns an object of the remote reference type, CompactDiscAccess
  CompactDiscAccess access = (CompactDiscAccess) home.create();
  // access the search methoddefined within the remote interface
  Collection  cds = access.searchCatalog("Coldplay");
  Object[] array = cds.toArray();

  for (int i=0;i<array.length; i++) {
    CompactDiscProduct cd = (CompactDiscProduct) array[i];
    out.println("CD " + cd.getId() + " is called " +
            cd.getTitle() + " and is by " + cd.getArtist() + ".<br>");
  }
%>
</body>
</html>
```

There should be no surprises within Listing 15.17. It is accessing the session Bean, which then completes the search, and returns references to serialized JavaBeans of type CompactDiscProduct to the client; the client can then iterate through them and display them on the page. If you want to try this application for yourself, you can either modify the entity Bean application, redeploying the application on WebLogic, or you can download the application from the book Web site (`www.samspublishing.com`) and deploy it as per the instructions for the entity Bean application.

Web Application EJB Access Architecture

Throughout this chapter, all the EJB access has been carried out from scriptlets within JavaServer Pages. If you have read Chapter 7, "JSP Application Architecture," however, you will be aware that putting excessive scriptlets into JSPs is not necessarily good practice. You have seen it done in the book examples deliberately to keep the examples simple.

In practice, however, where should the EJB access code go? There are a number of possibilities, and the best places for the EJB access code are either in tag libraries or Beans.

This would fit the MVC pattern discussed in Chapter 7, where the JavaBeans or tag libraries act as the model, the JSP is the view, and the servlet acts as the controller.

Figure 15.20 demonstrates the classic model 2 architecture, but with the JavaBeans interacting with the session Beans, and then making that data available to the client applications.

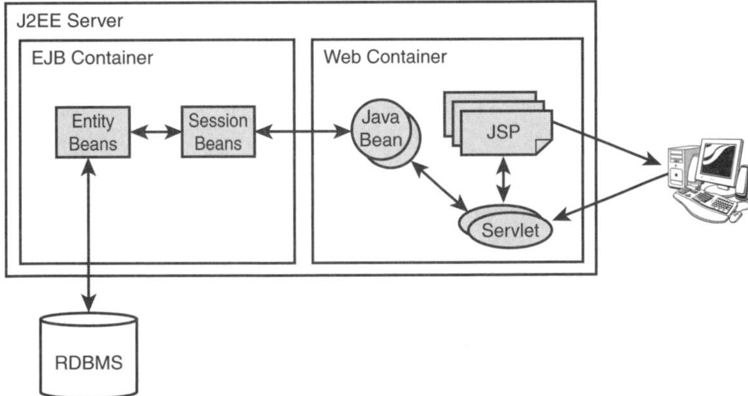

Figure 15.20 Web application/EJB interaction architecture.

The final set of code examples will demonstrate how this can be set up. First, Listing 15.18 is a controller servlet, which sets up the collection of locally available JavaBeans.

Listing 15.18 ControllerServlet.java

```
import javax.ejb.CreateException;
import java.util.Collection;
import javax.rmi.*;
import java.rmi.RemoteException;
import java.io.IOException;
import javax.servlet.*;
import javax.servlet.http.*;
import javax.naming.*;
import com.conygre.cd.*;
public class ControllerServlet extends HttpServlet {

  // this variable will hold the servlet context
  private ServletContext application;

  public void init(ServletConfig config) throws ServletException {
      super.init(config);
      // get the servlet context
      application = getServletContext();
      try {
      // create the context
      Context context = new InitialContext();
      // look up the EJB using its JNDI name
      Object obj = context.lookup("java:comp/env/ejb/CompactDiscAccess");
      // cast the returned reference to the
      // home interface type using the narrow() method
      CompactDiscAccessHome home
                  = (CompactDiscAccessHome)
                  (PortableRemoteObject.narrow
                      (obj, CompactDiscAccessHome.class));
    // call the create() method on the home interface referece
    // that returns an object of the remote reference type, CompactDiscAccess
    CompactDiscAccess access = (CompactDiscAccess) home.create();

    // now invoke the business method to obtain
    // all of the compact discs as local beans
    // of type CompactDiscProduct (see the CompactDiscAccess session bean)
    Collection cds = access.getProducts();
    // assign the returned collection to have application scope
    application.setAttribute("stock",cds);
    }
    catch (NamingException e) {
      System.out.println("Naming exception " + e);
    }
    catch (RemoteException e) {
        System.out.println("Remote exception " + e);
      }
```

Listing 15.18 **Continued**

```
    catch (CreateException e) {
        System.out.println("Create exception " + e);
      }
  }

  public void doGet(HttpServletRequest req, HttpServletResponse res)
                throws ServletException, IOException {
    // as other pages were added, they could be forwarded to in the usual way
    RequestDispatcher rd =
       application.getRequestDispatcher("/model2/welcome.jsp");
    rd.forward(req, res);

  }
}
```

Within the `init()` method, the `CompactDiscProduct` Beans returned from the session Bean are now placed into an application-scoped attribute called `stock`. The `doGet()` method acts as the controller. In our basic example, it forwards to just one page, but obviously in a more complex environment, there would be additional entries here for search pages and such like.

The controller forwards to a page called `welcome.jsp`, and that is shown next in Listing 15.19.

Listing 15.19 `welcome.jsp`

```
<%@taglib uri="http://java.sun.com/jstl-el/core" prefix="c" %>
<html>
<head>
<title>List of all Compact Discs</title>
</head>
<body>
<h1>All Available CDs Accessed Via Model 2 Architecture</h1>

<c:forEach var="item" items="${stock}">
  <br>
  Id: <c:out value='${item.id}'/><br>
  Title: <c:out value="${item.title}"/><br>
  Artist: <c:out value="${item.artist}"/><br>
  No. of tracks: <c:out value="${item.tracks}"/><br>
  Price: <c:out value="${item.price}"/><br>
  <hr>
</c:forEach>

</body>
</html>
```

The `welcome.jsp` page is a very simple JSP because all the complexity is now hidden away from the page developer. Any additional JSPs can now either use the same `stock` application-scoped attribute, or they can go back to the session Bean and get up to date data. This is the one danger of using local Beans in this way—if the data at the back changes, your Beans will not reflect those changes. You should, therefore, consider carefully when you are going to use local Beans, and when you are going to go back to the EJB container to get up to date data.

Summary

In this chapter, you have seen the role of the entity Bean to represent your data and the session bean to represent your business logic and act as a façade to your entity Beans. You have also seen how Web applications can interact with EJBs. If you have deployed the sample application, you have seen how complete J2EE applications can be deployed in the WebLogic 7 application server.

In the next chapter, you will see how Web applications can be secured using the J2EE security model. Up to now in our example applications anyone can access anything, but securing aspects of any Web application is vital.

16

Security and JSP

SECURITY IS CRITICAL TO SO MANY WEB applications. It is the one thing that most Internet users are most concerned about, and it is those concerns about security that often prevent them from making purchases online, thus hindering your ability to make any money (if your site is a commerce site)! It is also of utmost importance to the Web application developer—especially in distributed environments where disparate application components need to interact with one another.

In this chapter, you will be exposed to the security requirements of a Web application. I will then explain the different terms used when defining security in Web applications, which can be somewhat bewildering when first encountered. You will then learn how Web applications can be made secure, and you will be exposed to the security features within Tomcat.

Security Requirements

We'll start with a question: What are the security requirements of a Web application?

The answer depends on your perspective. If you are a user, you will have one set of concerns. If you are running the site, you will need to consider those concerns, plus a number of other concerns of your own. This question, therefore, will be answered from two perspectives: first from the site user's perspective, and second from the developer's perspective.

Security—From a Site User Perspective

If you have been working through this book sequentially, you should be familiar by now with our shopping cart application. In this application, users are able to browse DVDs, books, and compact discs, and add them to their shopping cart. However, there is no purchase functionality in the Web site. If there were, this would have some security implications. Simply browsing the site and adding items to a cart is not a problem. The problems come when users want to purchase the products using their credit card or pass other sensitive information over the Internet.

From a user's perspective, the concerns are

- When my creditcard number travels across the Internet, how can I be sure that no one will intercept it?
- Is the Web site really the Web site it says it is?

There is another concern, although not particularly focused on by commerce site users:

- How can I be sure that my data has not been tampered with?

These three issues are the main concerns that need to be addressed when securing Web applications. Fortunately, technologies exist to address each of these issues.

Security—From the Site Perspective

As well as requirements that are foremost in a user's mind, there can be other such security requirements from a developer or business analyst perspective:

- Restricting user access to resources
- Confirming that users are who they say they are (particularly for banking and financial services sites)
- The passing of security credentials through to different parts of a disparate application

Table 16.1 shows a summary of the various security requirements.

Table 16.1 **Security Requirements of Web Applications**

Requirement	Description (from the Servlet 2.3 Spec)
Authentication	The means by which communicating entities prove to one another that they are acting on behalf of specific identities authorized for access.
Access control for resources	The means by which interactions with resources are limited to collections of users or programs for the purpose of enforcing integrity, confidentiality, or availability constraints.
Data Integrity	The means used to prove that a third party has not modified information while in transit.
Confidentiality	The means used to ensure that information is made available only to users who are authorized to access it.

The J2EE Security Model

To implement authentication, access control, data integrity, and confidentiality from a J2EE platform you need to understand a number of important concepts discussed in the following sections.

Roles and Principals

Within any Web application, there can be different types of users: some might be registered users, some are premium users, and some are entry-level users. These different types of users will have different access levels within a Web application, and these different types of users can be referred to as *roles*. Individual users can then be assigned to these different roles; the *principal* is the actual user. So a principal could be in one or more roles.

To put it in concrete terms, I am a registered user of a Web site, my username is `johndoe`, and I am a premium user. My principal is `johndoe`, and the role could be `PremiumUser`.

The principal and role information can be stored in a variety of ways. They could be in an LDAP directory, an NT domain, or in a database, and a server can be configured to interact with them. WebLogic, for example, has out-of-the-box support for all these.

Declarative and Programmatic Security

Within the J2EE standard, you can implement security in two ways:

- Declarative security—security information is defined within the various deployment descriptors, whether they be EJBs, Web folders, or other resources. This is handled by the deployer of the application as opposed to the developer of the application.
- Programmatic security—security information is hard-coded into the application using the security APIs. This is handled by the developer of the application as opposed to the deployer of the application.

As we explore how security is actually implemented in Web applications, you'll see examples of roles and principals, and also examples of declarative and programmatic security. We'll start with declarative security via authentication.

Authentication

Authentication is the validation of users against user information. Users are validated to have access to resources within domains, referred to as authentication domains. The authentication domain is the context into which the user has been authenticated. So, in a Web site the domain could be the Web site domain `www.yourdomainname.com`. In Web applications, the authentication of users is typically done by checking usernames and passwords.

Four kinds of authentication can be set up declaratively in Web applications:

- HTTP basic authentication
- HTTP digest authentication
- Form-based authentication
- HTTPS client authentication

Resources can be specified as requiring authentication from within `web.xml`. The structure of the security component of `web.xml` is shown in Listing 16.1.

Listing 16.1 **Defining Security Constraints in `web.xml`**

```
<security-constraint>
  <web-resource-collection>
    <web-resource-name>Protected Area</web-resource-name>
    <url-pattern>/protected</url-pattern>
  </web-resource-collection>
</security-constraint>
```

This extract from `web.xml` is used to define a part of the Web application that will have a security constraint. How this area is protected is defined using additional elements. For basic-, form-, and digest-based authentication, the following is also present in `web.xml`:

```
<login-config>
  <auth-method>BASIC | DIGEST | FORM | CLIENT-CERT</auth-method>
  <realm-name>The Name of the Realm</realm-name>
</login-config>
```

The `<login-config>` element defines the authentication mechanism that is to be used. You will notice that HTTPS is missing as an option. This is because HTTPS is set up slightly differently as you'll see.

If you are using Tomcat, you can set up the user information in a file called `tomcat-users.xml`, which is located in the `<tomcat-home>\conf` folder. Although it is not a good idea to use this file to store user information in a real application, it is ideal for testing, which is what it is there for. The default entries for `tomcat-users.xml` are shown here:

```
<tomcat-users>
    <user name="tomcat" password="tomcat" roles="tomcat"/>
    <user name="role1" password="tomcat" roles="role1"/>
    <user name="both" password="tomcat" roles="tomcat,role1"/>
</tomcat-users>
```

For our purposes, two users will be added, one called `alex` with a realm of `customer`, and one called `abigail` with a role of `guest`. Both can have the password set to `password`.

You will need to modify your user list as shown:

```
<user name="alex" password="password" roles="customer"/>
<user name="abigail" password="password" roles="guest"/>
```

HTTP Basic Authentication

This is authentication at its most basic (as the name implies!). It involves the sending of a clear-text username and password to a server to access a protected resource. The mechanism is defined by the HTTP/1.0 specification. This is very insecure, and not to be recommended.

Listing 16.2 shows a complete `web.xml`-deployment descriptor that could be used to set up basic authentication for our `protected` folder.

Listing 16.2 `web.xml` **for Basic Authentication**

```
<web-app xmlns="http://java.sun.com/xml/ns/j2ee"
   xmlns:xsi="http://www.w3.org/2001/XMLSchema-instance"
   xsi:schemaLocation="http://java.sun.com/xml/ns/j2ee
   http://java.sun.com/xml/ns/j2ee/web-app_2_4.xsd" version="2.4">

  <security-constraint>
    <web-resource-collection>
      <web-resource-name>Protected Area</web-resource-name>
      <url-pattern>/protected/*</url-pattern>
    </web-resource-collection>
    <auth-constraint>
      <role-name>guest</role-name>
      <role-name>customer</role-name>
    </auth constraint>
  </security-constraint>

  <login-config>
    <auth-method>BASIC</auth-method>
    <realm-name>The Name of the Realm</realm-name>
  </login-config>

</web-app>
```

Note

If you want to try this application, you will need to rename `webBasicAuth.xml` to `web.xml` in the sample application.

If a basic HTML file were placed in the `protected` folder, you would access it by asking for the username and password in a dialog box similar to that shown in Figure 16.1.

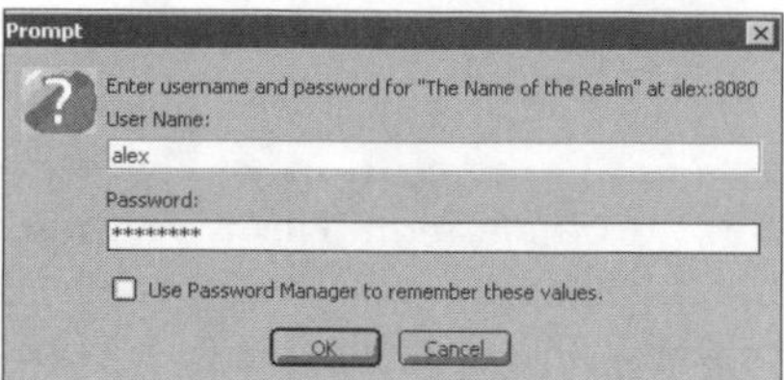

Figure 16.1 Basic authentication prompt displayed in Netscape 6.2.

A similar prompt to that shown in Figure 16.1 comes up in Internet Explorer when protected resources are requested. Figure 16.2 shows what Tomcat 4 displays if incorrect credentials are supplied.

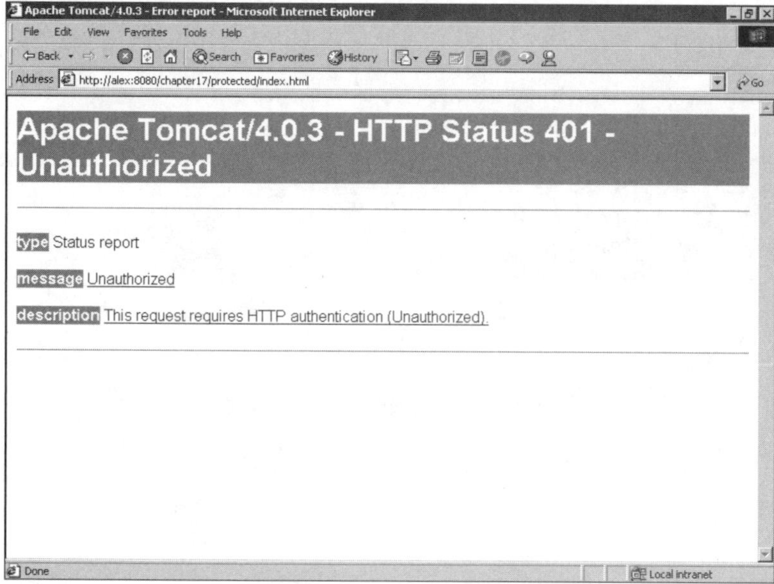

Figure 16.2 Result of supplying incorrect credentials in Tomcat 4.

If your clients are all using Internet Explorer browsers, you have an alternative to basic authentication. Internet and Extranet applications are often restricted to Internet Explorer, and in those situations you can take advantage of the *digest authentication method*.

Digest Authentication

The difference between digest authentication and basic authentication is that in digest authentication, the username and password are never sent over the wire. Instead, a hash is created made up of the following pieces of information:

- The username
- The password
- The URL
- The randomly generated string (the nonce)
- The HTTP method being used

The *nonce* is a randomly generated string that is sent to the client when he first requests a protected resource.

Caution

Remember, not all browsers support this authentication method, so use it with caution. When tested with Netscape 6.2, users were automatically refused access. Note also that servlet containers are only *encouraged* to provide support for it – they do not have to.

Note

Hashing is the process of taking some characters, using an algorithm, and creating a String or number from them. This created value should be unique to every set of characters that is hashed. The algorithm used here by default is called *MD5*. Hashing algorithms will be discussed again in the section entitled "HTTPS Client Authentication and SSL" later in this chapter.

For a full discussion of digest authentication, visit `http://www.ietf.org/rfc/rfc2617.txt`.

Figure 16.3 summarizes what happens in digest authentication:

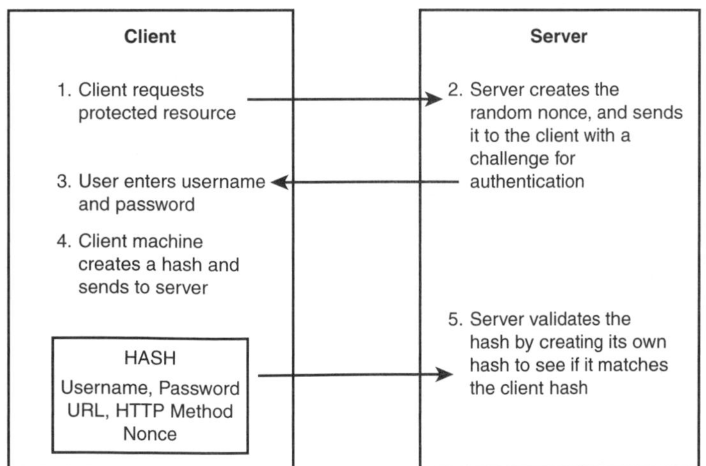

Figure 16.3 Digest authentication.

Transforming our existing Web application to use digest authentication is simply a matter of modifying the `<auth-method>` element of `web.xml` so that it contains `DIGEST`:

```
<auth-method>DIGEST</auth-method>
```

> **Caution**
>
> If you are trying this out using the provided sample application or by creating the files yourself, remember that modifications to `web.xml` require a restart of Tomcat.

Due to the limited browser support, this mechanism is only really only useful in intranet and extranet environments where the Web browser being used can be controlled.

Form-Based Authentication

With both basic and digest authentication, the user is presented with a rather aesthetically unattractive dialog box! What are usually somewhat easier on the eyes are username and password fields within an HTML form. This can then be built into your Web pages with your own look and feel, and will be less obtrusive within the context of the Web application.

The J2EE specifications recognize this fact, and have provided an alternative way of collecting usernames and passwords that takes advantage of a standard HTML form. What is unusual about this mechanism, however, is how the form is constructed within the HTML. There is a standard way of defining the form in terms of the field names, and the action attribute of the form. Listing 16.3 shows an example of an HTML form that can be used in form-based authentication.

Listing 16.3 `login.html`

```
<html>
<head>
<title>Login Form</title>
</head>
<body>
<h1>Please log in</h1>
You must log in before you can access the protected area.
<hr>
<form method="POST" action="j_security_check">
Username: <input type="text" name="j_username"><br>
Password: <input type="password" name="j_password"><br>
<input type="submit" value="Continue">
</form>
</body>
</html>
```

Notice that the file does not have to be a JSP, it is just a standard piece of HTML. The username has to be `j_username`, the password has to be `j_password`, and the action attribute has to specify the value `j_security_check` as shown in Listing 16.3.

For this form to work, there also needs to be a login failure page, which can be any HTML page. The one in our example is shown in Listing 16.4.

Listing 16.4 `loginFailed.html`

```
<html>
<head>
<title>Login Form</title>
</head>
<body>
<h1>Sorry</h1>
You are not a valid user.
<hr>
</body>
</html>
```

Finally, the form and the failure pages need to be specified within `web.xml`. Listing 16.5 shows how the `<login-config>` element must be modified.

Listing 16.5 **Extract from `web.xml` for Form-Based Authentication**

```
<login-config>
  <auth-method>FORM</auth-method>
  <form-login-config>
    <form-login-page>/login.html</form-login-page>
    <form-error-page>/loginFailed.html</form-error-page>
  </form-login-config>
</login-config>
```

When a protected resource is requested from within a browser while using form-based authentication, the server redirects the browser to the login form. Figure 16.4 shows the browser after our protected content has been requested.

If the correct username and password are supplied, the browser will redirect to the originally requested resource, which in our case is

```
http://alex:8080/chapter16/protected/index.html
```

If the incorrect credentials are supplied, the browser redirects to the error page as specified in `web.xml`. This can be seen in Figure 16.5.

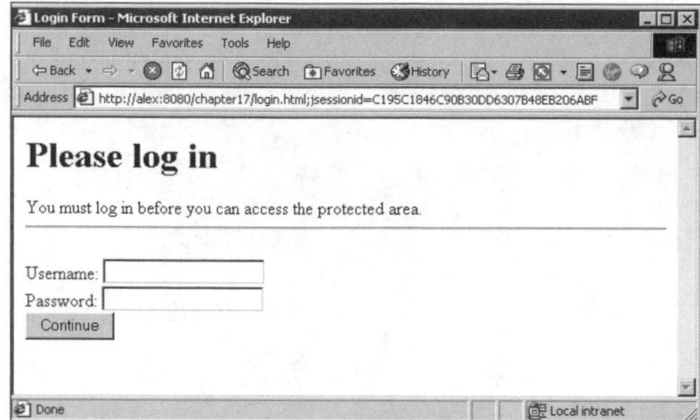

Figure 16.4 `login.html` presented to clients who request protected resources.

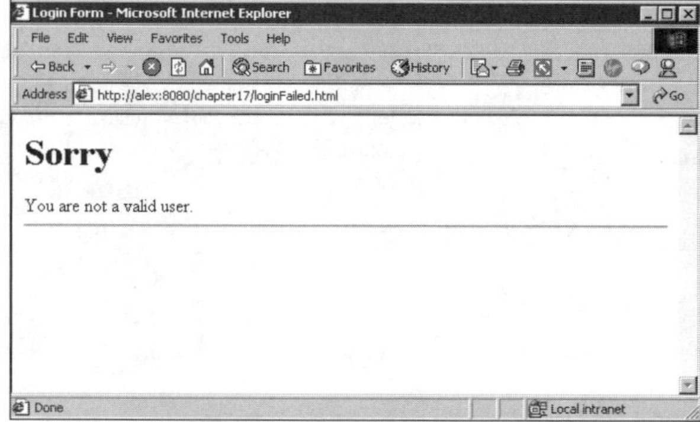

Figure 16.5 `loginFailed.html`.

The process can be summarized as follows, as specified in the Servlet 2.4 specification:

1) The login form is sent to the client when the user requests a protected resource. The URL to the resource that the user was after is maintained by the container.
2) The user returns a completed form to the server.
3) The Web container attempts to authenticate the user, and if successful, the principal is checked to ensure that they are allowed access to a particular resource. If they are, then the originally requested URL is used to deliver a response to the client.
4) If they are not authenticated, then the error page is displayed using either redirection or forwarding. The status code of the response is set to 401 (Access denied).

That completes our discussion of the first three forms of authentication: basic-, digest-, and form-based. The fourth and final form of authentication is more complex, and also is core to many Web applications, so we'll discuss it next.

HTTPS Client Authentication and SSL

HTTPS is short for HTTP over Secure Socket Layer (SSL), so we'll begin with a discussion on SSL.

Secure Socket Layer is used ubiquitously in Web applications when security is required, and it can be taken care of by the browser and Web server automatically. It can provide a secure connection between a client and a server. Secure socket layer is in fact a combination of several security technologies:

- Symmetric key encryption
- Asymmetric key encryption
- Digital signatures
- Digital certificates
- Secure digest

Let's see what these technologies are, and how they can be combined to create a secure connection.

> **Note**
>
> Secure Socket Layer as a technology is used in conjunction with HTTP, and is referred to as HTTPS (Hypertext Transfer Protocol over Secure Socket Layer).

Symmetric Key Encryption

The concept of encryption is not a new one; it has been around for centuries, and has come a long way! *Encryption* is the process of converting data into a format that is not understood by unauthorized individuals. The encrypted data is referred to as *ciphertext*. *Decryption* is the conversion of the ciphertext back to the original data. The *key* contains the algorithm that is used to encrypt the data. The term *symmetric key encryption* is used to describe encryption and decryption that relies on the same key at both the encrypting and decrypting ends of the communication. See Figure 16.6.

Symmetric key encryption is very simple in principle. Both the client and the server use the same key to encrypt and decrypt messages. Thus, as long as they are the only holders of the key, the messages are secure.

There is a fundamental problem with symmetric key encryption, however. Imagine a typical Web application where the server selects a key to be used by the client. How is the server going to get the key to the client? This is where another form of encryption can help us—asymmetric encryption.

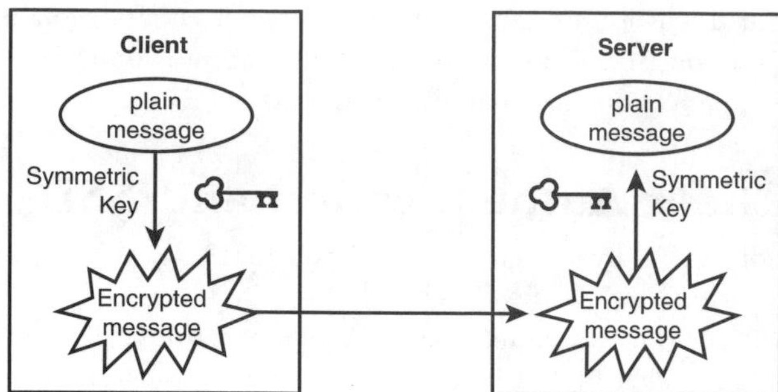

Figure 16.6 Symmetric key encryption.

Asymmetric Encryption

Asymmetric encryption is similar to symmetric key encryption, except that there are two keys involved. You need a different key to unlock encrypted messages. It is analogous to a bank night safe, where you as a bank customer have one key to open the safe to put stuff in, but you cannot use the same key to get stuff out! The bank staff then uses a different key to retrieve the contents of the night safe. In Web applications, the two keys are referred to as the *public key* and the *private key*. An individual owns the key pair, and one key, the private key, is kept private to them. The other one, the public key, is distributed as necessary (see Figure 16.7). This means that individuals can send messages to the key pair owner, encrypted with the owner's public key. Only the owner can decrypt the messages because he is the only one with the other key of the pair, the private key.

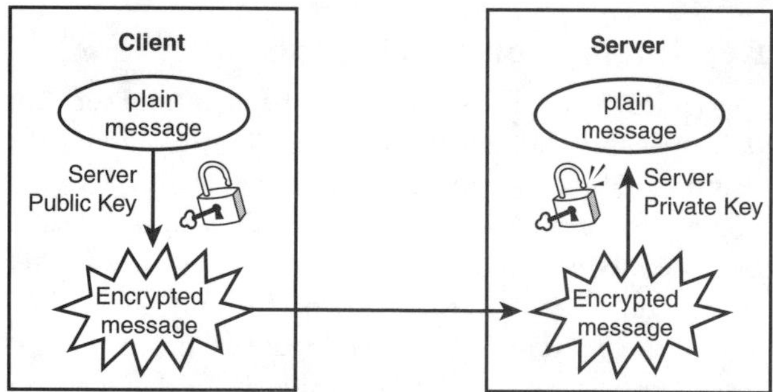

Figure 16.7 Asymmetric key encryption.

As you can see from Figure 16.7, this mechanism is great for one-way communication because the owner of the keys cannot get messages to the client. To do so, she would have to use her own private key to encrypt. This would create messages that can be decrypted by anyone with the public key, which is freely available. There are two possible ways around this:

- The client could also have a private/public key pair, so that both parties can interact using asymmetric encryption.
- Asymmetric and symmetric encryption could be combined to form a secure connection.

The first option is not really viable because, although this would be very secure, asymmetric encryption and decryption is a great deal slower than using symmetric key encryption. The difference can be up to 100 times.

SSL works by combining symmetric and asymmetric encryption, as follows:

1. The client makes a request to the server for a resource that needs to be secure.
2. The server sends to the client its *public* key. The client then generates a symmetric key, and encrypts the symmetric key using the server's public key. This encrypted symmetric key is then sent back to the server.
3. The server decrypts the symmetric key with its own *private* key.
4. Both the client *and* the server now have a symmetric key, which can be used to encrypt data that is sent back and forth.

This process is shown in Figure 16.8, and is at the core of SSL.

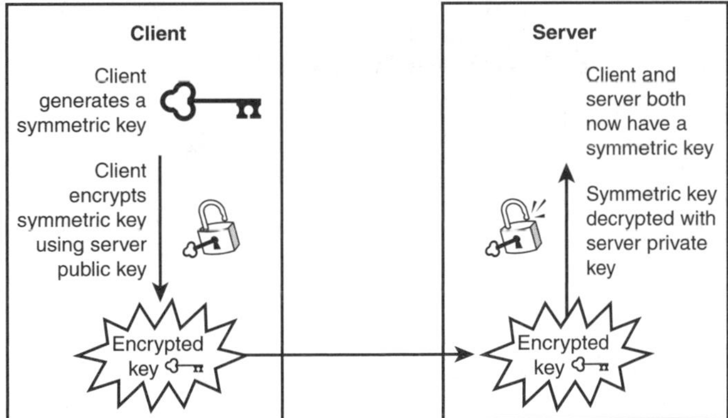

Figure 16.8 SSL using symmetric and asymmetric encryption.

There are two other factors to consider though. How do we guarantee that the server is who you think it is? Anyone could set up an official-looking Web site and rip people off. The way that sites confirm that they are who they say they are is with the use of digital certificates.

Digital Certificates

Digital certificates are the equivalent of a passport. When you board a plane for an international destination, you show your passport; a third party (in my case, the British

Passport Agency) vouches that you are who you say you are. To get my passport, I had to provide various forms of evidence that I really am Nick Todd.

A digital certificate serves the same function, but in this case for a Web site. It is a third party vouching for the site, saying that the site is who it says it is. Various companies provide these certificates such as Verisign, Xcert, and many others.

> **Note**
>
> If you are using Internet Explorer, you can view all the certificate providers that your browser implicitly trusts through the Internet Options panel and the Content tab. Select the Certificates button.

The digital certificate is essentially your public key, but provided with a certificate stating that the user is who he says that he is. Figure 16.9 shows the digital certificate information from the Sun Microsystems Web site. Notice that the public key information forms part of the certificate.

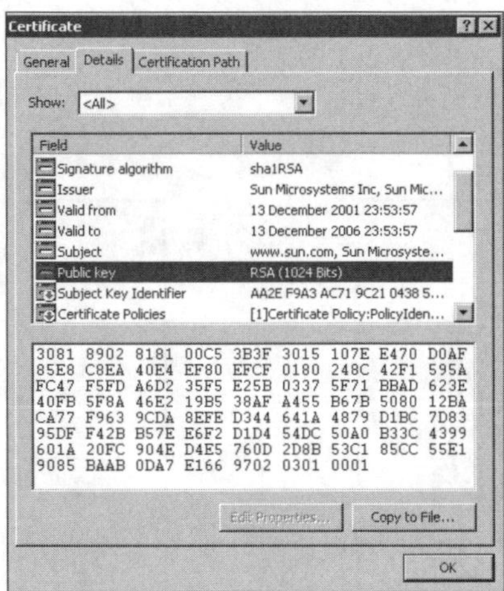

Figure 16.9 The digital certificate.

Finally, it also needs to be ensured that the message that has been sent has not been tampered with in any way. This is the role of the *digital signature.*

Digital Signatures

Digital signatures are the last piece of the SSL framework. When messages are sent, you know that they can be encrypted, but they could be tampered with. To prevent this, a hash is taken of a message before it is encrypted, which is then encrypted along with the original message. The encrypted message and the encrypted hash are then sent to the recipient. The recipient should find that when he decrypts the message and hashes it for himself that the hashes match. The hash is sometimes referred to as the *message digest.* The algorithms used currently, include MD2, MD4, and MD5.

All these technologies combine to make up SSL, and the entire process of making and using this kind of connection is done by the browser and the Web server. It is transparent to the developer, including the JSP developer. So, why have I spent so long on it? The reason is because a Web developer can interact with this process.

Java and SSL

J2EE application servers must support SSL since it is part of the J2EE specifications. Servlet containers that are not J2EE-compliant do not need to support SSL. However, Tomcat does support SSL, and if you create your own private/public key pair, Tomcat can be configured to use it. You will see how to do this next.

> **Caution**
>
> You do not normally need to configure Tomcat to run SSL because this is taken care of by the Web server that Tomcat is configured to run with (such as Apache). You will, however, need to configure Tomcat if you are planning to run it on its own without a Web server.

Creating a Private/Public Key Pair

The API for working with security in Java is the Java Secure Socket Extension (JSSE). It is a part of the JSDK 1.4 and higher. If you are using an earlier version of the JDK, you will need to download JSSE as a separate API from `http://java.sun.com/products/jsse/`

To create the key store, use the `keytool` that is provided with JSDK 1.4 or from the JSSE with the following command on Windows:

```
%JAVA_HOME%\bin\keytool -genkey -alias tomcat -keyalg RSA
```

On Unix, the command is

```
$JAVA_HOME/bin/keytool -genkey -alias tomcat -keyalg RSA
```

Figure 16.10 shows the command prompt window on Windows XP that comes up when running the keystore utility. You are prompted for several pieces of information that need to be provided.

```
C:\WINDOWS\SYSTEM32\CMD.EXE
Microsoft Windows XP [Version 5.1.2600]
(C) Copyright 1985-2001 Microsoft Corp.

C:\Java\j2sdk1.4.0\bin>keytool -genkey -alias tomcat -keyalg RSA
Enter keystore password:  changeit
What is your first and last name?
  [Unknown]:  Nick Todd
What is the name of your organizational unit?
  [Unknown]:  Conygre
What is the name of your organization?
  [Unknown]:  ContentMaster
What is the name of your City or Locality?
  [Unknown]:  Bristol
What is the name of your State or Province?
  [Unknown]:  S. Gloucs
What is the two-letter country code for this unit?
  [Unknown]:  NA
Is CN=Nick Todd, OU=Conygre, O=ContentMaster, L=Bristol, ST=S. Gloucs, C=NA corr
ect?
  [no]:  yes

Enter key password for <tomcat>
        (RETURN if same as keystore password):

C:\Java\j2sdk1.4.0\bin>
```

Figure 16.10 Running the keystore tool.

Configuring Tomcat for SSL

After you have done this, the `server.xml` configuration file for Tomcat needs to be modified. Listing 16.6 shows the section of `<tomcat-home>\conf\server.xml` that needs to be uncommented. This section sets up the SSL port and connector.

Listing 16.6 **Excerpt from `server.xml`**

```
    <Connector className="org.apache.coyote.tomcat4.CoyoteConnector"
               port="8443" minProcessors="5" maxProcessors="75"
               enableLookups="true"
           acceptCount="10" debug="0" scheme="https" secure="true"
               useURIValidationHack="false">
      <Factory className="org.apache.coyote.tomcat4.CoyoteServerSocketFactory"
               clientAuth="false" protocol="TLS" />
    </Connector>
```

> **Caution**
>
> Tomcat versions 4.0 and earlier use a different Connector. Connectors are discussed in Appendix H, "Configuring Tomcat."

We now have SSL configured on our Tomcat server, but it is not being used by any Web applications. Additional configuration information specific to a Web application now goes in the appropriate `web.xml` file.

We will modify our application to use form-based authentication, but over SSL. The `web.xml` will now be amended as shown in Listing 16.7.

Listing 16.7 **`web.xml` Customized for SSL**

```
<web-app xmlns="http://java.sun.com/xml/ns/j2ee"
   xmlns:xsi="http://www.w3.org/2001/XMLSchema-instance"
   xsi:schemaLocation="http://java.sun.com/xml/ns/j2ee
   http://java.sun.com/xml/ns/j2ee/web-app_2_4.xsd" version="2.4">
  <security-constraint>
    <web-resource-collection>
      <web-resource-name>Protected Area</web-resource-name>
      <url-pattern>/protected/*</url-pattern>
    </web-resource-collection>
    <auth-constraint>
      <role-name>guest</role-name>
      <role-name>customer</role-name>
    </auth-constraint>

    <user-data-constraint>
      <transport-guarantee>CONFIDENTIAL</transport-guarantee>
    </user-data-constraint>
  </security-constraint>
```

Listing 16.7 **Continued**

```
  <login-config>
    <auth-method>FORM</auth-method>
    <form-login-config>
      <form-login-page>/login.html</form-login-page>
      <form-error-page>/loginFailed.html</form-error-page>
    </form-login-config>
  </login-config>
</web-app>
```

> **Caution**
> To run this demo successfully, you must be running Tomcat in a Java Runtime of 1.4 or higher. Earlier versions of Java do not come with the Java Secure Socket Extensions, which are required for this to work.

The element that you need to pay particular attention to here is the `<transport-guarantee>` element found within the `<user-data-constraint>` element. The possible values for this element are

- `CONFIDENTIAL`—the data must be transmitted in a way that prevents others from intercepting the data
- `INTEGRAL`—the data must be transmitted in such a way that it cannot be tampered with (remember the message digest?)
- `NONE`—there are no transport guarantees required

Both `CONFIDENTIAL` and `INTEGRAL` will typically result in the use of SSL.

After you have set up the `web.xml` file as shown, you can now visit the protected resource in a browser. Note the fact that now the port number is `8443`, which is the Tomcat default SSL port, and also note that the URL prefix is `https` as opposed to `http`. Assuming that you are using the Web application from the book Web site (put the ISBN number of this book into the search box at `www.samspublishing.com`), the URL to reach the protected resource is `https://localhost:8443/chapter16/protected/index.html`.

When the URL is visited, you should be prompted by your browser to agree to accept the certificate. This is because you issued the certificate, about 10 minutes ago if you are following through on your own machine, not by an authorized certification authority.

You can view your own certificate from the browser. Figure 16.11 shows the certificate that was created earlier in Figure 16.10.

When you have accepted the certificate, you will be asked for your username and password using the `login.html` page shown in Figure 16.4. This time, however, the username and password will be sent over HTTPS.

As you have now seen, there are four kinds of authentication that can all be set up declaratively from within the various deployment descriptors—basic, digest, form-based, and client-based over HTTPS.

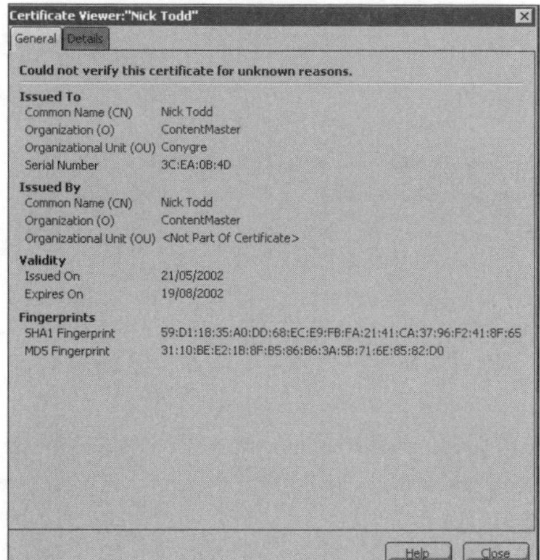

Figure 16.11 Certificate as viewed in Netscape 6.2.

Programmatic Security

We will now turn our attention to how your security implementation can not only include declarative security as you have seen, but also programmatic security. Consider the following scenario: You want to build up a JSP using fragments, and fragments A and B are interchangeable. Users from one role should be shown one fragment, and users from within a different role should see an alternative fragment. The security API is required to implement this kind of security.

You don't need to be fully competent with the entire security API to implement security from within a Web application, but you can take advantage of some of the methods that are found within the `HttpServletRequest` object.

The methods along with their functions are shown in Table 16.2.

Table 16.2 `HttpServletRequest` **Security-Related Methods**

Method	Description
`boolean isUserInRole(String roleName)`	This method can be used to identify whether the current user is within a specific role or not. If there is no current logged in user, the method returns `false`.
`Principal getUserPrincipal()`	This method returns the principal object representing the current user. This method will return `null` if there is no current logged in user.

Table 16.2 **Continued**

Method	Description
`String getRemoteUser()`	This method will return the username of the current user as a string. If there is no user, `null` will be returned.
`String getAuthType()`	This method returns the authentication type that was used to access the resource as a string. The possible values are `BASIC_AUTH`, `DIGEST_AUTH`, `FORM_AUTH`, or `CLIENT_CERT_AUTH`, corresponding to the four certification methods discussed earlier in the chapter.
`boolean isSecure()`	This method returns `true` if the resource is being accessed across a secure connection, typically SSL.

We'll now see a basic-worked example of how this API can be utilized. Three JSPs will be created: one containing one of two possible fragments, and then the two fragments. Which fragment will depend on the user's role.

If you have been following through the chapter demos on your machine, you will already have the files within your `<tomcat-home>\webapps\chapter16\protected` folder.

The three files are called `fragmentForGuests.html`, `fragmentForCustomers.html`, and `main.jsp`.

The two fragments simply contain one line of HTML as follows:

```
fragmentForGuests.html: <h1>You are a welcome guest at our site</h1>
fragmentForCustomers.html: <h1>You are a welcome customer at our site</h1>
```

The `main.jsp` file is the one to take note of. It is shown in Listing 16.8.

Listing 16.8 `main.jsp`

```
<html>
<head>
<title>Protected Page</title>
</head>
<body>
<h1>Welcome to our protected area</h1>

<% if (request.isUserInRole("guest")) { %>
  <jsp:include page="fragmentForGuests.html"/>

<%
    }
    else if (request.isUserInRole("customer"))  { %>
```

Listing 16.8 **Continued**

```
     <jsp:include page="fragmentForCustomers.html"/>
<% } %>


Your user name is <%=request.getRemoteUser()%> <br>
<hr>
<% if (request.isSecure()) { %>
    This page is being accessed over a secure connection.
<% } %>

</body>
</html>
```

Notice that the user information is being accessed from within this page, and different fragments are being included depending on the role of the users. Earlier in the chapter we set up two users within Tomcat by adding the following two entries to `<tomcat-home>\conf\tomcat-users.xml`:

```
<user name="alex" password="password" roles="customer"/>
<user name="abigail" password="password" roles="guest"/>
```

Assuming that these two users are set up as shown, the browser will incorporate one of the two fragments, depending on who you are logged in as. Figure 16.12 shows the output in the browser when you log in as user `abigail`, who is in the role of `guest`. The URL for `main.jsp` is shown here:

```
https://localhost:8443/chapter16/protected/main.jsp
```

Figure 16.12 Output from `main.jsp`.

There is one fundamental weakness with this approach, which is that the role names `guest` and `customer` are now hard-coded into the JSP. If you did this in numerous servlets and JSPs, you would have all sorts of problems if the role names changed. One way around this is to define some role names within `web.xml` that can act as parameters that will be resolved if they are referred to in the JSPs. This means that if the role names changed, you would only have to change their mappings within the `web.xml` deployment descriptor.

Listing 16.9 shows how `web.xml` could be modified to define these additional parameters. In the example, we have created two new names, `visitor` and `registeredUser`. These names are mapped to the actual role names `guest` and `customer`. Notice that they are defined for a specific servlet or JSP.

Listing 16.9 `web.xml` **with Parameterized Roles**

```
<web-app xmlns="http://java.sun.com/xml/ns/j2ee"
   xmlns:xsi="http://www.w3.org/2001/XMLSchema-instance"
   xsi:schemaLocation="http://java.sun.com/xml/ns/j2ee
   http://java.sun.com/xml/ns/j2ee/web-app_2_4.xsd" version="2.4">
  <servlet>
    <servlet-name>mainWithParameters</servlet-name>
    <jsp-file>/protected/mainWithParameters.jsp</jsp-file>
    <security-role-ref>
      <role-name>visitor</role-name>
      <role-link>guest</role-link>
    </security-role-ref>
    <security-role-ref>
      <role-name>registeredUser</role-name>
      <role-link>customer</role-link>
    </security-role-ref>
  </servlet>

  <servlet-mapping>
    <servlet-name>mainWithParameters</servlet-name>
    <url-pattern>/protected/mainWithParameters</url-pattern>
  </servlet-mapping>

<!-- content as in Listing 16.7 -->

</web-app>
```

The JSP, `main.jsp`, would be amended as shown in Listing 16.10, where the role checks now use the new names, `visitor` and `registeredUser`.

Listing 16.10 **Extract from** `mainWithParameters.jsp`

```
<% if (request.isUserInRole("visitor")) { %>
  <jsp:include page="fragmentForGuests.html"/>

<%
```

Listing 16.10 **Continued**

```
    }
    else if (request.isUserInRole("registeredUser"))  { %>
     <jsp:include page="fragmentForCustomers.html"/>
<% } %>
```

Security in J2EE Applications

So far in this chapter you have seen how to build security into a Web application, but what if that Web application is part of a much larger J2EE application? What if EJB resources, for example, are also required? Within EJBs the same security model is used, in the sense of principals and roles.

For EJBs, the access rights can be defined declaratively or programmatically. If you are defining access declaratively, additional entries are added to the EJB deployment descriptor `ejb-jar.xml`.

Security roles are defined and then used for EJBs in `ejb-jar.xml` as shown in Listing 16.11.

Listing 16.11 `ejb-jar.xml`

```
<ejb-jar>
  <enterprise-beans>
     <!--all the beans are defined here ▼
  </enterprise-beans>
  <assembly-descriptor>
    <security-role>
       <description>
        This is a registered user who can make
        purchases from the site
       </description>
       <role-name>customer</role-name>
    </security-role>

    <method-permission>
      <role-name>customer</role-name>
      <method>
        <ejb-name>CompactDiscAccessBean</ejb-name>
        <method-name>*</method-name>
      </method>
    </method-permission>

    <container-transaction>
      <!--all of the transactions are defined here ▼
    </container-transaction>
  </assembly-descriptor>
</ejb-jar>
```

If you look at Listing 16.11, you will see that there is some similarity with the deployment entries in the various `web.xml` examples that you have seen in this chapter. The example shown builds on the J2EE application that was created in the previous chapter. Notice the role is defined within the assembly descriptor. This will map to a role that is defined within the application server, typically through a visual interface of some kind. Figure 16.13 shows the user interface for the configuration of roles within the WebLogic 7 Application Server.

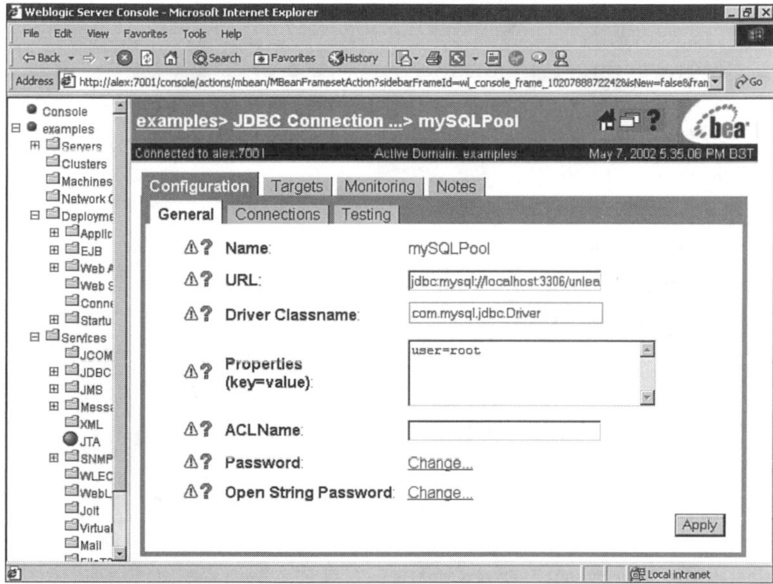

Figure 16.13 Web logic role configuration screen.

Look again at Listing 16.11. You can see the security roles being defined. To then relate those to specific EJB methods, you use the `<method-permission>` elements as shown. These are also located within the `<assembly-descriptor>` element. The roles used within these method-permissions must be declared within the `<security-role>` elements as in the example.

A helpful thing to consider is that when your Web applications are interacting with EJBs, the user information is made available to the EJB application. Therefore, the EJB container will have access to the principal object that the Web container is using to identify the user. This means that users that have authenticated themselves within the context of the Web application will also be authenticated for the EJB container as well. However, there is a slight complication. There is a difference between how a web container and an EJB container handle unauthenticated users.

Unauthenticated Users

In a Web application, the principal can be identified with a call to the `HttpServletRequest.getUserPrincipal()` method. If no user has authenticated, it returns `null`. However, if you call the equivalent method `EJBContext.getCallerPrincipal()`, it must return a Principal object. This must not be `null`.

The J2EE 1.4 specification does not specify how a J2EE server must address this issue, but there a number of options open to application server vendors, including the following recommended in the J2EE specification:

1) Use the same principal throughout the application.
2) Use a different principal for each server instance, or each session, or each application.
3) Use the <run-as> element enabling the application deployer to specify the principal to be used.

The <run-as> element

The `<run-as>` element can be used in both `web.xml` and `ejb-jar.xml` deployment descriptors. This allows the principal to be set at deploy time for a particular Web or J2EE application. A `<run-as>` element contains a `<role-name>` as shown below.

```
<run-as>
  <role-name>fred</role-name>
</run-as>
```

It is used in web.xml when defining a `<servlet>` element.

```
<servlet>
  <servlet-name>SomeServlet</servlet-name>
  <servlet-class>SomeServletClass</servlet-class>
  <run-as>
    <role-name>fred</role-name>
  </run-as>
</servlet>
```

If this servlet then invoked an EJB, the principal 'fred' will be passed on to the invoked EJB.

You can also declare a `<run-as>` element for the EJB itself. This is done within a `<security-identity>` element which contains the `<run-as>` element. This can then be used in the declaration elements for entity, session, and message-driven beans. An example of an entity bean using <run-as> is shown below. Message-driven and session beans are also done in the same way:

```
<entity>
  ...
  <security-identity>
    <run-as>
```

```
      <role-name>wilma</role-name>
    </run-as>
  </security-identity>
  ...
</entity>
```

This entity bean will now be accessed with the principal 'wilma' being used, which means that if called by a Web application from an unauthenticated user, the `EJBContext.getCallerPrincipal()` method will not return `null`.

Java Authentication and Authorization Service (JAAS)

Within J2EE 1.3–compliant application servers, there is also a security API called the Java Authentication and Authorization Service (JAAS). This API is an extension to the security APIs already available. This API essentially provides application developers with the ability to enforce access control based on who is *running* code.

The key benefit that this brings to J2EE applications is that the Java developer is no longer concerned with how the underlying authentication takes place. So, the user information may be coming from a Win2K domain, an LDAP directory, or an Oracle database. The Java application is shielded from the detail.

The authentication is done by what are referred to as pluggable modules. These are also referred to as *login modules*, and will normally request a username and password.

There are two core functions of JAAS:

- Authentication
- Authorization

The core classes for authorization are

- *Subject*—the subject represents a user or users, plus any security-specific attributes referred to as *credentials*.
- *Principal*—the principals represent the subject identities. You have seen these earlier in the chapter.
- *Credentials*—these are the security-specific attributes, which are represented by Java classes that optionally implement either the `Refreshable` or the `Destroyable` interfaces.

For authentication there is a `LoginContext`, which contains references to the `LoginModules` that contain the actual logic for the authentication process.

WebLogic 7 has full support for JAAS, and a URL containing more information on JAAS in WebLogic 7 is `http://e-docs.bea.com/wls/docs70/security/cli_apps.html#1042212`.

For a more generic overview of JAAS, you can also visit the JAAS Developers Guide at `http://java.sun.com/security/jaas/doc/api.html`.

Single Sign On

No chapter on security would be complete without a mention of single sign on. Just consider for a moment how many different usernames and passwords that you have for different Web sites that you visit. How do you remember them all? Do you use the same one everywhere (a very unsafe practice)? The idea of single sign on goes some way to reduce some of this hassle.

Imagine if you could manage your user information in one place, have one username and password, and have various sites of your choice use that sign-on information to provide you access to their resources. This could also be applied to technologies such as Web services, where applications can also have a single sign on that can then be used to authenticate them with various Web services.

You may well have come across Microsoft Passport (`www.microsoft.com/passport`), which provides a single sign on for various Microsoft offerings.

There is also the Liberty Alliance (`http://www.projectliberty.org/`), which is looking at developing an open standard that can also be used for single sign on.

Liberty Alliance is an organization made up of companies such as Sun, HP, Sony, AOL, and Nokia. There were around 40 sponsoring companies as of May 2002.

A further development along this line is that of Security Assertions Markup Language (SAML). SAML is an XML markup that can be used for passing sign-on information between different domains. More information can be found at `http://java.sun.com/features/2002/05/single-signon.html`.

One product that uses SAML is SiteMinder 5 from Netegrity. This product does the authentication of users for you. For more information on this product, visit `http://www.netegrity.com/`.

This discussion has so far been fairly high level. What can you do with what is currently available? In short, not a lot! Although you can have single sign on within a J2EE application as you have seen in the sense of a Web application login being passed to an EJB container, it is still not easily possible to propagate this to disparate J2EE applications.

Summary

In this chapter, you have seen how security can be implemented from Web applications, both in a declarative way and also in a programmatic way. You have also seen how security credentials within a Web container can be passed to an EJB container. You have also seen how a secure socket layer works, and how it can be implemented using the Tomcat Web container, if required.

Finally, two more recent technologies were discussed, namely JAAS and the concept of single sign on.

17

Personalization and Web Applications

PERSONALIZATION IS BECOMING KEY FOR MANY WEB applications in use today. For many large companies, a customer's perception of them is often shaped substantially by the quality of their Web site. Companies and organizations need to do all they can to drive repeat business through their site, and personalization is one of the tools that is used to achieve this. In this chapter, we'll explore what personalization is, and you will learn how Web applications built for the Java platform can incorporate personalization.

Introduction to Personalization

Personalization is, in essence, providing a personalized experience for the users who access your Web site. In other words, different users see different things within the site based on things such as their user preferences, previous visiting behavior, or buying habits.

Good examples of personalized sites include the following:

- `http://www.amazon.com`
- `http://my.yahoo.com`
- `http://www.msn.com`

Take Amazon for example; I use Amazon on a fairly regular basis to purchase books on a range of subjects. I buy a good number of technical books, so when I visit Amazon my personal page contains books on the technical subjects.

Another example would be if you frequently visited a cinema-listing site. If you register your details about which cinema you personally use with the site, your local cinema listing could be put on the home page for when you return. If you had a choice between two sites showing cinema listings, one with your local listings on the home page and another where you had to do a search every time, you would probably choose to visit the one that showed your local listings. This is one of the key benefits of personalization. The more people that visit your site, the more likely they are to purchase something. Hence, your site revenue increases either through advertising or direct sales.

Having said all this about the benefits of personalization, it is also worth sounding a note of caution. Just because you *can* do personalization, doesn't mean that you always should. If you personalize everything, it can get very confusing for your users! Before incorporating personalization into a Web site, consider carefully what benefits that your proposed personalization will bring to the end users experience. If you cannot really think of anything, you might be in danger of building in personalized content because you *can* rather than because you *should*. You also need to consider the legal implications of what you are doing. Gathering user information, and then using it to selectively promote products to them has legal implications that cannot be ignored. This must be considered before you go headlong into personalizing your site. One Web site that has some interesting reviews and articles on how personalization can best be used is `http://www.appiancorp.com/`. So, how can you gather information about your users? You can solicit information from visitors a number of ways, which are described in the following sections.

Using Persistent Cookies

One way of personalizing content is to use persistent cookies. These were discussed in Chapter 8, "Session Tracking Using JSP." When a user visits your site, a persistent cookie can be left on the client machine. As the user is browsing the site, you can track his movements and store the information in a database of some description. When the user returns at some later date, you can use this browsing information to decide what content to display within the site.

For example, I had to get a baby buggy for my son Alex, so I visited an online baby store. I was somewhat overwhelmed by the number of different buggies that were available, so I browsed about, but never bought anything. When I returned to the site a few days later the home page was showing a number of buggies at special prices. I had never registered with the site; it was simply using a persistent cookie in my browser.

This mechanism alone has limitations, however. You cannot tell if users are male or female, how old they are, how much money they have to spend, and what their interests are. You will need to ask them for these answers, and this is where site registration comes in.

Using Registration and Forms

If you are going to provide a personalized experience for your user that goes beyond simply tracking what they do in your site, you will need to provide some kind of registration mechanism. Users will need to explicitly tell you certain pieces of information. You can encourage this by making some parts of the site only available to registered users, which is common practice among many sites today.

The information gleaned can be as complex or as basic as you want. You simply need to consider what it is you are going to do with this data that you are collecting. You do need to seriously consider, however, how much information you are going to collect. How do you feel when you are presented with a screen full of compulsory form fields to fill in, simply to enable you to register for a Web site?

After the information is collected, however, you can use it to create personalized content for users based on what they have specified in their user profile information.

After a user profile has been created, you can store much more than the information that they provided from the fill-in form. You can add the pages that they have visited, the content they have seen, the promotions that they clicked, and so on, to this profile.

A Personalized Application Example

A comprehensive example of a user profile is used in the case study of our fictitious training company in Chapter 9, "Developing Custom Tag Libraries." For this chapter, we will use a basic profile of our users. It will simply contain their favorite product type.

> **Note**
>
> If you want to install the demo application that is being referred to in this chapter you will need to download the Web application called `chapter17Personalization.war` from the Sams Web site (`http://www.samspublishing.com`). This contains the database script required for this application to work in MySQL.

The URL for the home page is

`http://localhost:8080/chapter17Personalization/shopping/welcome`

Our demonstration is a variation of the shopping-cart application that you have been exposed to in various chapters in this book. Essentially, the shop provides users with the ability to purchase DVDs, CDs, and books from a Web site. The product information comes from a database. No information has been stored about the users in all the previous applications shown. The application has been changed to also maintain user information in a database and allow people to register with the site.

The User Profile

The user profile is shown by the SQL listing in Listing 17.1. This listing is an extract from the database set up script `tablesSetUp.sql` in the `chapter17Personalization.war` demonstration site.

Listing 17.1 **Extract from** `tablesSetUp.sql`

```
create table users (name varchar(50) primary key,
                                    password varchar(30));
insert into users values('John','password');
```

Listing 17.1 **Continued**

```
insert into users values('Janet','password');
insert into users values('Fred','password');
insert into users values('Jane','password');
insert into users values('Mel','password');
insert into users values('Mark','password');

create table interests(
          username varchar(50) not null,
          interest varchar(10) not null);
-- now set up some dummy data. This would normally be collected via
-- an HTML form
insert into interests values('guest', 'CD');
insert into interests values('John','DVD');
insert into interests values('Fred','book');
insert into interests values('Jane','DVD');
insert into interests values('Mel','book');
insert into interests values('Mark','CD');
insert into interests values('Janet','CD');

create table user_roles (
          name varchar(50) not null,
          rolename varchar(50) not null,
          primary key (name, rolename));

-- add some user and role mappings
insert into user_roles values('guest', 'none');
insert into user_roles values('John','customer');
insert into user_roles values('Fred','customer');
insert into user_roles values('Jane','customer');
insert into user_roles values('Mel','customer');
insert into user_roles values('Mark','customer');
insert into user_roles values('Janet','customer');
```

The table called `interests` in Listing 17.1 is used to contain the users' core interest, which as you can see is `CD`, `DVD`, or `book`. It could be a great deal more complex, storing all sorts of information about the user, but for this example, we'll keep it simple. The usernames and passwords are stored in another table called `users`.

> **Note**
>
> The interests are in a separate table to keep our options open. If desired, the application could be modified to allow more than one interest per user.

Setting Up Login Using the Database

When the provision of usernames and passwords was discussed in Chapter 16, "Security and JSP," the usernames and passwords were maintained in the `tomcat-users.xml` file. This was because we were not adding or modifying user information. We are now using a database because you are storing more than just the usernames and passwords, and you also want to be able to dynamically add users as they register.

To configure Tomcat to use your database to contain user information, you will need to add the following entry to `server.xml`:

```
<Realm  className="org.apache.catalina.realm.JDBCRealm" debug="99"
    driverName="org.gjt.mm.mysql.Driver"
    connectionURL="jdbc:mysql://localhost:3306/jsphandbook?user=root"
    userTable="users" userNameCol="name" userCredCol="password"
    userRoleTable="user_roles" roleNameCol="rolename" />
```

You will then need to locate and comment out the following entry:

```
<Realm className="org.apache.catalina.realm.MemoryRealm"/>
```

This is how Tomcat was specifying to use `tomcat-users.xml` to contain user information.

> **Caution**
>
> If you are building this demonstration on your machine, you must make this change yourself because it is not part of the Web application.

If you notice from the additional entry in `server.xml`, there is a reference to the `users` table and also a reference to a `user_role` table. This table maps users to roles, as did the `tomcat-users.xml` discussed in Chapter 16. We have used a single role called `customer`, and the SQL for that table is also shown in Listing 17.1.

The Login Page

We need a login page to enable users to log in, and we need a registration form to enable users to register. This is shown in Figure 17.1 with its code shown in Listing 17.2.

Listing 17.2 `login.html`

```
<html><head>
<title>
Welcome to Ashdown.com - The best deals for Books, CDs and DVDs!
</title>
</head>
<body bgcolor="#FFCC99">
<h2>Log in</h2>

<form method="POST" action="j_security_check">
```

Listing 17.2 **Continued**

```
Username: <input type="text" name="j_username"><br>
Password: <input type="password" name="j_password"><br>
<input type="submit" value="Continue">
</form>

<hr>
Alternatively, please register:
<form method="post" action="registerServlet">
Your Username: <input type="text" name="name"><br>
Your Password: <input type="password" name="password"><br>
Please confirm password: <input type="password" name="password2"><br>
Your main interest: <br>
<input type="radio" name="interest" value="book"> Books<br>
<input type="radio" name="interest" value="DVD"> DVDs<br>
<input type="radio" name="interest" value="CD"> CDs<br>
<br>Once you submit this form, you will be redirected to this page. <br>
Please log in with your specified login name and password<br>
<input type="submit">
</form>

</body>
</html>
```

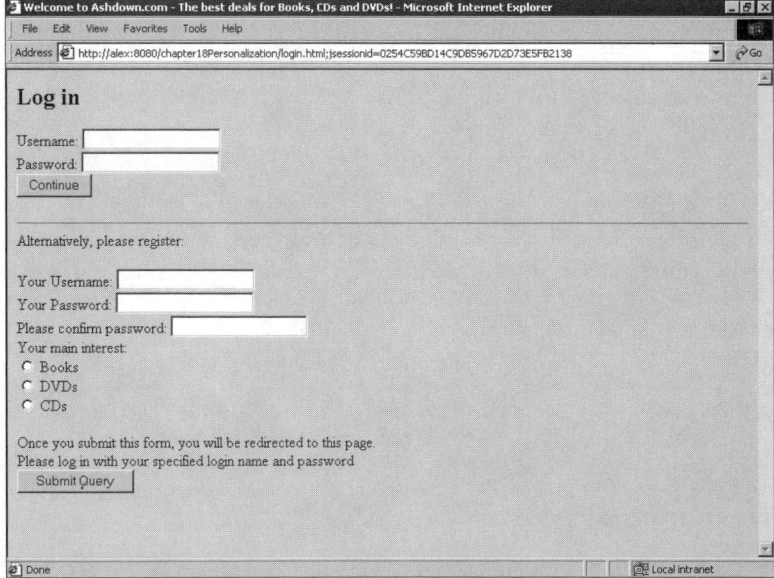

Figure 17.1 Login and registration form.

Note that in Listing 17.2 there are two forms: one for logging in and one for the registration process. This listing will look familiar if you have read Chapter 16, which covers the login process using form-based authentication. You will also know that there must be an entry in the `web.xml` file. Basically, all the shopping pages are in a folder called `shopping`, and it is this folder that is being protected by the form-based login. Listing 17.3 shows `web.xml` for our application. Various aspects of this will be referred to as we progress.

Listing 17.3 `web.xml`

```
<?xml version="1.0" encoding="ISO-8859-1"?>
<web-app xmlns="http://java.sun.com/xml/ns/j2ee"
   xmlns:xsi="http://www.w3.org/2001/XMLSchema-instance"
   xsi:schemaLocation="http://java.sun.com/xml/ns/j2ee
   http://java.sun.com/xml/ns/j2ee/web-app_2_4.xsd" version="2.4">
    <servlet>
        <servlet-name>
            controller
        </servlet-name>
        <servlet-class>
            com.conygre.ShoppingCartController
        </servlet-class>
    </servlet>
        <servlet>
        <servlet-name>
            registerServlet
        </servlet-name>
        <servlet-class>
            com.conygre.RegistrationServlet
        </servlet-class>
    </servlet>


    <servlet-mapping>
        <servlet-name>
            controller
        </servlet-name>
        <url-pattern>
            /shopping/welcome
        </url-pattern>
    </servlet-mapping>

        <servlet-mapping>
        <servlet-name>
            registerServlet
        </servlet-name>
```

Listing 17.3 **Continued**

```
        <url-pattern>
            /registerServlet
        </url-pattern>
    </servlet-mapping>


    <welcome-file-list>
        <welcome-file>/welcome</welcome-file>
    </welcome-file-list>
    <taglib>
        <taglib-uri>http://java.sun.com/jstl-el/core</taglib-uri>
        <taglib-location>/WEB-INF/c.tld</taglib-location>
    </taglib>
    <taglib>
        <taglib-uri>http://java.sun.com/jstl-el/sql</taglib-uri>
        <taglib-location>/WEB-INF/sql.tld</taglib-location>
    </taglib>
    <security-constraint>
        <web-resource-collection>
            <web-resource-name>Protected Area</web-resource-name>
            <url-pattern>/shopping/*</url-pattern>
        </web-resource-collection>
        <auth-constraint>
            <role-name>guest</role-name>
            <role-name>customer</role-name>
        </auth-constraint>
    </security-constraint>
    <login-config>
        <auth-method>FORM</auth-method>
        <form-login-config>
            <form-login-page>/login.html</form-login-page>
            <form-error-page>/loginFailed.html</form-error-page>
        </form-login-config>
    </login-config>
</web-app>
```

Note the security aspects toward the bottom of Listing 17.3. The `<security-constraint>` element and the `<login-config>` elements are specifying both the login form and also the fact that anything within the `shopping` subfolder is protected. It is this folder that contains our shopping Web site.

The Profile Object

For the application to access user information in a convenient way, an object used to encapsulate the user information will be used. This is set up for us with the help of a servlet and a Profile bean.

Notice from Listing 17.3, that there is a servlet called the `controller`. The controller servlet acts as the gateway into the Web application after people have logged in. The controller servlet source code is shown in Listing 17.4.

Listing 17.4 `ShoppingCartController.java`

```
// this servlet is used as the entry point into the application
// it sets up the profile object and the shopping cart for the current user
// it then finally forwards to the home page of the application, welcome.jsp

package com.conygre;
import java.io.*;
import javax.servlet.*;
import javax.servlet.http.*;

public class ShoppingCartController extends HttpServlet {

  public void doGet(HttpServletRequest req, HttpServletResponse res)
          throws ServletException, IOException {
    doPost(req, res);
  }

  public void doPost(HttpServletRequest req, HttpServletResponse res)
          throws ServletException, IOException {
    HttpSession session = req.getSession();
    ServletContext application = getServletContext();
    // if there is no profile object set up to represent the current user
    if (session.getAttribute("currentUser") == null){
      // create a new profile object, passing in the username
      Profile profile = new Profile(req.getRemoteUser());
      session.setAttribute("currentUser", profile);
      // create a shopping cart for them as well!
      session.setAttribute("cart", new com.conygre.Cart());
    }
    // everything set up, so forward to the home page
    RequestDispatcher rd =
            application.getRequestDispatcher("/shopping/welcome.jsp");
    rd.forward(req, res);
  }
}
```

The controller servlet has two main functions. It sets up the shopping cart (discussed in Chapter 14), and it also creates something that we have called the `profile` object, which represents the current user. The `profile` object used here is a very basic object in terms of its properties. It contains the username and the preferred product type, which are represented by the two properties, `name` and `interest`. The issue to consider is this; how does it know what the `interest` value should be? The value is within the database, and it needs to be looked up from there. The code is shown in Listing 17.5.

Listing 17.5 `Profile.java`

```
// this class represents the current user
// the user name is passed in to the constructor
// the other profile attribute for the interest is
// obtained from the database

package com.conygre;
import java.sql.*;

public class Profile {
    private String name;
    private String interest;

    public Profile(String name) {
        this.name = name;
        // now extract the interest from the database
        Connection conn = null;
        ResultSet result = null;
        Statement stmt = null;
        ResultSetMetaData rsmd = null;
        try {
          Class c = Class.forName("org.gjt.mm.mysql.Driver");
        }
        catch (Exception e) {
          System.out.println("Error occurred " + e);
         }
         try {
           conn = DriverManager.getConnection
                    ("jdbc:mysql://localhost:3306/jsphandbook", "root", "");
         }
         catch (SQLException e) {
            System.out.println("Error occurred " + e);
         }
         try {
            stmt = conn.createStatement();
            result =  stmt.executeQuery
                  ("SELECT * FROM interests where username=\"" + name + "\"");
            // move the cursor to the first and only row
            result.next();
            // set the interest variable
```

Listing 17.5 **Continued**

```
            interest = result.getString("interest");
            // close the connection
            conn.close();
        }
        catch (SQLException e) {
            System.out.println("Error occurred " + e);
        }
    }

    public String getName(){
        return name;
    }
    public void setName(String s){
        name = s;
    }
    public String getInterest(){
            return interest;
    }
    public void setInterest(String s){
            interest = s;
    }
}
```

When the `profile` object is created, the database is accessed and the `interest` value is obtained. Clearly, there could be many more profile properties. Note that the database access code is within the bean. This could be moved out and placed in a separate bean, but we left it in for simplicity so you could clearly see exactly what is going on.

Personalizing Pages

This profile bean was created in the controller servlet, and then placed into a session-scoped attribute called `currentUser`. This means that the pages now have convenient access to this data. The welcome page, `welcome.jsp`, uses this data for personalization. Figure 17.2 shows what `welcome.jsp` looks like when viewed in a browser, logged in as the user called Mel. This user has books as his preferred product type. Notice the circled part of the page.

The circled part of the diagram is personalized to the user based on his preferences. Figure 17.3 shows exactly the same the page, but for a different user.

Both users get different content presented. The source code for welcome.jsp is shown in Listing 17.6.

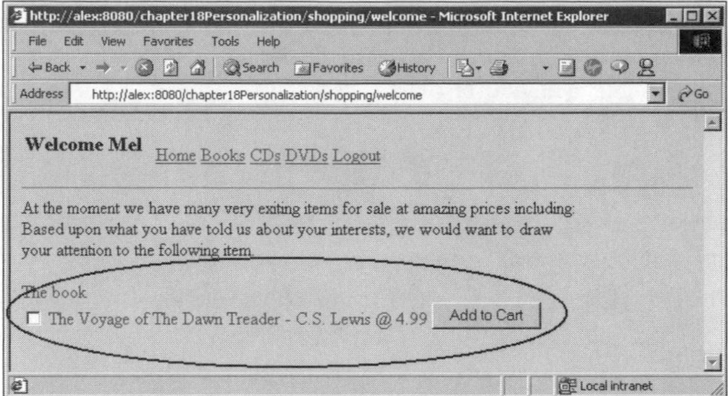

Figure 17.2 `welcome.jsp` as seen by user Mel.

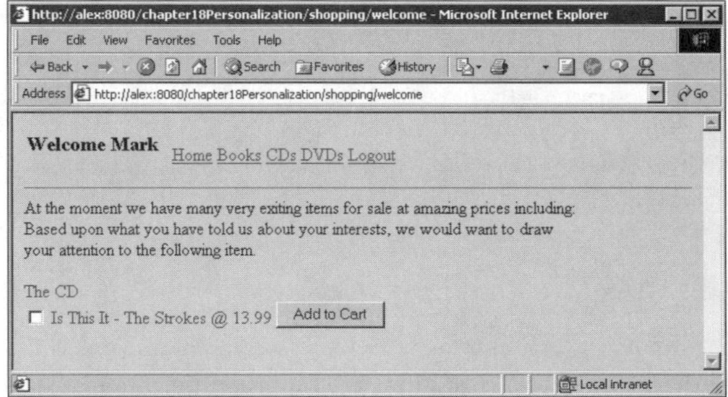

Figure 17.3 `welcome.jsp` as seen by a user Mark.

Listing 17.6 `welcome.jsp`

```
<%@ taglib uri="http://java.sun.com/jstl-el/core" prefix="c" %>
<%@ taglib uri="http://java.sun.com/jstl-el/sql" prefix="sql" %>
<jsp:include page="cache.jsp"/>
<sql:setDataSource var="handbookDb"
   user="root"
   url="jdbc:mysql://localhost:3306/jsphandbook"
   driver="org.gjt.mm.mysql.Driver"
   scope="application"
 />
<jsp:useBean id="stock" class="com.conygre.Stock" scope="application"/>
<html>
  <head>
    <title>Welcome to Ashdown.com -
     The best deals for Books, CDs and DVDs!</title>
```

Listing 17.6 **Continued**

```
  </head>
  <body bgcolor="#FFCC99">
    <c:import url="header.jsp" />
    At the moment we have many very exiting items for sale
    at amazing prices.
    <br>Based upon what you have told us about your interests,
    we would want to draw
    <br> your attention to the following item.<p>
    <font color="blue">

<form method="post" action="addToCart.jsp">
<%-- this content will vary depending upon the user --%>
<c:if test="${currentUser.interest == 'book'}">
    <p>The book<br>
    <input type="checkbox" name="id"
     value="<c:out value='${stock.books[0].id}'/>">
    <c:out value="${stock.books[0].title}" /> -
    <c:out value="${stock.books[0].author}" /> @
    <c:out value="${stock.books[0].price}" />
</c:if>

<c:if test="${currentUser.interest == 'DVD'}">
    <p>The DVD<br>
    <input type="checkbox" name="id"
     value="<c:out value='${stock.dvds[0].id}'/>">
    <c:out value="${stock.dvds[0].title}" /> -
    <c:out value="${stock.dvds[0].director}" /> @
    <c:out value="${stock.dvds[0].price}" />
</c:if>

<c:if test="${currentUser.interest == 'CD'}">
    <p>The CD<br>
    <input type="checkbox" name="id"
     value="<c:out value='${stock.cds[0].id}'/>">
    <c:out value="${stock.cds[0].title}" /> -
    <c:out value="${stock.cds[0].artist}" /> @
    <c:out value="${stock.cds[0].price}" />
</c:if>
<input type="submit" value="Add to Cart">
</form>
</body>
</html>
```

The most important part of this listing is the last section. It is querying the `currentUser.interest` property. Which `if` block gets output is dependent on the value of the `currentUser.interest` property. Mark preferred CDs and was presented with information about a CD, whereas Mel preferred books and was presented with a book.

> **Note**
> If you are wondering where all the data for the CDs, DVDs, and books is coming from, it is from the beans and tables referenced in the shopping cart application from Chapter 14, "Databases and JSP." It is included in the Web application provided for this chapter.

User Registration

Finally, we need to look at how users register with the Web site in the first place. The users that we have been working with were already set up.

Look again at Listing 17.2 for the `login.html` page, and Listing 17.3 for `web.xml`. The login page also has a form to enable new users to register, and the registration process is handled by a servlet configured in `web.xml`.

The registration servlet is shown in Listing 17.7.

Listing 17.7 `RegistrationServlet.java`

```
// this servlet is used for the registration of new users
// it is where the registration form in login.html submits
// its data

package com.conygre;
import java.io.*;
import javax.servlet.*;
import javax.servlet.http.*;
import java.sql.*;

public class RegistrationServlet extends HttpServlet {


  public void doPost(HttpServletRequest req, HttpServletResponse res)
           throws ServletException, IOException {
    // set up a connection
    Connection conn = null;
    ResultSet result = null;
    PreparedStatement stmt = null;
    PreparedStatement stmt2 = null;
    PreparedStatement stmt3 = null;

    try {
      Class c = Class.forName("org.gjt.mm.mysql.Driver");
    }
    catch (Exception e) {
```

Listing 17.7 **Continued**

```
      System.out.println("Error occurred " + e);
    }
    try {
      conn = DriverManager.getConnection
           ("jdbc:mysql://localhost:3306/jsphandbook", "root", "");
    }
    catch (SQLException e) {
       System.out.println("Error occurred " + e);
    }
    // create a prepared statement to create a new user
    // and set up their interests
    try {
       stmt = conn.prepareStatement
          ("INSERT into interests (username, interest) values (?,?)");
       stmt.setString(1, req.getParameter("name"));
       stmt.setString(2, req.getParameter("interest"));
       stmt.executeUpdate();

       stmt2 = conn.prepareStatement
          ("INSERT into users (name, password) values (?,?)");
       stmt2.setString(1, req.getParameter("name"));
       stmt2.setString(2, req.getParameter("password"));
       stmt2.executeUpdate();

       stmt3 = conn.prepareStatement
          ("INSERT into user_roles (name, rolename) values (?,?)");
       stmt3.setString(1, req.getParameter("name"));
       stmt3.setString(2, "customer");
       stmt3.executeUpdate();

       // close the connection
       conn.close();

    }
    catch (SQLException e) {
        System.out.println("Error occurred " + e);
  }
   // now redirect to the welcome servlet,
   // this will force a log in with their new username and password
   // because it is in the protected folder
   res.sendRedirect("shopping/welcome");
  }
}
```

Notice that a number of prepared statements are used in this registration servlet to update the database with the new entries. Three tables are modified—the `user` table, the `interests` table, and the `user_roles` table. Note that there is no error checking in this servlet. It has been left out for clarity.

A diagrammatic representation of our personalization can be seen in Figure 17.4.

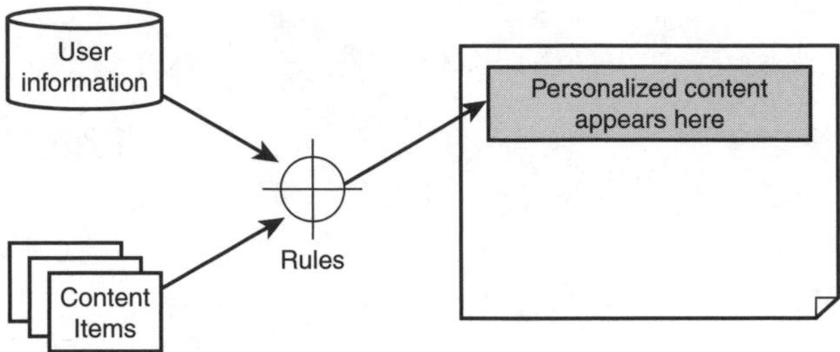

Figure 17.4 Rules-based personalization.

Essentially, the page uses rules to decide which content to show based on the user information provided.

Rule-Based Personalization Engines

You have now seen how a basic personalized application could be built to run in a standard Web-application container such as Tomcat. There are a number of weaknesses with this approach, however. Business people, not programmers, should decide the elements of personalization. So in this example, if the business user wanted to change the rules, she would have to get a JSP developer to go in and change the JSP pages. In more complex applications, changes could be required in beans as well, and the whole thing will not be particularly dynamic! By the time the personalization requirements are implemented they would probably change anyway. Also, how do you monitor how much difference your personalization has made to the profitability of your site? You invest money in personalization, but is it working? Are you showing the right content to the right people? Also, how is the personalized content added? In our example, we are using data from the database. How is new data added?

Personalization engines help to overcome these weaknesses. Business users, not programmers, set personalization rules; you can monitor how your personalization is working, and you can easily modify the personalized content.

To finish this chapter, we will present one such personalization product that comes from the application server vendor Art Technology Group. This vendor provides the Dynamo Personalization Server and the Dynamo Scenario Server products, which are specific to personalization. These products provide personalization that can be built in to your JSP pages.

Creating Rules

In our earlier example, the rules about who sees what and when were effectively placed directly into the JSP. When using ATG Dynamo, the rules are set up via a user interface—no programming code in sight! Figure 17.5 shows this interface.

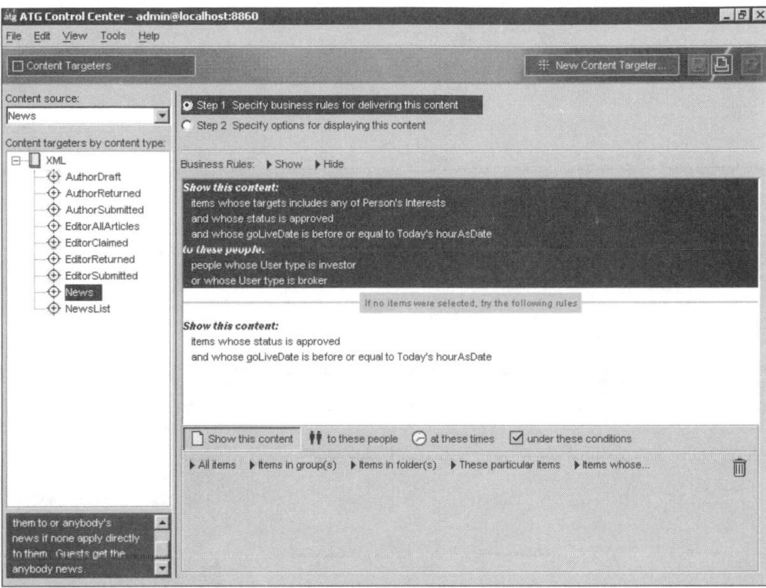

Figure 17.5 Setting up rules in the ATG control center.

As you can see, it is a fairly comprehensive interface allowing quite complex rules to be set up by a business user. This rule is taken from one of the demo applications that ship with the product.

You can also try out different aspects of personalization and log the user responses. So, for example, you might have two possible promotions, and you are unsure which one will work best. You can randomly present to different users one of the promotions, and then observe the take-up rate. Figure 17.6 shows how the Dynamo Scenario Server enables you to set this up. Again, it is all done through a visual interface.

The data collected can then be presented in a graphical format for business users to make strategic decisions about how to proceed with the promotion or whatever it is.

Finally, Listing 17.8 shows an example JSP page that takes advantage of these personalization rules. ATG has developed its own custom tag library to work with the personalization engine.

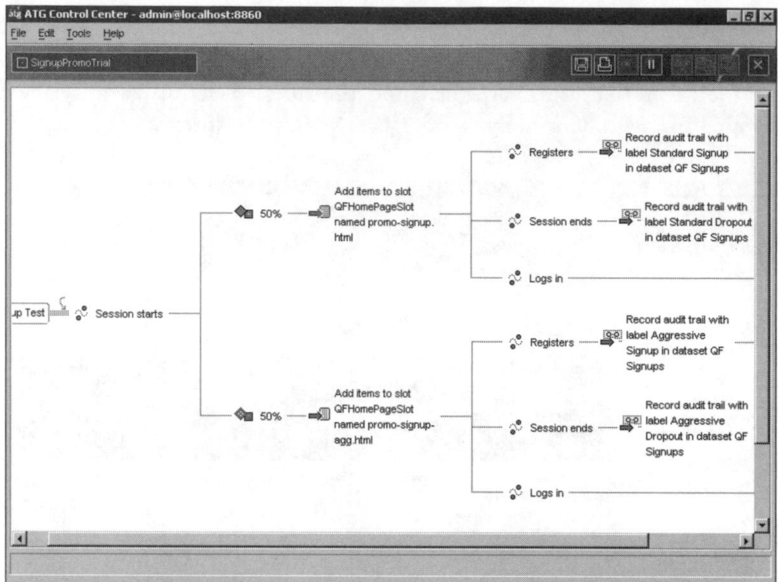

Figure 17.6 Logging user behavior in Dynamo.

Listing 17.8 **ATG dynamo personalized JSP.**

```
<%@ taglib uri="/dspTaglib" prefix="dsp" %>
<html>
<!-- other stuff -->

  <dsp:droplet name="/atg/targeting/TargetingRange">
    <dsp:param bean="/atg/registry/RepositoryTargeters/Features/BrokerFeatures"
                             name="targeter"/>
    <dsp:param bean="Profile.numberfeatureitems" name="howMany"/>
    <dsp:param name="sortProperties" value="+title"/>
    <dsp:oparam name="outputStart">
      <tr><td colspan=2><img src="images/d.gif" vspace=4></td></tr>
    </dsp:oparam>
    <dsp:oparam name="output">
      <tr valign=top>
        <td><dsp:a href="feature.jsp">
        <dsp:param name="ElementId" param="element.repositoryId"/>
        <img height="73" vspace="2" border="0" hspace="8" width="73"
           src="<dsp:valueof param="element.smallImageURL">
           images/features/noimage.gif</dsp:valueof>">
         </dsp:a></td>
        <td><dsp:a href="feature.jsp">
```

Listing 17.8 **Continued**

```
        <dsp:param name="ElementId" param="element.repositoryId"/>
        <b><dsp:valueof param="element.title"/></b></dsp:a><br>
        <dsp:valueof param="element.headline"/></td>
      </tr>
      <tr><td colspan=2><img src="images/d.gif" width=1 height=10></td></tr>
    </dsp:oparam>
    <dsp:oparam name="empty">
      <dsp:valueof bean="Profile.goals"/>
      <TD>.</TD> <TD><B>No Features found</B> </TD>
    </dsp:oparam>
  </dsp:droplet>

<!-- other stuff -->
</html>
```

We will not get into the details here, but notice the following. The number of features being displayed is coming from the `profile` object. This is the equivalent of our profile bean. Notice too that there is no Java code in the page; it is all done with tags. In fact, ATG was one of the first vendors to incorporate the facility to separate Java code from presentation logic.

One other feature that the personalization products offer is the ability to generate personalized email using JSP—those emails that come to you and include your name. They can be written in JSP, and then the engine will send the emails for you. These could be promotional emails, confirmation emails, and so on. Although you can do this yourself, it is quite a bit of work, and these tools make it relatively easy.

> **Note**
> To see an example of how to send personalized email to your users, visit the case study in Chapter 18, which demonstrates how to do this using the JavaMail API.

If you want to try the ATG product, you can download it from `www.atg.com`.

Summary

This chapter should whet your appetite for how you can personalize your Web applications. Whether you are going to use a product such as ATG Dynamo, or whether you are going to incorporate aspects of personalization using the methods outlined in this chapter, it is becoming increasingly important for Web applications to differentiate themselves by adding powerful personalization into their architecture.

18

Case Study

THROUGHOUT THIS BOOK, THERE ARE WORKING EXAMPLES of the various topics being discussed. Indeed, several of the chapters have miniapplications that demonstrate the technology discussed within that particular chapter. However, none of the chapters has an application that draws many of the different themes together in the form of a complete application. This is where the final case study chapter comes in. The aim of this chapter is to show you a more complete working application that incorporates technologies such as Struts, XML, XSLT, tag libraries, JavaBeans, database access, and so on. References will be made throughout the case study to where in the book the technologies used in the various component parts of the case study are discussed.

> **Note**
>
> If you want to deploy this application on your machine, it is available as part of the book download from `www.samspublishing.com`, where you can enter the ISBN (0672324385) in the search field. The WAR file is called `ormonds.war`. There is a `readme.txt` file in the root folder of this WAR file that explains how to set up the database and the environment. It has been tested with MySQL as the database, and the version of Tomcat should be 4.1.2 or higher.

Introduction to the Case Study

This case study is based on a fictitious technical training company called Ormonds. Ormonds is a small business and most of its clients have been obtained through word of mouth, and the company is looking to expand its client base by way of the Internet. After all, it trains people to use these technologies, and a showcase Web site advertising its courses wouldn't be a bad thing. The Web site should enable potential clients to view the available courses that are available through Ormonds, and then make inquiries online regarding the booking of these courses.

The Internet Service Provider (ISP) that Ormonds uses runs Tomcat; therefore, a Java-based Web application is the obvious choice. In fact, this was why Ormonds chose this particular ISP.

The home page of the new Ormonds Web site is shown in Figure 18.1.

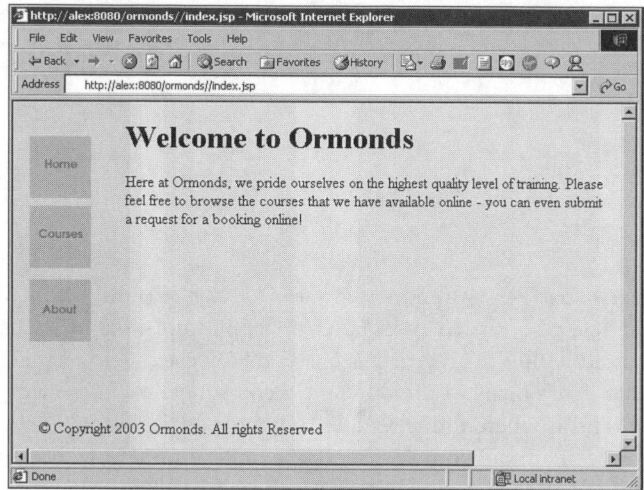

Figure 18.1 The Ormonds home page.

Case Study Architecture

The Ormonds Web site uses the following core technologies:

- JDBC
- JSTL
- Apache Struts
- XML
- XSLT
- Tomcat Security
- JavaMail

The Web site works in the following way. A user visits the home page and has the option of browsing the available courses. A user can view the outlines of the various courses, which at the bottom has a booking form that enables the user to request further information about booking. When the user submits this form, her information is put into a database, and the client receives an email confirming her request.

There is also an administration page that Ormonds employees can use to view the orders that have so far been submitted. A screen flow diagram is shown in Figure 18.2.

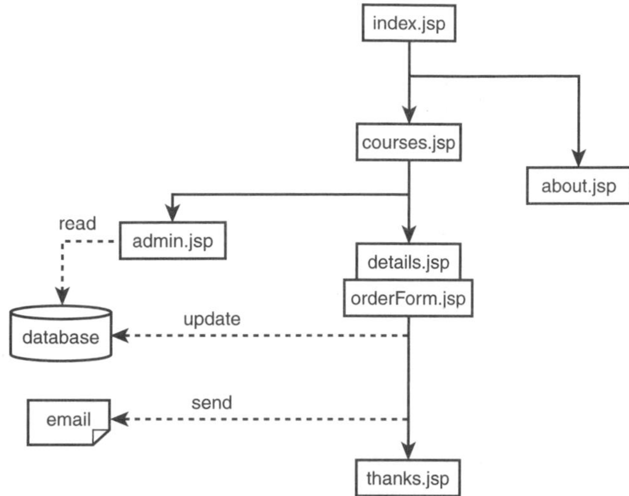

Figure 18.2 Screen flow diagram for Ormonds.

The application uses a Model 2 architecture approach throughout; there are two servlets. The form uses the Struts `ActionServlet`, and the other pages are delivered using a custom controller servlet. This has been done so that the case study demonstrates both a framework-based controller and also a custom controller.

The Page Architecture

The pages are built using templates, and tag libraries have been used throughout. The business logic has been kept within JavaBeans. The template structure for the pages is shown in Figure 18.3.

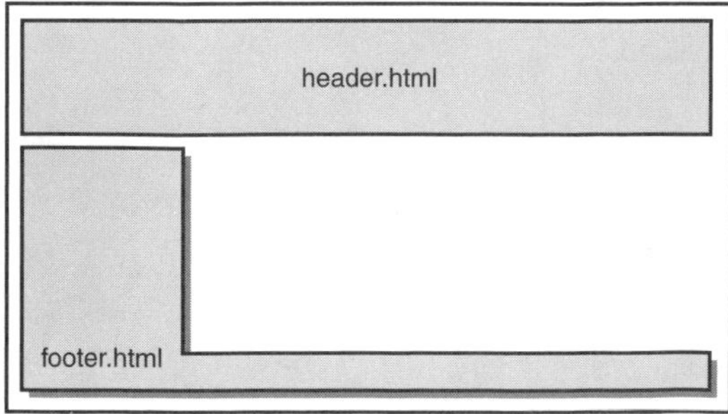

Figure 18.3 The page templates.

If you look at Figure 18.3 in conjunction with Figure 18.1, which shows the home page, you can see how the template is working. Each JSP has two includes, one for the header and one for the footer. The templates contain all the `<table>` tags and the menu bar, so the including pages simply add the two includes and put their content in between. The HTML for the two include files is shown in Listings 18.1 and 18.2.

Listing 18.1 `header.html`

```
<!-- the beginning of header.html -->
<table border="0" width="800">
    <tr>
    <td width="26" height="10"></td>
    <td width="500" height="290" rowspan="8" valign="top" align="left">
<!-- this is the end of header.html -->
```

Listing 18.2 `footer.html`

```
<!-- this is the start of footer.html -->
</td>
  </tr>
  <tr>
  <td valign="top" align="left" width="26">
<table border="0" cellpadding="0" cellspacing="0">
  <tr>
    <td align="left">
      <a href="gateway?page=/index.jsp">
      <img border="0" vspace="4" hspace="4"
      src="images/home.gif" width="64" height="64" align="top"></a>
    </td>
  </tr>
  <tr>
    <td>
      <a href="gateway?page=/courses.jsp">
      <img border="0" vspace="4" hspace="4"
      src="images/courses.gif" width="64" height="64"></a>
    </td>
  </tr>
  <tr>
    <td>
      <a href="gateway?page=/about.jsp">
      <img border="0" vspace="4" hspace="4"
      src="images/about.gif" width="64" height="64"></a>
    </td>
  </tr>
</table>
  </td>
```

Listing 18.2 **Continued**

```
  </tr>
</table>

<p>    © Copyright 2003 Ormonds. All rights Reserved</p>
<!-- this is the end of footer.html -->
```

Notice that comments have been placed into the included files to denote their beginning and end. This makes it much easier for page developers to edit and manage content because they can see what content has come from where when looking at the end result in a browser.

Listing 18.3 shows `index.jsp`, which is the home page and is one of the pages that uses these two includes.

Listing 18.3 `index.jsp`

```
<% if(application.getAttribute("urls") == null)
                          response.sendRedirect("gateway?page=/index.jsp");
%>
<html>
<head><title>Welcome to Ormonds</title></head>
<body background="images/background.jpg">
<jsp:include page="header.html" flush="true"/>
  <h1>Welcome to Ormonds </h1>
  <p>Here at Ormonds, we pride ourselves on the highest quality level
     of training.  Please feel free to browse the courses that we have
     available online - you can even submit a request for a booking online!
<jsp:include page="footer.html" flush="true"/>
</body>
</html>
```

The Course Information XML

The information about the courses is stored in an XML format, and there is an XSLT file that transforms this XML into a suitable HTML format for use in Web pages. Listing 18.4 shows an example of one of the course XML files. We have used XML since it will enable us to make use of the XML actions discussed in Chapters 10 and 11.

Listing 18.4 `course0.xml`

```
<course id="t1">
  <title>Java Programming for Developers</title>
  <technology>Java</technology>
  <duration>5 days</duration>
  <copyright>Conygre IT Ltd</copyright>
```

Listing 18.4 **Continued**

```
  <dates>
    <date>14th July 2003</date>
    <date>28th July 2003</date>
  </dates>
  <introduction>
    <paragraph>Java is fast becoming one of the most .. </paragraph>
  </introduction>
  <prerequisites>It assumes that delegates are already programmers.
  They will already understand the need for flow control, ..
    </prerequisites>
  <outline>
    <chapters>
      <chapter id="ch1">
        <heading>Introduction to Java</heading>
        <item>What is Java? </item>
        <item>The Java Virtual Machine</item>
        <item>The Java Runtime</item>
      </chapter>
      <chapter id="ch2">
        <heading>Java - the basics</heading>
        <item>Variable types in Java</item>
        <item>Java syntax </item>
        <item>  Java operators </item>
      </chapter>
      <!-- more chapters are in here in the actual application -->
      </chapters>
  </outline>
</course>
```

You'll see where this XML gets used later in the chapter.

Case Study Implementation

We'll start by looking at the home page and explaining Listing 18.3.

The Home page

Two items of special note are in Listing 18.3. One is the rather strange redirect at the top, which happens because in Tomcat welcome pages set up in `web.xml` cannot redirect to servlets, only JSP pages. Because this page needs to be visited via a controller servlet, the top of the JSP checks to see if this controller has been visited. This is because one of the roles of any controller is to initialize objects. The check at the top of the JSP simply queries one of these objects to see if it has been initialized. If it has not, the request is redirected to the controller.

The other notable feature of the home page shown in Listing 18.3, is the use of `<jsp:include>` rather than the `<%@include>` directive. The `<jsp:include>` action has been used to facilitate the straightforward modification of the HTML pages `header.html` and `footer.html`. If the include directive had been used, it would have meant that any changes to the pages would not have been represented in the output. The include directive results in the inclusion at compile time rather than runtime. This issue is discussed in Chapter 2, "The Basic Syntax of JSP."

Displaying the Course Information

When the user selects the Courses button from Figure 18.1, they are redirected to a page called `courses.jsp`. This page is shown in Listing 18.5.

Listing 18.5 `courses.jsp`

```
<%@ taglib uri="http://java.sun.com/jstl-el/core" prefix="c" %>
<%@ taglib uri="http://java.sun.com/jstl-el/xml" prefix="x" %>

<html>
<head><title>Welcome to Ormonds</title></head>
<body background="images/background.jpg">
<jsp:include page="header.html" flush="true"/>
<h2>Here is a list of the courses we provide:</h2>
  <c:forEach var="url" items="${urls}" varStatus="status">
    <c:import var="course" url="${url}"/>
    <x:parse var="xml" xml="${course}" />
    <p align="center">
    <a href="gateway?page=/details.jsp&index=<c:out value="${status.index}"/>">
                    <x:out select="$xml/course/title" />
    </a>
   </c:forEach>
<jsp:include page="footer.html" flush="true"/>
</body>
</html>
```

The output is shown in Figure 18.4.

In Listing 18.5, you can see that use is being made of both the core tags and the XML tags from the JSTL.

> **Note**
>
> The core tags are discussed in Chapter 5, "The JSP Standard Tag Library." The XML tags are discussed in Chapters 10, "Utilizing XML from JSP," and Chapter 11, "Transforming XML Using XSLT and XSLFO."

The property `urls` being used by this page is an array of URL objects that point to the XML files that contain the course information (as shown in Listing 18.4). You'll see how this is created when we look at the controller servlet.

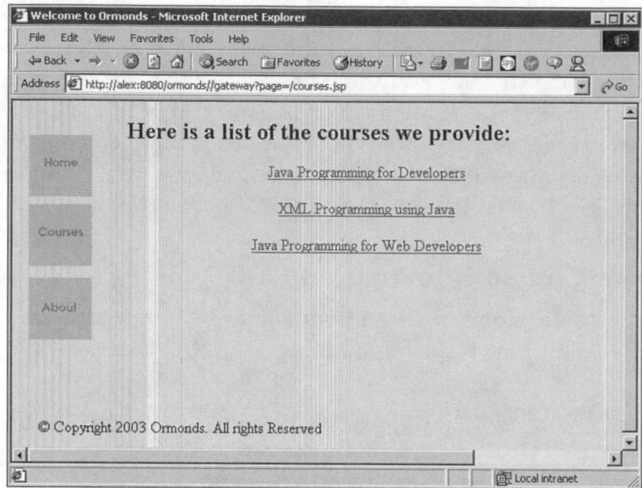

Figure 18.4 `courses.jsp` in a browser.

This page is looping through these URLs and creating hyperlinks to the controller servlet that also contains two parameters:

```
http://localhost:8080/ormonds/gateway?page=/details.jsp&index=0
```

The parameter `page` sets the JSP that should receive the forwarded request (in this case, `details.jsp`), and the parameter `index` specifies the index of the course that is to be displayed by `details.jsp`.

The text for the hyperlink is generated using the XML-specific tags of the JSTL, and they are processing the course XML files to extract the `title` of the course, and so on. This is displayed by the following code in Listing 18.5:

```
<a href="gateway?page=/details.jsp&index=<c:out value="${status.index}"/>">
        <x:out select="$xml/course/title" />
</a>
```

When a user clicks one of these hyperlinks, the next page to be displayed is `details.jsp`. This page has two functions: It presents the details of the specific course to the end user as HTML, and it provides a form for the user to request further information regarding the course. The top half of the output in the browser for `details.jsp` is shown in Figure 18.5.

At the base of the course details is the booking form. This is shown in Figure 18.6.

The JSP code for `details.jsp` is shown in Listing 18.6.

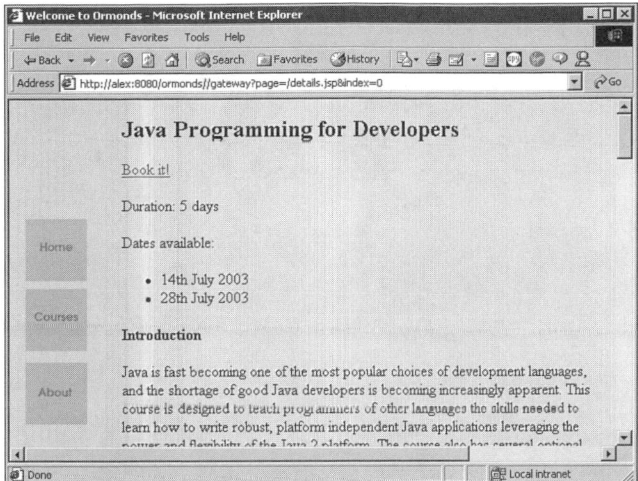

Figure 18.5 `details.jsp` in the browser showing course information.

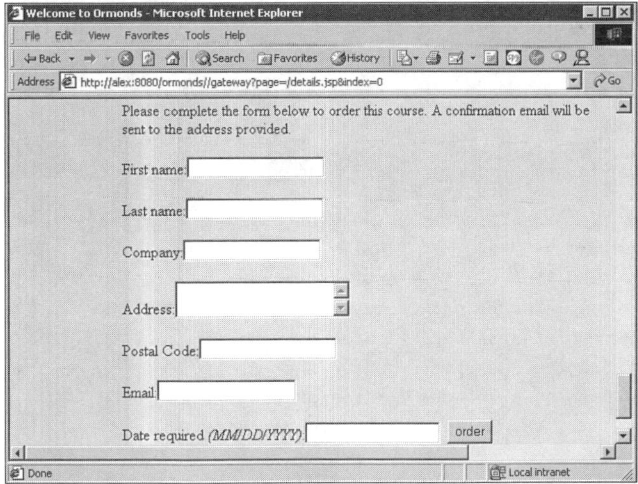

Figure 18.6 `details.jsp` in the browser showing the booking form.

Listing 18.6 `details.jsp`

```
<%@ taglib uri="http://java.sun.com/jstl-el/core" prefix="c" %>
<%@ taglib uri="http://java.sun.com/jstl-el/xml" prefix="x" %>

<html>
<head><title>Welcome to Ormonds</title></head>
```

Listing 18.6 **Continued**

```
<body background="images/background.jpg">
<jsp:include page="header.html" flush="true"/>
  <c:import var="xsl" url="${xsl}" />
  <c:forEach var="url" items="${urls}" varStatus="status">
     <c:if test="${status.index == param.index}">
       <c:import var="xml" url="${url}"/>
       <x:transform xml="${xml}" xslt="${xsl}"/>
       <x:parse var="content" xml="${xml}"/>
     </c:if>
   </c:forEach>

<jsp:include page="orderCourse.jsp" flush="true"/>

<jsp:include page="footer.html" flush="true"/>
</body>
</html>
```

This page also uses the XML tags from the JSTL tag libraries, and this time it is to complete an XSLT transformation. The stylesheet is set up as an attribute by the controller servlet and is accessed via the `xsl` attribute (the controller servlet will be discussed in the next section). The stylesheet being used is shown in Listing 18.7.

Listing 18.7 `courses.xsl`

```
<?xml version="1.0" encoding="UTF-8"?>
<xsl:stylesheet version="1.0" xmlns:xsl="http://www.w3.org/1999/XSL/Transform">
  <xsl:template match="/">
    <xsl:apply-templates select="/course/title"/>
    <xsl:apply-templates select="/course/duration"/>
    <xsl:apply-templates select="/course/dates"/>
    <xsl:apply-templates select="/course/introduction"/>
    <xsl:apply-templates select="/course/prerequisites"/>
    <xsl:apply-templates select="/course/outline"/>
  </xsl:template>
  <xsl:template match="dates">
    <p>Dates available:<ul>
        <xsl:apply-templates select="date"/>
      </ul>
    </p>
  </xsl:template>
  <xsl:template match="date">
    <li>
      <xsl:value-of select="."/>
    </li>
```

Listing 18.7 **Continued**

```
</xsl:template>
<xsl:template match="title">
  <h2>
    <xsl:value-of select="."/>
  </h2>
  <a href="#book">Book it!</a>
</xsl:template>
<xsl:template match="duration">
  <p>
    Duration: <xsl:value-of select="."/>
  </p>
</xsl:template>
<xsl:template match="introduction">
  <p>
    <b>
      Introduction
    </b>
  </p>
  <p>
    <xsl:apply-templates select="./paragraph"/>
  </p>
</xsl:template>
<xsl:template match="paragraph">
  <p>
    <xsl:value-of select="."/>
  </p>
</xsl:template>
<xsl:template match="prerequisites">
  <p>
    <b>
      Prerequisites
    </b>
  </p>
  <p>
    <xsl:value-of select="."/>
  </p>
</xsl:template>
<xsl:template match="outline">
  <p>
    <b>
      Outline
    </b>
  </p>
  <ol>
```

Listing 18.7 **Continued**

```
      <xsl:apply-templates select=".//chapter"/>
    </ol>
    <a name="book"/>
  </xsl:template>
  <xsl:template match="chapter">
    <li>
      <b>
        <xsl:value-of select="./heading"/>
      </b>
      <ul>
        <xsl:for-each select="./item">
          <li>
            <xsl:value-of select="."/>
          </li>
        </xsl:for-each>
      </ul>
    </li>
  </xsl:template>
</xsl:stylesheet>
```

Notice that the stylesheet has none of the outer HTML tags such as `<html>` or `<head>` and so on. This is because the output from the transformation is displayed within the context of the page template shown in Figure 18.3.

The Controller Servlet

You have already seen that the controller servlet is responsible for

- Setting up the `xsl` attribute—used by `details.jsp`.
- Setting up the `urls` attribute—this contains an array of the XML file URLs that contain the course information.
- Forwarding requests to the various pages based on the value of the `page` parameter.

The source for the controller servlet is shown in Listing 18.8.

Listing 18.8 `OrmondsControllerServlet.java`

```
package ormonds.servlet;

import javax.servlet.http.HttpServlet;
import javax.servlet.http.HttpSession;
import javax.servlet.http.HttpServletRequest;
import javax.servlet.http.HttpServletResponse;
import javax.servlet.RequestDispatcher;
```

Listing 18.8 **Continued**

```
import java.net.URL;
import java.util.Vector;
import java.sql.*;

public class OrmondsControllerServlet extends HttpServlet{

  public void doGet(HttpServletRequest request, HttpServletResponse response){

    HttpSession session= request.getSession();

    //prepare the XML, if not already done
    if ( getServletContext().getAttribute("urls") == null){
      setUpXMLURLs();
    }

    //declare a page variable to hold the value of page being requested
    // assign the default value
    String page = "/index.jsp";

    //retrieve the page requested
    String pageParam = request.getParameter("page");

    //if pageParam is not null, then set the page
    // to be the pageParam value
    if (pageParam != null){
      page = pageParam;
    }
    //get a request dispatcher
    RequestDispatcher dispatcher =
             getServletContext().getRequestDispatcher(page);

    //forward the user's request
    try {
      dispatcher.forward(request,response);
    }
    catch(javax.servlet.ServletException e){
      System.out.println("Could not forward to requested resource: " + e);
    }
    catch(java.io.IOException e){
      System.out.println("io error: " + e);
    }
    catch(Exception e){
      System.out.println("Unknown error occured - " + e);
    }
  }
```

Listing 18.8 **Continued**

```
  public void setUpXMLURLs(){
    // declare an array to hold all the urls to the XML
    URL[] xmlFiles;
    Vector v = new Vector(0);
    try {
      //Loop until there are no more XML files, adding each one to a vector
      for (int i=0;true;i++){
        URL previews =
            getServletContext().getResource("/previews/course" + i + ".xml");
        if (previews == null){
          break;
        }
        v.add(previews);
      }
      // assign the values of our vector to the array
      xmlFiles = (URL[])v.toArray(xmlFiles);
      //retrieve the XSL and bind it to the application
      URL xsl = getServletContext().getResource("/previews/courses.xsl");
      getServletContext().setAttribute("xsl",xsl);
    }
    catch(java.net.MalformedURLException e){
      System.out.println("could not retrieve the xml: " + e);
    }
    //add the array to the servlet context,
    // thus making it an "application" scoped object
    getServletContext().setAttribute("urls",xmlFiles);
  }
}
```

Note

The writing of controller servlets is discussed in Chapter 7, "JSP Application Architecture."

Every `GET` request will go through the controller servlets `doGet()` method. In this method, you can see that the first thing to be done is to initialize the `url` attribute if it is not already initialized. This is done by the private helper method `setUpXMLURLs()`. The XML files follow a basic naming convention, which means that they are named `coursex.xml`, where *x* is an incremental number. In the application, there are three courses represented by the three files: `course0.xml`, `course1.xml`, and `course2.xml`. The URLs are then placed into an array, which is then turned into an application-scoped attribute:

```
getServletContext().setAttribute("urls",xmlFiles);
```

The URL for the XSLT file is also set up as an application-scoped attribute from this helper method:

```
URL xsl = getServletContext().getResource("/previews/courses.xsl");
getServletContext().setAttribute("xsl",xsl);
```

After invoking `setUpXMLURLs()`, the remainder of the `doGet()` method is used to process the `page` parameter and forward the incoming request to the appropriate JSP. The relevant snippet of code is shown here:

```
String pageParam = request.getParameter("page");
. . .
RequestDispatcher dispatcher = getServletContext().getRequestDispatcher(page);
```

The processing of the data provided by the user needs to be looked at next.

So far, you have seen that the user first navigates to `courses.jsp` and is presented with a list of courses. Then, when a course is selected via a hyperlink, the next page, `details.jsp` generates output showing the details about the course selected using an XSLT transformation. The page `details.jsp` also contains a form to enable the user to request further information about booking a particular course. It is this form, and the processing of this form data, that is to be discussed in the next section.

Processing the Form

The form, although displayed as part of `details.jsp`, is actually contained within an include. Here is a snippet from `details.jsp`, shown in Listing 18.6:

```
<jsp:include page="orderCourse.jsp" flush="true"/>
```

Listing 18.9 shows the included page `orderCourse.jsp`.

Listing 18.9 `orderCourse.jsp`

```
<%@ taglib uri="http://java.sun.com/jstl-el/core" prefix="c" %>
<%@ taglib uri="/WEB-INF/struts-html.tld" prefix="html" %>

<hr>
<html:errors/>
Please complete the form below to order this course.
A confirmation email will be sent to the address provided.

<html:form action="order.do">
    <p>First name:<html:text property="firstName"/>
    <p>Last name:<html:text property="lastName"/>
    <p>Company:<html:text property="company"/>
    <p>Address:<html:textarea property="address"/>
    <p>Postal Code:<html:text property="postalCode"/>
    <p>Email:<html:text property="email" />
    <p>Date required <i>(MM/DD/YYYY)</i>:<html:text property="date"/>
```

Listing 18.9 **Continued**

```
    <c:if test="${param.index == 0}">
       <html:hidden property="course" value="Java Programming for Developers"/>
    </c:if>
    <c:if test="${param.index == 1}">
      <html:hidden property="course" value="XML Programming using Java"/>
    </c:if>
    <c:if test="${param.index == 2}">
     <html:hidden property="course" value="Java Programming for Web Developers"/>
    </c:if>
    <html:submit value="order"/>
</html:form>
```

Caution

At the time of writing, dynamic values could not be used in the `value` attributes in the above Listing. By the time the book is out, containers will support the use of dynamic attribute values here. We were using Tomcat 4.1.2 beta.

Listing 18.9 takes advantage of the Apache Struts framework, and therefore uses tags from the Struts framework to build the HTML form.

Note

The Struts framework is discussed in Chapter 7, "JSP Application Architecture."

When the form is submitted, an object of a type that subclasses `ActionForm` is populated with the properties from the form. The subclass is `ormonds.struts.OrderForm`. This is shown in Listing 18.10.

Listing 18.10 `ormonds.struts.OrderForm.java`

```
package ormonds.struts;

import javax.servlet.http.HttpServletRequest;
import org.apache.struts.action.*;

public class OrderForm extends ActionForm{

  private ActionErrors errors= new ActionErrors();
  private String lastName, firstName, email, company, address,
                 date, course, postalCode;

  // get and set methods for all the properties go in here
  // they have been omitted from the listing for brevity
```

Listing 18.10 **Continued**

```
  public ActionErrors validate(ActionMapping map, HttpServletRequest req){
    ActionErrors errors = new ActionErrors();

    if((firstName == null)||(firstName.equals(""))||(lastName == null)
        ||(lastName.equals("") )) {
      errors.add("Name", new ActionError("errors.name"));
    }
    if((company == null)||(company.equals(""))){
      errors.add("Company", new ActionError("errors.company"));
    }
    if((email == null)||(email.equals(""))){
      errors.add("Email", new ActionError("errors.email"));
    }

    //Checks to see that the final . of the email is after the @
    //a very basic email validation, -1 is returned if a character
    // does not exist
    if((email.indexOf(".") < 2) && (email.indexOf("@") < 0)){
      errors.add("Invalid", new ActionError("errors.invalidEmail"));
    }
    if ((date == null)||(date.equals(""))){
      errors.add("Date", new ActionError("errors.date"));
    }
    return errors;
  }
}
```

After a form is submitted the various `set` methods are invoked to populate the various `OrderForm` properties with the values from the form. After this has occurred, the `validate()` method is invoked, and this method will validate the form field values. So for example, the email address is checked to make sure it contains the `@` and `.` in the right places because it will be used to send an email later.

The population of this `OrderForm` object happens because of the setup of the Struts application within the `WEB-INF\struts-config.xml` file. The key entries are shown here:

```
<form-bean name="orderForm" type="ormonds.struts.OrderForm"/>
. . .
<action path="/order" type="ormonds.struts.OrderAction"
        name="orderForm" scope="request" input="/orderCourse.jsp">
  <forward name="success" path="/thanks.jsp"/>
</action>
```

It is here, for example, that the `/orderCourse.jsp` form is linked to the `OrderForm` class. The form property names must match the Bean property names for the values in the `OrderForm` Bean to be populated from the form. If you look carefully at Listings 18.9 and 18.10 you can see that this is indeed the case.

If an error is detected during validation, `orderForm.jsp` is displayed in the browser, but this time there is no surrounding content, and error messages are displayed at the top of the page. You can see this in Figure 18.7.

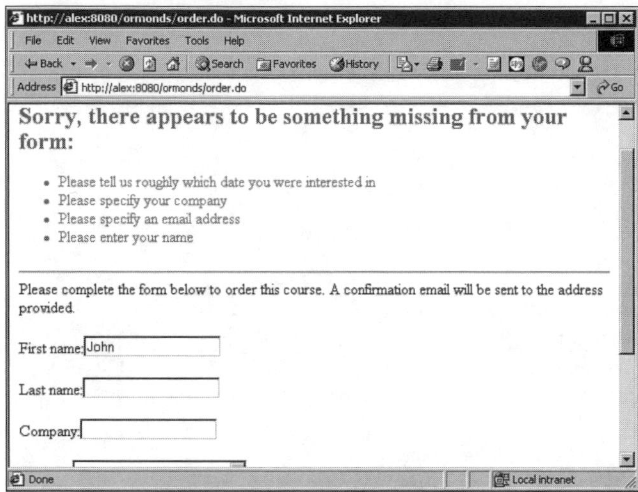

Figure 18.7 Displaying error messages.

After the `OrderForm.validate()` method has been invoked, the appropriate `Action` object is invoked (as specified in `struts-config.xml`). In our example, the `Action` subclass is an instance of the `ormonds.struts.OrderAction` shown in Listing 18.11.

Listing 18.11 `ormonds.struts.OrderAction`

```
package ormonds.struts;

import javax.servlet.http.*;
import org.apache.struts.action.*;
import ormonds.jdbc.OrmondsDataAccess;

public class OrderAction extends Action{

  public ActionForward perform(ActionMapping map,
                               ActionForm reqForm,
                               HttpServletRequest req,
                               HttpServletResponse res){
    OrderForm form = (OrderForm)reqForm;
    HttpSession session = req.getSession();
```

Listing 18.11 **Continued**

```
    session.setAttribute("form",form);

    // update the database
    OrmondsDataAccess access = new OrmondsDataAccess();
    access.update(form);

    // create email message content for the customer
    StringBuffer messageContentBuffer =
  new StringBuffer("Thankyou for your order.\n This is to inform you that\n ");
    messageContentBuffer.append(form.getFirstName() + " " +
                               form.getLastName() +
                               " from " +
                               form.getCompany() +
                               ", has ordered \n");
    messageContentBuffer.append(form.getCourse() +
                                " course on " +
                                form.getDate() + ".");
    messageContentBuffer.append("If you have any queries,
                                please email enquiries@ormonds.com.");
    String messageContent = messageContentBuffer.toString();
    // send the customer an email
    ormonds.mail.OrmondsEmail sender =
                new ormonds.mail.OrmondsEmail(form.getEmail(),
                                              messageContent,
                                              "Course ordering confirmation");
    boolean success = sender.sendMail();

    // return the success mapping
    return(map.findForward("success"));
  }
}
```

The `OrderAction` class initiates two main functions. One is to create, and then send an email to the customer. The second is to update a MySQL database.

Sending the Email

After the `OrderForm.validate()` method has returned with no errors, the `OrderAction.perform()` method is invoked. To enable the sending of an email there is the creation of a `StringBuffer` object that is to contain the text of the mail:

```
StringBuffer messageContentBuffer =
  new StringBuffer("Thankyou for your order.\n This is to inform you that\n ");
messageContentBuffer.append(form.getFirstName() + " " + form.getLastName() +
                           " from " + form.getCompany() +  ", has ordered \n");
```

```
messageContentBuffer.append(form.getCourse() + " course on " +
                            form.getDate() + ".");
messageContentBuffer.append("If you have any queries,
                             please email enquiries@ormonds.com.");
```

The text could have been extracted from a file or a property somewhere, but to keep it simple for now we have embedded it in the Java code. This message now needs to be sent. An additional Bean will do that for us.

If you have read the section of Chapter 7 about Apache Struts, you will appreciate that the `Action` objects invoke the business logic, but do not normally contain it.

The email is actually sent by an object of type `ormonds.email.OrmondsEmail`. This is shown in Listing 18.12, and it merits some explanation.

Listing 18.12 `OrmondsEmail.java`

```
package ormonds.mail;
import ormonds.struts.*;
import javax.servlet.http.*;
import org.apache.struts.action.*;
import javax.mail.*;
import javax.mail.internet.*;
import java.util.Properties;

public class OrmondsEmail {

  private String address;
  private String contents;
  private String subject;

  public OrmondsEmail(String address, String contents, String subject) {
    this.address = address;
    this.contents = contents;
    this.subject = subject;
  }

  public boolean sendMail() {
    try {
      Properties properties = new Properties();
      Session mailSession = Session.getInstance(properties,null);
      MimeMessage message = new MimeMessage(mailSession);
      message.setText(contents);
      message.setSubject(subject);
      Address address = new InternetAddress(this.address);
      Address fromAddress = new InternetAddress("from@address.goeshere");
      message.setFrom(fromAddress);
      message.addRecipient(Message.RecipientType.TO,address);
```

Listing 18.12 **Continued**

```
      message.saveChanges();
      Transport transport = mailSession.getTransport("smtp");
      transport.connect("mail.server.goes.here","username","password");
      transport.sendMessage(message, message.getAllRecipients());
      transport.close();
      // no exceptions, so return true
      return true;
    }
    catch(MessagingException e){
      System.out.println("could not send mail" + e);
      // something went wrong so return false
      return false;
    }
  }
}
```

The classes used to send email are all from the `javax.mail` and `javax.mail.internet` packages, and they are commonly referred to as JavaMail, which is part of the J2EE platform. The classes and interfaces are within the Web application as part of the `WEB-INF\lib\mail.jar` archive. This archive is available as a separate download from `http://java.sun.com/products/javamail/index.html`.

It also relies on the JavaBeans Activation Framework (JAF). This is available from `http://java.sun.com/products/javabeans/glasgow/jaf.html`.

The process of creating and sending an email when using JavaMail is as follows:

Create a `javax.mail.Session`

The first step is to create a `javax.mail.Session` object, which is often used to hold the server name, username, password, and from address. Do not confuse this with the `HttpSession`! The `Session` object is obtained by invoking the static `getInstance()` method. A `Properties` object can be used to hold this information. Our values are set later in the code as you will see:

```
Properties properties = new Properties();
Session mailSession = Session.getInstance(properties, null);
```

Create a `javax.mail.internet.MimeMessage`

After the session is created, we can now create the email message that is to be sent. Because this message is to be sent as a MIME message, an object of type `javax.mail.internet.MimeMessage` will be used:

```
MimeMessage message = new MimeMessage(mailSession);
```

Working with Addresses

After the message has been created, it needs to be configured with a FROM address, a TO address, a subject, and the contents from the `StringBuffer` created by the `OrderAction` object. To set the TO and FROM addresses, we use another class, the `javax.mail.internet.InternetAddress` class:

```
Address address = new InternetAddress(this.address);
Address fromAddress = new InternetAddress("from@address.goes_here");
```

The addresses, the subject, and the message contents are then set on the `MimeMessage` using a series of `set` methods. After all the properties have been set, the headers of the message can be set based on the contents of the message. This is done using the `saveChanges()` method:

```
message.setText(contents);
message.setSubject(subject);
message.setFrom(fromAddress);
message.addRecipient(Message.RecipientType.TO,address);
message.saveChanges();
```

Sending the Message

To send the message, a `javax.mail.Transport` object is required which is obtained from the `javax.mail.Session`. This can then be used to send the message to the recipients:

```
Transport transport = mailSession.getTransport("smtp");
transport.connect("mail.server.goes.here","username","password");
transport.sendMessage(message, message.getAllRecipients());
transport.close();
```

> **Note**
> If you want to test this, you will need to provide a genuine username, password, and server name.

The `send()` method is used to send the message. After it has been sent, the transport should be closed using the `close()` method.

The `OrmondsEmail` sender class, although appropriate for low-volume Web sites such as Ormonds, would not be appropriate for all sites. Many sites send out email regularly to clients, and it is not usually good for performance to have this process being carried out by the same server that is serving up the Web content. However, a basic class like this would be appropriate for confirmation emails such as this. If Ormonds were using a high-end application server such as ATG Dynamo, which has a specialized personalization engine, this class would be redundant because this functionality is built in to the product.

Note

Personalization is discussed in Chapter 17, "Personalization and Web Applications."

Finally, we need to look at how the database is updated, and then how the Ormonds staff can access this information.

Interacting with the Database

The database schema used by this application is shown in Listing 18.13.

Listing 18.13 `tablesSetUp.sql`

```
CREATE DATABASE IF NOT EXISTS ormonds;

-- this table will contain all the order information
use ormonds ;

DROP table if exists orders;
create table orders (
  id INTEGER (2)    PRIMARY KEY NOT NULL AUTO_INCREMENT,
  surname varchar (20),
  firstname varchar (20),
  company varchar (20),
  address varchar (50),
  postalCode varchar (12),
  email varchar(30),
  date varchar (10)
);

-- creates a users table used for the administrators
DROP table if exists user_table;
create table user_table (
  name varchar(20) primary key,
  password varchar(10)
);

insert into user_table values('Ormonds','password');

-- create a table to contain the admin role
DROP table if exists user_roles;
create table user_roles (
          name varchar(20) not null,
          rolename varchar(10) not null,
          primary key (name, rolename)
          );

insert into user_roles values ('Ormonds', 'admin');  );
```

The database used is MySQL and there are three tables in this schema; two are associated with the administration of users, which we will discuss later. The table that we need to pay attention to now is the `orders` table. There are fields for each of the values supplied by the online form shown in Figure 18.6.

The `OrderAction` class shown in Listing 18.11 shows that another class is being used to populate the database:

```
// update the database
ormonds.jdbc.OrmondsDataAccess access = new ormonds.jdbc.OrmondsDataAccess();
access.update(form);
```

It is this `OrmondsDataAccess` class that we need to look at. This class has a method called `update()` that is invoked every time a form is submitted. It is shown in Listing 18.14.

Listing 18.14 `OrmondsDataAccess.java`

```
package ormonds.jdbc;

import java.sql.*;
import javax.sql.*;
import ormonds.struts.*;
import javax.naming.*;

public class OrmondsDataAccess
{
  private DataSource source=null;

  public OrmondsDataAccess()
  {
    try {
      InitialContext context = new InitialContext();
      source = (DataSource)context.lookup("java:comp/env/jdbc/ormonds");
    }
    catch (NamingException e) {
      System.out.println("Naming Exception " +  e);
    }
  }

  public void update(OrderForm form) {
    PreparedStatement statement = null;
    Connection connection = null;
    try
    {
      connection = source.getConnection();
      statement = connection.prepareStatement("insert into orders ➥
          (surname, firstname, company, address, postalCode, email, date) ➥
          VALUES (?, ?, ?, ?, ?,?,?)");
```

Listing 18.4 **Continued**

```
      statement.setString(1, form.getLastName());
      statement.setString(2, form.getFirstName());
      statement.setString(3, form.getCompany());
      statement.setString(4, form.getAddress());
      statement.setString(5, form.getPostalCode());
      statement.setString(6, form.getEmail());
      statement.setString(7, form.getDate());
      statement.executeUpdate();
      statement.close();
      connection.close();
    }
    catch (SQLException e) {
      System.out.println("Something went wrong with the database update" + e);
    }
    finally {
     try {
      if (statement != null)
       statement.close();
      }  catch (SQLException e) {}
      try {
       if (connection != null)
        connection.close();
       } catch (SQLException e) {}
   }
  }
}
```

The code in this class is basic JDBC code that will update the database using a `PreparedStatement`. Most of this code should make sense to you because it is JDBC code, which was discussed in Chapter 14, "Databases and JSP."

The database is then accessible via a page in the site that is only available to authorized Ormonds staff. The page is a protected resource called `admin.jsp`. It is shown in Listing 18.15.

Listing 18.15 `admin.jsp`

```
<%@ taglib prefix="sql" uri="http://java.sun.com/jstl-el/sql" %>
<%@ taglib prefix="c" uri="http://java.sun.com/jstl-el/core" %>
<sql:setDataSource
  var="conn"
  dataSource="jdbc/ormonds"
/><html>
<head><title>Ormonds Administration</title></head>
<body background="../images/background.jpg">
<jsp:include page="../header.html" flush="true"/>
```

Listing 18.15 **Continued**

```
<h1>Orders To Date</h1>
<sql:query dataSource="${conn}" var="orders">
    SELECT * FROM orders
</sql:query>
<table width="90%" border="1">
<tr>
<!-- add the table column headings -->
<c:forEach var="columnName" items="${orders.columnNames}">
  <th> <c:out value="${columnName}"/> </th>
</c:forEach>
</tr>
<!-- add the table rows from the result set -->
<c:forEach var="row" items="${orders.rowsByIndex}">
  <tr>
    <c:forEach var="column" items="${row}">
      <td><c:out value="${column}"/></td>
    </c:forEach>
  </tr>
</c:forEach>
</table>
<jsp:include page="../footer.html" flush="true"/>
</body>
</html>
```

This listing uses the JDBC tags discussed in Chapter 14 to access the table and interact with the database. What the page is doing is simply accessing the database table and displaying the results in an HTML table. It can be seen in Figure 18.8.

Securing the Administration Pages

Authorized users are the only ones with access to the administrative area; these users have been set up with the role of `admin` in the `user_roles` and `user_table` tables in the MySQL database.

> **Note**
> Setting up these tables and the configuration of security is discussed in Chapter 16.

For this to be configured, the following entry has been added into `server.xml`:

```
<Realm className="org.apache.catalina.realm.JDBCRealm"
       debug="99"
       driverName="com.mysql.jdbc.Driver"
       connectionURL="jdbc:mysql://localhost:3306/ormonds?user=root"
       userTable="user_table" userNameCol="name" userCredCol="password"
       userRoleTable="user_roles" roleNameCol="rolename"/>
```

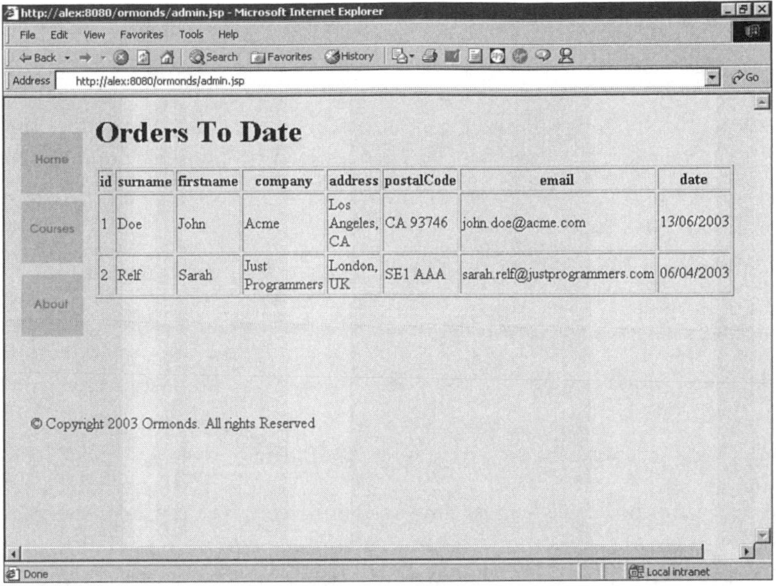

Figure 18.8 `admin.jsp` in a browser.

> **Caution**
>
> If you are planning to run this application on your machine, you will need to locate the `<Realm ..>` element after the `<Engine name="Standalone . . ."/>` element, comment it out, and replace it with the `<Realm>` element shown above. See the `readme.txt` in the root folder of the Web application for more information.

The resources are then protected by the following entry in `web.xml`. In our application it is a single JSP:

```
<!-- set up the secure area for Ormonds staff-->
<security-constraint>
  <web-resource-collection>
    <web-resource-name>Administrative Pages</web-resource-name>
    <url-pattern>/admin.jsp</url-pattern>
  </web-resource-collection>
  <auth-constraint>
    <role-name>admin</role-name>
  </auth-constraint>
</security-constraint>
<login-config>
  <auth-method>BASIC</auth-method>
  <realm-name>Realm</realm-name>
</login-config>
```

Summary

In this example application, many of the subjects discussed in this book have been drawn together to create a complete Web application. Our aim in adding this chapter at the end is to show how a complete application might look. There are many ways that these applications can be built, but this case study has adhered to the following in its design:

- The use of controller servlets to instantiate Beans and forward requests to the appropriate JSP.
- A high level of delegation, with each component having discrete roles.
- JSPs containing no business logic.
- Minimal use of scriptlets in the JSPs. There are only two lines of code on the home page, which is there because of a Tomcat issue. The other pages contain no code at all.
- XML/XSLT Technology used to present XML data to clients.

If you have read this book all the way through, you have now been exposed to a comprehensive set of technologies that you can take advantage of in the building of your own Web applications using JSP technology. We wish you every success in your JSP endeavors!

III

Appendices

A An XSLT and XPath Checklist

B An Overview of XML Schema

C A Checklist of the Tags in the JSP Standard Tag Library

D Basic JSP Syntax Checklist

E Debugging Tomcat and Running the Examples

F The Java Community Process

G J2EE Application Servers

H Configuring Tomcat

I Installing MySQL and WebLogic Server

J Glossary

An XSLT and XPATH Checklist

THIS APPENDIX CONTAINS THE MOST FREQUENTLY USED XSLT tags and XPATH expressions along with relevant descriptions and examples of their use. For an exhaustive XSLT reference, you can visit the XSLT home page at the W3C web site `http://www.w3.org/TR/xslt`.

XSLT Checklist

This section shows the syntax and use of the most common XSLT tags.

<xsl:apply-templates>

```
<xsl:apply-templates [select="XPATH expression"] [mode="name"]>
  <!-- can contain either <xsl:sort> or <xsl:with-param> elements -->
</xsl:apply-templates>
```

Attribute Name	Meaning
`select` (optional)	Contains an XPATH expression to specify which node set is to be processed. If this attribute is omitted, all children of the current node will be processed.
`mode` (optional)	Any template that has a matching mode and also matches the nodes specified with the select attribute will be matched. Useful for applying different transformations to similar nodes; for example, a different mode could be matched depending on the result of a Boolean test. The nodes processed would be the same either way, but the result could be quite different.

In the following example, any nodes called address that are found directly under a customer node will be selected for processing. Any template that has a match for an address node and a mode of Europe will process them. This would most logically come as a result of an <xsl:when> element that would test to see if the customer was living in Europe:

```
<xsl:apply-templates select="customer/address" mode="Europe" />
```

<xsl:call-template>

```
<xsl:call-template name="name">
  <!-- may contain <xsl:with-param> elements -->
</xsl:call-template>
```

Attribute Name	Meaning
name	The name of the template to be called.

The following `<xsl:call-template>` will call a template whose name attribute has a value of `header`. The `<xsl:call-template>` element does not change the current context node, it remains exactly the same. In the previous example, this means that within a template called `header` the current context node would be considered whatever the context node was when the `<xsl:call-template>` element was reached:

```
<xsl:call-template name="header" />
```

<xsl:choose>

```
<xsl:choose>
  <!-- contains one or more <xsl:when> elements and, optionally, an
<xsl:otherwise> element which must come last if it is included -->
</xsl:choose>
```

This element has no attributes. `<xsl:choose>` provides the equivalent of `if/else` or `switch/case` functionality. It contains one or more `<xsl:when>` elements, which have `test` attributes. If the `test` attribute of any of the `<xsl:when>` elements returns `true`, the content of that `<xsl:when>` element is processed. If none of the `<xsl:when>` elements has a `test` attribute that evaluates to `true`, the content of an `<xsl:otherwise>` element is processed if the `<xsl:otherwise>` element is included. This should be used instead of the `<xsl:if>` element whenever a default value is required. With `<xsl:if>` there is no provision for a default value, whereas `<xsl:otherwise>` provides us with that option when `<xsl:choose>` is used.

The following example displays a flag, depending on the value of a person's country attribute. If the country is unknown, or not included in the list of countries whose flags are available, a neutral image is displayed:

```
<xsl:choose>
  <xsl:when test="@country = 'Japan'">
```

```
    <img src="japFlag.jpg"/>
  </xsl:when>
  <xsl:when test="@country = 'United Kingdom'">
    <img src="ukFlag.jpg"/>
  </xsl:when>
  <xsl:otherwise>
    <img src="neutral.jpg"/>
  </xsl:otherwise>
/<xsl:choose>
```

Obviously, in a real-world example there would be many more countries than the two used here. The example does not actually specify that the `country` attribute belongs to a `person` element; normally you would consider that it was simply an attribute of the current node.

<xsl:if>

```
<xsl:if test="Boolean XPATH expression">
  <!-- contains a template body that will be used
        if the value of the test attribute returns true -->
</xsl:if>
```

Attribute Name	Meaning
`test`	The Boolean expression to be evaluated.

In the following example, the content of the `<xsl:if>` will be included in the resulting document only if the `carnivore` attribute of the current node has a value of `true`:

```
<xsl:if test="@carnivore = 'true'">
  <b>Carnivore</b>
</xsl:if>
```

<xsl:otherwise>

```
<xsl:otherwise>
  <!-- contains a template body that will be used if none of the test
 attributes from proceeding <xsl:when> elements have returned true-->
</xsl:otherwise>
```

There are no attributes for this element.

The following example displays a flag, depending on the value of a person's `country` attribute. If the `country` is unknown, or not included in the list of countries whose flags are available, a neutral image is displayed:

```
<xsl:choose>
  <xsl:when test="@country = 'Japan'">
```

```
    <img src="japFlag.jpg"/>
  </xsl:when>
  <xsl:when test="@country = 'United Kingdom'">
    <img src="ukFlag.jpg"/>
  </xsl:when>
  <xsl:otherwise>
    <img src="neutral.jpg"/>
  </xsl:otherwise>
/<xsl:choose>
```

Obviously, in a real-world example there would be many more countries than the two used here. The example does not actually specify that the `country` attribute belongs to a `person` element; normally, you would consider that it was simply an attribute of the current node.

<xsl:param>

```
<xsl:param name="name" [select="XPATH expression"]>
  <!-- may contain content that will provide the value of the
   parameter if the select attribute is missing -->
</xsl:param>
```

Attribute Name	Meaning
`name`	The name of the parameter.
`select` (optional)	Matches a node (or nodes) that will provide the value of this parameter.

The following example declares a parameter called `Name` with a value of the `customer` node's `name` attribute:

```
<xsl:with-param name="Name" select="customer/@name" />
```

If this element was found at the top level, that is, as a child of the `<xsl:stylesheet>`, it can be local to a template. In the former case, the parameter is visible to the entire stylesheet, in the latter case the parameter's visibility is limited to the template.

<xsl:sort>

```
<xsl:sort [select="XPATH expression"] [order="ascending|descending"]
[case-order="upper-first|lower-first"] [lang="language code"]
[data-type="text|number|name"] />
```

Attribute Name	Meaning
select (optional)	Defines the node upon which the sort will be based. For example, if this XPATH expression returned a name attribute of the current node, the sort would be based on the node's name.
order (optional)	Defines whether the nodes are to be processed in ascending or descending order. The default is ascending.
case-order (optional)	Defines whether lowercase letters are to be collated before or after uppercase letters.
lang (optional)	This specifies the language of the key being used. The values are in the same value space as the xml:lang attribute. The default is the language of the system. The values are defined by RFC 1766. Acceptable values would be en or en-US, for example. Visit http://www.ietf.org/rfc/rfc1766.txt for more information.
data-type (optional)	Defines whether the sort should be based on numerical values (using a value of number), alphabetically (using a value of text, which is the default) or a user-defined data-type (using a value that is a valid Name).

In the following example, templates matching customer nodes will be processed in order of the value of their age attributes. This will be done on their numerical value (as opposed to alphabetical!) in descending order:

```
<xsl:apply-templates select="employee">
  <xsl:sort select="@age" order="descending" data-type="number" />
</xsl:apply-templates>
```

<xsl:stylesheet>

```
<xsl:stylesheet [id="id"] version="version number"
[extension-element-prefixes="namespaces"]
[exclude-result-prefixes="namespaces"]>
</xsl:stylesheet>
```

Attribute Name	Meaning
id (optional)	Used to identify this <xsl:stylesheet> element. Used when this element is contained within another XML Document.
version	Specifies the version of XSLT used within this stylesheet. A value of 1.0 will enable the stylesheet to be processed by either XSLT 1.0 or XSLT 1.1 processors. However, if features from XSLT 1.1 are required, this attribute must have a value of 1.1 and cannot be used with XSLT 1.0 processors.
extension-element-prefixes (optional)	If there are any extension elements used within this stylesheet, their namespaces are defined in this attribute. Values are separated with whitespace.
exclude-result-prefixes	If any namespaces are used in this stylesheet, but are not required in the resulting document, their namespaces should be included as values of this attribute. Namespaces included here will only be copied to the resulting document if they are used in the resulting document. Values are separated with whitespace.

The <xsl:stylesheet> element is the document element in any XSLT stylesheet. The content of the stylesheet is contained in this element.

This following example is a stylesheet element with a version number of 1.1. This means that the stylesheet will contain features found in XSLT 1.1:

```
<xsl:stylesheet version="1.1">
```

<xsl:template>

```
<xsl:template [name="name"] [match="XPATH expression"] [mode="name"]
[priority="number"]>
</xsl:template>
```

Attribute Name	Meaning
name (optional)	Templates can be named in the order that they can then be called using the <xsl:call-template> element. Must be present if there is no match attribute.
match (optional)	Contains an XPATH expression, which determines the nodes processed by this template. Must be present if there is no name attribute.

Attribute Name	Meaning
`mode` (optional)	Only templates with a matching mode to that specified in the `<xsl:apply-templates>` element will be processed. See `<xsl:apply-templates>` for a fuller explanation.
`priority` (optional)	When multiple templates match the same node, this attribute specifies which template takes priority.

This example of a template will match any nodes called `products`, which is at any level beneath an order element. If there are multiple templates matching these nodes, the template with the highest priority will be matched. In this case, a template would require a priority higher than 5 to be matched in priority over this one:

```
<xsl:template match="order//products" priority="5">
```

<xsl:value-of>

```
<xsl:value-of select="XPATH expression"
 [disable-output-escaping="yes|no"] />
```

Attribute Name	Meaning
`Select`	Matches a node (or nodes) whose textual content will be output.
`disable-output-escaping` (optional)	Defines whether or not special characters should be output as they are (with a value of `yes`) or transformed into the appropriate entity reference(with a value of `no`), such as `>`.

In this example the content of the `description` element will be output to the resulting document:

```
<xsl:value-of select="book/description"/>
```

<xsl:when>

```
<xsl:when test="boolean XPATH expression">
  <!-- contains a template body that will be used
       if the value of the test attribute returns true -->
</xsl:when>
```

Attribute Name	Meaning
`test`	The Boolean expression to be evaluated.

The following example will display the relevant flag depending on the value of a person's `country` attribute:

```
<xsl:choose>
  <xsl:when test="@country = 'Japan'">
```

```
    <img src="japFlag.jpg"/>
  </xsl:when>
  <xsl:when test="@country = 'United Kingdom'">
    <img src="ukFlag.jpg"/>
  </xsl:when>
  <xsl:otherwise>
    <img src="neutral.jpg"/>
  </xsl:otherwise>
/<xsl:choose>
```

The example does not actually specify that the `country` attribute belongs to a `person` element; normally, you would consider that it was simply an attribute of the current node.

<xsl:with-param>

```
<xsl:with-param name="name" [select="XPATH expression"]>
  <!-- may contain content that will provide the value of the
   parameter if the select attribute is missing -->
</xsl:with-param>
```

Attribute Name	Meaning
`name`	The name of the parameter.
`select` (optional)	Matches a node (or nodes) that will provide the value of this parameter.

This example will pass a parameter called `Age` to the template matching `legalRights`. The value of this parameter will be the value of the `customer` node's `age` attribute. This parameter can be accessed from an `<xsl:param>` element in the template that is called:

```
<xsl:apply-templates select="legalRights">
  <xsl:with-param name="Age" select="customer/@age" />
</xsl:apply-templates>
```

XPATH Checklist

This section contains the syntax for the most commonly used Xpath expressions.

anElementName

You can match an element directly by its name. The following example matches a node called `Customer`:

```
Customer
```

/

This is a child operator or the root operator. The following example shows it working as a child operator. This example will match a node called `date` under an `Order` node:

```
Order/date
```

//

This is the descendant operator. This operator matches any nodes with the specified pattern at any level beneath the named node. The following example will match all `paragraph` nodes underneath the `Library` node:

```
Library//paragraph
```

.

This operator matches the current node. The following example will match all `fruit` nodes under the current node:

```
.//fruit
```

..

This is the parent path operator, useful for finding sibling nodes. This example will match a node called `animal` that is a sibling of the current node:

```
../animal
```

*

This is the wildcard path operator, which can be used to match any element nodes. In this example, all element nodes beneath the current node will be matched:

```
.//*
```

@

This is the attribute path operator. The example will match an attribute node called `gender`:

```
@gender
```

The following example will match all attributes of the current node:

```
@*
```

node()

This is a method that will match any node except an attribute or the root node. In this example, all nodes beneath the current node will be matched:

```
.//node()
```

|

The OR operator will, as in the following example, match one of a choice of nodes. In this instance, either `postcode` or `zipCode` will be matched:

```
postcode|zipCode
```

Predicates

An XPATH expression can have what is called a predicate on the end. A predicate is essentially a filter for a returned node set. So, a predicate could be used to test for the presence of sub elements or attributes. A predicate is always within `[]` brackets. The first example will match an `animal` node that has a `mammal` child:

```
animal[mammal]
```

The predicate works by first returning all matching nodes from the left part of the expression (in this case, `animal`), and then filtering the result using the contents of the expression within the square brackets. So, in this case, the filter is based on the presence of a `mammal` child.

In this second example, the test is for the presence of a `carnivore` attribute:

```
animal[@carnivore]
```

You can also match a node by index. For example, the following will match only the third `animal` node. Be aware that the index starts at 1:

```
animal[3]
```

To match the last element, you can use the XPATH method `last()`. This method matches the index of the last element. In the example, only the last `animal` node will be matched:

```
animal[last()]
```

B

An Overview of XML Schema

TO ACHIEVE THE BENEFITS OF USING XML as a data format, you must understand the rules of how an XML document needs to be structured, and what it should contain. The order that elements and attributes should be placed within an XML document, along with the name of elements and attributes, need to be specified.

The first W3C recommendation for defining XML structure was Document Type Definitions (DTDs). XML Schema is a more recent recommendation, finalized in May 2001; schemas are more powerful and can describe the content and structure of XML more specifically than DTDs.

XML Schema is important to Web application developers not only because of the extensive role schemas play in Web services, but also because they are now used to define the deployment descriptors for J2EE applications.

> **Note**
>
> This appendix will help you to read and understand basic XML Schemas. For a more detailed discussion of the XML Schema recommendation, the following book from Sams Publishing will be helpful:
>
> *The XML Schema Complete Reference* by Cliff Binstock et al (ISBN 0672323745).

DTDs

DTDs are written in EBNF (extended Backus-Naur form) and they look a little like XML. An example of a DTD is shown here:

```
<!ELEMENT cd (artist+, title, price)>
<!ELEMENT artist (#PCDATA)>
<!ELEMENT title (#PCDATA)>
<!ELEMENT price(#PCDATA)>
<!ATTLIST cd quantity CDATA #REQUIRED>
```

This basic DTD declares that an element named `cd` must contain one or more artist elements (denoted by + symbol), followed by a `title` element, and then a `price` element. The commas after the child elements indicates that a valid XML document must contain them in the order specified. Each child element of `cd` is then defined; the definitions declare that the data type `PCDATA` (Parsed Character Data) is required as a value, which means that a textual value is expected. As such, an XML document could contain `fred` as the price and this value would be valid.

The `<!ATTLIST ..>` entry is declaring an attribute for the element `cd`. The attribute is required, and contains character data (`CDATA`).

DTDs will not be discussed in any more detail here. From now on, our attention will turn to the subject of the appendix, XML Schema.

XML Schema Introduction

XML Schema has a very rich set of data types indeed. In fact, this is one of the most powerful advantages that XML Schema has over DTDs. In addition to this, the schema developer can develop his own custom data types.

XML Schemas are also written in XML, which enables them to be manipulated or displayed with any XML-aware tool. This also gives you the advantage of not having to learn another syntax.

Another major advantage that XML Schemas have over DTDs is that they provide full namespace support. This will be discussed further later in this appendix. Listing B.1 shows a basic schema example.

Listing B.1 **Basic XML Schema Example**

```
<xs:schema xmlns:xs="http://www.w3.org/2001/XMLSchema" >
  <xs:element name="cd">
    <xs:complexType>
      <xs:sequence>
         <xs:element name="artist" type="xs:Name" maxOccurs="10"/>
         <xs:element name="title" type="xs:string"/>
         <xs:element ref="price" maxOccurs="1"/>
      </xs:sequence>
      <xs:attribute name="quantity" type="xs:double" use="required"/>
    </xs:complexType>
  </xs:element>
  <xs:element name="price" type="xs:int"/>
</xs:schema>
```

The basic XML Schema shown in Listing B.1 describes the structure and content in a very similar way to the previous DTD example. However, one crucial difference is that there are now more specific data types. For example, the `price` element is defined as containing a `double`.

It is important to note that the root element of the schema document is `<schema>`.

The rest of the syntax contained in this example will be explained later in this appendix.

One other thing to note is that the schema is more complex than the corresponding DTD. This is simply a result of the fact that XML Schemas are more powerful and can give a finer-grained definition; they will therefore always have the potential to be more complex documents.

XML Schema Namespaces

> **Note**
> An XML *namespace* is a unique name assigned to a particular XML vocabulary. For a detailed discussion of namespaces, visit `www.w3c.org`, where the specification is managed.

The namespace for an XML Schema needs to be declared in the root `<schema>` element:

```
<xs:schema xmlns:xs="http://www.w3.org/2001/XMLSchema">
    .....
</xs:schema>
```

> **Note**
> You might be wondering why the XML Schema datatype's namespace is not used. This is because it is included in the XML Schema namespace.

The prefix indicating that the W3C XML Schema namespace is being used is typically `xs` or `xsd`, although it can be anything you want.

This example declares the W3C standard XML Schema namespace, indicating that elements and attributes defined in this namespace are to be used.

It is worth noting that XML authoring tools such as XML Spy have the W3C XML Schema specification built-in, which can greatly assist in writing XML Schemas providing autocomplete mechanisms.

XML Schema Structure

Figure B.1 displays the relationship of some of the other elements to the root `<schema>` element.

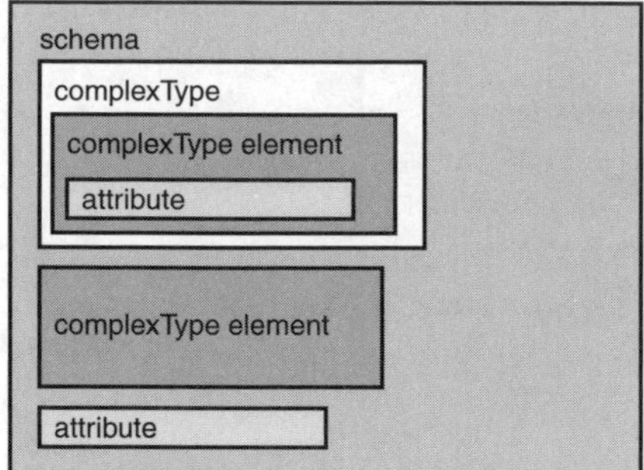

Figure B.1 Basic structure of an XML Schema.

This diagram demonstrates the following:

- Every XML Schema has a root element of `<schema>`.
- This element can contain *globally defined* `<element>` elements.
- The `<element>` elements can contain one or more definitions for an `<attribute>`, a `complexType`, or further element tags.
- The `<schema>` element can contain one or more globally defined `<complexType>` elements.
- This `<complexType>` element can contain one or more definitions for an `<attribute>` or an `<element>`.
- The `<schema>` element can contain one or more globally defined `<attribute>` elements.

Defining Elements

Elements within XML Schema are defined using the `<element>` tag.

Within each `<element>` tag, two attributes need to be defined. The `name` of the element needs to declared, followed by the `type`—that is the datatype—of the element:

```
<xs:element name="price" type="xs:int"/>
```

This example is declaring an element that has the name attribute of `price`, and is of type `int`, which indicates that an `Integer` is its expected value. So, where was the datatype `int` defined?

Datatypes

In XML Schema there are 47 built-in datatypes. These types are very useful for restricting values to be something more precise than just strings or IDs, as DTDs provide. A full list of these datatypes can be found at `http://www.w3.org/TR/xmlschema-2/`.

Coupled with this advantage, datatypes can also be self-defined as `simpleType` or `complexType` elements:

```
<xs:element name="price" type="price"/>
<xs:simpleType name="price">
  <xs:restriction base="xs:int">
    <xs:minExclusive value="5" />
    <xs:maxExclusive value="40" />
  </xs:restriction>
</xs:simpleType>
```

In this example, an element named `price` has been defined as type `price`. This datatype is then defined, based on the existing built-in datatype `int`, and the value is constricted to be between 5 and 40 exclusive. There are 12 constraining facets defined in the XML Schema Datatypes specification, including `minExclusive` and `maxExclusive` used in this example. Further details can also be found at `http://www.w3.org/TR/xmlschema-2/`.

`simpleType` and `complexType`

An element that does not contain any child elements and has no attributes is said to be a *simple type* (unless it is a completely empty element), and is declared as follows:

```
<xs:element name="artist" type="xs:Name"/>
```

Any elements that contains child elements or attributes are considered to be complex type elements:

```
<xs:element name="cd">
    <xs:complexType>
        <xs:sequence>
            <xs:element ref="artist" type="xs:Name" maxOccurs="unbounded"/>
            <xs:element name="title" type="xs:string"/>
            <xs:element ref="price" maxOccurs="1"/>
        </xs:sequence>
    </xs:complexType>
</xs:element>
```

This `complexType` example is *anonymous*. This means that it does not contain a `name` attribute. Anonymous `complexTypes` cannot be used elsewhere in the schema because they are declared within the scope of an element, in this case, the `cd` element definition.

Naming a `complexType` ensures that it can be used elsewhere in the schema. This is referred to as being *globally defined*. The following example shows how this is done:

```
<xs:element name="cd" type="cd"/>
    <xs:complexType name="cd">
        <xs:sequence>
            <xs:element name="artist" type="xs:Name" maxOccurs="unbounded"/>
            <xs:element name="title" type="xs:string"/>
            <xs:element ref="price" maxOccurs="1"/>
```

```
        </xs:sequence>
    </xs:complexType>
<xs:element name="price" type="xs:int"/>
```

On the same note, the child element `price` within the `complexType` does not include the `name` attribute, but has a `ref` attribute instead. The `price` element is globally defined later including the `name` attribute. Any element declared globally in this way can be used elsewhere in the schema as long as it is referenced using the `ref` attribute.

Within a `complexType`, the `compositor` must also be specified. This is used to set how the child elements must be composed, that is, in what sort of order. In the previous example `xs:sequence` is used, meaning that the child elements must appear in the order that they are shown. The other options for compositor are `xs:all` and `xs:choice`. If `xs:all` is specified, all the child elements are required, but can appear in any order. If `xs:choice` is used, one or more of the child elements specified can be used.

Attributes

Attributes are declared within the `complexType` element using `xs:attribute`:

```
<xs:element name="cd">
  <xs:complexType>
    <xs:sequence>
      ..............
    </xs:sequence>
    <xs:attribute name="quantity" type="xs:int" use="required"/>
  </xs:complexType>
</xs:element>
```

The `xs:attribute` tag can contain a `ref` attribute if it is being declared globally. If it is being declared locally, or in the global attribute definition, the `type` attribute needs to be defined in element declarations. Another mandatory attribute is the `use` attribute. This can be set to `required`, `optional`, or `prohibited` depending on how the attribute is to be used.

Assigning XML Schemas

To associate an XML document with a particular schema, there are certain steps to be taken:

1. In the instance document declare the `schema instance` namespace and associate it with a prefix, typically `xsi`:

   `http://www.w3.org/2001/XMLSchema-instance/`

2. In the root element in the XML instance document use either the `schemaLocation` attribute or the `noNamespaceSchemaLocation` attribute to assign the schema. Table B.1 illustrates their differences and uses.

Table B.1 **The Uses of `schemaLocation` and `noNamespaceSchemaLocation`**

Attribute Name	Description	Content
`noNamespaceSchemaLocation`	If the schema you are using has no namespace, you can use this attribute to specify the location of the schema that is associated with the elements and attributes of your XML document.	The location of the schema. This can be a relative path, an absolute path, or a URL. For example: `C:\Schemas\MySchema.xsd`.
`schemaLocation`	This is used for schemas that do belong to a namespace. It specifies both a namespace URI and schema location. The effect being that any content belonging to the specified namespace should be validated using the specified schema.	A namespace URI and a schema location. These two values are separated by whitespace. An example value could be `http://MyNamespace.com/MyXMLProject C:\Schemas\MyShema.xsd`.

The following examples demonstrate the assignment of an XML schema:

```
<cds xmlns:xsi="http://www.w3.org/2001/XMLSchema-instance"
xsi:noNamespaceSchemaLocation="c:\XMLSchemas\cds.xsd">
```

The W3C `XMLSchema-instance` namespace is defined for schema-specific attributes that appear in instance documents usually prefixed by `xsi`.

The previous example shows how a schema is attached to an XML instance document that does not make use of namespaces. It attaches the schema to the instance document by using the `noNamespaceSchemaLocation` attribute, declared inside the `<schema>` element opening tag.

If namespaces are used, the `namespaceSchema` location attribute is used:

```
<cds  xmlns ="http://www.samspublishing.com/cds"
  xmlns:xsi="http://www.w3.org/2001/XMLSchema-instance"
  xsi:schemaLocation="http://www.samspublishing.com/cds c:\XMLSchemas\cds.xsd">
```

The `schemaLocation` attribute contains two values separated by whitespace. The previous example will indicate to the parser that the `http://www.samspublishing.com/cds` namespace is defined by a file called `cds.xsd`, and gives the actual schema location. In this case the absolute path is specified although the relative path can also be used.

Multiple Schemas

An XML instance document can have more than one XML Schema associated with it. Figure B.2 shows a representation of a document that is separated into three distinct areas. Each of these areas of content could be validated against a different XML Schema. Area A would be validated against Schema A, Area B against Schema B, and so on. An example of this in practice is shown in Listing B.2.

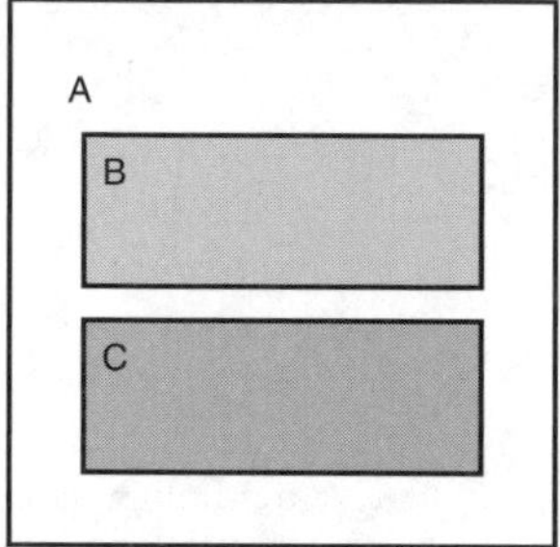

Figure B.2 XML with content validated against multiple Schemas.

Listing B.2 **An XML File Using** `noNamespaceSchemaLocation`

```
<?xml version="1.0" encoding="UTF-8"?>
<SOAP-ENV:Envelope xmlns:SOAP-ENV="http://schemas.xmlsoap.org/soap/envelope/"
   xmlns:xsd="http://www.w3.org/2001/XMLSchema"
   xmlns:xsi="http://www.w3.org/2001/XMLSchema-instance">
 <SOAP-ENV:Body>
 <getFavoriteColorResponse
     xsi:noNamespaceSchemaLocation="/home/user/schemas/color.xsd"
     SOAP-ENV:encodingStyle="http://schemas.xmlsoap.org/soap/encoding/">
   <getFavoriteColorReturn xsi:type="xsd:string">
     red
   </getFavoriteColorReturn>
 </getFavoriteColorResponse>
</SOAP-ENV:Body>
</SOAP-ENV:Envelope>
```

> **Note**
>
> For more information on SOAP, check out Chapter 12, "Invoking Web Services from JSP," which explains SOAP messages in more detail.

Here is a real-world example of a SOAP message. In the example, you can see that there are two distinct sections of XML: content belonging to the `SOAP-ENV` namespace and content belonging to no namespace at all. The latter is being validated against a schema located at `/home/user/schemas/color.xsd`. In this case the SOAP-ENV content is not being validated against any schema at all, although this is simply because it never is in the case of a SOAP message. There is no reason why both areas of content could not be validated against two different schemas. All that would be required would be to add an `xsi:schemaLocation` attribute to the `Envelope` element specifying a schema to validate all the content belonging to the `SOAP-ENV` namespace.

`Import` and `Include`

Two elements can be used in an XML Schema to include the content of other XML Schemas: `import` and `include`.

The key difference between the two is that `import` is used to import a schema for a different target namespace, whereas `include` includes a schema with the same namespace or adopts a schema with no target namespace at all.

Tables B.2 and B.3 illustrate the various attributes and values of the two elements.

Table B.2 **Attributes of the `import` Element**

Attribute Name	Description	Content
`id`	Unique id for this element	ID
`schemaLocation`	The Location of the schema to be imported	Any URI
`namespace`	The target namespace URI for the imported schema	Any URI

Table B.3 **Attributes of the `include` Element**

Attribute Name	Description	Content
`id`	Unique id for this element	ID
`schemaLocation`	The Location of the schema to be imported	Any URI

Example Element Definition

To conclude this appendix, we will take a brief look at an element definition in a real-world schema. The following is taken from the servlet 2.4 specification public draft:

```
<xsd:simpleType name="auth-methodType">
    <xsd:restriction base="j2ee:string">
        <xsd:enumeration value="BASIC"/>
        <xsd:enumeration value="DIGEST"/>
        <xsd:enumeration value="FORM"/>
        <xsd:enumeration value="CLIENT-CERT"/>
    </xsd:restriction>
</xsd:simpleType>
```

You can see in this example that a `simpleType` has been defined with a global scope. Any element or attribute that has a type of `auth-methodType` will only be able to contain the values: `BASIC`, `DIGEST`, `FORM`, or `CLIENT-CERT`. This is defined by the `enumeration` elements. These enumerations are defined within a restriction element that has a string as its base. This means that the developer is about to define a datatype based on a string, and that datatype will be a restriction from the original string datatype. In this case, the restriction is to limit the string to certain values, although it could be to restrict the length of the string as well as several other options. In the next example you can see an element definition that declares itself to have a type of `auth-methodType`. Therefore, this element will only have a value that matches one of the values specified in the enumeration:

```
<xsd:element name="auth-method" type="j2ee:auth-methodType" minOccurs="0"/>
```

An example of legitimate instance XML would be

```
<auth-method>DIGEST</auth-method>
```

Invalid content would be

```
<auth-method>BRIBE</auth-method>
```

C

A Checklist of the Tags in the JSP Standard Tag Library

THIS APPENDIX IS A SUMMARY OF THE actions that the JSP Standard Tag Library (JSTL) provides. You can find further information on the core actions and internationalization actions in Chapter 5, "The JSP Standard Tag Library." You can also find examples of the SQL actions in Chapter 14, "Databases and JSP," and the XML actions are used in Chapters 10, "Utilizing XML from JSP," and 11, "Transforming XML Using XSLT and XSLFO."

Tag Library URIs

Table C.1 lists the URIs for the different functional areas provided by JSTL 1.1. The URIs shown are for those libraries that support the JSTL Expression Language (EL). The commonly used prefixes are also shown, although you can use any prefixes you want in JSP. The JSTL 1.0 URIs for the EL-based libraries were the same as in Table C.1, except that they contained the substring jstl rather than jstl-el.

Table C.1 **JSTL 1.1 Tag Libraries**

Functional Area	URI	Prefix
Core	http://java.sun.com/jstl-el/core	c
XML	http://java.sun.com/jstl-el /xml	x
Internationalization-capable formatting	http://java.sun.com/jstl-el /fmt	fmt
SQL (relational database access)	http://java.sun.com/jstl-el /sql	sql

Table C.2 lists the URIs for the JSTL 1.0 libraries that support RT expressions.

Table C.2 **JSTL 1.0 RT-Based Tag Libraries**

Functional Area	URI	Prefix
Core	http://java.sun.com/jstl/core_rt	c_rt
XML	http://java.sun.com/jstl/xml_rt	x_rt
Internationalization-capable formatting	http://java.sun.com/jstl/fmt_rt	fmt_rt
SQL (relational database access)	http://java.sun.com/jstl/sql_rt	sql_rt

Note

Tables C.1 and C.2 list the URIs that the tag libraries use. Note that these are not URLs, and do not resolve to anything on the Web. However, the `http://java.sun.com/jstl` URL is an alias for the JavaServer Pages Standard Tag Library homepage (`http://java.sun.com/products/jsp/jstl`).

Core Actions

You can find more detailed information about, and examples of, the core actions in Chapter 5.

The `c:out` action

The `c:out` action is similar to the JSP expression tag (`<%= ... %>`). It evaluates the expression supplied in the `value` attribute. If the value evaluates to an instance of `java.io.Reader`, then data is read from that `Reader` and written to the current `JspWriter`. If the `value` attribute does not evaluate to a `Reader`, then the result is converted to a string, and the result is displayed in the output from the JSP. The reason for this behavior is to speed up the reading of large amounts of data that is displayed in the JSP.

The `c:out` action can be supplied with a default value that can be displayed if the supplied expression cannot be evaluated, or if it evaluates to `null`. The default value can be specified either as an attribute, or as body content of the action. The body content is any valid JSP code.

Note

In this appendix, all of an action's attributes that have a default value have that value marked in bold type.

The two forms of the syntax are

```
<c:out value="expression"
      [escapeXml="{true | false}"]
      [default="default_value"] />
```

and

```
<c:out value="expression"
       [escapeXml="{true | false}"]
>
    default value
</c:out>
```

The attributes of the c:out action have the following properties:

- The value attribute is the expression to evaluate.
- The default attribute is the value used if the supplied expression cannot be evaluated, or if it evaluates to null.
- The escapeXML attribute indicates whether to convert any of the characters <, >, &, ', and " to their character entity codes (default value is true).

The c:set Action

You can set the value of a target object's property, or the value of a scoped variable, with the c:set action. As is covered in Chapter 6, you can also use the c:set action to invoke JavaBean setter methods. The value can be specified using either an attribute or body content of the action. The body content is any valid JSP code. To set the value of a scoped variable by using body content, use

```
<c:set var="variable_name"
       [scope="{page | request | session | application}"]
>
    body content
</c:set>
```

To set the value of a scoped variable by using an attribute, use

```
<c:set var="variable_name"
       value="some_value"
       [scope="{page | request | session | application}"] />
```

To set the value of a property of a target object by using body content, use

```
<c:set target="target_object_name"
       property="property_name"
>
    body content
</c:set>
```

To set the value of a property of a target object by using an attribute, use

```
<c:set target="target_object_name"
       property="property_name"
       value="some_value"
/>
```

The attributes of the `c:set` action have the following properties:

- The `value` attribute is the expression to evaluate.
- The `var` attribute is the name of the exported scoped variable. The `scope` attribute is the scope of the exported scoped variable. The default value is `page`.
- The `target` attribute specifies the target object whose property is to be set. The `property` attribute is the name of the target object's property.

The `c:remove` Action

You can use the `c:remove` action to delete a scoped variable. The syntax of the `c:remove` action is

```
<c:remove var="variable_name"
        [scope="{page | request | session | application}"] />
```

The attributes of the `c:remove` action have the following properties:

- The `var` attribute specifies the name of the scoped variable that is to be removed.
- The optional `scope` attribute dictates which method is used to remove the scoped variable. If the `scope` attribute is specified, the `PageContext.removeAttribute(variable_name, scope)` method is used. Otherwise, the `PageContext.removeAttribute(variable_name)` method is used instead.

The `c:catch` Action

The `c:catch` action enables you to catch objects of type `java.lang.Throwable` from any nested actions, without them being handled by the JSP error-page mechanism. The syntax of the `c:catch` action is

```
<c:catch [var="variable_name"]>
    nested actions
</c:catch>
```

The `var` attribute is optional, and if specified, is used to store a `page`-scoped reference to the error. If the `var` attribute is specified, but no errors occur within the nested actions, any existing scoped variable is removed.

If the `var` attribute is not specified, any error is caught, but not stored.

The `c:if` Action

This action enables you to conditionally process the action's body content depending on whether a Boolean test condition evaluates to `true`. The test condition is specified through the `test` attribute.

Alternatively, you can expose a scoped variable that contains the result of the expression rather than evaluate body content of the action. In this case, the name of the scoped variable is set through the `var` attribute, and its scope through the `scope` attribute. The syntax of the `c:if` action without body content is

```
<c:if test="test _condition"
      var="variable_name"
      [scope="{page | request | session | application}"]
/>
```

With body content the syntax is

```
<c:if test="test _condition"
      [var="variable_name"]
      [scope="{page | request | session | application}"] >
    body content
</c:if>
```

Notice in this second form of the syntax that you can optionally export the result of the test condition. However, if you specify a value for the `scope` attribute, you must also specify a value for the `var` attribute.

The `c:choose` Action

The `c:choose` action is like Java's `if/else if/else` construct, or the `switch` construct, in that it enables you to perform the processing of mutually exclusive conditions. It can contain one or more `c:when` actions and zero or one `c:otherwise` actions, which are described in the following sections. If you have a child `c:otherwise` action, it must be the last nested action with the enclosing `c:choose` action.

The syntax of the `c:choose` action is

```
<c:choose>
    nested <c:when> and <c:otherwise> actions go here
</c:choose>
```

The `c:when` Action

You can use the `c:when` action to represent a particular branch of execution within a `c:choose` action. The `c:when` action can only appear as a child element of a `c:choose` action.

The syntax is

```
<c:when test="test_condition">
    body_content
</c:when>
```

The Boolean condition is set using the `test` attribute. The `test` attribute's value can be dynamic, for example:

```
<c:when test="${user.age > 30}">
```

The `c:otherwise` Action

Within a `c:choose` action, the `c:otherwise` action enables you to specify an alternative to any `c:when` action whose `test` conditions did not evaluate to `true`. The `c:otherwise` action must be the *last* element of a `c:choose` action.

The syntax is

```
<c:otherwise>
    body_content
</c:otherwise>
```

The body content can be any valid JSP.

The `c:forEach` Action

The `c:forEach` action iterates over its body content either a fixed number of times or once for each item in a specified collection. When you want to iterate a fixed number of times, the syntax is

```
<c:forEach begin="begin_index"
           end="end_index"
           [step="step_value"]
           [var="variable_name]
           [varStatus="varStatus_name"]
>
    body_content
</c:forEach>
```

Note that the `begin` and `end` values are inclusive. For example, this code prints out the numbers 1 to 10:

```
<c:forEach var="counter" begin="1" end="10">
    <c:out value="${counter}" />
</c:forEach>
```

The `var` attribute can be used to store the value of the current index in a nested variable for use within the body of the `c:forEach` action, and the `step` attribute can be used to indicate by how much the index should be incremented after each iteration. Also, the status of the iteration can be accessed through a nested scoped variable set using the `varStatus` attribute. The scoped variable is of type `javax.servlet.jsp.jstl.core.LoopTagStatus`. See Chapter 5 for details.

The syntax for iterating over a collection of objects is essentially the same as when iterating a fixed number of times as in the example a moment ago, except that you specify the collection through an `items` attribute:

```
<c:forEach items="collection"
           [begin="begin_index"]
           [end="end_index"]
           [step="step_value"]
           [var="variable_name"]
           [varStatus="varStatus_name"]
>
    body content
</c:forEach>
```

The c:forTokens Action

This action enables you to iterate over a list of tokens (set with the items attribute). The tokens are separated by tokens that you can specify using the delims attribute. The syntax is

```
<c:forTokens items="string_of_tokens"
             delims="delimiters"
             [begin="begin_index"]
             [end="end_index"]
             [step="step_value"]
             [var="variable_name"]
             [varStatus="varStatus_name"]
>
    body_content
</c:forEach>
```

The other attributes work the same way as for the c:forEach action.

The c:import Action

The c:import action enables you to embed content from a specified URL into the current JSP, or export the content as a string. The syntax is of the c:import action for embedding content inline is

```
<c:import url="url_of_resource"
          [context="context"]
          [var="variable_name"]
          [scope="{page | request | session | application}"]
          [charEncoding="character_encoding"]
>
    body content
</c:import>
```

The body content of the c:import action can contain c:param actions to add arguments to the query string. The c:param action is described later in this appendix.

You use the `context` attribute when you want to include content from another Web application. For example, to access a resource called `/someFile.jsp` in a context called `otherWebApp`, you would use the following code:

```
<c:import url="/someFile.jsp"
        context="/otherWebApp"
/>
```

If you want to cache the results as a string instead of embedding the content within the current JSP, you can do so by using the `var` and `scope` attributes. The `charEncoding` attribute enables you to specify the character encoding of the external resource.

It is also possible to expose the external resource through a `java.io.Reader` object by specifying a `varReader` attribute using this syntax:

```
<c:import url = "url_of_resource"
        varReader = "variable_name"
        [context = "context"]
        [charEncoding = "character_encoding"]>
    body content
</c:import>
```

See Chapter 5 for examples of both approaches.

The `c:import` action is very powerful. For example, you can use a `c:import` action with `c:param` actions to access a data source and assign the result to a variable. If the data source emits XML, such as a database or an RSS syndication stream, you can use the JSTL XML actions to process the results.

The `c:url` Action

If you need to build a rewritten URL that contains a user's session ID, you can use the `c:url` action. This has the same effect as the `javax.servlet.http.HttpServletResponse.encodeURL()` method defined in the Servlet API.

The `c:url` action can take two forms, depending on whether you want to set query-string arguments on the URL. If you do not want to set arguments, the syntax is

```
<c:url value="value"
      [context="context"]
      [var="variable_name"]
      [scope="{page | request | session | application}"
/>
```

As with the other actions that use it, the `context` attribute is used to specify a foreign context for another Web application, and the result can be stored in a scoped variable identified through the `var` and `scope` attributes; otherwise, it will be written to the output.

If you want to set query string arguments on the URL, the following form is useful:

```
<c:url value="value"
       [context="context"]
       [var="variable_name"]
       [scope="{page | request | session | application}"
>
    body content contains c:param actions
</c:url>
```

The `c:param` action is described later in this appendix.

The `c:redirect` Action

This action causes the processing of the current JSP to be aborted, and an HTTP redirect to be sent back to the client. As with the `c:url` action, the syntax of the `c:redirect` action allows for optional body content containing `c:param` actions that add arguments to the query string:

```
<c:redirect url="url_value"
            [context="context"]
>
    optional c:param actions
</c:redirect>
```

Note that you cannot use the `c:redirect` action after any content has been written out by the JSP; for example, if you have used the `out.flush()` method from within a scriptlet. If you do, then you do not see any more output from the JSP after the `c:redirect` action.

The `c:param` Action

You can nest `c:param` actions within the body of `c:url`, `c:redirect`, and `c:import` actions to add request parameters to their query strings. There are two forms for the syntax of the `c:param` action:

```
<c:param name="parameter_name"
         value="parameter_value"
/>
```

and

```
<c:param name="parameter_name">
    parameter_value
</c:param>
```

The values for both the `name` and `value` attributes can be dynamically computed. If the `name` is `null`, the parameter is ignored. On the other hand, if the value equates to `null`, an empty value is passed instead of the `value` attribute.

If you use the second form of the syntax, the `c:param` action strips any leading and trailing whitespace from the parameter value.

XML Actions

You can find more information about, and examples of, the XML Actions in Chapters 10 and 11.

The `x:parse` Action

This action enables you to parse an XML document. You can specify the document either through body content or through a `String` or `Reader` object. The syntax for body content is

```
<x:parse {var="variable_name" [scope="scope"] | varDom="var" [scopeDom="scope"]
         }
         [systemId="systemId"]
         [filter="filter"]>
    XML content to be parsed
</x:parse>
```

In this case, the body content is parsed. You have a choice about whether you want the parsed content to be exported through an implementation-dependent scoped variable (by using the `var` and `scope` attributes), or through a scoped instance of type `org.w3c.dom.DOMDocument` (through the `varDom` and `scopeDom` attributes).

If the XML is stored in a `String` or `Reader` object, you can parse that content with the following syntax:

```
<x:parse doc="XML_content"
        {var="variable_name" [scope="scope"] | varDom="var" [scopeDom="scope"]}
        [systemId="systemId"]
        [filter="filter"]>
```

The `doc` attribute specifies the XML content to be parsed. In JSTL 1.0, you could use the `xml` attribute instead, but since names that begin with "xml" in any combination of case are reserved by the XML Specification, the "xml" attribute has been deprecated in JSTL 1.1.

In both cases, the `systemId` attribute specifies a URI that is the system identifier for the input XML document. The `filter` attribute is used to set a filter (of type `org.xml.sax.XMLFilter`) that is applied to the input document.

When you use the parsed document in XPath expressions, you use syntax such as the following:

```
<c:import url="http://www.foo.com/data.xml"
          var="someXML"
/>
<x:parse doc="${someXML}" var="parsedDocument" />
<x:out select="$parsedDocument/people/person/name" />
```

In this example, the `c:import` action makes the XML source available through a variable called `someXML` so that the `x:parse` action can parse it. The `x:parse` action stores the parsed document in the `parsedDocument` variable for use by the `x:out` action. Now here is the important bit: The variable name you choose represents the root of the InfoSet of the parsed document. Thus, the `x:out` action does not simply use the XPath location path `/people/person/name`, but `$parsedDocument/people/person/name`.

The x:out Action

If you want to evaluate an XPath expression and output the result as a string, you can use the `x:out` action. Apart from the fact that this action works with XPath expressions, it is very similar to the `c:out` action and the JSP expression tag (`<%= ... %>`). Its syntax is

```
<x:out select="XPath_expression"
       [escapeXml="{true | false}"]
/>
```

The optional `escapeXml` (default value of `true`) allows you to specify whether the `&`, `<`, `>`, `'`, and `"` characters should be replaced with their character entity codes in the output.

The x:set Action

This action enables you to evaluate an XPath expression, and store the result in a scoped variable. Its syntax is

```
<x:set select="XPath_expression"
       var="variable_name"
      [scope="{page | request | session | application}"
/>
```

The x:if Action

This action is similar to the `c:if` action, except that the test condition uses an XPath expression. If the XPath expression evaluates to `true`, the `x:if` action's body content is evaluated. You can optionally store the result of evaluating the XPath expression in a scoped variable. The syntax is

```
<x:if select="XPath_expression"
      [var="variable_name"]
      [scope="{page | request | session | application}"]
>
    body_content
</x:if>
```

The x:choose Action

As with the c:choose action, the x:choose action enables you to perform conditional processing of nested x:when and x:otherwise actions (these actions are described in the next two sections of this appendix). The syntax is

```
<x:choose>
    body_content (nested x:when and x:otherwise actions)
</x:choose>
```

The x:when Action

This action represents a particular branch of execution within an x:choose action. It is similar to the c:when action, except its test condition is specified through an attribute called select rather than test. Also, the x:when action's select attribute must contain an XPath expression. The syntax is

```
<x:when select="XPath_expression">
    body_content
</x:when>
```

Make sure that the x:when action has a parent element that is an x:choose action, and also that your x:when actions appear before an x:otherwise action (if present).

The x:otherwise Action

As with the c:otherwise action, the x:otherwise action can be optionally placed as the last nested action within an x:choose action. It is processed if none of the x:when actions evaluates to true. The syntax is

```
<x:otherwise>
    body_content
</x:otherwise>
```

The x:forEach Action

The x:forEach action evaluates the XPath expression supplied in the select attribute, and processes its body content for each node in the result set from the XPath expression:

```
<x:forEach select="XPath_expression"
           [var="variable_name"]
           [begin="begin_index"]
           [end="end_index"]
           [step="step_value"]
           [varStatus="varStatus_name"]
>
    body_content
</x:forEach>
```

You can use the var attribute to specify the name of a nested visibility variable that holds the current iteration item.

Within the body content of the x:forEach action, the XPath context is set to the current iteration item.

The begin, end, step, and varStatus attributes work in the same way as for the c:forEach action.

The x:transform Action

This powerful action enables you to apply a specified XSLT transformation to an XML document. The result of processing the transformation can be either written to the page (the default behavior) or stored in a scoped variable.

The syntax takes three forms. The first form has no body content, and the XML document and the XSLT transformation are both specified by attributes:

```
<x:transform doc="XML_document"
             xslt="XSLT_stylesheet"
             [docSystemId="XML_System_Identifier"]
             [xsltSystemId="XSLT_System_Identifier"]
             [var="variable_name"
              scope="page | request | session | application"]
/>
```

The attributes are self-explanatory:

- doc is the XML document to be transformed. Its value can be a Reader, a String, a javax.xml.transform.Source, or an object exported by any of the x:transform, x:parse, or x:set actions. In JSTL 1.0, you could use the xml attribute instead of doc. xml is now deprecated in JSTL 1.1.
- xslt is the transformation stylesheet that is to be applied to the XML document. Similarly, to the xml attribute, the xslt document can be specified as a String, a Reader, or a javax.xml.transform.Source object.
- docSystemId is an optional attribute. If used, its value is a URI that identifies the XML document. JSTL 1.0 used the now deprecated xmlSystemId instead of JSTL 1.1's docSystemId.
- xsltSystemId is an optional attribute. If used, its value is a URI that identifies the XSLT stylesheet.
- Instead of writing the transformed document to the JSP, you can store it in an exported variable of type org.w3c.dom.Document. You can specify the name of the exported variable by using the var attribute, and its scope through the scope attribute with the usual values available (page, request, session, and application). The default level is page.

The second form of the syntax is identical to the first form, except that it has body content where you can specify transformation parameters (see the next section on `x:param` actions).

The third form is very similar to the second form, except that the XML document is specified in the body content of the action rather than through the `xml` attribute:

```
<x:transform xslt="XSLT_stylesheet"
             [xmlSystemId="XML_System_Identifier"]
             [xsltSystemId="XSLT_System_Identifier"]
             [var="variable_name"
              scope="page | request | session | application"]
>
    XML document
    optional x:param actions
</x:transform>
```

For all three forms of the syntax, you can specify an object that controls how the result is to be processed. In the latter case, simply replace the two attributes, `var` and `scope`, with an attribute called `result` whose value is an object of type `javax.xml.transform.Result`. This object is then responsible for building the transformation result tree.

The `x:param` Action

The `x:param` action can be nested within the `x:transform` action to pass transformation parameters to the XSLT stylesheet. The value of the parameter can be set either through an attribute called `value`, or as body content of the `x:param` action:

```
<x:param name="XSLT_parameter_name"
         value="parameter_value"
/>
```

or

```
<x:param name="XSLT_parameter_name">
    XSLT_parameter_value
</x:param>
```

Internationalization Actions

JSTL provides actions for the internationalization of Web applications based on the standard Java concepts of locales, time zones, and resource bundles. The actions include those to facilitate the formatting of dates, times, numbers, and currencies. There is an overview of some of these actions in Chapter 5.

The fmt:setLocale Action

You can use the fmt:setLocale action to provide a value for the javax.servlet.jsp.jstl.fmt.locale configuration variable. This is useful in situations where you already know what the client's preferred locale is, perhaps because they registered a preference that you stored in a database during an earlier visit to the Web application.

The fmt:setLocale action has one mandatory attribute called value, and two optional attributes called variant and scope:

```
<fmt:setLocale value="locale_string"
               [scope="{page|request|session|application}"]
               [variant="variant_string"]
/>
```

The scope attribute controls the scope of the configuration variable, and the variant is a browser-specific or vendor-specific code such as MAC for Macintosh, POSIX for POSIX, and WIN for Microsoft Windows. Variants are defined in the documentation for the java.util.Locale class.

The fmt:bundle Action

This action enables you to create a context that you can load a resource bundle into. The resource bundle can then be used by nested actions, such as the fmt:message action. The syntax of the action is

```
<fmt:bundle basename="resource_bundle_base_name"
            [prefix="message_key_prefix"]
>
    body content
</fmt:bundle>
```

You use the basename attribute to specify the fully qualified name of the resource bundle (similar to fully qualified class names). The prefix attribute is simply a type-saving feature: It enables you to specify a string that is prepended to any message keys that are used in nested fmt:message actions.

The fmt:setBundle Action

This action creates a context and enables you to store it in one of two places, either a scoped variable or the javax.servlet.jsp.jstl.fmt.localizationContext configuration variable (if you omit the var attribute). The syntax of the action is

```
<fmt:setBundle basename="resource_bundle_base_name"

               [var="variable_name"]
               [scope="{page|request|session|application}"]
/>
```

The `scope` attribute dictates the scope of the created context, regardless of where it is stored.

The `fmt:message` Action

The `fmt:message` action looks up a message in a resource bundle that corresponds to a key that you supply. You can specify the key either through an attribute (`key`) or as body content:

```
<fmt:message key="message_key"
             [bundle="resource_bundle"]
             [var="variable_name"]
             [scope="{page|request|session|application}"]
/>
```

You can nest the `fmt:message` action within a `fmt:bundle` action, or you can specify another resource bundle through the optional `bundle` attribute.

Regardless of which way you pass the value for the message key, you can also pass parameter values for any variables used in the message by nesting `fmt:param` actions. Here is the syntax for passing both the message key and parameters in the body of the action:

```
<fmt:message [bundle="resource_bundle"]
             [var="variable_name"]
             [scope="{page|request|session|application}"]
>
    message_key
    nested_fmt:param_actions
</fmt:message>
```

The result of formatting the value can be stored in a scoped variable (by using the `var` and `scope` attributes in the usual way), or the action writes it to the page if you omit the `var` attribute.

The `fmt:param` Action

You can nest `fmt:param` actions within a `fmt:message` action to pass parameters to a compound message (one that uses variables). You can specify the value of the parameter either as body content or through the `value` attribute:

```
<fmt:param name="parameter_name">
    parameter_value
</fmt:param>
```

or

```
<fmt:param name="parameter_name" value="parameter_value" />
```

The `fmt:requestEncoding` Action

This action enables you to set the name of the character encoding that is used to decode request parameters. Most Web browsers fail to include a `Content-Type` header in the requests that they send to servers, so if you know what the encoding is in advance, you can set it on the page before you retrieve any parameters (using the EL, or explicitly). The syntax is

```
<fmt:requestEncoding value="character_set_name" />
```

The `value` attribute simply sets the name of the character encoding that has to be used when decoding any request parameters.

If you do not know in advance what to specify for the `value` attribute, you should omit the `value` attribute. In this case, the `fmt:requestEncoding` action checks the `Content-Type` header for a character set. If it does not find one, it looks for the session-scoped variable called `javax.servlet.jsp.jstl.fmt.request.charset`. If this variable is not found, the `ISO-8859-1` character set is used as the default.

The `fmt:setTimezone` Action

This action is similar to the `fmt:setBundle` action in that it stores a time zone either in a scoped variable or in the `javax.servlet.jsp.jstl.fmt.timeZone` configuration variable. The syntax is

```
<fmt:setTimezone value="time_zone_identifier"
                 [var="variable_name"]
                 [scope="{page|request|session|application}"]
/>
```

Here is an example of storing a time zone for later use:

```
<fmt:setTimeZone value="GMT+2:00" var="timeZone" scope="page" />
```

In the next section on the `fmt:timezone` action, there is an example that uses this time zone.

You can find information on time-zone identifiers in the documentation of the `java.util.TimeZone` class.

The `fmt:timezone` Action

This action enables you to set the time zone that is used by the `fmt:formatDate` and `fmt:parseDate` actions. Its syntax is

```
<fmt:timezone value="time_zone_name">
    body_content
</fmt:timezone>
```

You can explicitly specify a time zone, such as `GMT+2:00`. Alternatively, you can use a time zone that was stored using the `fmt:setTimeZone` action as in the previous section. Here is an example JSP that retrieves the current time and date, and formats it using both techniques:

```
<%@ taglib uri="http://java.sun.com/jstl/fmt" prefix="fmt" %>

<html>
  <body>
    <jsp:useBean id="currentDate" class="java.util.Date" />

    <fmt:timeZone value="GMT-7:00">
      <fmt:formatDate value="${currentDate}"
                      type="both"
                      dateStyle="full"
                      timeStyle="full"
      />
    </fmt:timeZone>
    <hr />
    <fmt:setTimeZone value="GMT+2:00" var="timeZone" scope="page" />
    <fmt:timeZone value="${timeZone}">
      <fmt:formatDate value="${now}" type="both"
                      dateStyle="full" timeStyle="full" />
    </fmt:timeZone>
  </body>
</html>
```

The first `fmt:timeZone` action specifies a time zone of `GMT-7:00`, which is used by the nested `fmt:formatDate` action. The second `fmt:timeZone` action uses a time zone of `GMT+2:00`, which is stored by the `fmt:setTimeZone` action in a page-scoped variable called `timeZone`.

The `fmt:formatNumber` Action

If you need to format a number for a particular locale, you can use the `fmt:formatNumber` action. The number to be formatted can be specified either through an attribute (`value`) or as body content of the action. The syntax when using the attribute to set the value is

```
<fmt:formatNumber value="number_to_format"
                    [var="variable_name"]
                    [scope="{page | request | session | application}"]
                    [type="number | currency | percent"]
                    [pattern="custom_pattern"]
                    [currencyCode="currency_code"]
                    [currencySymbol="currency_symbol"]
                    [groupingUsed="{true | false}"]
```

```
                    [maxIntegerDigits="number_of_digits"]
                    [minIntegerDigits="number_of_digits "]
                    [maxFractionDigits="number_of_digits "]
                    [minFractionDigits="number_of_digits "]
/>
```

You use the `type` attribute to indicate whether the value to be parsed is a number, a currency, or a percentage. For numbers you can additionally specify a custom formatting pattern through the `pattern` attribute if the number is not formatted according to the page's locale. If you are formatting a currency, you can override the locale's currency code and currency symbol if you provide values for the `currencyCode` and `currencySymbol` attributes.

The `groupingUsed` attribute enables you to specify whether you want grouping separator characters to be used in the result, whereas the four attributes `maxIntegerDigits`, `minIntegerDigits`, `maxFractionDigits`, and `minFractionDigits` control how many digits appear in the integer and fractional parts of the result value.

The result of formatting the value can be stored in a scoped variable (by using the `var` and `scope` attributes in the usual way), or the action writes it to the page if you omit the `var` attribute.

The `fmt:parseNumber` Action

You use this action when you need to parse a number, a percentage, or a currency for a given locale (which you can set through the `parseLocale` attribute) or one that is in a custom format. The value that you want to parse can be specified either as an attribute (`value`) or as body content of the action. The syntax when using an attribute is

```
<fmt:parseNumber value="value_to_parse"
                 [type="{number | currency | percent}"]
                 [pattern="custom_pattern"]
                 [var="variable_name"]
                 [scope="{page | request | session | application}"]
                 [parseLocale="parse_locale"]
                 [integerOnly="{true | false}"]
/>
```

The `type` attribute indicates how the value should be parsed, and for numbers you can specify a pattern that is different from the locale's default through the `pattern` attribute. Also for numbers, you can indicate that you only want to have the integer part of a number parsed by setting the `integerOnly` attribute to `true`.

You can store the result in a scoped variable by using the `var` and `scope` attributes in the usual way. If you omit the `var` attribute, the result is simply displayed.

The `fmt:formatDate` Action

This action enables you to format dates for a specific time zone (which you can set through the `timezone` attribute). The syntax of the `fmt:formatDate` action is

```
<fmt:formatDate value="date_to_format"
                [var="variable_name"]
                [scope="{page | request | session | application}"]
                [type="{date | time | both}"]
                [dateStyle="{default | short | medium | long | full}"]
                [timeStyle="{default | short | medium | long | full }"]
                [pattern="custom_pattern"]
                [timezone="time_zone"]
/>
```

The body content is always empty, and the date to format is set through the `value` attribute. The result is written to the page, unless you explicitly store the result in a scoped variable by providing values for the `var` and `scope` attributes.

Providing a value for the `type` attribute controls whether only the date or time parts (or both) of the `value` you provide are formatted. The `dateStyle` and `timeStyle` attributes follow the rules defined by the `java.text.DateFormat` class, although you can specify your own formatting pattern through the `pattern` attribute.

The `fmt:parseDate` Action

You use this action when you need to parse a date that is formatted for a given locale (which you can set through the `parseLocale` attribute) or in a custom format. The value that you want to parse can be specified either as an attribute (`value`) or as body content of the action, and the `timezone` attribute indicates for which time zone the value is to be interpreted.

The syntax of the action when you use an attribute to specify the date is

```
<fmt:parseDate value="date_to_parse"
               [type="{date | time | both}"]
               [parseLocale="parse_locale"]
               [timezone="time_zone"]
               [dateStyle="{default | short | medium | long | full}"]
               [timeStyle="{default | short | medium | long | full }"]
               [pattern="custom_pattern"]
               [var="variable_name"]
               [scope="{page | request | session | application}"]
/>
```

The `type` attribute indicates whether the date that is to be parsed contains a date, a time, or even both. If the value to be parsed is formatted using a custom pattern, you can specify the pattern through the `pattern` attribute.

The dateStyle and timeStyle attributes are exactly the same as for the fmt:formatDate action.

You can store the result in a scoped variable by using the var and scope attributes in the usual way. If you omit the var attribute, the result is simply displayed.

SQL Actions

JSTL provides SQL actions that enable you to:

- Update a database through SQL DELETE, INSERT, and UPDATE statements.
- Query a database and process the results.
- Use transactions to group together database operations.

When you use a JSTL SQL action, the database connection is closed by the time its owning action has completed executing.

The sql:setDataSource Action

You can set the data source for the SQL actions by using the sql:setDataSource action (see Chapter 14 for other ways to set the data source).

This action exports the data source as a scoped variable, or as a configuration variable (called javax.servlet.jsp.jstl.sql.DataSource) if a variable name is not supplied (through the optional var and scope attributes).

The syntax can take several forms. The first takes a dataSource attribute that sets the data source:

```
<sql:setDataSource dataSource="data_source"
                   [driver="JDBC_driver_class_name"]
                   [user="user_name"]
                   [password="password"]
                   [var="variable_name"]
                   [scope="{page | request | session | application}"]
/>
```

The value of the dataSource attribute is either a String or a javax.sql.DataSource object. See Chapter 14 for examples of the different forms that the datasource attribute can take.

The second form of the syntax for the sql:setDataSource action enables you to specify a JDBC URL to the datasource, rather than use the datasource attribute:

```
<sql:setDataSource url="JDBC_URL"
                   [driver="JDBC_driver_class_name"]
                   [user="user_name"]
                   [password="password"]
                   [var="variable_name"]
                   [scope="{page | request | session | application}"]
/>
```

Notice with both forms of the syntax that you can also optionally specify the JDBC driver class, along with a username and password, to make the connection.

The `sql:param` Action

You can use the `sql:param` action to pass SQL parameters to the `sql:query` and `sql:update` actions. The `sql:param` action simply specifies a value either through the `value` attribute or as body content. Names are not required for parameters because the order in which the `sql:param` actions are nested within `sql:query` or `sql:update` actions matches the order of the parameters in the SQL statement (denoted by the `?` character).

The two forms of the syntax are

```
<sql:param value="parameter_value" />
```

and

```
<sql:param>
    SQL_parameter_value
</sql:param>
```

The `sql:query` Action

You can use the `sql:query` action to query a database. The results of the query are exported in a scoped variable in the usual way, through the `var` and `scope` attributes.

You can specify the SQL query string either using an attribute called `sql` or as body content of the action. You can also specify SQL `PreparedStatement` parameters to the query using `sql:param` actions nested within the body of the `sql:query` action. Thus, there are three forms that the syntax can take. The first has no body content, and uses the `sql` attribute to set the SQL query string:

```
<sql:query sql="SQL_query_string"
           var="variable_name"
           [scope="page | request | session | application"]
           [dataSource="data_source"]
           [maxRows="maximum_number_of_rows_to_return"]
           [startRow="start_row_value"]
/>
```

The `dataSource` attribute sets the data source to be queried. The `maxRows` attribute sets the maximum number of rows that are included in the result set. You can use the `startRow` attribute to indicate the first row from the result set that is to be included in the result generated by the action. These rules apply to all three forms.

Rows in the result set are indexed from `0`. So, if you specify a value of `0`, or omit the `startRow` attribute, then results are returned starting with the first row. The `maxRows` attribute specifies the maximum number of rows that can be returned from the action. If you omit the maxRows attribute, or specify a value of -1, then there is no limit on the number of rows that are returned.

The second form of the action is the same as the first, except that there is body content, which contains sql:param actions to pass parameters to the query. The syntax is therefore:

```
<sql:query sql="SQL_query_string"
           var="variable_name"
           [scope="page | request | session | application"]
           [dataSource="data_source"]
           [maxRows="maximum_number_or_rows_to_return"]
           [startRow="start_row_value"]
>
    <sql:param> actions
</sql:query>
```

The third form is very similar to the second, except that the SQL query string is passed as body content rather than through the sql attribute:

```
<sql:query var="variable_name"
           [scope="page | request | session | application"]
           [dataSource="data_source"]
           [maxRows="maximum_number_or_rows_to_return"]
           [startRow="start_row_value"]
>
    SQL_query
    optional sql:param actions
</sql:query>
```

The result of the query implements an interface of type javax.servlet.jsp.jstl.sql.Result. This interface declares the following methods:

```
public java.util.SortedMap[]     getRows()
public Object[][]          getRowsByIndex()
public int               getRowCount()
public String[]           getColumnNames()
public boolean          isLimitedByMaxRows()
```

The getRows() and getRowsByIndex() methods provide access to the rows in the result set, while the getRowCount() method returns the number of rows in the result. The getColumnNames() method simply returns the column names from the database, and the isLimitedByMaxRows() method indicates whether the query action had a maxRows attribute with a value that was not -1.

The `sql:update` Action

If you need to execute SQL DDL instructions, or SQL `UPDATE`, `DELETE`, or `INSERT` statements, you can use the `sql:update` action.

There are three forms of the syntax. You use the first form when you do not need to specify any update parameters because this form of the action has no body content:

```
<sql:update sql="SQL_statement"
            [dataSource="data_source"]
            [var="variable_name"]
            [scope="{page|request|session|application}"]
/>
```

The `sql` attribute contains the SQL update statement, and the other attributes are the same as in the previous action. That is, the database to be updated is specified through the `dataSource` attribute, and the result of updating the database is stored in the scoped variable identified by the `var` and `scope` attributes.

The second form of the syntax for this action enables you to set SQL parameters for the update statement using nested `sql:param` actions:

```
<sql:update sql="SQL_statement"
            [dataSource="data_source"]
            [var="variable_name"]
            [scope="{page|request|session|application}"]
>
    sql:param actions
</sql:update>
```

The third and final form of the syntax for the `sql:update` action is very similar to the previous form, except that the SQL update statement is specified in the body content of the action, along with any parameters:

```
<sql:update [dataSource="data_source"]
            [var="variable_name"]
            [scope="{page|request|session|application}"]
    SQL_update_statement
    sql:param actions
</sql:update>
```

The `sql:transaction` Action

If you need to group the `sql:query` and `sql:update` actions into a transaction, you can nest them inside a `sql:transaction` action. The `sql:transaction` action is responsible for setting the data source, and any nested actions are not allowed to do so.

The `sql:transaction` action performs the following steps:

- Checks to see that the data source supports transactions and throws an exception if not. If transactions are supported, the next step depends on whether the user has supplied a value for the `isolation` attribute. If they have, the current transaction isolation is stored for subsequent restoration when the action ends. If not, the current data source isolation level is used.

- Ignores its body content, and instead enables the JSP container to process it. This processing will normally consist of nested `sql:update` and `sql:query` actions.
- If an exception is thrown while processing the action, an SQL rollback is performed. Otherwise, when the action ends, an SQL commit is executed. In either case, the original transaction isolation level is restored, the connection is set to autocommit for any subsequent SQL commands, and the connection is closed.

The syntax for this action is

```
<sql:transaction [dataSource="data_source"]
                 [isolation="isolation_level"]
>
    nested sql:update and sql:query actions
</sql:transaction>
```

The possible values for the `isolation` attribute are `read_committed`, `read_uncommitted`, `repeatable_read`, and `serializable`.

The `sql:dateParam` Action

This is a utility action that you can use to convert an instance of the `java.util.Date` class to any of the `java.sql.Time`, `java.sql.TimeStamp`, or `java.sql.Date` classes. This action is used to supply date parameters to SQL actions, such as `sql:query` and `sql:update`, by nesting the `sql:dateParam` actions within their body content.

You do not need to nest a `sql:dateParam` within a `sql:param` action. It is acceptable for you to place a `sql:dateParam` action anywhere that a `sql:param` action can appear.

The syntax for the `sql:dateParam` action is

```
<sql:dateParam value="parameter_value" type="[timestamp | time | date]"/>
```

The type of the `value` attribute is `java.util.Date`, and the default value for the `type` attribute is `timestamp`, which corresponds to the `java.sql.TimeStamp` datatype. The other values for the `type` attribute indicate that you want the `java.util.Date` instance to be converted to a `java.sql.Time` instance (if you specify a value of `time` for the `type` attribute), or `java.sql.Date` (if you specify a value of `date`).

D

Basic JSP Syntax Checklist

THIS APPENDIX IS A SUMMARY OF THE material covered in Chapter 2, "The Basic Syntax of JSP," and Chapter 3, "Further JSP Syntax." Further information can be found in those two chapters.

JSP Directives

Directives are tags that you can insert into a JSP document to give the JSP container information about the JSP. These tags directly affect the servlet code that is generated. The three directives that can be used in a JSP are `include`, `page`, and `taglib`.

The `include` Directive

The `include` directive is used to include text from another file. The included file's content is embedded when the JSP is translated into a servlet. Thus, before the usual translation phase occurs, the included content is inserted into the JSP, and the result is translated into a servlet before compilation and execution occurs. See Chapter 1, "JSP, J2EE, and the Role of the Servlet," for details of the translation, compilation, and execution process.

The content that is included can contain JSP tags. Multiple `include` directives can be used in a JSP.

The syntax for the `include` directive is

```
<%@ include file="relative_url_to_included_file" %>
```

However, the `include` directive has a drawback. If the included content changes, this change is not seen unless the time stamp on the including file also changes. An alternative to using the `include` directive is to use the `include` action.

The `include` action makes a dynamic call at *runtime* when the page is requested. This means that any changes in the included file are reflected in the including page. The syntax of the action is:

```
<jsp:include page="/include/header.html" />
```

The page Directive

You can set properties for a JSP with the page directive and its associated attributes. These properties affect the generated servlet.

The syntax of the page directive is

```
<%@ page page_attribute_list %>
```

See Table D.1 for a description of the various attributes that can be used with the page directive.

Table D.1 **The page Directive Attributes**

Attribute Name	Value	Description
autoFlush	Boolean true or false	Defines the behavior expected when the output buffer is full. If the value is true, the buffer is automatically flushed when full. If false, an exception is thrown when the buffer overflows. Default value: true Example: <%@ page autoFlush="true" %>
buffer	none, or a number of kilobytes (for example, 64kb)	Enables you to set the size of the output buffer. Default value: 8kb Examples: <%@ page buffer="none" %> <%@ page buffer="64kb" %>
contentType	A MIME type, with an optional character encoding	Sets the MIME type for the output: text/html, text/xml, or text/plain. Default value: text/html; charset=ISO-8859-1 Examples: <%@ page contentType="text/html" %> <%@ page contentType="text/plain;UTF-8"%>
errorPage	Relative URL	Sets the JSP page to which any Java exceptions thrown by the current page should be passed. Example: <%@ page errorPage="myErrorPage.jsp" %>

Table D.1 **Continued**

Attribute Name	**Value**	**Description**
extends	Fully qualified class name	Specifies the superclass of the servlet that is generated for the current JSP. *Use with care because the container may already be using its own class here.* Example: <%@ page extends="com.foo.MyClass"%>
import	Classes and interfaces to import	Enables you to import from standard Java packages. Examples: <@ page import="java.net.URL" %> <@ page import="java.util.Calendar, java.io.*" %>
info	Textual message	Sets an informational string that can be retrieved from the generated servlet by invoking the getServletInfo() method that is defined in the javax.servlet.Servlet interface. Example: <%@ page info="A Currency Converter" %>
isErrorPage	Boolean true or false	Indicates whether the current page will receive exceptions from other pages. If so, the exception intrinsic is made available. Default value: false Example: <%@ page isErrorPage="true" %>
isThreadSafe	Boolean true or false	Dictates whether the generated servlet implements the SingleThreadModel interface. Use a value of false if your code handles multiple threads safely. Default value: true Example: <%@ page isThreadSafe="true" %>

Table D.1 **Continued**

Attribute Name	Value	Description
language	Programming language name	At the moment, there is only one valid name (java) for the programming language that can be used for the generated servlet. Thus, this attribute can be safely left to default to the value java. Default value: java Example: `<%@ page language="c" %>`
session	Boolean true or false	This attribute indicates whether the page needs access to an HTTP session. If the value is `true` (the default), then a `session` object of type `javax.servlet.http.HttpSession` is available. If the value is `false`, then any reference to this object causes a translation error.
pageEncoding	Character encoding name	The value must be an IANA character encoding name. If a value is not specified for this attribute, then the `contentType` attribute is used (if present). If neither `pageEncoding` nor `contentType` is present, then `ISO-8859-1` is used.
isScriptingEnabled	Boolean `true` or `false`	If scripting is disabled (`false`) for this translation unit or page, then any declarations, scriptlets, or scripting expressions cause a translation error.Default value: `true`
isELEnabled	Boolean `true` or `false`	If the EL is disabled (`false`), then any EL expressions are ignored for this translation unit or page. If the EL is enabled (`true`), then any EL expressions are evaluated where they appear in either action attributes, or in template text.

The `taglib` Directive

You can use your own custom tags, or third-party tags, in a JSP. A set of predefined, common tags is described in Chapter 5, "The JSP Standard Tag Library." You can find information about how to define your own tags in Chapter 9, "Developing Custom Tag Libraries."

A custom tag must have some associated handler code, known as a *tag handler*. This mapping is defined in an XML document known as a *tag library descriptor* (TLD).

The syntax for the `taglib` directive is

```
<%@ taglib (uri="URI_TO_TAG_LIBRARY" | tagDir="TAG DIRECTORY")
           prefix="TAG_PREFIX" %>
```

The `uri` attribute specifies the location of the tag library descriptor (TLD), using either a relative or absolute path. The `prefix` attribute is an arbitrary string of text that is used to uniquely identify the custom tags you want to use. The page developer chooses the prefix. This avoids the situation where a tag library developer chooses a prefix that could clash with one that is already being used on the page.

An example document could be

```
<%@ taglib uri="MyCustomTags.tld" prefix="foo" %>
<html>
  <head><title>Chapter 2: Tag Library Usage</title></head>
  <body>
    ...
    <foo:processResultSet />
    ...
  </body>
</html>
```

Instead of specifying a `uri` attribute, you can instead use a `tagDir` attribute. Its value must begin with `/WEB-INF/tags/`. See Chapter 9, "Developing Custom Tag Libraries," for more details.

Comments in JSPs

There are three types of comments that can be used in a JSP: HTML, Java, and JSP. See Table D.2 for a description of the effect that each type of comment has on the generated servlet, and the output that the client sees.

Table D.2 **Comments in JSPs**

Comment type Type	Syntax	Description
HTML	<!-- comment text -->	An HTML comment. This type of comment appears in the content that is sent back to the client.

Table D.2 **Continued**

Comment type Type	Syntax	Description
Java	// single-line comment /* multiple line comment */ /** Javadoc comment */	These three comment types are for documenting any Java code that appears on a page inside declaration or scriptlet tags. These comments appear inside the generated servlet, but do not appear in the content that is sent back to the client.
JSP	<%-- comment text --%>	A JSP comment. This style of comment is used to document the JSP itself.

JSP Predefined Variables

Nine variables are made available for a JSP to use. The JSP does not need to declare or initialize them in any way. However, the `exception` and `session` variables must be made available by using the `page` directive. See Table D.3 for a description of each variable.

Table D.3 **JSP Predefined Variables**

Variable	Description
application	An object that implements the javax.servlet.ServletContext interface. This interface provides methods that enable a servlet to query for information about its environment, as well as write messages and errors to log files.
config	The ServletConfig object for the current page. The config object provides methods that allow access to any initialization information provided to a servlet.
exception	This is the error object that is available only to error pages. An error page uses the page directive, with a value of true for the isErrorPage attribute (see Table D.1).
out	An object of type javax.servlet.jsp.JspWriter. Can be used to write text content back to the client.
page	This variable corresponds directly to the this reference in the generated servlet. The page object is not typically used when writing a JavaServer Page.
pageContext	The pageContext provides methods that enable you to retrieve references to the other implicit objects; to store and retrieve objects via an attribute mechanism that uses a name/value pair; and to forward and redirect requests.
request	The object that models the incoming client request; for example, request parameters and session information. Usually implements the javax.servlet.http.HttpServletRequest interface.

Table D.3 **Continued**

Variable	Description
response	The object that models the outgoing response. For example, it enables you to manage user sessions and write content. Usually implements the javax.servlet.http.HttpServletResponse interface.
session	This object provides methods that enable you to store named objects in the user's session. These named objects can be accessed across multiple client requests.

The JavaServer Pages Standard Tag Library

The JavaServer Pages Standard Tag Library (JSTL) provides a set of tested and reliable tags. These tags cover four areas of functionality, as described in Table D.4. Because the tags are standard, you can use them in multiple JSP containers.

Table D.4 **JSTL Functional Areas**

Area	Description
Core	The core tags provide support for flow control and expressions. There are also tags for accessing URL-based resources whose content can then be processed or embedded within the JSP page.
XML	The JSTL XML tag set is based on XPath, and provides functionality for parsing, accessing, and transforming XML. There are also flow control tags.
Internationalization	This set of tags helps page authors tailor content to a particular locale. The tags cover setting the locale; creation of messages that can be adapted to available locales; and date and number formatting.
SQL	You can use these tags for quick applications and prototypes. The SQL tags enable you to specify a JDBC driver, and execute queries and updates.

The SQL tags are not recommended for production use. Instead, you are encouraged to use JavaBean components.

The JSP Expression Language

The JSP Expression Language (EL) is discussed in Chapter 3, "Further JSP Syntax." This section presents a summary of the Expression Language. It can be used in conjunction with the JSTL tag library, and in JSP 2.0 containers, it can be used inline in JSP pages. Expressions are enclosed in the following enclosing elements:

```
${EL Expression}
```

So, for example, an expression could be used in a JSTL tag in the following way:

```
<c:out value="${shoppingCart.total}" />
```

In this example, `shoppingCart` is a variable that will be available through one of the four scoped contexts (page, request, session, or application). The EL will automatically locate the variable by moving sequentially through the scopes until it locates the name `shoppingCart`. It will start with the innermost scope first which is page, and then work outward.

The EL can also be used in JSP pages inline, so you could have something like this in a JSP:

```
<p>Here is the quote of the day ${quotes.monday}
```

There are also a number of operators that can be used in the EL. These are listed in Table D.5.

Table D.5 **Expression Language Operators**

Operator	Description
`+, -, *, /, %, div, mod`	Arithmetic operators.
`&&, ||, !, and, or, not, empty`	Logical operators.
`.`	Used for accessing objects.
`[]`	Used for accessing objects and collections.
`==, <, >, <=, >=, !=, eq, ne, lt, gt, le, ge`	Relational operators.

These operators enable the use of the expression language in tags like the `if` tag as shown here:

```
<c:if test="${pageScope.signalStrength < 5}">
  <c:set var="signalFailure" value="true" scope="page" />
</c:if>
```

The variable `pageScope` used in the previous example is an implicit variable that is available to developers using the EL. Table D.6 shows a summary of the implicit objects that are available using the EL.

Table D.6 **The Implicit Objects of the Expression Language**

Implicit Objects	Description
`pageContext`	This is the page context object.
`pageScope`	Page scoped attributes can be accessed by name using this variable.
`requestScope`	Request scoped attributes can be accessed by name using this variable.

Table D.6 **Continued**

Implicit Objects	Description
`param`	The `param` object is a `Map` which contains any request parameters that are normally accessed using the `request.getParameter(String paramName)` method.
`paramValues`	This object represents the result of the call to `request.getParameterValues(String paramName)`.
`header`	This implicit variable contains a `Map` of all the headers along with their values.
`headerValues`	This object represents the result of the call to `request.getHeaders(String headerName)`.
`sessionScope`	Session-scoped attributes can be accessed by name using this variable.
`cookie`	This variable provides access to the Cookies array.
`applicationScope`	Application-scoped attributes can be accessed by name using this variable.
`initParam`	This variable gives access to the JSP initialization parameters.

Standard Actions

The standard actions are used within JSP to perform things like forward requests to other JSPs or servlets, or include nested JSPs, or interact with JavaBeans. They can also be used to set up the Java Plugin HTML for the inclusion of Java applets within Web pages.

The standard actions are discussed in detail in Chapter 3. Table D.7 lists the standard actions and their functions.

Table D.7 **A Summary of the Available Standard Actions**

Name	Description
`<jsp:forward>`	This standard action is used to forward requests on to another URL.
`<jsp:include>`	This allows a page to include another page based upon a specified URL.
`<jsp:useBean>`	This specifies a particular JavaBean that is to be used within a page.
`<jsp:setProperty>`	This action is used to set the property of a JavaBean available to the page.
`<jsp:getProperty>`	This action is used to retrieve a JavaBean property that has been set on the page.
`<jsp:param>`	This action sets a parameter that can be passed to other pages.
`<jsp:params>`	The params action is used to set parameters for use by the plugin action (see following).

Table D.7 **Continued**

Name	Description
`<jsp:plugin>`	The plugin action enables the appropriate HTML to be embedded to enable the use of the Java Plugin to be used by browsers to run Java applets within pages.
`<jsp:fallback>`	This element is used within the Java plugin action to specify what happens if the browser does not support the plugin.
`<jsp:attribute>`	Allows for the setting of attributes for tags within the body of an XML tag rather than the value of an XML attribute.
`<jsp:body>`	Allows for the explicit setting of the body content of a tag. This is required when `jsp:attribute` actions are used and body content is required.
`<jsp:invoke>`	This action can ONLY be used in a tag file, or a translation error occurs. It enables you to invoke a fragment, with optional parameters. The result can be written to the `JspWriter`, or to a page-scoped variable for manipulation.
`<jsp:doBody>`	This action can ONLY be used in a tag file, or a translation error occurs. It enables you to invoke the body of a tag, and write the result to the `JspWriter`, or to a scoped variable for manipulation.

Adding Java Code to JSPs

There are three different ways in which you can add Java code to a JSP. The first way is through a declaration tag, which enables you to declare variables and methods that are available to the page. The second way is through an expression tag that evaluates a Java expression, and outputs a string value to the page. The third way is to use a scriptlet tag that enables you to embed Java code directly into the page for execution.

The next three sections describe these three tags.

The Declaration Tag

Variables and methods can be declared inside a declaration tag in a JSP. The rest of the JSP code on the page can access such variables and methods by name. Variables can be optionally initialized inline.

Multiple declaration blocks can exist in a JSP. The syntax is

```
<%! Variable_and_method_declarations %>
```

The variables and methods are copied into the generated servlet at member level, that is, outside of the `_jspService` method. For variables, and any objects they reference, this could be a problem when multiple clients access the page. This is because each client request runs under a separate thread. Thus, it is necessary to either synchronize access to the shared variables in code, or to use the `isThreadSafe` attribute of the `page` directive, with a value of `false`. See Chapter 1 for more details of this.

Here is an example that declares a variable and a method:

```
<html>
  <head><title>Declaration tags</title></head>
  <body>
    <%!
      int upperLimit = 10;

      int getRandomNumber()
      {
        return (int)(Math.random() * upperLimit);
      }
    %>

    A new random number between 0 and 10 is <%= getRandomNumber() %>.<br>
    Refresh this page to see another.
  </body>
</html>
```

This example simply displays a random number in the range 0 to 10 each time that it is viewed. The `upperLimit` variable defines the maximum value that can be displayed, and you can see that it is initialized inline with the value 10.

The `getRandomNumber()` method uses the `upperLimit` variable, and returns a new random number.

The example uses an expression tag to invoke the `getRandomNumber()` method. Expression tags are explained in the next section.

The Expression Tag

A JSP expression is a piece of JSP code that is converted to a string and inserted into the output. Variables can be referenced by name, whereas methods can be invoked on objects, inside an expression tag.

Expressions do *not* terminate with a semicolon character. This is because the expression is passed as a parameter to the `out.write()` method inside the generated servlet's `_jspService` method.

The syntax for the expression tag is

```
<%= expression %>
```

Objects are converted to a string by invoking their `toString()` method. Primitives are handled automatically.

Referring back to the example given in the previous section on declaration tags, you saw this:

```
A new random number between 0 and 10 is <%= getRandomNumber() %>.
```

This expression tag invoked the `getRandomNumber()` method that was declared in a declaration tag.

The Scriptlet Tag

Java code can be embedded into a JSP using a `scriptlet` tag. The default scripting language for a page is Java (see Table D.1, `language` attribute), although other languages could be supported in the future.

Any code inside a scriptlet is copied into the generated servlet's `_jspService` method. Scriptlets have access to the predefined variables, as well as any variables or methods declared in declaration tags.

The syntax for the `scriptlet` tag is

```
<% scriptlet_code %>
```

Here is an example that displays a list of names:

```
<html>
  <head><title>Scriptlet tags</title></head>
  <body>
    <%!
      String[] names = {"Mark", "Tracy", "Joshua", "Samuel"};
    %>

    <h1>A list of names</h1>

    <% for (int i=0; i<names.length; i++)
      {
    %>
        Name <%= i %> is <%= names[i] %> <br>
    <% } %>
  </body>
</html>
```

The names are set up inside the declaration tag, in an array called `names`. The scriptlet consists of a `for` loop that iterates over the names in the array.

Notice that it is legal to have partial statements within a scriplet:

```
<% for (int i=0; i<names.length; i++ )
   {
%>
```

Debugging Tomcat and Running the Examples

THIS APPENDIX IS DESIGNED TO HELP YOU with the examples found in the book. Each section comprises a number of issues that you might come across while running the examples. The guidance in this appendix might also help you when you are debugging and running your own Web applications.

Debugging Web Applications and Tomcat

Chapter 1, "JSP, J2EE, and the Role of the Servlet," gives instructions for the installation of Tomcat. In this appendix, we will start with some of the more common problems that occur with the installation of Tomcat.

When I Start Tomcat, It Disappears After a Few Seconds

This can be caused by a number of things. The following sections form a checklist you can run through.

The Java Version

We recommend that you use J2SDK 1.4 or higher to run Tomcat. You can check this by running a command prompt or console and typing

```
java -version
```

This will return the version of Java that your platform is using as a runtime. If you are using an earlier version, and you also installed the light edition of Tomcat (that is, the version that does not come with the XML APIs), Tomcat will fail to start successfully.

Environment Variables

Tomcat uses two important environment variables. It does guess them, but if you are having problems it can be helpful to set them directly. The variables are `JAVA_HOME`, which should point to your Java install directory, and `CATALINA_HOME`, which should point to your Tomcat install directory. Figure E.1 shows the variables set up on a Windows XP system.

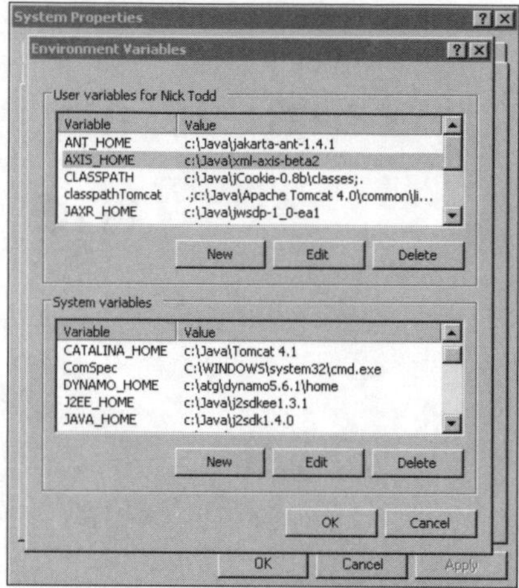

Figure E.1 Setting the environment variables.

> **Caution**
>
> On Windows machines where you are not the administrator, you might need to log out and log back in for these changes to take effect.

To access the dialog box shown, simply right-click the My Computer icon and select Properties. There will be a button called Environment Variables on Windows XP, or an Advanced tab on Windows 2000. If you are using Windows 98, you will need to add these variables to the `autoexec.bat` file found in the root of your boot disk. An example is shown here:

```
set JAVA_HOME=c:\j2sdk1.4
set CATALINA_HOME=c:\Tomcat x.x
```

On a Unix System, you will need to set the environment variables as follows:

```
export JAVA_HOME=/usr/java/j2sdk1.4
export CATALINA_HOME=/home/user/jakarta-tomcat-x.x.x
```

On a Linux system, you will probably find it easier to add these lines to either your `.bashrc` or your `.bash` profile file. This will take effect for any bash consoles that you open in the future.

On Windows 98, you will also need to increase the environment space to 1096. The easiest way to do this is to right-click a command prompt window, select Properties, and then under the Memory tab, set the initial environment to at least 1096.

If neither of these issues solve the problem, you can visit the Tomcat home page and locate the FAQs and mailing lists there. The URL is `http://jakarta.apache.org/tomcat`.

When I Try to Start Tomcat, It States That Port Number 8080 Is in Use

If, when you installed Tomcat, you opted for the NT service to be installed on an NT-based Windows platform such as NT/Win2K/WinXP, this service is started automatically when the install is complete. This means that when you try and start Tomcat for yourself you get a port conflict because port 8080 is already in use by the service. To identify if this has happened on your machine, locate the Services within your Control Panel and stop the Tomcat service, setting it to Manual Startup at the same time. The Tomcat service can be seen in Figure E.2, which shows the services on Windows XP.

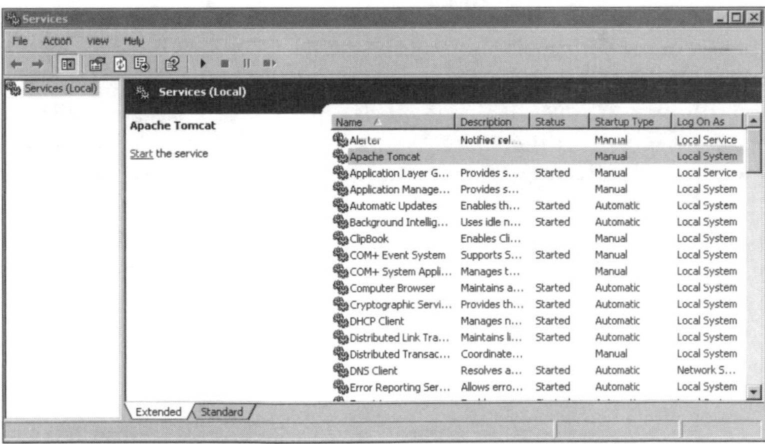

Figure E.2 The Tomcat service on XP.

Tomcat Is Running, But I Cannot Get a Web Application to Work

This can be caused by a number of things. We'll go through this based on the type of error you are getting.

File Not Found Errors

File not found errors appear in the browser, as shown in Figure E.3.

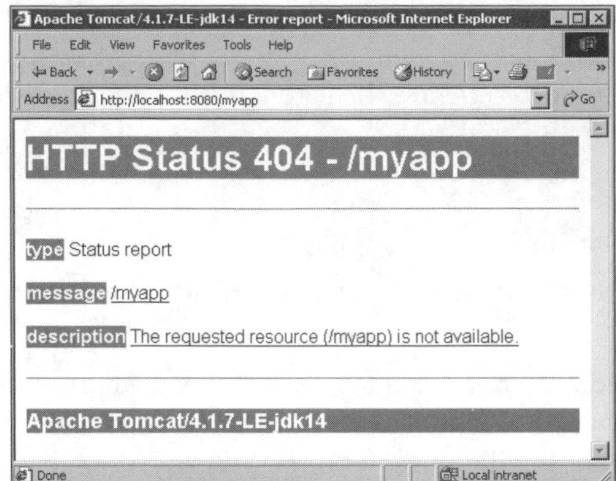

Figure E.3 File Not Found Response from Tomcat.

The first thing to check is your URL. Remember, these URLs are case-sensitive, which is something that's easily forgotten if you're used to a Windows platform.

If the URL is definitely right, you might want to check that the resource you have requested is part of the Web application specified. This is easy for JSP because they should simply be in the Web application folder structure. If the JSP is there, you might need to restart Tomcat. It could be that the Web application has not been picked up by Tomcat because you put it in the `<tomcat-home>\webapps` folder. For servlet resources, you might want to double-check that your `web.xml` file has correctly set up the servlet mapping. This is described in Chapter 1.

One last thing to check here is that the `web.xml` file is correct. If this file has any errors in it, the application will not be accessible, and 404 errors are returned. To identify this, look at the startup window for Tomcat. There will be a listed error here for your Web application if there is a configuration problem with it. An example is shown in Figure E.4.

```
Start Tomcat
INFO: Jk running ID=0 ... init time=310 ms
Starting service Tomcat-Standalone
Apache Tomcat/4.1.7-LE-jdk14
31-Jul-2002 12:21:40 org.apache.commons.digester.Digester fatalError
SEVERE: Parse Fatal Error at line 70 column -1: End of entity not allowed; an en
d tag is missing.
org.xml.sax.SAXParseException: End of entity not allowed; an end tag is missing.

        at org.apache.crimson.parser.Parser2.fatal(Parser2.java:3182)
        at org.apache.crimson.parser.Parser2.fatal(Parser2.java:3170)
        at org.apache.crimson.parser.Parser2.content(Parser2.java:1837)
        at org.apache.crimson.parser.Parser2.maybeElement(Parser2.java:1507)
        at org.apache.crimson.parser.Parser2.parseInternal(Parser2.java:500)
        at org.apache.crimson.parser.Parser2.parse(Parser2.java:305)
        at org.apache.crimson.parser.XMLReaderImpl.parse(XMLReaderImpl.java:442)

        at org.apache.commons.digester.Digester.parse(Digester.java:1284)
        at org.apache.catalina.startup.ContextConfig.applicationConfig(ContextCo
nfig.java:282)
        at org.apache.catalina.startup.ContextConfig.start(ContextConfig.java:63
9)
        at org.apache.catalina.startup.ContextConfig.lifecycleEvent(ContextConfi
g.java:243)
        at org.apache.catalina.util.LifecycleSupport.fireLifecycleEvent(Lifecycl
eSupport.java:166)
```

Figure E.4 Tomcat Response to configuration errors in `web.xml`.

Page Errors

Page errors fall into three categories: parser errors, compiler errors, and runtime errors. Parser errors are caused by markup errors within the JSP, so the page cannot be parsed correctly. Missing closing tags or poorly nested JSP tags are examples of what causes these exceptions. Page compile errors mean that the requested page cannot be compiled into a Java class and are caused by errors in JSP pages. This can be because of Java code errors within scriptlets or incorrect use of standard actions, directives, or tag libraries. Runtime errors occur from pages that have compiled fine, but then throw exceptions for other reasons such as `NullPointerExceptions`, and so forth. Either way, these errors come up in the browser, as shown in Figure E.5.

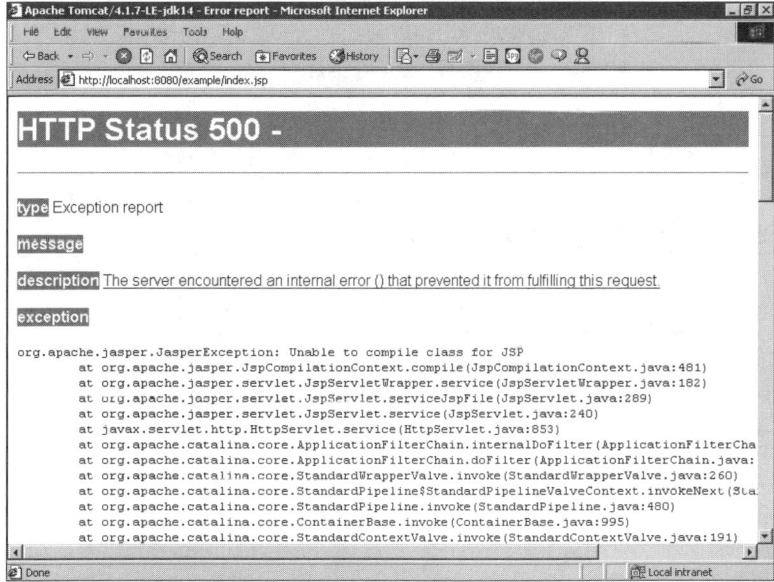

Figure E.5 Page errors in the browser.

Some containers send error 500 messages directly to your browser, and Internet Explorer does not show the resultant error page. Instead, it shows its own generic "This page cannot be displayed" screen. This means that you cannot identify the source of the error! To get the proper error messages, you need to uncheck the Show Friendly HTTP Error Messages option in the Internet Options of Internet Explorer. This is shown in Figure E.6.

If you scroll down these Tomcat error pages, you should see the root cause specified. The process of fixing compiler errors is very similar to fixing compiler errors in Java classes.

Fixing runtime errors can be more difficult, especially when pages are dependent on scoped variables that are initialized by other parts of the Web application.

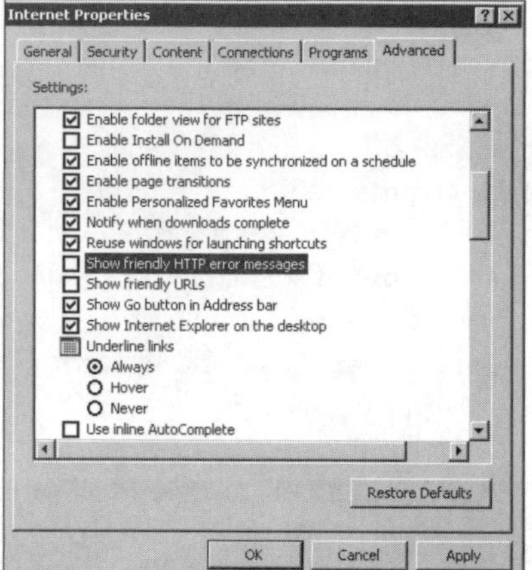

Figure E.6 Internet options in Internet Explorer.

General Debugging Tips

Following is a list of things that you can do to help debug your pages. Some of these are generic to the debugging of Java applications generally, whereas others are specific to JSP:

- Use `System.out.print()` statements within your JSP pages. These will come out in the Tomcat console. These can be used to display variable values and also to signify that specific points have been reached within flow control sections, such as `System.out.println("Got this far");`.
- Using <c:out> tags. If you are the JSTL on pages, you can use this tag to output variables that you are passing as parameters and such to make sure that they actually have the value you expect. This technique was used a great deal when building the demonstration applications.
- Make sure that you indent and write your JSPs in an easy-to-read manner so that you can identify the sources of your problems more easily.
- Look for references to line numbers in the presented error messages. Be aware that if they are compiler errors, the line number will be the number in the autogenerated servlet, not the JSP page itself. Don't be nervous about looking at the Java version of the JSP. It can be very helpful when trying to identify compiler errors.
- Make good use of `try/catch` blocks in areas of your code that seem to be problematic.

- Try to incorporate good design within your application, separating the different roles of the parts of the application cleanly. This is discussed in Chapter 7, "JSP Application Architecture." This makes it easier to identify where the error is coming from.
- If you have one, take advantage of the debugging facilities within your IDE.

F

The Java Community Process

WHAT EXACTLY IS THE JAVA COMMUNITY PROCESS? Here is the definition from the Java Community Process Web site (`http://jcp.org`):

The Java Community Process (JCP) is the way the Java platform evolves. It's an open organization of international Java developers and licensees whose charter is to develop and revise Java technology specifications, reference implementations, and technology compatibility kits.

The Web site home page is shown in Figure F.1.

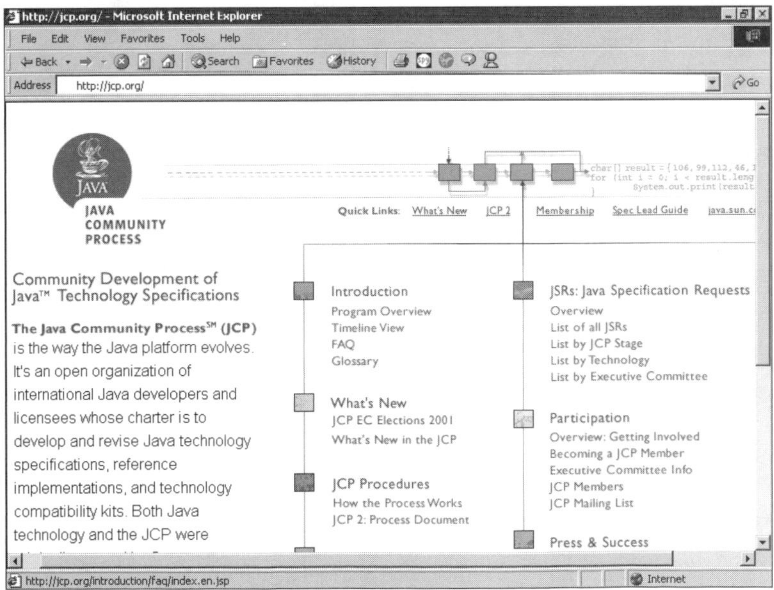

Figure F.1 The Java Community Process home page.

> **Note**
> Before you read any more of this appendix, it is worth browsing around the JCP Web site. It will help put this material into context.

Why Do We Need the Java Community Process?

Throughout this book a whole raft of standards have been discussed and explained. The JCP is the mechanism by which these standards evolve and develop. The JCP was started in 1998 by Sun Microsystems as a formalization of a review process used by Sun since the inception of Java in 1995. Each potential new standard is referred to as a Java Specification Request (JSR).

This process has been pivotal to the success of the Java platform. Experts from various vendors work together with individual experts to form new standards that can be incorporated into the Java platform.

Who Is Involved?

In short, the answer is everyone who wants to be! It's not only for the experts. There are several levels of involvement in the community process:

- The public
- Community members
- Expert group members
- Executive committee

The Public

At some of the stages in the review process, the public can make comments and contribute to the various JSRs. The public has a significant amount of access to the JCP via the Web site. The public can also view various JSRs online.

Community Members

Community members can participate at earlier stages in the lifecycle of a JSR, and they can also view all the new standards in the *community review stage*.

A company, organization, or an individual can become a community member. To become a community member, Sun Microsystems requires that the party sign a Java Specification Participation Agreement and pay a fee.

Expert Group Members

Each JSR has an expert group. These are the individuals and companies that will actually flesh out the proposed JSR. When a JSR is first suggested, a specification lead is suggested. This individual will then identify and invite individuals and companies to join the expert group for a specific JSR.

Executive Committee Members

The executive committee is made up of 16 voting JCP members, plus a chair, who does not vote. The chair is from the project management office based in Sun Microsystems. The committee has a specific set of functions, including the following:

- Select the JSRs that are to be developed within the JCP.
- Approve the draft specifications before they go for public review.
- Give the final approval to completed specifications.

Individuals are on the committee for a period of three years and there is a mechanism that enables the gradual rotation of committee members. For more details on the executive committee, visit `http://jcp.org/procedures/jcp2/#A`.

How Does a New JSR Evolve?

The process is similar to the process used by the World Wide Web Consortium, as it develops new standards for the Internet and XML world. For the JCP, a JSR goes through four discrete stages that make up the process. The stages are as follows:

1. Initiation—A community member or group of community members propose a new JSR. This proposal is then reviewed and either accepted or rejected by the executive committee. This process takes 14 days.
2. Community draft—An expert group is formed after a JSR has been accepted by the executive committee. The expert group puts together the first draft for the specification, which when completed, is made available to community members for review. After this review, the draft can be adapted and modified as necessary. The JSR once again goes before the executive committee, which decides whether the JSR should go to the next stage. This process can take up to 90 days.
3. Public draft—After the community review has taken place and the necessary changes have been made, the JSR goes into the public draft phase. This is where the specification is made available to the public so that they can have their input. After this phase, any additional changes are made before the JSR goes for final approval by the executive committee. This process can also take up to 90 days.
4. Maintenance—This last phase is where the JSR is tweaked and clarified as issues come up. The executive committee decides if issues are small enough to be fixed immediately or whether an expert group is required to make the necessary changes. This process takes around 30 days.

You can see the process timeline at the JCP Web site (`http://jcp.org/introduction/timeline/`).

A Case Study—The JSP 2.0 Specification

As an example, we will finish with a look at how the JSP 2.0 specification emerged. The JSR for this specification is JSR-152.

On October 20, 2001, the executive committee unanimously agreed upon the specification, which meant it could be commenced. Figure F.2 shows the voting result. Incidentally, Figure F.2 also shows the 16 executive committee members! The expert group was formed on October 23, 2001.

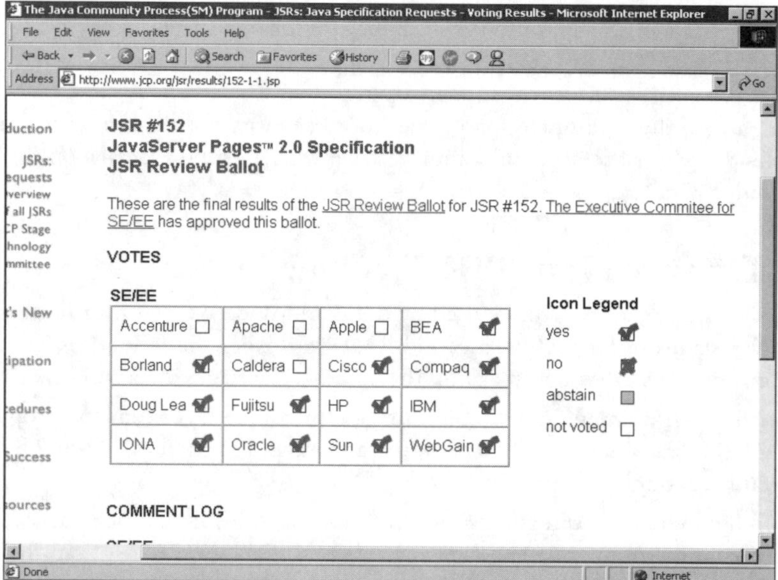

Figure F.2 Voting on JSP 2.0, JSR-152.

The JSR then went into community review until June 17, 2002, about eight months after the formation of the expert group.

The public review took place until July 29, 2002; just over one month after the community review was closed.

The home page of the specification shows the dates for the JSP 2.0 specification. The URL is `http://jcp.org/jsr/detail/152.jsp`.

G

J2EE Application Servers

THE APPLICATION SERVER MARKET IS VOLATILE and ever changing, and it can be very confusing as well. Since the dot-com bubble burst in 2001, the market is no longer growing like it was, and the vendors have to work extremely hard to maintain their market share. The challenge for the developers is to get through all the marketing hype and try and find out exactly what a particular product offers.

This appendix aims to explain what to look for in a server, explain the various types of server product available, and to look at some of the offerings currently on the market.

It is important to recognize that this appendix is a snapshot of the application server market at a particular point in time (Q2 2003). The market is a rapidly changing one, so some of the detail in this appendix will clearly go out of date. The point of this appendix is not to give bang up to date information on the servers available, but to discuss some of the principles involved in choosing a server, and to give an idea of what kinds of server are available. Note too that this appendix focuses on J2EE 1.3, since this was the version of J2EE that was current at the time of writing. By the time you read this, the current version will probably be 1.4, or higher!

> **Note**
>
> Because JavaServer Pages 2.0 is part of the J2EE 1.4 release, many JSP 2.0 enhancements (such as the expression language) will not run under a J2EE 1.3-compliant application server. Until vendors release J2EE 1.4 implementations of their products, we recommend running JSP 2.0 web applications under Apache Tomcat 5.0. Alternatively, if you wish to run JSP 2.0 in an application server, you can use the J2EE 1.4 reference implementation from Sun.

What to Look for in a Server

Choosing an application server can be tricky. Here are some various factors that can influence your decision:

- What existing systems does it need to integrate with?
- How much money do you want to spend, and what are the licensing arrangements for the product you are looking at?

- How concerned are you about support for the very latest J2EE standards?
- Do you require extra functionality such as personalization, commerce, or portals?
- Did you want to integrate with a particular development environment?
- Scalability
- Failover

Integration

Different server vendors provide, or have provided by third parties, integration products for their particular server. So, for example, the SilverStream eXtend (`www.silverstream.com`) platform has full support for a whole range of different database vendors and also SAP, CICS RPC, and many other data sources. The Oracle 9i Application server, along with integrating with a range of data sources, has full integration with the Oracle database products, which results in excellent performance when they are used together.

If you are using a content management system, different vendors will provide connectors into those content management engines. For example, if you are using the Documentum or Interwoven products, the ATG Dynamo Application server has connectors available for those specific content engines.

It is important to complete your research on these kinds of issues, because some of the available connectors are significantly lacking in flexibility and/or performance, and they are of little use.

> **Note**
>
> The Web site `www.serverwatch.com` is an excellent source of information on application servers. It has reviews on many of the servers and provides all sorts of articles on how different server products are best used.

Money, Money, Money!

These servers can cost big bucks, and the licensing arrangements can add to the expense. The application server vendors are very good at selling functionality that customers do not actually require. For example, many will sell on the J2EE promise, but then when you look closely, the product is hardly using anything from the J2EE platform. According to research from Gartner (`www.gartner.com`), companies have overspent about $1 billion on application servers since 1998, and companies will overspend an additional $2 billion by 2003.

The number of clients I've worked with who have purchased application server technology that is frankly beyond their requirements is quite shocking. Remember, Tomcat and the Apache Web server are free.

One non-J2EE compliant application server that bucks the trend in terms of cost is the JBoss Application Server, which can be downloaded from `www.jboss.org`. This one is free! Not only is it free, but the developers state that it implements most if not all of the J2EE specifications, and there is a substantial base of organizations that are using it successfully in production. Note that JBoss is not officially recognized as J2EE compliant by Sun Microsystems as it has not been certified. You also need to bear in mind with JBoss, that although the server is free, there is limited documentation with it – this is one of the things you end up paying for.

For developers, there are also a number of vendors who are making certain versions of their application server products available for free. One such vendor is Sun Microsystems, who allow you to use the Sun ONE Application Server 7 Platform Edition for free. This can be downloaded from:

`http://wwws.sun.com/software/products/appsrvr_pe/home_appsrvr_pe.html`

Standards Support

Nearly all the application server vendors will mention J2EE support on their home pages, but you need to dig a little deeper. There are different versions of J2EE, and there is a big difference between full support and partial support. Almost all the major vendors have J2EE 1.3 compliant servers now, and you can always check which servers are fully J2EE compliant by visiting the following URL:

`http://java.sun.com/j2ee/compatibility.html`

This web page lists all the current compatible servers. In my experience, vendor web sites are not always clear as to which version of J2EE they support, and whether they have been certified as such by Sun. This URL from the Sun web site is therefore very useful when trying to identify J2EE compatible servers.

The following list was accurate when the book was written, and is based upon the compatibility list on the Sun web site:

- ATG Dynamo 6
- BEA WebLogic Server 7.0
- Borland Enterprise Server, AppServer Edition & JBuilder 6.0
- Fujitsu INTERSTAGE Application Server
- IBM WebSphere Application Server 5.0
- IONA Orbix E2A Application Server
- Macromedia JRun 4
- Oracle 9i Application Server
- Pramati Server 3.0 & Studio 3.0
- SAS AppDev Studio 2.0.2 Preview Release
- SilverStream eXtend App Server 4.0 Beta

- SpiritSoft
- SunTM ONE Application Server
- SunTM ONE Studio 4
- Sybase EAServer 4.1
- Tmax Soft JEUS 4.0
- Trifork Application Server 3.1
- J2EE SDK 1.3

As you can see, there are quite a few! There is another list for J2EE 1.2, and there will be a further list for J2EE 1.4.

One server that does deserve a mention here is the J2EE Reference Implementation from Sun Microsystems. We have not used it in the book because it is not used for commercial implementations, but it is free and can be downloaded from the Sun Web site `http://java.sun.com/j2ee/`.

If you simply want to check out the latest standards on a no-frills application server, this definitely is an option. There are versions available for J2EE 1.2, 1.3, and 1.4. When new standards are being released, it is the reference implementation that is the first available supporting the new standard. The reference implementation also comes with a deployment tool, which, although some would argue is a bit clunky, it can be used quite effectively to create EAR files that can then be deployed on other servers.

Extra Functionality

This is one area where the server vendors increasingly differentiate themselves. Because J2EE is a standard, customers can shop around for, and even change, application server vendors, deploying their portable J2EE applications elsewhere.

Some vendors offer very rich layers in addition to the J2EE standard platform. These can be personalization, discussed in Chapter 17, "Personalization and Web Applications." Many now provide a portal framework of some kind, and many provide commerce frameworks also. One of the best examples of this would be the ATG Dynamo Application Server. ATG has a very rich product set that comprises:

- J2EE 1.3-compliant application server
- A personalization engine
- A portal framework
- A commerce engine

This is in stark contrast to server products such as JBoss, which is essentially an application server (albeit a very good one). Obviously, you pay more for these additional application components, but they are tried and tested and run within the context of the application server. Interestingly, ATG now supports other application servers, so its product set does not even require its application server to be the foundation. Figure G.1 shows the user interface for part of the ATG Dynamo personalization offering called *scenarios*.

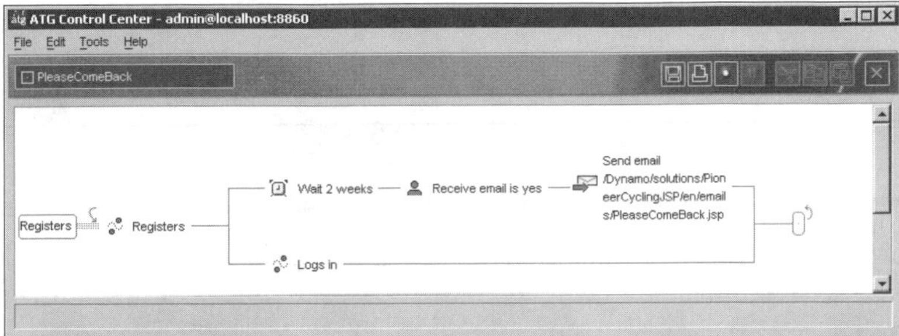

Figure G.1 ATG Dynamo Scenario Server.

Other vendors that offer similar product stacks include Oracle, which has a highly developed set of offerings that forms the Oracle 9i Application Server. Sun has a portal product, called SunONE Portal Server, which enables the building of portal applications. These are obviously just a few, but it is worth checking these things out because using one of these products can save you a significant amount of development time.

> **Note**
>
> A *portal* is a Web front end to a whole host of information and application components. Examples would include the MSN site from Microsoft, where one page acts as a gateway to all sorts of functionality. Visit `www.msn.com` to see an example of a portal. One of the key things about portals is that they can be personalized. See Chapter 17 for more information.

One thing that you need to be aware of with these feature-rich servers is the lock-in to the server product, meaning that you cannot switch server vendors without a considerable amount of work—you are locked in to a particular supplier. If you take full advantage of the available features, it will shorten the development time, but you will be stuck with the platform unless you are prepared to rebuild it.

Integration with Development Environments

Many products now have IDE support built in. Two such products would be:

- Borland Application Server and the Enterprise Studio development tool
- IBM WebSphere and WebSphere Studio

Both Borland and IBM have a significant advantage in that they have proven Java Integrated Development Environments (IDEs) that have been in use for several years now. Both vendors have capitalized on this by integrating them with their application server products. When using the Borland Enterprise Studio in conjunction with the Borland Application Server, you can run your applications within a debug mode, which is a very useful and rare feature for the J2EE developer.

Many IDE products have support for application servers, and it is worth checking which servers they integrate with if this is an important issue for you.

Some servers ship with development environments as well, and have rich interfaces to aid with the development and deployment processes. You will see some of these in Chapter 15, "Enterprise JavaBean and JSP Interaction," and Chapter 17.

Scalability

Scalability is crucial to enterprise Web applications, and application server vendors always use the word *scalable* when describing their products. Scalability is the capability of your application to cope with an increasing volume of clients at any one time without losing any significant performance. Scalability also refers to the capability of an application to cope with an increasing number of concurrent transactions taking place. For many applications, a basic implementation of Tomcat with Apache will suffice, but for sites with high traffic, banks of servers are required to cope with the high number of users.

The core way to address scalability is to employ *clustering*. Clustering is having groups of application servers working together to process client requests. A scalable infrastructure should allow for the addition of servers to a cluster as load increases. Assuming that there are no bottlenecks within your application logic, clustering should allow *linear scalability*. Linear scalability refers to how you should be able to go on supporting increasing numbers of clients with additional servers. See Figure G.2 to see what this means.

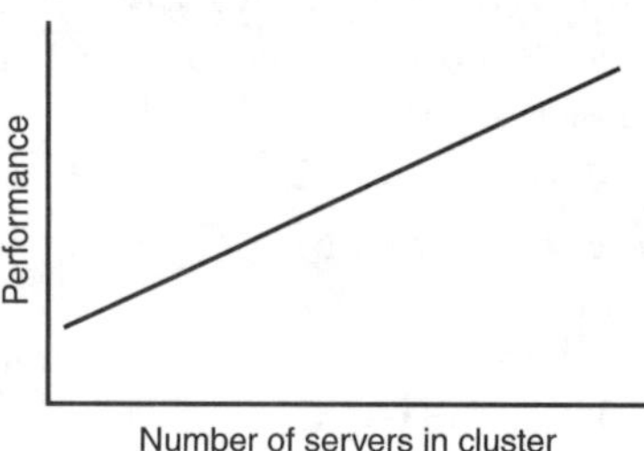

Figure G.2 Linear scalability.

Application servers have convenient administration consoles so that additional servers can be set up in a straightforward manner. The vendors also provide monitoring tools to help you view the performance of your clusters. Figure G.3 shows the clustering monitor from the WebLogic 7 server.

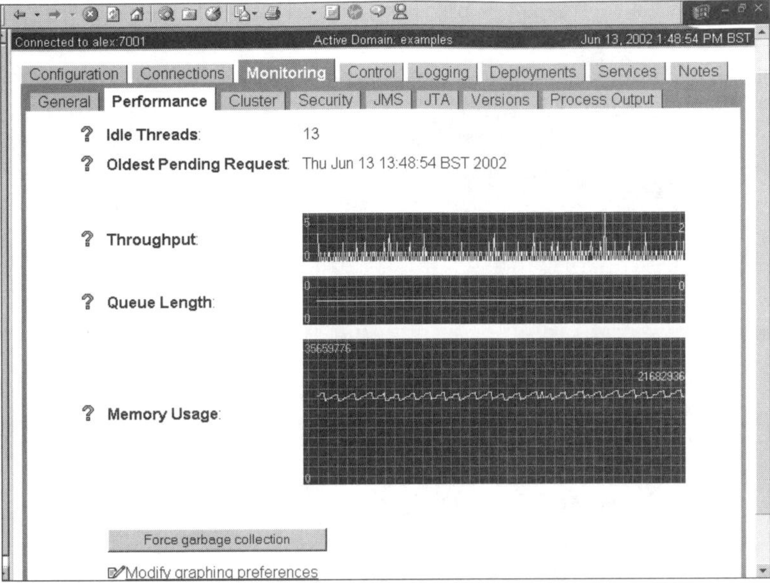

Figure G.3 The cluster monitor from the Web Logic 7 application server.

Other vendors provide similar interfaces to enable the effective clustering of servers to provide scalability.

The free application server, JBoss, also provides for clustering. This is achieved by the configuring of deployment XML files. The following features are available to users of the JBoss Application Server:

- Automatic discovery. Clustered nodes can find each other with no additional configuration required.
- The JNDI tree is replicated across the entire cluster.
- There is support for distributed deployment of EJBs and JBoss services across servers within a cluster.

For more information on JBoss clustering, you can visit `http://telia.dl.sourceforge.net/sourceforge/jboss/JBoss.3.0QuickStart.pdf` and download the JBoss Quick Start PDF file.

Failover

What happens when a server fails for some reason? You would hope that another server from the cluster would take over. This is what happens in configurations that have session failover. If a server goes down for whatever reason, you would expect another server to automatically pick up the pieces. Session failover is available within many of the application servers on the market. It is discussed in detail in Chapter 8, "Session Tracking Using JSP."

All the application server vendors I have come across provide this facility, although the Tomcat Web container does not.

Configuring Tomcat

THIS APPENDIX COVERS THE MOST COMMON ISSUES that you face when working with the Tomcat Web container.

The Configuration File server.xml

Most of the configuration for the Tomcat container is found within an XML file called server.xml. This is found in <tomcat-home>\conf. Listing H.1 shows an example of server.xml.

Listing H.1 server.xml

```
<Server port="8005" shutdown="SHUTDOWN" debug="0">
  <Listener
   className="org.apache.catalina.mbeans.ServerLifecycleListener"
   debug="0"/>
  <Listener
   className="org.apache.catalina.mbeans.GlobalResourcesLifecycleListener"
   debug="0"/>
  <GlobalNamingResources>
    <Environment name="simpleValue" type="java.lang.Integer" value="30"/>
    <Resource name="UserDatabase" auth="Container"
     type="org.apache.catalina.UserDatabase"
     description="User database that can be updated and saved"/>
    <ResourceParams name="UserDatabase">
      <parameter>
        <name>factory</name>
        <value>org.apache.catalina.users.MemoryUserDatabaseFactory</value>
      </parameter>
      <parameter>
        <name>pathname</name>
        <value>conf/tomcat-users.xml</value>
```

Listing H.1 **Continued**

```
      </parameter>
    </ResourceParams>
  </GlobalNamingResources>
  <Service name="Tomcat-Standalone">
    <Connector className="org.apache.coyote.tomcat4.CoyoteConnector"
     port="8080" minProcessors="5" maxProcessors="75" enableLookups="true"
     redirectPort="8443" acceptCount="10" debug="0" connectionTimeout="20000"
     useURIValidationHack="false"/>
    <Connector className="org.apache.coyote.tomcat4.CoyoteConnector"
     port="8009" minProcessors="5" maxProcessors="75" enableLookups="true"
     redirectPort="8443" acceptCount="10" debug="0" connectionTimeout="20000"
     useURIValidationHack="false"
     protocolHandlerClassName="org.apache.jk.server.JkCoyoteHandler"/>
    <Engine name="Standalone" defaultHost="localhost" debug="0">
      <Logger className="org.apache.catalina.logger.FileLogger"
       prefix="catalina_log." suffix=".txt" timestamp="true"/>
      <Realm className="org.apache.catalina.realm.UserDatabaseRealm"
       debug="0" resourceName="UserDatabase"/>
      <Host name="localhost" debug="0" appBase="webapps" unpackWARs="true"
       autoDeploy="true">
        <Logger className="org.apache.catalina.logger.FileLogger"
         directory="logs" prefix="localhost_log." suffix=".txt"
         timestamp="true"/>
        <Context path="/example" docBase="c:\JSPHandbook\appendixH\example"
         debug="0" reloadable="true"/>
      </Host>
    </Engine>
  </Service>
</Server>
```

Listing H.1 actually shows the default `server.xml` with a few minor alterations and the comments removed for brevity. It is helpful to see what the configuration file looks like, and this appendix seeks to explain the content of it.

> **Note**
>
> For a detailed description of how Tomcat can be configured, read the book *Tomcat Rapid Working Knowledge* by Martin Bond and Debbie Law, from Sams Publishing, ISBN 0-672-32439-3.

Configuring Individual Applications

Most of the configuration for individual Web applications is done in the `web.xml` file. However, there are some aspects that are configured within `server.xml`. This is done within individual `Context` elements:

```
<Context path="/example" docBase="c:\JSPHandbook\appendixH\example"
 debug="0" reloadable="true"/>
```

A <Context> element represents a Web application within the container. If you recall from Chapter 1, "JSP, J2EE, and the Role of the Servlet," there is a ServletContext object that represents your Web application and the <Context> element in server.xml enables you to configure Web applications that are deployed within a container. Each context is basically a Web application. The values defined within server.xml are then complemented by the Web applications deployment descriptor web.xml.

The Context element has a number of attributes, which have been outlined in Table H.1.

Table H.1 **Attributes of the** Context **Element**

Attribute	Function
docBase	The docBase (Document base) specifies the path to the location of the Web application. It could also be a path to a WAR file. In the previous example, it is an absolute path. It can also be a path relative to the base folder used by the container for Web applications; that is <tomcat-home>\webapps.
path	The path is the name to be used for the folder when visiting the application from a client. So, for example, to visit the application specified in the example, the URL would be http://localhost:8080/example/ In this URL, example is the value of path. The values of path for each of the contexts must be unique. If you want your web Web application to appear at the server root, then set the path to be an empty string, "". This will mean that your application would now be found at http://localhost:8080
reloadable	The reloadable attribute specifies whether changing classes can be reloaded dynamically at runtime. This is particularly useful for the development process as it enables you to develop servlets and other classes without constantly restarting the container. This is not recommended for live sites because of the processing overhead it entails.
cookies	This specifies whether session tracking should involve cookies for a particular Web application. Cookies are discussed in Chapter 8, "Session Tracking Using JSP." The default value is true.
privileged	If privileged is true, the application can access container-wide servlets. There are some management servlets that come with Tomcat that would be included.

Table H.1 **Continued**

Attribute	Function
`wrapperClass`	Servlets running in Tomcat are wrapped within a wrapper class. There is a class provided by default, but you could specify an alternative. It must implement `org.apache.catalina.Wrapper`.
`className`	This is the class name of the `Context`. It must implement `org.apache.catalina.Context`. The default implementation is `org.apache.catalina.core.StandardContext`. This has the two additional attributes defined at the end of the table.
`useNaming`	This enables Tomcat to create a JNDI context for a Web application that is compatible with the J2EE platform. Web applications that interact with the J2EE platform are discussed in Chapter 15, "JSP and EJB Interaction."
`override`	The attribute values set in each `Context` element being discussed here inherit default values from an element called `DefaultContext`. This element can be found either within a `Host` or an `Engine` element. If `override` is set to `true`, any values set in a specific context will override values from the `DefaultContext`.
`crossContext`	Setting this attribute to `true` will enable Web applications deployed within the same container to interact with one another. They will both need to have `crossContext` set to `true`.
`debug`	The numerical value of this attribute determines the level of detail that will go into any error logs for the application. The default is `0`. The higher the number, the more the level of detail. Level 0 is fatal errors, level 1 is errors, level 2 is warnings, level 3 is information, and level 4 is debug.
`workDir`	This is used to specify a working directory for your Web applications. So, if a servlet or JSP wanted to create a file to contain some data, for instance, it would be placed into this working directory.

The use of the `docBase` and `path` attributes enables you to set up virtual directories for your Web applications.

If you have worked with Web server software before, you may well be familiar with the concept of setting up virtual directories that you can place your Web applications in. A virtual directory is where you set up a system in such a way that a folder is located in one physical location, but is mapped to another location such as the `webapps` folder for Tomcat. So, for example, you could have a folder on your machine. This virtual directory could contain a Web application, but not be physically placed within the Tomcat folder structure at all. Figure H.1 shows this.

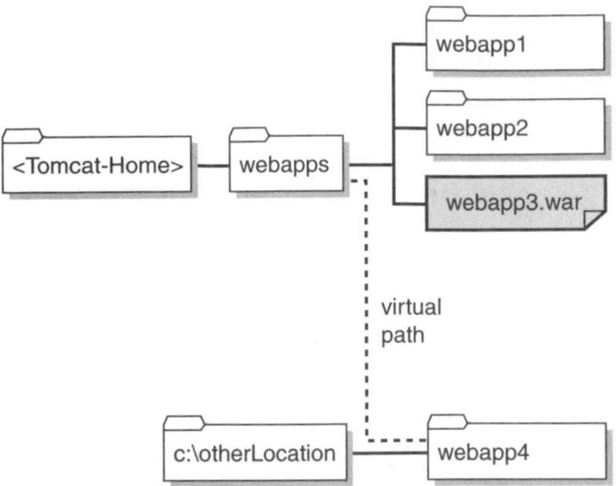

Figure H.1 Using virtual directories.

In Figure H.1, `webapp1` and `webapp2` are folders containing complete Web applications. The `WAR` file `webapp3.war` contains a complete Web application. The folder `webapp4` is not located within the Tomcat folder structure at all, but is mapped as a virtual folder within Tomcat.

So far, you have seen what can be configured for individual Web applications. There are also a number of configuration changes that can be made for the container itself.

Configuring the Container

This is done within the remaining elements of the `server.xml` configuration file. The overall structure of the elements of `server.xml` is shown in Figure H.2.

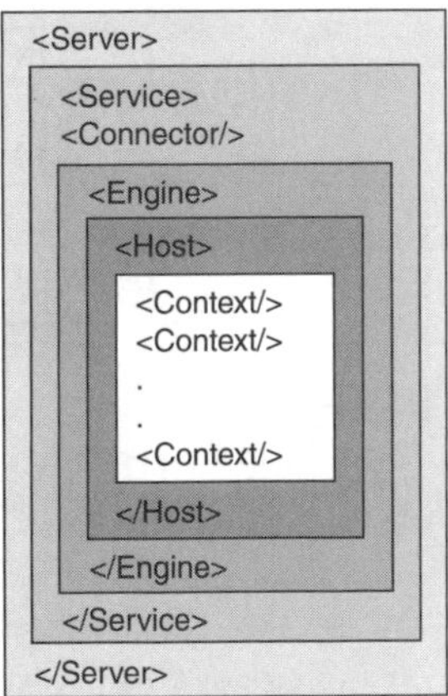

Figure H.2 Elements of `server.xml`.

The Server Element

The root element for server.xml is Server. The attributes of this element define properties for the entire Tomcat server. Two attributes you need to be aware of are found in this element.

- port—This is the port number on which Tomcat listens for shutdown commands to the Tomcat server.
- shutdown—This attribute contains the command that is used for shutting down the Tomcat server.

> **Note**
> You will see the references to *Catalina* throughout the Tomcat documentation. Catalina is the name given to the servlet container within Tomcat 4 versions. This is because for Tomcat 4, the servlet container was completely rewritten.

The Service and Connector Elements

The Service element is there to define the service that will handle client requests. This will consist of one or more Connector elements and an Engine element. A Connector defines a connection into Tomcat. These are referred to as Jakarta Tomcat Connectors or JTC Connectors in the documentation. They could be direct from a client browser, or they could be from Web server software. Figure H.3 shows the connector architecture.

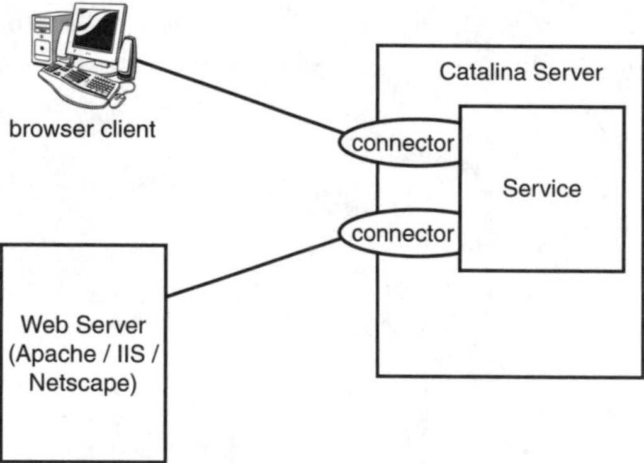

Figure H.3 Connectors and Tomcat.

The Service element from server.xml that is being used when you connect directly to Tomcat is the one called Tomcat-Standalone. This Service element is shown here:

```
<Service name="Tomcat-Standalone">
  <Connector . . ./>
```

```
  <Engine . . .> . . . </Engine>
</Service>
```

Each connector is configured for a particular type of connection. That may be an HTTP 1.1–compliant browser, which you have been using if you have been trying the examples, or for a live Web site, the connector will probably be a Web server, which will forward requests to the service within Tomcat.

The `Connector` element from within our `Tomcat-Standalone` service is shown here:

```
<Connector className="org.apache.coyote.tomcat4.CoyoteConnector"
 port="8080" minProcessors="5" maxProcessors="75" enableLookups="true"
 redirectPort="8443" acceptCount="10" debug="0" connectionTimeout="20000"
 useURIValidationHack="false"/>
```

A number of connectors are available that connect into Web servers. These are built from a combination of Java code and C code that interfaces into the Web server software. Other server vendors provide similar connectors for their products, so servers such as WebLogic from BEA and JBoss, to name a few, all provide their equivalents of these connectors.

Notice the large number of attributes. These attributes are connector-dependent, so depending on the connector being used, they will be different. In the previous example, the one that should make immediate sense is the `port`. The value is 8080, the port number you use when you connect into Tomcat directly from a browser. The Tomcat-Standalone service uses a connector called the `Coyote HTTP/1.1 Connector`.

Caution

If you are using a version of Tomcat older than 4.1, you will be using the `HTTP/1.1 Connector`. This connector has been deprecated in favor of the Coyote connector.

Table H.2 lists the main attributes of the `Coyote HTTP/1.1 Connector` Element.

Table H.2 **The Main Attributes of the Coyote HTTP/1.1** `Connector` **Element**

Attribute	Function
`className`	This is the class name being used by the connector. When using the Coyote connector the value must be `org.apache.coyote.tomcat4.CoyoteConnector`.
`port`	This is the port number on which the connector receives requests. The default is `8080`.
`acceptCount`	In busy periods, the server will queue requests that cannot be handled immediately. The `acceptCount` specifies how many requests will be queued. The default value for this attribute is `10`.
`connectionTimeout`	This is the number of milliseconds that the connector will wait for a URL to be processed. The default timeout is 60000 ms (60 seconds).
`maxProcessors`	This specifies the maximum number of processors that are to be available to handle requests. The default is `20`.

Table H.2 **Continued**

Attribute	Function
minProcessors	This is the minimum number of processors available to handle requests. The default is 5.
redirectPort	If a request comes in that requires SSL, and the connection is not an SSL connection, this is the port that such requests should be redirected to. The initial value in server.xml is 8443, which refers to the port number used by a commented commented-out SSL connector. This will need to be uncommented if it is to be used. This is discussed in more detail in Chapter 16, "Security and JSP."

You have now seen that the `Service` element contains one or more `Connector` elements. The `Service` element also contains an `Engine` element.

The `Engine` Element

The `Engine` element, in general terms, defines the part of Tomcat that actually processes the requests that come in. The `Engine` element can then contain multiple `Host` elements that correspond to the hostnames that the Tomcat implementation must support. Two main attributes can be set in the `Engine` element:

- `defaultHost`—This is the host to use when requests come in for hostnames that are not explicitly declared to be supported by the container.
- `name`—This is the name that you give to the engine. This will be used in error messages and such.

The remaining attributes can be located in the Tomcat documentation. These nested `Host` elements will be discussed next.

The `Host` Element

The `Host` element is used to define the settings for a specific hostname, typically set up in the Domain Name Service (DNS) to refer to the machine that Tomcat is running on. So, if your domain name is `www.contentmaster.com`, you would set up the properties for this domain name within the `host` element. In Listing H.1, the hostname is `localhost`, so the configuration is for the local machine:

```
<Host name="localhost" debug="0" appBase="webapps" unpackWARs="true">
 . . .
</Host>
```

Some of the main attributes that can be set up for the host are shown in Table H.3.

Table H.3 **The Main Attributes of the Host Element**

Attribute	Function
appBase	The appBase (Application base) specifies the path to the location of the Web applications for this host name. This is <tomcat-home>\webapps by default. But it can be changed to a different folder if required.
name	The name is the host name that is being referred to, so in the URL: http://alex:8080/example/ The name would be alex.
className	This is the class to be used to define the host within Tomcat.
debug	See the debug attribute in Table 4.1.
unpackWARs	This specifies whether WAR files should be extracted. The default value is true.
liveDeploy	Earlier in the appendix, the capability to deploy applications on a live Tomcat server was discussed. This attribute controls this capability, and it is only possible when this attribute is set to true. The default is true.

For more information on the Host element, and specifically more advanced issues such as how you can set up multiple hostnames for the same machine, visit the following page in the documentation on your local Tomcat installation:

```
http://localhost:8080/tomcat-docs/config/host.html
```

The Tomcat Servlets

To configure all the elements within server.xml, Tomcat 4.1 and higher comes with an administration servlet to make this a whole lot easier. A manager servlet that helps with the deployment process also exists. These two servlets will be discussed next.

The Tomcat Administration Servlet

The administration servlet provides an interface into server.xml. It is available at the following URL:

```
http://localhost:8080/admin/index.jsp
```

As with the manager servlet, you will need to log on to use this servlet. Figure H.4 shows the interface that this servlet provides when using Tomcat 4.1.

Other containers also provide similar interfaces to help with the deployment of Web applications, and it is with the other Web containers that we will finish this appendix.

Using the Tomcat Manager Servlet

A Tomcat manager can be used when using Tomcat 4.1 or higher. Figure H.5 shows the Tomcat Manager; it can be accessed from your Tomcat home page.

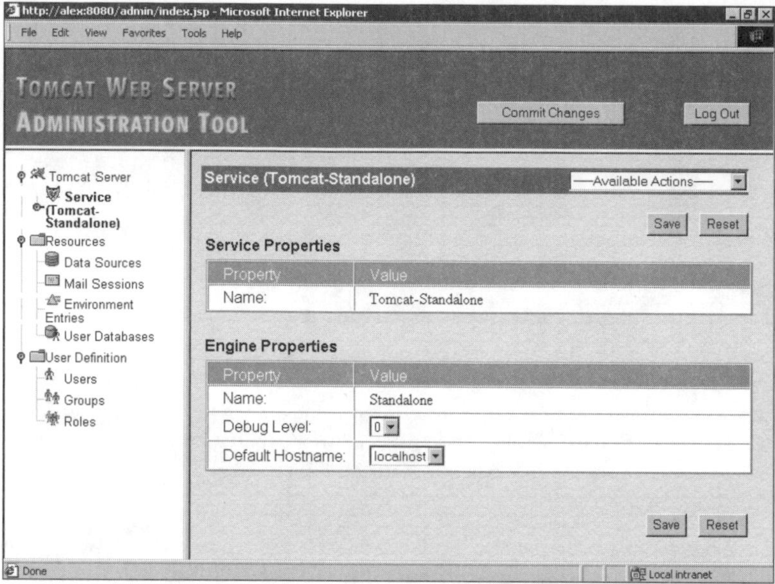

Figure H.4 The Tomcat administration servlet.

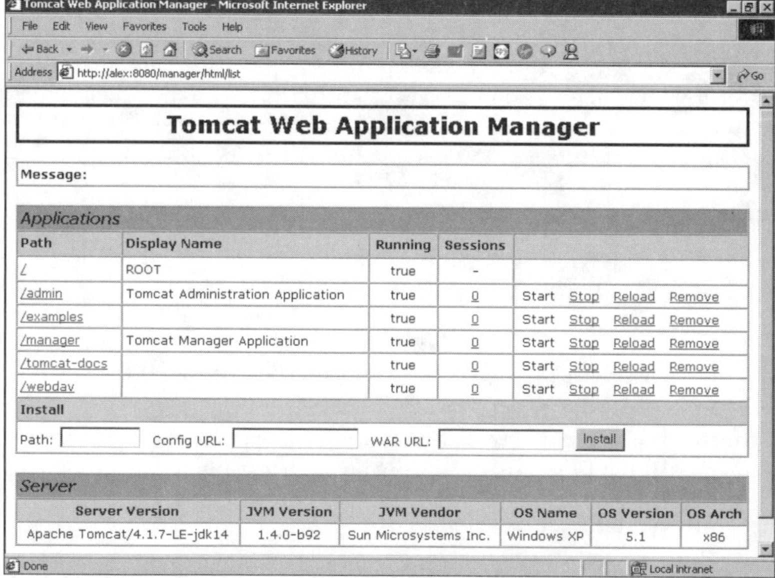

Figure H.5 The Tomcat Manager.

> **Caution**
> You will need to log in as the administrator to view this page. The username is admin with no password unless you changed it at installation.

The URL for the manager servlet is as follows:

```
http://localhost:8080/manager
```

Various query string parameters can be placed onto this URL to allow for the various functions that the management servlet can be used to perform. The functions of the management servlet are as follows:

- The deployment and removal of Web applications.
- The starting and stopping of Web applications.
- To provide a list of the deployed applications currently on the server.
- List the sessions that are currently running for a particular application.
- The refreshing of a Web application when changes have been made to the contents of the WEB-INF classes and JAR files.
- Provide a list of all the available security roles that have been set up (these roles are discussed in Chapter 16, "Security and JSP."

So for example, to deploy and start a new application using the manager servlet, the parameters could be as follows:

```
http://localhost:8080/manager/install?path=/myapplication&
                                  war=file:/c:/JSPHandbook/chapter04/example
```

The results of entering this URL in a browser will be as follows:

```
OK - Installed application at context path /myapplication
```

This will have deployed a Web application located in the folder c:\JSPHandbook\chapter04\example.

The application will not have been started automatically. To start the application, you can then enter the following URL:

```
http://localhost:8080/manager/start?path=/myapplication
```

The application will then be available via the URL:

```
http://localhost:8080/myapplication
```

> **Caution**
> The previous URL does not work with Tomcat 4.1.2 beta. This should be fixed in later versions of Tomcat, but we were unable to test it at the time of writing.

If you look carefully at the URLs that the manager servlet uses, you will see that they comprise the following:

```
http://<host-name>:<port-number>/manager/<command>?<parameter list>
```

The commands are shown in Table H.4.

Table H.4 **The Commands of the Manager Servlet.**

Command	Parameters and Function
`install`	The `install` command is for the installation of Web applications. It uses the following parameters: `path`—the path of the Web application that you want to interact with. `war`—the location of the Web application that is to be deployed to the previous path. Our earlier example demonstrated this: http://localhost:8080/manager/install?path=/myapplication& war=file:/c:/JSPHandbook/chapter04/example Note that this does not copy the Web application into the `<tomcat-home>\webapps` folder. It sets up a new `Context` element in `server.xml`. This is discussed in the "Configuring Individual Applications," section at the start of this appendix.
`remove`	This is the opposite of `install`. It uses the `path` parameter to specify the `Context` that you want to be removed from `server.xml`.
`deploy`	Note that this command uses the `HTTP PUT` method because it physically copies a Web application from the `war` location into the `<tomcat-home>\webapps` folder. It then installs it and starts it. It uses the same parameters as the `install` command.
`undeploy`	This is the opposite to `deploy`. This command deletes the application from the `<tomcat-home>\webapps` folder. Therefore, it must be used with care! The parameter used is `path`.
`start`	This command uses the `path` parameter to specify the application you want to start. Applications that are deployed using the manager servlet are not started automatically.
`stop`	This command uses the `path` parameter to specify the application you want to stop. It is the opposite of the `start` command.
`reload`	This command uses the `path` parameter to specify the name of an application to reload. This is useful if you have changed the `web.xml` deployment descriptor or one of your Bean classes, for example. This can be used with applications where the `reloadable` attribute has been set to `false` in the `Context` element for the particular application.
`list`	The `list` command takes no parameters, but returns a list of all the currently deployed Web applications.
`resources`	This command lists all the available JNDI resources that are available to all your applications. JNDI is discussed in Chapter 13, "Locating Resources Using JNDI." This command has an optional `type` parameter where you can specify what type of resource you are interested in.

Table H.4 **Continued**

Command	Parameters and Function
`roles`	This command lists all the security roles set up for this application. Security roles are discussed in Chapter 16.
`session`	This uses the path parameter and will tell you how many active sessions are currently running on the application specified.

The reason that query parameters are used in this way, and not simply a friendly HTML-based interface, is that applications as well as people to deploy applications can use this servlet. The error and success messages, for example, are very concise, which enables applications to easily process them. Future releases of Tomcat should also provide a browser interface in conjunction with this URL-based interface.

I

Installing MySQL and WebLogic Server

THIS APPENDIX HAS BEEN INCLUDED TO HELP you with the installation of the database MySQL and the BEA WebLogic server, which are both used in some of the examples.

MySQL

The database used for the database and EJB chapters is MySQL. This is a freeware database available from `http://www.mysql.com`.

The following instructions show how to set up and install MySQL on both a Linux and a Windows platform. The version used for the book was 3.23.49. First, you will need to download the MySQL installation files from the previous URL.

Windows Installation and Setup

To install MySQL on Windows, follow these steps:

1. Extract the downloaded `.zip` file to a temporary location.
2. Launch `setup.exe`, which is a part of that `.zip` file.
3. Click the Next button twice, and then choose your installation folder. The default is `c:\mysql`.
4. Select a Typical installation, and click Next.
5. Select Finish to complete the setup.

An optional GUI comes as a separate download for MySQL, and it is available from the MySQL Web site. This is not essential for working with the demos in the book, but if you prefer using GUIs instead of command-line tools, you might want to try it out.

Linux Installation and Setup

These instructions will concentrate on installing and running MySQL on Linux. For instructions on installing MySQL on other Unix platforms, please see the documentation on the MySQL Web site.

By far the best way to install MySQL on Linux is to download the appropriate RPM file. If there is an RPM made available for your Linux distribution, this would be the preferred file to use. Otherwise, simply download the latest stable RPM from the MySQL Web site. There will be at least two RPMs to install—one for the server and one for the clients.

Install the RPM as follows:

```
shell> rpm -I MySQL-X.X.X-1386.rpm  MySQL-client-X.X.X.rpm
```

If you only want to install the client, simply install the latter RPM. Data will be placed in /var/lib/mysql and the appropriate scripts will be placed in /etc/rc.d/, which will cause MySQL to be started at boot time. The MySQL daemon should also be running immediately after installation. You will need to use whatever tools that are provided by your distribution for controlling services if you want to modify this behavior.

All the scripts, which will be discussed later, should have been installed on your $PATH and can therefore be run from the shell without needing to navigate to specific directories.

Creating a Database

On a Windows platform, locate your <my-sql-install>\bin folder, and then launch the winmysqladmin.exe application. This will launch the WinMySqlAdmin console. It then disappears, and puts a set of traffic lights in your system tray. If you right-click it and select Show Me, it comes back! The console is shown in Figure I.1.

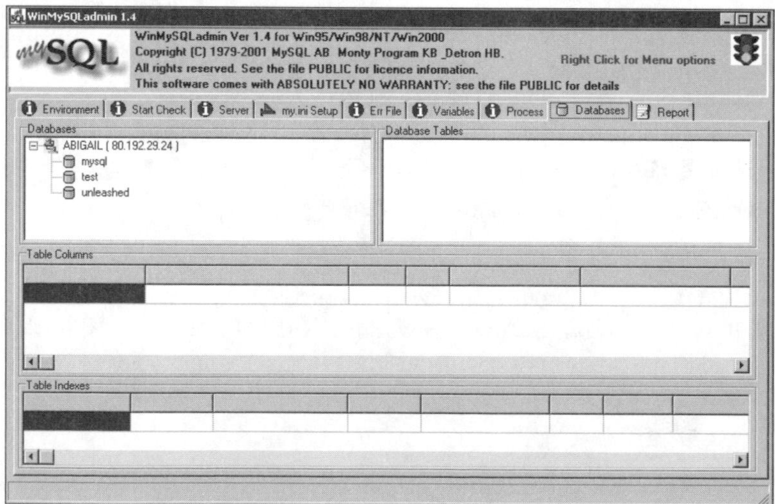

Figure I.1 The SQL Admin tool.

Using this tool, you can visit the Database tab, and then create a database by right-clicking the machine name (ABIGAIL is the name in the example). You can then select the Create Database option, and provide the name for your database.

On a Linux platform the mysqladmin script must be run from the shell for each command. For example, to confirm that MySQL is running on localhost with user root and no password, the following command would be required:

```
shell> mysqladmin -h localhost -u root ping
```

If the server was running, you would see the following:

```
mysqld is alive
```

Running the Provided SQL Scripts

On Windows, to run the scripts provided that create the tables for the various chapters, you can use a command-line utility. Get a command prompt in the folder <mysql-install>\bin, and then type **mysql**. This should give you the result shown in Figure I.2.

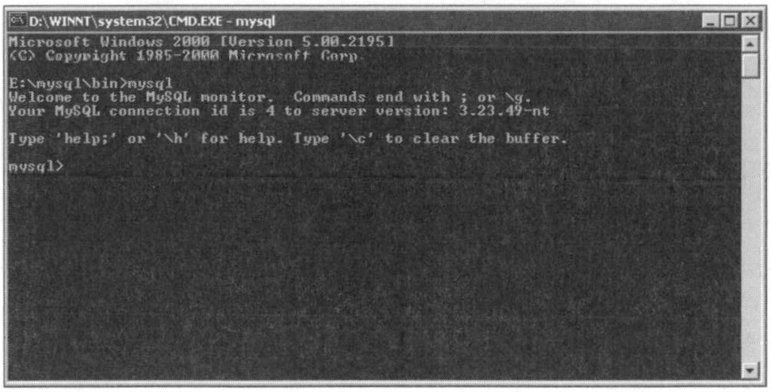

Figure I.2 Running the mysql command-line tool.

To then run a SQL script, you can enter the following command:

```
.\ c:\path\to\file\filename
```

The .\ is the command to run a SQL script. To see the other commands, you can simply enter **help**. When you are finished, type **quit**.

The procedure on Linux is similar. As mentioned earlier, the MySQL script can be run from anywhere in a shell—there is no need to navigate to a directory. Simply typing the following will log you in as the user root:

```
mysql -u root
```

To run a script, use the source command:

```
source /path/to/file/filename
```

Setting Up the JDBC Driver

This has been done for you in most of the sample applications, but if you want to obtain the latest driver, this is the process.

A JDBC driver is available from:

```
http://www.mysql.com/downloads/api-jdbc.html
```

Download and extract the `.zip` file. This should give you a folder called `mysql-connector-java-3.x.x-stable` . Within this folder there will be a `.jar` file of a similar name to the folder that contains the driver. The `.jar` used when the book was written is `mysql-connector-java-3.0.6-stable-bin.jar`. This will then need to be put into your `WEB-INF\lib` folder.

If you are configuring a Tomcat `DataSource`, then it will need to be placed into `<TOMCAT_HOME>\common\lib`. See Chapter 14, "Databases and JSP," for more information.

For WebLogic, if you are using the JDBC driver, then it needs to be put into your classpath. One easy way to do this for WebLogic is to place it into the <bea_install>\jdk131_03\jre\lib\ext folder.

MySQL Issues

You may find, as you try to run JDBC applications that access MySQL, that you sometimes get the following error:

```
Server Configuration Denies access to Data Source
```

This is due to the fact that there is sometimes a difficulty in resolving names. The solution is to change the hostname in your JBDC URL to either an IP address or a different hostname. So, for example:

```
jdbc:mysql://localhost:3306/jsphandbook
```

could become either

```
jdbc:mysql://127.0.0.1:3306/jsphandbook
```

or, if your hostname was "nigel"

```
jdbc:mysql://nigel:3306/jsphandbook
```

Experiment with different references to your host machine until you are able to access MySQL.

BEA WebLogic

The following instructions relate to WebLogic 7 server. The example applications should run in later versions, but they have not been tested.

Windows Installation and Setup

> **Caution**
> You will not be able to install WebLogic on Windows 95/98/Me platforms.

First, you will need to download an evaluation version of WebLogic from `www.bea.com`. Launch the downloaded executable. For the Windows NT/2000/XP platform, this will be `weblogic700_win.exe`. Now, follow these steps:

1. Launch the executable, and at the Welcome screen, click Next.
2. Read and accept the licence agreement, and if you agree, select Yes.
3. Select an install directory; the default is `c:\bea`. Click Next.
4. Select Typical Installation, and click Next.
5. Leave the installation directory as it is, and click Next again, and the installation will complete.

To test your installation, you can now launch the WebLogic server. You will find it under:

```
Start/Programs/BEA WebLogic Server Platform 7.0/WebLogic Server 7.0/
Server Tour and Examples/Launch Examples Server
```

This will now launch the server and open the WebLogic welcome screen in a browser.

> **Tip**
> If you are a Windows XP user, you might find that your browser does not display the console applet correctly. To fix this, you will need the Java Plugin for the XP platform. This is available from `http://java.sun.com/getjava/download.html`.

Linux Installation and Setup

To install WebLogic on Linux, follow these steps:

1. From `www.bea.com`, navigate to the download for Red Hat Linux and download the Net installer.
2. Change the permissions for the file with

   ```
   shell> chmod u+x net_platform700_linux.bin
   ```

3. Run the script with

   ```
   ./net_platform700_linux.bin
   ```

4. A wizard will now launch, and the installation from here is exactly as with Windows.

To launch the server and test your installation, simply change the directory to `<weblogic-installation-directory>/common/bin` and run `./quickstart.sh`.

If you are having any problems with the WebLogic server, the best place to start is the WebLogic documentation, which is available online at `http://www.bea.com/support/index.shtml`.

Glossary

Apache Web Server A free, open source, HTTP Server. Apache is now the most widely used HTTP Server. It is available from the Jakarta project at `http://jakarta.apache.org`.

applet A Java program that runs in the context of an HTML page, providing dynamic content. Commonly used for games or situations where real-time data transfer or interaction is required.

CGI Common Gateway Interface. An approach to server programming that predates Java servlets. Often it is not multithreaded. Typically, CGI scripts, as they are called, are written in Perl because of its capability to process textual data.

client The originator of requests to a server. In the context of JavaServer Pages, the client most often refers to a browser. *Client* is a relative term because the JSP server can be a client to a database server for example.

cookie Small piece of data passed from a server to a client. This is then returned by clients with subsequent requests to identify the client. Most often used to maintain a session.

deployment descriptor An XML file used to configure aspects of J2EE applications. It contains information necessary to deploy an application. For example, the deployment descriptor can be used to pass parameters to servlets and JSPs at initialization.

distributed environment An environment where applications might be running across multiple physical or virtual machines. For example, a cluster of WebLogic servers interacting with an Oracle database.

DTD Document Type Definition. Used to define structure for XML, so element names, content, attributes, and so on, will be defined here. Because of various limitations of DTDs, XML Schemas are starting to supercede them.

dynamic content Content that varies according to user, time, location, and so on. One URL can display different content at different times to different users. This content is generated on the server using technologies such as JSP, CGI, and ASP.

EJB Enterprise JavaBean. JavaBeans that have been designed for use in a distributed environment. They can be either Session Beans, which represent business logic, or Entity Beans, which represent data; for example, a registered user. In conjunction with the container, EJBs are capable of managing their own persistence and the handling of transactions.

HTML Hypertext Markup Language. A markup language that is used to define the presentation and structure of Web pages.

HTTP Hypertext Transfer Protocol. The protocol used on the Internet for browser requests and responses; the current version is 1.1. This can be used for HTML pages, MP3 files, and other media that are accessed via the Internet.

J2EE Java 2 Enterprise Edition. There are three versions of the Java Platform: the Micro Edition, which is targeted at embedded systems; the Standard edition, which contains all the APIs used for most Java applications; and the Enterprise Edition. The Enterprise Edition contains many extra APIs for use in an enterprise context. These include Transaction Management, Security, JNDI, and many others. JavaServer Pages and Servlets are part of the Java 2 Enterprise Edition.

JAAS Java Authentication and Authorization Service. Enables applications to provide user authentication and enables them to provide the ability to impose restrictions and access controls on the user.

JAF JavaBeans Activation Framework. JAF provides the capability to determine a type for a piece of data and activate an appropriate object to work with that data.

Java Community Process An international organization of Java developers who drive, revise, and develop the Java Platform. See `http://jcp.org`.

JavaBeans A Java class that follows certain conventions. A JavaBean must follow the naming conventions within the Java Programming Language. It should also have `get` and/or `set` methods for any instance variables. A JavaBean must have a no argument contructor. JavaBeans should also implement the `Serializable` interface.

JavaMail An API for sending and receiving electronic mail. Designed specifically with email clients in mind.

JAXP Java API for XML Processing. A set of Java APIs used to read, manipulate, and create XML. A part of J2SDK 1.4.

JDBC Java Database Connectivity. A set of interfaces to enable the interacting with databases from Java applications. A driver is required for the database connection. Drivers are available for most database implementations such as Oracle or SQL Server.

JMS Java Messaging Service. Provides an API for passing business data between objects using messaging. These objects can be distributed across multiple environments and platforms. Messages can be broadcast to multiple objects at once.

JNDI Java Naming and Directory Interface. Allows for the registration and location of objects. These objects can be distributed across multiple environments and platforms.

JSP JavaServer Page. A text file that is compiled into a Java servlet by a server. Used in Java-based Web applications to deliver dynamic content. They typically contain HTML, XML, and custom tags, and they can also contain Java programming language code.

JSTL JavaServer Pages Standard Tag Library. Provides commonly required Java functionality in the form of a tag library for use within JSP. These tag libraries cover such requirements as XML interaction, database access and formatting, as well as standard programming constructs such as looping and branching.

JTA Java Transaction API. JTA provides an API for transaction management between applications and data sources.

Linux A free, open source, Unix-based operating system originally developed by Linus Torvalds.

MIME Multipurpose Internet Mail Extensions. Enables applications to determine data types for data and process them accordingly. HTML has a MIME type of text/html, for example.

multithreading The capability to run multiple paths of execution within an application at one time. Each thread will have a specific role or task within the application. Java is a multithreaded programming language and Servlets (and therefore JSPs) are multithreaded by default. Every request for a JSP or servlet will launch a new thread, unless the JSP or servlet implements the `SingleThreadModel` interface.

RMI Remote Method Invocation. An API enabling Java applications to interact across separate JVMs.

Schema *See* XML Schema.

server Refers to either the hardware or the software that receives the request and generates a response to the client. In some quarters, the software is referred to as a service.

servlet A Java class capable of processing a request and generating a response. These are typically HTTP requests and responses, although the Servlet API does allow for non-HTTP servlets. Requires a Web container, such as Tomcat, to run.

ServletRequest An interface representing the request made by the client. In Web applications, the subinterface, `HttpServletRequest` is used.

ServletResponse An interface representing the response made to the client. In Web applications, the subinterface, `HttpServletResponse` is used.

SQL Structured Query Language. A text-based query language used for querying and manipulating databases.

Swing A set of classes used in the Java programming language for building Graphical User Interfaces (GUIs). More configurable/customizable than the standard GUI classes found in the Abstract Windowing Toolkit (AWT).

tag Library A way of representing complex Java functionality in the form of tags that can be used on pages. This facilitates the separation of presentation from business logic.

Tomcat A free, open source implementation of the Servlet and JSP specifications. A very popular Web container, which is often used in a commercial context. Available from the Jakarta project at `http://jakarta.apache.org`.

Unix An operating system that was invented in 1969. Many "flavors" of Unix now exist, including Linux, Solaris, FreeBSD, and OpenBSD.

URI Uniform Resource Identifier. A reference to a specific resource. Most often found as a Web address, in the form of a URL, which is a subset of URI.

URL Uniform Resource Locator, which is a subset of URI. A URL is used to specify the location of a specific resource. Commonly found in the context of the Internet, where it can be used to request many resources, including HTML, images, video, and audio.

Web application An application consisting of HTML pages, graphics, and all the other components that make up a Web site. In Java Web applications, they will additionally consist of JSP, servlets, tag libraries, and JavaBeans.

Web container Software that runs servlets and JSP. Tomcat is a good example of a Web container. A Web container is the minimum required to run servlets or JSP.

Web service A Web service is a software component that has methods invoked over a network such as HTTP. This invocation is done using XML technology, and the platform and language of the software component should be transparent to the invoker of the component.

WML Wireless Markup Language. A subset of XML used for presenting content in a WAP browser, typically found on a mobile phone.

XML eXtensible Markup Language. A subset of the Standard General Markup Language (SGML). XML is a simple, flexible, and powerful way of marking up data (usually text) using tags similar to those in HTML.

XML Schema Supercedes DTDs as a means of defining an XML data structure. XML Schema is a very powerful mechanism for defining XML structure because unlike DTDs, it is written in XML. The structure can be defined in great detail, even down to the data types that XML elements and attributes can contain.

XPath A pattern-matching language for use with XML. It is used to match and retrieve nodes within the XML tree. It is used extensively within XSLT.

XSLT eXtensible Stylesheet Language for Transformations. An XML vocabulary used to describe how XML can be transformed into any other text-based format. It requires a processor that will use both the XML and XSLT to produce a result in the format defined in the XSLT.

Index

Symbols

& (ampersand), XML element names, 322
* (asterisk), methods, 531, 643
@ (at sign), 54, 643
: (colon), XML element names, 322
$ (dollar sign), 85, 368
. (dot operator), 103
"" (double quotation marks), attributes, 323
/ (forward slash), 322, 349
- (hyphen), XML element names, 322
? (question mark), 469
. (period), XML element names, 322
| (pipe), OR operator, 644
; (semicolon), 54, 124, 569
' (single quotation mark), attributes, 323
[] (square brackets operator), 103
[] (square brackets), XPath predicates, 644
<%@ include> directive, 231, 611
&apos built-in entity, 323
" built-in entity, 323
* wildcard path operator, 643
. operator, 643
.. parent path operator, 643
.\ command, 729
/ child operator, 643
// descendant operator, 643
<ResourceParams> element, name attribute, 477
@ attribute path operator, 643
< (left angle bracket), XML element names, 322
< (open angle bracket), 322
> (close angle bracket), 322
> (right angle bracket), XML element names, 322
_ (underscore), XML element names, 322
{ } (curly braces), 85, 124
| OR operator, 644

Numbers

1.0 specification (XML), 317

A

absolute location paths (XPath), 349
acceptCount attribute, 719
access control for resources, Web applications, 560
accessing
- actions, 481-491
- collections, 103-104, 688
- connections (connection pools), 493
- databases, 479-481, 507
- EJBs, 514-515
- objects, 103-104, 688
- Web services using stubs, 419
- WSDL, 423

Action, Struts framework, 215
action attribute, 224
Action objects, 218
- business logic, encapsulating, 231
- Struts applications, 227-230

ActionForm, 215, 218, 224-227
ActionMapping, 215, 218
actions
- averager, Averager.java file (code), 308-309
- core, 132

core (conditional), 140-144
core (general-purpose), 132-140
core (iterator), 144-150
core (URL-related), 150-156
core (XML), 156-159
custom
body content, 297-303
scripting variables, exporting, 304
tag libraries, 97-98
custom iteration, 293-295
custom tags, 131
empty, 276-283
empty with attributes, 283-288
Tag interface lifecycle, 289-292
c:catch, code, 139
c:choose, Java pseudo-code, mapping to, 143
c:for-each, 304
c:forEach, code, 146
c:forTokens, code, 149
c:if, code, 141-142
c:import, 361
c:out, 133-134, 304
c:set, attributes, 135
defineObjects, EmptyTagWithAttrsExport.java file (code), 305-306
displayResult, DisplayResult.java file (code), 309-310
flow-control (XML), 159-160
formatting, 160-161
global attributes (standard tag library), 490-491
Internationalization, 160-161, 668-675
<jsp: forward>, 210
<jsp:include>, 231, 611
JSTL XML, code, 332
nested, averager.jsp file (code), 308
SQL
grouping, 488
sql:dateParam action, 679
sql:param action, 676
sql:query, 160, 676-677
sql:setDataSource action, 675-676
sql:transaction, 160, 678-679
sql:update, 160, 678
sql:param (standard tag library), 487-488
sql:query, stock beans, populating, 503
sql:query (standard tag library), 482-485
sql:setDataSource (standard tag library), 481-482
sql:transaction (standard tag library), 488-490
sql:update (standard tag library), 486-487
standard, 87-98
standard tag library, 481
tags interacting, 303
transform (XML), 160
XML, 664-668
x:forEach, 363
x:out, 363
x:set, 365
x:transform, 365
actions, JSTL, 657-664. *See also* standard actions
ActionServlet, Struts framework, 215
activating entity Beans, 526
Active Server Pages (ASP), 41, 80-82
addCookie(Cookie cookie) method, 236
addnewAddress.html, code, 474-475
addresses, email (Ormonds case study), 626
AddToCart.java file (code), 270
addToCart.jsp file (code), 269
Admin tool (SQL), 728
admin.jsp file, 629-630
administration consoles, WebLogic 7, 537
administration pages, email (Ormonds case study), 630-631
administration servlets (Tomcat), 721
algorithms
descriptions, 321
hashing, definition, 565
Amazon Web site, personalization (Web applications), 585
ampersand (&), XML element names, 322

ancestor axis identifier, 352
ancestor-or-self axis identifier, 352
ancestor-or-self location path, 353
ancestor::* location path, 353
anElementName expression, 642
angle brackets
- left <, XML element names, 322
- right >, XML element names, 322
- < (open angle bracket), 322
- > (close angle bracket), 322

anonymous complexType element, 649
Ant project (Jakarta), 162
Apache
- FOP (Formatting Objects Processor) Web site, 381
- Web site, Xalan, 348

Apache API (Apache Web Server API), 8
Apache Axis (Apache eXtensible Interaction System)
- averager services, 392
- installing, 390
- Release Candidate 1 version, 390
- Web services, deploying to, 391-393
- Web site, 389-390

Apache Software Foundation Web site, 162
Apache Struts, source code, 224
Apache Struts framework, 620
Apache Web Server API, 8
Apache Web site, bean tags, 224
APIs (Application Programmer's Interfaces)
- Apache Web Server API, 8
- Connector 1.0, 11
- DOM (Document Object Model), XML, parsing, 326-333
- EJB (Enterprise Java Beans) 2.0, 10
- J2EE 1.3, 10-11
- JAAS (Java Authentication and Authorization Service) 1.0, 10
- JAF (Java Activation Framework) 1.0, 11
- Java IDL, 11
- Java Mail 1.2, 11
- JavaBeans, 166
- JAXP (Java API for XML Processing), 11, 325
- JDBC (Java Database Connectivity) 2.0 extensions, 11, 426, 462, 475
- JMS (Java Messaging Service) 1.0, 10
- JNDI (Java Naming and Directory Interface), 11, 441
- JSP 1.2, 10
- JTA (Java Transaction API) 1.0, 10
- RMI (Remote Method Invocation over IIOP), 11
- SAX (Simple API for XML), 325, 333-340
- Servlets 2.3, 10
- single-threaded CGI and multithreaded ISAPI/NSAPI, contrasting, 8
- UDDI, 428-430, 433
- Web applications, 8

appBase attribute, 721
applet.html file (code), 93-94
applets, 7-8
application flow, Model 2 architecture, 211
application folders, J2EE, structure, 531
application object, predefined variables, 70-73
application predefined variable, 686
Application Programmer's Interface. *See* APIs
application scope, 176-177
application servers
- caching, 506
- J2EE, 705-712

application.xml file (code), 535-536
ApplicationResources.properties file (code), 223
applications. *See also* Web applications
- ATG Dynamo application server, Session Manager, 256
- J2EE (Java 2 Enterprise Edition)
  - containers, 13-14
  - deploying, 17, 540
  - EJB container, 14-15

JAAS (Java Authentication and Authorization Service), 583
JMS (Java Messaging Services), 14
JNDI (Java Naming and Directory Interface), 14
layers, 13
running, 536-539, 541
security, 580-581
security services, 14
transaction services, 14
Web container, 15-16
JBoss Application Server, Web site, 711
JNDI, 445-446
server-side, 8
shopping cart case study
controller servlets, 262-265
Java beans, 259-262
JSPs, 265-272
shopping-cart, 496-506

applications (JSP)
<%@ include> directive, 231
business logic, encapsulating, 231
code, duplicating, 231
comments, 232
CSS (Cascading Style Sheets), 232
exception handling, 232-233
HTML and Java, separating, 231
include mechanisms, 231
JSF (JavaServer Faces), 230
<jsp:include> action, 231
Model 1 architecture, 201-202, 212
Model 2 architecture, 212
application flow, 211
CD JSP, 206-208
controller servlets, 208-211
frameworks, 213-214
included files, 208
MVC (Model View Controller) design, 202-203
requests, 203
Stock Bean, 204-206
Web site, demonstration of, 204
structure, 232
Struts applications
Action objects, 227-230
ActionForm objects, 224-227
architecture, 218
bean tag library, 224
building, 216-218
data validation, 226-227
error messages, 222
HTML tag library, 221-224
mappings, setting up, 219-220
tag libraries, 220-221
Web pages, 220-224
Struts framework, 214-216
style, 232

applications (Struts)
Action objects, 227-230
ActionForm objects, 224-227
architecture, 218
bean tag library, 224
building, 216-218
data validation, 226-227
error messages, 222
HTML tag library, 221-224
mappings, setting up, 219-220
tag libraries, 220-221
Web pages, 220-224

applicationScope, 132

applicationScope implicit object, 108

applicationScope object, 689

architectures
Cocoon, 382-384
directory naming services, 438
EBJ access, 555-558
JNDI, 436-438, 441
Model 1, 201-202, 212
Model 2, 212
application flow, 211
CD JSP, 206-208
controller servlets, 208-211
frameworks, 213-214
included files, 208
MVC (Model View Controller) design, 202-203
requests, 203

Stock Bean, 204-206
Web site, demonstration of, 204
Model-View-Controller, 167
Ormonds Web pages, 607-609
session failovers, 256
Struts applications, 218
systems, not using JNDI, 441
archives, WEB-INF\lib\mail.jar (Web site), 625
arithmetic operators, 101, 688
array objects, SortedMap, 485
ASPs (Active Server Pages), 41, 80-82
<assembly-descriptor> element, 531, 581
asterisk (*)
methods, 531
* wildcard path operator, 643
asymmetric key encryption, 570-571
at sign (@)
@ attribute path operator, 643
toString method, 54
ATG Dynamo
caching, 506
control center, rules, setting up, 601
downloading, 603
personalized JSP (code), 601-603
user behavior, logging, 601
ATG Dynamo Application Server, 256-258, 708-709
ATG Dynamo Framework Web site, 233
ATG Dynamo Portal Server, portal home page, 408
ATG Dynamo Web site, 258
attribute axis identifier, 352
attribute element, child elements, 288
attribute instruction (XSLT), 357
Attribute interface, 443
attribute path operators, @ (at sign), 643
<attribute> element, 648
attributes
"" (double quotation marks), 323
' (single quotation mark), 323
acceptCount, 719
action, 224
appBase, 721
autoFlush, 64, 682
basename (JSTL), 669
buffer, 64, 682
Cart, 265
case-order (optional) (XSLT), 639
charEncoding (JSTL), 662
className, 716, 719, 721
com.conygre.ShoppingCartController class, 264-265
connectionTimeout, 719
contentType, 64, 682
context (JSTL), 662
cookies, 715
Coyote HTTP/1.1 Connector Element, 719-720
crossContext, 716
curencyCode (JSTL), 673
curencySymbol (JSTL), 673
CurrentUser, 265
c:out action properties, 657
c:remove action properties, 658
c:set action, 135, 658
data-type (optional) (XSLT), 639
dataSource, 481-483, 486-490, 493, 675-676
dateStyle (JSTL), 674-675
debug, 716
debut, 721
declaring, 650
default (JSTL), 657
defaultHost, 720
delims (JSTL), 661
disable-output-escaping (optional) (XSLT), 641
docBase, 715
driver, 481
dynamic values, 620
empty custom-tag actions, 283-288
EmptyTagWithAttrs.java file (code), 284-285

emptyTagWithAttrs.jsp file (code), 283-284
errorPage, 65, 682
escapeXML (JSTL), 657
exclude-result-prefixes (XSLT), 640
extends, 65, 683
extension-element—prefixes (optional) (XSLT), 640
formatting objects, Web site, 379
global, actions (standard tag library), 490-491
groupingUsed (JSTL), 673
Guest, 265
howMany, custom tags, 284
id (optional) (XSLT), 640
import, 65, 683
info, 65, 683
interOnly (JSTL), 673
isErrorPage, 65, 683
isolation, 489
isThreadSafe, 65, 683
JNDI directory services, 438
<jsp:include> standard action, 91
key (JSTL), 670
lang (optional) (XSLT), 639
language, 66, 684
liveDeploy, 721
match, 360, 640
maxFractionDigits (JSTL), 673
maxIntegerDigits (JSTL), 673
maxProcessors, 719
maxRows, 483, 490, 676
minFractionDigits (JSTL), 673
minIntegerDigits (JSTL), 673
minProcessors, 720
mode(optional) (XSLT), 635, 641
name, 477, 636-642, 663, 720-721
noNamespaceSchemaLocation, XML Schemas, 650-651
of Context element, 715-716
of Host element, 721
of import element, 653
of include element, 653
of page directive, 682-684
of scope, 174
order (optional) (XSLT), 639
override, 716
page directive, 64-68
pageEncoding (page directive), 66
parseLocale (JSTL), 673-674
password, 481
path, 715
pattern (JSTL), 673
port, 718-719
prefix (JSTL), 669
priority (optional) (XSLT), 641
privileged, 715
redirectPort, 720
reloadable, 715
schemaLocation, XML Schemas, 650-651
scope, 481-483, 486, 658, 667, 670
scoped, 136
select (optional) (XSLT), 635, 638-639, 642
Select (XSLT), 641
ServletContext object, 35-37
session (page directive), 66
session-scoped, 137-138
shutdown, 718
sql, 483, 486, 676
sql:query action, 483
sql:setDataSource action, 481
sql:update action, 486
startRow, 483, 676
step (JSTL), 660
Stock, 265
systemId (XML), 664
target (JSTL), 658
test (XSLT), 637, 641
timeStyle (JSTL), 674-675
timezone (JSTL), 674
TLD files, 287
trans-attribute, 531
type (JSTL), 673-674

unpackWARs, 721
url, 481
useNaming, 716
User, 265, 481
value, 487
value (JSTL), 657-658, 663
var, 481-483, 486, 658, 667
varReader (JSTL), 662
version (XSLT), 640
workDir, 716
wrapperClass, 716
XML, 323-324, 667
XML documents, 322-324
xmlSystemId (XML), 667
xslt (XML), 667
xsltSystemId (XML), 667

attribute::* location path, 353

attrs parameter, 334

<auth-method> element, 566

authentication, 561
digest, 564-566
form-based, 566-569
http (Hypertext Transfer Protocol), 563-564
Internet Explorer, 564
<login-config> element, 562
login.html file (code), 566
loginFailed.html file (code), 567
Tomcat, incorrect credentials, result of, 564
Web applications, 560
web.xml file, 562-563

authorization, JAAS (Java Authentication and Authorization Service) classes, 583

Authorization function (JAAS), 583

autoexec.bat file, environment variables, 694

autoFlush attribute, 64, 682

autogenerated sources, <jsp:forward> standard action (code), 88

averager action, Averager.java file (code), 308-309

averager services, 392

Averager Web service SOAP response (code), 396

Averager.java file (code), 308-309, 388-389

averager.jsp file (code), 308

AveragerClient.java file (code), 396-397

AveragerDeploymentDescriptor.wsdd file (code), 391

AveragerFaultHandler.java file (code), 400-401

axis identifiers, 351-353

axis identifiers (XPath), 351-353

Axis. *See* Apache Axis

B

backups of sessions, configuring, 258

basename attribute (JSTL), 669

bases, search, 439

basic authentication, 563-564

basic XML Schemas example (code), 646

basic.jsp file (code), 42-45

BasicFormProcessor servlet, 31-32

BasicFormProcessor.java file (code), 30

BasicServlet, 27

BasicServlet.java file (code), 21

BEA Web Logic Web site, 258, 536

BEA WebLogic, downloading, 731

BEA WebLogic server
documentation (Web site), 732
installing, 730-732
Linux, installing, 731-732
online help, 732
Web applications, deploying, 121
Web site, 731
Windows, installing, 731

<bea-install> element, 536

Bean Managed Persistence (BMP), 518

bean tag library, Struts applications, 224

bean tags, Web site, 224

beanAlreadyExists.jsp file (code), 191

beanAlreadyExists2.jsp file (code), 192

beans. ***See also*** **EJBs; entity Beans; JavaBeans; session Beans**
business logic, encapsulating, 231
dynamic discovery, 170
Entity Beans for Data Access, 14
events, 168
message-driven, 511
Message-Driven Beans for Asynchronous Messaging, 15
no-argument constructors, 170
persistence, 168-170
properties, 168-170
role in component-based development, 167-170
stock, populating, 503
Stock Bean, Model 2 architecture, 204-206
behavior of users, logging in ATG Dynamo, 601
bind() method, 452
binding
JNDI objects, 450-453
objects to names (code), 450-451
Binding class, 442
<binding> element (WSDL), 417-418
bindings (JNDI), 436-438
<bindingTemplate> element (XML), 427
BindObject.java file (code), 450-451
Binstock, Cliff, 645
blocks
finally, 467
try/catch, Tomcat and Web applications, 698
blueprints, J2EE Blueprints
EJBs, 510
session Beans, 542
Web site, 511
BluePrints Web site, 212
BMP (Bean Managed Persistence), 518
body content
custom actions, 297-303
manipulating in custom tags, 300
repeated processing, 292-297
<body> tag, 394
BodySupport class, methods, 297-298
BodyTag interface, 274, 298-299
BodyTagSupport class, 274
Bond, Martin, 714
Book.java file (code), 171-172, 402-403, 500-501
BookClient.java file (code), 406-407
BookClientServlet.java file (code), 410-411, 421-422
bookEntryForm.jsp file (code), 193-194
Bookns (WSDL namespace), 415
bookProcess.jsp file (code), 195
bookProcessBean.jsp file (code), 196
bookProcessBeanAllParams.jsp file (code), 199
bookProcessBeanNamedParams.jsp file (code), 197-198
BookRetriever.java file (code), 404
books.jsp, code, 505-506
BookSearchDeploymentDescriptor.wsdd file (code), 404-405
BookService, SOAP, 405-406
bookservice.wsdl file, 413-415
BookserviceSoapBindingStub.java file (code), 420-421
bookstores, online (Web services), 385
boolean absolute (int row) method, 470
boolean first() method, 470
boolean isNew() method, 252
boolean isSecure() method, 577
boolean isUserInRole(String roleName) method, 576
boolean last() method, 470
boolean next() method, 469
boolean previous() method, 469
boolean relative (int rows) method, 470
Boolean type, EL (Expression Language), 101
bound objects, looking up (code), 453-454
bound properties (JavaBeans), 173
braces, curly ({ }), expressions, 85

brackets
> (close angle bracket), 322
< (open angle bracket), 322
[] (square), XPath predicates, 644
left angle (<), XML element names, 322
right angle (>), XML element names, 322
square, operator ([]), 103
Brownell, David, 333
browser-specific transformations, 370-376
BrowserDependentServlet.java file (code), 373-375
browsers. *See* Web browsers
buffer attribute, 64, 682
builder tool. *See* IDEs
building
Java clients, 396-402
Struts applications, 216-218
built-in entities, 323
built-in templates, 362-363
bundles, resource, 160
business logic
Action, Struts framework, 215
encapsulating, 166, 231
presentation logic, separating, 124
businesses, finding, 423
<businessEntity> element (XML), 426
<businessService> element (XML), 426
buttons
Certificates, 572
Configure and Deploy, 541
onClick method, 165
properties, 165

C

c.tld file, code, 128-129
cache tag, 495
Cache taglib project (Jakarta), 163
cache.jsp, code, 501-503
caching
application servers, 506
ATG Dynamo, 506
content, 495-496
DataSource, 498
CallableStatement, 469
Cart attribute, 265
Cart.java file (code), 261-262
Cascading Style Sheets (CSS), 232
case sensitivity, XML namespaces, 355
case studies. See also Ormonds case study
JSP 2.0 specification, 704
shopping cart application, 259-272
case-order (optional) attribute (XSLT), 639
Catalina (Tomcat), 718
catchWithIf.jsp file (code), 141
<categoryBag> element (XML), 427
CD JSP, Model 2 architecture, 206-208
cd.jsp file, 206-207, 267-268
cdBrowse.jsp file (code), 207-208
certificates
digital, 571-572
providers, viewing on Internet Explorer, 572
viewing, 575
Certificates button, 572
CGI (Common Gateway Interface), 7-8
chapter sample code Web site, 165
chapter18Personalization.war file, downloading, 587
characters
$ (dollar sign), 368
/ (forward slash), XPath location paths, 349
special, XML (Extensible Markup Language), 322
XML element names, 322
characters() method, 339
charEncoding attribute (JSTL), 662
checkout.jsp file (code), 270-271
child axis identifier, 351
child elements
of attribute element, 288
of variable element, 307
child operator, / (forward slash), 643
child::* location path, 353

choose instruction (XSLT), 357
ciphertext, decryption, 569
class files, 119
.class files, roles, 513
Class.forName(), 463-464
classes
BasicServlet, web.xml file (code), 27
Binding, 442
BodySupport, methods, 297-298
BodyTagSupport, 274
com.conygre.Cart, methods, 262
com.conygre.ShoppingCartController, attributes, 264-265
Credentials (JAAS), 583
diagrams, home, remote and implementation classes, 514
DocumentBuilder, 325
DocumentBuilderFactory, 325
EBJObject wrapper, 522
ElFunctions, 275
ELFunctions.java file (code), 275
EmptyTag, 278
exception, java.sql.SQLException, 467
home, 514
implementation, 512-514,
entity Beans, 521-524
session Beans, 546, 550
JAAS (Java Authentication and Authorization Service) authorization, 583
Java
Averager.java file (code), 389
JavaBeans, 166
stylesheets, compiling, 358
java.lang.Math, random() method, 54
java.lang.Object, toString method, 54
java.lang.Throwable, 40
javax.naming.Binding, 442
javax.naming.event.NamingEvent, 444-445
javax.naming.Reference, 443
javax.servlet.http.Cookie, 236
javax.servlet.http.HttpServlet, 17
javax.servlet.jsp.PageContext, methods, 78-79
Jspwriter, 77
MyHandler, code, 336-339
NamingEvent, 444
OrderAction, 623, 628
org.apache.axis.AxisFault, 401
org.apache.struts.action.Action, 215
org.apache.struts.action.ActionForm, 215
org.apache.struts.action.ActionMapping, 215
org.apache.struts.action.ActionServlet, 215
org.uddi4j.client.UDDIProxy, 429
OrmondsEmail sender, 626
primary key, 513
Principal (JAAS), 583
Reference, 443
remote, 514
SAXParser, 325
SAXParserFactory, 325
ServletConfig, methods, 34
skeleton, EJBs, 512
StreamResult, 359
StreamSource, 359
stub, EJBs, 512
Subject (JAAS), 583
Swing, Java tutorial Web site, 203
TagSupport, 274, 278
UDDIProxy, 429
UML diagram, 274
Web applications, 119
WEB-INF\classes folder, Web applications, 118
wrapper, Java primitive datatypes, 197
className attribute, 716, 719, 721
CLASSPATH environment variable (J2EE), 446
client views of EJBs, 515-517
clients
ejbClient.jsp file (code), 516
EJBs, 511

Java, 396-402
objects, instance data, 171
protected resources, login.html file, 567-568
XML Spy, 395-396
close() method, 467, 626
cluster monitor, WebLogic 7 server, 710
clustering, definition, 710
CMP (Container Managed Persistence), 518
Cocoon, 381-384
cocoon.war file Web site, 382
code. *See also* static initializers
addnewAddress.html, 474-475
AddToCart.java file, 270
addToCart.jsp file, 269
admin.jsp file, 629-630
Apache Struts source code, downloading, 224
applet.html file, 93-94
application.xml file, 535-536
ApplicationResources.properties file, 223
ASP (Active Server Page) example, 81
ATG Dynamo, personalized JSP, 601-603
Averager Web service SOAP response, 396
Averager.java file, 308-309, 388-389
averager.jsp file, 308
AveragerClient.java file, 396-397
AveragerDeploymentDescriptor.wsdd file, 391
AveragerFaultHandler.java file, 400-401
basic.jsp file, 42-45
BasicFormProcessor servlet, 32
BasicFormProcessor.java file, 30
BasicServlet.java file, 21
beanAlreadyExists.jsp file, 191
beanAlreadyExists2.jsp file, 192
BindObject.java file, 450-451
Book.java, 171-172, 402-403, 500-501
BookClient.java file, 406-407
BookClientServlet.java file, 410-411, 421-422
bookEntryForm.jsp file, 193-194
bookProcess.jsp file, 195
bookProcessBean.jsp file, 196
bookProcessBeanAllParams.jsp file, 199
bookProcessBeanNamedParams.jsp file, 197-198
BookRetriever.java file, 404
books.jsp, 505-506
BookSearchDeploymentDescriptor.wsdd file, 404-405
bookservice.wsdl file, 413-414
BookserviceSoapBindingStub.java file, 420-421
bound objects, looking up, 453-454
BrowserDependentServlet.java file, 373-375
c.tld file, 128-129
cache.jsp, 501-503
Cart.java file, 261-262
catchWithIf.jsp file, 141
cd.jsp file, 206-207, 267-268
cdBrowse.jsp file, 207-208
chapter samples, Web site, 165
checkout.jsp file, 270-271
comments, HTML (Hypertext Markup Language), 52-53
CompactDisc.java file, 519
CompactDiscAccess.java file, 544
CompactDiscAccessBean.java file, 546
CompactDiscAccessHome.java file, 543
CompactDiscBean.java file, 521-522
CompactDiscHome.java file, 519-520
CompactDiscProduct.java file, 544-546
configuring, 497
ControllerServlet.java file, 555-557
cookies.jsp file, 237-238
course0.xml file, 609-610
courses.jsp file, 611
courses.xsl file, 614-616
createPerson.jsp file, 133
createURL.jsp file, 154
custom tags, 131

c:catch action, 139
c:forEach action, 146
c:forTokens action, 149
c:if action, 141-142
c:out action, 133-134
DataBean.java file, 228-229
declarationTag Method.jsp, 57
details.jsp file, 613-614
displayAttributes.jsp file, 136
displayDetails.jsp file, 133-134
DisplayResult.java file, 309-310
displaySubset.jsp file, 363-364
displayValues.jsp file, 155
displayYourRequest.jsp file, 246-247
doLogin.jsp file, 271-272, 504-505
duplicating, 231
ejb-jar.xml file, 527-528, 552-553, 580
ejbClient.jsp file, 516
EJBs, getHello() method, 455-456
EL (Expression Language) expressions, 98-99
ELFunctions.java file, 275
elFunctions.jsp file, 276
embedding, 59-61
embeddingCode.jsp file, 59
EmptyTag.java file, 277-278
emptyTag.jsp file, 276-277
emptyTags.tld file, 281
EmptyTagWithAttrs.java file, 284-285
emptyTagWithAttrs.jsp file, 283-284
EmptyTagWithAttrsExport.java file, 305-306
emptyTagWithAttrsExport.jsp file, 303-304
error-handling pages, 76
exception handling, 232-233
exceptions, 74-76
footer.html file, 608-609
forEach.jsp file, 146
ForwardingServlet.java file, 39
generateError.jsp file, 74
globalParam.jsp file, 368-369
globalParam.xsl file, 369-370
header.html file, 608
header.jsp file, 208, 266
HelloWorld.jsp file, 456-457
HelloWorldBean.java file, 455-456
HTML
  creating with plugin.jsp file, 95-96
  files, 319
  forms, 28-29
  Java, mixing, 123-124
  output, 82
  storing, 124
  user details, 133
index.jsp file, 221, 409-410, 609
IndexAction.java file, 228
IndexForm.java file, 225-226
information, prompting for, 153-154
init() method, modified, 36
initialization parameters, passing, 116
initialization.jsp file, 116-117
iterations with scriplets, 83
IterationTag.java file, 294-295
iterationTag.jsp file, 293
Java
  comments, 50-51
  declaration tag, 690-691
  embedded, 181
  expression tag, 691
  scriptlet tag, 692
  tag handlers, 68
javax.servlet.jsp.jstl.sql.Result, 483
jdbc.drivers property, 464
jdbcConnection.jsp, 466-467
JSP (JavaScript Page) example, 81-82, 456-457
jspService method, 55, 60-61, 190
  application object, 72
  include directive, 63
  predefined variables, 69-70
  shared objects, retrieving, 72-73
<jsp:forward> standard action, autogenerated sources, 88

JSTL iteration example, 84
JSTL XML actions, 332
localhost.BookRetriever.java file, 421
LoggerServlet.java file, 37
login.html file, 566, 589-590
login.jsp file, 271
loginFailed.html file, 567
logout.jsp file, 248, 272
LookupObject.java file, 453-454
LookupObjectSubContext.java file, 454-455
main.jsp file, 577-578
mainWithParameters.jsp file, parameterized roles, 579-580
methods, 57-59
moreCourseInfo.htm file, 244
MoreInfoRequest.java file, 245-246
moreInformationRequest.jsp file, 245
moreInformationRequestWithBean.jsp file, 247
multiTemplate.jsp file, 360-361
MyAccount.jsp file, 62
MyHandler class, 336-339
MyHandler.java file, 336-339
MyHandler.jsp file, 335-336
named parameters, 367
named templates, 367
namedTemplate.xsl file, 366
newAddressForm.html, 473
objects, 450-455
orderCourse.jsp file, 619-620
ormonds.struts.OrderAction, 622-623
ormonds.struts.OrderForm.java file, 620-621
OrmondsControllerServlet.java file, 616-618
OrmondsDataAccess.java file, 629
OrmondsEmail.java file, 624-625
PageDirective.jsp file, 66-68
param.xsl file, 367
parameters, passing to stylesheets, 368-369
ParameterServlet.java file, 33-34
parseDoc JSTL.jsp file, 332
parseDoc.jsp file, 328-329
parseJDOM.jsp file, 342-343
people.xml file, 317-318, 355
people.xslt file, 355-356
peopleAttrs.xml file, 323-324
plugin.jsp file, 94-96
preparedStatement.jsp, 468-469
processError.jsp file, 76
productSearch.jsp file, 554
Profile.java file, 594-595
prompt.jsp file, 153-154
pseudo-code (Java), mapping to c:choose action, 143
public static method, implementing, 275
RegistrationServlet.java file, 598-599
removeAttribute.jsp file, 138
resultSetDisplay.jsp, 471-472
resultSetDisplayQueryTag.jsp, 484
resultSetDisplayWithTagLibrary.jsp, 480
SAX (Simple API for XML), 335-336
scoped attributes, 136
server.xml, 476, 574, 713-714
ServletLifeCycleMethods.java file, 18-19
servlets, generated, 51-52, 75-76
session-scoped attributes, 137-138
SessionCount.java file, 254
setAttributes.jsp file, 136-137
shared objects, 70-71
ShoppingCartController.java file, 209-210, 262-263, 593
shoppingCartTables.sql, 496-497
simplePage.jsp file, 53-54
SOAP, 398-399, 405-406
SOAP requests, 394
SortedMap[] property, 485
source, generated servlets, 50
stock beans, populating, 503
Stock.java file, 204-206, 260-261, 498, 500
struts-config.xml file, 219-220
stylesheets, global parameters, 369-370

tablesSetUp.sql file, 587-588, 627
tag libraries, mapping, 127
tag library usage, 69
TagLifecycle.java file, 289-291
tariffs.fo file, 377-378
tariffs.xml file, 370-371
tariffsFO.xslt file, 379-381
tariffsHTML.xslt file, 371-372
tariffsWML.xslt file, 372-373
TDL, JSTL tags, 128-129
tranformSubset.jsp file, 364-365
transform.xsl file, 361
UDDI, entries in IBM Test Registry, 424-425
uddiClient.jsp file, 428-429
URL mapping, setting up, 114-115
URLs, 154-155
useAndSet1.jsp, 186-189
useBean1 scriptlet.jsp, 179-180
useBean1.jsp, 181-183
useBean2 scriptlet.jsp, 180
useBean2.jsp, 184-185
usingDataSource.jsp, 477-479
usingEL.jsp file, 99
usingIncludes.jsp file, 90-91
usingIncludesWithParameters.jsp file, 92
usingParamTag.jsp, 487-488
usingTransactions.jsp, 488-489
usingUpdateTag.jsp, 486-487
usingXalan.jsp file, 358-359
variables, declaring, 56-57
Web application parameters, setting, 35-36
web.xml (for session bean) file, 553-554
web.xml files, 411-412, 534-535
- application parameters, setting, 35-36
- BasicFormProcessor servlet, 32
- BasicServlet class, 27
- customized for SSL (Secure Socket Layer), 574-575
- form-based authentication, 567
- initialization parameters, passing, 116
- parameterized roles, 579
- personalization (Web applications), 591
- servlet initialization parameters, 33-34
- tag libraries, mapping, 127
- URL mapping, setting up, 114-115
- welcome files, setting up, 114

weblogic-cmp-rdbms-jar.xml file, 533-534
weblogic-ejb-jar.xml file, 532-533, 553
welcome files, setting up, 114
welcome.jsp file, 210-211, 266-267, 557, 595, 597
welcomeText.html file, 62
WishList.java file, 251
wishList.jsp file, 250-251
XML
- attributes, 323-324
- data files, 370-373
- document subsets (code to display), 363-364
- documents, 317-318, 328-329, 342-343, 349, 352
- elements, 323-324
- files, 319
- input documents, 355
- output documents, 355

XML Schemas, 646, 652
xmlExample.html file, 319
XPath expressions, transforming, 364-365
XSLT, 360-361
XSLT single templates, 355-356

collections
- accessing, 688
- accessing in EL, 103-104
- personNodes, 330

colon (:), XML element names, 322
com.conygre.Cart class, methods, 262
com.conygre.ShoppingCartController class, attributes, 264-265
command-line tools, mysql, 729
commands
- .\, 729
- deploy, 724

install, 724
list, 724
Manager servlets (Tomcat), 724-725
reload, 724
remove, 724
resources, 724
roles, 725
session, 725
start, 724
stop, 724
undeploy, 724

comment instruction (XSLT), 357

comments
cookies, 239-240
generated servlets, code, 51-52
HTML (Hypertext Markup Language), 52-53, 685
Java, 50-51, 686
JSP, 686
Web pages, 232
XML documents, 324

committees, executive members, 703

Common Gateway Interface (CGI), 7-8

commons-dbcp.jar, 477

commons-pool.jar, 477

communications, EJBs, 512

community draft stage, JCP (Java Community Process), 703

community members, involvement with JCP (Java Community Process), 702

community review stage, 702

CompactDisc entity Bean, 543

CompactDisc.java file (code), 519

CompactDiscAccess.java file (code), 544

CompactDiscAccessBean.java file (code), 546

CompactDiscAccessHome.java file (code), 543

CompactDiscBean.java file (code), 521-522

CompactDiscHome.java file (code), 519-520

CompactDiscProduct.java file (code), 544-546

compiler errors, 697

compilers, XSLTC (XSLT Compiler), 358

compiling stylesheets into Java classes, 358

complexType element, 649-650

<complexType> element, 648

component-based development (JavaBeans), 166-170

component-based systems, 167

components, 166-167, 215

composite names, 454

compositors, complexType element, 650

conditional core actions, 142-144

CONFIDENTIAL value (<transport-guarantee> element), 575

confidentiality, Web applications, 560

config object, predefined variables, 73

config predefined variable, 686

configuration files, server.xml, code, 476

configuration screens, WebLogic 7 Application Server, 581

Configure and Deploy button, 541

configuring
containers, 717-721
data sources, 475
DataSource, Tomcat, 497-498
JNDI service providers, 448-450
JSP in web.xml, 114-116
session backups, 258
Tomcat, 589
- administration servlets, 721
- Connector element, 718-720
- containers, configuring, 717-721
- Engine element, 720
- Host element, 720-721
- Manager servlets, 721-725
- Server element, 718
- server.xml file (code), 713-714
- Service element, 718-720
- servlets, 721
- Web applications, configuring, 714-717

Web applications, web.xml file, 714-717
XA DataSources, 539

Connection object, 465
connection pools, 491-492
ConnectionEventListener interface, 494
ConnectionPoolDataSource interface, 493
performance, 475
PooledConnection interface, 493-494
ConnectionEventListener interface, 494
ConnectionPoolDataSource interface, 493
connections
accessing (connection pools), 493
databases, closing, 467
JDBC, 464-469, 482
connectionTimeout attribute, 719
Connector 1.0 API, 11
Connector element, 718-720
consoles
WebLogic 7 administration, 537
WebLogic server, 458
constrained properties (JavaBeans), 173
constraints, security, (code), 562
constructors, no-argument, (JavaBeans), 170-171
Container Managed Persistence (CMP), 518
containers. *See also* **directives; Web containers**
configuring, 717-720
EJB, 14-16, 509-510
generated servlets, source code, 50
J2EE applications, 13-14
Jakarta Tomcat, 23-25
JSPs, 50
translating to servlets, 127
content. *See* **body content**
content, JSPs (JavaServer Pages), 49-50
content caching, 495-496
content file, Web applications, 118
content validation, XML Schemas, 652
contentType attribute, 64, 682
context attribute (JSTL), 662
Context element, attributes, 715-716
Context interface, 442
<Context> element, 715
<context-root> element, 536
Context.bind() method, 451
Context.INITIAL_CONTEXT_FACTORY environment property, values, 449
Context.lookup() method, 453
Context.rebind() method, 451
Context.rename() method, 453
Context.unbind() method, 452
contexts
initial, J2EE RI (Reference Implementation), 447
JNDI, 454-455
objects, looking up from subcontexts (code), 454-455
control centers, ATG Dynamo rules, 601
controller servlets, 202, 593
Model 2 architecture, 208-211
Ormonds case study, 616-619
shopping cart application case study, 262-265
controllers
ActionServlet, Struts framework, 215
Ormonds case study, 607
ControllerServlet.java file (code), 555-557
conventions, naming (Java Naming and Directory Interface), 439-440
convertBean() method, 550
converting tariffs.fo file to PDF, 378
cookie implicit object, 108
cookie object, 689
cookies
comments, 239-240
Internet Explorer, 238
lifetime, 238
limitations, 241
maxAge property, 240
maxAge value, 238
Netscape, 238
persistence, 240, 586
security, 239-240
session tracking, 235-238
standards, Web site, 238
URLs, rewriting, 241-243
versions, 238-239

cookies attribute, 715
cookies.jsp file, 237-239
Cookie[] getCookies()method, 22
cooperating actions of tags, 303
copy instruction (XSLT), 357
CORBA Common Object Services (COS) Naming Service, 437
core actions
- conditional, 140-144
- general-purpose, 132-140
- iterator, 144-150
- JSTL
  - c:catch, 658
  - c:choose, 659
  - c:forEach, 660-661
  - c:forTokens, 661
  - c:if, 658
  - c:import, 661-662
  - c:otherwise, 660
  - c:out, 656-657
  - c:param, 663-664
  - c:redirect, 663
  - c:remove, attribute properties, 658
  - c:set, 657-658
  - c:url, 662-663
  - c:when, 659
- URL-related, 150-156
- XML, 156-159

core components, Struts framework, 215
core JSTL tags, TDL (code), 128-129
core structures, WSDL documents, 415
Core tag library, 131
- actions, 160
- core actions
  - conditional, 140-144
  - general-purpose, 132-140
  - iterator, 144-150
  - URL-related, 150-156
  - XML, 156-159
- EL (expression language), 132
- flow-control actions (XML), 159-160
- transform actions (XML), 160

core tags, 84, 611, 687
core technologies, Web services, 385
COS Naming Service, Web site, 437
costs, J2EE application servers, 706-707
counters, session, 255
course information (Ormonds), 609-616
course0.xml file (code), 609-610
courses.jsp file, 611
courses.xsl file (code), 614-616
Coyote HTTP/1.1 Connector Element, attributes, 719-720
crashes of servers, resolving, 257
create methods, 520, 543
createPerson.jsp file (code), 133
createURL.jsp file (code), 154
Credentials class (JAAS), 583
crossContext attribute, 716
CSS (Cascading Style Sheets), 232
CTLX (Custom Tag Library extension) (Jakarta), 163
curencyCode attribute (JSTL), 673
curencySymbol attribute (JSTL), 673
curly braces ({ }), 85, 124
CurrentUser attribute, 265
currentUser.interest property, 597
custom actions
- body content, 297-303
- defineObjects, EmptyTagWithAttrsExport.java file (code), 305-306
- scripting variables, exporting, 304
- tag libraries, 97-98

custom iteration actions, 293-295
custom objects, passing, 402-408
custom tag libraries, 273
- custom tags
  - body content, custom actions, 297-303
  - body content, repeated processing, 292-297
  - EL (Expression Language) functions, 274-276
  - empty actions, 276-283

empty actions with attributes, 283-288
Tag interface lifecycle, 289-292
writing, 274
importing, 126-130
Tag Extensions, 273-274
tags, 303-311
Custom Tag Library extension (CTLX) (Jakarta), 163
custom tags, 125, 130
actions, 131
body content, 292-303
body-content element, 282
code, 131
cooperating actions, 303
description, 282
EL (Expression Language) functions, 274-276
empty actions, 276-288
emptyTag, 277
EmptyTag.java file (code), 277-278
emptyTag.jsp file (code), 276-277
emptyTags.tld file (code), 281
emptyTagWithAttrs, 283
EmptyTagWithAttrs.java file (code), 284-285
emptyTagWithAttrs.jsp file (code), 283-284
howMany attribute, 284
interacting, 303-311
name element, 282
tag handlers, 277
Tag interface, 276, 289-292
tag-class element, 282
writing, 274
customizing, web.xml file for SSL (Secure Socket Layer) (code), 574-575
c:catch action, 138-140, 658
c:choose action, 142-143, 659
c:for-each action, 304
c:forEach action, 145-148, 660-661
c:forTokens action, 149-150, 661
c:if action, 140-142, 658
c:import action, 150-152, 361, 661-662
c:otherwise action, 144, 660
c:out action, 133-135, 304, 656-657
<c:out> tags, 698
c:param action, 152, 663-664
c:redirect action, 155-156, 663
c:remove action, 137-138, 658
c:set action, 135-137, 657-658
c:url action, 152-155, 662-663
c:when action, 143-144, 659

D

data
instance, making private to objects, 171
integrity, Web applications, 560
portable (XML), 315-316
XML files, code, 370-373
data sources, configuring, 475
data validation, Struts applications, 226-227
data-type (optional) attribute (XSLT), 639
***Database Programming with JDBC and Java, 2nd Edition*, 462**
databases
accessing, 479-491, 507
caching, 495-496
connection pools, 491-494
connections, closing, 467
creating on MySQL servers, 728-729
email (Ormonds case study), interacting with, 627-630
modifying, JDBC drivers, 473-475
MySQL, downloading, 727
RDBMS (Relational Database Management Systems), 439
statements, closing, 467
Tomcat, configuring, 589
DataBean object, 228
DataBean.java file (code), 228-229
DataSources, 497-498
attribute, 481-483, 486-490, 493, 675-676
interface, 475
object, 475, 493

TX, 539
XA, configuring, 539
datatypes
defining in XML Schemas, 648-650
primitive, wrapper classes, 197
W3C Web site, 648
dateStyle attribute (JSTL), 674-675
debug attribute, 716
debugging
Tomcat
compiler error, 697
<c:out> tag, 698
designing effectively, 699
environment variable, 693-695
error message line number, 698
File Not Found error, 695-696
J2SDK 1, 693
JSPs, writing clearly, 698
page error, 697
parser error, 697
port 808, 695
runtime error, 697
System.out.print() statement, 698
try/catch block, 698
web.xml file, 696
Web applications
compiler errors, 697
<c:out> tags, 698
designing effectively, 699
environment variables, 693-695
error message line numbers, 698
File Not Found error, 695-696
J2SDK 1.4, 693
JSPs, writing clearly, 698
page errors, 697
parser errors, 697
port 8080, 695
runtime errors, 697
System.out.print() statements, 698
try/catch blocks, 698
web.xml files, 696
debut attribute, 721
declaration tag, 55, 690-691
methods, 57-59
variables, declaring (code), 56-57
declarations, XML documents, 320-321
declarationTag Method.jsp (code), 57
declarative security, J2EE security model, 561
declarative template programming (XSLT), 360-361
procedural programming, 366-370
subsets, 363-365
templates built in, 362-363
declare element, 307
declaring
attributes, 650
methods, code, 57-59
no-argument constructors as public, 171
variables, code, 56-57
XML Schemas namespaces, 647
decryption of ciphertext, 569
default attribute (JSTL), 657
defaultHost attribute, 720
defineObjects custom action, EmptyTagWithAttrsExport.java file (code), 305-306
defining
complexType element in XML Schemas, 649-650
datatypes in XML Schemas, 648-650
elements in XML Schemas, 648
globally defined, complexType element, 649
JSPs (JavaServer Pages), 49
listeners, 254
security constraints in web.xml file (code), 562
simpleType element in XML Schemas, 649-650
tags in JSTL (JavaServer Pages Standard Tag Library), 83
delims attribute (JSTL), 661
deploy command, 724

deploying
averager services, 392
entity Beans, 526-528
deployment descriptor, 529-531
deployment folder structure, 531-532
J2EE applications, running, 536-541
transaction demarcation mode, 531
with Web applications, 534-536
in WebLogic, 532-533
folder structures, 120
J2EE (Java 2 Enterprise Edition), 16-17, 540
session Beans, 552-555
WAR files, 120-121
Web applications, 119-121
Web services to Apache Axis, 391-393
deployment descriptor, 16, 529-531
deployment folders, structure, 531-532
descendant axis identifier, 352-353
descendant location path, 353
descendant operator, // (double forward slash), 643
descendant-or-self axis identifier, 352-353
descendant-or-self location path, 353
description element, 288
description languages, WSDL (Web Services Description Language), 387
descriptions
algorithms, 321
custom tags, 282
tag library, 282
descriptors, deployment, 16, 529-531. ***See also*** **TLD**
designs, MVC (Model View Controller), 202-203
destroy() method, 20
details.jsp file, 612-614
***Developing Java Servlets*, 264**
developments, component-based (JavaBeans), 166-170
diagrams
class, home, remote, and implementation classes, 514
screen flow, Ormonds, 607
UML, 274
digest authentication, 564-566
digests, message, 572
digital certificates, 571-572
digital signatures, 572-573
digits, XML element names, 322
DirContext interface, 444
directives
<%@ include>, 231
<%@include>, 611
include, 61-63, 681
page, 63-68, 682-684
syntax, 61
taglib, 68-69, 274, 685
directories
javax.naming.directory package, 443-444
NDS (Novell Directory Services), 437
structure for Web applications, 281
<TOMCAT HOME>/common/lib, 281
virtual, 716
/WEB-INF, 281
/WEB-INF/CLASSES, 281
/WEB-INF/LIB, 281
Directory Information Tree (DIT), 439
directory naming services, architecture, 438
directory services (JNDI), 438-439
dirty reads, 490
disable-output-escaping (optional) attribute (XSLT), 641
discovery, dynamic discovery, 170
displayAttributes.jsp file (code), 136
displayDetails.jsp file (code), 133-134
displaying
admin.jsp file in Web browsers, 630
courses.jsp file in Web browsers, 611
details.jsp file in Web browsers, 612

error messages, 622
Ormonds course information, 611-616
scoped attributes (code), 136
session-scoped attributes (code), 138
shared objects, 72
subsets of XML documents, 363-364
XML document subsets, code, 363-364

displayResult action, DisplayResult.java file (code), 309-310

DisplayResult.java file (code), 309-310

displaySubset.jsp file (code), 363-364

displayValues.jsp file (code), 155

displayYourRequest.jsp file (code), 246-247

distinguished names, 439

DIT (Directory Information Tree), 439

DNS (Domain Name Service), 437

doAfterBody() method, 293, 296, 301-303

docBase attribute, 715

document element information item (XML), 319. *See also* top-level element

Document Object Model. *See* DOM

Document Type Definitions. *See* DTDs

documentation
BEA WebLogic server (Web site), 732
Cocoon, Web site, 384
JavaBeans, Web site, 173

DocumentBuilder class, 325

DocumentBuilderFactory class, 325

DocumentBuilderObject, 326

documents
subsets, 363
well-formed (XML), 317-319
WSDL, core structures, 415
XML, DTDs, 27

documents (XML)
attributes, 322-324
code, 317-318, 349, 352
comments, 324
declarations, 320-321
DOM (Document Object Model) trees, 326
elements, 321-322
InfoSet, 320
input, code, 355
malformed, viewing in Internet Explorer, 318
output, code, 355
parsing, 333, 342-343
processing, code, 328-329
processing output, 331, 340
structure, 319-320
subsets, displaying, 363-365
tags, expanding and collapsing, 318
well-formed, 317-319
XML Schemas, 650-651

documents (XML) well-formed, viewing in Internet Explorer, 318

doEndTag() method, 303

doGet() method, 19, 210, 557, 618-619

doInitBody() method, 298

dollar sign ($), 85, 368

doLogin.jsp file (code), 271-272, 504-505

DOM (Document Object Model), 325
APIs, XML, parsing, 326-333
methods, 326-327
trees, XML documents, 326

Domain Name Service (DNS), 437

domains, DNS (Domain Name Service), 437

DOMBuilder, 344

doPost() method, 19, 264

doStartTag() method, 278, 296, 299, 303, 306

dot operator (.), 103, 643

double dots (..) parent path operator, 643

double forward slash, // descendant operator, 643

double getTotal() method, 262

double quotation marks (""), attributes, 323

Double.parseDouble method, 197

downloading
Apache Struts source code, 224
ATG Dynamo, 603
BEA WebLogic, 731

chapter18Personalization.war file, 587
J2SE VM, 23
Jakarta Tomcat, 23
Jakarta-Taglibs project, 82
Java Web Services Developer Pack, 83
JAXP, 358
JBoss Application Server, 707
JDK 1.2, 445
jdom.jar file, 344
JSSE (Java Secure Socket Extension), 573
MySQL database, 727
Net installer, 731
Ormonds case study, 605
Red Hat Linux, 731
Struts framework, 216
tag libraries, 163
Tomcat VM, 23
drafts, JCP (Java Community Process), 703
dragging and dropping with mouse, 165
driver attribute, 481
Driver Manager (JDBC)
Class.forName(), 463-464
connections, 464-469
database modifications, 473-475
javax.sql.DataSource interface, 475-479
jdbc.drivers property, 464
ResultSet interface, 469-473
ResultSetMetaData interface, 469-473
statements, 465-469
drivers, JDBC
setting up on MySQL servers, 730
static initializers, 463-464
Type 1 JDBC-ODBC Bridge, 462
Type 2 Native API, 462
Type 3 JDBC Net Pure Java Driver, 463
Type 4 Native Protocol Pure Java Driver, 463
dropping. *See* dragging and dropping
DTDs (Document Type Definitions), 315
EBNF (extended Backus-Naur form), 645
entities, 322
XML documents, 27, 324-325
XML Schemas, 645-646
duplicating code, 231
dynamic attribute values, 620
dynamic discovery, 170

E

.ear file extension, 16
EBJ containers, ejb-jar.xml file, 16
EBNF (extended Backus-Naur form), 645
ECMAScript, EL (Expression Language), 100
EJB (Enterprise Java Beans) 2.0 API, 10
EJB container, 14-15
EJB QL Web site, 531
ejb-jar.xml file, 16, 527-528, 552-553, 580
<ejb-link> element, 535
<ejb-ql> element, 531
<ejb-ref> element, 535
<ejb-ref-name> element, 535
ejbActivate() method, 526
ejbClient.jsp file (code), 516
ejbCreate() method, 523, 550
ejbLoad() method, 525
EJBObject wrapper class, 522
ejbPassivate() method, 525-526
ejbPostCreate() method, 523
ejbRemove() method, 526, 550
EJBs (Enterprise JavaBeans)
access architecture, 555-558
accessing, 514-515
.class files, roles, 513
client views, 515-517
clients, 511
communications, 512
containers, 509-510
ejb-jar.xml file (code), 580
entity Beans, 511
finder methods, 516
getHello() method (code), 455-456
home class, 514
home interface, 512-514
implementation class, 512-514
interfaces, parameters, marshaling and unmarshaling, 512

J2EE Blueprints, 510-511
lifecycle methods, 525-526
local home interface, 513-514
local remote interface, 513
message-driven Beans, 511
MyHelloWorld, looking up (code), 456-457
primary key class, 513
remote class, 514
remote interface, 512-514
session Beans, 511
skeleton class, 512
stub class, 512
writing, 517-518

ejbStore() method, 525

EL (Expression Language), 687
applicationScope, 132
Boolean type, 101
collections, accessing, 103-104
Core tag library, 132
ECMAScript, 100
ELFunctions.java file (code), 275
elFunctions.jsp file (code), 276
expressions, 98-99
features, 100
FloatingPointLiteral type, 101
functions, 110, 274-276
implicit objects, 688-689
IntegerLiteral type, 101
Internationalization tag library, 132
JSTL, 131
JSTL URIs, 655
literal types, 101
NullLiteral type, 101
objects, 103-104, 107-108
operators, 101-102, 688
pageScope, 132
requestScope, 132
reserved words, 108
RT (runtime expression values), 131
scope, 132
sessionScope, 132
SQL tag library, 132
String type, 101
XML tag library, 132
XPath, 100

element instruction (XSLT), 357

element names, XML, 322

<element> element, 648

elements
<assembly-descriptor>, 531, 581
attribute, child elements, 288
<attribute>, 648
<auth-method>, 566
<bea-install>, 536
<binding> (WSDL), 417-418
<bindingTemplate> (XML), 427
body-content, custom tags, 282
built-in templates, overriding, 363
<businessEntity> (XML), 426
<businessService> (XML), 426
<categoryBag> (XML), 427
child, 288, 307
complexType, 649-650
<complexType>, 648
Connector, 718-720
Context, attributes, 715-716
<Context>, 715
<context-root>, 536
Coyote HTTP/1.1 Connector Element, attributes, 719-720
declare, 307
defining in XML Schemas, 648
description, 288
<ejb-link>, 535
<ejb-ql>, 531
<ejb-ref>, 535
<ejb-ref-name>, 535
<element>, 648
Engine, 720
<entity>, 529
formatting objects, Web site, 379
Host, 720-721
<html:errors> element, 227
import, 653
include, 653

<login-config>, 562, 567, 592
<message> (WSDL), 416
<method-permission>, 581
name, 282, 288
name-from-attribute, 307
<operation> (WSDL), 417
<persistence-type>, 529-530
person, 356
<portType> (WSDL), 416
<prim-key-class>, 530
<query>, 531
<query-method>, 531
required, 288
<ResourceParams>, name attribute, 477
rtexprvalue, 288
<schema>, 647-648
scope, 307
<security-constraint>, 592
<security-role>, 581
Server, 718
server.xml file, 717
Service, 718-720
<service> (WSDL), 418
<servlet>, 114
<servlet-mapping>, 114
simpleType, defining in XML Schemas, 649-650
standard action, 177
tag-class, custom tags, 282
taglib, 282
<tModel> (XML), 427-428
<tModelInstance> (XML), 427-428
top-level, 129
<transport-guarantee>, values, 575
type, 288
<type-storage>, 533
<types> (WSDL), 415-416
<user-data-constraint>, 575
variable, child elements, 307
variable-class, 307
<welcome-file-list>, 114
XML, 321-324
of XML Schemas, definition example, 653-654

ELFunctions class, 275
elFunctions.jsp file (code), 276
email
JavaMail, 625
javax.mail package, 625
javax.mail.internet package, 625
MIME, (Multipart Internet Mail Extensions), 23
Ormonds case study
addresses, 626
administration pages, securing, 630-631
databases, interacting with, 627-630
javax.mail.internet.MimeMessage, creating, 625
javax.mail.Session, creating, 625
messages, sending, 626-627
sending, 623-625
StringBuffer object, 623
WEB-INF\lib\mail.jar archive (Web site), 625
EMBED tag, 96
embedded Java code, 181
embedding code, 59-61
embeddingCode.jsp file (code), 59
empty custom-tag actions, 276-282
Tag interface lifecycle, 289-292
with attributes, 283-288
EmptyTag class, 278
emptyTag custom tag, 277
EmptyTag.java file (code), 277-278
emptyTag.jsp file (code), 276-277
emptyTags.tld file (code), 281
emptyTagWithAttrs custom tag, 283
EmptyTagWithAttrs.java file (code), 284-285
emptyTagWithAttrs.jsp file (code), 283-284
EmptyTagWithAttrsExport.java file (code), 305-306
emptyTagWithAttrsExport.jsp file (code), 303-304
emulators, Nokia 7110, 376

encapsulating business logic, 166, 231
encoded URLs, processing (code), 153-155
encodeURL(String url) method, 242
encryption, 569-571
endDocument() method, 340
endElement() method, 340
Engine element, 720
engines, rule-based personalization (Web applications), 600-603
Enterprise Java Beans (EJB). ***See*** **EJBs**
entities, 322-323
entity Beans, 511
- activating, 526
- <assembly-descriptor> element, 531
- <bea-install> element, 536
- BMP (Bean Managed Persistence), 518
- CMP (Container Managed Persistence), 518
- CompactDisk, 543
- <context-root> element, 536
- creating, 518-519
- deploying, 526-541
- <ejb-link> element, 535
- <ejb-ql> element, 531
- <ejb-ref> element, 535
- <ejb-ref-name> element, 535
- <entity> element, 529
- home interface, 519-524
- implementation class, 521-524
- lifecycle, 524-526
- passivating, 526
- persistence, 518
- <persistence-type> element, 529-530
- <prim-key-class> element, 530
- <query> element, 531
- <query-method> element, 531
- remote interface, 519
- state of, 524
- <type-storage> element, 533

Entity Beans for Data Access, 14
<entity> element, 529
Enumeration getAttributeNames() method, 252
<envelope> tag, 394
environment properties, Context.INITIAL_CONTEXT_FACTORY, values, 449
environment variables
- adding to autoexec.bat file, 694
- CLASSPATH (J2EE), 446
- HOME (J2EE), 446
- Tomcat, debugging, 693-695

error handling SOAP, 398-401
error messages
- displaying, 622
- line numbers, Tomcat and Web applications, 698
- MySQL servers, 730
- Struts applications, 222

error pages, 73
error-handling pages, code, 76
errorPage attribute, 65, 682
errors, 40, 695-697
escapeXML attribute (JSTL), 657
Essential XML Quick Reference**, 354**
EVAL_BODY_BUFFERED field, 298
EVAL_BODY_INCLUDE, 296
EVAL_BODY_INCLUDE variable, 298
events
- components, frameworks, 167
- JavaBeans, 168
- javax.naming.event package, 444-445
- listeners, 444
- sessions, 248-252
- source, 444

exception classes, java.sql.SQLException, 467
exception handling, 39-41, 232-233
exception object, 73-76
exception predefined variable, 686
exceptions
- generating, 74-75
- handling, 73
- java.io.IOException, 39
- java.lang.Throwable class, 40

java.servlet.ServletException, 40-41
java.servlet.UnavailableException, 41
RemoteException, 401
ServiceException, 401
ServletException, throwing (code), 40-41
throwing, 75

exceptions, Web pages, 77
exclude-result-prefixes attribute (XSLT), 640
executeQuery() method, 466
executeUpdate() method, 473
executive committee members, 703
exemplars, 354-361
existing tag libraries, 126
expert group members, involvement with JCP (Java Community Process), 702
exported variables, naming, 667
Expression Language. *See* EL
expression tags, 53-55, 691
expressions
{ } (curly braces), 85
$ (dollar sign), 85
[] (square brackets), 364-365, 644
anElementName, 642
EL (Expression Language), 98-99
RT (runtime expression values), 131, 655
XPath, 643-644

extended Backus-Naur form (EBNF), 645
extended readers, scope, 152
extends attribute, 65, 683
Extensible Markup Language. *See* XML
eXtensible Stylesheet Language: Transformations. *See* XSLT
extension-element-prefixes (optional) attribute (XSLT), 640
extensions, Tag extensions, 273-274
extensions of files
.ear, 16
.jar, 16, 730
.java, 50
.war, 16, 120

F

Faces, JSF (JavaServer Faces), 230
factory classes, 325
faffing, definition, 94
failover
J2EE application servers, 711-712
of sessions, 256-258

Fasosin, Michael, 231
fields, 280, 298
File Not Found error, 695-696
file objects, 169
file systems, JNDI naming services, 437
files
AddToCart.java (code), 270
addToCart.jsp (code), 269
admin.jsp, 629-630
applet.html (code), 93-94
application.xml (code), 535-536
ApplicationResources.properties (code), 223
autoexec.bat, environment variables, adding, 694
Averager.java (code), 308-309, 388-389
averager.jsp (code), 308
AveragerClient.java (code), 396-397
AveragerDeploymentDescriptor.wsdd (code), 391
AveragerFaultHandler.java (code), 400-401
basic.jsp (code), 42-45
BasicFormProcessor.java (code), 30
BasicServlet.java (code), 21
beanAlreadyExists.jsp (code), 191
beanAlreadyExists2.jsp (code), 192
BindObject.java (code), 450-451
Book.java (code), 171-172, 402-403
BookClient.java (code), 406-407
BookClientServlet.java (code), 410-411, 421-422
bookEntryForm.jsp (code), 193-194
bookProcess.jsp (code), 195
bookProcessBean.jsp (code), 196

bookProcessBeanAllParams.jsp (code), 199
bookProcessBeanNamedParams.jsp (code), 197-198
BookRetriever.java (code), 404
BookSearchDeploymentDescriptor.wsdd (code), 404-405
bookservice.wsdl, 413-415
BookserviceSoapBindingStub.java (code), 420-421
BrowserDependentServlet.java (code), 373-375
c.tld, code, 128-129
Cart.java (code), 261-262
catchWithIf.jsp (code), 141
cd.jsp, 206-207, 267-268
cdBrowse.jsp (code), 207-208
chapter18Personalization.war, downloading, 587
checkout.jsp (code), 270-271
.class, roles, 513
class, 119
cocoon.war Web site, 382
CompactDisc.java (code), 519
CompactDiscAccess.java (code), 544
CompactDiscAccessBean.java (code), 546
CompactDiscAccessHome.java (code), 543
CompactDiscBean.java (code), 521-522
CompactDiscHome.java (code), 519-520
CompactDiscProduct.java (code), 544-546
configuration, server.xml, code, 476
content, Web applications, 118
ControllerServlet.java (code), 555-557
cookies.jsp, 237-239
course0.xml (code), 609-610
courses.jsp, 611
courses.xsl (code), 614-616
createPerson.jsp (code), 133
createURL.jsp (code), 154
DataBean.java (code), 228-229
details.jsp (code), 613-614
details.jsp, displaying in Web browsers, 612
displayAttributes.jsp (code), 136
displayDetails.jsp (code), 133-134
DisplayResult.java (code), 309-310
displaySubset.jsp (code), 363-364
displayValues.jsp (code), 155
displayYourRequest.jsp (code), 246-247
doLogin.jsp (code), 271-272
.ear extension, 16
ejbClient.jsp (code), 516
ejb-jar.xml, 16, 527-528, 552-553, 580
ELFunctions.java (code), 275
elFunctions.jsp (code), 276
embeddingCode.jsp (code), 59
EmptyTag.java (code), 277-278
emptyTag.jsp (code), 276-277
emptyTags.tld (code), 281
EmptyTagWithAttrs.java (code), 284-285
emptyTagWithAttrs.jsp (code), 283-284
EmptyTagWithAttrsExport.java (code), 305-306
emptyTagWithAttrsExport.jsp (code), 303-304
footer.html (code), 608-609
forEach.jsp (code), 146
ForwardingServlet.java (code), 39
generateError.jsp (code), 74
globalParam.jsp, code, 368-369
globalParam.xsl, code, 369-370
header.html (code), 608
header.jsp (code), 208, 266
HelloWorld.jsp (code), 456-457
HelloWorldBean.java (code), 455-456
HTML, code, 319
include, HTML markups, 92
included files, Model 2 architecture, 208
includedPage.jsp, 174
index.jsp, 118, 142
index.jsp (code), 221, 609, 409-410
IndexAction.java (code), 228
IndexForm.java (code), 225-226

initialization.jsp (code), 116-117
INSTALL, 216
IterationTag.java (code), 294-295
iterationTag.jsp (code), 293
.jar extension, 16, 730
jar, 118-119, 477
*.java extension, 50
jdom.jar, downloading, 344
jstl.jar, 130
library, Tomcat, 119
localhost.BookRetriever.java (code), 421
LoggerServlet.java (code), 37
login.html, 566-568, 589-590
login.jsp (code), 271
loginFailed.html, 567-568
logout.jsp (code), 248, 272
LookupObject.java (code), 453-454
LookupObjectSubContext.java (code), 454-455
main.jsp, 577-578
mainWithParameters.jsp, parameterized roles (code), 579-580
moreCourseInfo.htm (code), 244
MoreInfoRequest.java (code), 245-246
moreInformationRequest.jsp (code), 245
moreInformationRequestWithBean.jsp (code), 247
multiTemplate.jsp (code), 360-361
MyAccount.jsp (code), 62
MyHandler.java (code), 336-339
MyHandler.jsp (code), 335-336
namedTemplate.xsl, 366-368
orderCourse.jsp (code), 619-620
ormonds.struts.OrderForm.java (code), 620-621
OrmondsControllerServlet.java (code), 616-618
OrmondsDataAccess.java (code), 629
OrmondsEmail.java (code), 624-625
PageDirective.jsp (code), 66-68
param.xsl, code, 367
ParameterServlet.java (code), 33-34
ParameterServlet.java, init() method, modified (code), 36
parseDoc JSTL.jsp (code), 332
parseDoc.jsp (code), 328-329
parseJDOM.jsp (code), 342-343
people.xml (code), 317-318, 355
people.xslt (code), 355-356
peopleAttrs.xml (code), 323-324
plugin.jsp, 94-96
processError.jsp (code), 76
productSearch.jsp (code), 554
Profile.java (code), 594-595
prompt.jsp (code), 153-154
RegistrationServlet.java (code), 598-599
removeAttribute.jsp (code), 138
requestedPage.jsp, 174
server.xml, 573-574, 713-721
ServletLifeCycleMethods.java (code), 18-19
SessionCount.java (code), 254
setAttributes.jsp (code), 136-137
ShoppingCartController.java (code), 209-210, 262-263, 593
simplePage.jsp (code), 53-54
standard.jar, 130
Stock.java (code), 204-206, 260-261
storing in Tomcat, 50
struts-blank.war, 216, 221
struts-config.xml (code), 219-220
tablesSetUp.sql (code), 587-588, 627
TagLifecycle.java (code), 289-291
tariffs.fo, 377-378
tariffs.xml (code), 370-371
tariffsFO.xslt (code), 379-381
tariffsHTML.xslt (code), 371-372
tariffsWML.xslt (code), 372-373
TLD, attribute section, 287
<TOMCAT_HOME>\work, 50
tranformSubset.jsp (code), 364-365
transform.xsl (code), 361
uddiClient.jsp, 428-430
useAndSet1.jsp (code), 186-189

useBean1 scriptlet.jsp (code), 179-180
useBean1.jsp (code), 181-183
useBean2 scriptlet.jsp (code), 180
useBean2.jsp (code), 184-185
usingEL.jsp (code), 99
usingEL.jsp, output, 99
usingIncludes.jsp (code), 90-91
usingIncludesWithParameters.jsp (code), 92
usingIncludesWithParameters.jsp, output, 92
usingXalan.jsp (code), 358-359
.war extension, 16, 120
WAR, deploying, 120-121
web.xml (code), 411-412
WEB-INF\lib\mail.jar archive (Web site), 625
web.xml
 basic authentication, setting up (code), 563
 customized for SSL (Secure Socket Layer) (code), 574-575
 form-based authentication (code), 567
 initialization parameters, passing (code), 116
 parameterized roles (code), 579
 personalization (Web applications) (code), 591
 security constraints, defining (code), 562
 session bean (code), 553-554
 tag libraries, mapping (code), 127
 taglib-uri, 128
 Tomcat and Web applications, debugging, 696
 URL mapping, setting up (code), 114-115
 Web applications, 118
 Web applications, configuring, 714-717
 welcome files, setting up (code), 114
web.xml (code), 534-535
 application parameters, setting, 35-36
 BasicFormProcessor servlet, 32
 BasicServlet class, 27
 servlet initialization parameters, extracting, 33-34
 servlet initialization parameters, setting, 33
weblogic-cmp-rdbms-jar.xml (code), 533-534
weblogic-ejb-jar.xml (code), 532-533, 553
welcome, setting up (code), 114
welcome.jsp (code), 210-211, 266-267, 557, 595-597
welcomeText.html (code), 62
WishList.java (code), 251
wishList.jsp (code), 250-251
XML, 16, 319, 370-373
xmlExample.html (code), 319

filters, search, 439

finally block, 467

findAll method, 516

findAncestorWithClass() method, 310

finder methods, 516, 520-521

findForward() method, 229

find_service method, 430

FloatingPointLiteral type, EL (Expression Language), 101

flow-control actions, XML, 159-160

flush attribute, <jsp:include> standard action, 91

fmt:bundlee action, 669

fmt:formatDate action, 161, 674

fmt:formatNumber action, 161, 672-673

fmt:message action, 161, 670

fmt:param action, 670

fmt:parseDate action, 674-675

fmt:parseNumber action, 673

fmt:requestEncoding action, 671

fmt:setBundle action, 669

fmt:setLocale action, 669

fmt:setTimezone action, 671

fmt:timezone action, 671-672
folders
deployment, structure, 531-532
J2EE application, structure, 531
mm.mysql-2.x.x, 730
Root, Web applications, 118
structures, deploying, 120
<tomcat-home> (Tomcat installation folder), 24
WEB-INF, Web applications, 118
webapps (Tomcat), 26
following axis identifier, 352-353
following location path, 353
following-sibling axis identifier, 352
following-sibling location path, 353
footer.html file (code), 608-609
FOP (Formatting Objects Processor) Web site, 381
for-each instruction (XSLT), 357
for-each tag, 84, 356
forEach.jsp file (code), 146
form data, HTML
processing, 28-32
requests, forwarding to servlets, 38-39
servlet initialization, 32-34
ServletContext object, 35-38
form-based authentication, 566-569
formats. ***See also*** **XSLFO**
presentation, XML, transforming into, 347
XML, Ormonds course information, 609-610
XPath location paths, 349
formatting objects
syntax, 381
tariffs.fo file (code), 377-378
tariffsFO.xslt file (code), 379-381
Web site, 379
formatting actions, 160-161
Formatting Objects Processor (FOP) Web site, 381
formed-based authentication, web.xml file (code), 567
forms
ActionForm, Struts framework, 215
bookEntryForm.jsp file (code), 193-194
error messages, displaying, 622
HTML (Hypertext Markup Language)
code, 28-29
JavaBeans, 193-200
user details (code), 133
login, 589
of jsp:setProperty tag, 186
of jsp:useBean tag, 178-179
parameter values, bookProcessBean.jsp file (code), 196
parameters, bookProcess.jsp file (code), 195
personalization (Web applications), 586-587
processing for Ormonds case study, 619-623
registration, 589
forward (standard action), 88-90
forward slash (/)
/ child operator, 643
double, // descendant operator, 643
XML element names, 322
XPath location paths, 349
forward() method, 88
forwarding requests to servlets, 38-39
ForwardingServlet.java file (code), 39
frameworks
ATG Dynamo Framework Web site, 233
components, 166-167
Model 2 architecture, 213-214
RealMethods Web site, 233
Struts, 214-216
Struts (Apache), 620
XSLT multitemplate program (code), 360
functionality, J2EE application servers, 708-709
functions
Authentication (JAAS), 583
EL (Expression Language), 274-276
in EL, 110

ELFunctions.java file (code), 275
elFunctions.jsp file (code), 276
node(), 353
not(), 354
OrderAction class, 623
static Java in EL, 110

G

Gartner Web site, 706
general-purpose core actions, 133-140
generated servlets
code, 51-52, 75-76
instance variables, 57
PageDirective.jsp file (code), 67-68
source code, 50
generateError.jsp file (code), 74
generating
exceptions, 75
Java from WSDL, 419-422
WSDL, 419
GET method, 31, 171-173, 444
GET requests, 618
getAll method, 444
getAttribute() method, 175-176, 246
getAverage method, 394
getChildNodes() method, 327
getConnection() method, 493
getDocumentElement() method, 327
getElementsByTagNames(String) method, 327
getFirstChild() method, 327
getHello() method, code, 455-456
getLastChild() method, 327
getMetaData() method, 470
getNextSibling() method, 327
getParameter(String name) method, 31
getParameterValues(String name) method, 31
getParentNode() method, 327
getPreviousSibling() method, 327
getRandomNumber() method, 691
getRowsByIndex() method, 504
getServletContext method, 34, 70
getServletName() method, 34
getValue() method, 246
global attributes, actions (standard tag library), 490-491
global locations, Web applications, 119
global parameters, stylesheets, code, 369-370
globally defined, complexType element, 649
globalParam.jsp file, code, 368-369
globalParam.xsl file, code, 369-370
Goodwill, James, 264
grammar, XML, 387
grouping SQL actions, 488
groupingUsed attribute (JSTL), 673
groups, expert members (Java Community Process), 702
Gudgin, Martin, 354
Guest attribute, 265

H

handlers. *See* tag handlers
handlers, EmptyTagWithAttrs.java file (code), 284-285
handling exceptions. *See* exception handling
hashes, message digests, 572
hashing algorithms, definition, 565
header implicit object, 108
header object, 689
header.html file (code), 608
header.jsp file (code), 208, 266
headerValues implicit object, 108
headerValues object, 689
HelloWorld.jsp file (code), 456-457
HelloWorldBean.java file (code), 455-456
help. *See also* resources
online, BEA WebLogic server, 732
standards support, J2EE application servers, 707
hierarchical tag structures, 307-311

home class, 514
HOME environment variable (J2EE), 446
home interfaces, 512-514
  entity Beans, 519-521
  session Beans, create methods, 543
home pages
  Apache Axis, 390
  Cocoon, 382
  Jakarta Tomcat, 25
  JCP (Java Community Process), 701
  Ormonds, 606, 610-611
  portal, 408
  shopping Web sites, 265
  UDDI, 424
  XPath, Web site, 157
Host element, 720-721
howMany attribute, custom tags, 284
HTML (Hypertext Markup Language), 52
  code, storing, 124
  comments, 52-53, 685
  creating with plugin.jsp file (code), 95-96
  files, code, 319
  forms
    code, 28-29
    JavaBeans, 193-200
    user details (code), 133
  <html:checkbox> tag, 222
  <html:errors> tag, 222
  <html:form> tag, 222
  <html:option> tag, 222
  <html:radio> tag, 222
  <html:select> tag, 222
  <html:submit> tag, 222
  <html:text> tag, 222
  Java, 123-124, 231
  markups, in include files, 92
  output, code, 82
  tag library, Struts applications, 221-224
  XML documents, code, 355
HTML form data
  processing, 28-32
  requests, forwarding to servlets, 38-39
  servlet initialization, 32-34
  ServletContext object, 35-38
<html:checkbox> tag, 222
<html:errors> element, 227
<html:errors> tag, 222
<html:form> tag, 222
<html:option> tag, 222
<html:radio> tag, 222
<html:select> tag, 222
<html:submit> tag, 222
<html:text> tag, 222
HTTP (Hypertext Transfer Protocol), 235
  authentication, 563-564
  requests, 19
  W3C, Web site, 19
HTTPS (Hypertext Transfer Protocol over Secure Socket Layer)
  asymmetric key encryption, 570-571
  digital certificates, 571-572
  digital signatures, 572-573
  Java, 573-575
  private key encryption, 570
  public key encryption, 570
  security, 569
  SSL (Secure Socket Layer), 572-575
  symmetric key encryption, 569
HttpServletRequest interface, 79
HttpServletRequest object, methods, 576-577
HttpServletRequest parameter, 21-23
HttpServletResponse parameter, 21-23
HttpSession getSession() method, 22
HttpSession object, summary, 252-253
HttpSessionBindingListener, sessions, 251
http://localhost:8080/axis/services/bookservice (WSDL namespace), 415
http://schemas.xmlsoap.org/soap/encoding (SOAP namespace), 394
http://schemas.xmlsoap.org/soap/encoding/ (WSDL namespace), 414
http://schemas.xmlsoap.org/soap/envelope (SOAP namespace), 394

http://schemas.xmlsoap.org/wsdl/ (WSDL namespace), 414
http://schemas.xmlsoap.org/wsdl/http/ (WSDL namespace), 415
http://schemas.xmlsoap.org/wsdl/mime/ (WSDL namespace), 415
http://schemas.xmlsoap.org/wsdl/soap/ (WSDL namespace), 414
http://www.w3.org/2001/XMLSchema (SOAP namespace), 395
http://www.w3.org/2001/XMLSchema-instance (SOAP namespace), 395
http://www.w3.org/200l/XMLSchema (WSDL namespace), 414
Hypertext Markup Language. *See* HTML
Hypertext Transfer Protocol over Secure Socket Layer. *See* HTTPS
Hypertext Transfer Protocol. *See* HTTP
hyphen (-), XML element names, 322

I

I18N (Internationalization), Web site, 160
IBM Web site, UDDI registry, 424
IBM Test Registry, UDDI entry (code), 424-425
IBM Web Services Test Area, 424
id (optional) attribute (XSLT), 640
id attribute, 653
identifiers, 351-353
IDEs (integrated development environments), 166, 170
IE (Internet Explorer). *See* Internet Explorer
if instruction (XSLT), 357
implementation class, 512-514, 524
  entity Beans, 521-524
  session Beans, 546, 550
implementing public static method (code), 275
implicit objects, 69, 80-81, 107-108, 688-689
import attribute, 65, 683
import element, 653
importing custom tag libraries, 126-130
include (standard action), <jsp:include>, 90-92
include directive, 61-63, 681
include element, 653
include files, HTML markups, 92
include mechanisms, code duplication, 231
include method, 39
included files, Model 2 architecture, 208
includedPage.jsp file, 174
index.jsp file, 221, 409-410, 609
  appearance in Web browsers, 412
  Web applications, 118
IndexAction.java file (code), 228
indexed properties (JavaBeans), 173
IndexForm.java file (code), 225-226
info attribute, 65, 683
information
  in UDDI registries, 430
  prompting for (code), 153-154
InfoSet (XML Information Set), 319-320
init() method, 210, 557
  modified (code), 36
  ServletException, throwing (code), 40-41
initial contexts, J2EE RI (Reference Implementation), 447
initialization parameters, 33, 116
initialization.jsp file (code), 116-117
initializing servlets, 32-34
initiation stage, JCP (Java Community Process), 703
initParam implicit object, 108
initParam object, 689
input, XSLT (eXtensible Stylesheet Language: Transformations), 348-349
input documents (XML), code, 355
install command, 724
INSTALL file, 216
installers, Net, 731
installing
  Apache Axis, 390
  BEA WebLogic server, 730-732

Jakarta Tomcat, 23-24
Java Plugin, 94
Linux on BEA WebLogic server, 731-732
MySQL server, 727-730
Struts framework, 216
Tomcat, <tomcat-home> (Tomcat installation folder), 24
Unix on MySQL servers, 728
WebLogic 7, 536
Windows, 727, 731
instance data, making private to objects, 171
instance variables, 57
instantiating JavaBeans from JSPs, 177-183
instructions (XSLT), 357, 368
int getMaxInactiveInterval() method, 252
IntegerLiteral type, EL (Expression Language), 101
INTEGRAL value (<transport-guarantee> element), 575
integrated development environments (IDEs), 166, 170
integration, J2EE application servers, 706
integrity of data, Web applications, 560
interacting tags, 303-377
interacting with databases, Ormonds case study, 627-630
interfaces. *See also* APIs; JNDI
Attribute, 443
BodyTag, 274, 298-299
ConnectionEventListener, 494
ConnectionPoolDataSource, 493
Context, 442
DataSource, 475
DirContext, 444
home (entity Beans), 512-514, 520-521
home (session Beans), create methods, 543
HttpServletRequest, 79
IterationTag, 274, 292
java.io.Externalizable, 168-169
java.io.Serializable, 168-169
javax.naming.Context, 442-443
javax.naming.directory.Attribute, 443-444
javax.naming.directory.DirContext, 444
javax.naming.event.NamingListener, 445
javax.naming.Name, 443
javax.servlet.http.HttpSession, methods, 252
javax.servlet.jsp.jstl.core.LoopTagStatus, methods, 147-148
javax.servlet.jsp.tagext.BodyTag, methods, 298
javax.servlet.jsp.tagext.Tag, 279-280
javax.servlet.Servlet, 17
javax.servlet.ServletContext, 70
javax.servlet.ServletResponse, 79
javax.sql.DataSource, 475-479
local home, 513-514
local remote, 513
Name, 443
NamingListener, 445
org.xml.sax.helpers.DefaultHandler, methods, 335
parameters, marshaling and unmarshaling, 512
PooledConnection, 493-494
remote, 512-514, 519, 544-546
ResultSet, 469-473
ResultSetMetaData, 469-473
SessionListener, 253-256
SPIs (Service Provider's Interfaces), 441
Statement, 465
Tag
custom tags, 276
fields, 280
lifecycle, 289-292
methods, 279
TagLifecycle.java file (code), 289-291
UML diagram, 274
tag handlers, 274
XML Spy, 395
Internationalization (I18N), Web site, 160

Internationalization actions, 160-161
internationalization actions (JSTL)
fmt:bundlee, 669
fmt:formatDate, 674
fmt:formatNumber, 672-673
fmt:message, 670
fmt:param, 670
fmt:parseDate, 674-675
fmt:parseNumber, 673
fmt:requestEncoding, 671
fmt:setBundle, 669
fmt:setLocale, 669
fmt:setTimezone, 671
fmt:timezone, 671-672
internationalization tag, 84
Internationalization tag library, EL (expression language), 132
internationalization tags (JSTL), 687
Internet Explorer (IE)
basic authentication, 564
certificate providers, viewing, 572
cookies, 238
Internet options, 697
malformed documents (XML), viewing, 318
OBJECT tag, 96
well-formed documents (XML), viewing, 318
XML document tags, expanding and collapsing, 318
interOnly attribute (JSTL), 673
intrinsic objects, ASP variables, 80-81
invalid SOAP requests (code), 398-399
invalidate tag, 495
invalidate() method, 248
invocations, out.print method, 185
invoking Web services, 385
iPlanet, sessions, 253
iPlanet Web site, 258
ISAPI/NSAPI, multithreaded and single-threaded CGI, 8
isErrorPage attribute, 65, 683
isolation attribute, 489
ISPs, Ormonds case study, 606
isTextNode() method, 330
isThreadSafe attribute, 65, 683
iterations
custom iteration actions, 293-295
JSTL, example (code), 84
scriptlets (code), 83
IterationTag interface, 274, 292
IterationTag.java file (code), 294-295
iterationTag.jsp file (code), 293
iterator core actions, 144
c:forEach, 145-148
c:forTokens, 149-150

J

J2EE (Java 2 Enterprise Edition), 7
application folder structure, 531
application servers, 705-712
applications
containers, 13-14
deploying, 17
deploying in WebLogic, 540
EJB container, 14-15
JMS (Java Messaging Services), 14
JNDI (Java Naming and Directory Interface), 14
layers, 13
running, 536-541
security services, 14
transaction services, 14
Web container, 15-16
Blueprints, 510-511, 542
CLASSPATH environment variable, 446
deploying, 16-17
HOME environment variable, 446
HTML form data, 28-39
J2EE 1.3 core APIs, 10-11
Jakarta Tomcat, 23-25
Java servlets, 17-23, 39-41
JSPs (JavaServer Pages), 41-46
platform, 12

servers, 446
standards, 10-13
Web applications, 26-27, 46-48
J2EE 1.3 core APIs, 10-11
J2EE applications, JAAS (Java Authentication and Authorization Service), 583
J2EE BluePrints Web site, 212
J2EE Reference Implementation, Sun Microsystems Web site, 708
J2EE RI (Reference Implementation), 446
initial contexts, 447
JNDI, 448-455
transient services, 451
J2EE security model, 560-561
J2SDK 1.4, 693
J2SE (Java 2 Standard Edition), 10
J2SE VM, downloading, 23
JAAS (Java Authentication and Authorization Service), 10, 583
JAF (JavaBeans Activation Framework) Web site, 11, 625
Jakarta, 162-163
Jakarta Struts framework, 214-216
Jakarta Taglibs project, 162-163
Jakarta Tomcat, 23-25
Jakarta Web site, 163, 224
Jakarta-Taglibs project, downloading, 82
JAR files, 118-119, 477
.jar file extension, 16, 730
Java
applets, 7-8
classes, 166, 358, 389
clients, 396-402
code, 123-124, 690-692
comments, 50-51, 686
embedded code, 181
exception handling, 73
generating from WSDL, 419-422
HTML, separating, 231
Plugin for the XP platform, 731
primitive datatypes, wrapper classes, 197
pseudo-code, mapping to c:choose action, 143
servlets, 17-23
single-threaded CGI and multithreaded ISAPI/NSAPI, contrasting, 8
SSL (Secure Socket Layer), 573-575
static functions in EL, 110
tag handlers, 68
Web applications, 7-10
Web site, Swing classes, 203
Java 2 Enterprise Edition. *See* J2EE
Java 2 Standard Edition (J2SE), 10
Java Activation Framework (JAF) 1.0 API, 11
Java API for XML Processing (JAXP) 1.1 API. *See* JAXP
Java API for XML Registries (JAXR), 431-433
Java Authentication and Authorization Service (JAAS) 1.0 API, 10, 583
Java beans, shopping cart application case study, 259-262
Java Community Process (JCP), 701-704
Java Database Connectivity (JDBC) 2.0 extensions API, 11. *See* JDBC
Java Development Kit (JDK), 166
Java IDL API, 11
Java Mail 1.2 API, 11
Java Messaging Service (JMS) 1.0 API, 10
Java Naming and Directory Interface (JNDI), 11, 475. *See* JNDI
Java Petstore, 511
Java Plugin, 93-96
Java Secure Socket Extension (JSSE), 573
Java servlets, exception handling, 39-41
Java Specification Request (JSR), 702
Java Transaction API (JTA) 1.0, 10
Java Tutorial Web site, 168
Java virtual machine (JVM), 7
Java Web Services Developer Pack, downloading, 83
***.java file extension, 50**

java.io.Externalizable interface, 168-169
java.io.InputStream getResourceAsStream(String path) method, 35
java.io.IOException, 39
java.io.ObjectInputStream, 168
java.io.ObjectOutputStream, 168
java.io.PrintWriter getWriter() method, 22
java.io.Serializable interface, 168-169
java.io.ServletOutputStream getOutStream() method, 22
java.lang.Math class, random() method, 54
java.lang.Object class, toString method, 54
java.lang.Throwable class, 40
java.net.URL getResource(String path) method, 35
java.servlet.ServletException, 40-41
java.servlet.UnavailableException, 41
java.sql package (JDBC API), 475
java.sql.SQLException exception class, 467
java.util.Enumeration getHeaders() method, 22
JavaBeanAllParamss, bookProcessBeanAllParams.jsp file (code), 199
JavaBeanNamedParamss, bookProcessBeanNamedParams.jsp file (code), 197-198
JavaBeans, 165
- beanAlreadyExists.jsp file (code), 191
- beanAlreadyExists2.jsp file (code), 192
- beans, 167-170
- Book.java file (code), 171-172
- bookEntryForm.jsp file (code), 193-194
- bookProcess.jsp file (code), 195
- bookProcessBean.jsp file (code), 196
- bound properties, 173
- business logic, encapsulate, 166
- buttons, properties, 165
- chapter sample code Web site, 165
- component-based development, 166-170
- constrained properties, 173
- DataSource, caching, 498
- documentation, Web site, 173
- file objects, 169
- get method, 171-173
- HTML forms, 193-200
- IDEs (integrated development environments), 166
- indexed properties, 173
- instantiating from JSPs, 177-183
- J2EE Web container, 15
- Java classes, 166
- java.io.Externalizable interface, 168-169
- java.io.ObjectInputStream, 168
- java.io.ObjectOutputStream, 168
- java.io.Serializable interface, 168-169
- <jsp:attribute> standard action, 97
- <jsp:body> standard action, 98
- jsp:getProperty tag, 177, 183-185
- <jsp:getProperty> standard action, 97
- jsp:setProperty tag, 177, 185-189
- <jsp:setProperty> standard action, 97
- jsp:useBean tag, 177-183, 186-193
- <jsp:useBean> standard action, 97
- no-argument constructors, 170-171
- Ormonds case study, 607
- properties, accessing and setting from JSPs, 183-189
- RAD (rapid-application development), 165
- server-side components, 166
- set method, 171-173
- specification, 166-168
- streams, 168
- thread objects, 169
- useAndSet1.jsp file (code), 186-189
- useBean1 scriptlet.jsp file (code), 179-180
- useBean1.jsp file (code), 181-183
- useBean2 scriptlet.jsp file (code), 180
- useBean2.jsp file (code), 184-185
- using from JSPs, standard action elements, 177
- Web application scope, 174-177

JavaBeans Activation Framework (JAF), 11, 625
JavaBeans API, 166
JavaMail, 625
JavaServer Faces (JSF), 230
JavaServer Pages Standard Tag Library. *See* JSTL
JavaServer Pages. *See* JSPs
javax package, Web applications, 119
javax.ejb package, 518
javax.mail package, 625
javax.mail.internet package, 625
javax.mail.internet.MimeMessage, creating, 625
javax.mail.Session object, 625
javax.naming package, 442-443
javax.naming.Binding class, 442
javax.naming.Context interface, 442-443
javax.naming.directory package, 443-444
javax.naming.directory.Attribute interface, 443-444
javax.naming.directory.DirContext interface, 444
javax.naming.event package, 444-445
javax.naming.event.NamingEvent class, 444-445
javax.naming.event.NamingListener interface, 445
javax.naming.ldap package, 445
javax.naming.Name interface, 443
javax.naming.Reference class, 443
javax.naming.spi package, 445
javax.servlet package, 17
javax.servlet.http package, 17
javax.servlet.http.Cookie class, 236
javax.servlet.http.HttpServlet class, 17
javax.servlet.http.HttpSession interfaces, methods, 252
javax.servlet.jsp.jstl.core.LoopTagStatus interface, methods, 147-148
javax.servlet.jsp.jstl.sql.Result, code, 483
javax.servlet.jsp.PageContext class, methods, 78-79
javax.servlet.jsp.tagext.BodyTag interface, methods, 298
javax.servlet.jsp.tagext.Tag interface, 279-280
javax.servlet.Servlet interface, 17
javax.servlet.ServletConfig object, 33
javax.servlet.ServletContext interface, 70
javax.servlet.ServletResponse interface, 79
javax.sql package (JDBC API), 475
javax.sql.DataSource interface, 475-479
javax.xml.parsers package, 325
javax.xml.parsers.DocumentBuilder Factory property, 326
javax.xml.parsers.SAXParserFactory property, 325
JAXP (Java API for XML Processing), 11, 325-326, 358
JAXR (Java API for XML Registries), 431-433
JBoss Application Server, 707, 711
JCP (Java Community Process), 701-704
JDBC (Java Database Connectivity), 11, 461
  API, 462, 475
  connections, dataSource attribute, 482
  Driver Manager
    Class.forName(), 463-464
    connections, 464-469
    database modifications, 473-475
    javax.sql.DataSource interface, 475-479
    jdbc.drivers property, 464
    ResultSet interface, 469-473
    ResultSetMetaData interface, 469-473
    statements, 465-469
  drivers, setting up on MySQL servers, 730
  URLs, 465
JDBC driver, 462-464
jdbc.drivers property, 464
jdbcConnection.jsp, code, 466-467
JDK (Java Development Kit), JavaBeans API, 166

JDK 1.2, downloading, 445
JDOM
DOMBuilder, 344
SAXBuilder, 344
Web site, 341
XML, 341-345
jdom.jar file, downloading, 344
JEE applications, security, 580-581
JJ2EE Java Petstore, 511
JMS (Java Messaging Service) 1.0 API, 10, 14
JNDI (Java Naming and Directory Interface), 435, 440, 475
APIs (Application Programmer's Interfaces), 441
applications, 445-446
architecture, 441
Context.INITIAL_CONTEXT_FACTORY environment property, values, 449
contexts, 454-455
directory services, 438-439
J2EE, 14, 446
J2EE RI (Reference Implementation), 446-455
javax.naming package, 442-443
javax.naming.directory package, 443-444
javax.naming.event package, 444-445
javax.naming.ldap package, 445
javax.naming.spi package, 445
JDK 1.2, downloading, 445
JSP, 455-458
name lookups, 453-454
naming conventions, 439-440
naming services, 435-440
objects, binding, 450-453
packages, 441
Service Providers, 440, 448-450
size of, 442
SPIs (Service Provider's Interfaces), 441
systems not using JNDI, architecture, 441
JSF (JavaServer Faces), 230
JSP 1.2 API, 10
JSP 2.0 specification, 95, 704
JSP Standard Tag Library. *See* JSTL
***JSP Unleashed*, Sams Publishing Web site, 204**
<jsp-file> tag, 114
JspRuntimeLibrary.handleGetProperty() method, 185
JspRuntimeLibrary.introspecthelper() method, parameters, 189
JspRuntimeLibrary.toString() method, 185
JSPs (JavaServer Pages), 41, 46. *See also* applications (JSP)
basic.jsp file (code), 42-45
code, embedding, 59-61
comments, 50-53, 686
configuring in web.xml, 114-116
containers, 50, 127
content, 49-50
declaration tags, 55-59
declarationTag Method.jsp (code), 57
defining, 49
directives, 61-69
EJBs, MyHelloWorld, looking up (code), 456-457
embedded Java code, 181
embeddingCode.jsp file (code), 59
expression tags, 53-55
J2EE Web container, 15
JavaBeans, 177-189
JNDI, 455-458
jspService method (code), 55, 60-61
lifecycle, 42
output, caching, 495
personalized (code), 601-603
SAX (Simple API for XML) output, 340
servlets, generated, source code, 50
shopping cart application case study, 265-272
simplePage.jsp file, 54
simplePage.jsp file (code), 53-54
SOAP, 408-413

syntax, 49
variables, 80-82
variables (predefined)
application object, 70-73
config object, 73
error-handling pages (code), 76
exceptions, 73-77
generated servlets (code), 75-76
generateError.jsp file (code), 74
implicit objects, 69
jspService method (code), 69-73
out object, 77-78
page object, 78
pageContext object, 78
processError.jsp file (code), 76
request object, 79
response object, 79-80
roles, 69-70
session object, 80
shared objects, 70-72
XML documents, processing output, 331, 340
writing, Tomcat and Web applications, 698

jspService method, 59, 125
code, 60, 72-73
useAndSet1.jsp file (code), 187-189

jspService method (code), 55, 60-61
include directive, 63
predefined variables, 69-70

jspService() method, 45, 190

JspWriter class, 77

<jsp:attribute> standard action, 97, 690

<jsp:body> standard action, 98, 690

<jsp:fallback> standard action, 95-96, 690

<jsp:forward> actions, 210

<jsp:forward> standard action, 88-89, 689

jsp:getProperty tag, 177, 183-185

<jsp:getProperty> standard action, 97, 689

<jsp:include> action, 231, 611

<jsp:include> standard action, 90-92, 689

<jsp:param> standard action, 89-90, 689

<jsp:params> standard action, 95, 689

<jsp:plugin> standard action, 94-95, 690

jsp:setProperty tag, 177, 185-189

<jsp:setProperty> standard action, 97, 689

jsp:useBean tag, 177, 180-183, 190-193
forms of, 178-179
syntax, 178-179
useAndSet1.jsp file (code), 186-189

<jsp:useBean> standard action, 97, 689

JSR (Java Specification Request), JCP (Java Community Process), 702

JSSE (Java Secure Socket Extension), downloading, 573

JSTL (JavaServer Pages Standard Tag Library), 49
Apache Software Foundation Web site, 162
attribute properties, 657-659, 662-664
basename attribute, 669
charEncoding attribute, 662
code mixtures, reading, 83
context attribute, 662
core actions, 656-662
Core tag library, 131
applicationScope, 132
conditional, 140
core actions, 132
c:catch action, 138-140
c:choose action, 142-143
c:forEach action, 145-148
c:forTokens action, 149-150
c:if action, 140-142
c:import action, 150-152
c:otherwise action, 144
c:out action, 133-135
c:param action, 152
c:redirect action, 155-156
c:remove action, 137-138
c:set action, 135-137
c:url action, 152-155
c:when action, 143-144
EL (expression language), 132

fmt:formatDate action, 161
fmt:formatNumber action, 161
fmt:message action, 161
formatting actions, 160-161
general-purpose, 132
Internationalization actions, 160-161
iterator core actions, 144-145
pageScope, 132
requestScope, 132
sessionScope, 132
SQL actions, 160
sql:query action, 160
sql:transaction action, 160
sql:update action, 160
URL-related, 150
XML core actions, 156-157
XML flow-control actions, 159-160
XML transform actions, 160
x:choose action, 159-160
x:forEach action, 159-160
x:if action, 159-160
x:otherwise action, 159-160
x:out action, 158-159
x:param action, 160
x:parse action, 157-158
x:set action, 159
x:transform action, 160
x:when action, 159-160
core tags, 128-129, 611, 687
curencyCode attribute, 673
curencySymbol attribute, 673
dateStyle attribute, 674-675
default attribute, 657
delims attribute, 661
EL, 131
escapeXML attribute, 657
Expression Language, 85
groupingUsed attribute, 673
HTML and Java code, mixing, 123-124
internationalization actions, 669-675
Internationalization tag library, EL (expression language), 132
internationalization tags, 687
interOnly attribute, 673
iteration example (code), 84
iterations with scriptlets (code), 83
Jakarta Web site, 163
Jakarta-Taglibs project, downloading, 82
Java Web Services Developer Pack, downloading, 83
key attribute, 670
maxFractionDigits attribute, 673
maxIntegerDigits attribute, 673
minFractionDigits attribute, 673
minIntegerDigits attribute, 673
name attribute, 663
parseLocale attribute, 673-674
pattern attribute, 673
prefix attribute, 669
pseudo-code (Java), mapping to c:choose action, 143
scope attribute, 658, 670
servlets, 123-124
SQL actions, 675-679
SQL tag library, EL (expression language), 132
SQL tags, 687
step attribute, 660
tag libraries, 125-131
tags, 83-84
target attribute, 658
templates, 124
third-party tag libraries, 162-163
timeStyle attribute, 674-675
timezone attribute, 674
type attribute, 673-674
URIs, 655-656
value attribute, 657-658, 663
var attribute, 658
varReader attribute, 662
XML actions, 332, 664-668
XML tag library, EL (expression language), 132
XML tags, 611, 687

jstl.jar file, 130
JTA (Java Transaction API) 1.0, 10
JVM (Java virtual machine), Java applets, 7

K

Kay, Michael (Saxon Web site), 348
key attribute (JSTL), 670
key stores, creating, 573
keys, 569-571
keystore tool, running, 573
keywords, transient, 169

L

lang (optional) attribute (XSLT), 639
language attribute, 66, 684
languages. ***See also*** **EL; HTML; XML; XPath**
- ECMAScript, 100
- Expression Language (JSTL), 85
- meta-language, definition, 317
- SAML (Security Assertions Markup Language), 584
- SGML (Standard Generalized Markup Language), 317
- SQL (Structured Query Language), 465
- WML (Wireless Markup Language), 370
- WSDL (Web Services Description Language), 387

Law, Debbie, 714
layers, J2EE applications, 13
LDAP (Lightweight Directory and Access Protocol), 439
left angle bracket (<), XML element names, 322
letters, XML element names, 322
Liberty Alliance Web site, 584
libraries. ***See also*** **Core tag library; custom tag libraries; JSTL; TLD**
- bean tag, Struts applications, 224
- HTML tag, Struts applications, 221-224
- Internationalization tag library, 132
- standard tag library, 479-491
- SQL tag library, 132
- tag
  - custom actions, 97-98
  - custom tag libraries, importing, 126-130
  - custom tags, 125, 130-131
  - description, 282
  - downloading, 163
  - existing libraries, 126
  - J2EE Web container, 16
  - Jakarta Taglibs project, 162-163
  - mapping (code), 127
  - Struts applications, 220-221
  - third-party, 162
- tag library usage (code), 69
- Web applications, 119
- XML tag library, 132

library files, Tomcat, 119
lifecycles
- entity Beans, 524-526
- Java servlets, 18-20
- JSPs (JavaServer Pages), 42
- methods, 524-526
- session Beans, 550-552
- Tag interface, 289-292

lifetimes, cookies, 238
Lightweight Directory and Access Protocol (LDAP), 439
limitations, cookies, 241
line numbers, error messages (Tomcat and Web applications), 698
linear scalability, definition, 710
Linux, 731-732
list command, 724
list method, 442-443
listBindings method, 442
listeners, 254, 444
listing, averager service methods, 392
listings. ***See*** **code**
lists, mailing lists, 333

literal types, EL (Expression Language), 101
liveDeploy attribute, 721
loading drivers, 463-464
local home interface, 513-514
local remote interface, 513
locales, 160
localhost.BookRetriever.java file (code), 421
localName parameter, 334
locateCDHomeInterface() method, 550
location paths, 349-350, 353
locations, global (Web applications), 119
LoggerServlet.java file (code), 37
logging
ServletContext object, 37-38
user behavior in ATG Dynamo, 601
logic, business, 124, 215, 231
logical operators, 102, 688
login forms, 589
login pages for personalization (Web applications), 589-592
.login-config element, 562, 567, 592
login.html file, 566-568, 589-590
login.jsp file (code), 271
loginFailed.html file, 567-568
logins, setting up for personalization (Web applications), 589
logout.jsp file (code), 248, 272
long getCreationTime() method, 252
long getLastAccessedTime() method, 252
LookupObject.java file (code), 453-454
LookupObjectSubContext.java file (code), 454-455
lookups (JNDI), 436, 453-454

M

Mailer taglib project (Jakarta), 163
mailing lists, XML-DEV Web site, 333
main.jsp file, 577-578
maintenance stage, JCP (Java Community Process), 703
mainWithParameters.jsp file, parameterized roles (code), 579-580
malformed documents (XML), viewing in Internet Explorer, 318
Manager servlets (Tomcat), 721-725
managers. *See* Driver Manager
map variable, 229
mapping
Java pseudo-code to c:choose action, 143
JDBC APIs, 462
requests, ActionMapping (Struts framework), 215
tag libraries (code), 127
mappings
Struts applications, 219-220
URL (uniform resource locator), 114-116
Mark, welcome.jsp file, 595
markup languages. *See also* HTML; XML
SAML (Security Assertions Markup Language), 584
SGML (Standard Generalized Markup Language), 317
WML (Wireless Markup Language), 370
marshaling parameters, unmarshaling, 512
match attribute, 360
match (optional) attribute (XSLT), 640
maxAge property (cookies), 240
maxAge value (cookies), 238
maxFractionDigits attribute (JSTL), 673
maxIntegerDigits attribute (JSTL), 673
maxProcessors attribute, 719
maxRows attribute, 483, 490, 676
McClanahan, Craig, 214, 230
Mel, welcome.jsp file, 595
members of committees, 702-703
members of expert groups, involvement with JCP (Java Community Process), 702
message digests, 572
message tag, 224
<message> element (WSDL), 416
message-driven Beans, 511

Message-Driven Beans for Asynchronous Messaging, 15
messages
email (Ormonds case study), sending, 626-627
error, 222, 622, 698, 730
SOAP, tcpmon tool, 401-402
meta-language, definition, 317
<method-permission> elements, 581
methods
* (asterisk), 531
addCookie(Cookie cookie), 236
averager services, 392
bind(), 452
BodySupport class, 297-298
BodyTag interface, 298
boolean absolute (int row), 470
boolean first(), 470
boolean isNew(), 252
boolean isSecure(), 577
boolean isUserInRole(String roleName), 576
boolean last(), 470
boolean next(), 469
boolean previous(), 469
boolean relative (int rows), 470
characters(), 339
close(), 467, 626
com.conygre.Cart class, 262
components, frameworks, 166
ConnectionEventListener interface, 494
Context.bind(), 451
Context.lookup(), 453
Context.rebind(), 451
Context.rename(), 453
Context.unbind(), 452
convertBean(), 550
Cookie[] getCookies(), 22
create, 520, 543
declarationTag Method.jsp (code), 57
destroy(), 20
doAfterBody(), 293, 296, 301-303
doEndTag(), 303
doGet(), 19, 210, 557, 618-619
doInitBody(), 298
DOM (Document Object Model), 326-327
doPost(), 19, 264
doStartTag(), 278, 296, 299, 303, 306
double getTotal(), 262
Double.parseDouble, 197
EJB lifecycle, 525-526
ejbActivate(), 526
ejbCreate(), 523, 550
ejbLoad(), 525
ejbPassivate(), 525-526
ejbPostCreate(), 523
ejbRemove(), 526, 550
ejbStore(), 525
encodeURL(String url), 242
endDocument(), 340
endElement(), 340
Enumeration getAttributeNames(), 252
executeQuery(), 466
executeUpdate(), 473
find service, 430
findAll, 516
findAncestorWithClass(), 310
finder, 516, 520-521
findForward(), 229
forward(), 88
GET, 31, 444
get (JavaBeans), 171-173
getAll, 444
getAttribute(), 175-176, 246
getAverage, 394
getChildNodes(), 327
getConnection(), 493
getDocumentElement(), 327
getElementsByTagNames(String), 327
getFirstChild(), 327
getHello(), code, 455-456
getLastChild(), 327
getMetaData(), 470

getNextSibling(), 327
getParameter(String name), 31
getParameterValues(String name), 31
getParentNode(), 327
getPreviousSibling(), 327
getRandomNumber(), 691
getRowsByIndex(), 504
getServletContext(), 34, 70
getServletName(), 34
getValue(), 246
HttpServletRequest object, 576-577
HttpServletRequest parameter, 22
HttpServletResponse parameter, 22
HttpSession getSession(), 22
include, 39
init(), 36, 40-41, 210, 557
int getMaxInactiveInterval(), 252
invalidate(), 248
isTextNode(), 330
java.io.InputStream getResourceAsStream(String path), 35
java.io.PrintWriter getWriter(), 22
java.io.ServletOutputStream getOutStream(), 22
java.net.URL getResource(String path), 35
java.util.Enumeration getHeaders(), 22
javax.servlet.http.HttpSession interfaces, 252
javax.servlet.jsp.jstl.core.LoopTagStatus interface, 147-148
javax.servlet.jsp.PageContext class, 78-79
javax.servlet.jsp.tagext.BodyTag interface, 298
javax.servlet.jsp.tagext.Tag interface, 279
JspRuntimeLibrary.handleGetProperty(), 185
JspRuntimeLibrary.introspecthelper(), parameters, 189
JspRuntimeLibrary.toString(), 185
jspService, 55, 59-61, 125, 187-189
  application object, 72
  include directive, 63
  predefined variables, 69-70
  shared objects, retrieving, 72-73
jspService(), 45, 190
lifecycle, 524
list, 442-443
listBindings, 442
locateCDHomeInterface(), 550
long getCreationTime(), 252
long getLastAccessedTime(), 252
node(), 644
Object getAttribute(String name), 35, 252
onClick, buttons, 165
org.xml.sax.helpers.DefaultHandler interface, 335
out.flush(), 89
out.print, invocation, 185
out.print(), 78
pageContext.findAttribute(), 185
pageContext.getAttribute(), 303
pageContext.setAttribute(), 303
parse(), 326
perform(), 227-229
PooledConnection interface, 493
PortableRemoteObject.narrow(), 457, 517
POST, 31
Principal getUserPrincipal(), 576
public abstract java.io.Reader getReader(), 298
public abstract java.lang.String getString(), 298
public abstract void writeOut(java.io.Writer w), 298
public boolean isFirst(), 148
public boolean isLast(), 148
public int doEndTag() throws JspException, 279
public int doInitBody() throws JspException, 298
public int doStartTag() throws JspException, 279
public int getBegin(), 148
public int getCount(), 148

public int getEnd(), 148
public int getIndex(), 148
public int getStep(), 148
public java.lang.Object getCurrent(), 148
public JspWriter getEnclosingWriter(), 298
public static, 274-275
public Tag getParent(), 279
public void clearBody(), 297
public void flush(), 297
public void release(), 279
public void setBodyContent(BodyContent b), 298
public void setPageContext(PageContext p), 279
public void setParent(Tag t), 279
random(), java.lang.Math class, 54
readObject, 169-170
rebind(), 452
registerTypeMapping(), 408
remove, 521
RequestDispatcher getRequestDispatcher(), 35
RequestDispatcher object, 38
ResltSet interface, 469-470
reverse(), 275
saveChanges(), 626
search, 444
searchCatalog(), 550
send(), 626
service(), 19
ServletConfig class, 34
ServletConfig getServletConfig(), 34
ServletContext getServletContext(), 252
ServletContext object, 35
session objects, 252
set (JavaBeans), 171-173
setAttribute(), 175-176, 246, 303
setBodyContent(), 299
setEntityContext(), 526
setString, 469
setStylesheet(), 375
setUpXMLURLs(), 618-619
setValue(), 246
startElement(), 334, 340
Statement interface, 465
String encodeURL(String url), 22
String getAuthType(), 577
String getHeader(String name), 22
String getId(), 252
String getInitParameter(String name), 35
String getMimeType(String file), 35
String getParameter(String name), 22
String getRealPath(String relativePath), 35
String getRemoteAddr(), 22
String getRemoteUser(), 577
String getServerInfo(), 35
String[] getParameterNames(), 22
Tag interface, 279
toString, 54
transform(), 375
trin(), 135
unbind(), 452
unsetEntityContext(), 526
validate(), 226, 621
valueBound(), 251
valueUnbound(), 251
void addCookie(Cookie cookie), 22
void addHeader(String name, String value), 22
void afterLast(), 470
void beforeFirst(), 470
void characters(char[] ch, int start, int length), 335
void endDocument(), 335
void endElement(String namespaceURI, String localName, String qName), 335
void endPrefixMapping(String prefix), 335
void error(SAXParseException e), 335
void fatalError(SAXParseException e), 335
void ignorableWhitespace(char[] ch, int start, int length), 335

void init(ServletConfig config), 263
void invalidate(), 252
void log(String message), 35
void notationDecl(String name, String publicID, String systemID), 335
void processingInstruction(String target, String data), 335
void resolveEntity(String publicID, String systemID), 335
void sendRedirect(String location), 22
void setAttribute(String name, Object value), 35, 252
void setContentType(String mime), 22
void setDocumentLocator(…), 335
void setItems(), 262
void setMaxInactiveInterval(int interval), 252
void setReset(), 262
void setStatus(int status), 22
void skippedEntity(String name), 335
void startDocument(), 335
void startElement(String namespaceURI, String localName, String qName, Attributes attrs), 335
void startPrefixMapping(String prefix, String namespaceURI), 335
void warning(SAXParseException e), 335
writeObject, 169-170

Microsoft
Passport Web site, 584
Web site, 348, 424

MIME (Multipart Internet Mail Extensions), 23, 625
minFractionDigits attribute (JSTL), 673
mini studies, shopping-cart application, 496-506
minIntegerDigits attribute (JSTL), 673
minProcessors attribute, 720
mm.mysql-2.x.x folder, 730
mode(optional) attribute (XSLT), 635, 641
Model 1 architecture, 201-202, 212
Model 2 architecture, 212
application flow, 211
CD JSP, 206-208
controller servlets, 208-211
frameworks, 213-214
included files, 208
MVC (Model View Controller) design, 202-203
requests, 203
Stock Bean, 204-206
Web site, demonstration of, 204

Model View Controller (MVC), 202-203
Model-View-Controller architecture, 167
models
J2EE security, 560-561
processing, XSLFO (XSL Formatting Objects), 377
servlet processing, 9

modes, transaction demarcation, 531
monitors, cluster (WebLogic 7 server), 710
moreCourseInfo.htm file (code), 244
MoreInfoRequest.java file (code), 245-246
moreInformationRequest.jsp file (code), 245
moreInformationRequestWithBean.jsp file (code), 247
Morgan, Brian, 264
mouse, dragging and dropping, 165
MSN Web site, personalization (Web applications), 585
MSXML Web site, 348
Multipart Internet Mail Extensions (MIME), 23, 625
multitemplate program (code), 360-361
multitemplate stylesheet (code), 361
multiTemplate.jsp file (code), 360-361
multithreaded ISAPI/NSAPI and single-threaded CGI, contrasting, 8
multithreading Java servlets, 20-21
MVC (Model View Controller) design, 202-203
MyAccount.jsp file (code), 62
MyHandler class, code, 336-339

MyHandler.java file (code), 336-339
MyHandler.jsp file (code), 335-336
MyHelloWorld EJB, looking up (code), 456-457
MySQL
database, downloading, 727
passwords, 476-477
server, 728-730
usernames, 477
mysql command-line tool, 729

N

name (optional) attribute (XSLT), 640
name attribute, 477, 720-721
JSTL, 663
XSLT, 636, 638, 642
name element, 282, 288
Name interface, 443
name lookups (JNDI), 453-454
name persistence, JNDI objects, 451
name resolution, MySQL servers, 730
name-from-attribute element, 307
named parameters (code), 367
named templates (code), 366-367
namedTemplate.xsl file, 366-368
names
composite, 454
distinguished, 439
objects, binding to (code), 450-451
usernames, MySQL, 477
XML elements, 322
namespace attribute, 653
namespace axis identifier, 352
namespaces
bookservice.wsdl file, 414-415
definition, 647
SOAP, 394-395
W3C Web site, 647
W3C XMLSchema-instance, 651
WSDL, 414-415
XML, case sensitivity, 355
XML Schemas, declaring, 647
XSLT, W3C Web site, 354
namespaceURI parameter, 334
namespace::* location path, 353
naming
exported variables, 667
struts-blank.war file, renaming, 216
naming conventions, JNDI (Java Naming and Directory Interface), 439-440
naming services (JNDI), 435-440
NamingEvent class, 444
NamingListener interface, 445
NDS (Novell Directory Services), 437
nested actions, averager.jsp file (code), 308
nested scoping, 307
Net installer, downloading, 731
Netscape
cookies, 238
EMBED tag, 96
vulnerabilities, Web site, 241
Netscape 6.2
basic authentication prompt, 563-564
browser-specific transformations, 375
certificates, viewing, 575
Network Information Service (NIS), 437
networks, NIS (Network Information Service), 437
newAddressForm.html, code, 473
NIS (Network Information Service), 437
no-argument constructors, 170-171
node() function, 353
node() method, 644
nodes
axis identifiers, 351-353
personNodes collection, 330
nodes of trees, DOM (Document Object Model) methods, 326-327
nodesets, 349
Nokia 7110 emulator, 376
Nokia WAP Toolkit, Web site, 375-376
noNamespaceSchemaLocation attribute, XML Schemas, 650-651
nonce, definition, 565

NONE value (<transport-guarantee> element), 575
nonrepeatable reads, 490
not() function, 354
Novell, NDS (Novell Directory Services), 437
Novell Directory Services (NDS), 437
NSAPI/ISAPI, contrasting multithreaded and single-threaded CGI, 8
NullLiteral type, EL (Expression Language), 101
numbers, error message lines (Tomcat and Web applications), 698

O

Object getAttribute(String name) method, 35, 252
OBJECT tag, 96
objects. *See also* XSLFO
accessing, 103-104, 688
Action, 218
business logic, encapsulating, 231
Struts applications, 227-230
ActionForm, 218, 224-227
ActionMapping, 218
application, 70-73
applicationScope, 689
arrays, SortedMap, 485
attributes of scope, 174
binding to names (code), 450-451
bound, looking up (code), 453-454
config, predefined variables, 73
Connection, 465
cookie, 689
custom, passing, 402-408
DataBean, 228
DataSource, 475, 493
DocumentBuilderObject, 326
exception, 73-76
file, 169
formatting, 377-381
header, 689
headerValues, 689
HttpServletRequest, methods, 576-577
HttpSession, summary, 252-253
implicit, 69, 80-81, 107-108, 688-689
initParam, 689
instance data, making private to objects, 171
intrinsic, ASP variables, 80-81
javax.mail.Session, 625
javax.servlet.ServletConfig, 33
JNDI, binding, 450-453
looking up from subcontexts (code), 454-455
OrderForm, populating, 621
ormonds.email.OrmondsEmail, 624
out, predefined variables, 77-78
page, predefined variables, 78
pageContext, 78-79, 278, 688
pageScope, 688
param, 689
paramValues, 689
profile, 592-595
Properties, 625
request, predefined variables, 79
RequestDispatcher, methods, 38
requestScope, 688
response, predefined variables, 79-80
ServiceInfo, 430
ServletConfig, 19
ServletContext, 35-38
session, 243-247, 625
methods, 252
predefined variables, 80
SessionListener interface, 253-256
sessions and events, 248-252
sessions, terminating, 248
tracking, 253
sessionScope, 689
shared, 70-72
Statement, 465
StringBuffer, email, 623
tag handler, 125

thread, 169
Throwable, 40
obtain a context (JNDI), 436
ODBC (Open Database Connectivity), JDBC API, 462
onClick method, buttons, 165
online bookstores, Web services, 385
online help, BEA WebLogic server, 732
Open Database Connectivity (ODBC), JDBC API, 462
<operation> element (WSDL), 417
operators
. (dot), 103, 643
arithmetic, 688
attribute path, @ (at sign), 643
child, / (forward slash), 643
descendant, // (double forward slash), 643
EL (Expression Language), 101-102, 688
logical, 688
OR, | (pipe), 644
parent path, .. (double dots), 643
relational, 688
wildcard path, * (asterisk), 643
[] (square brackets), 103
OR operators, | (pipe), 644
order (optional) attribute (XSLT), 639
OrderAction class, 623, 628
orderCourse.jsp file (code), 619-620
OrderForm object, populating, 621
org.apache.axis.AxisFault class, 401
org.apache.struts.action package, 215
org.apache.struts.action.Action class, 215
org.apache.struts.action.ActionForm class, 215
org.apache.struts.action.ActionMapping class, 215
org.apache.struts.action.ActionServlet class, 215
org.uddi4j.client.UDDIProxy class, 429
org.xml.sax.helpers.DefaultHandler interface, methods, 335
Ormonds case study
controller servlets, 616-619
controllers, 607
course information, 609-616
downloading, 605
email, 623-631
forms, processing, 619-623
home page, 606, 610-611
ISP (Internet Service Provider), 606
JavaBeans, 607
screen flow diagram, 607
Struts ActionServlet, 607
Web page architecture, 607-609
Web page templates, 607
Web site, technologies, 606
ormonds.email.OrmondsEmail object, 624
ormonds.struts.OrderAction (code), 622-623
ormonds.struts.OrderForm.java file (code), 620-621
OrmondsControllerServlet.java file (code), 616-618
OrmondsDataAccess.java file (code), 629
OrmondsEmail sender class, 626
OrmondsEmail.java file (code), 624-625
out object, predefined variables, 77-78
Out predefined variable, 686
out.flush() method, 89
out.print method, invocation, 185
out.print() method, 78
output
BasicFormProcessor servlet, 31
BasicServlet, 27
cookies.jsp file, 239
EL (Expression Language) expressions, 99
HelloWorld JSP, 457
JSP, 331, 340-341
main.jsp file, 578
namedTemplate.xsl file, 368
usingEL.jsp file, 99
usingIncludesWithParameters.jsp file, 92
XSLT (eXtensible Stylesheet Language: Transformations), 348-349

output documents (XML), code, 355
override attribute, 716

P

packages
javax, Web applications, 119
javax.ejb, 518
javax.mail, 625
javax.mail.internet, 625
javax.naming, 442-443
javax.naming.directory, 443-44
javax.naming.event, 444-445
javax.naming.ldap, 445
javax.naming.spi, 445
javax.servlet, 17
javax.servlet.http, 17
javax.xml.parsers, 325
JNDI, 441
org.apache.struts.action, 215
page attribute, <jsp:include> standard action, 91
page directive, 63
attributes, 64-66, 682-684
autoFlush attribute, 64
buffer attribute, 64
contentType attribute, 64
errorPage attribute, 65
extends attribute, 65
import attribute, 65
info attribute, 65
isErrorPage attribute, 65
isThreadSafe attribute, 65
language attribute, 66
PageDirective.jsp file (code), 66-68
pageEncoding attribute, 66
session attribute, 66
page errors, 697
page object, predefined variables, 78
Page predefined variable, 686
page scope, 174-176
pageContext implicit object, 107
pageContext object, 78-79, 278, 688
pageContext predefined variable, 686
pageContext.findAttribute() method, 185
pageContext.getAttribute() method, 303
pageContext.setAttribute() method, 303
PageDirective.jsp file (code), 66-68
pageEncoding attribute (page directive), 66
pages. *See also* home pages; JSPs; Web pages
administration pages, email (Ormonds case study), 630-631
ASPs (Active Server Pages), 41, 80-82
error, 73
pageScope, 132
pageScope implicit object, 107
pageScope object, 688
param implicit object, 107
param object, 689
param.xsl file, code, 367
parameterized roles, web.xml file (code), 579
parameters
attrs, 334
creating URLs (code), 154
forms, bookProcess.jsp file (code), 195
global, stylesheets (code), 369-370
globalParam.jsp file, code, 368-369
globalParam.xsl file, code, 369-370
HttpServletRequest, 21-23
HttpServletResponse, 21-23
initialization, passing (code), 116
JspRuntimeLibrary.introspecthelper() method, 189
localName, 334
mainWithParameters.jsp file (code), 579-580
marshaling and unmarshaling, 512
named, code, 367
namespaceURI, 334
param.xsl file, code, 367
passing, 89-90, 368-369
qName, 334
request, 197-199

servlet initialization, setting (code), 33
ServletContext object, 35-37
startElement() method, 334
url, 464
values, bookProcessBean.jsp file (code), 196
Web applications, setting (code), 35-36
ParameterServlet.java file, init() method, 36
ParameterServlet.java file (code), 33-34
paramValues object, 108, 689
parent axis identifier, 351
parent path operators, .. (double dots), 643
parent::* location path, 353
parse() method, 326
parseDoc JSTL.jsp file (code), 332
parseDoc.jsp file (code), 328-329
parseJDOM.jsp file (code), 342-343
parseLocale attribute (JSTL), 673-674
parser errors, 697
parsing XML (Extensible Markup Language), 325
code, 342-343
DOM (Document Object Model) APIs, 326-333
JDOM (Java Document Object Model) APIs, 341-345
SAX (Simple API for XML) APIs, 333-340
passing
custom objects, 402-408
initialization parameters (code), 116
parameters, 89-90, 368-369
passivating entity Beans, 526
Passport Web site, 584
password attribute, 481
passwords, MySQL, 476-477
path attribute, 715
paths, 349-350, 353. *See also* XPath
pattern attribute (JSTL), 673
PDFs, tariffs.fo file, 378
Peng, Alan, 231
people.xml file (code), 317-318, 355
people.xslt file (code), 355-356
/people/person/name location path, evaluation of, 350
peopleAttrs.xml file (code), 323-324
perform() method, 227-229
performance, connection pools, 475
period (.), XML element names, 322
persistence
CMP (Container Managed Persistence) and BMP (Bean Managed Persistence), comparing, 518
cookies, 240
JavaBeans, 168-170
<persistence-type> element, 529-530
persistence, name persistence, (JNDI), 451
persistent cookies, personalization (Web applications), 586
person element, 356
personalization (Web applications)
forms, 586-587
login pages, 589-592
logins, setting up, 589
persistent cookies, 586
profile object, 592-595
registration, 586-587
rule-based, 600
rule-based personalization engines, 600-603
user profiles, 587-588
user registration, 598-600
Web pages, 595-598
Web sites, 585-586
web.xml file (code), 591-592
personalized JSP (code), 601-603
personNodes collection, 330
phantom reads, 490
pipe, | OR operator, 644
PIs (processing instructions), 320
platforms
J2EE, (Java 2 Enterprise Edition), 12
XP, Java Plugin, 731

plugin.jsp file, 94-96
plugins, Java Plugin, 93-96
PooledConnection interface, 493-494
populating OrderForm object, 621
port 8080, Tomcat, 695
port attribute, 718-719
portable data (XML), 315-316
PortableRemoteObject.narrow() method, 457, 517
portal home pages, 408
portals, 709
<portType> element (WSDL), 416
POST method, 31
preceding axis identifier, 352-353
preceding location path, 353
preceding-sibling axis identifier, 352
preceding-sibling location path, 353
predefined variables
- application, 70-73, 686
- config, 73, 686
- exception, 73-77, 686
- implicit objects, 69
- jspService method (code), 69-70
- Out, 686
- out object, 77-78
- Page, 78, 686
- pageContext, 78, 686
- request, 79, 686
- response, 79-80, 687
- roles, 69-70
- Session, 80, 687

predicates (XPath), 354, 644
prefix attribute (JSTL), 669
PreparedStatement, 468, 487
preparedStatement.jsp, code, 468-469
presentation formats, XML, 347
presentation logic and business logic, separating, 124
<prim-key-class> element, 530
primary key class, 513
primitive datatypes, wrapper classes, 197
Principal class (JAAS), 583
Principal getUserPrincipal() method, 576
principals, J2EE security model, 561
PrintWriter, 31
priority (optional) attribute (XSLT), 641
private key encryption, 570
privileged attribute, 715
procedural programming, XSLT declarative template programming, 366-370
process timelines, JCP Web site, 703
processError.jsp file (code), 76
processes, XSLT (XSL Transformations), 348
processing
- body content, 292-297
- encoded URLs (code), 155
- forms, for Ormonds case study, 619-623
- HTML form data, 28-31
  - requests, forwarding to servlets, 38-39
  - servlet initialization, 32-34
  - ServletContext object, 35-38
- XML documents, 328-331, 340

processing instructions (Pis), 320
processing models
- servlets, 9
- XSLFO (XSL Formatting Objects), 377

processing-instruction instruction (XSLT), 357
processors
- Xalan (XSLT), 357-359
- XSLT, Web sites, 348

processPerson template, 368
productSearch.jsp file (code), 554
profile object, 592-595
Profile.java file (code), 594-595
profiles, user (Web applications), 587-588
programmatic security
- HttpServletRequest object methods, 576-577
- J2EE security model, 561
- main.jsp file, 577-578
- mainWithParameters.jsp file, code, 579-580
- web.xml file, code, 579

programming
declarative template programming (XSLT), 360-361
procedural programming, 366-370
subsets, 363-365
templates built in, 362-363
procedural, XSLT declarative template programming, 366-370
single template programming (exemplar), 354-359
programs, XSLT multitemplate (code), 360-361
projects, 162-163
prompt.jsp file (code), 153-154
prompting for information (code), 153-154
prompts, basic authentication in Netscape 6.2, 563-564
properties
buttons, 165
components, frameworks, 166
Context.INITIAL_CONTEXT_FACTORY environment, values, 449
currentUser.interest, 597
c:out action, attributes, 657
c:remove action, attributes, 658
c:set action, attributes, 658
JavaBeans, 168, 170
accessing and setting from JSPs, 183-189
bound, 173
constrained, 173
indexed, 173
javax.xml.parsers.DocumentBuilderFactory, 326
javax.xml.parsers.SAXParserFactory, 325
jdbc.drivers, 464
maxAge (cookies), 240
request parameters, 197-199
SortedMap, code, 485
Properties object, 625
protected resources
clients, login.html file, 567-568
Web site, 575
protocols. ***See also*** **HTTP**
LDAP (Lightweight Directory and Access Protocol), 439
SOAP (Simple Object Access Protocol), 387
providers of certificates, viewing on Internet Explorer, 572
pseudo-code (Java), mapping to c:choose action, 143
public
involvement with JCP (Java Community Process), 702
no-argument constructors, declaring as, 171
public abstract java.io.Reader getReader() method, 298
public abstract java.lang.String getString() method, 298
public abstract void writeOut(java.io.Writer w) method, 298
public boolean isFirst() method, 148
public boolean isLast() method, 148
public draft stage, JCP (Java Community Process), 703
public int doEndTag() throws JspException method, 279
public int doInitBody() throws JspException method, 298
public int doStartTag() throws JspException methods, 279
public int getBegin() method, 148
public int getCount() method, 148
public int getEnd() method, 148
public int getIndex() method, 148
public int getStep() method, 148
public java.lang.Object getCurrent() method, 148
public JspWriter getEnclosingWriter() method, 298
public key encryption, 570
public static final int EVAL_BODY_INCLUDE field, 280

public static final int EVAL_PAGE fields, 280
public static final int SKIP_BODY field, 280
public static final int SKIP_PAGE field, 280
public static method, implementing (code), 275
public static methods, 274
public Tag getParent() method, 279
public void clearBody() method, 297
public void flush() methods, 297
public void release() method, 279
public void setBodyContent(BodyContent b) method, 298
public void setPageContext(PageContext p) method, 279
public void setParent(Tag t) method, 279

Q

qName parameter, 334
queries
- SQL, 465, 469
- strings, 195

<query> element, 531
<query-method> element, 531
question mark (?), 469
quotation marks, 323

R

RAD (rapid-application development), JavaBeans, 165
random() method, java.lang.Math class, 54
rapid-application development (RAD), JavaBeans, 165
RDBMS (Relational Database Management Systems), JNDI directory services, 439
readers, extended, 152
readObject method, 169-170
reads, 489-490
RealMethods framework Web site, 233
rebind() method, 452
rebindings (JNDI), 437, 451-452
Red Hat Linux, downloading, 731
redirecting (standard action), 88
redirectPort attribute, 720
Reference class, 443
reference implementation. ***See*** **RI**
Regexp tablib project (Jakarta), 163
registerTypeMapping() method, 408
registration, personalization (Web applications), 586-587, 598-600
registration forms, 589
RegistrationServlet.java file (code), 598-599
registries
- IBM, 424
- IBM Test Registry, UDDI entry (code), 424-425
- Microsoft, 424
- RMI registry, JNDI naming services, 437
- UDDI, information, setting up, 430

Relational Database Management Systems (RDBMS), JNDI directory services, 439
relational operators, 101-102, 688
relative location paths, 350
Release Candidate 1 version (Apache Axis), 390
reload command, 724
reloadable attribute, 715
remote class, 514
remote interfaces, 512-514, 519, 544-546
Remote Method Invocation over IIOP (RMI) API, 11
RemoteException, 401
remove command, 724
remove methods, 521
removeAttribute.jsp file (code), 138
renaming JNDI objects, 453
request object, predefined variables, 79

request parameters
- bookProcessBeanAllParams.jsp file (code), 199
- bookProcessBeanNamedParams.jsp file (code), 197-198

request predefined variable, 686
request scope, 175-176
RequestDispatcher getRequestDispatcher() method, 35
RequestDispatcher object, methods, 38
requestedPage.jsp file, 174
requests
- GET, 618
- HTTP, 19
- mapping, ActionMapping (Struts framework), 215
- Model 2 architecture, 203
- servlets, 20, 38-39
- SOAP, 398-399, 405

requestScope, 132
requestScope implicit object, 107
requestScope object, 688
required element, 288
reserved words, in EL, 108
resolutions, name (MySQL servers), 730
resource bundles, 160
resources
- access control, Web applications, 560
- *Developing Java Servlets*, 264
- *Essential XML Quick Reference*, 354
- protected, 575, 567-568
- *Sams Teach Yourself XML in 21 Days*, 315
- *Tomcat Rapid Working Knowledge*, 714
- *XML and Web Services Unleashed*, 354
- *XML Bible*, Second Edition, 381

resources command, 724
response object, predefined variables, 79-80
response predefined variable, 687
responses
- Averager Web service SOAP response (code), 396
- SOAP from BookService (code), 406
- to SOAP invalid requests (code), 399

ResultSet interface, 469-473
resultSetDisplay.jsp, code, 471-472
resultSetDisplayQueryTag.jsp, code, 484
resultSetDisplayWithTagLibrary.jsp, code, 480
ResultSetMetaData interface, 469-473
reverse() method, 275
rewriting URLs (uniform resource locators), 241-243
RI (Reference Implementation) (J2EE), 446
- initial contexts, 447
- JNDI, 448-455

right angle bracket (>), XML element names, 322
RMI (Remote Method Invocation over IIOP) API, 11
RMI registry, JNDI naming services, 437
roles
- .class files, 513
- J2EE security model, 561
- parameterized, web.xml file (code), 579
- predefined variables, 69-70
- scope in Web applications, 174
- session Beans, 542
- SOAP (Simple Object Access Protocol), 387
- UDDI (Universal Description, Discovery, and Integration), 387
- WSDL (Web Services Description Language), 387

roles command, 725
root elements, <schema>, 647
Root folder, Web applications, 118
RT (runtime expression values), 131
RT expressions, JSTL URIs, 655
rtexprvalue element, 288
rtexprvalues, 131
rule-based personalization (Web applications), 600
rule-based personalization engines, personalization (Web applications), 600-603
rules, ATG Dynamo control center, 601

running
J2EE applications, 536-541
Jakarta Tomcat, 25
keystore tool, 573
SQL scripts, on MySQL servers, 729
Tomcat, 573-575
runtime errors, debugging, 697
runtime expression values (RT), 131

S

SAML (Security Assertions Markup Language), Web site, 584
Sams Publishing Web site, 26, 238, 514, 575
chapter sample code, 165
chapter18Personalization.war file, downloading, 587
JSP Unleashed, 204
Ormonds case study, downloading, 605
***Sams Teach Yourself XML in 21 Days*, 315**
saveChanges() method, 626
SAX (Simple API for XML), 325
APIs, XML, parsing, 333-340
code, 335-336
Web site, 333
XML documents, parsing, 333
SAXBuilder, 344
Saxon Web site, 348
SAXParser class, 325
SAXParserFactory class, 325
scalability, 710-711
scenarios, ATG Dynamo Application Server, 709
<schema> element, 647-648
schemaLocation attribute
of import element, 653
XML Schemas, 650-651
schemas. *See* XML Schema
Schmelzer, Ron, 354
scope
application, 47, 176-177
assigning to extended readers, 152
attributes, 174
EL (expression language), 132
includedPage.jsp file, 174
page, 48, 174-176
request, 48, 175-176
requestedPage.jsp file, 174
session, 47-48, 175-177
trees, 439
Web applications, 46
application scope, 47, 176-177
page scope, 48, 174-176
request scope, 48, 175-176
role of, 174
session scope, 47-48, 175-177
scope attribute, 481-483, 486, 658, 667, 670
scope element, 307
scoped attributes, 136
scoping nested, 307
screen flow diagrams, Ormonds, 607
screens
c:forEach action, 147
WebLogic 7 Application Server, configuration, 581
scriplets
code, embedding, 59-61
iterations, code, 83
scripting languages, EL (Expression Language), 100
scripting variables
emptyTagWithAttrsExport.jsp file (code), 303-304
exporting, 304
tags interacting, 303-307
scriptlet tag, 692
scripts, SQL, 729
search bases, 439
search filters, 439
search methods, 444
searchCatalog() method, 550

Secure Sockets Layer. ***See*** **SSL**
security
administration pages (Ormonds case study), 630-631
<assembly-descriptor> element, 581
<auth-method> element, 566
authentication, 561
digest, 564-566
form-based, 566-569
HTTP (Hypertext Transfer Protocol), 563-564
web.xml file, 562-563
certificates, viewing, 575
CONFIDENTIAL value (<transport-guarantee> element), 575
constraints, defining in web.xml file (code), 562
cookies, 239-240
declarative, J2EE security model, 561
ejb-jar.xml file (code), 580
HTTPS (Hypertext Transfer Protocol over Secure Socket Layer)
asymmetric key encryption, 570-571
digital certificates, 571-572
digital signatures, 572-573
Java, 573-575
private key encryption, 570
public key encryption, 570
SSL (Secure Socket Layer), 572-575
symmetric key encryption, 569
INTEGRAL value (<transport-guarantee> element), 575
J2EE applications, 580-583
J2EE security model, 560-561
JSSE (Java Secure Socket Extension), 573
key stores, creating, 573
keystore tool, running, 573
Liberty Alliance Web site, 584
<login-config> element, 562, 567
message digests, 572
<method-permission> elements, 581
Microsoft, Passport Web site, 584
NONE value (<transport-guarantee> element), 575
programmatic
HttpServletRequest object methods, 576-577
J2EE security model, 561
main.jsp file (code), 577-578
main.jsp file output, 578
mainWithParameters.jsp file (code), 579-580
web.xml file (code), 579
protected resources, Web site, 575
requirements, 559
SAML (Security Assertions Markup Language), Web site, 584
Sams Publishing Web site, 575
<security-role> element, 581
server.xml file (code), 574
single sign on, 584
SSL (Secure Socket Layer), 569
<transport-guarantee> element, values, 575
<user-data-constraint> element, 575
Web applications, 560
Web sites, 559-560
web.xml file, customized for SSL (Secure Socket Layer) (code), 574-575
WebLogic 7 Application Server, configuration screen, 581
Security Assertions Markup Language (SAML), Web site, 584
security services, J2EE containers, 14
<security-constraint> element, 592
<security-role> element, 581
securityhashing algorithms, definition, 565
select (optional) attribute (XSLT), 635, 638-639, 642
Select attribute (XSLT), 641
self axis identifier, 351
self::* location path, 353
semicolon (;), 54, 124
send() method, 626

Server element, 718
Server Watch Web site, 706
server-side applications, 8
server-side components (JavaBeans), 166
server.xml
code, 476
DataSource, configuring, 497
server.xml file, 573-574
Connector element, 718-720
containers, configuring, 717-721
elements, 717
Engine element, 720
Host element, 720-721
Server element, 718
Service element, 718-720
Tomcat, configuring (code), 713-714
servers. ***See also*** **BEA WebLogic server**
application, caching, 506
ATG Dynamo Application, 256-258
ATG Dynamo Application Server, 708-709
crashes, resolving, 257
J2EE, 446
J2EE application, 705-711
JBoss Application Server, Web site, 711
MySQL, 727-730
Web applications, 8-10
welcome pages, WebLogic examples, 537
Service element, 718-720
Service Provider's Interface (SPIs), JNDI, 441
service providers, JNDI, 440, 448-450
<service> element (WSDL), 418
service() method, 19
ServiceException, 401
ServiceInfo object, 430
services
DNS (Domain Name Service), 437
EJB containers, 509
J2EE containers, 14
JNDI directory, 438-439
JNDI naming, 435-440
NDS (Novell Directory Services), 437
NIS (Network Information Service), 437
RMI registry, 437
transient, 451
<servlet> element, 114
<servlet> tag, 114
<servlet-mapping> element, 114
servlet.https, javax.servlet.http package, 17
ServletConfig class, methods, 34
ServletConfig getServletConfig() method, 34
ServletConfig object, 19
ServletContext getServletContext() method, 252
ServletContext object, 35-38
ServletException, throwing (code), 40-41
ServletLifeCycleMethods.java file (code), 18-19
servlets
ActionServlet, Struts framework, 215
Apache Axis, averager services methods, listing, 392
BrowserDependentServlet.java file (code), 373-375
controller, 202, 593
Ormonds case study, 616-619
shopping cart application case study, 262-265
controller servlets, Model 2 architecture, 208-211
generated
code, 51-52, 75-76
PageDirective.jsp file (code), 67-68
source code, 50
HTML code, storing, 124
instance variables, 57
JSPs, 50, 127
jsp:getProperty tag, useBean2.jsp file (code), 185
JSTL, 123-124
Tomcat, 721-725

useBean1.jsp file (code), 182-183
void init(ServletConfig config) method, 263
servlets (Java), 10
basic.jsp file (code), 43-45
BasicFormProcessor, 30-32
BasicServlet, output, 27
BasicServlet.java file (code), 21
exception handling, 39-41
ForwardingServlet.java file (code), 39
HttpServletRequest parameter, 21-23
HttpServletResponse parameter, 21-23
initialization parameters, setting (code), 33
initializing, 32-34
J2EE Web container, 15
javax.servlet package, 17
javax.servlet.http.HttpServlet class, 17
javax.servlet.Servlet interface, 17
lifecycle, 18-20
LoggerServlet.java file (code), 37
multithreading, 20-21
ParameterServlet.java file (code), 33-34
processing model, 9
requests, forwarding to, 38-39
requests for, 20
ServletException, throwing (code), 40-41
ServletLifeCycleMethods.java file (code), 18-19
web.xml file (code), 27
Servlets 2.3 API, 10
session attribute (page directive), 66
session Beans, 511, 541
creating, 543
deploying, 552-555
home interface, create methods, 543
implementation class, 546, 550
J2EE Blueprints, 542
lifecycle, 550-552
remote interface, 544-546
role of, 542
stateful, 542-543, 550
stateless, 542-543, 550
Session Beans for Business Logic, 14
session command, 725
Session Manager, ATG Dynamo application server, 256
session objects, 243-247, 625
methods, 252
predefined variables, 80
SessionListener interface, 253-256
sessions, 248-253
tracking, 253
Session predefined variable, 687
session scope, 175-177
session tracking
cookies, 235-241
session failover, 256-258
session objects, 243-247
HttpSession object summary, 252-253
SessionListener interface, 253-256
sessions and events, 248-252
sessions, terminating, 248
tracking, 253
shopping cart application case study
controller servlets, 262-265
Java beans, 259-262
JSPs, 265-272
URLs (uniform resource locators), rewriting, 241-243
session-scoped attributes, 137-138
SessionCount.java file (code), 254
SessionListener interface, 253-256
sessions
backups, configuring, 258
counters, 255
events, 248-252
failover, 256-258
HttpSessionBindingListener, 251
iPlanet, 253
javax.mail.Session, creating, 625
terminating, 248
Tomcat, 253
Web Logic, 253
sessionScope, 132

sessionScope object, 108, 689
set method, JavaBeans, 171-173
setAttribute() method, 175-176, 246, 303
setAttributes.jsp file (code), 136-137
setBodyContent() method, 299
setEntityContext() method, 526
Sets, definition, 250
setString method, 469
setStylesheet() method, 375
setUpXMLURLs() method, 618-619
setValue() method, 246
SGML (Standard Generalized Markup Language), 317
shared objects, 70-72
shopping cart application case study
- controller servlets, 262-265
- Java beans, 259-262
- JSPs, 265-272

shopping Web sites, homepages, 265
shopping-cart application, 496-506
ShoppingCartController.java file (code), 209-210, 262-263, 593
shoppingCartTables.sql, code, 496-497
shutdown attribute, 718
signatures
- digital, 572-573
- getAttribute() method, 175-176
- readObject method, 169
- setAttribute() method, 175-176
- writeObject method, 169

SilverStream eXtend Web site, 706
Simple API for XML. ***See*** **SAX**
Simple Object Access Protocol. ***See*** **SOAP**
simplePage.jsp file, 53-54
simpleType element, defining in XML Schemas, 649-650
single quotation mark ('), attributes, 323
single sign on (security), 584
single template programming (exemplar), 354-359
single templates (XSLT), code, 355-356
single-threaded CGI and multithreaded ISAPI/NSAPI, contrasting, 8
SiteMinder 5 Web site, 584
skeleton class, EJBs, 512
SKIP_BODY, 296
Skonnard, Aaron, 354
slashes
- / (forward), 322, 349, 643
- double forward, // descendant operator, 643

SOAP (Simple Object Access Protocol)
- Averager Web service response (code), 396
- messages, tcpmon tool, 401-402
- namespaces, 394-395
- requests (code), 394
  - BookService (code), 405-406
  - invalid (code), 398-399
- roles, 387
- Web services, 393-394
  - custom objects, passing, 402-408
  - error handling, 398-401
  - Java clients, building, 396-402
  - JSP, 408-413
  - tcpmon tool, 401-402
  - XML Spy, 395-396
- Web services and XML, 387
- XML, 394
- XML Schemas, 652-653

software components, 166
SortedMap array object, 485
SortedMap property, code, 485
source code
- Apache Struts, downloading, 224
- generated servlets, 50

sources
- autogenerated, 88
- data, configuring, 475
- events, 444

special characters, XML (Extensible Markup Language), 322
specifications
- JavaBeans, 166, 168
- JSP 2.0, 95, 704

JSR (Java Specification Request), 702
XPath, W3C Web site, 349
XSLT, W3C Web site, 348
specifications XML 1.0, 317
SPIs (Service Provider's Interfaces), JNDI (Java Naming and Directory Interface), 441
Spy 4.3 (XML), ejb-jar.xml file structure, 528
Spy (XML), 395-396
SQL (Structured Query Language)
actions, grouping, 488
Admin tool, 728
dataSource attribute, 675-676
maxRows attribute, 676
queries, 465, 469
scripts, running, 729
sql attribute, 676
startRow attribute, 676
SQL actions
global attributes (standard tag library), 490-491
JSTL, 676-679
sql:param (standard tag library), 487-488
sql:query, 160
sql:query (standard tag library), 482-485
sql:setDataSource (standard tag library), 481-482
sql:transaction, 160
sql:transaction (standard tag library), 488-490
sql:update, 160
sql:update (standard tag library), 486-487
standard tag library, 481
sql attribute, 483, 486, 676
SQL tag library, EL (expression language), 132
SQL tags, 84
JSTL, 687
standard tag library, 480
sql:dateParam action, 679
sql:param (standard tag library), 487-488
sql:param action, 676
sql:query (standard tag library), 482-485
sql:query action, 160, 503, 676-677
sql:setDataSource action, 481-482, 675-676
sql:transaction (standard tag library), 488-490
sql:transaction action, 160, 678-679
sql:update (standard tag library), 486-487
sql:update action, 160, 678
square brackets ([]), XPath predicates, 644
square brackets operator ([]), 103
SSE, JSSE (Java Secure Socket Extension), 573
SSL (Secure Socket Layer)
asymmetric key encryption, 571
Java, 573-575
security, 569
symmetric key encryption, 571
web.xml file, customized (code), 574-575
stages, JCP (Java Community Process), 703
standard action elements, 177
standard actions, 87
custom actions, tag libraries, 97-98
forward, 88-90
include, <jsp:include>, templating Web pages, 90-92
Java Plugin, 93-96
JavaBeans, 97-98
<jsp:attribute>, 97, 690
<jsp:body>, 98, 690
<jsp:fallback>, 95-96, 690
<jsp:forward>, 88-89, 689
<jsp:getProperty>, 97, 689
<jsp:include>, 90-92, 689
<jsp:param>, 89-90, 689
<jsp:params>, 95, 689
<jsp:plugin>, 94-95, 690
<jsp:setProperty>, 97, 689
<jsp:useBean>, 97, 689
parameters, passing, 89-90

redirecting, 88
Web pages, templating with <jsp:include> standard action, 90-92
Standard Generalized Markup Language (SGML), 317
Standard taglib project (Jakarta), 163
standard tag library,actions, 479
global attributes, 490-491
sql:param, 487-488
sql:query, 482-485
sql:setDataSource, 481-482
sql:transaction, 488-490
sql:update, 486-487
standard.jar file, 130
standards
cookies, Web sites, 238
J2EE (Java 2 Enterprise Edition), 10-13
standards support, J2EE application servers, 707
start command, 724
startElement() method, 334, 340
startRow attribute, 483, 676
state of entity Beans, 524
stateful session Beans, 542-543, 550
stateless session Beans, 542-543, 550
Statement interface, 465
Statement object, 465
statements
CallableStatement, 469
databases, closing, 467
JDBC drivers, 465-469
PreparedStatement, 468, 487
System.out.print(), Web applications, 698
states, community review, 702
static initializers, 463-464
static Java functions, in EL, 110
step attribute (JSTL), 660
STL, EL, RT (runtime expression values), 131
Stock attribute, 265
Stock Bean, Model 2 architecture, 204-206
stock beans, populating, 503
Stock.java file (code), 204-206, 260-261, 498, 500
stop command, 724
stores, key (creating), 573
storing
files in Tomcat, 50
HTML code, 124
StreamResult class, 359
streams, 168
StreamSource class, 359
String encodeURL(String url) method, 22
String getAuthType() method, 577
String getHeader(String name) method, 22
String getId() method, 252
String getInitParameter(String name) method, 35
String getMimeType(String file) method, 35
String getParameter(String name) method, 22
String getRealPath(String relativePath) method, 35
String getRemoteAddr() method, 22
String getRemoteUser() method, 577
String getServerInfo() method, 35
String type, EL (Expression Language), 101
StringBuffer object, email, 623
strings, query, 195
String[] getParameterNames() method, 22
Structured Query Language (SQL), 465
structures
deployment folders, 531-532
directories for Web applications, 281
ejb-jar.xml file, 528
folder, deploying, 120
J2EE application folders, 531
tags, hierarchical, 307-311
Web applications, 117
Web pages, 232
WSDL documents, 415

XML (Extensible Markup Language), 317-324
XML Schemas, 647-648
Struts ActionServlet, 607
Struts, Apache, source code, 224
Struts applications
Action objects, 227-230
ActionForm objects, 224-227
architecture, 218
bean tag library, 224
building, 216-218
data validation, 226-227
error messages, 222
HTML tag library, 221-224
mappings, setting up, 219-220
tag libraries, 220-221
Web pages, 220-224
Struts framework, 214-216
Struts framework (Apache), 620
Struts project (Jakarta), 162
struts-blank.war file, 216, 221
struts-config.xml file (code), 219-220
stub class, EJBs, 512
stubs, Web services, accessing, 419
style, Web pages, 232
stylesheets. ***See also*** **XSLT**
compiling into Java classes, 358
CSS (Cascading Styl Sheets), 232
global parameters (code), 369-370
globalParam.xsl file, code, 369-370
parameters, passing to (code), 368-369
tariffsHTML.xslt file (code), 371-372
tariffsWML.xslt file (code), 372-373
subcontexts, objects (code), 454-455
Subject class (JAAS), 583
subsets, 363-365
summaries, HttpSession object, 252-253
Sun Microsystems. ***See also*** **J2EE RI (Reference Implementation)**
J2EE (Java 2 Enterprise Edition) standard, 13
J2EE Blueprints, EJBs, 510
NIS (Network Information Service), 437
Web site, 445, 449, 511
Sun Microsystems Web site, J2EE Reference Implementation, 708
Swing classes, Java tutorial Web site, 203
switches, -tt (trace templates), 362
symmetric key encryption, 569-571
syntax
comments, 685-686
directives, 61, 681-685
EL (Expression Language), 98, 687-689
formatting objects, 381
HTML comments, 685
Java code, 690-692
Java comments, 686
JSP comments, 686
JSPs (JavaServer Pages), 49
jsp:setProperty tag, 186
jsp:useBean tag, 178-179
JSTL
core tags, 687
c:catch action, 658
c:choose action, 659
c:forEach action, 660
c:forTokens action, 661
c:if action, 659
c:import action, 661
c:otherwise action, 660
c:out action, 656
c:param action, 663
c:redirect action, 663
c:remove action, 658
c:set action, 657
c:url action, 662
c:when action, 659
internationalization tags, 687
SQL tags, 687
XML tags, 687
JSTL internationalization
fmt:bundle action, 669
fmt:formatDate action, 674
fmt:formatNumber action, 672

fmt:message action, 670
fmt:param action, 670
fmt:parseDate action, 674
fmt:parseNumber action, 673
fmt:requestEncoding action, 671
fmt:setBundle action, 669
fmt:setLocale action, 669
fmt:setTimezone action, 671
fmt:timezone action, 671
named templates, 366
predefined variables, 686-687
SQL, 675-679
[] (square brackets), | OR operator, 644
standard actions, 689-690
XML (Extensible Markup Language), 317-319, 664-668
XPath, 642-644
XSLT, 635-642
System.out.print() statements, 698
systemId attribute (XML), 664
systems
component-based, 167
not using JNDI, architecture, 441

T

tablesSetUp.sql file (code), 587-588, 627
tag, <element>, 648
Tag Extensions, 273-274
tag handler objects, 125
tag handlers, 68
Averager.java file (code), 308-309
custom tags, 277
DisplayResult.java file (code), 309-310
interfaces, 274
Tag interface, 274
custom tags, 276
fields, 280
lifecycle, 289-292
methods, 279
TagLifecycle.java file (code), 289-291
tag libraries, 125. *See also* custom tag libraries
bean, Struts applications, 224
custom actions, 97-98
downloading, 163
existing libraries, 126
HTML, Struts applications, 221-224
J2EE Web container, 16
mappint (code), 127
Struts applications, 220-221
third-party, 162-163
tag library description, 282
tag library descriptor. *See* TLD
tag library usage (code), 69
tag-class element, custom tags, 282
taglib directive, 68-69, 274, 685
taglib element, 282
taglib-uri in web.xml file, 128
TagLifecycle.java file (code), 289-291
tags. *See also* custom tag libraries; directives; JSTL
bean, Web site, 224
<body>, 394
cache, 495
Core tag library, 132
core, 84, 611
custom, 125, 130
actions, 131
body content, 282, 292-303
code, 131
cooperating actions, 303
description, 282
empty actions, 276-288
emptyTag, 277
EmptyTag.java file (code), 277-278
emptyTag.jsp file (code), 276-277
emptyTags.tld file (code), 281
emptyTagWithAttrs, 283
EmptyTagWithAttrs.java file (code), 284-285
emptyTagWithAttrs.jsp file (code), 283-284

hierarchical structures, 307-311
howMany attribute, 284
interacting, 303
name element, 282
scripting variables, 303-307
tag handlers, 277
Tag interface, 276, 289-292
tag-class element, 282
writing, 274-276
<c:out>, Web applications, debugging, 698
declaration, 55-59, 690-691
defining in JSTL (JavaServer Pages Standard Tag Library), 83
EMBED, 96
emptyTag, 277
emptyTagWithAttrs, 283
<envelope>, 394
expression, 53-55, 691
; (semicolon), 54
for-each, 356
forEach, 84
handlers, 685
<html:checkbox>, 222
<html:errors>, 222
<html:form>, 222
<html:option>, 222
<html:radio>, 222
<html:select>, 222
<html:submit>, 222
<html:text>, 222
interfaces, UML diagram, 274
internationalization, 84
Internationalization tag library, 132
invalidate, 495
<jsp-file>, 114
jsp:getProperty, 177, 183-185
jsp:setProperty, 177, 185-189
jsp:useBean, 177-183, 186-193
JSTL (JavaServer Pages Standard Tag Library), 49, 84, 687
message, 224
OBJECT, 96
scriptlet, 692
<servlet>, 114
SQL, 84
SQL tag library, 132
standard tag library, 479
Tag Extensions, 273-274
TLD (tag library descriptor), 68, 685
<url-pattern>, 114
XML, 84, 318, 611
XML tag library, 132
<xsl:apply-templates>, 635-636
<xsl:call-template>, 636
<xsl:choose>, 636-637
<xsl:if>, 637
<xsl:otherwise>, 637-638
<xsl:param>, 638
<xsl:sort>, 638-639
<xsl:stylesheet>, 639-640
<xsl:template>, 640-641
<xsl:value-of>, 641
<xsl:when>, 641-642
<xsl:with-param>, 642
xs:attribute tag, 650

TagSupport class, 274, 278

target attribute (JSTL), 658

tariffs.fo file, 377-378

tariffs.xml file (code), 370-371

tariffsFO.xslt file (code), 379-381

tariffsHTML.xslt file (code), 371-372

tariffsWML.xslt file (code), 372-373

tcpmon tool, SOAP messages, 401-402

TDL, core JSTL tags (code), 128-129

technologies
Ormonds Web site, 606
Web services, 385

templates
built in (XSLT), 362-363
built-in, overriding, 363
declarative template programming (XSLT), 360-370
JSTL, 124

named, 366-367
namedTemplate.xsl file, 366-368
Ormonds Web pages, 607
param.xsl file, code, 367
processPerson, 368
single template programming (exemplar), 354-359
-tt (trace templates) switch, 362
Web pages, <jsp:include> standard action, 90-92
XML single, code, 355-356
XSLT multitemplate program (code), 360-361
XSLT multitemplate stylesheet (code), 361

test attribute (XSLT), 637, 641
third-party tag libraries, 162-163
thread objects, 169
threads, contrasting single-threaded and multithreaded ISAPI/NSAPI, 8
Throwable object, 40
throwing ServletException (code), 40-41
throwing exceptions, 75
timelines, JCP process, 703
timer (Visual Basic), 166
timeStyle attribute (JSTL), 674-675
timezone attribute (JSTL), 674
TLD (tag library descriptor), 68, 126, 274, 281, 287, 685
<tModel> element (XML), 427-428
<tModelInstance> element (XML), 427-428
Tomcat
Catalina, 718
class files, 119
configuring, 589, 713-714
DataSource, configuring, 497-498
debugging, 693-699
files, storing, 50
incorrect credentials, result of, 564
Jakarta, 23-25
javax package, Web applications, 119
library files, 119
Manager servlets, commands, 724-725
running, 573, 575
server.xml file, 713-721, 574
servlets, 721-725
sessions, 253
<tomcat-home> (installation folder), 24
virtual directories, 716
Web containers, 117
web.xml file, Web applications, 714-717
webapps folder, 26
Windows XP, 695

<TOMCAT HOME>/common/lib directory, 281
Tomcat project (Jakarta), 162
***Tomcat Rapid Working Knowledge*, 714**
Tomcat VM, downloading, 23
<tomcat-home> (Tomcat installation folder), 24
<TOMCAT_HOME>\work file, 50
tools
builder, IDEs, 166, 170
keystore, running, 573
mysql command-line, 729
Nokia WAP Toolkit, Web site, 375-376
SQL Admin, 728
tcpmon, SOAP messages, 401-402

top-level element, 129
toString method, 54
tracking sessions. *See* session tracking
tranformSubset.jsp file (code), 364-365
trans-attribute, 531
transaction demarcation mode, 531
transaction services, J2EE containers, 14
transactions, 488-489
transform actions, XML, 160
transform() method, 375
transform.xsl file (code), 361
transformations. *See also* XSLT
browser-specific, 370-376
BrowserDependentServlet.java file (code), 373-375

Netacape 6.2, browser-specific, 375
XSLT (XSL Transformations), 358
transformers, XSLT, 383
transforming
subsets of XML documents, 364-365
XML into presentation formats, 347
XML with XSLFO, 377
Cocoon, 381-384
objects, formatting, 377-381
XPath expressions, code, 364-365
transient keyword, 169
transient services, 451
translating JSP containers to servlets, 127
translets, stylesheets, 358
<transport-guarantee> element, values, 575
trees
DIT (Directory Information Tree), 439
DOM (Document Object Model), XML documents, 326
nodes, 326-327, 351-353
personNodes collection, 330
scope, 439
trim() method, 135
try/catch blocks, Tomcat and Web applications, 698
-tt (trace templates) switch, 362
tutorials
Java Tutorial Web site, 168
Java Web site, Swing classes, 203
TX DataSources, 539
Type 1 drivers, JDBC-ODBC Bridge, 462
Type 2 drivers, Native API (JDBC), 462
Type 3 drivers, JDBC Net Pure Java Driver, 463
Type 4 drivers, Native Protocol Pure Java Driver (JDBC), 463
type attribute (JSTL), 673-674
type element, 288
<type-storage> element, 533
types
Boolean, EL (Expression Language), 101
FloatingPointLiteral, EL (Expression Language), 101
IntegerLiteral, EL (Expression Language), 101
literal, EL (Expression Language), 101
MIME, Web site, 23
NullLiteral, EL (Expression Language), 101
String, EL (Expression Language), 101
<types> element (WSDL), 415-416

U

UDDI (Universal Description, Discovery, and Integration)
APIs, 428-430, 433
businesses, finding, 423
entries in IBM Test Registry (code), 424-425
registries, 424, 430
roles, 387
UDD14J Web site, 428
Web services, 387, 423-424
Web site, 424
XML, 424-428
UDDI4J Web site, 428
uddiClient.jsp file, appearance in Web browsers, 430
uddiClient.jsp file (code), 428-429
UDDIProxy class, 429
UltraDev project (Jakarta), 163
UML, simplified diagram, 274
unbind() method, 452
undeploy command, 724
underscore (_), XML element names, 322
uniform resource locators. *See* URLs
Universal Description, Discovery, and Integration. *See* UDDI
Unix, installing on MySQL servers, 728
unmarshaling parameters, 512

unpackWARs attribute, 721
unsetEntityContext() method, 526
upperLimit variable, 691
URIs, JSTL, 655-656
url attribute, 481
URL mapping, setting up (code), 114-115
url parameter, 464
<url-pattern> tag, 114
URL-related core actions, 150-156
URLs (uniform resource locators)
  creating from parameters (code), 154
  encoded, processing (code), 155
  encoding, 153
  JDBC, 465
  mappings, 114-116
  rewriting, 241-243
useAndSet1.jsp file (code), 186-189
useBean1 scriptlet.jsp file (code), 179-180
useBean1.jsp file (code), 181-183
useBean2 scriptlet.jsp file (code), 180
useBean2.jsp file (code), 184-185
useNaming attribute, 716
User attribute, 265, 481
user details, HTML forms (code), 133
user profiles, personalization (Web applications), 587-588
user registration, personalization (Web applications), 598-600
<user-data-constraint> element, 575
usernames, MySQL, 477
users
  behavior, logging in ATG Dynamo, 601
  Web sites, security perspective, 559-560
  welcome.jsp file, viewing, 595
usingDataSource.jsp, code, 477-479
usingEL.jsp file, 99
usingIncludes.jsp file (code), 90-91
usingIncludesWithParameters.jsp file, 92
usingParamTag.jps, code, 487-488
usingTransactions.jsp, code, 488-489
usingUpdateTag.jsp, code, 486-487
usingXalan.jsp file (code), 358-359

V

validate() method, 226, 621
validating XML Schemas content, 652
validation, data (Struts applications), 226-227
value attribute, 487, 657-658, 663
value-of instruction (XSLT), 357
valueBound() method, 251
values
  CONFIDENTIAL (<transport-guarantee> element), 575
  Context.INITIAL_CONTEXT_FACTORY environment property, 449
  dynamic attribute, 620
  INTEGRAL (<transport-guarantee> element), 575
  maxAge (cookies), 238
  NONE (<transport-guarantee> element), 575
  of parameters, bookProcessBean.jsp file (code), 196
  RT (runtime expression values), 131
  <transport-guarantee> element, 575
valueUnbound() method, 251
var attribute, 481-483, 486, 658
var attribute (XML), 667
variable element, child elements, 307
variable-class element, 307
variables
  ASPs (Active Server Pages), 80-82
  CLASSPATH environment (J2EE), 446
  environment, 693-695
  EVAL_BODY_INCLUDE, 298
  exported, naming, 667
  HOME environment (J2EE), 446
  instance, 57
  JSPs (JavaScript Pages), 80-81
  map, 229
  predefined
    application, 70-73, 686
    config, 73, 686
    error-handling pages (code), 76

exception, 73-77, 686
generated servlets (code), 75-76
generateError.jsp file (code0, 74
implicit objects, 69
jspService method (code), 69-73
Out, 686
out object, 77-78
Page, 78, 686
pageContext, 686
pageContext object, 78
processError.jsp file (code), 76
request, 79, 686
response, 79-80, 687
roles, 69-70
Session, 80, 687
shared objects, 71-72
scripting
emptyTagWithAttrsExport.jsp file (code), 303-304
exporting, 304
tags interacting, 303-307
upperLimit, 691
varReader attribute (JSTL), 662
version attribute (XSLT), 640
versions of cookies, 238-239
viewing
cd.jsp file in Web browsers, 268
certificates, 571, 575
malformed documents (XML) in Internet Explorer, 318
welcome.jsp file, 595
well-formed documents (XML) in Internet Explorer, 318
views, clients of EJBs, 515-517
virtual directories, 716
Visual Basic, 165-166
void addCookie(Cookie cookie) method, 22
void addHeader(String name, String value) method, 22
void afterLast() method, 470
void characters(char[] ch, int start, int length) method, 335
void endDocument() method, 335
void endElement(String namespaceURI, String localName, String qName) method, 335
void endPrefixMapping(String prefix) method, 335
void error(SAXParseException e) method, 335
void fatalError(SAXParseException e) method, 335
void ignorableWhitespace(char[] ch, int start, int length) method, 335
void init(ServletConfig config) method, 263
void invalidate() method, 252
void log(String message) method, 35
void notationDecl(String name, String publicID, String systemID) method, 335
void processingInstruction(String target, String data) method, 335
void removeAttribute(String name) method, 252
void resolveEntity(String publicID, String systemID) method, 335
void sendRedirect(String location) method, 22
void setAttribute(String name, Object value) method, 35, 252
void setContentType(String mime) method, 22
void setDocumentLocator(...) method, 335
void setItems() method, 262
void setMaxInactiveInterval(int interval) method, 252
void setReset() method, 262
void setStatus(int status) method, 22
void skippedEntity(String name) method, 335
void startDocument() method, 335
void startElement(String namespaceURI, String localName, String qName, Attributes attrs) method, 335

void startPrefixMapping(String prefix, String namespaceURI) method, 335
void warning(SAXParseException e) method, 335

W

W3C (World Wide Web Consortium)
id, 653
namespace
namespaces, 647
noNamespaceSchemaLocation attribute, 650-651
<schema> element, 648
schemaLocation attribute, 650-651
simpleType element, defining, 649-650
SOAP, 652-653
structure, 647-648
W3C XMLSchema-instance namespace, 651
schemaLocation, 653
Web site, 19, 157, 316
XML, 316
XML Schemas, 647
assigning, 650-651
<attribute> element, 648
attributes, declaring, 650
basic example (code), 646
code, 652
<complexType> element, 648-650
content validation, 652
datatypes, defining, 648-650
DTDs (Document Type Definitions), 645-646
element definition example, 653-654
<element>, 648
import element, 653
W3C XMLSchema-instance namespace, 651
WAR files, deploying, 120-121
.war file extension, 16, 120
Web applications
application scope, 47
classes, 119
configuring, web.xml file, 714-717
content file, 118
creating, 26-27
debugging, 693-699
deploying, 119-121
directories, structure, 281
EBJ access architecture, 555-558
entity Beans, deploying, 534-536
folder structures, deploying, 120
global locations, 119
index.jsp file, 118
JAR file, 119
Java, 7-10
javax package, 119
libraries, 119
page scope, 48
parameters, setting (code), 35-36
personalization
forms, 586-587
logins, 589-592
persistent cookies, 586
profile object, 592-595
registration, 586-587
rule-based, 600-603
user profiles, 587-588
user registration, 598-600
Web pages, 595-598
Web sites, 585-586
web.xml file (code), 591-592
request scope, 48
Root folder, 118
scope, 46, 174-177
security, 560
session scope, 47-48
structure, 117
WAR files, deploying, 120-121
WEB-INF folder, 118
WEB-INF\classes folder, 118
WEB-INF\lib folder, 118

web.xml file, 118
webapps folder (Tomcat), 26

Web browsers
admin.jsp file, 630
browser-specific transformations, 370-376
BrowserDependentServlet.java file (code), 373-375
cd.jsp file, viewing, 268
courses.jsp file, 611
details.jsp file, 612
digest authentication, 565
index.jsp file, appearance of, 412
Internet Explorer
basic authentication, 564
certificate providers, viewing, 572
Internet options, 697
malformed documents (XML), viewing, 318
well-formed documents (XML), viewing, 318
Netacape 6.2, browser-specific transformations, 375
page errors, 697
plugin.jsp file, 96
session counters, 255
uddiClient.jsp file, appearance of, 430
usingEL.jsp file, output, 99

Web containers
Jakarta Tomcat, 23-25
JavaBeans, 15
JSPs, 15
requests for servlets, 20
servlets, 15
tag libraries, 16
Tomcat, 117
Web applications, 117-121

Web Logic, sessions, 253

Web pages
applets, 7-8
comments, 232
error-handling, code, 76
exceptions, unhandled, 77
login, for personalization (Web applications), 589-592
Ormonds, 607-609
personalization (Web applications), 595-598
structure, 232
Struts applications, 220-224
style, 232
templating with <jsp:include> standard action, 90-92

Web servers, 8-9

Web services
accessing, using stubs, 419
Apache Axis, 389-392
averager, 392
Averager SOAP response (code), 396
core technologies, 385
definition, 385
deploying to Apache Axis, 391-393
invoking, 385
Java classes, Averager.java file (code), 389
online bookstores, 385
SOAP, 393
Averager Web service response (code), 396
custom objects, passing, 402-408
error handling, 398-401
invalid requests (code), 398-399
Java clients, building, 396-402
JSP, 408-413
namespaces, 394-395
requests (code), 394, 405
responses from BookService (code), 406
tcpmon tool, 401-402
XML Spy, 395-396
UDDI, 423-430, 433
WSDL, 413-423
XML, 386-387
XML Spy, interface, 395

Web Services Description Language. *See* WSDL

Web sites
Apache, 224, 348
Apache Axis, 389-390
Apache Software Foundation Web site, 162
Apache Struts source code, downloading, 224
ATG Dynamo, 258, 603
ATG Dynamo Framework, 233
BEA Web Logic, 258, 536, 732
Bookns (WSDL namespace), 415
Cocoon, 382-384
cookie standards, 238
COS Naming Service, 437
digest authentication, 565
DNS (Domain Name Service), 437
EJB QL, 531
EL operators, 101
FOP (Formatting Objects Processor), 381
formatting objects, 379
Gartner, 706
http://localhost:8080/axis/services/bookservice (WSDL namespace), 415
http://schemas.xmlsoap.org/soap/encoding (SOAP namespace), 394
http://schemas.xmlsoap.org/soap/encoding/ (WSDL namespace), 414
http://schemas.xmlsoap.org/soap/envelope (SOAP namespace), 394
http://schemas.xmlsoap.org/wsdl/ (WSDL namespace), 414
http://schemas.xmlsoap.org/wsdl/http/ (WSDL namespace), 415
http://schemas.xmlsoap.org/wsdl/mime/ (WSDL namespace), 415
http://schemas.xmlsoap.org/wsdl/soap/ (WSDL namespace), 414
http://www.w3.org/2001/XMLSchema (SOAP namespace), 395
http://www.w3.org/2001/XMLSchema-instance (SOAP namespace), 395
http://www.w3.org/200l/XMLSchema (WSDL namespace), 414
I18N (Internationalization), 160
IBM, UDDI registry, 424
IBM Web Services Test Area Web site, 424
Internet Explorer vulnerabilities, 241
iPlanet, 258
J2EE BluePrints, 212
J2SE VM, downloading, 23
JAF (JavaBeans Activation Framework), 625
Jakarta, 163, 216, 224
Jakarta Taglibs project, 82, 162
Java, Swing classes, 203
Java Community Process, 12, 125
Java Plugin, installing, 94
Java Tutorial, 168
Java Web Services Developer Pack, downloading, 83
JavaBeans documentation, 173
JavaBeans specification, 167
JAXP, downloading, 358
JAXR (Java API for XML Registries), 433
JBoss Application Server, 707, 711
JCP (Java Community Process), 701-703
JDOM (Java Document Object Model), 341
jdom.jar file, downloading, 344
JNDI service providers, 449
JSP 2.0 specifications, 95, 704
JSSE (Java Secure Socket Extension), downloading, 573
Liberty Alliance, 584
Microsoft, 348, 424, 584
MIME types, 23
Model 2 architecture demonstration, 204
MSXML, 348
MySQL database, downloading, 727
Netegrity SiteMinder 5, 584
Netscape vulnerabilities, 241
Nokia WAP Toolkit, 375-376
Ormonds, 605-606

personalization (Web applications), 585-586
portals, 709
protected resources, 575
RealMethods framework, 233
SAML (Security Assertions Markup Language), 584
Sams publishing, 26, 238, 514, 575
  chapter18Personalization.war file, downloading, 587
  JSP Unleashed, 204
  Ormonds case study, downloading, 605
Sams Publishing Web, chapter sample code, 165
SAX (Simple API for XML), 333
Saxon, 348
security, 559-560
Server Watch, 706
shopping, homepage, 265
SilverStream eXtend, 706
SiteMinder 5, 584
Struts framework, 214
Sun Microsystems
  J2EE Blueprints for EJBs, 511
  J2EE Reference Implementation, 708
  JDK 1.2, downloading, 445
  JNDI service providers, 449
Tomcat VM, downloading, 23
UDDI, 424
UDDI4J, 428
W3C, 647
  XML Schema, 325
  XPath homepage, 157
  XPath specification, 349
  XSLFO (XSL Formatting Objects), 381
W3C (World Wide Web Consortium), HTTP requests, 19
W3C Web, 348, 354
Web servers, 9
WEB-INF\lib\mail.jar archive, 625
Xalan, 348
  XML Bible, Second Edition, 381
  XML Spy, 32
  XML-DEV mailing list, 333
  XSLFO (XSL Formatting Objects), 381
  XSLT, 635
  XSLT processors, 348
  XSLTC (XSLT Compiler), 358
WEB-INF folder, Web applications, 118
/WEB-INF directory, 281
/WEB-INF/CLASSES directory, 281
/WEB-INF/LIB directory, 281
WEB-INF\classes folder, Web applications, 118
WEB-INF\lib folder, Web applications, 118
WEB-INF\lib\mail.jar archive (Web site), 625
web.xml file, 411-412, 534-535
  application parameters, setting, 35-36
  basic authentication, setting up (code), 563
  BasicFormProcessor servlet, 32
  BasicServlet class, 27
  code, personalization (Web applications, 591
  customized for SSL (Secure Socket Layer) (code), 574-575
  DataSource, configuring, 498
  form-based authentication (code), 567
  initialization parameters, passing (code), 116
  JSP, configuring, 114-116
  parameterized roles, code, 579
  security constraints, defining (code), 562
  servlet initialization parameters, 33-34
  session beans file (code), 553-554
  tag libraries, mapping (code), 127
  taglib-uri, 128
  Tomcat, debugging, 696
  URL mapping, setting up (code), 114-115
  Web applications, 118, 714-717
  welcome files, setting up (code), 114
webapps folder (Tomcat), 26

WebLogic
Configure and Deploy button, 541
entity Beans, deploying, 532-533
J2EE applications, 540
server console, 458
server welcome page examples, 537
WebLogic 7, 536-537, 710
WebLogic 7 Application Server, configuration screen, 581
weblogic-cmp-rdbms-jar.xml file (code), 533-534
weblogic-ejb-jar.xml file (code), 532-533, 553
welcome files, 114, setting up (code), 114
welcome pages, WebLogic examples, 537
<welcome-file-list> element, 114
welcome.jsp file (code), 210-211, 266-267, 557
welcomeText.html file (code), 62
well-formed documents (XML), 317-319
wildcard path operators, * (asterisk), 643
Windows
installing, 727, 731
Jakarta Tomcat, launching, 25
Windows XP, Tomcat, 695
Wireless Markup Language (WML), 370
WishList.java file (code), 251
wishList.jsp file (code), 250-251
WML (Wireless Markup Language), 370
words, reserved in EL, 108
workDir attribute, 716
World Wide Web Consortium. *See* W3C
wrapper classes
EJBObject, 522
Java primitive datatypes, 197
wrapperClass attribute, 716
writeObject method, 169-170
writing
custom tags
body content, 292-303
EL (Expression Language) functions, 274-276
empty actions, 276-288
Tag interface lifecycle, 289-292
EJBs, 517-518
JSPs, Tomcat and Web applications, 698
XSLT stylesheets, 356
WSDL (Web Services Description Language)
accessing programatically, 423
<binding> element, 417-418
documents, core structures, 415
generating, 419
Java, generating, 419-422
<message> element, 416
namespaces, 414-415
<operation> element, 417
<portType> element, 416
roles, 387
<service> element, 418
<types> element, 415-416
Web services, 387, 413-415
XML, bookservice.wsdl file namespaces, 414-415

X

XA DataSources, configuring, 539
Xalan
-tt (trace templates) switch, 362
Web site, 348
Xalan processor (XSLT), 357-359
XML. *See also* documents (XML)
& (ampersand), 322
: (colon), 322
/ (forward slash), 322
- (hyphen), 322
< (left angle bracket), 322
. (period), 322
> (right angle bracket), 322
_ (underscore), 322
1.0 specification, 317
actions, 332, 664-668
attributes, code, 323-324
<bindingTemplate> element, 427

<body> tag, 394
bookservice.wsdl file, namespaces, 414-415
<businessEntity> element, 426
<businessService> element, 426
<categoryBag> element, 427
course0.xml file (code), 609-610
data files, code, 370-373
digits, 322
document element information item, 319
DOM (Document Object Model), 325
DTDs (Document Type Definitions), 324-325
elements, code, 323-324
entities, 322-323
<envelope> tag, 394
files, 16, 319
formats, Ormonds course information, 609-610
grammar, 387
HTMLSerializer, 383
JAXP (Java API for XML Processing), 325-326
letters, 322
malformed documents, viewing in Internet Explorer, 318
messages, sending and receiving, 386
meta-language, definition, 317
namespaces, case sensitivity, 355
parsing, 325
  DOM (Document Object Model) APIs, 326-333
  JDOM (Java Document Object Model) APIs, 341-345
  SAX (Simple API for XML) APIs, 333-340
Pis (processing instructions), 320
portable data, 315-316
SAX (Simple API for XML), 325, 340
scope attribute, 667
SGML (Standard Generalized Markup Language), 317
SOAP (Simple Object Access Protocol), 387
special characters, 322
structure, 317-319
syntax, 317-319
systemId attribute, 664
tags, 611
<tModel> element, 427-428
<tModelInstance> element, 427-428
transforming into presentation formats, 347
UDDI (Universal Description, Discovery, and Integration), 387, 424-426
var attribute, 667
W3C (World Wide Web Consortium), 316
well-formed documents, 317-319
WSDL (Web Services Description Language), 387
XML (Extensible Markup Language), 315
xml attribute, 667
xmlSystemId attribute, 667
XPath, /people/person/name location path, 350
XSLFO (XSL Formatting Objects), 347
  Cocoon, 381-384
  objects, formatting, 377-381
  processing model, 377
  transformations, 376-377
XSLT (eXtensible Stylesheet Language: Transformations), 347
  attribute instruction, 357
  choose instruction, 357
  comment instruction, 357
  copy instruction, 357
  copy-of instruction, 357
  declarative template programming, 360-370
  element instruction, 357
  exemplar, 354-357
  for-each instruction, 357
  if instruction, 357
  input, 348-349
  instructions, 357

output, 348-349
procedural programming, 366-370
process, 348
processing-instruction instruction, 357
single template programming (exemplar), 354-359
StreamResult class, 359
StreamSource class, 359
subsets, 363-365
templates built in, 362-363
transformations, 358, 370-376
value-of instruction, 357
Xalan processor, 357-359
XPath, 349-354
xslt attribute, 667
xsltSystemId attribute, 667
***XML and Web Services Unleashed*, 354**
xml attribute (XML), 667
***XML Bible*, Second Edition, 381**
XML core actions, 156-159
XML flow-control actions, 159-160
XML Information Set (InfoSet) 319-320
***XML Schema Complete Reference*, 645**
XML Schema, 315, 324
assigning, 650-651
<attribute> element, 648
attributes, declaring, 650
basic example (code), 646
code, 652
<complexType> element, 648-650
content validation, 652
datatypes, defining, 648-650
DTDs (Document Type Definitions), 645-646
element definition examle, 653-654
<element> element, 648
import element, 653
include element, 653
namespaces, declaring, 647
noNamespaceSchemaLocation attribute, 650-651
<schema> element, 647-648
schemaLocation attribute, 650-651
simpleType element, defining, 649-650
SOAP, 652-653
structure, 647-648
W3C XMLSchema-instance namespace, 651
Web site, 325
XML Spy, 395-396
XML Spy 4.3, ejb-jar.xml file structure, 528
XML Spy Web site, 32
XML Stylesheet Language Transformations. *See* XSLT
XML tag, 84, 687
XML tag library, EL (expression language), 132
XML transform actions, 160
XML-DEV mailing list Web site, 333
xmlExample.html file (code), 319
xmlSystemId attribute (XML), 667
XP (Windows), Tomcat, 695
XP platform, Java Plugin, 731
XPath
@ attribute path operator, 643
/ child operator, 643
// descendant operator, 643
. operator, 643
.. parent path operator, 643
* wildcard path operator, 643
absolute location paths, 349
ancestor axis identifier, 352
ancestor-or-self axis identifier, 352
anElementName expression, 642
attribute axis identifier, 352
axis identifiers, 351-353
child axis identifier, 351
descendant axis identifier, 352-353
descendant-or-self axis identifier, 352-353
EL (Expression Language), 100
expressions, transforming (code), 364-365
following axis identifier, 352-353
following-sibling axis identifier, 352

homepage, Web site, 157
location paths, format, 349
namespace axis identifier, 352
node() function, 353
node() method, 644
nodesets, 349
not() function, 354
| OR operator, 644
parent axis identifier, 351
/people/person/name location path, evaluation of, 350
preceding axis identifier, 352-353
preceding-sibling axis identifier, 352
predicates, 354, 644
relative location paths, 350
self axis identifier, 351
specification, W3C Web site, 349
XSLT (eXtensible Stylesheet Language: Transformations), 349-351

XSL Formatting Objects. *See* XSLFO

XSL Transformations. *See* XSLT

XSLFO (XSL Formatting Objects), 347
Cocoon, 381-384
HTMLSerializer, 383
processing model, 377
Web site, 381
XML, 347, 376-381

XSLT (eXtensible Stylesheet Language: Transformations)
attribute instruction, 357
case-order (optional) attribute, 639
choose instruction, 357
comment instruction, 357
copy instruction, 357
copy-of instruction, 357
data-type (optional) attribute, 639
declarative template programming, 360-370
disable-output-escaping (optional) attribute, 641
element instruction, 357
exclude-result-prefixes attribute, 640
exemplar, 354-357
extension-element—prefixes (optional) attribute, 640
for-each instruction, 357
id (optional) attribute, 640
if instruction, 357
input, 348-349
instructions, 357
lang (optional) attribute, 639
match (optional) attribute, 640
mode(optional) attribute, 635, 641
multitemplate program (code), 360-361
multitemplate stylesheet (code), 361
name (optional) attribute, 640
name attribute, 636-642
namespaces, W3C Web site, 354
order (optional) attribute, 639
output, 348-349
priority (optional) attribute, 641
process, 348
processing-instruction instruction, 357
processors, Web sites, 348
select (optional) attribute, 635, 638-639, 642
Select attribute, 641
single template, code, 355-356
single template programming (exemplar), 354-359
specification, W3C Web site, 348
stylesheets, writing, 356
test attribute, 637, 641
transformations, 358, 370-376
transformers, 383
value-of instruction, 357
version attribute, 640
Web site, 635
Xalan, -tt (trace templates) switch, 362
Xalan processor, 357-359
XML, transforming into presentation formats, 347
XPath, 349-354
<xsl:apply-templates> tag, 635-636

<xsl:call-template> tag, 636
<xsl:choose> tag, 636-637
<xsl:if> tag, 637
<xsl:otherwise> tag, 637-638
<xsl:param> tag, 638
<xsl:sort> tag, 638-639
<xsl:stylesheet> tag, 639-640
<xsl:template> tag, 640-641
<xsl:value-of> tag, 641
<xsl:when> tag, 641-642
<xsl:with-param> tag, 642
xslt attribute (XML), 667
XSLTC (XSLT Compiler), 358
xsltSystemId attribute (XML), 667
<xsl:apply-templates> tag, 635-636
<xsl:call-template> tag, 636
<xsl:choose> tag, 636-637
xsl:if instruction, 368
<xsl:if> tag, 637
<xsl:otherwise> tag, 637-638
<xsl:param> tag, 638
<xsl:sort> tag, 638-639
<xsl:stylesheet> tag, 639-640
<xsl:template> tag, 640-641
<xsl:value-of> tag, 641
<xsl:when> tag, 641-642
<xsl:with-param> tag, 642
xs:attribute tag, 650
x:choose action, 159-160, 666
x:forEach action, 159-160, 363, 666
x:if action, 159-160, 665
x:otherwise action, 159-160, 666
x:out action, 158-159, 363, 665
x:param action, 160, 668
x:parse action, 157-158, 664-665
x:set action, 159, 365, 665
x:transform action, 160, 365, 667-668
x:when action, 159-160, 666

Y-Z

Yahoo Web site, 585

Content Master

www.contentmaster.com

Content Master is one of the world's leading technical authoring and consultancy organisations, working with key software vendors to provide leading-edge content to technical audiences. This content, combined with our business knowledge helps enable business decision makers, developers and IT Professionals to keep abreast of new initiatives, helping them build innovative enterprise solutions.

We also offer educational and content consultancy, identifying the most effective strategies for the development and deployment of materials. Our unique approach encompasses technical, business and educational requirements. This ensures that developed content not only offers the right level of specialist knowledge but that it addresses commercial requirements and is structured in the most effective way. This covers a range of media, including web, print and CD.

Other Content Master books:

Sams Teach Yourself J2EE in 21 Days
ISBN: 0-672-32384-2

Tomcat Kick Start
ISBN: 0-672-32439-3

JavaServer Pages 2.0 Unleashed
ISBN: 0-672-32438-5

Content Master
Tortworth House
Tortworth
Wotton-under-Edge
Gloucestershire
GL12 8HQ
http://www.contentmaster.com
Call +44 1454 269222

Content Master has worked with customers to develop strategies to address:

- Internal and external web sites
- Internal systems and business documentation
- Internal and external training materials
- Content development strategies
- Training business strategies

Our other core products and skills include the following;

- Books for publication: Working with the major publishing houses, we author books aimed at the technical and business decision maker audiences
- Content creation:
  - White papers
  - Case studies
  - Blueprints
  - Website Content
  - Deployment guides
  - Software development kits
  - Best practice documentation
  - Business Decision Maker seminars
  - Sales and marketing collateral
- Courseware: we write classroom based and multi-media training courses for leading software companies, usually under the brand of the commissioning vendor
- Resource: we regularly provide the following to our partners:
  - Program managers
  - Technical writers
  - Subject matter experts
  - Testing facilities and resource
  - Editors
  - Instructional designers
  - Consultants